The Lead Generation Handbook

Bernard A. Goldberg

DIRECT MARKETING PUBLISHERS

DEDICATION

To Sandy, Caren, Dawn and Wendy . . .
Without your support and patience, this book
would not have been possible.

Published by

Direct Marketing
Publishers

1304 University Drive
Yardley, PA 19067
(215) 321-3068 FAX (215) 321-9647

Printed in the United States of America.

Library of Congress Catalog Card Number: 91-78109

International Standard Book Number: 1-879644-02-9

Acknowledgments

An effort of this size couldn't have happened without the support and help of many people.

Marie Smith has been a godsend in editing. She has helped make each of my books clear, concise, and readable. Her efforts are often unheralded but she has my heartfelt thanks and this book would never have been completed without her support.

Tracy Emerick, Dick Vink, Lane Wolbe and Mel Jaffe contributed more than the material that is included under their bylines. As friends, they have been there when I needed guidance and advice. As professionals, they are without peers in their areas of expertise and have taught me a great deal.

Mark Mancini and his creative talents provided the cover for this book and my Telephone Selling Manual. His creative concepts really put the finishing touch on the books.

The direct marketing industry has an outstanding group of professionals who were always eager to help. Ned Johnston, Jim Kobs, Chuck Tannen, Mark Weinstein, Bob King, Mike Goodkin, Tony Keenen and Bob Borders were helpful in providing support and insight.

Without my clients I wouldn't have learned the lessons that are communicated in this book . . . they're terrific. Special thanks to Pat McVeigh, Dave Wenning, Kelly Brown, Tom Begush, Dave Smith, Jeff Kahn, Armand Phillippi, Doug Bowden, Clint Teegardin, Joe Love, Keith Barnette, Marty Flynn, Mike Cappeto, Jeff Weiner, Jan Deruiter, Skid Pirtle, Darci Maenpa, Kevin Keegan, Rob Crine, Peter Wells and Bob Dowdell.

About the Author

Bernard A. Goldberg

Bernie Goldberg spent ten years at IBM Corporation in marketing and sales of small to medium computer systems. Bernie was one of the top sales people and later a top sales manager for the company. In addition, he spent two years in sales training and marketing planning. In his last position with IBM in 1979, he managed a pioneering facility in direct marketing and telemarketing. Like most of us, he started in business-to-business direct marketing with no experience and no prior training. Because of Bernie's prior sales background he has empathy and understanding for the field sales organization.

Prior to IBM, Bernie spent four years in the army immediately after receiving his Bachelor of Arts degree from C.W. Post College.

After IBM, Bernie's entrepreneurial spirit fostered two different telemarketing companies. He has specialized in all aspects of business-to-business direct marketing. He is a frequent speaker at direct marketing and telemarketing meetings and has written numerous articles on both subjects. He has also served as Vice Chairman and Programming Chairman of the Business-to-Business Council of the Direct Marketing Association. In addition to this book, Bernie co-authored *Business-to-Business Direct Marketing*, now in its second edition, and wrote *How to Manage and Execute Telephone Selling*. He also publishes bi-monthly *The Business Marketing Note Pad*.

Bernie is currently president of his own consulting firm, B. A. Goldberg Consulting, in Yardley, Pennsylvania. A native of Amityville, New York, Bernie resides with his wife and three daughters in Yardley, Pennsylvania.

Table of Contents

Chapter One:

The Changing Business Market

The business world has experienced significant change in the last few years. Ask yourself why you're aggressively looking at alternative selling methods? What issues are causing you the greatest concern for the future?

Many companies are trying to find alternative methods, besides face-to-face selling, to reach smaller customers or sell less expensive products. The pressure to reduce selling costs and find alternative distribution techniques will continue. The real question is what has changed in the last few years to force business executives to focus on other distribution methods?

Over the last century, our economy has dramatically shifted from agriculture and manufacturing to services. In the late 19th century, services represented about 20% of the jobs in America. Most of our population was employed making or growing products. A recent report to the President of the United States contained Illustration 1–1. As you can see, today almost 80% of America's workers are employed in the services sector. This change, although gradual, has been most apparent in the last two decades.

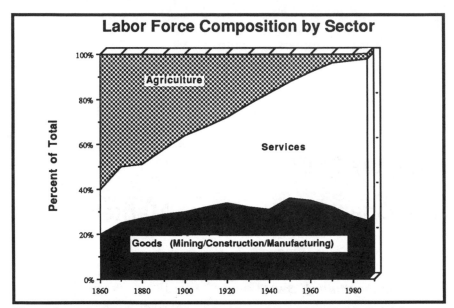

Illustration 1-1: Distribution of the labor force from *1988 U.S. Industrial Outlook*, U.S. Department of Commerce.

The gradual shift to a predominant service labor force has changed where people work, what they're doing and their required skill levels. Unions are less of a factor and working conditions are less important than in the past. Industry is less dependent on manual physical strength to get the job done.

There has been a dramatic increase in two income households because the labor effort required in the services arena is less dependent on brawn. America is finding out that women can be just as effective in the marketplace. Physical labor can be done less expensively in underdeveloped countries and therefore a great deal of our manufacturing has moved offshore. The change to a services-based economy continues unabated.

Our marketing and selling efforts have had to change as well. We are no longer selling mostly goods that have been made and developed in the USA. We are no longer selling primarily to men; many of our potential customers are women. More and more of our prospects and customers are working at desks in offices.

Perhaps one of the issues that causes you the greatest concern is competition. This area also has changed dramatically in the last two decades. The same report to the President I mentioned earlier, contained the following statement regarding foreign competition.

> *"Recent experience suggests that a persistent quality advantage of certain imported goods may be quite important to U.S. buyers. Also, to maintain market share and remain competitive, the Japanese and other exporters to the U.S. have lowered their profit margins to absorb part of the exchange rate and cost increases."*

Competition has always been an important element in our society. It has been one of the key elements to force product innovation and marketing changes. Foreign competition has forced American industry to recognize that quality is an important consideration in the products we buy. Recent advertising from all of the American automobile manufacturers demonstrates how important the quality issue has become. Ford emphasizes "Quality is Job #1" and you've probably observed Lee Iacocca extolling the significant quality advantage Chrysler has over the Japanese.

Foreign companies don't seem to have the same profit perspective as their American counterparts. They are not driven by quarterly goals and objectives and are much more willing to invest for the long-term. Besides lowering their profit objectives to deal with the exchange rate, many will even lose money to develop market share and awareness.

It has become much more expensive to sell to other businesses, yet foreign competition forces most companies to maintain existing prices while absorbing the higher costs. Technology is being introduced to more and more areas of American business to help reduce costs and allow companies to remain competitive. But as costs increase we are unable to pass them along to our customers. We just have to continue to improve productivity to remain competitive.

The cost of making a face-to-face sales call has dramatically increased in the last decade. Through 1987, McGraw-Hill conducted a biannual survey to determine selling costs and the cost of a face-to-face sales call. As you can see in Illustration 1-2, the cost of one call in 1977 was about $97. That same sales call in 1987 had increased to over $250.

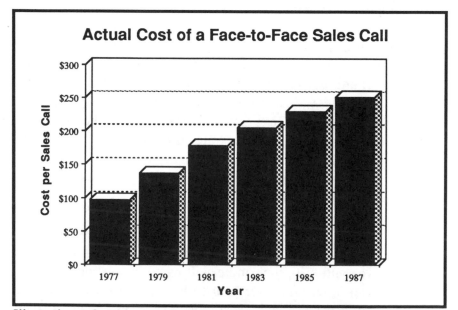

Illustration 1-2: The cost of a face-to-face sales call according to the McGraw Hill Laboratory for Advertising Performance.

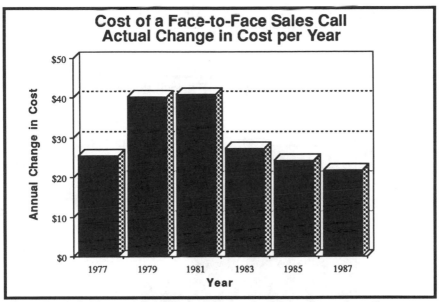

Illustration 1-3: The actual change in the cost of a face-to-face sales call per year.

There is good news and bad news about the cost of face-to-face selling.

First the bad news, the cost of a face-to-face sales call continues to increase at an alarmingly high rate. As you can see, the actual increase in the cost of a face-to-face sales call really took an enormous jump in 1979 and 1981. Although still increasing, it only grew about $20 between 1981 and 1987. The cost is not growing as rapidly as it was in the early 1980's, but it is still growing nevertheless. The most recent increase is almost 10% which is significantly higher than the prevailing inflation rate of only 3.5% per year.

The good news is that the percentage of growth of the total cost has continued to decline since 1979. Between 1977 and 1979 the cost of a sales call grew by over 40%, but between 1985 and 1987 it grew less than 10%. Although this decrease in the growth rate is encouraging, we should not lose sight that in 1987 a sales call costed

$251.00 compared to $97 in 1977. The actual cost of a sales call is much higher today than ever before.

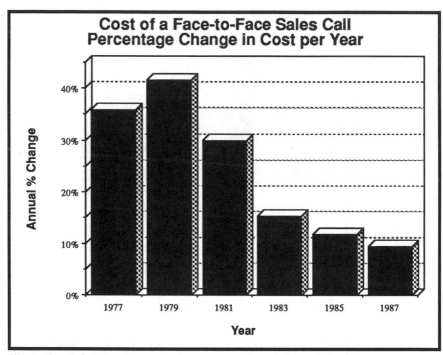

Illustration 1-3: The change in the cost of a face-to-face sales call per year represented in percentages.

Increased selling costs manifest themselves in all parts of our business. It makes it more difficult to sell products and services profitably, yet we cannot raise prices to compensate for the additional expenses because of the competitive nature of our environment. The increasing cost of a sales call has made it prohibitively expensive to sell certain less profitable products or to sell to smaller customers.

If we assume that you can afford to spend 20% of your gross revenue to sell your products or services, and a sales call costs $250, you have to generate at least $1,250 in revenue for each sales call you make. If a customer does not generate at least $1,250 in revenue you can't afford even one sales call! That is one of the primary reasons that so many of us are looking at direct marketing to help service and support smaller customers.

Consider the information salespeople keep on their customers and active prospects. It probably includes every letter created or received. In many cases the only complete file of communication between a company and customer is the file maintained by the salesperson. And the only file of activity between company and prospect will inevitably be that which is maintained by the salesperson. Companies tend to purge their communication and customer files each year. Salespeople tend to be like packrats; they never throw out anything.

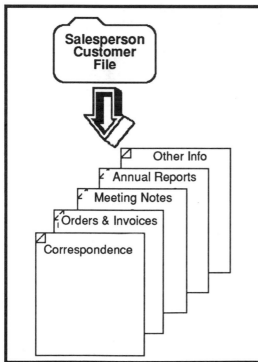

A typical salesperson probably has filed all the orders and invoices, and notes from any meetings he may have attended. Even the annual reports and financial statements about the customer or prospect company will often find their way into the salesperson's files. Most good salespeople use this information to record the sales activity thus far and to develop a strategy for future selling actions.

Illustration 1-4: The salesperson's customer and prospect database.

Salespeople know that the history of a relationship between their company and a customer can be useful in selling additional products and services. In business selling, the relationship is one of the most important criteria to continuing the selling effort. It can be used to develop and sustain a strategy to sell additional products and services. And salespeople are never sure when a piece of information will be important, therefore they tend to keep everything forever.

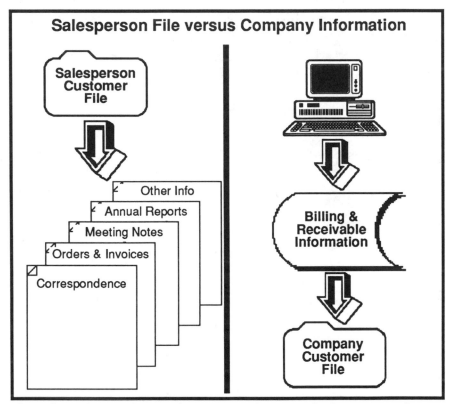

Salesperson File versus Company Information

Illustration 1-5: The salesperson's customer and prospect database compared to the company's information.

Contrast your files to those which are maintained by your company. Most company customer files are maintained by accounting and are used for billing and accounts receivable purposes. These files typically contain the name of the person responsible for paying the bill, often an individual in the accounts payable department. Most files are limited to only one contact and therefore will not contain the name of the person responsible for the buying decision. In addition, the account history will often be limited to the last few invoices and maybe a summary of annual sales activity.

These accounting files are limited in the amount of information that can be stored. It is difficult to change or modify the information because of the company's existing billing and invoicing computer programs.

The contrasting files developed and maintained by the salesperson and the company present an interesting enigma. Because of the escalating cost of the sales call, you can't afford to deal face-to-face with smaller customers, yet you have almost no information available about these companies in your existing data files.

As I mentioned earlier, the key to successful business selling is the relationship that exists between your company and the customer or prospect. As you eliminate face-to-face selling activity with smaller customers, any history of the business relationship will be lost unless you begin to develop a complete marketing database.

Many companies will often avoid the smaller customer opportunities because of the file limitations in their data processing department. It can be frustrating and defeating to request support from the data processing department. If you ask your DP organization to provide the capability to maintain and build a complete customer database, you'll probably get a snicker or even a full belly laugh. They will often tell you that it sounds like a good idea but it will take them about two years.

You need some form of database to sustain any marketing activity, and as we'll discuss soon, the availability of technology now makes it possible for you to solve this problem yourself. Desktop computers with database capabilities now make it relatively easy for you to develop and maintain your own database. There are even software solutions available specifically designed to support marketing communication.

Communication & Awareness		
	Company	
	Known	**Unknown**
Unique	Most desirable situation Use DM/Telephone Selling/Advertising	Communicate your solution to market Use DM
Commodity	Create uniqueness & communicate to market Use DM	Most difficult to sell Establish uniqueness & awareness Use DM

(Row/column axis label: **Product**)

Illustration 1-6: The communications challenge.

The communication challenge continues to change but the mission has basically stayed the same. As we change our target audience, the approach we take will change.

Look at Illustration 1-6 and determine which condition best reflects the position of your company and product or service. If you find yourself unknown and selling a commodity product, it will be almost impossible to sell. You have to change this situation relatively quickly in order to survive. You probably can't afford enough advertising to use advertising to change this situation significantly.

Direct marketing is probably your best alternative. A well targeted audience using direct mail with a dynamite offer may generate some success. This situation is a difficult one at best and you have to work to establish uniqueness and awareness at the same time.

If you have an unknown product or company but truly offer unique features and benefits, the communication mission is well defined -- make the marketplace aware of your solution. Again, direct marketing can be ideal.

A known commodity requires you to develop a unique proposition that allows your customers and prospect to understand why your are unique in your offering. You will have to establish uniqueness in your company or distribution approach.

The objective is to become known and unique. If you're a very large company with an unlimited budget, general broadcast advertising can be very effective to position your company and create awareness. This approach is typically effective in consumer product marketing. Business marketing narrows the target audience and requires better targeting of the message and the media. Direct mail, telephone selling and targeted space advertising seem to work best in the business universe.

No area has experienced more rapid change in the last decade than technology. The price of technology has continued to decline while performance continues to increase. These changes have distinct advantages to almost every company. Not only can you create your own database using personal computers, but spreadsheets enable you to analyze and evaluate the results of your efforts virtually immediately. Desktop publishing allows you to create high quality communications without the cost and hassle of using outside professionals. The use of computers permeates at almost every turn within virtually every company.

In 1983 you would have spent about $6,500 to purchase an IBM PC with 640K bytes of memory, a floppy disk drive, a hard disk drive, and a printer. If you were selling this equipment as a distributor, you were probably able to generate about a 30% profit margin and therefore had about $1,800 to pay for your selling and administrative expenses.

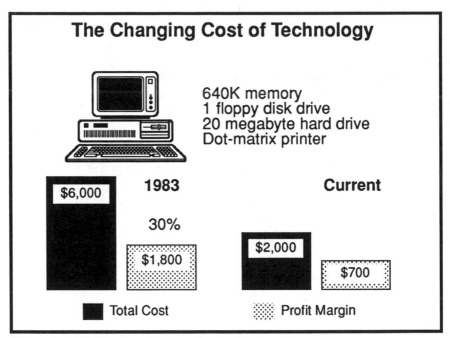

Illustration 1-7: The changing cost of technology.

Today you can buy almost the same computer for under $2,500. In fact, you can probably acquire a system with 1 megabyte of memory and 40 megabytes of disk space for under $2,000. This means that computers are even more available than ever before and continue to grow in their use in most companies.

The explosion of technology has also presented some interesting challenges. The reduction in the end-user cost has also reduced the profit margin dollars available to sell and support computer systems. Today, if the dealer is still able to generate a 30% profit margin, there is only about $800 to pay for selling and administrative expenses. Yet it hasn't gotten any easier or less expensive to sell that computer.

As I mentioned earlier, selling costs and the cost of face-to-face sales calls have continued to increase. The computer dealer analogy may not seem appropriate for you, but technology has affected almost every product sold. The same disadvantage experienced by the computer dealer because of the decline in price due to technology advancement, is felt by almost every company. Technology enhancements will often cause a decline in profit margin dollars leaving less money available for selling expenses. It's almost like a double whammy -- available margin dollars going down while selling expenses are going up.

People in the Past

- **Blue collar majority**
- **Little sophistication required**
- **Cost for acquisition, training and retention was reasonable**

Our employment of people has also changed dramatically. In the past, the people employed by companies were mostly blue collar. They worked in manufacturing or on farms. They made or grew the product and basically performed an element of the process. There was not a lot of sophistication required to get the job done. As a result the cost to acquire, train, and keep people employed and happy was reasonable.

Today, most people are employed in the service sector and tend to be white collar oriented. The people tend to specialize and develop unique skills. These specialized skills are more expensive to acquire. Training costs, which in the past were minimal, have become a major expense in many companies. Because companies are making major investments to teach new and advanced skills to their employees, it is even more important to retain these people over time, and therefore more expensive.

People - Current

- **Primarily white collar orientation**
- **Specialization required**
- **Cost for acquisition, training and retention has become moderate to expensive**

People expenses have continued to escalate. Obviously salary dollars have continued to grow but so have people associated expenses for training and benefits. Again, keep in mind that foreign competition doesn't allow us to increase prices to cover the increased cost. Business executives are looking to alternative selling techniques to reduce expenses and accommodate smaller customers to whom it is too expensive to make face-to-face sales calls. Business-to-business direct marketing is the fastest growing segment of the direct marketing industry. Many companies are developing catalogs and telephone selling operations to sell to smaller companies. Lead generation programs are becoming a necessity in order for companies to survive.

Consumer vs Business-to-Business Direct Marketing

Let's examine the difference in direct marketing to consumers and direct marketing to people in businesses. Let's first examine the difference in the two universes.

In consumer selling, you only have to deal with a three line address. The name, street address and city, state and zip code of the prospect or customer. And houses don't move, therefore you can develop marketing campaigns targeted to households. In fact, people don't buy houses; houses buy people. If you move today, someone who is basically just like you will probably buy your house and respond to similar marketing activity. When you move we get another prospect of similar quality to whom we can market, and as you'll see in a moment, we can still keep track of you.

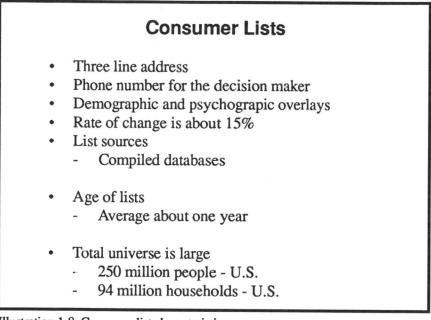

Consumer Lists

- Three line address
- Phone number for the decision maker
- Demographic and psychograpic overlays
- Rate of change is about 15%
- List sources
  - Compiled databases

- Age of lists
  - Average about one year

- Total universe is large
  - 250 million people - U.S.
  - 94 million households - U.S.

Illustration 1-8: Consumer list characteristics.

The phone number will typically be that of the decision maker. When I call you at home, you or your spouse will make a decision about my product or service. You will not refer me to someone else in the company.

Your last name will most often be recorded the same way by all companies and your address will also be handled similarly by most companies. Therefore, we can create coding techniques that are virtually foolproof which allow duplicate elimination and matching of one list to another. This matching capability allows us to create lists that are overlayed with additional information. We can combine subscription, membership, purchase and prior respondent information to develop your complete profile. It is unbelievable how effective we are at targeting because of the computer and match-code techniques developed over the years.

Consumer lists change about 15% each year. And the postal service offers the National Change of Address (NCOA) service that allows us to track where you've gone and update our mailing lists.   Thus we won't lose you when you move on to another location.

Most direct marketing in the consumer world is done from compiled lists that have had data overlayed to allow better and more accurate targeting.   Because most of these lists are updated only once each year, the average age of a consumer list is about one year old. As an aside, if the list is only changing about 15% per year, the list is 85% accurate even before using the NCOA service.

Finally, the consumer universe is large.   There are about 250 million people and 94 million households. You have an unbelievably large universe to market to before you have to reattempt the same record. Because of the size of the universe, many consumer programs are single-shot projects with no requirement to maintain a database and track the marketing activity. However, the larger and more sophisticated consumer direct marketers are using database tracking techniques with great success.

The business arena differences are immediately apparent. Business lists require anywhere from four to six lines of address information. Besides the person's name, you may even store a position title and perhaps a salutation. The company name requires another line. Many companies will have two lines for the street address to include a suite number, mail stop, or post office box. And the city, state and zip code will require still another line. Computer programs designed to handle consumer addresses are not effective for business direct marketing.

Duplicate company names and addresses are a fact of life in business marketing. Even if you're relatively certain that your house file doesn't contain exact duplicates, many companies are subsidiaries of other companies and you can have a duplicate company on your customer files and not even know it.

Different people will abbreviate company names differently. Many companies develop customer files with duplicate company names because of different spelling and abbreviation permutations. And the problem is compounded when multiple people order from the same company. Even if you have the most sophisticated system to screen duplicates, there is not a computer program or manual procedure that can identify duplicates if two individuals from the same company spell or abbreviate their company name differently.

As well as we manage information in consumer marketing, we haven't developed the same level of sophistication in match coding and duplicate elimination in the business-to-business world. Inconsistent company names and addresses as well as company hierarchy make overlays and matching almost impossible. If you send your company file to a computer service bureau to eliminate duplicate records or append phone numbers, it is unusual for more than 50% of the records to be matched.

If you decide to use telephone selling in the business-to-business environment, you will have to make many additional phone calls. Frequently one call will be referred to another person in the company requiring additional calls. Typically the phone number you have will be to the switchboard and you will have to be switched to the contact you're trying to reach. Once you finally get through be prepared to be told that the decision is made by someone else in the company and you will have to start all over again.

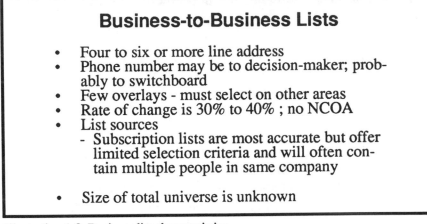

Business-to-Business Lists

- Four to six or more line address
- Phone number may be to decision-maker; probably to switchboard
- Few overlays - must select on other areas
- Rate of change is 30% to 40% ; no NCOA
- List sources
  - Subscription lists are most accurate but offer limited selection criteria and will often contain multiple people in same company

- Size of total universe is unknown

Illustration 1-9: Business list characteristics.

The average rate of address change in business is 30% to 40% per year. And there is no NCOA to help track and update our lists.

The frequency of change and imperfect matching techniques in business makes almost any list somewhat inaccurate. Even if the list is updated twice each year, it can still be 20% inaccurate. Most compiled lists are updated annually, therefore they are probably 40% inaccurate. In your direct marketing promotion, you should use title-addressing as well as name addressing to ensure that your package is delivered to the target you're trying to reach.

The most accurate lists are those that are used and updated frequently. Controlled circulation, a form of magazine subscription, will probably give you the most areas of selection and the most accurate name and address information. Unfortunately, these lists may not provide enough prospects to cover your maximum opportunity. These lists will also often contain multiple contacts within the same company.

The size of the business universe is a controversial subject that frequently creates lively debates at direct marketing meetings. Everyone seems to have a different estimate concerning how many businesses there are in America. Different list owners will have conflicting estimates of the size of the business universe. There really is no way to identify an accurate count.

Now let's explore the differences in the consumer and business selling environments.

The Consumer Selling Environment

- Target is the contact
- Target makes the decision
- Telemarketing hours
  - 5 to 9 p.m.
  - Weekends

- Direct mail gets through
- Average order is small - under $25
- A non-contact/decision is consumed
- The target is spending their own money
- Decision is frequently made on a counter near a trash can
- Telemarketing is frequently used
- Telesales is rarely used except in customer service.

Illustration 1-10: The consumer selling environment.

In consumer selling, typically the person we contact, either through the mail or on the phone, is the target we are attempting to reach. In addition, the target or contact is usually the decision-maker and doesn't need to get approval or advice before buying.

In telephone selling, the primary hours of contact are during evenings and weekends when consumers are at home.

Direct mail is typically delivered to the target. Whether the prospect reads the promotion will primarily depend on the creative approach used.

The target is typically spending their own money. No one will review their decision and they don't need approval to make the decision. Consumers are more concerned about cashflow and typically will be more inclined to buy products that cost under $25 per month.

Consumers will often make a decision about your offer where they open their mail. This is frequently done at the kitchen counter near a trash can. The creative approach has to create enough excitement and interest to encourage your target to read your promotion.

Telemarketing is often used to sell, meaning the callers follow a script and make a specific offer over the telephone.

The business environment is totally different.

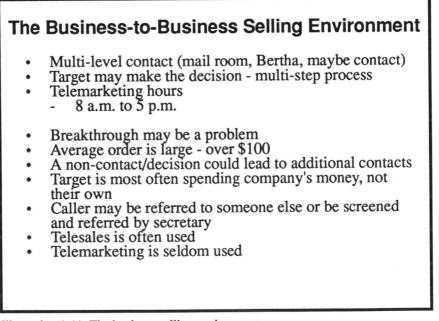

The Business-to-Business Selling Environment

- Multi-level contact (mail room, Bertha, maybe contact)
- Target may make the decision - multi-step process
- Telemarketing hours
  - 8 a.m. to 5 p.m.

- Breakthrough may be a problem
- Average order is large - over $100
- A non-contact/decision could lead to additional contacts
- Target is most often spending company's money, not their own
- Caller may be referred to someone else or be screened and referred by secretary
- Telesales is often used
- Telemarketing is seldom used

Illustration 1-11: The business selling environment.

Most business promotions will be seen by numerous people before they ever reach your target. Most businesses have mail rooms and receptionists responsible for directing communication to the appropriate target. Many business executives have professional screening personnel. Bertha Barrier's mission in life is to keep you and your communication away from her boss. Your creative approach will have to appeal to more than just your target. You have to first get the promotion through a series of screens before it is ever read by your target.

In many situations, your target may not be able to make the decision and there may be others involved. You may have to promote more than one person at the same time in the same company in order to affect a decision. In telephone selling, it is not unusual to have to make repeated calls to the same company before you connect with the appropriate decision-maker.

Because of the multi-level selling effort, your promotion may have a problem getting to your target and opened. Dimensional mailings, those of unusual size and/or shape, and first class business letters are often used to ensure breakthrough. Even before you make an offer to your prospect you have to sell a group of people to allow the offer to be delivered.

Most business decisions do not involve the prospect spending their own money. This makes the decision tougher because someone else will frequently scrutinize and question the value and quality of the decision. However, it is easier to get larger dollar sales because companies are less concerned with immediate cashflow and often purchase directly with no payment plan.

Telephone calling is done during business hours and often results in referrals to others within the company. It will take more attempts to reach the contact in the business arena. In addition, most telephone selling programs involve open dialogue telesales as opposed to fully scripted telemarketing.

The business selling environment is more difficult because of the multiple level contact and decision process. It is compounded by the inability to ensure that your target ever sees your promotion because of the natural screening done by most businesses. And the fact that most business people are not spending their own money tends to prolong the decision process and make it even more difficult.

But *well conceived and designed direct marketing does work in selling to other businesses*. This is particularly true where companies are developing and sustaining ongoing customer relationships. These relationships allow you to target promotions with several offers and ensure that they are received and read by your target. Most promotions will require more than one contact to present and get a decision about your offer.

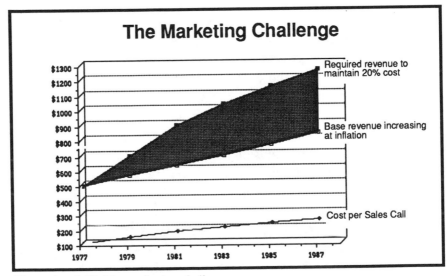

Illustration 1-12: The marketing challenge.

Things have really changed in the last few years and most of us are feeling tremendous pressure to improve selling productivity and reduce customer service expenses.

Illustration 1-12 shows the cost of the average sales call has been increasing dramatically during the last 10 years. If we assume an allowable selling expense of 20% of gross revenue, in 1977 you had to generate about $500 in revenue for each sales call made. As I mentioned earlier, in 1987 you had to generate about $1,250 in revenue to cover the $250 sales call.

If you examine the actual inflationary value of the 1977 revenue over the same 10 year period, the $500 in revenue was worth about $800 in 1987. The increased sales required to sustain the additional selling expenses have had to come from higher sales productivity.

The difference between the inflated 1977 revenue and the required 1987 revenue to cover the increased selling expense is the pressure we're all feeling. The shaded area has to be covered by increased productivity in order to maintain required profit margins.

Sales time was often taken for granted in the past. The expenses were fixed and it really didn't matter how a face-to-face salesperson spent their time. But the changing marketplace has forced most businesses to reexamine these misconceptions.

As we continue to change to a service based economy with more sophisticated workers, even greater pressure will be generated to increase sales productivity.

The cost of the sales call will continue to increase, forcing businesses to find less expensive alternatives to sell to smaller customers and to sell less expensive products. Direct marketing will become an even more important sales strategy.

Competition, especially foreign, will continue to restrict our ability to raise prices to cover additional expenses. We have to get better at everything we do. We especially have to find less expensive ways to sell and service customers. Again direct marketing may be the best alternative.

Sustaining your customer relationships may well be the key to your success in the future. The history of the relationship will require some form of database. The availability of desktop solutions now makes it possible for every company to build and maintain a marketing database independent of the data processing department.

Technology will continue to amaze us. Computer systems will become even smaller, less expensive and more powerful. We will see technology in every facet of our lives and our businesses. The good news is that technology may allow us to contain our costs and increase productivity. The downside is that technology has become an important ingredient of the products we sell and as its costs continue to decline, so do the available margin dollars.

As you look to direct marketing, and all of you need to examine this important channel of distribution, keep in mind how different business selling is when compared to selling to consumers. It is more difficult and more expensive to sell to other businesses.

Business lists are not as accurate as consumer lists because of inconsistent company names and addresses. The decision-maker is more difficult to establish and in most cases will need someone else's approval before making a buying decision.

Most direct marketing activity will have to go through several levels or layers before it finally reaches your target. Your creative approach will have to be designed to break through.

The pressure is definitely on! Those companies that deal with this pressure and find ways to reduce selling costs and improve customer service will succeed. Direct marketing may be your only alternative and that's what's really changed.

Chapter Two:

Business-to-Business Overview

Why use Lead Generation?

The cost of selling products and services has continued to increase unabated. The cost of making a face-to-face sales call has increased almost 300% in the last ten years. As indicated in Illustration 2-1, the average industrial face-to-face sales call costed $96.79 in 1979 and is estimated to cost over $250 in 1987. This information is no longer being published, but I estimate the cost in 1990 has probably exceeded $300.

This ever increasing cost has caused the business executive to examine alternative methods of delivering their sales message while still maintaining the personal contact afforded by the face-to-face sales call.

The escalating cost of the face-to-face sales call has been responsible for many new and exciting innovations in marketing in the last few years. Every business is examining alternative methods of

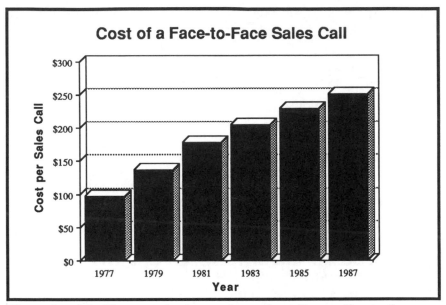

Illustration 2-1: The cost of a face-to-face sales call according to the McGraw Hill Laboratory for Advertising Performance.

identifying prospects and communicating their sales message in a mass sales situation. Well conceived lead generation programs are the ideal way to ensure message dissemination with management control before involving an expensive face-to-face contact.

Well conceived lead generation programs offer you an opportunity to ensure that your sales message is constant, of high quality, and is delivered when and where you desire to provide you with a business advantage. With a lead generation program you can ensure that the same message is given to a group of prospects and that there will be uniformity in the message delivered. Management gets to control and influence expectation levels directly with the prospect. Salespeople are only introduced to the highest quality sales opportunities.

Within lead generation you not only expand into new markets and reinforce your good standing with existing clients, you establish yourself as the authority and experienced supplier of solutions to business problems. By running a sustained lead generation effort you position yourself in the recipient's mind as a leader, decision-maker and "best contact" on the products promoted.

While lead generation efforts are not inexpensive to execute, they are much less expensive on a per call or per contact basis than one-on-one face-to-face sales calls. They should be designed as a step-by-step guide to the entire selling process.

Lead generation is a selling tool. Your goal is to sell more products and services to your current customers and add new customers. In the business-to-business arena, you should expect to spend over $100 per qualified sales lead. You could spend considerably more to promote and attract the proper person to buy your products or ser-vices. In return, you get your prospect's undivided attention for some amount of time, and you are assured that your message is pre-sented consistently.

Unfortunately, lead generation programs are the most difficult direct marketing efforts to execute. *No direct marketing program promis-es more and delivers less than lead generation.* And it is no wonder since, in many cases, novices to lead generation efforts are not even aware of the disciplines of direct marketing and how to measure and control the process. However, this book will give you the specific steps you need to know to make your lead generation program as effective as possible.

Direct Marketing Defined

There are many definitions for direct marketing. Many people con-fuse direct selling, like face-to-face calling, with direct marketing. Direct marketing is really everything exclusive of the face-to-face contact. I have simplified the definition into six understandable ele-

ments, described in Illustration 2-2. The first element of this definition explains that direct marketing is normally a part of a planned
marketing program and will often include a series of contacts.

The Definition of Direct Marketing

- **An organized and planned system of contacts**

- **Using a variety of media -- seeking to produce a lead or an order**

- **Developing and maintaining a database**

- **Measurable in costs and results**

- **Effective in all methods of selling**

- **Expandable with confidence**

Illustration 2-2:   A definition of direct marketing.

Direct marketing activity can employ various media forms but it
always seeks to produce a lead or an order. <u>Direct marketing will
call its identified target to perform some action.</u>

The creation and maintenance of a database is an integral aspect of
direct marketing. "Database" is perhaps the most misunderstood
and diversely defined word in business today. Data processing people have one definition, while direct marketers have their own
meaning.

As part of my simplified definition, I have adopted a definition
from *Direct Marketing Magazine* that is easy to understand.

Direct marketing will develop and maintain a database which:

- *Provides names of customers or prospects*
- *Is a vehicle for storing and measuring responses*
- *Is a vehicle for storing and measuring purchases*
- *Is a vehicle for continuing direct communication to the prospects, respondents and customers*

Let's examine each of the elements of this database definition and again differentiate business-to-business from consumer direct marketing.

- **A database provides names of customers or prospects.**

  People used to think that buying a mailing list was all that was necessary to create a database. The world has become more sophisticated, and technology allows us to do a much better job of building complete information repositories. The original mailing list is important and becomes a part of the database, but information involving the activity of that list is also essential.

  The U.S. consumer universe consists of over 240 million people in about 90 million households. The business world is not as easily counted. While it is safe to say that there are over 17 million business names in the U.S., each company may have several operating business names. Different company names and abbreviations for the same company complicate matters. For example, 3M Corporation has several identities:

  3M
  Three M
  Minnesota Mining and Manufacturing Company
  3M Company

3M Inc.
3M Corporation

These six identities for the same company do not include the seemingly endless name permutations on the divisional and subsidiary level. All of these company name variations make tracking a purchaser or a respondent much more difficult in the business-to-business universe. Addresses, executive names and phone numbers complicate the problem. Plus, list compilers each have different counts of businesses and business executives for the same type of business lists to be purchased.

As you can see a company may be a complex web of divisions and subsidiaries and purchasing decisions delineated in various ways. An extremely sophisticated database capable of tracking and reporting these relationships may be beyond your immediate grasp. But don't be daunted; always capture the information. It is still very difficult to maintain the hierarchy of business and who owns what, but as programming and hardware power advances you may need to establish the various relationships to target your offer to the appropriate universe. In fact, you're likely to need to reach both the decision makers and the influencers to sell your product or service, and you should start capturing that information immediately.

Business-to-business list management is more difficult than consumer list management. Business addresses may be 4, 5 or 6 lines long including internal 'mail stop' addresses. List selection by title - never a consideration in consumer list selection - can be tricky because an individual's title often carries different weight from company to company. By comparison, a consumer list normally has 3 line addresses and you can usually count on reaching the decision maker or key influencer.

- **A database is a vehicle for storing and measuring responses.**

Once you reach the target and get a response to your offer, create a record of that response and whether the prospect has purchased. The database should enable you to track each contact and each response.

Your customers have established a relationship with you and have a lower degree of fear, uncertainty and doubt (FUD). They know who you are, what you sell, and the quality of your products. More importantly, they have demonstrated a need for your products or services by purchasing in the past. The best source of additional business is former customers. Many companies forget that prospects who responded, but did not purchase from prior campaigns, are also excellent sources of additional business. They have established some relationship with you and should not be ignored.

In many lead generation programs the capturing of information stops with the response. It is difficult to get salespeople to cooperate and provide purchase information. Many managers become so frustrated with trying to capture purchase data that they simply "give up."

- **A database is a vehicle for storing and measuring purchases.**

Once prospects respond to a direct marketing program, you want to track their responses to see if they become buyers.

Direct marketing programs often use the initial response rate as the sole measurement criteria. Cost per respondent or lead, which is the effective measurement from initial response, is an important first part of the program's measurement criteria. By tracking and measuring the responses, cost per respondent or lead can be established. However, cost per respondent will not help you measure the *profitability* of your program. To evaluate the ultimate success of the program, you should measure the respondent through the entire sales cycle and determine the cost per order, average order size, and lifetime value.

When someone initially responds to a direct marketing program, it is referred to as the *front-end* of the program. The prospect has responded but whether they will actually purchase the product or service is still unclear. The **back-end** of the program refers to the conversion of a respondent to a buyer and a repeat buyer. In direct selling programs, where the response is actually an order, the front-end and back-end can be the same.

A program can seem attractive at the front-end in terms of cost per respondent. It may be a failure when the cost per order and average order size is reviewed.

• **A database is a vehicle for continuing direct communication to the prospects, respondents, and customers.**

The database should provide a sustained and complete ability to contact the:

a) Initial list of prospects
b) Respondents
c) Buyers

The need to track the status of each contact while measuring the results of each effort makes this process complicated.

Most companies rely on the salesperson to develop and maintain the company/customer relationship. There is limited information about customers and virtually no data about prospects. With this scenario, it is almost impossible to maintain sustained communication.

Direct marketing is measurable in both its costs and its results, (see Illustration 2-2). In the consumer universe, a buying decision usually occurs within one contact or call. A business-to-business transaction may have an *influencer* who selects a product, but a different person who makes the actual buying decision. The size of the expenditure can affect the length of time it takes to get a decision. This multilevel decision process often precludes a single contact from generating an order.

In lead generation programs, trying to establish buyers and cost per buyer can be very frustrating. Several factors affect this.

- The purchase may occur in the future.
- The respondent and the buyer may be different people.
- The name of the company that actually responds or buys can be difficult to track.

Direct marketing can serve in all methods of selling. In a retail setting, where the buyer seeks the seller, coupons and special offers can drive traffic into the retail center. Or a salesperson may use direct marketing as a lead generation vehicle in order to get a face-to-face appointment. Soliciting the prospects to buy through the telephone or mail, which is similar to the consumer mail order business, is another possibility.

One of the key benefits of direct marketing is that a successful technique can be expanded with confidence. Results should be predictable. If something worked before at a certain volume or rate, you should be able to get similar results, other factors being equal.

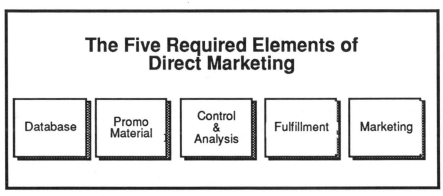

The Five Required Elements of Direct Marketing

| Database | Promo Material | Control & Analysis | Fulfillment | Marketing |

Illustration 2-3: The five elements of direct marketing.

Illustration 2-3 depicts the five basic functions or elements that must be controlled to effectively implement direct marketing.

*   **Database**

    We defined and discussed the elements of the database. A more detailed discussion will follow in Chapter 13.

*   **Promotional Material**

    Specialized promotional material that seeks to produce a response, either a lead or an order, is required. We have frequently seen programs in which technical specification material and brochures were redeployed for use in generating sales leads. This material was created as collateral to assist the field sales force; it was not designed to create a response, and is unlikely to do so.

A comment I often hear is, My business is different, I tried direct marketing, and it didn't work. When the prior attempts are examined, no effort to provide specialized promotional material is evident.

- **Controls and Analysis**

An effective direct marketing program measures both costs and results. Costs are usually pretty easy to monitor, but in the business-to-business environment it is surprisingly difficult to measure the results of the program.

The different company names and abbreviations make tracking difficult. It is not unusual to have a prospect fill out a response device while away from the office. They may or may not include their company name. If the company name is provided, it may be abbreviated or given differently than other names for the same company that are already on the list.

In several programs in which I participated, leads were given to the salespeople with company names listed and the orders were placed with different company names. The orders were actually placed through a leasing company and became impossible to link to the original lead.

The decision process frequently extends beyond the initial contact and the eventual order may not occur during the original time period designated by the campaign's planners. Lead programs in high technology industries can have selling cycles of months and years. Management wants to measure the success of the lead efforts in weeks, so the lead programs are never successful.

Frequently a company assigns purchasing agents. The respondent and the purchaser may be different people. This creates similar measurement problems to those I discussed earlier with different company names. Purchasing agents can further complicate the tracking process because ongoing direct marketing programs targeted to customers can be aimed at the wrong individual. The purchasing agent is normally told to place the order and may not have the money, authority, need, or desire for additional products or services.

Companies will often have different phone numbers for the corporate offices and the individual employees. Therefore, using a phone number as a controlling identifier will not work. Many companies use *direct-inward-dialing*. This service, available from your local phone company, will give people a direct line to their office that can still go through the company switchboard.

Companies have frequent changes in responsibility and a respondent today may not be the appropriate target tomorrow. This tends to be the most difficult problem in business marketing. It is worthwhile to retain title information on responses to help identify the appropriate target within the company as individuals move around.

It is possible to receive multiple responses from the same company that only generate one order. This can occur as purchase decisions are centralized and pooled to take advantage of volume discounts. Multiple influencers can also cause this to happen.

- **Fulfillment**

Delivering the offer made in the direct marketing promotion is called *fulfillment*. The ability to deliver your promise is key to successful direct marketing.

Providing fulfillment includes such simple yet essential steps as ensuring that the 800 number used in the promotion is answered. There have been situations where the advertising department forgot to notify the switchboard, customer service department, or outside service that a promotion had been run. You can imagine the way the incoming calls were handled.

Prospects might respond to your promotion and ask for additional information. Responding to this kind of inquiry is another form of fulfillment.

Sending leads to the salesperson and having them follow-up is, again, a form of fulfillment. This seems obvious enough, but in my experience, you can never assume anything when planning or instituting a lead generation program for a field sales force.

Within a true mail order operation, fulfillment involves shipping the product and handling billing, collections, returns, and inventory control.

- **Marketing**

Marketing has two distinct areas that must be addressed to ensure the success of direct marketing.

The first area to address in marketing is the integration of the direct marketing program into the existing marketing channel. This is the *tactical* use of direct marketing; how you will implement direct marketing with the current approach to selling.

The *strategic* use of direct marketing relates to the long term efforts and results that will be experienced.

Both the strategic and tactical ramifications of direct marketing should be evaluated and reviewed prior to beginning a direct marketing project.

A key to the success of the direct marketing effort is a complete and detailed business plan prior to the start of the project. You can't measure the success of a program if you're not certain of your objectives. This business plan should focus on each of the five elements of direct marketing.

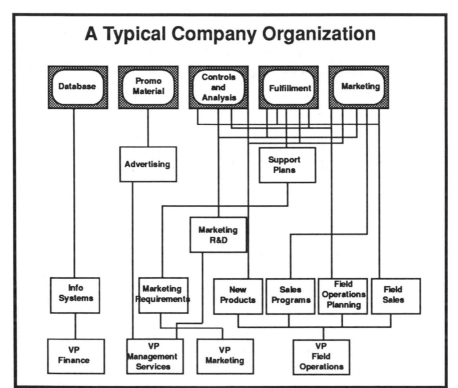

Illustration 2-4: A typical company and the organization that relates to the five elements of direct marketing.

Complete control over each element is required and you must have the ability to react to the changing business environment. In most businesses, the five elements report to different units of the organization and are controlled by managers and executives who are not directly involved in the direct marketing effort.

Look closely at Illustration 2-4 and you'll probably see shades of your own organization. With this 'spaghetti chart' organization, you tend to spend more time selling people internally than executing direct marketing. Plan a means to control these five elements of direct marketing prior to implementing a program.

The Universe

There are many definitions for the targets we are trying to reach with the direct marketing effort. Let's review the universe concept as it is pictured in Illustration 2-5.

Imagine the business-to-business universe as a funnel that you are viewing from above. The entire funnel is made up of suspects.

A *suspect* is no more than a business name. We understand that many businesses operate under more than one name; even an abbreviation of a name can be considered a different suspect.

Prospects comprise the next ring inside the funnel. A prospect is a suspect that meets your predetermined qualification criteria. You might want to include prospects in an ongoing marketing program. You probably only want to reach each establishment once, although it may do business under many different names. Your qualification criteria may also be specific to a certain decision maker or individual within the prospect's business.

Referrals are prospects of such high quality that you want to refer them to someone for immediate action. They form the next ring.

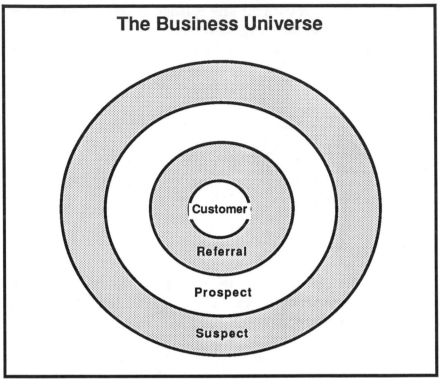

Illustration 2-5: A conceptual view of the business-to-business universe.

You may send the referral to a salesperson for disposition or try to generate an order immediately. In the past, I've found that the term 'lead' was used synonymously with referral. The referral term should not be confused with occasions when one prospect or customer refers you to another prospect or customer.

The *customer* is contained in the inner most ring and is the smallest group of the universe. This term describes individuals who have purchased products or services from you.

Most businesses spend a great deal of their resources attempting to locate prospects in the suspect universe (Illustration 2-6). In reality, each company should spend as little effort as possible on suspects and focus attention on:

1) Customers
2) Referrals
3) Prospects

An interesting point has been raised by some of my clients. Frequently, the individual responsible for implementing a direct marketing program has been instructed to eliminate customers and known referrals from the list. In the business-to-business arena, no computer program can eliminate all customers and active referrals from any list, due to the name variation problem. Some duplication and mistaken contacts are unavoidable.

I have graphically looked at the business-to-business universe as a funnel. As you know, as the neck of a funnel narrows, the pressure

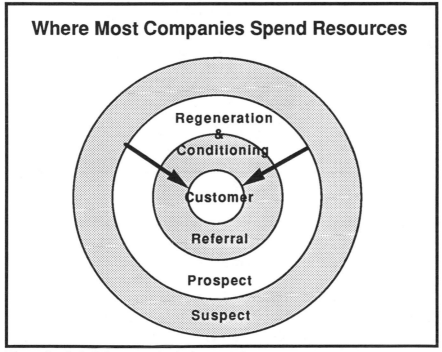

Illustration 2-6: Where most businesses spend resources.

increases. It is impossible not to get the rings towards the center of the funnel wet.

In other words, when designing a selective direct marketing program, anticipate that everyone will hear of your offer, not just a few.

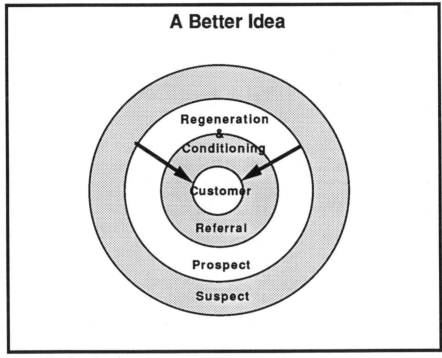

Illustration 2-7: Another way to generate customers.

A program that could have a negative effect on your customers and active referrals should be carefully evaluated. Direct marketing should generate a lead or an order, not hurt business.

When you attempt to eliminate certain names because of the impact direct marketing will have on selected groups, you're trying to avoid getting that group wet. You can restrict the offer to certain prospects or customers easier than you can eliminate their names. You should be able to explain or justify an offer that does not include your customers; it is not unusual to have special terms and conditions that restrict an offer from being used by certain people.

The Objective

Targets can fall into one of four categories (Illustration 2-8).

1) Prospects or suspects who are not qualified and not interested are relatively easy to eliminate from further activity. They will not respond to direct marketing contacts or advertising and require no further action at this time.

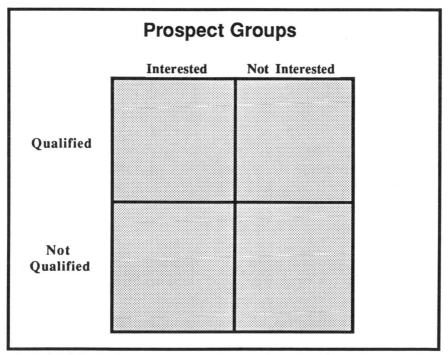

Illustration 2-8: Another way of looking at the business-to-business universe.

2) The not qualified yet interested group can be a terrible drain on resources if you are doing a lead generation program and sending the leads to a sales force for follow-up. These prospects tend to ask many questions with no intention to purchase the product or service you are offering. One of a sales manager's most difficult tasks is to ensure that sales people don't spend their time with this group. A salesperson has to deal with rejection all day long. This type of prospect is a false oasis in the desert of rejection. The prospect will talk to the salesperson and ask lots of questions, but rarely buy anything.

3) The not interested yet qualified prospect can be another big drain on resources. We often hear salespeople say they have found a great prospect. Which is a better place to spend time?

   a) Convincing a prospect who is interested in your product or service that they can actually use it; that is, taking the interested prospect and making them qualified.

   Or

   b) Convincing the prospect who is qualified that they *should be* interested in your product or service.

   Either situation is difficult and time consuming.

4) The group you need to work on is both qualified and interested in your product or service. We are all trying to find the qualified and interested prospect, the referral. You can apply our definitions to the four categories of prospects (Illustration 2-9).

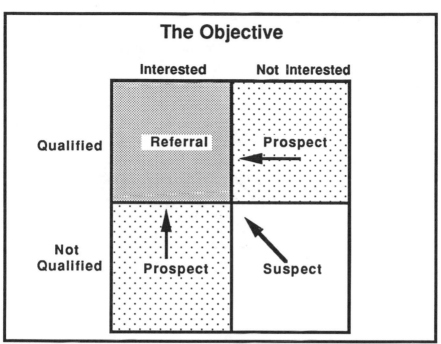

Illustration 2-9: The real objective of direct marketing.

The ideal situation is to expend your most expensive resource, sales-people, on the group in the upper left corner of the grid; the qualified and interested group. Cultivate the interested and not qualified group, and the not interested and qualified group, with various direct response promotional efforts that are less costly than a sales force. Develop a conditioning and regeneration program to move this group along through the sales cycle.

When a prospect becomes a referral, interested and qualified, the name should be turned over to the sales organization. The objective is to provide only referrals to the sales force. Bear in mind the other groups will provide future referrals. Your direct marketing program should convert these prospects into referrals.

The Buying Decision

People go through a number of steps when they decide to buy anything. Sometimes the buying decision is made very quickly and the prospect doesn't really understand the entire decision process. Focus on each step of the process to ensure you create an environment that will encourage your prospect or referral to purchase the product or service you are offering.

The buying decision can be visualized as a pyramid (Illustration 2-10). One of the cornerstones of the structure is Need. *Need* can be defined as a problem that a prospect has to address. For example, a

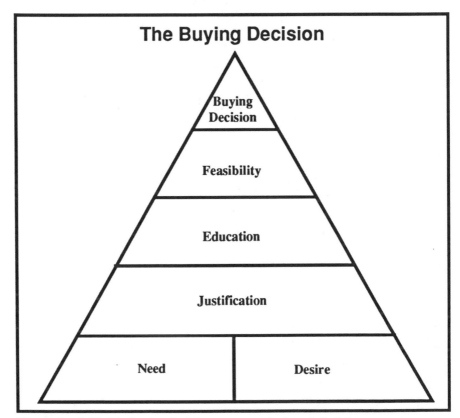

Illustration 2-10: The buying decision as created in the mind of the prospect.

prospect having difficulty generating invoices in a timely manner has a need for an invoicing system. The need is not for a particular product, but for a solution to a problem.

The other cornerstone of the buying decision is desire. Again, the desire is not for your product, but for a solution that will solve the problem or satisfy the need discussed earlier. In this case, the prospect wants to find a better way to invoice.

Once need and desire are established, your prospect must justify making a change to address the need. Justification is not always financial; emotion plays a very important role in the buying decision. Your prospect has to be assured that making a change is going to be worthwhile.

Your prospect will study various ways for meeting their need by examining solutions or various approaches. Thus far into the buying decision, the project has still not involved a specific vendor but has centered on how to solve a specific problem.

After your prospect understands their desire to fill a need, has justified making a change, and has researched alternatives, they must believe that making a change to meet their need is feasible within the environment. Will the change to meet the need adversely affect the company? Will the cure kill the patient?

Once your prospect has evaluated each element, they are prepared to make a buying decision. It may seem farfetched to expect each buying decision to be this complicated. The whole process may take only a few moments in the mind of your prospect. The order of activity may be different, but we all go through this process whenever we purchase anything.

It is after you make the buying decision that you select a vendor and a product. You may select product before vendor, but you always make the buying decision first. The following defines a process that prospects go through to make a purchase.

- **Decide to Buy**
  Need and interest must be established.

- **Select Vendor**
  Awareness, liking, and preference must be established.

- **Select Product**
  Need must be fulfilled and justified with the best possible solution.

Some direct marketing programs seem to be aimed at the vendor and product areas of the buying process. The assumption is that the prospect has already made the buying decision. In fact, most of the time, the material used in the direct marketing effort is all product oriented and isn't designed to produce a lead or an order. This is especially true in the technology product arena.

I believe it is always worthwhile to create or affirm the buying decision in all contacts. Need and desire are the cornerstones of the ultimate sale. Evaluate your existing mail pieces and advertising. See which of these areas you're addressing. You may be missing an important opportunity by not focusing on the buying decision.

Relationship Marketing

The pressure on businesses to find alternative methods for dealing with their business customers has increased substantially in the last decade. According to the latest McGraw-Hill statistics, the cost of an industrial face-to-face call has increased from around $97 in 1977 to over $251 in 1988. The Marketing Challenge (Illustration 2-11) shows that using a 20% cost of selling/marketing as an average percentage of gross revenue, reveals significant disparity between the rising cost of the sales call, and the revenue required to support that call.

In 1977 the revenue necessary to sustain the average sales call, assuming a 20% cost of selling, was less than $500. Today, more than $1,250 in revenue is required to support that same sales call using the 20% assumption criteria. Based on inflation, an order worth $500 in 1977, is worth about $800 today. The shaded area in Illustration 2-11 represents the *pressure* or disparity that businesses are faced with when selling to other businesses.

There are a number of ways to deal with this continuing problem.

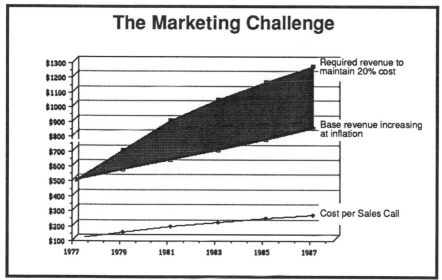

Illustration 2-11: The Marketing Challenge.

The easiest method is to increase prices to maintain profits. However, competitive pressures make it difficult to increase prices at a level high enough to offset the escalating costs of selling. Another more popular method, has been to curtail or abandon selling efforts to smaller customers, or for less expensive products.

As companies feel the pressure to address the escalating cost of sales, they begin to explore alternatives for selling to smaller customers and for selling less expensive products.   As Illustration 2-11 indicates, many companies cannot afford even one sales call to a customer who is spending less than $1,250.

Historically, it was the salesperson's responsibility to maintain the relationship with a company's customers. Successful salespeople maintain a vast inventory of information about their customers. Each sales representative maintains a file containing the historical relationship of his company and his customers. In fact, these files are handed down from one salesperson to another as territories or responsibilities change. In some cases, the salesperson's file is the most complete historical record available detailing the relationship between the customer and the company.

I've asked a number of salespeople in my seminars why they maintain extensive customer files. Here are some of their responses.

- I want a complete history of everything the customer has done with me, so I can understand how the customer thinks.
- My file contains letters, notes from calls, and copies of all orders, so I can reconstruct the activity between us.
- I don't trust my company to maintain files; they have lost orders and letters in the past.
- If I know all the activity that has transpired in the past, I can use that information to construct what I should do next.
- If I leave the company, I may want to market to my customers in my new job. A good customer file will give me a basis for future activity.

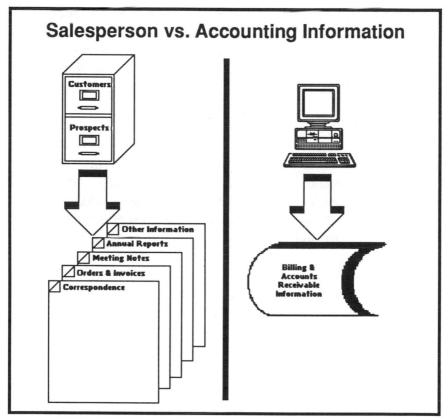

Salesperson vs. Accounting Information

Illustration 2-12: The salesperson's relationship file.

The answers run the gamut from security to opportunity. The under-lying reason for maintaining customer files is that salespeople know the key to selling is establishing and maintaining a relationship with their customers and prospects. The files document that sustained relationship.

Good salespeople will continue to maintain the history of their rela-tionships in their own files. The real question is: How can we, as companies, maintain the same historical record for all our cus-tomers? This question becomes more critical as we assess alterna-tive methods of dealing with various customer segments.

Some companies instruct their clerical staffs to develop and maintain complete customer files. Over time these files become too full and older information is often purged. In addition, these files often only contain contact information in which the customer initiated the contact. The file may not contain all contact initiated by the company.

It is quite common to have a customer file in accounting or administration detailing order and billing information. Another customer file in sales and marketing may contain correspondence and contacts with the customer. And still another customer file maintained by the salesperson has all the information above as well as notes and miscellaneous information the salesperson has developed concerning that customer.

The files maintained by accounting and sales administration will generally be well-organized and standardized. However, they will not be complete. The salesperson's files will be complete, but individualized by the salesperson making them difficult for someone else to use. There may be scarce information available about smaller customers.

It is interesting that there tends to be a direct relationship between how frequently a customer is contacted and how often they buy. The best customers are often those who have received the best sales and support services from the company.

As selling costs continue to grow, the number of customers that a company can afford to have salespeople call on will continue to decline. Smaller customers become too expensive to service with a salesperson. As a result, the historical record of the relationship with that customer, maintained by the salesperson, is lost.

It is almost a self-fulfilling prophecy that smaller customers remain small or even become non-customers over time. The company ultimately loses its relationship with these customers. Does this mean that businesses cannot afford to deal with smaller customers?

Not necessarily. Direct marketing, telemarketing, and telesales are ideal methods to sustain and enhance the relationship between a company and its customers; all customers, small and large. However, in business-to-business selling, some form of database will be required to record and identify the marketing relationships.

Traditional consumer selling is frequently a one-shot approach. That is, the company makes an offer for a product, and does or does not sell the product. Often, there is no need or desire to maintain a sustained relationship with the customer. Like retail selling, the consumer marketer will attempt to drive a new customer for each order. Because of the relatively large size of the consumer universe, it is both reasonable and affordable to drive a new customer for each order.

Business marketers can't afford to regenerate new customers for each order. Most businesses are selling to a limited universe, which tends to be relatively small. The best opportunity for a company is to establish long term relationships with their customers.

Some form of database is necessary to sustain the relationship in business-to-business marketing. This database can be as simple as the sales files described earlier. It doesn't always have to be executed on a large mainframe computer and cost hundreds of thousands of dollars. Earlier I stated that a direct marketing database will:

- Contain the names, addresses, titles, and phone numbers of contacts you want to reach via direct mail, telephone or some other direct marketing format.
- Have the capability to record all responses.
- Have the capability to record all purchases.

- Provide the capability to sustain communication and selling activity for all names on the database and record each contact.

This is done by the salesperson in his desk file. It just makes good business sense to develop a history of the relationship between a company and its customers. Unfortunately, as the company grows, the ability to maintain a manual database becomes impossible. And, because most companies have data processing report to the financial area of the company, computerized databases for marketing purposes become a low priority.

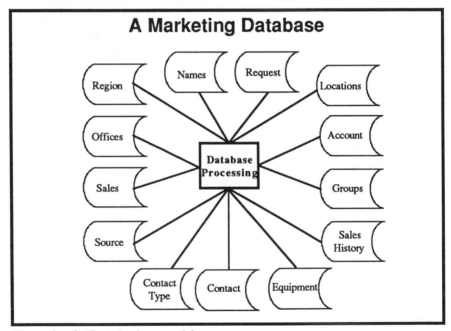

Illustration 2-13: A database model.

The direct marketing database can become very complex, as there are a large number of data elements related to the selling process. Illustration 2-13, identifies some of the tables in one database model.

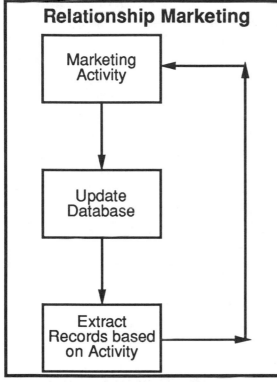

Relationship Marketing

Marketing Activity

Update Database

Extract Records based on Activity

Illustration 2-14: Relationship Marketing.

This is not to suggest that each company develop such a sophisticated database immediately. However, every business selling to other businesses should plan to develop a complete marketing database over time. It should not suspend any current marketing efforts to enhance general customer relationships for the sake of database development. It should be evolutionary.

Recently, a number of effective, inexpensive and easy-to-use computerized database programs have become available that allow the marketing and sales department to use personal or desktop computers to satisfy their database needs. These programs make it relatively easy to implement the database described above. Armed with a marketing database, whether manual or fully automated, relationship marketing can be expanded to include all customers.

As you'll note from Illustration 2-14 the results of one marketing activity should trigger the next marketing activity. The ongoing transactions in the relationship should control the ongoing marketing activity.

When a marketer knows all the products purchased by a customer, they can design a direct mail program or telesales program in which those customers are periodically contacted and solicited for additional sales based on what they have purchased in the past. Direct mail can be personalized and created via a word-processing system. Telesales contacts can be made which review prior activity and develop new needs based on the relationship. The customer can be made to feel like they are receiving personal attention. The 'relationship' is being sustained.

All customers can be scored based on the recency of their last purchase, how often they purchase and the total sales dollars expended. This *RFM* (recency, frequency and monetary) approach can be used to identify the best selling opportunities and periodic contact schedules can be established. For example, based on purchase history, the marketer can schedule each customer to receive a contact monthly, bi-monthly, quarterly, semi-annually, or annually. Telesales or telemarketing, as well as face-to-face selling, can be used to create a 'personal' contact.

In a recent project with a company that identified the need to focus on enhancing its customer relationships, all sales were made using telesales. Each customer was scored (A,B,C and D), and a planned contact level was identified for each category. Telemarketing and direct mail were used to enhance the relationship, but telesales was used as the fundamental selling channel. The company was able to double its sales and, as importantly, double the number of customers purchasing annually by simply increasing the contact level. The company focused on enhancing its relationship with its customers.

Business-to-business catalogs and telephone selling seem to be the most frequently used formats for dealing with smaller customers and lower average order sizes. These are effective approaches to continuing the concept of relationship marketing and they should enjoy continued success. Both formats capitalize on the customer relationship that has developed over time.

Another format that should be explored is a direct marketing newsletter. This newsletter has the ultimate objective of selling products and services. It shouldn't contain pictures of buildings and information about the personnel of the business. The newsletter should help the customer understand additional benefits they can derive by using the company's products and services. Most importantly, it should continue to ask the customer to order throughout the document. You may also want to consider using the newsletter as a mini-catalog followed by periodic telesales.

Database has become the most used and probably the most misunderstood term in marketing and direct marketing. In marketing, a *database* is the structure for storing and controlling the relationship information between a company and its customers. Obviously, the term has other meanings when used by data processing or administrative personnel.

Relationship marketing is not a new concept; successful salespeople have used it for years. What has changed is the cost of having salespeople deal with customers, the availability of high technology tools to enhance the sales relationship, and the increased level of competition forcing better relationships for business survival. Telesales and telemarketing are the ideal vehicles to enhance and sustain the relationship at an affordable cost-per-contact. The very survival of a business depends on its ability to enhance and sustain customer relationships.

Relationship marketing, and the increased costs of having a salesperson contact customers and prospects, is the driving force behind the phenomenal growth of telephone selling.

Business-to-Business Overview Summarized

So far I have reviewed the major distinctions between consumer and business direct marketing. Throughout the remainder of this book I will frequently contrast specific differences in marketing between these two universes. The fundamental differences in the two marketplaces are the accessibility of the prospect, and their financing or money sources.

Some definitions and concepts in direct marketing have also been established. Direct marketing has five basic elements and you must control all to succeed. The five elements -- database, promotional material, controls and analysis, fulfillment, and marketing -- were described in detail and will be covered at length throughout this book.

The business universe was defined and consists of four major groups:

- Suspects
- Prospects
- Referrals
- Customers

I defined these major groups and then explained the objectives of direct marketing.

The buying decision was explained - how prospects evaluate and ultimately decide on purchasing products. Central to this discussion is my belief that communications to the business universe should address the buying decision as well as vendor and product selection.

Finally, the concept of relationship marketing and improving customer sales was discussed in detail. Telemarketing and telesales are ideal ways to enhance and improve customer relationships. Some form of a database is required to use relationship marketing.

Throughout the remainder of this book, the focus will be on practical concepts that you can implement immediately. I'll use actual examples and case studies to illustrate my point. This chapter is my way of establishing common ground and definitions that will act as a foundation for other concepts and techniques.

Chapter Three:

Lead Generation Programs

Real World

As I said earlier, generating sales leads for a field sales force may be the most frustrating direct marketing program to launch. As the direct marketing manager, usually you have no control over the ultimate success of the project and it's almost impossible to measure the results. Let's see how you can increase your chances for success.

Virtually every business-to-business direct marketing professional can tell war stories of attempted lead generation projects that were never continued because the program's results couldn't be measured. The reason lead programs can be difficult to measure is due to not understanding the environment. We, the communications and direct marketing departments, perceive our mission to be to help the sales force by generating sales leads. Yet, the field organization frequently has a different perception of our role. They feel it's "the staff at headquarters, in their ivory towers" versus "the field force, where the rubber meets the road." If you examine the field's side of the story, their perception is often partially accurate.

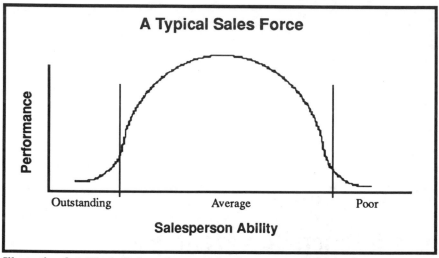

Illustration 3-1: The bell-shaped curve as it relates to a typical sales force.

Most lead generation program failures occur due to one or two fatal flaws. First, in many instances, the direct marketing program is designed with little or no input from the field sales force. As a result the field feels suspicious, distrustful and downright hostile. They think we have only encumbered them with additional reporting requirements and a lot of paperwork and supposed leads whose value has not been explained.

Second, lead generation programs are often designed for the outstanding performers of the sales force. We ask this group to qualify and sell the lead and then report back on the success of the lead program. This poor targeting has probably done more damage to lead programs than any other factor.

Why? The performance of a sales organization will normally fall into a bell-shaped curve, similar to Illustration 3-1. The left end of the curve, the outstanding salesperson, needs little or no help. However, if sent leads, this group is most likely to follow-up and even generate orders. They are not at all threatened by outside help and support.

The right end of the curve, the poor salesperson, wants help but has trouble accepting it. They are threatened and constantly look for excuses. Their excuse for failure will be directed at the poor leads we are sending to them.

The group in the middle, the average salesperson, is where your program should be targeted. If you can move this group to the left, even a small amount, you can have a dramatic impact on the success of your company.

My goals in this chapter are to explain the elements involved in a lead generation program and to pose the one question you have to answer to make a lead program successful.

The Use of Sales Time

The statement, "the only real resource we have in business is time," could not be more appropriately applied than in sales. The effective use of time is the key to the salesperson's success. The more time the salesperson has in front of a prospect or customer, the better the odds of making a sale.

Sales managers have to be very selective when they require the sales force to perform functions that take them away from contact with prospects or customers.

IBM measures their entire field force at least annually to determine how time is being used. The results are used to determine what resources are needed for products and services and how the organization might be improved. In 1979, it was discovered that only 33% of work time was being spent face-to-face with customers. It was alarming to find that two-thirds of the sales force's time was being spent in non-customer related activities.

This situation sounds extreme. Yet, you may be surprised to learn
that within your own company your sales force may actually spend
only half their time in front of customers. Vacations, holidays and
personal time off probably take more than one month out of every
year away from available time to sell. Consider the sales contests
and travel awards you run and you probably lose another week or
two. Education and product training time also take away selling
time from the sales force. Factor in the weekly sales meetings, and
time devoted to writing reports and special projects and it is easy to

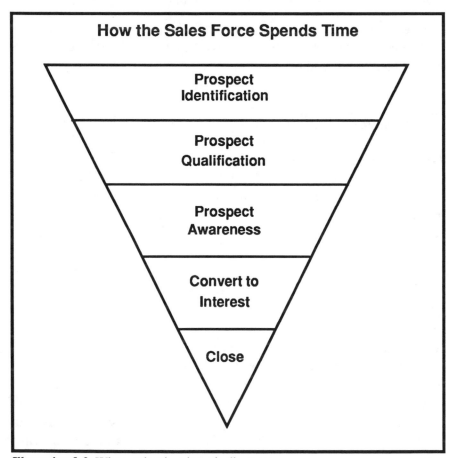

Illustration 3-2: Where sales time is typically spent.

see how as much as 50% of available selling time can be lost. In almost every situation I have been involved in the salespeople spend less than 50% of their time actually selling to customers and prospects.

As I mentioned earlier, the cost of making a face-to-face sales call has continued to increase virtually unabated. I estimate it to be around $300 and the $400 sales call isn't that far away. It is the rare situation I have been involved in that doesn't have a sales call cost over $300. Let me demonstrate:

Average annual earnings per salesperson	$50,000
Multiplier to include general and administrative expenses as well as support and other selling expenses.	3
Total cost per salesperson (multiplier x earnings)	$150,000
Average selling days per year	220
Average number of calls per day	2
Total calls per year (calls x days)	440
Cost per sales call (Total cost ÷ Total calls)	$340.00

I'll explain how you can arrive at your cost per sales call in more detail in Chapter 4. As you can see, it is not difficult to have a face-to-face sales call cost over $300.

When you couple this high cost with how little time salespeople actually spend in front of customers and prospects, Illustration 3-2 becomes even more meaningful. This diagram illustrates that most selling time is spent finding qualified prospects and making them aware of your offerings.

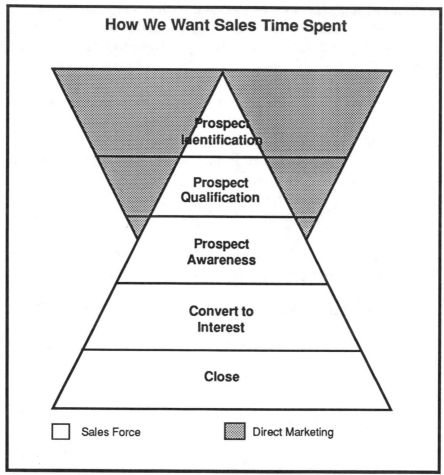

Illustration 3-3: Where we would like sales time spent.

Your objective is to invert the way sales time is spent to correspond with Illustration 3-3. Direct marketing should be used to move the prospect through the identification, qualification, awareness and interest stages. Of course the salesperson will not be completely eliminated during these stages, but their involvement should be reduced substantially.

If this is such a simple concept, why then isn't it happening naturally? Any salesperson will readily agree that prospect identification and qualification isn't something they like to do. The sales force would prefer to have these functions done for them. Why then do we have such a difficult time implementing lead generation programs with the sales force?

No one has a complete answer to this difficult question. I speculate that the sales force doesn't believe that anyone can perform this function as well as they do and their performance is ultimately based on new leads. They don't trust anyone else to do their job, especially staff generalists who don't have regular contact with the field. Also, often their prior experience with leads hasn't been good. Finally, the sales force typically creates the time to perform the identification and qualification phases. If the sales force had an adequate and ongoing supply of highly qualified referrals, their opinions and work habits might change. This is not a short-term problem with short-term answers.

Lead Generation Questions

As you begin to plan your lead generation program, you will need to resolve a number of critical questions. Illustration 3-4 identifies the six major issues.

1) What is a good lead?

Some of the experiences I had in designing a lead program at IBM will probably sound familiar to you.

The lead program was a test to support 90 salespeople in five branch offices. The salespeople were responsible for selling new account, first time users of computer systems. During the design phases of the project, we brought 16 of

Lead Program Questions to Resolve

1) What is a good lead?

2) How many leads are enough?

3) Which is worse -- no leads or too many?

4) How do you track leads?

5) What about turnover?

6) How do you get feedback?

Illustration 3-4: The six major issues involved in a lead generation program.

the salespeople together to get their opinions on several issues.

The 16 salespeople were asked to define what they felt to be a good lead. I wrote the definitions on charts as the salespeople gave their requirements. When we were finished there were 21 different definitions of a good lead.

It is intriguing that while the success of any lead program will ultimately be judged by the quantity and quality of the leads generated, we have yet to get a group of salespeople to agree on the definition of a good lead. On only one point do they agree: A good lead is one that closes. As direct marketers, salespeople feel we should be able to foretell that a specific lead will purchase a product or service.

Later, we will discuss some issues you need to address to establish the quality of a sales lead. During the IBM planning session, we ultimately agreed that a good lead was one that would specifically answer the following questions based on the sales group's predetermined qualifications:

- Were they evaluating a computer, bookkeeping machine or word processing equipment within the next 12 months?
- When were they planning to acquire the system?
- How many clerical people did they have?
- Had they added any clerical personnel in the last 12 months?
- Did they anticipate adding clerical people in the next 12 months?
- Did they have an Accounts Receivable problem?
- Did they have an Inventory Control problem?

Any prospect who was evaluating a product in the next 12 months was considered a lead and sent to the sales force. The salespeople had determined that they wanted an opportunity to sell any prospect who was in the process of product evaluation. This was a serious flaw in the structure of this program and will be discussed later.

2) How many leads are enough?

This question is also very difficult to get a consensus opinion from the sales force. They all agree that marketing should just send them the sales leads and they will handle them.

The same group of IBM salespeople originally said that they wanted as many as 20 leads per day. I had discussed with them our plan to use direct mail and telemarketing to generate the leads. Our plan was to give them their required number of leads every day. This was a new concept to the sales force; they had never experienced a sustained and ongoing flow of leads.

The sales force I was dealing with was selling computer products at a starting price of $14,000. It took at least three sales calls to sell the product. Given 20 leads per day, each salesperson would have to make 20 follow-up calls to qualify the lead and schedule an appointment. If each phone call took only five minutes, the sales force had just signed up for almost two hours of telemarketing every day. And this estimate assumes every dialing would result in a completed call which is totally unrealistic. We were able to convince the sales force to take only three sales leads per day.

This ultimately proved to be about three times as many leads as the salespeople could handle. A lot of the problems associated with the leads really tied back to our definition of a good lead. In a 90-day period, we generated over 12,000 leads.

The correct number of leads is directly related to the quality of follow-up required and the number of orders you want to generate as a result of the lead program. I will discuss in Chapter 4 the key to the success of any program is the expectation level. You'll never be able to completely replace the identification and qualification functions of the sales force. In the beginning, you should anticipate that only a small portion of the salesperson's business will come from the lead program. As the program gains credibility, you can expect a higher contribution from the leads.

3) Which is worse -- No leads or too many?

I have constantly asked this question of direct marketing executives and sales executives alike. The answers seem to follow a pattern.

The sales executive, sales manager, and salesperson always answer that no leads are the worse alternative. The sales force only wants an opportunity to sell; they never think about the issue of being unable to follow up on a lead. A lead to a salesperson means a potential order, and that is all they consider.

On the other hand, the direct marketer knows it's almost impossible to measure the results of a lead program. Generating excess leads only complicates the problem.

In addition, when you send too many leads to the sales force, all the leads become poor quality. The sales force can't handle the volume, therefore the leads can't be that good. Too many leads is normally a turn off to the sales organization. They perceive all the leads to be of lower quality and tend not to follow up, or they screen the leads and follow up selectively. This type of program tends to be non-recoverable; you can't expect the sales force to ever accept the leads positively in the future.

A final point about too many leads: a prospect who has been promised that a salesperson will call, expects to be contacted. When you fail to follow up, how do you think this prospect feels about your company and products? Quite probably they will be upset and may never do business with you. We call the concept of sending too many leads to follow up "poisoning your universe."

Obviously, the right number of leads is the amount on which the sales force can consistently follow up. No leads, although probably better from a direct marketing point of view, will yield no business. Too many leads can destroy the opportunity for the direct marketing program to succeed.

4) How do you track leads?

Within this issue are a number of points that need special attention for a successful generation program.

- **There must be specific objectives.**

    Lead programs frequently fail because of unrealistic expectations. For example, only a portion of the leads will actually be followed up and only a portion of the leads followed up will actually buy.

    My experience indicates you can expect only about 30% of the leads that are generated to be followed up. This sounds somewhat absurd, but nevertheless it's true. Salespeople will attempt to reach a prospect and if they are unable to contact the individual after several attempts, they will move on to someone else.

    In the best of programs I am surprised to receive a 60% follow up rate. I have seen follow up levels below 10%.

    Only a certain amount of leads actually followed up will buy. Perhaps you're expecting 25% of the leads to close. With excellent cooperation from the sales force you get 60% follow up. That means you will actually achieve 15% of the leads closing.   Not a bad program, but if you expected 25% to close, the program will be perceived as a failure.

    You must get everyone involved in the program to agree on very specific objectives .

- **There must be commitment.**

  Once you've established reasonable expectations for the lead program, everyone involved needs to commit to the project. Frequently, the direct marketer is behind a project, but sales and sales management haven't truly signed up. Only when everyone involved in the project agrees to meet specific expectations and responsibilities does the effort stand a chance to succeed.

  Commitment to the lead program must begin with the salesperson, and continue all the way up to the V.P. of sales. The best situation is to have the sales organization involved in the design of the program. The more the program belongs to them, the higher the odds for success.

  The lead program cannot succeed without feedback on the quality of the leads and how they can be improved. If management and the sales force aren't committed to giving feedback and helping to track the leads, the program will fail.

- **The system must be heuristic.**

  Heuristic means to teach yourself and to learn from experience. With specific agreement to realistic objectives, commitment to follow up the leads and provide feedback, the program can become heuristic. As you learn about the quality and quantity of the lead program, you can use the feedback to improve and make the program better. Similar to the computer in the movie *War Games*, the lead system can continue to learn from itself.

These issues truly affect our ability to track and understand the results of the lead generation program. Before you start the project, the issue of tracking the results needs to be resolved.

When we looked back on the IBM program, we ultimately made substantial changes because we didn't originally antici-pate these issues. However, we constantly had to return and resell management on why the project needed to be contin-ued and expanded. I wish I could say that these experiences were unique, but unfortunately, almost every lead program I've encountered suffers from the same problem.

5) What about turnover?

The real question is: What happens to your leads when the salesperson leaves? In most programs we've reviewed, the leads leave with the salesperson. It is not uncommon for sales representatives to keep copies of leads or enter the lead information into a computerized database.

Leads are expensive. After the lead has been followed up only once, it has become downright valuable. You probably have invested $300 to $500 in each lead. Part of designing your lead program must address the inevitable turnover within the field force and what will happen to the leads.

6) How do you get feedback?

As I mentioned earlier, feedback is one of the most critical elements in the ultimate success or failure of the lead pro-gram. The design of the lead document can radically affect the feedback of the program.

Lead Qualification Reporting

Disposition Codes

1) Actively working - prospect has agreed to further contacts.
2) Prospect not handled by this location.
3) Prospect referred to another location.
4) Prospect ordered.
5) Already a customer.
6) Prospect rejected us:
   a) They are too small
   b) We are too expensive
   c) We are not competitive
   d) Performance
   e) Deferred decision
   f) Satisfied with current
   g) Other
7) Prospect wants to be deleted from our files.
8) Prospect bought competition within the last year.
9) Unable to contact the prospect within the last 30 days.
10) Other - _____
    _____

Lead Quality Analysis

Likelihood to buy
1) Definitely will buy
2) Probably will buy
3) Uncertain
4) Probably won't buy
5) Definitely won't buy

Likelihood to buy from you
1) Definitely will buy
2) Probably will buy
3) Uncertain
4) Probably won't buy
5) Definitely won't buy

Timing to buy
1) Immediate
2) Less then 3 months
3) Less then 6 months
4) Less then 1 year
5) One year or more
6) Probably won't

☐ **Disposition Code**

☐ **Likelihood to buy**

☐ **Likelihood to buy from you**

☐ **Timing to buy**

Illustration 3-5: A typical lead quality reporting mechanism.

For example, the lead document must be easy for the sales-person to return, and since many sales reps work out of their briefcases or cars, copying the document can pose a problem. To facilitate analysis, once the document is returned, you may want to establish a coding plan to enable the sales-person to quickly identify the quality of the lead.

At IBM we established several questions with coded answers that allowed us to evaluate the lead and recognize any additional activity required to help convert the lead to an order. Illustration 3-5 depicts the reporting system I designed. Unfortunately, I had to change the salesperson's lead form three times to include this system. It is always difficult to change a program after it has started. By antici-pating how you'll receive feedback about the lead, you can avoid problems in the future.

The lead form I used was made up of four-part carbonless paper. The salesperson only had to fill in the appropriate codes and return the copies to the lead generation center. All the lead information was included on the form but the sales-person was asked to update outdated information. We antic-ipated giving the salesperson and the sales manager a copy of the lead, and the carbonless form made that task easy. As we all know, computers aren't sold on the first sales call. We provided an extra copy to report the initial call disposition and the final disposition of the lead. We even provided a binder with tabs to make territory organization easier.

The feedback on lead quality is as important as the lead gen-eration itself. Most times this is an area that is overlooked. You can't measure and control a program without informa-tion on the lead and the effectiveness of the program.

Lead Quality

Every salesperson has a different definition of a good lead. They rarely agree on criteria and have a difficult time expressing what qualities constitute a qualified lead.

To establish what makes a lead qualified, you must consider four categories. These categories are especially helpful if you're going to use telemarketing to qualify the lead prior to making a sales call.

As an aside, one of the problems in using telemarketing is the ease in which you can get additional information. Often people confuse lead generation and market research when performing the lead qualification process. Always ask yourself whether the information you're requesting is really necessary to establish if a prospect is qualified as a sales lead.

The major categories to use in lead qualification are :

Money
Authority
Need
Desire

As you may notice, the first letter of each word spells MAN with a D. This is a convenient way to remember the four qualification areas. It also spells DAMN!

Hopefully, if the prospect is interested in your product or service, they can afford to purchase from you. In reality, there are three areas that can help financially justify almost any business decision:

1) *Displaceable Expenses*: Dollars already being expended for similar or like services. You may find displaceable expenses

in related areas of the business, as well as in the primary area you're trying to address.

2) *Avoidable Expenses*: Dollars that the company can avoid having to spend in the future, if they buy your solution.

3) *Increased Revenue and Business Growth*: Dollars that the company might generate due to better procedures or approaches to their business. This area is often addressed as intangible. Many business decisions are made on emotion based on the intangible value to be derived. For example, a computer that allows instant access to order status will improve customer satisfaction and service. It is very difficult to attribute savings or revenue to improved customer service. However, we cannot overlook these 'intangibles' as a primary justification.

As you try to establish the ability of a company to buy your solution, don't get bogged down with unnecessary details. Sometimes it's nice to have additional facts, but they don't really improve the quality of the lead. Sales managers often forget that the salesperson will generate their own level of information. You invest too much time getting unnecessary details just to qualify the sales lead.

Authority is often difficult to establish. It is tough to determine if the person to whom you're trying to sell has the authority to buy from you. Ego being what it is, some business people cannot admit to people outside their own company that they have limited power. Lead quality normally suffers the most in this area. Many techniques can be tried to subtly establish buying authority. However, the best method is to ask the prospect directly if they can make the decision to buy your product or service.

Establishing need is the area we all tend to over complicate. Try to limit your questions and probes to one or two major criteria. Keep in mind that you're trying to qualify a sales lead that will be followed up by a salesperson. The salesperson will sell the product or service. Many companies perform too much market research under the guise of trying to determine prospect need. In most situations, the salesperson will want to establish the information and probably ask the same questions again.

Finally, a lead isn't qualified until the prospect has accepted the offer and agreed to see a salesperson. During the IBM program, we initially sent a prospect's name to the sales force when the prospect indicated plans to acquire a machine in the next 12 months. The prospect did not indicate any desire to talk to the salesperson. Obviously, when the salesperson called, the prospect wasn't certain of the purpose of the call. The quality of the lead was immediately questionable in the mind of the salesperson.

The whole process of establishing lead quality should be started on a blackboard with the salespeople. Write the four major categories on the board and ask the sales force what one single question in each area, if answered, would help to confirm the quality of the lead. You'll ultimately get more than one question. To eliminate the other questions, try to determine if the information is absolutely necessary to establish the qualification of the lead.

You can sometimes resolve the money, authority, and desire issues with one question that introduces the price of your product and an offer. Prospects may respond that they can't afford it or that they have to talk to someone else before deciding. Remember, a prospect isn't qualified unless they agree to become a referral.

The Sales Attitude

Illustration 3-6 lists the traits that make up a good salesperson. As sales managers, these are the characteristics we look for when hiring a salesperson. These traits are common in the successful salesperson.

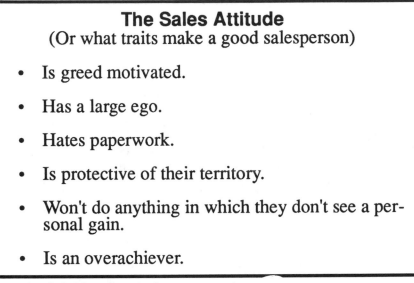

The Sales Attitude
(Or what traits make a good salesperson)

- Is greed motivated.

- Has a large ego.

- Hates paperwork.

- Is protective of their territory.

- Won't do anything in which they don't see a personal gain.

- Is an overachiever.

Illustration 3-6: The sales attitude.

Every sales manager has their own opinion regarding the characteristics desirable in the perfect salesperson. The list in Illustration 3-6

The Definition of Direct Marketing

- An organized and planned system of contacts

- Using a variety of media -- seeking to produce a lead or an order

- Developing and maintaining a database

- Measurable in costs and results

- Effective in all methods of selling

- Expandable with confidence

Illustration 3-7: The definition of direct marketing.

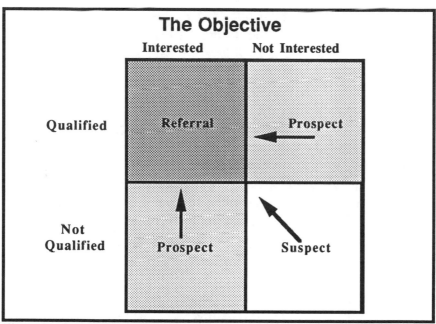

Illustration 3-8: The real objective of direct marketing.

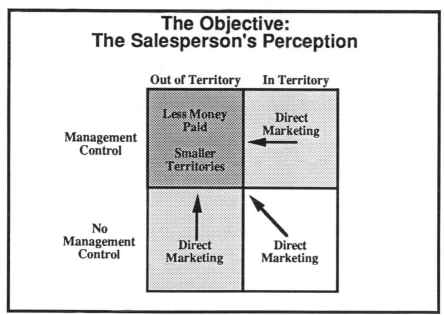

Illustration 3-9: The salesperson's perception of direct marketing.

reflects the characteristics mentioned by sales managers I have interviewed. The real issue is the difference between the actual definition of direct marketing (see Illustration 3-7) and the salesperson's attitude toward it.

Generalizations are always dangerous, but bear in mind the target is the center of the bell curve, the average salesperson. The sales attitude is built around a very large, yet fragile ego. It is hard for salespeople to accept that you can find a prospect in their territory that they didn't already know about. Your requirement to track the lead and determine its quality goes directly against the key elements of the sales attitude. An individual who hates paperwork, is protective of their territory and does nothing unless it produces a personal gain, is not likely to help you measure and control the lead program.

Direct marketing people and salespeople have very different views on the objectives of direct marketing. The grid in Illustration 3-8 shows how direct marketing views its mission. Now review Illustration 3-9 to see how the salesperson views the same objective.

The salesperson is not that far from wrong. Direct marketing's objective is to reduce the cost of selling. We want salespeople to spend more time in better selling opportunities. Clearly, part of the direct marketing program is to sell the sales staff on this objective.

The sales attitude can seriously affect the success of the direct marketing program. Without statistics, we will never be able to measure the success of the project. When you design the lead generation program, you should consider how the salesperson will perceive your efforts.

Lead Management

You must design your system to get information to measure and track leads. Over the years, many systems have been created and refined to generate information about lead disposition. It seems that every company initially goes through the same process. Illustration 3-10 shows the typical lead tracking approach.

The key element is the chastisement of the sales organization when the lead information isn't returned. This is especially difficult if more leads were generated than the sales organization could follow-up. The more pressure that is put on the organization to return the lead information, the more likely the data will be inaccurate.

Here's a typical scenario: The pressure is applied to the sales force to return the lead information. The sales force reacts to the pressure by taking all the leads and coding them as bad leads.

Lead management is frustrating and difficult. Many companies give up and send leads without any attempt to measure the results. In fact, the Direct Marketing Association's Business-to-Business Council conducted a survey in 1979, 1980 and 1981 to determine direct marketing effectiveness. The full survey is available in the DMA Fact Book and can be purchased from the Direct Marketing Association. Illustration 3-11 lists two of the questions which indicate typical lead measurement and follow-up.

Most of the time, when direct mailing to prospects, objectives are not set. And measurement is even less likely. The typical tracking system is only used in less than 50% of the leads generated. Remember that this survey represents a group of people who have tried to measure, and who have learned the harsh realities of trying to forward and track leads to a reluctant sales force.

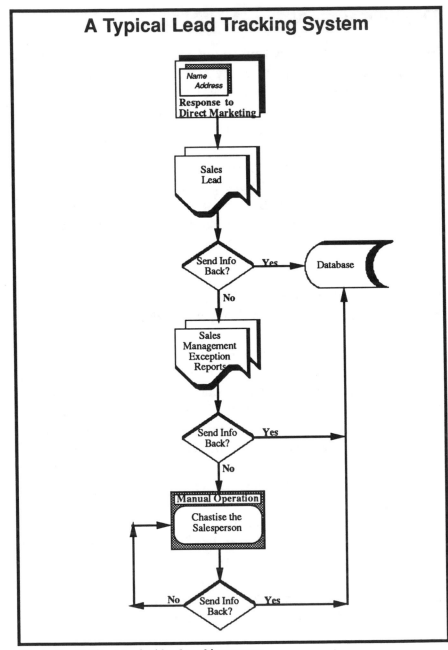

Illustration 3-10: A typical lead tracking system.

	1979 Office Equip Manufacturers	1980 Printing Industry	1981 Wholesale Durable Goods
Business/Industrial Council Research - 1986 Fact Book			
How frequently do you set objectives when mailing to prospects?			
Rarely	16.6%	27.8%	30.7%
Never	30.2%	27.7%	30.6%
Do you measure conversion of leads into actual sales?			
Yes	-	43.3%	27.3%
No	-	55.8%	72.7%

Illustration 3-11: Two questions from the market research survey conducted by the Business Industrial Council of the Direct Marketing Association.

We encourage people to continue to work with the sales force on measuring lead quality. However, you might consider also asking the *prospect* what finally happened. Illustration 3-12 indicates an approach that could give you the lead quality information you require.

It may be hard to believe, but when this approach has been used we have found less than 50% of the leads generated were ever followed up by the sales force. This really isn't a condemnation of the sales force, but a reflection on the reality of the environment. If more sales leads are generated than can be followed up, when we contact the prospect and find a vast majority not being attended to, we only confirmed that too many leads were generated. Additionally, the

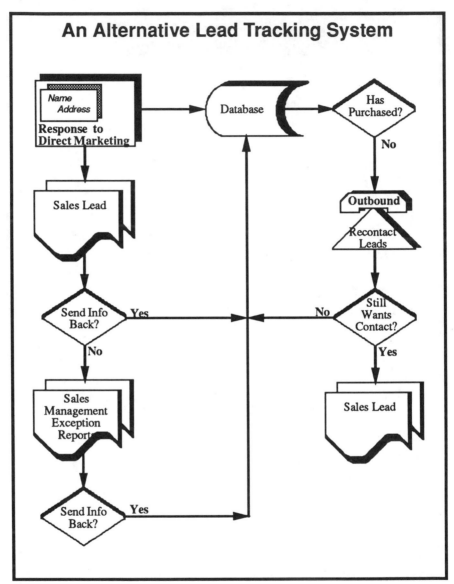

An Alternative Lead Tracking System

Illustration 3-12: An alternative lead tracking system.

salesperson probably tried to reach the prospect on more than one occasion. After several attempts, the salesperson pursued something else. In the crush of business, the lead may get lost. Following-up with the prospect allows you to determine the final outcome. If the lead wasn't contacted, you still may have a sales opportunity.

Lead measurement and tracking need to be considered in the initial program design. Establish a lead tracking system which is based on sales force interaction and direct contact with the prospect. You will get invaluable information on the quality and quantity of sales follow-up. You also will gain great insight into what and why prospects are buying, including your competition.

Scoring

With the IBM program, lead quality became a major issue. The sales force had asked for many more leads than they could possibly follow up. Ultimately we returned to the drawing table to try to define a good lead.

During the telemarketing effort I had the communicator input prospect responses directly into a computer. The computer was used to determine the quality of the prospect and to ensure only those prospects who qualified as leads or referrals were offered a salesperson visit.

The communicators were part-time employees who were not knowledgeable in the IBM product line. They had been trained in good telephone techniques and the telephone call was completely scripted. The script itself was manual using a flip card approach, but the scheduling and data capture were interactive with the computer. The following script was used during the telemarketing call. Keep in mind that all cards in the script are not printed here. *How to Manage and Execute Telephone Selling*, another book I have written, published by Direct Marketing Publishers, addresses the topic of scripts more extensively.

This script was developed with the sales staff and focused on screening prospects before the leads were sent to a salesperson for follow-up. Initially, a lead was sent out for any prospect that was in the process of evaluating a system within three months regardless of the prospect's desire to see a salesperson. We used binary decision-making; that is, by answering yes or no to a series of questions, the prospects qualified themselves. If the prospect was making a decision within six months, they were automatically qualified, and IBM offered to have a salesperson contact the prospect. If the decision was to be made within three months, the lead was sent to the salesperson, regardless of whether the prospect agreed to see a salesperson.

If a purchase was planned for the future, the other qualification criteria was examined to determine if the prospect should be offered a salesperson. Again, all the questions were binary. The prospect answered yes or no to meet the criteria. The prospect's answers to certain questions determined if a salesperson would call on that prospect.

When the IBM script was developed, we didn't understand or relate to the MAND concept (money, authority, need, desire) that was discussed earlier. The sales force asked for three sales leads per day. If the prospect had answered certain questions, the sales force wanted to have that prospect as a lead. We quickly had severe lead quality problems. Many prospects were evaluating 'personal computers' that cost approximately $2,000. The smallest IBM systems were then priced at about $15,000. The salespeople were unhappy with the leads.

Using the manual scripting technique, you really don't have many options on lead qualification. You can link different binary decisions, but the qualification process becomes more and more difficult to implement.

If name-directed: Good (morning/afternoon) (FIRST AND LAST NAME OF DECISION MAKER) please? IF NO LONGER AT FIRM, ASK FOR HIS/HER REPLACEMENT, (Record on screen).

If not name-directed: Good (morning/afternoon) Please connect me to your office manager -- but before you do, I need to know that person's full name and title.

If asks who is calling: This is (YOUR FULL NAME) calling on behalf of IBM. Is Mr(s) _____ in?

If not available: Will (He/She) be in later today -- or will (He/She) be in tomorrow at this time?

Introduction to switchboard - establish decision maker   **1**

Mr(s) _____? I'm (YOUR FULL NAME) and I'm calling on behalf of IBM. You are the (TITLE) for (COMPANY), right?

    If No: Please tell me, what is your correct title?

Then you're the person I should be talking to, because IBM has recently introduced a new line of computers that can now give companies the benefits of data processing at a cost far below what you may have associated with us in the past. I am not asking for any confidential information. The purpose of my call is to see if you're thinking about getting a small computer, a bookkeeping machine or perhaps word processing equipment? (PAUSE)

    If Yes or Unsure: Go to Define Decision Status - Card 3

    If No: Go to Gather Data - Card 4

Introduction to decision maker-verify title & establish interest 2

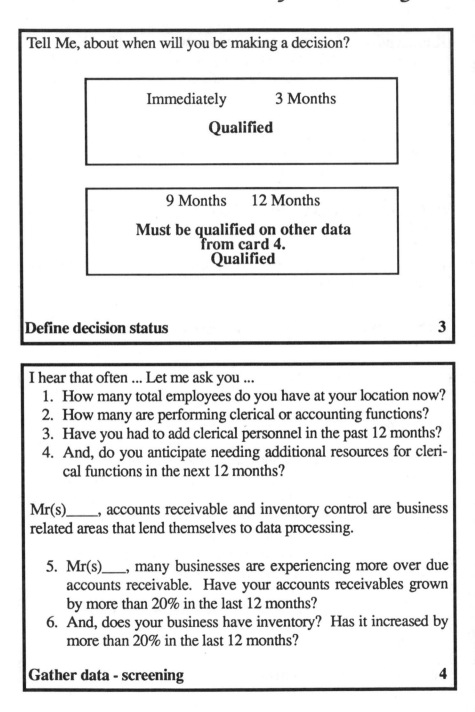

Tell Me, about when will you be making a decision?

Immediately   3 Months
Qualified

9 Months   12 Months
**Must be qualified on other data
from card 4.
Qualified**

Define decision status   **3**

I hear that often ... Let me ask you ...
1. How many total employees do you have at your location now?
2. How many are performing clerical or accounting functions?
3. Have you had to add clerical personnel in the past 12 months?
4. And, do you anticipate needing additional resources for clerical functions in the next 12 months?

Mr(s)____, accounts receivable and inventory control are business related areas that lend themselves to data processing.

5. Mr(s)___, many businesses are experiencing more over due accounts receivable. Have your accounts receivables grown by more than 20% in the last 12 months?
6. And, does your business have inventory? Has it increased by more than 20% in the last 12 months?

Gather data - screening   **4**

A. And do you use a computer now?

    If Yes: Is it your own?   **If Yes**: Do you rent it?
                                               Or did you purchase it?

B. Do you use a Service Bureau, Mr(s)____?
If No to both: Go to appropriate close based on qualifying instruction.
If Yes to either A or B: Continue

What Kind is that?
And how long have you used it/them?
About how much do you spend a month?
And, are you satisfied that you are getting all your data processing needs covered by your current procedures?

Go to correct close based on qualifying instructions.

Gather data - data processing experience   **5**

Thanks so much for talking with me today. Could I have one of our representatives call you to talk about your needs further?

> **If Yes**: Fine. You'll be hearing from us soon.
> * And, what would you like a computer to do to help your business, Mr(s)____?
> * What products or services does your company specialize in?
> * Could you give me a general idea of your company's annual sales volume?

If refuses rep call: Go to appropriate objection.

Making decision: Offer IBM rep contact   **6**

Mr(s) _____? Your business sounds like it is growing significantly and perhaps you're not aware that the cost of data processing has gone below what you might spend for a single clerk, or bookkeeping machine. Now may be the time to evaluate if data processing can help you.

IBM offers many services to help you determine your needs and implement the right solution for your business. May I have one of our representatives call to discuss this with you further?

> **If Yes**: Fine. You'll be hearing from us soon.
> * And, what would you like a computer to do to help your business, Mr(s)_____?
> * What products or services does your company specialize in?
> * Would you give me a general idea of your company's annual sales volume?

If No: Go to Gather Data - Card 4

Not making a decision but qualified: Offer IBM rep   7

Thanks so much for your courtesy. By the way, what products or services does your company specialize in?

We'd like to keep in contact with you, Mr(s) _____, so you'll be hearing from IBM from time to time -- and please give us a call when you feel you have to add equipment or personnel.

Thanks again -- have a very nice day. Good-bye.

Close: If not qualified or refuses all offers   8

The IBM salespeople asked for fewer leads that were of higher quality. We tried to define 'higher quality,' but had the same problem we had defining a good lead. Which was better: A prospect making a decision in 90 days or less who only had one clerical person; or a prospect not making a decision for more than six months who had eight clerical people?

We began to evaluate the relationship of the answers to the qualification questions. This relative lead qualification procedure was a tremendous breakthrough, and finally allowed us to differentiate between prospects and referrals.

Computer Decision		Clerical Employees		Total Employees	
Immediate	35	6 or more	15	100+	15
Less then 3 mos	25	3 to 6	10	50 to 99	10
3 to 6 mos	15	2	5	25 to 49	5
6 to 12 mos	10	1	0	less than 25	0
Unsure	5	0	(10)		
Not evaluating	0				
Added Clerical In Last Year		**Will Add Clerical**		**Accounts Rec'vble**	
Yes	10	Yes	15	Yes	10
No	0	No	0	No	0
Inventory Growth		**Using Data Proc**		**Annual Sales**	
Yes	10	Purch Sys>1 yr	5	25 million+	10
No	0	Purch Sys<1 yr	(10)	1 to 25 million	5
				500k to 1 mill	0
		Serv Bureau	15	less than 500k	(5)
		Not Satisfied	15		

Illustration 3-13: A lead scoring system.

I established point values for each answer and we were then able to score the lead. The scoring system in Illustration 3-13 is an example of the algorithms we used.

This system is almost impossible to implement with a manual script and a communicator trying to score manually while on the phone. The ideal situation would allow the prospect to be scored automatically during the phone call and enable the score to be used to determine the appropriate offer.

I worked with the sales force to establish the values for each answer. Bear in mind that the best scoring system will change and be modified as you learn from leads you've already generated. I went back and scored all the leads we generated prior to the scoring system introduction, and found the average lead to be worth about 20 points. Qualified leads required a score of at least 40 points.

I automated the scheduling process of the telemarketing calls and placed terminals in front of each communicator. I used a relative approach to determine lead quality and the appropriate offer that would be made to the prospect. The computer was programmed to evaluate the answers. If the prospect crossed a certain threshold, the offer was made. For the first time we could actually differentiate between prospects and referrals.

A prospect was one who scored between 20 and 39 points. Referrals had to score more than 39 points. IBM also decided that a single question could not qualify a referral. The average referral or lead had a score of 47 points after we introduced the scoring qualification system. More importantly, the salespeople now liked 65% of the leads and were unhappy with only 35%. Before we implemented the scoring system, the sales force disliked 65% of all leads generated. Order information is not released by IBM.

I have used scoring algorithms in many other programs with the same kinds of results. When I work with clients to define the values for scoring, no one question will qualify a prospect to be a referral. The MAND concept makes it easier to decide what questions to ask.

It is very difficult to implement a scoring system to determine the offer without being interactive with a computer during the telephone call. However, scoring after the fact can be valuable to determine lead quality, the results of your offers, and list usage.

Scoring solves many problems but creates a whole new set of opportunities. In the past, every prospect who met a certain criteria was sent to the sales force for action. With scoring, you identify the best referrals to send to the salespeople. You also identify a group qualified as prospects, but not qualified enough to be leads. What do you do with this group to ultimately turn them into leads and customers?

You can accomplish similar scoring results by using two step mailing techniques. Initial respondents are mailed a second piece which has qualification information that can be returned. After the second response, the prospect can be considered a lead. Obviously, this technique will substantially reduce the number of leads sent to the salespeople.

Lead Qualification - The prospect is the only one that counts!

Very often lead generation programs include a qualifying step to determine if the respondent merits a follow-up by a salesperson. This qualifying step is targeted to ensure that the prospect is qualified based on our criteria. When do we consider the interest and desire of the prospect?

There are four fundamental areas to consider in finding a good lead:
    Money
    Authority
    Need
    Desire

Does the prospect have the money to afford your proposition? The underlying assumption to this qualification issue is that the prospect has some expectation as to the cost of your product or service. In many lead generation programs, companies avoid price discussions for fear of reducing the response. You can introduce price in relation to monthly terms or the minimum price required for your basic unit. I am not advocating baiting your prospects, but by identifying some price point, you'll eliminate the totally unqualified response.

Does your respondent have the authority to participate in the buying decision for your product? Most leads are not qualified because the respondent doesn't have the authority. As many as 85% of unqualified leads are attributed to this area. I do not advocate asking prospects a lot of questions to empirically determine whether they are qualified. Authority is the exception. I suggest that all lead generation efforts include a basic question to determine the decision authority of the respondent. One question that works particularly well for me is:

Which of the following best describes your involvement in a decision to acquire _____?
   1) you make the decision
   2) you investigate and recommend
   3) the decision is made elsewhere in the company

Non-decision makers should not be sent to salespeople for follow-up activity. If the prospect answers with a 3, ask for the name and phone number of the person who is responsible. If the respondent is not involved in the decision, you'll never get a salesperson to follow-up. This group of respondents will require a fulfillment approach other than a face-to-face contact.

It always surprises me how often this qualification question is answered. This question does work effectively in establishing authority.

Does the prospect have a need or problem that your product can fulfill? In order to sell anything a prospect must have a problem or need that your product or service will address. Need is not necessarily product related. A company having a problem collecting accounts receivable may find a computer useful in helping to solve this problem. The need isn't for the computer but to improve accounts receivable.

Finally, does your prospect have a desire to find a solution to their need or problem. Once a prospect recognizes that a problem exists, unless they have demonstrated a desire to overcome the need, they are not qualified. A prospect must accept an offer to do something, demonstrating desire.

Many companies will develop sophisticated questionnaires to determine if a prospect should be contacted by a salesperson. These companies believe that to be considered a lead a prospect must meet certain pre-established criteria. The IBM program discussed earlier is an example of using data to qualify the prospect.

A few years ago I learned a very valuable lesson. Prospects who don't meet our qualification criteria will often buy. Back in the mid 70's while selling computers, we often thought that a business had to have at least one million in annual sales to afford a computer. We uncovered a prospect in the fuel oil business who was much smaller, yet he decided to buy a computer. Should we have refused the order?

This seems like an absurd question, yet so many lead programs focus on data like annual sales, instead of money, authority, need and desire. These programs try to capture information that will reveal if the prospect has money and need. If the criteria is met, these same lead generation programs will offer the prospect an opportunity to be contacted by a salesperson. Sometimes, the prospect will not even be offered the opportunity to accept or reject a sales call. Instead, a decision will be made by the empirical value of the data and the *lead* will be forwarded to the salesperson.

These kinds of respondents are not leads and will tend to destroy lead generation programs. **The prospect who doesn't acknowledge that they are a lead is not a lead.**

The key to successful lead generation efforts will often rest on the offer you make to the respondent. The most prevalent offer made in lead generation programs is to have a salesperson contact the prospect. The next most often used offer is to provide additional information. Neither of these offers alone will help qualify a lead.

The best leads will generate a respondent who recognizes a problem, wants to solve the problem, and has some understanding of how much a solution might cost. In addition, this respondent will have the authority to pursue a solution to the problem. Most qualifications can be resolved in a well-conceived offer.

An offer that promises a salesperson contact to describe XYZ computer will not generate well-qualified respondents. Similarly, promising information about the XYZ computer will generate questionable quality respondents. You can strengthen the quality of the respondent by identifying the price of the computer and how it will help the business.

For example: Our XYZ computer can help you reduce your accounts receivable by 20% and cost as little as $250 per month - Respond today for a free operations analysis of your business.

This offer establishes a potential benefit and cost in the mind of the prospect. You don't have to ask questions about sales or accounts receivable. By identifying a benefit and cost, respondents can determine if they are qualified.

As I mentioned earlier, I believe the most important consideration is whether the prospect thinks they are qualified. If a prospect is convinced they have a problem and can appreciate the cost of the solution and afford it, who cares what the data indicates? The prospect is going to buy -- not the data. Of course prospects who can't pass credit checks can be a problem, but I would rather deal with a few credit problems than prospects who have not indicated a desire to make a change.

In my early experiences in lead generation I was also enamored with using data to evaluate lead quality. I even sent prospects who only wanted additional information to the sales force as leads. These programs ultimately failed. How the prospect judges their level of interest and need are really the only important ingredients in developing high quality leads.

Telephone is an excellent medium for qualifying respondents to convert them to leads. Because this medium is so interactive, we will often go too far in data gathering and lose sight of the lead generation objective.

Lead generation programs will often become market research projects. Direct marketers have to guard against this phenomenon. I believe that telephone should be used to qualify respondents but only by making a well-conceived offer. Only questions that establish money, authority, need and desire should be asked. These issues can most often be established in the offer and one question about decision authority.

The best leads are those that have the prospect convinced they are qualified. Once you begin to focus on generating this kind of lead, the number of leads you send to the field will go down, but the number of leads that convert to orders will go up. Your sales force will be happier.

Conditioning and Regeneration

Most companies have a limited universe within the business-to-business arena. A prospect is very valuable and, even if they do not buy from you now, they may buy from you in the future. When you talk to the sales organization, you learn that a prospect takes time to nurture and sell. Selling through direct marketing is the same. Once a prospect is identified, you should continue to market this prospect even if they became a lead and were sent to the sales force. This sustained selling activity is a form of *conditioning* and repeated attempts to get the prospect to respond through direct mail and telephone selling is *regeneration*.

During the IBM lead program, we learned there is a difference between prospects and referrals. When operating a lead generation program, the referrals are sent to the sales force and prospects are nurtured and conditioned into referrals. We also know that not all the leads will be followed up with the same quality.

We designed a direct mail program that involved multiple contacts spread over a three to four month period. After the prospects or referrals were identified, they were mailed a conditioning series of mail pieces to move them along through the sales cycle. The series was not product oriented. It focused on the buying decision. Need and desire were the themes used throughout the series. Cost justification, application needs and identification, and computer uses were the topics of three of the pieces in the series. All the pieces asked the prospect to get involved with the material. They all contained involvement gimmicks.

Prospects and referrals were tested to determine the effectiveness of this approach. Lead quality improved dramatically and the sales force wanted to add their own prospects to the existing database to have them receive the mail series.

Conditioning and regeneration are key elements to continuing to work the prospect and referral universe. If you're unable to close the business today, this technique allows you to get the business in the future. Good salespeople perform this function independently. When a salesperson identifies a qualified prospect, they begin to work to sell that prospect over time. The salesperson will send literature, letters and make many phone calls until the prospect succumbs to their efforts. Tenacity is a trait we all look for in a good salesperson.

We should learn from our sales force. This repetitive activity works in direct marketing as well as in direct selling. The sales force should be consulted to determine those techniques that are successful. You should try to implement a uniform system to condition prospects to become referrals and to regenerate referrals into customers over time.

Lead Generation - Two Big Pitfalls

The vast majority of promotion expense in businesses selling to other businesses is in generating sales leads for the field salesperson. Lead generation is the most difficult direct marketing program to successfully implement. In fact, it is unusual to find a lead generation program that has sustained itself for more than a year or two.

Prospects will often respond to a direct marketing program and never receive additional information or follow-up. I have found that less than 30% of leads sent to salespeople are ever contacted. Illustration 3-14 demonstrates what can occur if information is not fulfilled in a timely manner to prospects and customers.

Illustration 3-14: The other side of fulfillment.

Lead generation programs often make promises but never deliver. I think there are two problems that you should be aware of before implementing a lead generation program. The first is the normal delay that the prospect will experience from response to receipt of information. The second is whether the salesperson ever contacts the prospect and how you'll measure their sales activity.

Even in the best scenario, a prospect who becomes interested in your product or service, and who responds to the promotion will have to wait two weeks or more before receiving the information they request.

Even in a well planned and executed fulfillment operation, a prospect will suffer some delay between response and receipt of information. There are obvious delays caused by fulfillment operations and postal handling. In other environments, information requests have not been completely planned for and are handled ineffectively.

Delays in handling responses will cause the prospect to cool or even forget that they responded. It is even possible for the prospect to pursue a competitive alternative while waiting to receive information.

The sooner information can be fulfilled, the higher the odds of closing the sale.

If you are generating sales leads for salespeople, you are never certain of the quality and timeliness of the follow-up. Many salespeople will pre-judge lead quality based on their own subjective evaluation. In some cases, those leads that the salespeople feel are poor quality may never receive any follow-up. In addition, a salesperson has their own priorities and may not execute a follow-up contact to your leads as quickly as you would like.

Most salespeople don't like sales leads. To prove this point, when was the last time you heard a salesperson say, Those were great leads, send me more! The more typical reaction seems to be, Those were awful leads, and the only good ones were prospects that I already knew about.

Most salespeople feel threatened by leads and will typically condemn lead generation activity as a waste of the company's money. It is very difficult to get the salesperson to return any information concerning lead disposition or follow-up.

You should design a fulfillment program that puts information in the hands of your prospects as soon as possible. If you can turn around information the same day, do it.

The information kit you use to fulfill information requests should be designed to generate a lead or an order. Existing material or brochures should not be mailed in an effort to save costs.

Even if you plan to send the respondent to your sales force as a lead, send a complete information kit to him as well. You are never certain that the sales force will follow up quickly or completely. I suggest to my clients that they not only send an information kit, but a letter explaining who the prospect can contact if they aren't contacted soon by the sales force.

As we mentioned earlier, lead management programs should be designed to have the prospect tell you about selling activity. So many lead programs ultimately fail because management is unable to get the salesperson to report on lead quality and disposition.

Prospects responding to direct marketing are indicating an interest in your company. Most respondents would like to start a relationship with the company, yet most businesses rely on the salesperson to develop and sustain that relationship. You can help the salesperson and your company if you also maintain some relationship with your respondents.

You can use direct mail promotion to fulfill the initial inquiry along with sending the lead to the salesperson. Even if the salesperson fails to follow-up, you'll be assured of a contact. A telephone call after the lead has been generated can be made in the guise of customer service to help measure the effectiveness of the lead program.

The sustained use of direct mail can also be used to maintain a relationship with the respondent and help move the prospect further towards buying your products or services.

There are many challenges in developing and executing lead generation programs. The two pitfalls described have traditionally created some of the most obvious reasons for failure. As you plan your next campaign, consider the timely follow-up of information to your respondents and how you will ensure that the salesperson fulfills as you have promised. As you plan on solutions to these troublesome areas, you will begin to take positive steps towards better lead generation efforts.

Lead Programs Summarized

In this chapter I talked about the inconsistencies in lead follow-up, the difficulty in lead definition, and how to implement leads with the sales force. Whenever you implement a lead program, you try to reduce the cost of selling by improving the effectiveness of the sales force. The lead program has to work as a tool for the sales force. It should not be perceived by the salespeople as an alternative to their efforts. Nothing will destroy the effectiveness of the project faster then if the salespeople feel that you are trying to replace them with direct marketing. Work with your sales organization to create the lead program to make their jobs easier rather than eliminate them.

When the decision is made to implement the lead program, do not reduce commissions or territories. For the lead program to be successful, you need the support of the salespeople. Anything that affects their perception of the direct marketing effort in a negative way, should be avoided at all costs. Sell the direct marketing program to the sales force. If mail is being used, send a copy of the piece to the homes of the salespeople. Put them on your list.

In order to measure the effectiveness of the lead program, you must have feedback. Salespeople perform a variety of activities. Unfortunately, their highest priority will not be to give you information on the quality of the leads. You should design a lead tracking and management system to control the distribution and reporting of the leads. Ask sales management to get involved and help with reporting. However, do not chastise the salespeople for not returning sales leads. Consider positive actions such as contests for the most leads followed-up. Make sure you publicize sales successes from the sales leads. Nothing will motivate a salesperson to follow-up the leads more than sales success.

Design a way to ask the prospect directly what has happened. Special offers that give a premium for buying as a result of the offer are an interesting method to measure the conversion of leads to orders. Giving a coupon or special discount to the prospect also will help measure some of the conversions.

A questionnaire or telephone call after the lead is generated is an ideal way to determine lead quality and lead conversion. Go directly to the referral and ask about the quality of the lead follow up. You can find out what the prospect bought, if anything; why the prospect bought or didn't buy; and you can determine if that prospect is still a sales opportunity for you.

Remember, most salespeople are operating from their briefcases or car trunks. They normally don't have a copier or filing cabinet with them. When you design the lead report format, help the salesperson organize and manage their territory. Use multiple copy formats if you want information returned, so the salesperson only has to fill in the blanks and return it. Make forms easy to use and understand. Give the salesperson an easy way to file and manage the information you're sending to them. All leads should be sent to the field in the same format. I prefer a three-ring binder, with pre-punched lead information. Cards and other formats are just as effective, as long as you think of the salesperson first.

One final point. Any information you have on the prospect or referral should be sent to the salesperson. Don't hide any data. Most salespeople are entrepreneurs and like to have complete control of their accounts.

Chapter Four:

Planning Lead Programs

Why Plan?

Planning a lead generation program starts with identifying the objectives or goals you want to achieve. These objectives should, if possible, be specific revenue and profit goals, but initially they will be identified as a specific number of leads.

Too many books on marketing, advertising, and direct marketing contain an obligatory chapter on business planning. Typical presentations on this subject tend to be about as exciting as watching paint dry. However, don't let past dull recitations on abstract business theory lessen your zeal to master the business plan. No subject is more vital in determining the success or failure of a marketing effort. I'll show you a practical guide on how to develop and execute a business plan for business-to-business direct marketing. I'll conclude this chapter with an actual business plan.

The best direct marketing business plans can be read and understood by someone who doesn't know a thing about your business. Perhaps the most difficult part of developing the plan is keeping it simple enough for your spouse or child to understand.

Writing a detailed business plan may not seem like the best use of your time because you probably already think that you know everything about your business. *Business planning* is putting on paper all the facts you have at your disposal.

In many instances, in order to implement your strategy and tactics you'll need outside help. The aid of an agency, consultant or list broker may be required. The business plan can be a tool to quickly and inexpensively bring these people up to speed on the specifics of your business.

There are many purposes for a business plan. Internal support will have to be briefed on your plans and assumptions. You can use it to remind you of your original objectives after the project is complete.

Your management should be given the completed plan prior to starting any activity. By ensuring that everyone has the same understanding and expectations, your project will have a higher chance of success.

The Tarzan Theory of Management

Why are so many decisions in business revolutionary as opposed to evolutionary? Management is never happy with the status quo and is always looking for new and better ways to do things. There is nothing so constant as change. But sometimes we initiate change without considering its impact on the current status quo.

So often, market research and other intelligence sources dictate that the company should change its current approach. These decisions to change are often made without considering the impact to existing procedures and approaches. The results of dramatic changes can create chaos and confusion.

The Tarzan Theory of Management dictates: **you never let go of one rope until you have the other rope firmly in your grasp.** Failing to follow this dictum can cause you to drop with no safety net to cushion your fall. In addition, if you survive the fall, there may be no way for you to climb back to where you were before.

Companies will sometimes find their current selling approach faltering and begin to look for new and better ways to increase market penetration. Lead generation, telephone selling and catalog sales are often considered panaceas. The mistake companies make is in abruptly replacing the current approach with these alternative distribution techniques rather than implementing the techniques in an evolutionary manner, testing and learning along the way. The results are often overwhelmingly negative. Besides losing customers, many of the existing sales force will also leave.

As you consider alternative selling techniques, keep the Tarzan Theory in mind. Whatever selling technique you have primarily used thus far must be considered successful until you find an alternative that works better.

I often work with clients who want to implement telephone selling as an alternative to using face-to-face activity. These companies frequently decide to reduce territories and move accounts and opportunities to the telephone selling operation. Little thought is given to the impact this change may have on the existing sales force.

Salespeople, like most people, don't accept change very well. Selling requires a lot of self confidence, and when territories and compensation programs are changed, salespeople often feel threatened. When telephone selling is added to traditional selling techniques, the sales force may want to see the effort fail. They will sense a loss of territory and an ultimate loss of compensation. It will be very hard to make the telephone selling effort or any lead generation program successful.

Companies that introduce telephone selling, or any alternative selling technique, without testing and coordinating the change with existing approaches are violating the Tarzan Theory of Management. The risks are great because the new selling approach may not work and implementing it may create far reaching negative implications.

It's not just direct marketing and lead generation approaches that you should consider in making decisions about the Tarzan Theory. Any significant change in your company should be evaluated as to the impact it will have on current procedures.

For example, if you plan to change compensation or product strategies, consider how the change will affect existing product sales. What will the impact of the compensation change be on the sales force and their current compensation plan?

You should create opportunities to test new concepts before you make revolutionary changes to your distribution approach. Reduce the risk of failure by developing concepts that allow you to test in complementary environments.

If you plan to reduce commissions on smaller customers and products because selling expenses have become too high, you'll have to prove to your sales force that they can make as much money as before. In order to prove this point, you'll probably have to know some history and have experience using the alternative approach. Therefore, construct tests that prove your theories before you introduce radical changes to the existing approach.

Obviously, testing alternatives will require money and time but doing so will buy you insurance against complete disaster. Even after you test and prove an alternative successful, you should still develop a plan to evolve to the new approach. Keep a firm grip on the existing rope until you're sure the new rope can support you.

The Tarzan Theory is appropriate for all business decisions. If you're considering adding a catalog to your promotional efforts, create the initial catalog as a sales support tool. Pay the salespeople full commissions on sales activity. The sales force will help the catalog gain acceptance and orders. After the catalog has developed customer support, you can consider gradually reducing commissions on sales generated from the catalog.

The cost of the initial catalog will add incremental expense, but if you can't make the catalog work with sales support, it will probably fail anyway. By introducing the catalog as a sales support vehicle, the sales force will feel less threatened and more comfortable. If the catalog fails, you will not have lost the support and loyalty of the field organization. The additional investment required to pay full commissions on sales generated by the catalog may be the least expensive insurance policy you'll ever buy.

If you have discovered that certain segments of your market are too expensive to sell with traditional techniques, make a gradual and evolutionary change. You cannot abruptly change direction and emphasis and ensure success.

Telephone selling can be successfully added to most sales strategies if it is introduced as a complementary extension of existing tactics. Create a teamed environment where the telephone salespeople and the field salespeople initially work as a team. Don't make any changes to current compensation programs.

As the telephone salespeople begin to establish relationships with customers and gain acceptance from the field organization, you can gradually shift sales emphasis and adjust compensation. If the effort is not successful, you still have the support of the field organization. You haven't let go of the original rope in case you miss the other rope.

We make most personal decisions with an understanding of the Tarzan Theory. We don't typically move without having identified another place to live and work. Most of us will not consider changing jobs before we identify another opportunity. Yet, business decisions that can affect significant change in your company are often made with little or no consideration of the Tarzan Theory.

As a direct marketing consultant, I am often asked whether a program will be successful. Even though I may be absolutely convinced that the effort should succeed, I will usually advise clients not to change their existing business until we are absolutely sure of success. And even after we test and determine the level of success, I will still caution clients to move slowly and gradually introduce change.

Keep in mind what has made you successful so far. As you move to different techniques, make sure the existing approach continues to work unchanged until you prove the new approach. Don't let go of the rope until you have the new rope firmly in your grasp. Before you make radical change, and any change is considered radical by salespeople, plan your program to ensure success.

The business plan will often contain several major sections that can be categorized into the following areas:

- Company Background
- Organization Charts
- Current Costs and Budgets for Sales

Outline of Business Background

1) Background
   A) History of the company

   B) Product overview
      1) Type of products
      2) Product mix
      3) Revenue by product

   C) Marketplace
      1) The market
      2) Target individuals by product
         a) Decision makers
         c) Influencers
      3) Revenue by market segment

   D) Competition

   E) Current and prior channels of distribution
      1) Current channels by product
      2) Salespeople overview
         a) Type of sales organizations
         b) Reporting structures
         c) Personalities
      3) Prior experience with direct marketing
      4) Pricing per channel
         a) Discounts allowed
         b) Pricing and strategy overview
      5) Revenue by channel of distribution

Illustration 4-1: Outline of Business Background.

- Direct Marketing
- Intensive Planning
- Strategies
- Measurements
- Tactics

Company Background

The background of the business encompasses many areas. Begin your plan with a brief history of your company and explain the key reasons for its success. Remember, you're trying to write a plan for someone who doesn't know anything about your company.

You'll be tempted to avoid writing the history of your company. You may think this subject is too basic and superfluous. I have found that by forcing a review of the past, you can build a better foundation for activity in the future. Founders of businesses had great ideas and products. As time goes by, many companies may stray from the things that made them successful in the past. Reviewing the past history of the business may open doors that were accidentally shut.

Next, write a review of the products or services offered by your company. Try to address product evolution and how you obtained your current product mix. If your business has product areas or groups, review the major areas as well as the specific types of products. Don't try to address the marketplace or current marketing strategy. Focus on the product, product features, and product benefits you offer your customers. You will focus on the marketplace and marketing strategy later. Again, keep in mind that whoever is reading your plan may not know your company, your industry, or the problem that your products are designed to solve.

If you ask your spouse or a close friend to read this section of the plan, pay close attention to the questions they ask. If the products are not clear, try redefining them again.

Don't try to describe every item of inventory. Focus on the major product categories and what these do for your customers.

Try to present the sales mix and percentage of sales for which each major product group is responsible. Real dollars and percentages of the total are very helpful. A comparison of the last few years of activity can help to show product trends. The average order size and number of orders by product group are important data to analyze in establishing strategy.

Now that you've examined the products and share of revenue, review the market and marketplace. A thorough study of the market is helpful in evaluating strategies and objectives. Review the markets for your products and product groups without focusing on your current marketing strategy. Just as you avoided strategy discussions in the product review, focus on the market and marketplace separately.

The purpose of the market section is to explain the size and composition of your marketing opportunity. You want to review the size of the market and the number of opportunities for you to sell your product. Business counts by Standard Industry Classifications (SIC), geography, and business size are important. List brokers can be helpful in quantifying your marketing opportunity.

Within the marketplace overview, a section should identify the individuals you're trying to reach. Each product group's target individuals should be identified. Focus on the potential customers for your products; how they think and act; and how they make buying decisions.

Include a description of each major decision maker, including personality similarities and organization reporting structures. As discussed in Chapters 1 and 2, a unique characteristic of the business market is the multiple levels involved in the purchasing decision.

In your review of the individuals involved in the buying process, focus on influencers as well as decision makers. If selling your products involve both decision makers and influencers, try to describe their individual functions and how they interact. Describe how these players fit into the organization and how they affect the buying decision. Examining the general personalities of all of these individuals can help you evaluate new or existing strategies. Keep in mind that different product groups may have different buying decision structures.

Now write a similar analysis for your market and market distribution. Include total revenue by market segment and percentages of revenue from market segments. By listing comparative information over several years you will notice trends in the marketplace.

The revenue analysis by market may not always be appropriate. Some companies have an unusual distribution of business. For example, if 25% of your sales come from one or two accounts, your marketplace is different than a traditional company. This non-typical distribution will distort any analysis and will not be helpful in directing future marketing efforts. However, you should try to identify the unique characteristics of your offering that has caused the unusual distribution. There may be a special benefit that can allow you to expand your business substantially.

Try to review the average volume of a customer in both dollars sold and number of orders. Later, when we review the need for direct marketing, the customer volume data could become very important.

Competitive products and services can affect your ability to generate sales. Incorporate a detailed analysis of competition into your business plan. If possible, try to evaluate why the competition is succeeding or failing. Competitive pricing and offers can be key ingredients in the direct marketing program you develop. The competitive analysis should focus on the various product and market segments. If your competitors differ by region, be sure to review how this will affect your ability to sell in each area.

Now that you've examined the product and the market, evaluate the strategy and channels you've used to sell your products to that market. In this section, review your current and past approaches to selling to the market.

Relate how the current approach and channels of distribution have evolved. Each channel of distribution should be reviewed and explained. Understanding the current sales process and channels of distribution are critical to the success of your direct marketing efforts. How the current process works will be critical to any new programs you try.

If salespeople are involved, whether your own or other distributors, they can affect direct marketing. The sales force's personalities, compensation, and motivation, are important elements to consider when you implement direct marketing.

Describe the reporting structure of your sales organization. The way they are managed is critical to how you'll introduce and manage your direct marketing program. If you or your company has had a prior experience with direct marketing, document the program and results. Salespeople are like elephants, they never forget. More importantly, they never forgive.

An important and integral part of your business plan explains how you will introduce the direct marketing plan to the current channels of distribution. Prior activities can dramatically influence the reception of your current program. Remember the Tarzan Theory of Management.

As you discuss the different channels of distribution, review the pricing, discounts offered, and gross revenue by channel. Again, list comparative information for several years to help identify any trends. Average revenue per order and number of orders is useful information to include.

If pricing differs by channel of distribution, explain why. The different pricing structure can be an indication of how different offers may be received by your market. You should understand why different customers are paying different prices for the same products.

Similarly, if selling strategies differ by channel, explain why. These different strategies can indicate strategies to test within an integrated direct marketing program.

Organization Charts

After you've reviewed the background of the business, an explanation of the organization should be included in the business plan.

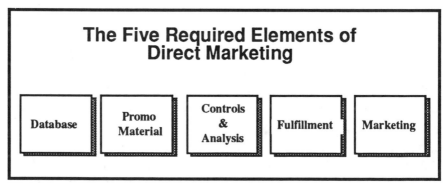

Illustration 4-2: The five required elements of direct marketing.

Develop a current organization chart that identifies your functions and where you fit into the company. More importantly, focus on the organization as it controls the five elements necessary for direct marketing. The five elements were presented in Chapter 2 and are restated in Illustration 4-2.

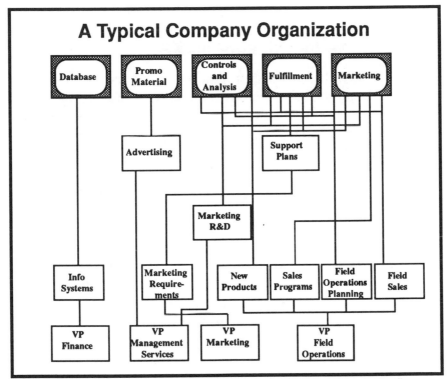

Illustration 4-3: A typical company and the organization that relates to the five elements of direct marketing.

Direct marketing will frequently report to multiple areas of a company. Illustration 4-3 shows how complicated a typical reporting structure can make implementing direct marketing. You may not be able to change the structure, but you should certainly be aware of it.

You'll have to coordinate support for all the functions prior to starting a direct marketing project. I have often seen direct marketing managers spend precious time trying to internally "sell" or gain the proper support from others in the company after the project has started. Measurement and implementation will become very difficult without support from data processing and controls and analysis personnel.

Current Costs and Budgets for Sales

So far, most of the information that you have been documenting should be easily available within your company. In fact, there may already be a business plan that you've been able to use. The budgets for the current sales approaches are also pretty easy to establish. Get as much detail as possible on this subject. The key measurement to the success of direct marketing is profitability. If you can produce an order for less than the current approach, the program will probably be considered successful.

Most companies do not measure sales costs on a cost per order or cost per item basis. On the other hand, direct marketing is measurable and normally focuses on the cost per order or cost per item sold. Striking a comparison to measure the success of your program against historical information can be difficult.

Once you've established the selling budget for the year, some simple math will help you establish the overall cost per order or cost per item.

Refer to your background section to get the total number of items sold for the last year. Then determine your total sales expense by reviewing the budget.

Sales Expense ÷ Number of Orders = Sales Cost per Order

By dividing the sales expense dollars by the number of orders, you can determine the overall cost per order. This is a good place to start. However, it can be seriously distorted by more expensive products.

Now, establish the percentage of revenue that is used for sales expense. Divide the sales expense by the total revenue. Again, reviewing both the product and market sections, you can establish the actual dollars of sales expense per order and per item sold. You'll probably be surprised at how expensive generating orders has become.

Sales Expense ÷ Total Revenue = % of Revenue used for Sales Expense

As I mentioned earlier, comparative results over several years can show interesting trends. Over time, you'll begin to get a better sense as to what has been happening to selling expenses.

I have always found that the less expensive products and smaller customers are allocated sales expenses that are not realistic. That is to say, you may find only fractions of a dollar allocated to certain products for sales expense. Certain customers may be allocated sales expenses that amount to less than the cost of one phone contact per year.

This exercise in establishing the cost per order or the cost per item often focuses attention on where you need direct marketing support. You will learn where costs have escalated to a point where profitable selling has become prohibitive. It is easy to get top level management to commit to a program to save money and reduce costs.

Try to establish the cost of the order, average order size and cost per sales call. This is difficult to do and will require you to convince management to agree with certain assumptions. If you can establish the cost per sales call, your direct marketing objectives will be easier to establish.

The advent of personal computers and spread sheets has made life a lot easier. We can model and change assumptions with ease and examine the impact of our changes. There are a number of ways to establish the cost per sales call. We'll examine one from which you may want to create a spread sheet model. This approach is an example that you can expand or contract based on your own requirements.

First, establish the total revenue and marketing costs for the period you will use to establish the cost per sales call. Try to use a 12 month period so you'll have to plan your results on an annual basis. Next identify the total number of salespeople you have in your company. Do not include management or field support personnel. These and other 'overhead' costs will be included within the total marketing costs.

Total Marketing Costs ÷ Number of salespeople = Cost per Salesperson

By dividing the total marketing costs by the number of salespeople, you'll establish the cost per salesperson per year. I have frequently encountered sales executives who maintain that they're paying their sales forces strictly on a commission basis, therefore the commissions are the only cost for the salespeople. This ignores the other costs involved in promoting and supporting the products.

If you're only using a sales force, the only time you have an opportunity to sell is when the salesperson makes contact with your customers or prospects. Marketing expenses should be apportioned to all of the salespeople, since this will give you a much better indication of your true selling costs.

Now use your background section to get the total number of orders generated. Establish the average order size next by dividing the total revenue by the number of orders.

Now determine the average revenue and the average number of orders per salesperson. To do this, divide the revenue by the number of salespeople. Then divide the total revenue by the total number of orders.

So far the data you've been creating has been based on numbers you can easily verify. You haven't made any assumptions, except to use all marketing expenses to determine the cost per salesperson per year. If your management is uncomfortable with this approach, ask them to give you the average earnings per year per salesperson. If you double this figure, to allow for support, expenses, fringe benefits, and general and administrative costs, it may be easier to develop your plan. This approach isn't as accurate as the first method, but it will still give you a basis from which to work. *Remember to document how you arrived at the cost per salesperson per year.*

Now that you know the average cost per salesperson, the average number of orders per salesperson, and the average revenue per order, you can begin to establish cost per sales call.

Much of the information you will generate on the cost per sales call will be based on assumptions that are difficult to verify. Try to be as conservative as possible. Use multiple sources for your data and be sure to document how and why you made a certain assumption. Review your assumptions with management and be flexible enough to make changes based on their suggestions.

You should also establish the average number of face-to-face sales calls made per business day. Most companies believe they average between three and four face-to-face sales calls per day. The same

McGraw-Hill research used to establish the cost of an average face-to-face sales call referenced in Chapter 1, also estimates an average of 2.1 sales calls per day per salesperson.

Salespeople spend time traveling to and from the call, planning the call and creating call reports and orders. When you consider all the other activities required of the salesperson, three to four calls per day may be overly optimistic.

The actual number of selling days per year is an interesting and sometimes very depressing fact of business. There are 365 days per year. 104 are weekends (52x2). This leaves 261 available selling days. When you subtract vacations (average 10 days) and holidays (average 10 days) and personal days (average 6 days) you'll have only 235 potential selling days per year.

This 235 days equals only 19.6 selling days per month. Now estimate the number of days taken from selling time for meetings, administrative work in the office, training, and recognition events and you'll probably end up with 200 to 220 days available for selling per year. And 220 days of selling per year equals only 18.3 selling days per month.

Using an average of three sales calls per day, the average salesperson makes 660 sales calls per year. Four sales calls per day would equal 880 sales calls per year. Although this number is usually far lower than the number of calls management thought were being made, it is probably overstated. Averaging three or four calls per day doesn't recognize the independence of the sales force and their tendency to play golf, tennis, and socially spend time with their customers.

The worksheet in Illustration 4-4 gives a simple format for establishing the cost per sales call. With this information you can also establish the cost per order by dividing total expenses by total

Salesperson Cost Worksheet

A) Total annual revenue   _____

B) Total annual marketing expenses   _____

C) Total number of orders   _____

D) Total number of salespeople   _____

E) Revenue per salesperson per year   _____
    $(A \div D = E)$
F) Cost per salesperson per year   _____
    $(B \div D = F)$
G) Average order size   _____
    $(A \div C = G)$
H) Average # of orders per salesperson   _____
    $(C \div D = H)$
I) Average # of sales calls per day   _____
    (Based on assumption)
J) Number of business days per year   _____
    per salesperson (Normally 200-220)
K) Number of sales calls per year per   _____
    salesperson $(J \times I = K)$
L) Cost per sales call   _____
    $(F \div K = L)$
M) Number of sales calls per order   _____
    $(K \div H = M)$
N) Closing rate   _____
    $(H \div K = N)$

Illustration 4-4: Salesperson Cost Worksheet.

orders. To determine your average cost per sales call, divide the average cost per salesperson per year by the average number of sales calls. To establish the number of sales calls per order, divide the number of sales calls per year by the number of orders per year. Finally, identify your closing rate by dividing the number of orders by the number of sales calls. *Closing rate* is the percentage of sales calls that result in an order.

Your cost per sales call may surprise you and your management. As I mentioned in Chapter 1, the average cost of an industrial sales call across most industries is over $250. In my experience this cost has frequently been much higher. Knowing how expensive it has become to make a sales call can help you establish where direct marketing can most help your company.

If the average cost of a sales call is $250, and your allowable sales expense was 20% of revenue, you would have to generate a $1250 order for every 5 sales calls. This is determined by dividing the cost per sales call by the allowable percentage of revenue for selling expenses. This assumes that you're experiencing a 100% closing rate -- an impossible objective. Therefore, you will probably determine that there are certain products and market segments to which you can no longer sell using the traditional salesperson.

Knowing the facts -- the costs and the budgets -- can help you establish a better direction for your program. You'll also establish some measurement criteria that can help evaluate the success of your program.

Direct Marketing: Section of Business Plan

The purpose of this section of your business plan is to establish why you're going to use direct marketing. You should identify the problem that direct marketing will solve. The product, market, and marketing strategy sections establish what and to whom you're selling. The budgets and costs section establishes your current costs and will probably highlight the areas that need support.

Describe in clear terms what you plan to do with direct marketing and why. If you're planning a lead generation program, describe what you're planning to do and what you hope to accomplish.

Make sure you describe the universe you're trying to reach (prospects), the group that you want to respond (referrals), and finally who will buy (customers). List brokers and list salespeople can help you understand the size and composition of your target universe.

There are some interesting techniques you can use to establish why and where you need direct marketing support. One approach is to use *Intensive Planning*. This a concept that encourages communication, problem definition, and problem resolution.

Intensive Planning

Intensive planning sessions normally involve all of the individuals in a particular function. It should be done off site in an informal and relaxed environment. Normally the session will take two full days. I have run sessions for all the top management in a company to identify programs that will allow the company to attain its objectives. The same type of session has effectively helped a sales unit identify programs to allow it to reach its objectives.

The planning session needs to be coordinated and controlled by an outside individual. Consultants experienced in this type of planning, are excellent session moderators. The moderator and senior manager or executive should meet prior to the planning session and estab-

Planning Session Rules

- Only one person may speak at a time.
- Everyone is equal; positions within the company are forgotten.
- All problems are to be stated in complete sentences -- no abbreviations -- and should state cause and effect.
- If anyone leaves the room, all planning stops.
- The person with the marker is in charge.
- All participants must unanimously agree to include a problem.

Illustration 4-5: Intensive Planning Session Rules.

lish who should participate and the short and long-term objectives to be planned during the session.

The planning session should convene off site where there can be no interruptions. Meals should be available at the site to keep breaks to a minimum. The rooms used for the planning sessions should have a lot of wall space, as you'll be writing on flip charts and hanging the results on the walls. You'll also need two flip chart easels, flip chart paper, masking tape and several different colored markers.

Once everyone is present, the senior manager or executive starts the session by reviewing the objectives for the unit. These objectives should be both short-term (next 12 months) and long-term (next 3 years). The objectives should be written on a flip chart prior to the session. The objectives are taped to the wall after they have been reviewed and explained by the senior manager. The senior manager will become a participant in the planning session after the objectives are presented. They will only have a single vote equal to any other member of the group.

The rules for the planning session are very simple:

- Each person has one vote, regardless of their level or position within the company.

- All problems are written in complete sentences stating a cause and effect.

- In order for a problem to be included in the final planning document, all participants must agree to include it.

- There is only one speaker at a time, and no side conversations.

- The person with the writing marker is in charge.

On the first day the members will identify only the problems that interfere with their objectives. On the second day, the participants will group the problems and create action programs to solve them.

After the objectives are reviewed, the group will define all the problems that prevent them from attaining their objectives. No problem is too small as long as the group unanimously agrees to include the problem.

One participant is appointed to act as moderator and given the marker. The moderator position is rotated periodically. Initially, the outside participant who controls the session should moderate the session. The two flip chart stands are set up in the front of the room. All problems the group agrees to include are listed on one chart. Each problem and each chart are numbered. The other easel is used as a scratch pad until the problem is written clearly, in a complete sentence, and is one the whole group agrees to include.

One speaker at a time states a problem in a complete sentence defining both its cause and effect. It is very difficult to discuss problems without trying to solve them; strong control must be exercised to focus only on identifying problems.

If the problem is that the sales force needs qualified leads, a more complete statement should be established. For example: The sales force needs qualified leads to sell in order to meet this year's sales objectives. The cause and effect are defined. When you read this problem later in the day or at some point in the future, it will be easy to understand what was meant.

The problem is written on the scratch flip chart. After clearly stating the problem, the group discusses whether or not the problem should be included. If there is unanimous agreement, the problem is copied to the final charts.

As a final chart fills, it is removed from the easel and taped to the wall. The charts and problems should be kept in order. By keeping the problems in clear view, the group can refer to the charts and ensure no duplication. The complete sentence, cause and effect, makes understanding the problem easy.

The problem definition phase is the longest and toughest part of the planning session. It should continue until all the problems are described and written on the charts. It is not unusual to have more than 100 problems. Frequently, the problem definition phase will go late into the evening because only one day has been allocated for this phase.

The group dynamics and communication forced during the problem definition phase can be as important as the actual problem resolution.

During the second day, all the problems are grouped into several broad categories. Training, Communication, Compensation, Personnel, and Engineering are some groups, but you should create

Sales Problems			
Problems	**Actions**	**Who**	**When**
2,41,43	Align sales compensation programs to ensure consistency.	SJ	12/1
4,6	Establish accurate forecasting system.	TM	5/1
1,21,89	Develop hiring program to add 1 salesperson per month starting 6/1.	SJ	6/1

Illustration 4-6: Example of action plans from planning session.

your own groups. There are no rules for which problem goes in which group. One problem can appear in more than one group. It is easier to use a specific colored marker to identify each group, and to write the group next to the problem number.

After each problem is grouped, you can begin to establish action programs to solve the problems. Every problem has to fall within a group, or have its own group. Some problems will be outside the sphere of control of the participants and cannot be solved. These are environmental issues and should be grouped within a special group called Environment.

Additional charts are then created for each group. Each problem number is listed. When the charts are later transposed and typed, the group resolution charts should contain the complete problem description.

Obviously, you can't solve the problems in a two day planning session. However, you can establish action programs with target dates for completion and the individuals who are responsible. The set of charts listing the action program, target dates and responsible individual becomes your activity plan for the future.

The planning session helps you identify all of the problems that prevent you from reaching your objectives. The activity programs that come from this session should resolve most of those interferences.

If a session like this is conducted with sales, advertising, data processing, and marketing, the reasons to use direct marketing will be very clear. More importantly, everyone signs up to be part of the solution. You will get great support for all the required elements of direct marketing and everyone will know why you're doing the project.

It is critical that all the parties who will be involved understand and agree to the direct marketing program. Throughout this book I continually stress the need to communicate why and how you'll implement direct marketing. *The biggest cause for failure in any direct marketing project is an unrealistic expectation level at the onset.*

Sales Advisory Council

An extremely effective technique to ensure communication and support for programs that involve the field sales force is to implement a sales advisory council. As you probably know, the fastest way to circulate a rumor in your company is to introduce it to one of your salespeople. The sales force has their own private network and they discuss almost everything among themselves.

Changes in territories and compensation become common knowledge almost immediately even without being formally announced. The sales grapevine is alive and well in almost every company.

Companies seem to develop a strong adversarial relationship between headquarters support personnel and the field selling organization. Most decisions by headquarters are examined with great suspicion by the field. Most field salespeople believe that headquarters doesn't understand their selling environment and isn't really trying to help.

In a recent meeting with several salespeople and sales managers, a comment was made that really describes the severity of the we/they syndrome between headquarters and the field sales force.

> While we were in the headquarters building one salesperson said, "There is a large vacuum on top of this building and as people work in this environment, the vacuum seems to suck their brains right out of their heads. And, I'm really concerned that while I'm sitting here today, my brains are being sucked away as well."

This may sound extreme but the situation exemplifies the feeling of distrust that seems to exist in most companies between the field and headquarters personnel.

I have often heard from headquarters people how bad their salespeople are. They often describe them as primadonnas who are totally self-centered. In most situations, the headquarters personnel don't feel that the salespeople work very hard. And they often characterize them as over-paid, greedy, and lazy.

Lead generation programs are frequently designed and implemented by headquarters people to support field sales. With the feeling I've just described, no wonder we can't make these programs work.

To ensure success, the field has to be part of the design and development of the program virtually from the beginning. The communication grapevine can be used to help make the program successful instead of helping to destroy another headquarters pipe dream.

I frequently suggest to my clients that they implement a sales advisory council consisting of several salespeople, sales managers and the appropriate support personnel. Four to six salespeople as well as a sales manager can provide invaluable feedback on the programs you're considering. The program will become their program and they will communicate their support to the rest of the field organization.

Run the meetings of the advisory council similar to the intensive planning session. Encourage everyone to participate and explain that no idea is a bad one. When you decide on a program, ensure that you have unanimous support from the council before moving forward.

The advisory council can also be used to recognize outstanding sustained performance. Putting the best people on the council will help win the support of the rest of the field and most programs developed by the group will be readily supported by the rest of the organization.

Although the sales advisory council may add some additional expense to your promotion efforts and prolong the development cycle slightly, everyone wins. The salespeople will feel as if the program is their program. And a group of field people can only make a traditional headquarters program better. The salespeople will help you ensure that your offers are timely and exciting. They will also help you select the best lists and keep you pointed in the right direction.

Strategies

The primary differences between strategies and tactics are scope and the dimension of the undertaking. *Tactics* are the things we do to execute a strategy. A *strategy* defines where you would like to go over the longer term. The strategy is the war, while tactics are the individual battles.

So far you have identified the background of your company, its organizational structure, its current costs, and why you need direct marketing. You are now ready to establish long-term goals and objectives. For example, you may decide to reduce sales expenses from 20% of revenue to 18%. More realistically, you may only want to hold sales expenses at a certain rate, while costs are escalating. Several high technology companies have been trying to address the dual problem of increasing selling expenses and decreasing revenue per product. Retail distribution, catalog selling, direct mail and telephone selling are becoming more common in the high technology area because of reduced revenue per product.

As you establish your strategy, remember that you must consider its long-term implications. You may want to test and evaluate whether another channel of distribution is appropriate. Direct marketing or direct mail and/or telemarketing to sell the product may be reasonable, but you may have to introduce these programs in steps.

During the strategy review, focus only on determining the direction in which you want to move over the long term. Avoid establishing media and direct marketing applications; they are the tactics. For example, you may want to establish a database for ongoing direct contacts. This is a strategy. Buying database software, writing procedures to enter the data, and deciding which names will go into the database are all tactics.

To help you focus on your strategies, review the section of your business plan in which you stated why you needed direct marketing. Now you must establish a plan for testing and evaluating whether direct marketing can work for your company.

If you don't know where you're going, any road will get you there.

Establishing Lead Objectives

Lead generation programs frequently fail because companies do not establish reasonable and realistic objectives for the number of leads required. If you ask a sales executive how many leads they would like to see provided from a lead generation program, the answer will inevitably be as many as possible. . . the more the better. With 'concrete' objectives like this, is it any wonder that so many lead programs never get beyond the test phase?

You can plan better lead generation programs and establish objectives based on the number of orders and revenue required.

Using the Lead Requirements Worksheet (Illustration 4-7), you can quickly establish the leads required per salesperson and, by multiplying that number by the number of salespeople, the total number of leads required for the program.

It is unreasonable to expect a lead generation program to account for all of the business generated by the salespeople. Most salespeople will continue to generate their own opportunities and close business regardless of lead activity.

The place to start to establish the lead volume that will be required is with the annual quota or sales objective expected from each salesperson.

You should estimate the percentage of the annual quota that the salesperson will close without a lead generation program. Prior average sales performance can often indicate the sales that can be obtained without a new lead program.

Simple math will allow you to calculate the revenue you can anticipate from the sales force and the amount of revenue you will require from a lead program.

Lead Requirements Worksheet

A) Annual sales quota/objective per salesperson   _____

B) Percent sales quota achieved without leads   _____

C) Sales revenue achieved without leads *(B x A)*   _____

D) Sales revenue required from leads *(A - C)*   _____

E) Average revenue per order from leads   _____

F) Number of orders required from leads *(D÷ E)*   _____

G) Percentage of leads that order   _____

H) Number leads required per salesperson *(F ÷ G)*   _____

Illustration 4-7: Lead Requirements Worksheet.

List selection and offer can significantly influence the size of the average order generated from leads. If the lead program promotes a specific product or service, orders generated from respondents to the promotion will typically order products similar to the offer. Regardless of what your average order has been in the past, a different offer can change its size.

The Lead Requirements Worksheet needs a planned average order to determine the number of leads required. You can use your current average order as determined using the Salesperson Cost Worksheet on page 129, or the average order expected from the offer made in the direct marketing program.

By dividing the required revenue from the lead program by the average order, you'll establish the number of orders required from your lead program.

You can establish the number of leads that are required per salesperson by estimating the percentage of leads that order. This will give you a better set of lead objectives than might have been set in the past.

When you complete the Lead Requirements Worksheet, you also identify the quality of the leads you require. By establishing the anticipated closing rate and size of the order, you have identified a substantial part of the direct marketing program. You have established the list and offer requirements and probably even the promotional concept that you'll use.

A word of caution: Earlier I identified the number of available sales calls per salesperson per year as well as the cost per sales call. As you plan the lead generation program, you should evaluate the number of sales calls that a salesperson can make per year. It is not unusual to initially plan a lead program that requires more sales resources than might be available. If this occurs, you'll have to modify the closing ratio of your leads or the size of the order.

Plan your lead programs to produce results that are realistic and attainable. If you establish a required number of orders and revenue, you'll establish a program that can be measured and controlled. The program will have a chance to succeed.

Measurements

How you will measure your direct marketing program must be determined before you define all the elements that must be executed. In selling to the consumer, marketers appreciate that most buying decisions are made in a relatively short period. Most of the time, the targeted consumer can make the decision. The environment for selling to businesses is quite often more complicated. A single selling cycle can span many weeks and months.

If you won't find out whether a prospect has purchased for several months, how will you measure the success of your efforts? Simply design a program that allows you to measure the project in stages, and evaluate your success against interim objectives. Your business plan should contain these complete objectives for front and back-end results. Measuring response expectations and actual results to the initial offering can indicate whether your program will succeed. Keep in mind, however, that the ultimate measurement will be purchases.

First prepare a complete financial operating plan for each aspect of your direct marketing program. Include the costs and expected results of the program. As you execute different parts of the plan, you can compare results to expectations.

I have seen companies execute programs that could never succeed because of impossibly high expectations. It seems as if every executive expects a 20% response in the mail. High results (20% response is extremely high) may be possible, but shouldn't be required in order for a program to be successful.

Another gratifying result of all of your planning is that you don't have to implement a program with unreasonable expectations. Just take your ultimate objective, and plan backwards. If you need an order cost of $200, you can establish a financial and operating plan that produces that kind of result.

You may not realize how low a response rate you actually need to create a successful program.

Let's look at a direct response ordering program:

Average order	$400.00
Allowable sales expense rate	20%
Allowable sales expense dollars	$80.00
Cost per 1000 pieces mailed	$750.00
Required response rate ($.75/$80)	.94%

Let's assume that we are trying to sell a $400 average order. If our planned sales expense is 20%, we can spend $80 per order. If we're spending $750 per 1000 pieces to mail to the universe, a 1% response will produce 10 orders per 1000 pieces mailed. The total selling expense will be $75 per order. To arrive at the minimum acceptable response rate, you establish the cost per contact ($750 ÷ 1000 = $.75) and then divide by the allowable sales expense dollars. In our example this is 0.94%.

This was a very simple example that didn't consider returned orders, bad payment or any other fulfillment factors to complicate matters. However, it does illustrate how as little as a 1% response may be all you need to conduct a successful direct response ordering program.

Lead generation programs, or those campaigns that have multiple steps before closing the sale, are more difficult to measure but can also be planned using the same techniques. Along with the previous measurements given, you must add the cost of sales calls and the anticipated closing rates to arrive at the complete cost per order.

Here is a simple example of lead objectives that identifies a measurement plan for lead generation:

a)	Average order (estimate)	$5,000.00
b)	Allowable sales expense rate (estimate)	20%
c)	Allowable sales expense dollars (a • b)	$1,000.00
d)	Cost per sales call (estimate)	$250.00
e)	Closing rate (estimate)	30%
f)	Salesperson cost per order (d + e)	$833.33
g)	Allowable cost per direct mktg lead (c - f)	$166.67
h)	% Respondents qualified as leads (estimate)	40%
i)	Allowable cost per respondent (g • i)	$66.67
j)	Cost per 1,000 pieces mailed (estimate)	$750.00
k)	Number of leads required (j ÷ i)	11.25
l)	Required response rate (k ÷ 1,000)	1.13%

A number of elements will have to be measured to verify whether this plan succeeded. The first and easiest piece will be to establish the response rate to the mailing. If you get 1.13% response or better, you're ahead of your planned expectations. If 40% of the respondents qualify as referrals and are sent to the sales force, you again are ahead of the plan. If your initial response rate was higher, but your qualification rate lower, you can still be ahead of the plan. As long as you produce a qualified lead for $166.67 or less, you are meeting the plan.

In both examples, the program was successful if we could produce about 1% response. This response rate is reasonable and attainable for most programs. If you present a detailed plan that focuses on cost per order, you'll probably succeed. Lead programs have their own set of measurement problems that will be discussed later in Chapter 5.

XYZ Coffee Service Business Plan

If this approach to planning seems a little far-fetched or difficult to grasp, let's look at a real life example. I recently created a business plan that established the required response rates in a lead generation program for a sales force using only telemarketing. The company sold a coffee service to other businesses. Their objective was to generate sales leads that were interested in trying the coffee service.

XYZ Coffee Service Current Sales Approach

Average Earnings per Salesperson	$25,000
Multiplier to include General, Administrative & Management Costs in Average Earnings	2.00
Total Cost per Salesperson per year	$50,000
Average Customer Expenditures per year	$1,200
Annual New Sales Quota per Salesperson	$144,000
Average New Customers per Month per Salesperson	10
New Customers per Year per Salesperson	120
Average Face-to-Face Sales Calls per Week	21
Sales Calls per Year (Assume 48 Weeks allowing for Vacation and Holidays)	1,008
Sales Calls per Month	84
Closing Ratio (Orders per Month/Sales Calls per Month)	11.90%
Cost per Sales Call	$49.60
Cost per Order	$416.67

<u>Lifetime Value of the Customer</u>

% Loss of Customers per Year		30.00%
Value Year 1	$1,200	
Value Year 2	$840	
<u>Value Year 3</u>	<u>$588</u>	
Total for 3 Years		$2,628

% Cost of Sales of 1st Year Revenue   34.70%

% Cost of Sales of Total Revenue   15.90%

Anticipated Results with Telemarketing

Planned Closing Ratio of Leads Generated From
Telemarketing   30.00%

Number of Calls to Non-Ordering Prospects   1
    (Trial Service is delivered by Service Rep
Salesperson calls near end of trial to convert)

Number of Calls to Purchaser   2
    (Sales Rep has to make a second call to get contract
signed)

Total Face-to-Face Sales Calls per Order   4.3
    (Prospect Calls/Closing Ratio less one Call who
became a purchaser plus Purchaser Calls)

Total Salesperson Cost per Order $213.28
    (Total Face-to-Face Calls multiplied by Current Cost
per Sales call)

Cost of Trial of Service $35.00
    (Cost to deliver & pick up equipment and cost of cof-
fee)

Total Cost of Trials per Order $116.67
    (Cost of Trials divided by Closing Ratio)

Total Selling Cost per Order $329.95
    (Cost of Salesperson plus Cost of Trials)

Allowable Direct Marketing Cost per Order $86.72
    (Current Cost per Order less Total Selling Cost with
Telemarketing)

Telemarketing Cost per Hour	$30.00
(This assumes a $3.00 cost per follow-up phone call)	
Names Consumed per Hour	10
% of Consumed Calls that are Completed	65.00%
Number of Completed Calls per Hour	6.5
Required Orders per Hour	0.35
Required Response Rate of Original List	3.50%
Required Response Rate of Completed Calls	5.38%

In creating this business plan, management was unable or unwilling to reveal the entire marketing budget so we used the average earnings of the salespeople for our budgeting calculations. The cost of one salesperson was estimated at $25,000 per year. This number was doubled to $50,000 to approximate the true cost of the average salesperson per year. It was interesting to observe that even with this company's extremely low cost per sales call figure, the average cost of an order was still fairly high.

The average customer historically spent about $100 per month or $1,200 annually.

Each salesperson had an annual sales quota for new business of $144,000. We divided the above $1,200 by this $144,000 to get the annual new customer objective of 120 customers per salesperson. We then divided 120 by 12 months to get the monthly quota of 10 new customers.

Given that the average salesperson made 21 sales calls per week we then multiplied 21 by 48 weeks to establish 1,008 sales calls per year. The 48 weeks allowed for vacations and holidays. It really didn't allow for sick, personal, and other time off. Although somewhat overstated, these were management's numbers, and the credibility of our plan meant getting management to agree to a more conservative estimate. Finally, we divided the 1,008 calls per year by 12 to establish the monthly sales call volume of 84 calls per month.

Once we knew the total number of calls and the total number of orders per month, it was fairly easy to establish the closing ratio, cost per sales call, and cost per order. The closing ratio is established by dividing the number of orders by the number of sales calls (10 ÷ 84 = 11.90%). The cost per sales call is established by dividing the annual cost per salesperson by the number of sales calls made per year ($50,000 ÷ 1008 = $49.60). The cost per order can be established two different ways to yield the same results. (1) Divide the annual cost of the salesperson by the number of orders per year ($50,000 ÷ 120 = $416.67). (2) Divide the cost of the sales call by the closing ratio ($49.60 ÷ 11.90% = $416.81). There is a slight difference due to rounding.

Many businesses fail to examine the costs of acquiring a customer against the lifetime value of that customer. It is unfair to judge a program against only the first year's sales of a customer if that customer will continue to purchase products for a longer period. In this example, customer turnover or attrition rate was about 30% per year. Therefore, the average customer will last somewhat longer than three years. When considering turnover and lifetime values of customers, keep in mind that the turnover rate is always on the remaining balance, therefore it will never drop completely to zero.

The turnover rate of 30% was used to establish the value of the customer for the next three years. Although this was understating the lifetime value of the customer, it did allow us to work with a more realistic estimate of revenue from each customer. In addition, we didn't use present value techniques to establish the real return on investment. So being a little off in the value estimate was balanced against the missing factors of cash flow and net present value of money.

In year 1 the customer contributes $1,200 in revenue. The year 2 value is 70% (100% - 30% = 70%) of the $1,200 or $840. Year 3 is 70% of the $840 or $588. As you can see, the number will never equal zero. For our example we stopped the revenue, for evaluation purposes, after three years and totaled the revenue at $2,628.

The cost of selling can now be compared to both the annual revenue and the lifetime revenue of each customer. The annual revenue comparison shows that the cost of selling is almost 35% of the first year's revenue. This would make the cost of selling prohibitive in most businesses and suggests that you can't afford to sell. When the comparison is extended to include the lifetime value, it is about 16% of sales. This is a more realistic selling expense.

As you can see, it takes a great deal of work to establish the costs of current approaches to selling before you begin to develop the direct marketing approach. But you really should be armed with sales costs on a current basis to objectively compare them with your direct marketing results. Most sales executives are not aware of how expensive it has become to close an order.

XYZ Coffee Telemarketing Plan

We first established that the quality of the lead we wanted to generate should be able to close at a 30% rate. After some prospect qualification on the telephone, we were planning to telemarket an offer for a one month free trial of the coffee service. Prior experience with trial service had shown these offers to close at about 30%. The trial service would be delivered by the sales representative. If a prospect didn't order, it was felt that the salesperson would only have to make a single sales call to determine that the prospect would not become a customer. Prospects that became customers required a second call to have the service contract signed.

To establish the total number of face-to-face calls required for this program we added together the total number of prospecting calls that didn't order and the number of calls to customers who did order. It took one call to determine the quality of the prospect and 30% of the calls made would yield a customer. Therefore, 1 ÷ 30% = 3.33 sales calls to qualify prospects and one additional call to the customer who bought. The total number of sales calls required was 4.3 per sale.

To establish the cost of the sales calls we multiplied the current sales call cost by the total number of sales calls required per customer. Therefore, 4.3 x $49.60 = $213.28 in salesperson selling costs for each order. In addition, there was a cost to have the trial coffee service installed. The cost per trial service was $35.00. The total cost for trial service was established by dividing the single cost per service by the closing ratio. The total cost of the trials was $116.67 ($35.00 ÷ 30%).

The total sales expense per order was the sum of the salesperson costs and the cost of the trials. The total sales expense was $329.95 ($213.28 + $116.67). We then established the allowable direct marketing expense, $86.72, by subtracting the total planned selling expense from the current selling expenses ($416.67 - $329.95).

Because telemarketing was going to be used to generate the trials, we had to establish its cost. (I go into more detail in Chapter 9 on how to plan a telemarketing program.) For this example, we used the cost per telemarketing hour of $30.00. We expected to consume 10 names per hour of activity and 65% of the consumed names were completed contacts. Therefore, we anticipated 6.5 completed contacts per hour. A *completed contact* is contacting the prospect and getting a decision on the offer.

We then established how many acceptances we needed to generate for each hour of activity by dividing the cost per hour by the allowable direct marketing expense. We needed to generate .35 orders per hour ($30.00 ÷ $86.72). Once we knew the completed number of contacts per hour, and the number of orders required per hour, we established the required response rate for both the total number of records used, and the actual number of people contacted with telemarketing. From the original list, this program required a 3.5% response rate (.35 ÷ 10) or 5.4% (.35 ÷ 6.5) of the total contacts.

This was a program designed only for telemarketing and the response rate required to make the program successful was modest. This type of planning can defuse expectation levels that may not be realistic.

Even before you get into the specifics of your program, measurement has to be considered and evaluated. First, you have to determine how you'll measure the program, and how much you can afford to spend. With a firm understanding of the tolerable selling costs, you can design and plan the direct marketing effort.

Tactics

As you define the actual direct marketing tactics you will use, be sure you document and chart the flow of the program. *The biggest single problem we've encountered in direct marketing programs is not anticipating all the necessary and possible alternative steps.* A complete flowchart will force you to consider all of the alternatives.

You're designing an operating system when you design a direct marketing program. The database, promotional material, controls and analysis, fulfillment and marketing integration must be anticipated. By developing a complete flow of the activities, you will be forced

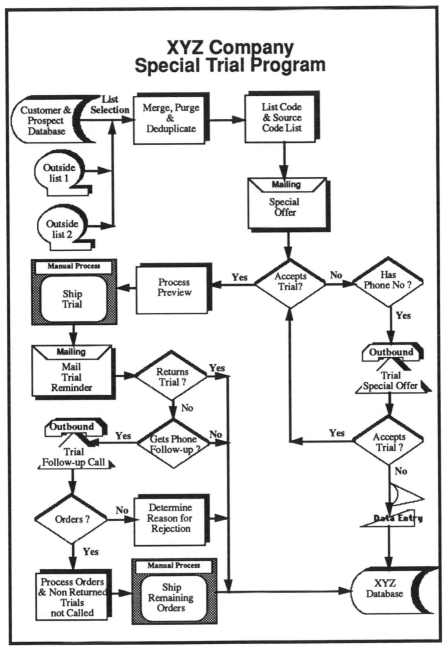

Illustration 4-8: A Sample Flowchart.

to anticipate all of the possible alternatives. As part of the flowchart, you should consider time frames and contingencies that can affect the program.

As you can see in Illustration 4-8, you should first anticipate what lists you will use and where you will get them. These lists will then be merged to create a single mailing list. Eliminate the duplicate names on this list. Duplicates are expensive and can have a seriously adverse effect on your prospects, especially if you will be using telemarketing. Illustration 4-9 identifies typical flowchart symbols that you might use to design programs.

At the same time that the lists are merged and the duplicate records are eliminated, the list should be source coded to allow measurement. In our example, we planned to test three groups of customer lists and two outside lists for the direct marketing project. Each of the five lists had to be coded with special sourcing information to allow measurement.

The mail was then dropped to all of the prospects. The prospect could respond by mail or through an inbound 800 number. These respondents were processed and, if possible, eliminated from the telephone marketing list. We recognized that a prospect who had already responded might still receive a phone call. The script was designed to address this situation.

Acceptances were sent a trial of the product and a portion of those who accepted were scheduled for a follow-up telephone selling call 14 days after the trial was mailed. The trials that did not receive a phone call received mail reminders. This was a method to test the impact of the second phone call. The second phone call also provided information on why the prospect was rejecting the trial and not purchasing the product. Any prospect that decided to purchase the product was shipped the remainder of the order and added to the customer file.

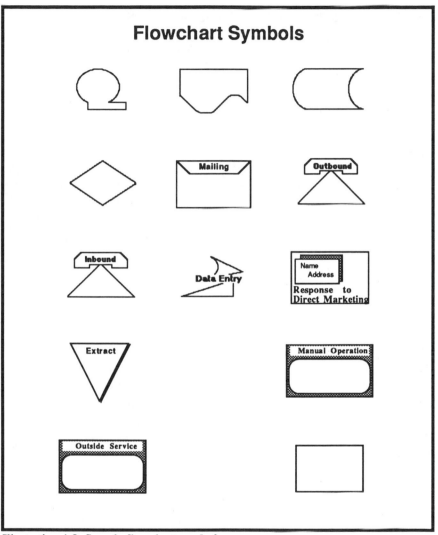

Illustration 4-9: Sample flowchart symbols.

Prospects who did not respond to the mailing and who had a phone number, received a telemarketing call 15 days after the mail was dropped. If the prospects accepted the offer, they were processed similarly to the mail acceptances as described in the preceding paragraph.

From the acceptances, telemarketing and follow-up telephone calls, and other information, a complete prospect database was established for future activity.   A business plan was developed from the flowchart to establish a methodology to measure the program.

XYZ Direct Marketing Program

	Cust A	Cust B	Cust C	List 1	List 2	Total
Mail Activity						
Tot Rec on list	1,299	6,500	6,500	4,500	2,500	21,299
Mail Response Rate	3.00%	2.00%	2.00%	1.00%	1.00%	1.73%
Total Resp/Trials	39	130	130	45	25	369
Proj Conv Mail Trial	25.00%	20.00%	20.00%	20.00%	20.00%	20.60%
Mail Orders	10	26	26	9	5	76
Mail Cost/1000	$400	$400	$400	$400	$400	
Mail Costs	$520	$2,600	$2,600	$1,800	$1,000	$8,520
Cost per Responder	$13.33	$20.00	$20.00	$40.00	$40.00	$23.09
Cost per Order	$52.00	$100.00	$100.00	$200.00	$200.00	$112.00
Phone Activity						
% of List Contactable	70.00%	70.00%	0.00%	0.00%	0.00%	70.00%
Total Contacts	909	4,550	0	0	0	5,459
% Request Trials	30.00%	25.00%	25.00%	20.00%	20.00%	25.85%
Telemktg Trials	273	1,138	0	0	0	1,411
% of Trials Converting	20.00%	20.00%	20.00%	20.00%	20.00%	20.00%
Number of Orders	55	228	0	0	0	283
Telemktg Contact/Hour	8	8	8	6	6	
No. of Init Telemktg Hrs	114	569	0	0	0	683
No. Prev F/U Telemktg Hrs	34	142	0	0	0	176
Total Telemktg Hrs	148	711	0	0	0	859
Cost/Telemktg Hr	$35.00	$35.00	$35.00	$35.00	$35.00	$35.00
Total Telemktg Costs	$5,180	$24,885	$0	$0	$0	$30,065
Cost per Trial	$18.97	$21.87	$0.00	$0.00	$0.00	$21.31
Cost per Order	$94.18	$109.14	$0.00	$0.00	$0.00	$106.24
Mail & Phone Combined						
Total Previews	312	1,268	130	45	25	1,780
Total Orders	65	254	26	9	5	359
Costs						
Direct Marketing	$5,700	$27,485	$2,600	$1,800	$1,000	$38,585
Goods	$4,875	$19,050	$1,950	$675	$375	$26,925
Previews	$6,240	$25,360	$2,600	$900	$500	$35,600
Commissions	$3,510	$13,716	$1,404	$486	$270	$19,386
Total Costs	$20,325	$85,611	$8,554	$3,861	$2,145	$120,496
Cost per Order	312.69	337.05	329	429	429	335.64
Revenue per Order	$900	$900	$900	$900	$900	$900
Gross Revenue	$58,500	$228,600	$23,400	$8,100	$4,500	$323,100
Contribution	$38,175	$142,989	$14,846	$4,239	$2,355	$202,604
% Rev as Contribution	65.00%	63.00%	63.00%	52.00%	52.00%	63.00%

The business plan for direct mail is done based on experience and known costs. Begin the business planning process with the total number of records on each list. You have to know how many of each group will be used for direct marketing. If you already have had experience with a particular list segment, use those results during the planning process. Certain segments of the customer list may perform better than others. In our example, the different response rates were based on our experience with that type of list. The total response rate, which is the weighted average for all of the list segments, was also calculated by dividing the total number of responses by the total number mailed. The total response is the sum of the response for each list category.

The total responses by list segment and total for the test are easily established using the projected response rates. Again, experience with various list segments can be used to project the closing ratio of each group of respondents. You can determine the weighted average closing ratio by dividing the total number of orders by the total number of respondents. The total number of orders is the sum of the orders for each group.

The cost for the mail is used to calculate the mailing cost for each segment of the list. The total cost is the sum of the costs by list category. Now you can easily establish the cost per responder and the cost per order.

Now that you have planned your direct mail campaign you can use a similar approach to plan your telemarketing and telephone sales activity. As you'll note from the plan, only a small portion of the list (Cust A & Cust B) had phone numbers and could be used for telemarketing. From those records that are contacted via telephone, we establish the respondents and orders from telemarketing by using the same methodology employed for direct mail. As I discuss in Chapter 6, only a percentage of the list we start with will be able to

be contacted with telemarketing. Note that only the total number of
records used for telemarketing is included in the Totals column. As
you'll note in the phone activity portion of the plan, the totals column reflects 5,459 total contacts, 1,411 total trials and 283 total
orders.

Now let's return to our XYZ Direct Marketing example. After the
initial offer to try XYZ's coffee, we planned follow-up phone calls
to those prospects who accepted the offer, to try to convert the trials
into orders. We used the number of anticipated contacts per hour to
determine the number of calling hours required for both the initial
and subsequent follow-up calls. Using the $35.00 per calling hour
cost, we established the cost per responder (trial) and the cost per
order.

At this point, we have established the combined anticipated results
of the program. Next, we combined the results by list segment, and
then calculated totals for the entire program. We summarized the
total number of orders and previews by type of media and list segment.

We then figured the costs for the direct marketing effort. We also
calculated the cost of goods for orders, the cost of goods for the previews, and any commissions paid for orders by list segment.

Finally, we totaled all the costs for the project by list segment. We
determined the cost per order by dividing the costs per order by the
total number of orders. The gross revenue was calculated by multiplying the revenue per order by the total number of orders. The
costs are subtracted from the revenue to determine the contribution
by list segment. By dividing the contribution by the gross revenue
we determined the percent of contribution.

Contribution is the amount of gross profit made by a specific
activity. In many companies, this is the method of measuring the

effectiveness of any marketing program. In essence, it is the gross profit of a project after allowing for cost of goods and cost of selling including commissions. It doesn't normally include general and administrative expenses or other overhead items. The concept of contribution is more fully described in Chapter 8.

By tracking the costs and results by list segment, the effectiveness of each list and facet of the marketing program can be accurately evaluated. You'll be able to determine if the overall program was a success or failure, and which portions of your target audience produced more orders than others.

Documenting the Plan

Once you have established the background and strategy for your direct marketing programs, each new program you execute is much easier to plan. You still want to define the prospect, offer, and universe you're trying to contact, but you don't have to spend much time on the historical issue. In addition, most of your anticipated results will be based on the experiences you've had in other direct marketing efforts.

On the following pages I have included a sample plan of an ongoing program for you to use as a model.

Acme Computer Corporation
Marketing and Sales Department
Sales Operating Guide

Section: **Sales Programs**
Subject: Shared Data Program   Subject #: 20-05

This guideline identifies and explains a special marketing program to generate sales leads and expand the customer base. The program uses direct marketing to make the offer to an appropriate group of prospects, and then leads are given to the salesperson for follow-up.

1.0 Objective

This program is designed to develop qualified sales leads for the salespeople to pursue. A special offer is used to get the prospect involved and interested in Acme Computer. Because it has been determined that selling a relational database as a concept is very difficult, this promotion emphasizes the need to share information when several computers are involved. The concept of purchasing equipment has a higher perceived level of risk and is more difficult to sell. This promotion is targeted to reduce risk and make the decision to try an ACC system virtually painless. The offer is targeted to make the prospect feel accepting the offer is similar to accepting the free 30-day post installation trial they receive when they acquire software.

After indicating an interest and concern in sharing information, the prospect is offered the opportunity to install an Acme Computer AC300 system for 30 days and discover how easy and flexible sharing data is with an Acme Computer System.

The Acme Computer system will be installed by the customer after some training and assistance by Acme Computer personnel. The system will be installed using RS-232 communication and the initial target audience will be primarily the DEC VAX user who is also using PCs.

2.0 The Universe.

    2.1 The universe of prospects for this promotion consists of three unique groups of people.

        2.1.2 Businesses that have only an IBM host system installed and are also sharing information with a network of PCs.

        2.1.2 Businesses that have an IBM host system, DEC VAX system, and a network of PCs sharing information.

        2.1.3 Businesses that have a DEC VAX host system installed, and are also sharing information with a network of PCs.

    2.2 The primary target in each group of prospects is the executive or manager responsible for the data processing installation.

    2.3 The prospect's objectives in accepting the free trial offer are to:

        2.3.1 Determine if they can share data across multiple hosts and users.

        2.3.2 Decide if Acme Computer has a potential solution for sharing data problems.

2.3.3   Test new technology and a relational database easily by installing the AC300.

2.3.4   Educate themselves and their staff on an available approach for solving both current and future problems.

2.3.5   Enable users to see their own applications running with the AC300.

2.3.6   Be shown how to use simple query and 4GL approaches to access data without having to write application programs.

2.3.7   Learn first hand what is required to install hardware.

Installing hardware has been perceived as difficult. The trial program will give the prospect an opportunity to disprove this perception.

3.0   Prospect Qualification

A qualified prospect is one who:

3.1   Is currently using PCs and any of the following hosts:
DEC VAX
Sun
Apollo
AT&T

3.2   Can provide a block multiplexor channel connection and additional programmer support to implement the AC system if they are using an IBM VM/CMS host.

3.3   Can identify an application that will be used for data sharing after the trial.

3.4   Has reasonable credit worthiness.

3.5   Is an end-user. VARs and resellers are excluded.

3.6   The ACC salesperson will obtain the following additional qualification information:

     3.6.1   Types of hosts.

     3.6.2   Number of hosts at the site.

     3.6.3   Number of hosts to be used during the trial installation.

     3.6.4   The application for data sharing after the trial.

     3.6.5   A schedule to implement the trial and the application.

     3.6.6   Application alternatives other than the ACC solution.

     3.6.7   The method of payment for the solution after the trial. (The availability of funding.)

     3.6.8   Agreement from the prospect that they understand the costs associated with continuing to use the ACC system.

     3.6.9 The authority of the prospect to accept the trial.

3.6.10 The decision criteria and names of those who will decide to purchase the AC system after the trial.

3.6.11 A letter of commitment signed by the prospect. This letter will identify the ACC responsibilities for the trial, and prospect responsibilities to implement the trial.

3.6.12 The criteria for evaluating the trial and what it will take to convince the prospect to continue using an AC system.

4.0 Offer

4.1 Free trial of AC300 for 30 days.

4.2 System will be installed for sharing of data between PCs and supported hosts.

4.3 ACC will provide training, system, installation support and guidance on conversion of data files to the AC300.

4.4 Prospect will provide:

4.4.1 Files for use on the AC300.

4.4.2 Users who will be trained by the prospect with ACC assistance.

4.4.3 Site and site preparation including electrical and environmental changes if needed.

4.4.4 Communication facilities.

4.4.5　Host and PCs to work with the AC300. The PC will have a minimum configuration of at least an XT with 4 megabytes free.

5.0　Direct Marketing Approach

5.1　Flowchart Explanation

5.1.1　Lists will be acquired for targeting the offer and the direct marketing program. The internal lists of prior respondents and customers will be used as the base list to start all activities. The Computer Intelligence Corporation (CIC) list of VAX systems will also be used. A subscription list of VAX systems will be acquired for direct mail and telemarketing activities.

The DEC Professional list or Gary Slaughter Compiled list will be used.

The lists will be name-directed whenever possible. The target contact will be the director or manager of data processing.

Additional lists will be tested to include IBM VM/CMS sites. The same list sources will be used but will specifically be targeted for IBM. During the initial mailings, only DEC users and Telco managers will be used.

If possible, sites that have both IBM and DEC hosts will be identified and coded on the list to allow testing of all types of prospects.

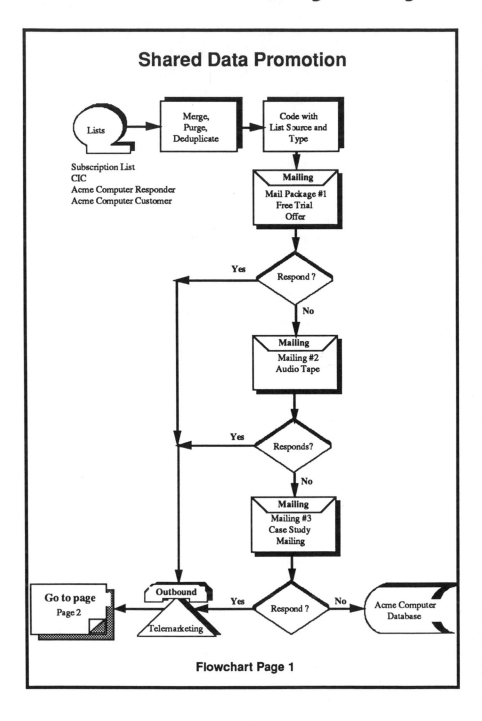

Shared Data Promotion

Lists

Subscription List
CIC
Acme Computer Responder
Acme Computer Customer

Merge, Purge, Deduplicate

Code with List Source and Type

Mailing
Mail Package #1
Free Trial
Offer

Respond ? — Yes / No

Mailing
Mailing #2
Audio Tape

Responds? — Yes / No

Mailing
Mailing #3
Case Study
Mailing

Respond ? — Yes / No

Outbound
Telemarketing

Go to page
Page 2

Acme Computer
Database

Flowchart Page 1

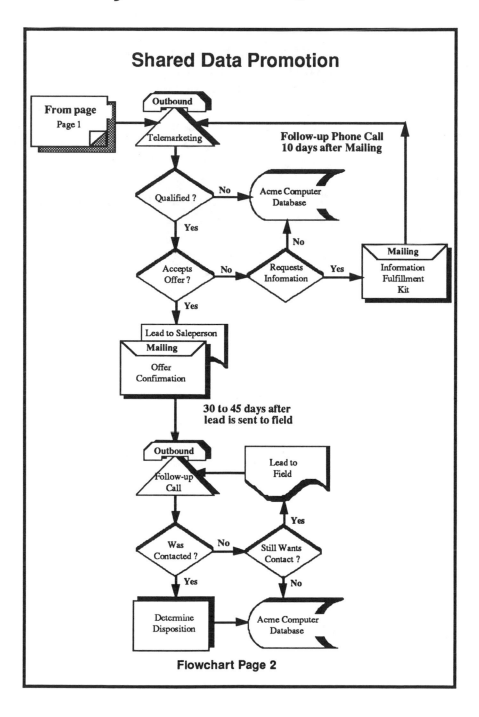

Shared Data Promotion

From page — Page 1

Outbound — Telemarketing

Follow-up Phone Call 10 days after Mailing

Qualified? — No → Acme Computer Database

Yes

Accepts Offer? — No → Requests Information

No → Acme Computer Database

Yes → **Mailing** — Information Fulfillment Kit

Yes → Lead to Saleperson

Mailing — Offer Confirmation

30 to 45 days after lead is sent to field

Outbound — Follow-up Call ← Lead to Field

Yes

Was Contacted? — No → Still Wants Contact?

Yes → No

Determine Disposition → Acme Computer Database

Flowchart Page 2

If telemarketing is used, the combined undupli-
cated list will be sent to a service bureau specializing in appending phone numbers to the record.
This will be done in parallel to the mailing. This
process normally takes about two weeks and is
about 50% effective on the list supplied to the
service bureau.

5.1.2   The lists will be sent to an outside service bureau
and combined to eliminate duplicate names and
sites. The primary list will be the Acme
Computer customer list, followed by the former
respondent list. The CIC list will be next in the
hierarchy and the subscription lists will be last.

5.1.3   The service bureau will code each record with
the list source:

List Source	System	Code
Acme Computer Customer	Unknown	ACC0
Acme Computer Customer	VAX	ACC1
Acme Computer Customer	IBM	ACC2
Acme Computer Customer	AT&T	ACC3
Acme Computer Customer	Other	ACC4
Acme Computer Prospect	Unknown	ACP0
Acme Computer Prospect	VAX	ACP1
Acme Computer Prospect	IBM	ACP2
Acme Computer Prospect	AT&T	ACP3
Acme Computer Prospect	Other	ACP4
CIC	Unknown	CIC0
CIC	VAX	CIC1
CIC	IBM	CIC2
CIC	AT&T	CIC3
CIC	Other	CIC4

Name of Publication	Unknown	SU10
Name of Publication	VAX	SU11
Name of Publication	IBM	SU12
Name of Publication	AT&T	SU13
Name of Publication	Other	SU14

Acme Computer will only offer complete coverage in selected cities. The list will be extracted to only include selected sectional centers that are geographically within the covered areas. This will be explained in a memo prior to the mailing.

5.1.4 All of the un-duplicated names will be mailed package number 1.

5.1.5 Respondents to the first mailing will be sent to the local sales office for telemarketing and actual follow-up.

5.1.6 Nonrespondents to the mailing will be mailed package number 1 again. This will be mailing #2.

5.1.7 Respondents to the second mailing will be sent to the local sales office for telemarketing and face-to-face sales follow-up.

5.1.8 Nonrespondents to the second mailing will be mailed a third mailing package. This will be mailing #3.

5.1.9 A database will be developed and only those records that are the property of Acme Computer will be included (Acme Computer Customers, Acme Computer Prospects, CIC).

5.1.10 If the prospect is qualified during the telemarketing effort, the prospect will be offered a visit from an ACC salesperson to review the free trial program and discuss how it can be implemented. The mail solicitations will offer the prospect the opportunity to try the AC system for 30 days free. The salesperson will determine the prospect's qualification level in order to receive the free trial.

5.1.11 The prospect may refuse the offer and ask for additional information. This group will be fulfilled with an information package.

Ten days after the information package is mailed, this group will be recontacted via telemarketing to try to convert them into sales leads.

5.1.12 The names of unqualified prospects and those prospects that refuse the offer will be updated on the database and held for possible future activity.

5.1.13 Accepters of the offer will receive a letter confirming their acceptance, and giving the name of the salesperson or sales manager by whom they will be contacted.

A sales lead will be sent to the salesperson. Both the confirmation letter and lead will be mailed within two business days of the initial contact.

5.1.14 All leads will be recontacted via telemarketing 30 to 45 days after they were mailed to determine the disposition of the situation. If the lead wasn't contacted by a salesperson, he will be offered the opportunity to be contacted.

5.1.15 If the prospect wants to be recontacted, the lead's name will be telephoned to the regional director and mailed the same day.

5.1.16 If the prospect was contacted, the disposition will be determined and the database updated.

6.0 Financial Projections

Anticipated Results

Number of Records for Analysis	20,000
% of Records lost via merge, purge, de-duplicate	25.00%
Number of records lost via merge, purge, de-duplicate	5,000
Records receiving pre-mailing	15,000

Group	AC Prosp	DEC Prof	CMP Publ	Total
Mail				
Total Records - Mail #	3,000	10,000	2,000	15,000
Mail Resp Rate	1.00%	1.00%	1.00%	1.00%
Total Respondents	30	100	20	150
% Leads of Respondents	60%	60%	60%	60%
Leads	18	60	12	90
% Trials of Leads	60%	60%	60%	
Trials	11	36	7	54
% Orders of Trials	30%	30%	30%	
Orders	3	11	2	16
Total Records - Mail #2	2,970	9,900	1,980	14,850
Mail Resp Rate	1.00%	1.00%	1.00%	1.00%
Total Respondents	30	99	20	149
% Leads of Respondents	60%	60%	60%	60%
Leads	18	59	12	89
% Trials of Leads	60%	60%	60%	
Trials	11	35	7	53
% Orders of Trials	30%	30%	30%	
Orders	3	11	2	16
Total Records - Mail #3	2,940	9,801	1,960	14,701
Mail Resp Rate	1.00%	1.00%	1.00%	1.00%
Total Respondents	29	98	20	147
% Leads of Respondents	60%	60%	60%	60%
Leads	17	59	12	88

	AC Prosp	DEC Prof	CMP Publ	Total
% Trials of Leads	60%	60%	60%	
Trials	10	35	7	52
% Orders of Trials	30%	30%	30%	
Orders	3	11	2	16

Total Mail Results (3 Mailings)

	AC Prosp	DEC Prof	CMP Publ	Total
Respondents	89	297	60	446
Leads	53	178	36	267
Trials	32	106	21	159
Orders	9	33	6	4

Total Mail Results (2 Mailings)

	AC Prosp	DEC Prof	CMP Publ	Total
Respondents	60	199	40	299
Leads	36	119	24	179
Trials	22	71	14	107
Orders	6	22	4	32

Costs

Mail Costs - (Per piece mailed in all programs)

Cost per Direct Mail Piece for Package 1 (w/postage)	$1.89
Cost per Direct Mail Piece for Package 2 (w/postage)	$2.89
Cost per Direct Mail Piece for Package 3 (w/postage)	$1.89
Cost per Literature Fulfillment Kit	$3.00
Cost per Lead Confirmation Mailing	$1.50

List Costs - (Per name acquired in all programs)

Cost per Name with Processing	$0.15
Cost per Name for Phone number	$0.30
Cost per Lead Processed	$1.50

Telemarketing Costs - (Per telephone contact made in all programs)

Cost per Telephone Call	$5.00

One Time Costs

Development	$20,000

List	AC Prosp	DEC Prof	CMP Publ	Total
Initial Name	$0.00	$4,500.00	$900.00	$5,400.00
Phone Number	$0.00	$0.00	$0.00	$0.00
Lead Processing	$79.50	$267.00	$54.00	$400.50
Total List Costs	$79.50	$4,767.00	$954.00	$5,800.50

Direct Mail	AC Prosp	DEC Prof	CMP Publ	Total
Package #1	$5,670.00	$18,900.00	$3,780.00	$28,350.00
Package #2	$8,670.00	$28,900.00	$5,780.00	$43,350.00
Package #3	$5,670.00	$18,900.00	$3,780.00	$28,350.00
Lit Req Fulfill	$51.00	$177.00	$36.00	$264.00
Lead Confirmation	$79.50	$267.00	$54.00	$400.50
Total Mail Costs	$20,140.50	$67,144.00	$13,430.00	$100,714.50

Telemarketing Costs	AC Prosp	Dec Prof	CMP	Total
Lead F/U Call	$445.00	$1,485.00	$300.00	$2,230.00
Tot Telemktg Cost	$445.00	$1,485.00	$300.00	$2,230.00
Development Costs				$20,000.00
Total Costs	$20,665.00	$73,396.00	$14,684.00	$128,745.00
Total Leads	53	178	36	267
Total Trials	32	106	21	159
Total Orders	9	33	6	48
Cost per Lead	$389.91	$412.34	$407.89	$482.19
Cost per Trial	$645.78	$692.42	$699.24	$809.72
Cost per Order	$2,296.11	$2,224.12	$2,447.33	$2,682.19
Avg Order Size	$95,000	$95,000	$95,000	$95,000
Total Revenue	$855,000	$3,135,000	$570,000	$4,560,000
% Rev/Direct Mktg	2.42%	2.34%	2.58%	2.82%

List				
Initial Name	$0.00	$3,000.00	$600.00	$3,600.00
Phone Number	$0.00	$0.00	$0.00	$0.00
Lead Processing	$54.00	$178.50	$36.00	$268.50
Total List Costs	$54.00	$3,178.50	$636.00	$3,868.50

Direct Mail				
Package #1	$5,670.00	$18,900.00	$3,780.00	$28,350.00
Package #2	$8,583.30	$28,611.00	$5,722.20	$42,916.50
Package #3	$0.00	$0.00	$0.00	$0.00
Lit Req Fulfill	$72.00	$240.00	$48.00	$360.00
Lead Confirmation	$54.00	$178.50	$36.00	$268.50
Total Mail Costs	$14,379.30	$47,929.50	$9,586.20	$71,895.00

Telemarketing Costs				
Lead F/U Call	$300.00	$995.00	$200.00	$1,495.00
Tot Telemktg Cost	$300.00	$995.00	$200.00	$1,495.00
Development Costs				$20,000.00
Total Costs	$14,733.30	$52,103.00	$10,422.20	$97,258.50
Total Leads	36	119	24	179
Total Trials	22	71	14	107

	AC Prosp	Dec Prof	CMP	Total
Total Orders	6	22	4	32
Cost per Lead	$409.26	$437.84	$434.26	$543.34
Cost per Trial	$669.70	$733.85	$744.44	$908.96
Cost per Order	$2,455.55	$2,368.32	$2,605.55	$3,039.33
Revenue per Order	$95,000	$95,000	$95,000	$95,000
Total Revenue	$570,000	$2,090,000	$380,000	$3,040,000
% Rev/Direct Mktg	2.58%	2.49%	2.74%	3.20%

7.0 Direct Mail Copy Platforms

7.1 Package #1 - Initial Free Trial Offer

Purpose:

- Create powerful impact.
- Introduce shared data concept.
- Help envision data sharing problem.
- Help prospect identify data sharing problem in their environment.
- Motivate prospect to want more information on how AC system can help solve their problem.
- Ask prospect to call AC to find out more.

Considerations:

How will you create impact?

- Three-dimensional impact
- Personalized format
- High quality brochure

How will you emphasize the magnitude of the problem to motivate your prospect to respond?

- Focus the DP manager on the Proliferation of PCs in their organization.
- Is the prospect losing money?
- Is the prospect losing customers?

How will you ensure that Package #1 breaks through the mail room clutter?

- Personal addressing with no teaser copy on the envelope looking like a first class package.
- Size and shape will be different.
- Package will convey quality and expense and make it difficult for the mail room to discard without delivering.

How will you ask the prospect to respond?

- Business Reply Card
- Business Reply Envelope
- 800#
- FAX

7.2 Package #2 - Audio tape free trial offer

Same criteria as Package #1, with the following additional parameters.

- Package #2 will follow the mailing of Package #1 by about three weeks.

- Package #2 might be tested as a stand-alone mailing.

7.3 Package #3 - Offering Free Trial of AC300

Same criteria as Package #2, with the following additional parameters.

- Package #3 will follow the mailing of Package #2 by about three weeks.

- Package #3 might be tested as a stand-alone mailing.

7.4 Lead Confirmation Mailing

Purpose:

- To tell the prospect that they will be contacted by an AC salesperson soon and will explain the free trial of the AC300 system.

- To open the door of communication if the salesperson has not responded promptly to the prospect.

- To acknowledge that AC knows the prospect has accepted their offer.

7.5 Send Literature Fulfillment

Package #1 initially will be used to fulfill literature requests. Ultimately a separate package to fulfill literature requests will be developed.

I used an outlining format for this business plan in order to make additional programs easy to test and document. You should try to establish a consistent format for developing your own follow-up programs.

Planning Summarized

By now your business plan looks like a major tome. It contains as much as you'll ever want to know about your company, why you need direct marketing, and what results you expect from the direct marketing program. As I said at the start of this chapter, reading about business planning isn't very exciting. Most of the information is common sense and has probably already been developed within your company.

The development of the program you're going to implement is the only fun part of planning. It may seem easier to just start writing the program, but without prior planning, your chances for failure are very high. Much of the remainder of this book describes different tactical approaches to implementing business-to-business direct marketing.

By forcing yourself to examine the basics of your business, you'll ensure that the implementation of direct marketing will have the highest chance to succeed. Your company organization may require unique implementation considerations and reporting programs. Establishing the current selling costs will allow you to effectively measure and evaluate the direct marketing effort. Finally, the overall planning phase will help clarify why you need direct marketing and what results you should expect.

Once you've developed a documented direct marketing business plan, it will be easy to communicate your program to others within your company and to outside vendors you might need. In addition, the documented plan will give you a basis from which to build new programs.

I know how hard it is to read about planning, but using some of the examples I've given, I hope you find the actual planning phase easier to accomplish. Don't sell business planning short. The effort you spend up front could be the best investment you'll make to ensure that your program is successful.

Chapter Five:

Measuring Lead Programs

Perhaps the most frustrating element in any lead generation effort is measuring the results. Salespeople will often ignore management attempts to track and measure the results of lead programs. After repeated efforts to gain sales information about leads that were sent to the sales force, most managers responsible for the lead generation program simply give up and measure only response and lead results. They never find out if their program was successful.

Part of the enigma in measuring lead programs starts with how programs are planned and executed. Lead generation programs frequently fail because companies do not establish reasonable and realistic objectives for the number of leads required. If you ask a sales executive how many leads they would like to see provided from a lead generation program, the answer will inevitably be as many as possible. . . the more the better. With 'concrete' objectives like this, is it any wonder that so many lead programs never get beyond the test phase?

You can plan better lead generation programs and establish objectives based on the number of orders and revenue required. As I discussed in the last chapter, using the Lead Requirements Worksheet, you can quickly establish the leads required per salesperson and the total number of leads required for the program.

Salespeople and their managers are extremely tactical in their approach to business. They are only concerned with making their sales objectives now! Sales leads are viewed as opportunities to help them meet their immediate goals and even if they can't follow-up on all opportunities, those they do contact might convert to an order now.

Don't confuse activity with results!

One of the biggest mistakes made by the sales force is believing activity or effort are measurements of results. While it is true that hard work will often produce high results, misdirected activity can actually be counterproductive. The most glaring example of this phenomenon is the generation of poor quality sales leads. Another classic example is when more sales leads are generated than can be contacted by your sales force.

Seminars are often a classic example of misdirected effort. Management will want to fill a show or seminar with warm bodies on the seats. Their logic is that the more people that hear the message, the better the odds to close an order. Very often, because of management pressure, the salespeople will invite their customers or friends to attend the seminar even though their "warm bodies" represent little opportunity to sell additional products or services.

After the seminar, management will want to assess the ultimate results from the seminar and will create reports and follow-up programs which create lots of activity but do not produce sales. The seminar appears to have been successful. However seminars should generate sales -- not merely activity.   I'll discuss seminars in more detail in Chapter 10.

Remember: any program you design should produce orders preferably, lots of orders.   Design programs to achieve the most measurable results in terms of sales.   In fact the best programs will require the least effort and meet the sales goals.

Unfortunately, most people responsible for lead generation efforts, never establish order objectives.   The sales executive responsible has expectations that are never communicated to you.   The result is often a good lead program that is discarded because it didn't meet unrealistic objectives.

The Ill-Informed Walrus

The following anecdote may describe a situation you may find yourself in when you measure your lead efforts.   I am uncertain who authored this anecdote but it is quite appropriate in any discussion about measuring lead programs.

> "How is it going down there?" barked the big walrus from his perch on the highest rock near the shore. He waited for the good word.
>
> Down below, the smaller walruses conferred hastily among themselves. Things weren't going well at all, but no one wanted to break the news to the Old Man. He was the biggest and wisest walrus in the herd, and he knew his business -- but he did hate to hear bad news. And he had such a terrible temper that every walrus in the herd was terrified of his ferocious bark.

"What will we tell him?" whispered Basil, the second-ranking walrus. He well remembered how the Old Man had raved and ranted at him the last time the herd caught less than its quota of herring, and he had no desire to go through that experience again. Nevertheless, the walruses had noticed for several weeks that the water level in the nearby Arctic Bay had been falling constantly, and it had become necessary to travel much farther to catch the dwindling supply of herring.

Finally, Basil spoke up: "Things are going pretty well, Chief," he said. The thought of the receding waterline made his heart feel heavy, but he went on: "As a matter of fact, the beach seems to be getting larger."

The Old Man grunted. "Fine, fine," he said. "That will give us a bit more elbow room." He closed his eyes and continued basking in the sun.

The next day brought more trouble. A new herd of walruses moved in down the beach, and with the supply of herring dwindling, this invasion could be dangerous. No one wanted to tell the Old Man, though only he could take the steps necessary to meet this new competition.

Reluctantly, Basil approached the big walrus, who was still sunning himself on the large rock. After some small talk, he said, "Oh, by the way Chief. A new herd of walruses seems to have moved into our territory." The Old Man's eyes snapped open, and he filled his great lungs in preparation for a mighty bellow. But Basil added quickly, "Of course, we don't anticipate any trouble. They don't look like herring-eaters to me -- more likely interested in minnows. And as you know, we don't bother with the minnows ourselves."

The Old Man let out the air with a long sigh. "Good, good," he said. "no point in our getting excited over nothing, then, is there?"

Things didn't get any better in the weeks that followed. One day, peering down from the large rock, the Old Man noticed that part of his herd seemed to be missing. Summoning Basil, he grunted peevishly, "What's going on, Basil? Where is everybody?"

Poor Basil didn't have the courage to tell the Old Man that many of the younger walruses were leaving every day to join the new herd. Clearing his throat nervously, he said, "Well, Chief, we've been tightening things up a bit. You know, getting rid of some of the dead wood. After all, a herd is only as good as the walruses in it."

"Run a tight ship, I always say," the Old Man grunted. "Glad to hear that everything's going so well."

Before long, everyone but Basil had left to join the new herd, and Basil realized that the time had come to tell the Old Man the facts. Terrified but determined, he flopped up to the large rock, "Chief," he said, "I have bad news. The rest of the herd has left you."

The old walrus was so astonished that he couldn't even work up a good bellow. "Left me?" he cried. "All of them? But why? How could this happen?" Basil didn't have the heart to tell him, so he merely shrugged helplessly.

"I can't understand it," the old walrus said. "And just when everything was going so well!"

Moral: What you like to hear isn't always what you need to know.

Measuring lead programs can place the person responsible in a role similar to Basil's. Reporting results to your superior when the expectations are unreasonable can be a painful experience.

In the last chapter I discussed planning your program. If you have established and documented the expectations for your program, measurement may be possible.

Any discussion on measuring lead programs has to start with the objectives and goals. There is no reason to measure the results if you haven't set objectives for the effort. As I said earlier, if you don't know where you are going, any road will get you there.

It is unreasonable to expect a lead generation program to account for all of the business generated by the salespeople. Most salespeople will continue to generate their own opportunities and close business regardless of lead activity.

The place to start in establishing the required lead volume is with the annual quota or sales objective expected from each salesperson.

Estimate the percentage of the annual quota that the salesperson will close without a lead generation program. Prior average sales performance can often indicate the sales that can be obtained without a new lead program.

Simple math will allow you to calculate the revenue that can be anticipated from the sales force and the amount of revenue that will be required from your lead program.

List selection and offer can significantly influence the size of the average order generated from leads. If the lead program promotes a specific product or service, orders generated from respondents to the promotion will typically order products similar to those in the offer. Regardless of what your average order has been in the past, a different offer can change its size.

The Lead Requirements Worksheet needs a planned average order to help you determine the number of leads required. You can use your current average order or the average order expected from the offer you make in your direct marketing program.

By dividing the required revenue from the lead program by the average order, you'll establish the number of orders required from your lead program.

By estimating the percentage of leads that will order, you can also establish the number of leads that are required per salesperson. This will give you a better set of lead objectives than you might have had in the past.

When you complete the Lead Requirements Worksheet, you are also identifying the quality of the leads you require. By establishing the anticipated closing rate and order size, you are identifying a substantial part of the direct marketing program. You have established the list and offer requirements and probably even the promotional concept that you'll use.

In the Salesperson Cost Worksheet in Chapter 4, I identified the number of available sales calls per salesperson per year as well as the cost per sales call. As you plan your lead generation program, evaluate the number of sales calls that a salesperson can make per year. It is not unusual to initially plan a lead program that requires more sales resources than might be available. If this occurs, you'll have to modify the closing ratio of your leads or the order size.

The Company - Prospect Relationship

Plan your lead programs to produce results that are realistic and attainable. If you establish a required number of orders and revenue you'll establish a program that can be measured and controlled. The program will have a chance to succeed.

The measurement of lead programs often depends on information provided by the salesperson. Managers will frequently design elaborate tracking and reporting systems that require the field force to provide information about their selling activity and the quality of the leads. This approach will fail.

As I mentioned in Chapter 3, the personality of most salespeople works against reporting systems and lead tracking. The salesperson's ego makes it difficult for them to acknowledge that you have identified a sales opportunity in their territory that they weren't already aware of. They can't acknowledge that you can prospect more effectively in their territory.

Most lead management, tracking and reporting systems work the same way. Illustration 5-1 shows that leads are generated by advertising or direct marketing and then forwarded to the field force.

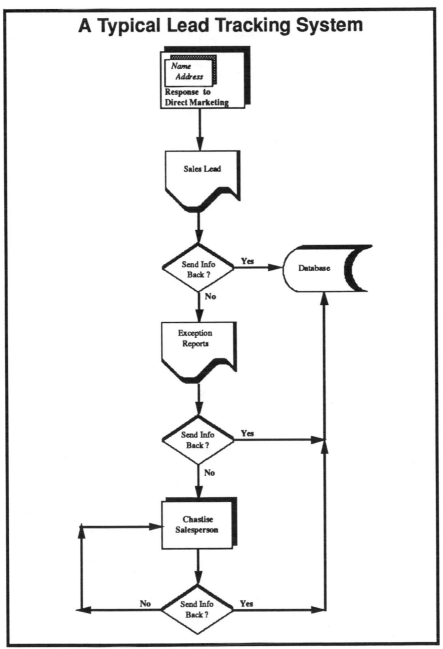

Illustration 3-10: A typical lead tracking system.

As the salespeople do not supply the information, exception reports are generated that identify open leads. This information is sent to management for action and disposition. The pressure is really applied to the salesperson to report their activity.

Most salespeople manage their territories from their cars and tend to be somewhat disorganized. Their prior experience with leads often causes them to have a negative opinion about lead quality. Leads may not be regarded as having value and may be treated with disdain.

You have probably spent $100 to $200 for each lead that has been provided to the salespeople. The salespeople may not appreciate the value of your leads, but you have made a significant investment in generating them. Very often, companies will give leads to the salespeople without maintaining a copy or computerized record of the lead.

If you give a salesperson a cash advance and they leave your employ today, you will probably recover the cash from any outstanding wages due the employee.

If that same person has a company car and leaves your employ, you will certainly require the car to be returned before you allow the employee to leave.

If the person leaves your employ, what happens to the lead?

The lead will probably leave with the individual. If each salesperson has only 10 leads and you only spend $100 per lead, that's $1,000 that the salesperson removes from your company. You probably wouldn't allow the cash to leave and you certainly wouldn't allow a physical asset, like a car, to leave. Yet the leads seem to vanish without notice.

Many companies haven't created a database of lead information. Leads are simply forwarded to the salesperson for activity. These

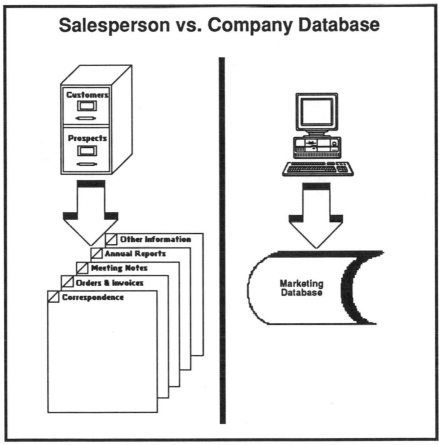

Illustration 5-2: The salesperson's relationship file.

companies assume that the salesperson will keep track and maintain appropriate information on each prospect.

As you may recall from my previous discussion, salespeople tend to create the only complete relationship file. Their files are maintained for prospects as well as customers. It is unlikely that a salesperson will yield their desire and responsibility to build and maintain information about their territory to any management or headquarters function.

The salesperson files are mostly paper records that they have built and continue to maintain. They are comfortable with the format and contents of the information base. You will probably have a tough time getting them to support a different approach in this area.

Companies that attempt to develop prospect databases often go too far and doom their effort from the start. I have witnessed several companies that have provided lap-top computers with complete contact history as well as database information about every prospect and customer. These companies expect the salesperson to update the database via the lap-top after each contact. Most salespeople will resist this approach. They will suspect management of attempting to monitor every move they make and their egos will force them to reject the effort.

I often ask audiences if a company's relationship with its customers and prospects is a relationship between a salesperson and the prospect company or between their company and the prospect company?

Did a prospect respond to your lead generation effort because of a relationship with a salesperson? Probably not. They are responding because of an interest in your company and products. Why not maintain the essence of this relationship from the beginning?

As leads are received, enter the contact information into a centralized database. The ideal situation is to create a database of all leads and respondents. This information will provide you with a house file that will become a critical element in future lead programs.

The Territory Management System

Salespeople hate paperwork. They tend to treat all communication, both external and internal, with equal disdain. Odds are good that most communication material will be piled in several stacks and often discarded without ever being read. Leads can often fall into this category, especially if you send different types of leads in different formats.

All leads should be formatted to look the same. When designing the lead form, consider how the salesperson will report the lead's disposition and status.

I prefer to create leads in a format that will help the salesperson manage their territories. I often suggest that leads be printed on 8-1/2" x 11" paper. The lead form should be pre-punched to allow insertion in a binder and contain multiple copies to facilitate reporting.

The lead form can be one of the key elements in a territory management system. By providing a binder with sectional tabs, similar forms for customer information and blank forms for salesperson generated prospects, there is a complete territory management system.

The lead form should be consistently created for any prospect sent to the field for activity. In many systems I've designed, I've suggested that a three-part form be sent to the salesperson. Each form of the set should be printed in a different color to make it easier to control the reporting process.

Only capture the basic information about the prospect. The information you really require from the salesperson is:

> What is the likelihood of the prospect to buy?
> What is the likelihood of the prospect to buy from you?
> When is the prospect likely to buy?

It is easier to convince salespeople to give you a minimum amount of information. With the appropriate contact information and this sales-generated buying information, you can mount sustained marketing

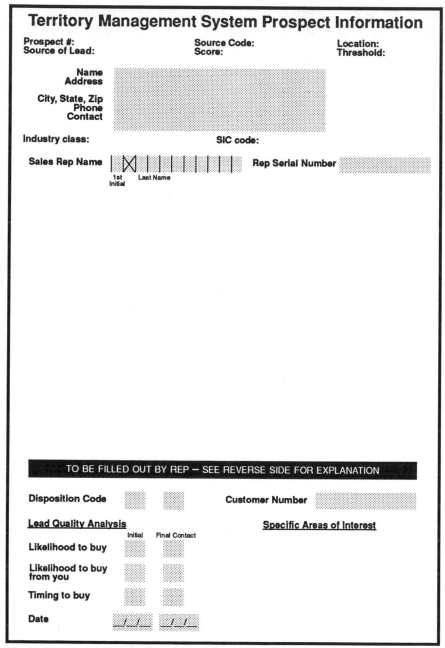

Illustration 5-3: Territory Management Form (front side of form).

HOW TO USE THE TERRITORY MANAGEMENT SYSTEM PROSPECT INFORMATION FORM

GENERAL INFORMATION

1. CONTACT THE PROSPECT - Make any required corrections/additions to the shaded areas on the front of this form. This includes filling in the information requested at the bottom of the form.

2. RETURN the initial contact copy to the Territory Management System (TMS), within 30 calendar days.

   Subsequent communication with TMS – Whenever the disposition of the prospect is established, notify TMS by completing the final contact copy with updated information. You should always keep the territory management copy. Periodically TMS will issue updated forms with additional information at which time you can dispose of your outdated form.

The information and sample below are provided for your assistance.

• •

A. DISPOSITION CODES

1. ACTIVELY WORKING – PROSPECT HAS AGREED TO FURTHER CONTACTS
2. PROSPECT NOT HANDLED BY THIS LOCATION
3. REFERRED PROSPECT TO ANOTHER LOCATION
4. PROSPECT ORDERED (Insert cust # on front)
5. ALREADY A CUSTOMER (Insert cust # on front)
6. PROSPECT REJECTED BECAUSE
   a. They are too small
   b. We are too expensive
   c. We are not competitive
   e. Deferred decision
   f. Satisfied with current approach
   g. Other
7. PROSPECT WANTS TO BE DELETED FROM OUR FILES
8. PROSPECT BOUGHT COMPETITION WITHIN THE LAST YEAR
9. UNABLE TO CONTACT PROSPECT WITHIN LAST 30 DAYS
10. OTHER

B. LEAD QUALITY ANALYSIS

LIKELIHOOD TO BUY	LIKELIHOOD TO BUY FROM YOU
1. Definetly will buy	1. Definetly will buy
2. Probably will buy	2. Probably will buy
3. Uncertain	3. Uncertain
4. Probably won't buy	4. Probably won't buy
5. Definetly won't buy	5. Definetly won't buy

TIMING TO BUY
1. Immediate
2. Less than 3 months
3. Less than 6 months
4. 1 year or more
5. Probably won't

• •

A. DISPOSITION CODE – Select and record appropriate disposition code. If you select code 5, include the appropriate letter code. If you sell the prospect or find he is already a customer, include the customer number. In order to establish the best prospect, we need to learn from those prospects that become customers. If the prospect orders via a different customer name, we will never learn how to improve your leads! **Include the customer number!**

B. LEAD QUALITY ANALYSIS – Even those prospects that don't buy can help us learn how to improve lead quality. Your analysis of the prospect's interest is critical. **Select the proper codes and answer the three questions!**

C. DATE – Insert the appropriate date for the transaction as you return the information.

B. SPECIFIC AREAS OF INTEREST – Future marketing activity can and should be tailored and directed at specific prospect needs. Your analysis of the prospects requirements is critical. **Select the proper Interest codes!**

Territory Management System Prospect Information

Illustration 5-4: Territory Management Form (rear side of form).

campaigns to various segments of the database. In addition, you can evaluate the quality of the lead program.

Print all leads in the same format using the same size paper. Think about how you can help the salesperson better manage their territories. Many of the lead management service bureaus offer lead formats that make it easier for the salesperson to manage their territories and also to provide you with information to measure and manage your program.

Illustration 5-3 is a lead form I have used effectively with many different companies. The form was created using 4-part carbonless paper. The large blank area on the front of the form allows for a great deal of varied information to be distributed depending on the various lead programs.

The rear of the form, Illustration 5-4, contains coding and completion instructions. This approach makes it easier for the salesperson to understand what is expected.

The first copy is kept by the first line sales manager. Many managers create a binder with separate sections for each salesperson. An administrative assistant will then file each lead alphabetically by salesperson. The leads can be annotated with date of receipt.

Because sales territories are extremely dynamic, I don't suggest that most companies attempt to assign leads to specific salespeople as they are generated. As the lead is received by the local manager, they can assign the salesperson. When the lead is returned to the territory management system (TMS), the salesperson information can be updated.

The remaining three copies are provided to the salesperson. Within 30 days the salesperson returns one copy with disposition information. One of the disposition codes means the salesperson was not able to contact the lead within 30 days.

Many business transactions will take longer than 30 days. The additional copies of the lead information provide a method for the salesperson to permanently retain a copy of the lead information and a way to report on the final disposition of the prospect. One copy should be permanently kept in the salesperson's territory management binder. The fourth and final copy can be returned when the salesperson achieves a final result for the prospect.

No matter what method you ultimately select to measure the effectiveness of the lead effort you will have to rely on the salesperson to provide information and feedback. As I mentioned in Chapter 3, you can use the salesperson to provide information or you can go directly to the prospect to evaluate the disposition of the lead. The lead information has to be communicated to the salesperson. I am a firm believer that you should require salespeople to provide feedback about lead quality. As you design the lead program decide how you will provide the information and capture feedback.

You can achieve better support from the sales force if you provide a mechanism that helps them manage and organize their territories. A system that helps to manage territories and also provides you with feedback is a better alternative to merely trying to police the system.

In addition to providing leads in the territory management format, you should also provide customer information in a similar form.

The final element of the territory management resource is a blank form that will allow the salesperson to include their own prospects and leads that they generate. If you design this blank form to also be multi-part, the salesperson can provide additional prospects to your central database.

Two of the biggest advantages of this approach are portability and ease of use. The binder containing complete territory information will travel well and operate effectively on desks, in cars, at home or while traveling via commercial transportation.

Although I do advocate requesting feedback from salespeople, I don't believe in chastising and using high pressure tactics to ensure that information is returned. If you force the salespeople to provide information, all of the leads will be coded as bad or uncontacted. The key to getting information returned is to provide high quality leads from the beginning.

I advocate designing lead reporting and management systems that help salespeople. The more we do to support their efforts, the higher the likelihood they will support our programs.

Several lead management firms have designed reporting systems that contact the salesperson periodically via telephone or direct mail and ask for the status of an open lead.

In one of my clients situations, we FAX the lead directly to the sales office. An outside fulfillment service maintains a complete database and handles all of the prospect inquiries. The same day we create and forward the lead, we also print a double post card that is mailed to the salesperson. The post card contains a pre-paid business reply card that the salesperson completes and mails back to the fulfillment service. The information is added to the prospect database and if the lead has not been finally disposed of in a reasonable period of time, another post card is sent to the salesperson to complete when a final disposition is established.

In both approaches we have designed response vehicles that are easy for the salesperson to use. The data is relatively easy to capture and return to the lead management control point. If you are asking the sales force to capture and return an abundance of information they will resist. If you design a reporting mechanism that is easy to use and requires virtually no additional effort you will probably succeed.

Later we will discuss techniques to maintain contact and enhance the company - prospect relationship directly with the prospect. This technique can ensure complete reporting and measurement. If you go directly to the prospect and find out what has happened and ask the salesperson for their feedback, you'll have a complete closed loop reporting system.

The information from the salesperson will allow you to generate a series of reports to track all leads provided to the sales manager. You'll know every lead sent to the field and how many have been returned with disposition information. It will be relatively easy to generate a series of reports to managers aging the open leads and requesting further disposition information.

If you decide to track prospects that have been contacted as well as those leads that have not reached a final disposition, you can also generate an open opportunity report.

All too frequently, managers lose sight of the objective in the lead program and place undo pressure on the salespeople to return lead information. This creates suspicion within the organization and heightens the natural adversarial relationship between management and sales. Exception reports are effective in allowing the field managers to control the lead effort but should not be used to force reporting and compliance.

Very often it becomes extremely frustrating trying to get the salespeople to return information about sales leads. Many companies give up and only measure response rates. Lead quality, which would be determined from the returned sales data and order information is virtually unknown.

The evaluation of each lead on a scale of likelihood to buy and timing to buy will allow you to evaluate lead programs on an ongoing basis.

Remember the ultimate objective in any lead generation effort is to close orders. Interim measurements about lead quantity and lead quality are just a way to review activity, they don't measure results.

Using the Prospect to Control and Measure

As I mentioned in Chapter 3, the best source of measuring lead programs is the respondent. You will learn the effectiveness of the lead program and the effectiveness of the selling effort by the field sales force.

Every time I have contacted leads after they have been sent to the field force, I am surprised at the high number that were never contacted by salespeople. This is often caused by several factors:

- The salespeople are not happy with the quality of leads from prior programs. They have pre-judged the current leads and determined it is not in their best interest to waste time contacting poor quality leads again.

- The salespeople have received too many leads to follow-up. This is one of the most common problems. The salespeople do not have enough time to contact all of the leads and will often make arbitrary judgments about lead quality. For some unknown reason, they will elect to contact only a few prospects. The rest will never be contacted and are often returned coded as bad leads.

- The salespeople have unsuccessfully attempted to contact the prospect several times.

  I know from my experiences in telephone selling only about 25% of dialings in the business world will result in a completed call. Most salespeople will call prospects at convenient times during the day. Convenient to the salesperson, not to the prospect. If they leave a return phone number, the salesperson will probably not be available when the prospect does call back. And if a salesperson makes 3 or 4 attempts and doesn't get through, they will probably give up and move on to other opportunities.

Leads that the salesperson is unable to contact will often be returned as poor quality leads.

- The salesperson is already aware of the lead. Some leads will be returned by the salesperson because he is familiar with the company. He may never contact the respondent and simply returns the lead, often coding it as poor quality.

Salespeople have difficulty acknowledging that you can find a prospect in their territory they didn't already know about. They feel that to do so is to admit someone else has done a better job than they have. It is an ongoing struggle to convince the sales force that you are working -- not competing -- with them.

Once you execute a lead generation program and make an offer to a prospect, that prospect deserves your continued attention. If you have made a significant offer and a prospect has accepted, failure to contact the prospect can do great long-term harm to your company.

It is important your company develop and maintain a direct relationship with the prospect as well as asking a salesperson to do so.

Mail or FAX the prospect a confirmation of their response and tell them which sales office you have asked to contact them. By doing so, you are building the relationship between your company and the prospect. You will also gain the ability to go back directly to the prospect to find out if a salesperson contacted them. The prospect probably responded to your promotion because they had an interest in your company and products -- not because of a relationship they had with a salesperson. You should maintain the relationship the prospect started.

Cellular Company Case Study

Let's examine a lead generation program that evolved to the extent that we actually measured the relationship with the prospect.

Cellular Company is a major supplier of cellular telephone equipment. They were interested in generating sales leads for their independent distributors in several market areas. Broadcast, radio, television, space ads in both newspapers and magazines, and direct mail were used to generate responses. Illustration 4-10 shows how the responses were handled by an independent telemarketing service bureau. The independent firm was fully automated and handled both mail and phone responses. If the prospect responded via telephone, the inbound communicators used a script to guide their conversation. As they obtained information from the prospect, they entered it directly into a computer.

Those prospects who did not provide a company name were considered lower quality. They were sent a less expensive fulfillment package. Cellular Company did not feel that a salesperson could effectively follow-up on prospects who responded from their homes. Salespeople have a tendency to prejudge the quality of leads. Respondents who only provide their home address are frequently categorized tire kickers, not buyers.

All respondents were added to a database and each contact was tracked. New respondents were checked against the database to ensure that their inquiries hadn't already been handled in the last 90 days. Quite often, a prospect who hasn't received a timely follow-up will respond a second time. Cellular Company was selling

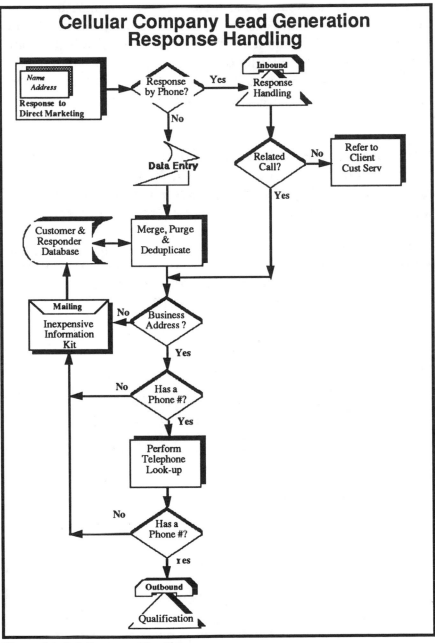

Illustration 5-4: Response Handling.

through outside distributors and there were several distributors in each market. We tried to ensure that the same prospect wasn't sent to two different distributors. We also tried to eliminate prior respondents to avoid entering duplicate names into the database when people responded more than once. As discussed earlier, de-duplication routines for business-to-business lists are not very effective.

All respondents were qualified via telephone. If a mail respondent did not provide a telephone number, and the number wasn't available through directory assistance, the respondent was considered not qualified and sent the less expensive information package.

At the onset of the project, Cellular Company recognized that their

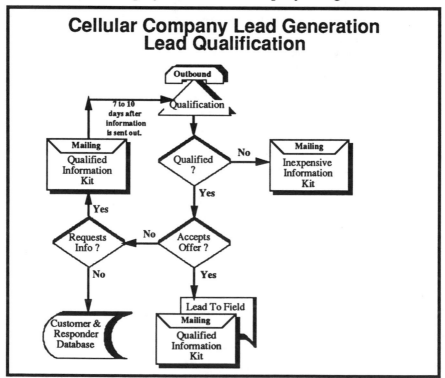

Illustration 5-5: Lead Qualification (Telephone Screening Method).

product was unique and there would be a lot of interest from people who were not qualified. In addition, Cellular Company had a limited geographic area in which they offered services. A less expensive generic fact kit was developed for unqualified prospects.

The qualified prospects, those with business addresses and phone numbers, were contacted via outbound telemarketing. Each prospect was screened for qualification and offered a call by a salesperson. The same lead qualification script was used for both inbound and outbound telemarketing. The telephone screening method is detailed in Illustration 5-5.

In every program some respondents will refuse to see a salesperson without first receiving some additional information. We know that many prospects request literature before they agree to be contacted by a salesperson. We also know that a substantial percentage of those prospects who request information can be converted to a lead if they are contacted after they receive the material.

Some respondents may be interested in your offer but may not be ready to commit to a purchase or to spending time with a salesperson. They may respond to your telephone offer by requesting additional information. In my experience, prospects who request additional information are legitimate prospects. About 25% of all prospects who request literature are genuinely interested in buying and may ultimately be converted into leads and customers.

Keeping track of who requested literature, when the literature was fulfilled, and when the prospect should be re-contacted will require some form of database. Small volumes will only require a manual database. However as the volumes become larger, the database will require a computerized approach.

Initially, Cellular Company management wasn't concerned about the the sales force returning lead information. Management was convinced that the sales force would follow-up on every lead and pro-vide feedback about lead quality. Cellular Company didn't feel that a lead management and control system was necessary.

After several months of lead generation and several thousand leads, only 5% of the leads had been returned with any information. Cellular Company couldn't evaluate the success of the lead program. Senior management received verbal feedback that lead quality was not very good. They were considering shutting down the project.

To evaluate the success of the lead program, a mail questionnaire was sent to all leads to determine their disposition. The respondent database made re-contacting the leads very easy.

The results were startling. Forty percent of the leads had been con-tacted by the sales force. In our experience, this is a good follow-up rate. We have seen lead follow-up as low as 8% in other campaigns. In this instance, the leads proved to be very high quality. Of the leads contacted by a salesperson, over 60% had purchased a prod-uct.

Management was alarmed about the business opportunity that had been lost because the sales force had not followed-up on the other 60% of the leads. Several action programs were implemented to ensure that Cellular Company could capitalize on the opportunity within their current and future respondent database.

A complete lead management and tracking system was implement-ed to ensure that the sales force followed up on all leads. The leads were only given to the third-party distributor salesperson for 30 days. Cellular Company used telemarketing to re-contact prospects 30 days after the leads were generated. The telemarketer asked the prospects if they had received the information requested, and if they had been contacted by a salesperson. If the prospect had not been contacted, the lead was regenerated and sent to another distributor

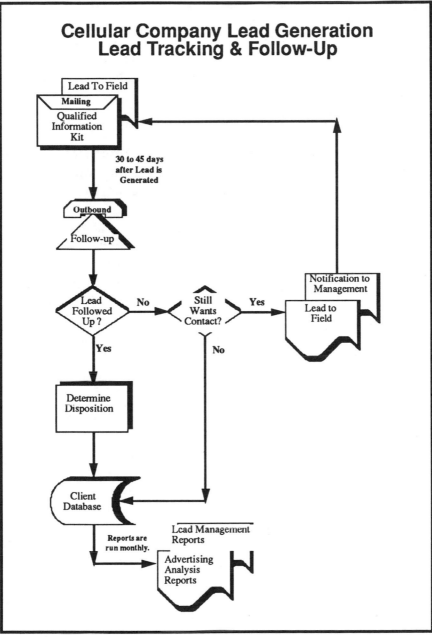

Illustration 5-6: Lead Tracking and Follow-up.

salesperson. Illustration 5-6 reflects the flow of activity in the lead tracking and follow-up system.

The results of the project were very rewarding. Almost 80% of generated leads were contacted. More importantly, 30% of all generated leads resulted in orders. The cost per lead and cost per order were substantially less than originally anticipated.

The database allowed ongoing contact with the respondent. It also enabled Cellular Company to develop an accurate measurement system and evaluate the success of the lead generation program.

The prospect was the best source of information about the sales activity that had occurred. It was interesting to compare feedback from the salespeople with the information provided by the prospects. Very often the information was contradictory. Salespeople indicated a prospect had been contacted and was not planning to buy. The prospect said that they had never been contacted and would like to buy. Although you can rationalize why this situation occurs, good business sense dictates that the prospect is never wrong. Management needed to correct the situation.

I think there are two reasons that a prospect and a salesperson's feedback would conflict:

    1)   The salesperson returned the lead because:

- The were not happy with the quality of the leads from prior programs.

- They had received more leads than they could follow-up.

- They had repeatedly tried unsuccessfully to contact the prospect.

In this case management can work with the salesperson to ensure they don't stop trying to contact the prospect too soon. Management can also create a follow-up letter to maintain direct contact with the prospect. This option gives the prospect a central facility they can contact if they are not contacted by a salesperson.

2)   The salesperson did speak with the prospect, but the prospect doesn't remember the contact. This is a training and sales quality issue that local management should address.

One technique we have successfully implemented in many situations is to call the prospect 10 to 30 days after the lead was sent to the salesperson. In this case, the prospect is contacted via telemarketing and asked:

Have you received the information you requested?

Were you been contacted by a salesperson?

Those prospects that weren't contacted give management an opportunity to correct the problem. The lead can be assigned to a different salesperson or territory, or local management can ensure that someone contacts the prospect immediately.

As an aside, it is interesting how lead quality immediately improves if you give uncontacted leads to another salesperson. The original salesperson will often complain about being deprived of an important sales opportunity in their territory. Even after they have returned the lead as poor quality.

Apple Computer Prospect Qualification System

Recently Apple Computer tested a program to determine lead quality and follow-up activity by their computer dealers. As you may know, the computer industry continues to offer higher performance products at ever decreasing prices. As you may recall from Chapter 1, Illustration 5-7 depicts this phenomenon.

The decreasing cost of technology has reduced the dollars available to sell each system. There is less money to pay salespeople for basically the same sale they made only a few years ago. The better salespeople are leaving the industry because they can't make as much money.

Analysis of prior lead generation efforts has demonstrated that only about 30% of leads are contacted by a dealer. Most prospects

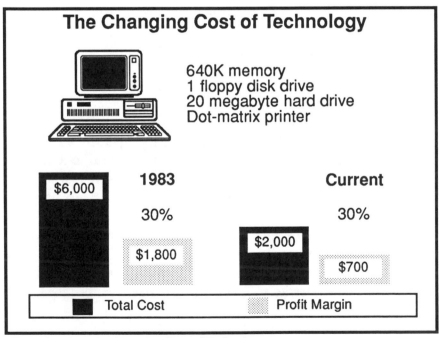

Illustration 5-7: The Changing Cost of Technology.

never receive adequate attention and follow-up. In addition, the quality of the dealer sales organization has continued to deteriorate and the lead follow-up problem is expected to continue in the future.

A program was needed to help prospects understand the Apple solution before they visited a computer dealer. The prospect needed to be convinced that the Macintosh solution was the leading alternative to meet their needs. A quality demonstration of the Macintosh's capabilities was required to convince the prospect that it was the best solution. Unfortunately, because of changing personnel, Apple was never certain of the quality of the demonstration given by the computer dealer.

In addition, computer vendors were compounding the problem by continually developing and executing other lead programs. Dealers are often overwhelmed by leads and sales programs developed by the manufacturers. As a result, many dealers do not assign enough resources to follow-up leads and inquiries. Many dealers presort or prequalify leads and inquiries before any follow-up is performed.

Seminars are also used extensively by dealers as a promotion activity. Many of the attenders are not qualified and have little or no understanding of how much a solution will cost. The lower quality of the attenders tends to demotivate the dealer sales force and further exacerbate the lead follow-up problem.

In a recent national program executed by Apple for Desktop Media, prospects were offered an opportunity to receive a video tape. The video tape showed two small businesses using Macintosh computers to perform desktop publishing. It showed how easy it was to use the Macintosh to produce high quality publications. The video ended by encouraging prospects to visit their Apple dealer to see and use the Macintosh themselves.

The respondents created from the video tape offer were sent to dealers for follow-up. In a subsequent program designed to measure the quality of the dealer's follow-up, Apple discovered that less then 15% had been contacted.

Another program was designed and tested to ensure follow-up and produce an even higher quality lead. The program included a method for Apple to control the follow-up to those respondents who requested the video. Only those prospects that were truly interested and qualified were turned over to the dealers.

Prospects who would be turned over to the dealers for follow-up had to meet the following qualifications.

1)   They had approved the money or had the authority to approve enough funds to cover the cost of a solution. The prospect had been told how much a solution would cost and still wanted to investigate further.

2)   The prospect had the authority to make a decision or would be involved in making the decision to acquire a computer system.

3)   The prospect understood what an Apple solution would do for their business. They had identified a problem and wanted to solve it.

4)   The prospect had been made an offer to find out how to acquire a computer system for $250 per month and wanted to take the next step deciding to acquire an Apple solution.

I don't believe it is important that salespeople think a prospect is qualified; it is only important that the prospect believe they are qualified. A qualified prospect has money, authority, need, and desire.

Prospects received a direct mail letter offering them the opportunity to receive a complete set of materials that had been personalized and customized. The materials consisted of six separate documents produced using desktop publishing software on the Macintosh. These materials showed how effective desktop media could be for their business, as well as the quality of the product.

The mailing encouraged prospects to FAX their responses. The letter created need by asking the prospect to complete a questionnaire which subtly sold the benefits of desktop publishing.

The response form also asked the prospect for the following information:

- Company name and address including phone number and FAX phone number.

- The respondent's full name and title.

- Either actual or fictitious sales and profit information that could be used to develop the personalized materials. The prospect was asked to provide data for last year, this year, and next year.

Those prospects that didn't respond to the initial mailing received a second mailing with the same offer about two weeks after the initial promotion. The list of respondents who had previously requested the video was used and both promotions were targeted to enhance the relationship with Apple Computer.

Respondents to the mailing were entered into a respondent database and fulfilled with a complete information kit. This kit included six personalized pieces that demonstrated the effectiveness of desktop publishing.

1) Proposal cover

2) Sales and profit graph

3) Operating statement

4) Overhead transparency

5) Newsletter first page

6) Sample invoice form

The fulfillment kit contained the complete package of materials and a personalized cover letter explaining the benefits of desktop publishing. The letter offered the prospect an opportunity to visit an Apple dealer for an even more personal demonstration of the Macintosh. The letter explained that the prospect could have a complete system, capable of developing all the materials included in the kit, for under $250 per month.

A telemarketing phone call was made two days after the fulfillment kit had been sent to the prospect. The kit had been shipped via overnight delivery. The call was timed to reach the prospect one day after they had received the information.

Using a script, the telemarketers offered prospects an opportunity to visit a computer dealer to see first hand how easy desktop publishing could be performed using the Apple Macintosh. The telemarketer again stated that the prospect could lease a system for under $250. This ensured that the prospect understood how much money was required to acquire an system. The prospect was also

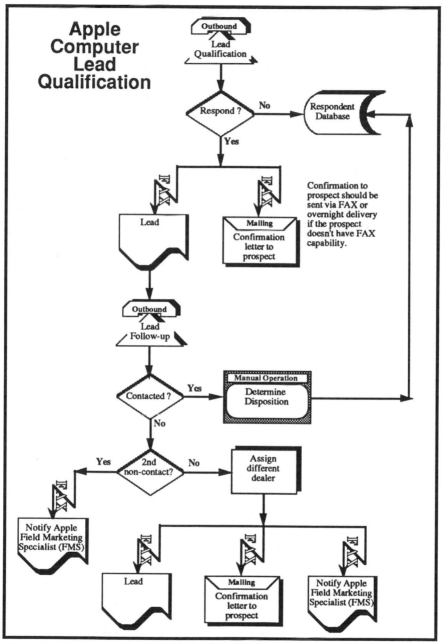

Illustration 5-8: Apple Computer Lead Qualification.

asked if they would be involved in a decision to acquire a computer.

Illustration 5-8 shows the flow of activities following a prospect's acceptance of the telemarketer's offer. Leads were sent to dealers who were assigned based on respondent's zip code.

⌘   Apple Computer, Inc.
        PO Box 751630
        Memphis, TN 38175-9967

Date: Wednesday, December 5 1990, 1:30 p.m.

To: Professional Computer Center
             Summit Square Center
             Langhorne, PA 19047
             Phone: (215) 860-5200

From: Pat McVeigh
             (800) 642-8550 Facsimile (800) 537-9199

Pages: Including this cover sheet: 1

The following prospect has responded and would like a personal demonstration of desktop publishing on the Macintosh.

            Bernie Goldberg, President
            Direct Marketing Publishers
            1304 University Drive
            Yardley, PA 19067
            Phone: (215) 321-3068
            Facsimile: (215) 321-9647

This lead responded to a direct mail letter on December 3, 1990. He requested a personalized Business Communication Kit. This kit was delivered to him the next day via Federal Express. In both the original letter and the Business Communication Kit, the prospect was told that he could acquire a complete Macintosh system, including software, for as little as $250 per month. A Mac II with LaserWriter and RagTime 3 were used at suggested retail of $11,500 to establish the $270 per month lease for 60 months.

The lead was contacted today by telemarketing and has accepted our offer to visit an authorized dealer to see first hand a complete demonstration of the Macintosh and learn how to acquire a system. He should be contacted ASAP.

Illustration 5-9: Apple Computer FAX Lead.

Leads were not permanently allocated to a dealer. Instead, leads were rented to dealers at a fixed fee per lead. A follow-up call was made to the prospect 14 days after the lead was sent to the dealer. If the prospect had not been contacted by the dealer, a reminder was forwarded to the dealer, and the lead was scheduled for another follow-up call in 14 days. If the second contact indicated that the prospect had still not been contacted, the lead was forwarded to another dealer for disposition. Later, the program was modified slightly so that leads that were not contacted were sent to dealer management for immediate attention. In addition, Apple was notified and kept track of the non-contacted leads.

 Apple Computer, Inc.
PO Box 751630
Memphis, TN 38175-9967

Date: Wednesday, December 5, 1990, 1:30 p.m.

To: Bernie Goldberg, President
Direct Marketing Publishers
1304 University Drive
Yardley, PA 19067
Phone: (215) 321-3068
Facsimile: (215) 321-9647

From: Pat McVeigh
(800) 642-8550 Facsimile (800) 537-9199

Pages: Including this cover sheet: 1

I am delighted that you've decided to visit one of our authorized dealers to learn more about business communication and the Apple® Macintosh®. You should be contacted directly by:

     Professional Computer Center
     Summit Square Center
     Langhorne, PA 19047
     Phone: (215) 860-5200

The sales manager at Professional Computer Center is Dennis Mehta. If you have not been contacted within the next two days, please call him or call us at (800) 642-8550.

Illustration 5-10: Apple Computer Prospect Lead Acknowledgement.

During the follow-up calls, the leads were sent to the prospect via FAX. Prospects also received a FAX confirmation of the phone call. The appropriate Apple Field Marketing Specialist (FMS) was also notified of the status of the lead via FAX.

For those prospects who accepted the opportunity to visit a dealer a lead form shown in Illustration 5-9 was sent via FAX to the appropriate deaaler. Leads were FAXed directly to the dealer the same day they were created by the telemarketing service bureau. The FAX lead was used to make them look different from leads generated through other programs.

When the lead form was sent to the dealer, the prospect was also sent a letter via FAX identifying the allocated dealer (Illustration 5-10). The letter was intended to make the prospect feel that Apple cared. The direct communication kept the dialogue open between Apple and the prospect.

Two weeks after the lead had been sent to the dealer, the prospect was again contacted by telemarketing to determine the disposition. Prospects who had been contacted were asked if they were planning to buy a Macintosh. Some limited market research information was captured. This call may have been too early in the selling cycle to expect orders, and therefore a subsequent phone call was made 30 to 60 days later to determine actual sales results. Direct mail could have also been used to measure the ultimate result.

The flavor of these calls were customer service. The prospect was reminded that they had requested information and a personal demonstration of the Macintosh. The prospect was told this call was to ensure that all of their questions had been answered.

Here is the follow-up script that was used when the prospect was contacted.

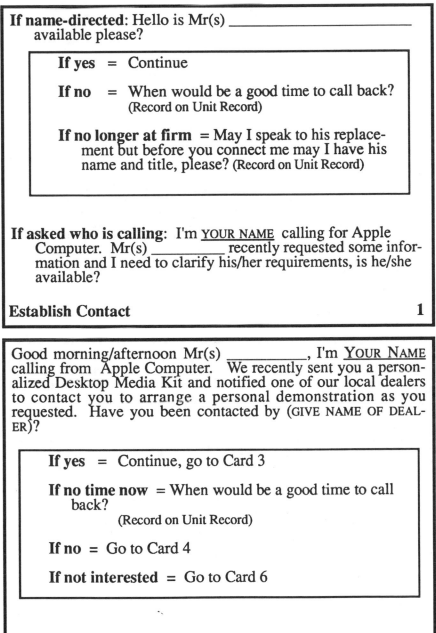

If name-directed: Hello is Mr(s) _____
   available please?

> **If yes** = Continue
>
> **If no** = When would be a good time to call back?
>   (Record on Unit Record)
>
> **If no longer at firm** = May I speak to his replace-
>   ment but before you connect me may I have his
>   name and title, please? (Record on Unit Record)

If asked who is calling: I'm YOUR NAME calling for Apple
   Computer. Mr(s) _____ recently requested some information and I need to clarify his/her requirements, is he/she
   available?

Establish Contact   **1**

Good morning/afternoon Mr(s) _____, I'm YOUR NAME
calling from Apple Computer. We recently sent you a personalized Desktop Media Kit and notified one of our local dealers
to contact you to arrange a personal demonstration as you
requested. Have you been contacted by (GIVE NAME OF DEAL-
ER)?

> **If yes** = Continue, go to Card 3
>
> **If no time now** = When would be a good time to call
>   back?
>   (Record on Unit Record)
>
> **If no** = Go to Card 4
>
> **If not interested** = Go to Card 6

Open Call   **2**

Great! Have you already received your personal demonstration?

If yes:

> Did you buy a Macintosh? (1=yes, 2=no, 3=in the process, 4=planning to buy)
>
> **If no** = Are you planning to buy ?
>
> **If Yes** = When?
>
> **If No** = Can you tell me why? (1=too expensive, 2=too complicated, 3=didn't like dealer, 4=prefer another machine, 5=bought different machine, 6=couldn't do my job)

If no: When are you scheduled to visit? (record date on unit record)

Go to Card 6.

Establish Disposition   **3**

I apologize and would be happy to arrange for a different dealer to contact you immediately. I'll also notify the local Apple dealer manager to ensure that you are not mishandled again. Would you like me to arrange another demonstration?

If yes:

> We have several dealers in your area, which of the following would you like to visit?
>
> > *Use the dealer locator system to identify local dealers participating in this program. If the prospect identifies a specific dealer he prefers to deal with that is not participating in this program, that dealer should still be used.*
>
> Go to Card 5.

If no = go to card 6.

Establish different dealer   **4**

I'll contact (NAME OF DEALER) and inform them of your interest in a personal demonstration. You should be contacted by them in the next day or so. I'll confirm my discussion with them to you with a FAX or letter, may I have your FAX phone number, please?

If you are not contacted by (IDENTIFY 2ND BUSINESS DAY) please call the dealer or us at (800) 642-8550.

Thanks for your time and have a nice day.

Close call - assign new dealer   **5**

We really appreciate your interest in Apple Computer and the Macintosh. From time to time we would like to stay in contact with you.

Will you verify that I have your correct mailing address? (Verify the name, title and address information on the unit record - ensure the name is spelled correctly)

Thanks for your time and have a nice day.

Close Call   **6**

You will notice that the script references a **unit record**. A unit record is a form used to track the disposition of telephone selling calls. Unit records are discussed at length in Chapter 9.

If the prospect was not contacted, the communicator apologized and offered to have the prospect contacted while informing Apple management. If the prospect accepted the offer, another dealer was assigned to the account. The lead was then FAXed to the new dealer and a confirmation was sent to the prospect. The appropriate Apple Marketing Manager was also notified. The dealer was requested to contact the prospect that day.

The follow-up call was made to all leads, even those that were generated a second time because they had not been contacted by a dealer. Leads not contacted after being referred to a second dealer were referred to Apple directly for attention.

This program was primarily designed to provide a personal demonstration of the benefits of desktop publishing to prospects. The prospects understood approximately how much the solution would cost. They also agreed to pursue the next logical step in evaluating their own system. The use of FAX and Federal Express demonstrated Apple's intense interest in their business, and established a very high level of customer service and commitment.

Apple remained in control of the sales effort. Apple's follow-up directly to the prospect assured 100% follow-up on all respondents.

Both the Cellular Company and Apple Computer examples demonstrate an approach to measuring lead programs that eliminates the need to pressure the sales force to provide feedback. Both programs requested the salesperson to provide the feedback, but the ultimate measurement was through the prospect.

As you'll note, every respondent and lead name was included on a central database which was available and used to maintain an ongoing relationship with the prospect.

Measuring Lead Programs Summarized

Perhaps the most frustrating element in any lead generation effort is measuring the results. Salespeople will often ignore management attempts to track and measure the results of lead programs.

Measuring any lead generation effort starts with developing objectives for the program. Often lead programs are an attempt to generate activity for a floundering sales force. Sales management reacts to declining sales by generating leads activity without defining what will be done with them or the number of orders required. Even if the program is measured, success is virtually impossible because the expectations weren't clearly defined.

The Ill Informed Walrus anecdote demonstrated the difficulty in communicating lead results to senior managers.

The planning approach suggested in Chapter 4 was emphasized again as a methodology to establish realistic lead objectives that can be used to measure results.

Leads are people who respond to offers made by a company. The respondents typically have an interest in the company and its products that is not based on a prior relationship with specific salespeople. As lead programs are designed, the company - prospect relationship should be developed and maintained even after a salesperson is introduced to the prospect.

Leads are extremely valuable and companies will often invest hundreds of dollars to create a lead. This valuable asset shouldn't be lost when a salesperson leaves the company. Salespeople are often the only ones maintaining any information about prospects. At a minimum, companies should establish a database of prospects, generate leads, and maintain the relationship initiated with those prospects after the leads are generated.

Salespeople have specific personality traits and often refuse to provide information about their leads. You can use these traits to your advantage if you recognize how salespeople manage their territory and prospects.

I believe it is useful to ask salespeople for feedback, but it is futile to chastise them if they do not provide the information. As you design your lead reporting system, consider doing something to help the salespeople manage their territories. The Territory Management System (TMS) demonstrated one way to provide a workable system that salespeople could use to manage their territory.

Lead forms should be created for any prospect that is sent to the field for activity. Only capture the basic information about the prospect from your salespeople. The information you require from the salesperson is:

> What is the likelihood of the prospect to buy?
> What is the likelihood of the prospect to buy from you?
> When is the prospect likely to buy?

Several service bureaus provide lead reporting mechanisms that use post cards to track the status of leads. This can be an effective approach to measuring and controlling lead activity.

The best source of lead information is the prospect. If you ask prospects what has occurred, they'll tell you.

Many leads sent to the sales force are never contacted by salespeople. This is often caused by several factors:

- The salespeople are not happy with the quality of leads from prior programs.

- The salespeople have received too many leads to follow-up.

- The salespeople have unsuccessfully attempted to contact the prospect several times.

- The salesperson is already aware of the lead in their territory.

Once you execute a lead generation program and make an offer to a prospect, that prospect deserves your continued attention. If you have made a significant offer and a prospect has accepted, failure to contact the prospect can do great long-term harm to your company.

It is important that your company develop and maintain a direct relationship with the prospects, as well as asking a salesperson to do so.

Two different lead programs illustrated how the program could be managed and controlled through the prospect. Both programs were extremely effective and virtually eliminated the frustration typically associated with lead measurement.

As you design and plan your lead program, consider using a two pronged approach to measurement. Ask the salespeople to provide feedback without chastising them, and ask the prospect what has happened. You'll be surprised at the results you'll achieve.

Chapter Six:
Generating Leads

The Good, the Bad and the Ugly

There are three kinds of direct marketing programs: good, bad, and ugly.

A good direct marketing program is one that worked. The program produced the anticipated results in line with the strategy and with the proper fulfillment.

Most direct marketing experts love to talk about their good programs. Everything worked great. Unfortunately, most lead generation programs don't produce desired results or yield the proper fulfillment, therefore a good lead generation program is rare.

Sure there are lots of awards given to creative lead generation programs. There are Direct Marketing Association (DMA) Echo winners every year. However, on further investigation, most of these award winning programs are no longer being utilized.

A few years ago, I began to give presentations describing programs that failed as well as those that succeeded. I think you can learn as much from a failure as a success. Unfortunately, most direct marketing professionals don't have a lot of enthusiasm for failed efforts. They love to talk about success. Don't we all?

One of the basic tenants of direct marketing is to test new creative concepts against your current best producing promotion as a control. Very often the control package will out-perform the new creative approach. Even when a program doesn't succeed, you can learn a lot about your market, products, and methods of promotion. The whole purpose of direct marketing testing is to find a more efficient method. In most situations several variables are tested and only one or two may succeed. Most of the effort results in failure.

You can become an expert in direct marketing after about 1-1/2 years of experience. Most of this time will be spent working on programs that fail.

> *A bad direct marketing program is one that didn't work. The program failed to produce the anticipated results.*

A bad direct marketing program is easy to understand, evaluate, and learn from. It is relatively simple; the direct marketing didn't work. You mailed or called a group of customers or prospects, made an offer, and didn't generate enough response to justify the cost of the program.

I have found that there are other direct marketing programs that are not successful, even though the direct marketing produced results higher than those anticipated. I refer to these direct marketing programs as ugly.

*An ugly direct marketing program uses effective direct mar-
keting but ultimately fails because another essential element
was not properly planned or executed.*

Illustration 6-1 shows the five required elements of direct marketing
discussed at length in Chapter 2. If one of these elements is absent
or improperly controlled, the entire direct marketing program
becomes ugly. Many lead programs are not successful because the
direct marketing was bad, but more fail because the program was
ugly.

The Five Required Elements of Direct Marketing

Database	Promo Material	Controls & Analysis	Fulfillment	Marketing

6-1: The five elements of direct marketing.

Lead programs that produce more leads than the sales staff can follow up will usually become ugly. The direct marketing activity produces adequate response, but the resources are insufficient to handle
the fulfillment. Seminars with unusually high attendance can also
create ugly results.

Many lead programs are initiated by the senior sales executive and
require a mailing to prospects to generate activity. In these programs there is no clear order objective for the lead activity and one
of two things happens:

- The response is lower than the executive expected and the
  program is considered a failure.

- More leads are generated than the sales staff can respond to causing the salespeople to classify the leads as poor quality. The program fails.

In the first situation, there was no plan or strategy for the direct marketing. Marketing, one of the elements of direct marketing, has not been controlled and executed properly. If a lead program has no clear lead or order objectives established as a marketing strategy, the program will most often fail. Controls and analysis can be developed to measure the effectiveness of the program, but judging success will be totally subjective.

The second situation is caused by failing to plan correctly as well as poor fulfillment. If you generate more leads than can be followed up by the sales force, you will almost always have an ugly program. Leads should be generated in a quantity that allows proper follow-up. If there are too many leads, the salespeople will challenge the lead quality. Fulfillment will become a problem.

Ugly programs are caused by improper control and execution of the five elements of direct marketing. In the preceding chapters I've discussed how to effectively plan and control direct marketing. Let's now turn our attention to the elements in creating direct marketing material to generate sales leads.

Using direct marketing to generate leads is a form of promotion. Bad or ugly direct marketing programs are caused by improper promotion execution.

<u>Promotion Defined</u>

Promotion can be defined as the further development and encouragement of prospects and customers to purchase one's products or services without the aid of a sales representative. A promotion can be as simple as a brief letter to a gala event. It can also be the generation of response to be used as sales leads.

Promotion may be viewed as having two aspects:

- Technical
- Creative

In advertising the vast amount of effort is spent on developing the creative concept that will entice the prospect to act. Direct marketing relies less on the creative and more on the technical aspects of the promotion.

> *Technical elements* are those elements that are a must if you are going to execute successful direct marketing: product information, a reply device, pricing, and an acceptable format for the media being used. In addition, the approach must conform to legal and trade practices as well as internal product and credit requirements.

> *Creative aspects* are the big ideas that clothe your information to make it more appealing to its market. Big ideas can be serious, funny, direct, or oblique in product positioning.

The technical aspects of direct marketing can influence as much as 70% of the success of the effort. Rather than discussing the creative elements which have less impact and, in many cases are a discussion of personal taste, we'll focus on the technical elements where you can have the greatest impact.

A direct marketing promotion has four parts:

1) List
2) Offer
3) Format
4) Copy/Graphics

Lists represent those people, from whatever source you select, you have chosen to target. The action you want the prospect to take is your *offer*. The method you select to deliver the offer to the prospect is the *format*, and the *copy/graphics* is how you say or show it. Understanding these parts of promotion will provide you with a basis to evaluate and implement the direct marketing concept.

If you were to weigh the four elements of the direct marketing effort, based on the relative value of each to the ultimate success of the project, they would appear like this:

List	50%
Offer	25%
Format	15%
Copy/Graphics	10%

These percentages do not reflect what most of us do most of the time. Most of us spend 80% of our effort on copy, 15% on format, 5% on list (generally a last minute detail) and 0% on offer.

As I mentioned earlier, in ugly programs, typically one of the five elements of direct marketing was not planned or controlled properly. Bad direct marketing programs are caused by one of the elements of promotion not being executed properly.

In *Business-to-Business Direct Marketing*, I discussed the process for creating direct marketing programs. Most developers of direct marketing spend most of their time and effort creating the words and pictures to present their product.

Even after the lengthy and complete effort to get the words and pictures just right, the program still fails. Prospects don't respond. They are not interested in your products and services. But it's not their fault, it's yours. You have spent 80% of your allotted time on just 20% of the areas needed in a direct marketing program.

Look through some promotional pieces you've received. How much of each do you read? 10%? 30%? 50%? 100%? And the parts you do read are the headline, graphics, captions, call-outs and subheads - - and maybe 10% to 15% of everything else.

How do you get people to pay attention to your message? Talk with trained successful salespeople and learn what they do to succeed. After conducting a number of interviews, develop a model and approach similar to the one used by a successful salesperson.

Initially the salesperson develops an understanding of the best market to sell to by trying the pitch on anybody who will listen. After a few thousand "nos" the salesperson learns who not to pitch. However, a good salesperson does not limit their sales by assuming that if a need isn't obvious, the prospect doesn't need their product. For example, while screen doors are, seemingly, a little used item in the manufacture of submarines, they may be great inside a submarine. Listen to your instincts, but don't be afraid to test a new market from time to time.

Like the salesperson, spend time seeking out the right market. Define the correct individual to market to within the market. You may have to market to both a decision-maker and an influencer. This is one of the most important aspects of the technical preparation of the direct marketing program. The list work makes the difference between success and failure. If you don't spend the effort to understand and evaluate your list, you'll experience thousands of "nos" in terms of non-response.

Let's again review the four elements of promotion:

List -   The customers or prospects to whom you plan to target your marketing effort.

Offer -   The proposition you are making to your customers or prospects in order to get them to respond. It is the action you want the prospect to take.

Format -   The vehicle for delivering the offer to your market: mail, phone, print, broadcast.

Copy/Graphics -   The words and pictures you use to communicate your offer to the market.

For a promotion to be effective, follow the same steps the sales force uses to develop a sale. Use your promotion as a surrogate salesperson.

An easy acronym to help you remember the elements of direct response promotion is *AIDA* -- Attention, Interest, Desire, Action. While general advertising has attention and interest as its goal, direct marketing goes further to include desire and action. These last two elements separate general advertising from direct marketing.

Just as an experienced salesperson does not bother trying to gain the attention of the wrong people, you should not use the wrong list.

Lists

The list is probably the most important element in any direct marketing promotion. In lead generation efforts the list can mean the difference between qualified leads and a satisfied sales force, or poor leads and a morale problem within the sales ranks.

There are basically four kinds of lists:

- House or Customer lists
- Compiled lists
- Respondent lists
- Subscription or Membership lists

Each list has different characteristics that may make it a worthwhile list for your business to use. The lists you select for your direct marketing effort will be the single most important decision in determining the success or failure of the project.

In real estate, there are three things that are important in a piece of property:

1) Location
2) Location
3) Location

Direct marketing has a similar series of important elements:

1) List
2) List
3) List

To underscore the importance of the list, carefully consider this direct marketing axiom: an outstanding offer made in an outstanding package to a poor list will produce poor results. On the other hand, a mediocre offer, in a mediocre package made to a good list will probably produce good results.

Let's look at the different kinds of lists and their characteristics:

House or Customer Lists: These are people that have previously responded to you or have already become customers. This is the most valuable list source you have and will produce the highest results when used in a direct marketing project. Even in lead generation efforts, this list will probably produce strong results even if the house list only contains customers.

Develop as much geographic, demographic and psychographic information as possible about your house lists. The more information you have on people who have already bought from you, the easier it will be to select prospects who may buy from you. There is a scientific computer method, called regression analysis, available to review customers and determine their areas of similarity. This technique will use mathematical algorithms to determine the important similar traits exhibited by a group of customers. If you have about 1,000 or more customers, regression analysis can be an interesting and exciting approach to help determine what your customers have in common. You can get additional information about regression analysis techniques from your local college statistics department or by contacting the Direct Marketing Association, 6 East 43rd Street, New York, NY 10017.

The existing sales force, if you have one, can be very helpful in establishing a profile of likely prospects to purchase your products or services. Again, people who have already purchased your products are the best indicator of others who should be your customers.

House lists, particularly if you're billing the customer, are fairly current and up to date. These lists will normally contain phone numbers and name and title information. Depending on the product you're selling the contact name and title may or may not be appropriate for your needs. Depending on your company's credit policies, your house lists may not contain industry and sizing information. Your customer list may contain 'ship to' and 'bill to' information and may not contain the contact you're looking for.

Evaluate your house lists for applicability to your needs. House lists are excellent sources for cross-selling, upgrading, and generating repeat business. They consist of customers with whom you have already established a working relationship. Some of these customers may not be buying from you today and can become valuable sales leads. Capitalize on that relationship in your direct marketing programs.

Many house lists will also contain respondents to prior direct marketing programs who may not have become customers. These prior respondents usually offer an excellent opportunity to generate additional sales leads in the future.

One of the big advantages of your house list is that it is in a format that you can use. It is probably a computer file already maintained within the company. Many times you won't even have to create special computer programs to use the house file. You own the house file and can use it as often as you want without having to get permission or pay a fee to the list owner.

The biggest disadvantage of your house file is its size and density. The house list doesn't contain all of the opportunities of businesses that can be your customers. The lead generation effort is designed to generate new opportunities and your house file will rarely provide you with the entire selling opportunity universe.

Compiled Lists: There are many companies that compile and develop lists as their primary business. You're probably familiar with the largest, Dun and Bradstreet (D&B), a well-known business information provider. Some list compilers have specialized in specific market niches. They may use direct mail and telephone interviewing to build and verify the information. You can even contract with a list compiler to build a unique list to meet your special needs.

Compiled lists are typically used by marketers to fulfill a unique requirement, so compiled list owners normally append some additional information to the basic name and address. Most use SIC codes as a primary segmentation tool. Frequently, compiled lists will have more than one contact per business. Some of the major list compilers have built total lists of all available businesses with some sizing and other demographic information.

Compiled lists are normally updated on a periodic basis, usually annually or bi-annually. Some lists are compiled from the yellow pages, therefore they are only updated once per year. With the frequent changes of title and position in American industry, compiled lists tend to be outdated 20% to 40%.   The basic sizing and segmentation data doesn't change significantly.

Compiled lists are excellent resources when you are looking for additional information to help you target a promotion. If you want to reach a segment of the market that can only be identified by very specific criteria, compiled lists are probably your best source.   These lists tend to offer the widest coverage and selection criteria. If you are looking for the greatest number of businesses in a particular industry or geographic area, a compiled list will probably be the best source.

Because most list compilers are in the business to sell their lists, they offer great flexibility in their ability to sell you the list in almost any format you desire. Most can send you the list on labels, lists, cards, magnetic tape, and diskettes. Some of the larger list compilers even make their lists available interactively through terminals or micro-computers in your office.

Compiled lists are developed to serve a particular function and not to identify a propensity to respond to direct marketing. These lists will not allow you to attribute any affinity to the names nor have they demonstrated any likelihood to respond to direct marketing.

Most compiled lists are created and updated annually. Many use the yellow-page directories as the primary source of new and additional names. As I mentioned in Chapter 2, the business universe is always in a high level of change and as much as 40% of the information in it can change each year. Therefore compiled lists tend to contain inaccurate and outdated information.

Compiled lists may not contain the appropriate contact information for your needs. Many compiled lists will contain individual contact name and title information appropriate for the compiler, but not necessarily appropriate for your promotional efforts.

Respondent Lists: People who have previously purchased or responded to direct marketing are more likely to respond to direct marketing again. The more people that respond, the more likely it is that they will respond again. Direct marketers commonly weigh the value of a respondent in terms of how *recently* they have responded, how *frequently* they respond, and the *monetary* value of their purchase. This concept is called **RFM (*Recency, Frequency and Monetary*)**. Catalog marketers are very familiar with this concept and frequently score their lists using RFM techniques.

Other direct marketers will frequently rent their respondent lists to others. Renting lists can provide excellent opportunities for you to sell your products or services. You will have to evaluate the type of products the respondents purchased on these lists, and the similarity between those products and yours. Business list brokers can provide valuable insight into list usage by other marketers and recommendations based on their years of experience in the list rental business.

In most cases, respondent lists do not contain very much additional information concerning the prospect or company beyond RFM. It is unusual for the respondent list to contain a phone number.

Respondent lists can be fairly current, depending on the group that you decide to rent. The more recently the respondents purchased, the more accurate the list will be. If the list is aged, you run the risk of not being able to reach many names on the list. This is commonly called a *Nixie*.

A respondent list is another company's house file. It is in their format designed for their use. These lists typically are available in only limited formats. The company is not in business to sell their list and therefore will be less responsive to your data needs.

In addition, as is the case with your house file, the list will typically only contain a small percentage of the universe you're trying to contact.

Subscription and Membership Lists: This group of lists consists of people who have demonstrated an affinity with a common set of interests. In the business community, a group that subscribes to a trade journal probably has an interest in that activity. By advertising, mailing, or phoning the members of this group, you are targeting the identified interest. This type of affinity is called a *psychographic characteristic* -- how people feel about things. Membership and subscription lists consist of people who have made a conscious decision to participate. They raised their hands and said, I want to belong.

Membership lists may contain industry, sizing, and other pertinent information. Most frequently, these lists only contain name and address data, though telephone numbers may be available. These lists may be out of date. Frequently, the name and address information on membership lists are not purged and kept current.

Subscription lists usually only contain name, title, and address information. The publication is being sent to the name on a periodic basis, and therefore the name and address information is accurate. Most subscription lists do not include telephone numbers, titles or industry information.

There are two types of subscriptions:

Paid Subscription: The subscriber has paid to receive the publication. Although there is very little additional information available about the subscriber, they paid to belong to this group. Paid subscriptions might also be classified as respondent lists because they are direct response purchasers.

Paid subscription lists contain virtually no information about the individual. You know that the subscriber has paid a fee to receive the publication which is a strong indicator of their interest in the subject. However, the list information is usually stored to allow the publisher to create a label to fulfill the subscription and mail renewal notices. Name and address information has very few data standards and can create substantial problems in duplicate elimination. There is little if any demographic or psychographic data which can be used to enhance the promotion effort.

Controlled Subscription: This is a free subscription. The reader fills out an application to qualify to receive the publication. Controlled subscription publication lists have additional information and can be segmented and targeted better than paid subscription lists. Although, because it is free, the reader may not have as strong an affinity towards the product as the paid subscriber.

Controlled circulation lists require the subscriber to certify that they want to continue receiving the publication annually. As part of the initial subscription and with each subsequent renewal the subscriber is asked to provide information about their company and their job. This data becomes an inherent part of the list that the publisher makes available to list purchasers. You can use the information to target promotions to the appropriate individuals.

Selecting the appropriate type of list will depend on the direct marketing promotion. Each list type has its own advantages. As you design your direct marketing program, I suggest you test different lists and list types to determine your most effective list source.

The lists you select are clearly the most important part of your direct marketing efforts. Unfortunately, the list is often the item you spend the least amount of time evaluating.

Earlier, during the planning phase, you should have identified the characteristics of your customers and prospects. During the identification phase you should have written a detailed description of the specific individual and types of individuals you intended to reach.

In the consumer universe, you can select prospects by demographic and geographic characteristics. Several firms specialize in creating complete lists of households with selected similar demographic characteristics. Some of these firms attempt to overlay lifestyle characteristics with demographic and geographic information. In essence, you can select households meeting almost any criteria.

Business list selection does not enjoy the same luxury of having finite selection information. Business demographics do not exist, even though this concept is frequently discussed. The demographics are those characteristics that are available based on the business itself. The concept of lifestyle would be applicable if we could analyze the corporate culture of all businesses.

However, here are some characteristics of businesses that are available that can improve your ability to select lists:

- Annual sales or revenue

- Number of employees

- Standard Industrial Classification (SIC)

- Location geography - state, ZIP, SCF (Sectional Center Facility - first three digits of the ZIP code)

- Assets

- Credit rating

- Types of equipment being used

- Expenditures above a certain value in any specific area

- Area of business activity: (regional, national, international)

- Number of locations

- Titles of employees

- Functions of employees

As you can see, the business list selection variables are quite different from those in the consumer world. The above list may not be complete for your needs. Only by evaluating your customers and prospects and the products you are trying to sell can you arrive at the criteria you should use for list selection. All the characteristics you feel are necessary may not be available on every list you evaluate. This problem is compounded by the limited size of business lists; you might use an entire list just testing it.

A lack of standards in company names and abbreviations, and numerous telephone numbers per company prevent elimination of duplicates. No matter how hard you try, you will never be able to eliminate all of your own customers from a prospect mailing. In addition, you will probably have duplicate mailings and contacts to a single individual, even when you use a single list source.

Subscription and membership lists may be a poor selection when you are planning to market in a small geographic area. The publication or organization may not have enough people in the selected area. Tight geographic marketing may necessitate the use of compiled lists.

On the other hand, compiled lists may not have complete contact names so you may be forced to solicit a title or function. This may not be so bad since testing has indicated that there is not a marked difference between title addressing and name addressing. Obviously, it is better to use the name if you have it. However, mailings to the wrong name may never get delivered.

The rate of change in contact name and address in the consumer world runs about 15% to 20% per year. In the business environment, change can run as high as 60%. Compiled lists tend to be about one year old and can have a substantial error rate in the contact name. Responder and subscriber lists may be updated more frequently and the contact name might be more accurate, but remember: you don't have the same number of selection criteria for these lists.

Some final thoughts on lists: Even after you have done a relatively good job of identifying the characteristics of the universe you want to solicit, the actual list selection is still going to be a gamble. There are many list brokers, direct marketing agencies, and list compilers who can help you select and test list alternatives.

A good list broker can be an important addition to any direct marketing resource team. Most brokers are paid a standard industry commission of 10% to 15% by the list owners, therefore you incur no fee. List brokers have experience with many lists and can recommend specific lists to meet your needs. The Direct Marketing Association can provide the names of list brokers in your area.

Lists are the most important ingredient in any direct marketing campaign. In face-to-face selling, the list may be more subtle because the salesperson builds and maintains his own list, but it just as critical.

Direct Marketing versus Sales

Looking back at the salesperson's style I discussed earlier, once they have identified a valid prospect, they will try to generate a sale. The salesperson's presentation will include a complete assessment of the prospect's needs. A good salesperson will find out the prospect's problems.

As a surrogate salesperson, your direct marketing promotional material must exhibit knowledge and empathy to gain the prospect's interest. Like a salesperson, you have to ask for the order or tell the prospect what you want him to do . . . make an offer.

The salesperson's presentation will include a complete assessment of the prospect's needs. A good salesperson will find out the prospect's problems.

In your direct marketing program, you should perform the same function by proposing to solve problems you already know exist. Format and copy should focus the prospect on their need and how your product will solve their problem. This is the first part of your offer.

Like any good salesperson, you must ask for the order. This is the second part of the offer. Move the prospect to action. Desire and action are easily affected when the offer is compressed by limitations of time, quantities, or pricing for a period of time.

A salesperson may make several contacts within an organization before finding out with whom to speak. Keep this in mind when contacting a company; it is a little presumptuous to believe a single promotional effort will reach the right person in any given company. Depending on the price of the product you are offering, it may even be presumptuous to believe the second effort will get the order.

An initial contact may merely be a probe to discover the name or title of the best person to establish a relationship with in a company. This can be accomplished by contacting a receptionist or switchboard attendant and asking that person the name of the most appropriate person to make a decision to buy your product. This kind of information can be obtained by mail or phone.

Such an effort could be a waste of time and money if your product is easily understood, inexpensive, and generates a strong contribution to overhead and profit. In this case, broad based promotion can be most cost effective; the shotgun approach.

If your product is expensive and requires more than one individual to make a buying decision, direct marketing can be an effective enhancement to the selling effort. It may be worthwhile to spend the time and money to make sure you are speaking with the person that will act as a "champion" for your product during the review and buy-in cycles.

You can also use direct marketing to sell many individuals within the company on the advantages and benefits of your product. While a salesperson can't talk to more than one person at a time, direct marketing will allow your message to reach as many individuals as needed on the same day.

Whatever approach you select, direct marketing can be used effectively as a lead generator for your sales force after you've established awareness, interest, and desire. The action can be the opportunity to be visited by a salesperson.

Before discussing offers, let's explore the major difference between corporate life and entrepreneurial life. Many of the offers received in the business environment are designed to save the prospect time and/or money. This can be expanded into the trite combination: efficiency and effectiveness. In truth, people who work for a corporation don't care much about the company's time and money. They say and act as they do because that is the company line. In many corporate environments, time and money are not personal needs.

To make an effective offer to employees, appeal to them as people. In general, corporate employees are interested in three things:

1. Getting promoted
2. Reducing hassles
3. Covering their rears

Let's review these interests in terms of life as an employee in a medium to large corporation. Getting promoted means having more status, more money, more power and all the reasons people hang around a corporation. If offered an opportunity to be promoted as a result of making a buying decision, an employee would find a way to make that decision.

Reducing hassle is a game frequently played by the corporate employee. If a promotion is not attainable, then most employees will try to reduce the chaos they experience on the job. If this can be done by making a buying decision, most people will take advantage of hassle reduction, so they can spend more time trying to get promoted.

Covering the rear is the avoidance process most people in corporate environments practice. They get others to share the risk of decisions so that no one can pin the tail on them. It is also the process of making decisions that can be revised in the event things don't work out as planned. Also, making decisions that reflect the industry choice will probably allow one to stay clear of ridicule. As a rear cover, most employees will respond to suggestions from others within the company -- especially from persons ranked above them in the organization. Other reasons to make a decision might be guarantees with a right of return, or offers that are supported by industry belief.

If an employee's rear is exposed, they won't have time to reduce hassle and get promoted. If your offer is aimed at the personal motivation of the company employee you're trying to reach, your odds of success are increased.

The *owner* of a business will be interested in how you can save them time and money. Business owners are saving their own money rather than the money of a corporation. The business owner often has better skills at using time. While the corporate employee is willing to delay decisions, the business owner makes decisions fast, especially when there is a way to save time or money. They don't need committee support to make a decision.

Offers

The *offer* is the proposition you make to your prospects to motivate them to respond to your promotion. Whether you are selling a notebook or a lifetime of financial counseling, you must get your prospect to take the first step that will achieve your objectives. You need to get the prospects to feel good about your offer so they can overcome fear, uncertainty and doubt (FUD) about your company and its product.

The biggest failure of most lead generation programs is their failure to make meaningful offers.

Your offer will include your product, price, payment terms, and any incentive you are willing to include. You might also attach special conditions to offer. In his book, *Profitable Direct Marketing*, Jim Kobs listed the following 99 direct response offers. This list comprehensively covers consumer and business offers.

BASIC OFFERS

1) **Right Price** - The starting point for any product or service being sold by mail. Consider your market and what's being charged for competitive products. And make sure you have sufficient margin for your offer to be profitable. Most products sold by mail require at least a three-time mark-up.

2) **Free Trial** - If mail order advertisers suddenly had to standardize all their efforts on one offer, this would no doubt be the choice; it's widely used for book and merchandise promotions. Looking at it like a consumer, the free trial relieves the fear that you might get stuck buying by mail because the advertiser is willing to let you try *their* product before they get *your* money. Most free trial periods are 10 or 15 days, but the length of the trial period should fit the type of product or service being offered.

3) **Money-Back Guarantee** - If for some good reason you can't use a free trial offer, this is the next best thing. The

main difference is you ask the customer to pay part or all of the purchase price *before* you let them try your product. This puts inertia on your side. The customer is unlikely to take the time and effort to send a product back unless they're really unhappy with it.

4) **Cash With Order** - This is the basic payment option used with a money-back guarantee. It's also offered with a choice of other payment options. Incentives (such as paying the postage and handling charge) are often used to encourage the customer to send their check or money order when they order.

5) **Bill Me Later** - This is the basic payment option used with free trial offers. The bill is usually enclosed with the merchandise or follows a few days later, and it calls for a single payment. Because no front-end payment is required by the customer, the response can be as much as double that of a cash offer.

6) **Installment Terms** - This payment option is similar to the Bill Me Later Option, except that it usually involves a bigger sale price and installment terms are set up to keep the payments around $10 to $20 per month. It is usually necessary to offer installment terms to sell big ticket items by mail to consumers.

7) **Charge Card Privileges** - Offers the same advantages of Bill Me Later and Installment plans, but the seller doesn't have to carry the paper. This option can be used with bank charge cards, travel and entertainment cards, and specialized cards (like those issued by the oil companies).

8) **C.O.D.** - This is the Postal Service acronym for Cash-On-Delivery. The mail carrier collects when they deliver the package. This option is not widely used today because of the added cost and effort required to handle C.O.D. orders.

FREE GIFT OFFERS

9) **Free Gift For An Inquiry** - Provides an incentive to request more information about a product or service. Usually increases inquiries, though they become somewhat less qualified.

10) **Free Gift For A Trial Order** - Commonly called a "keeper" gift - because the customer gets to keep the gift just for agreeing to try the product.

11) **Free Gift For Buying** - Similar to Number 10, except the customer only gets to keep the gift if they buy the product or service. The gift can be given free with any order, tied to a minimum purchase, or used as a self-liquidator.

12) **Multiple Free Gifts With A Single Order** - If one gift pays out for you, considering offering two or more. You may even be able to offer two inexpensive gifts and spend the same as you would on one more expensive item. The biggest user of multiple gifts is Fingerhut Corporation. At last count, they were up to four free gifts for a single order!

13) **Your Choice Of Free Gifts** - Can be a quick way to test the relative appeal of different gift items. But this will seldom work as well as the best gift offered on its own.

The choice may lead to indecision on the consumer's part.

14) **Free Gifts Based On Size Of Order** - Often used with catalogs or merchandise that lends itself to a quantity purchase. You can offer an inexpensive gift for orders under $10.00; a better gift for orders totalling between $10.00 and $25.00; and a deluxe gift for orders over $25.00.

15) **Two-Step Gift Offer** - Offers an inexpensive gift if customer takes the first step and a better gift if they take the second step. For example, you might offer a free record album for *trying* a new stereo set, and a deluxe headset if you elect to *buy* it.

16) **Continuing Incentive Gifts** - Used to get customers to keep coming back. Book clubs often give bonus coupons which can be used to purchase additional books. This option is also suitable for silverware, where you give one place setting per order.

17) **Mystery Gift Offer** - Sometimes works better than offering a specific gift. It helps if you can give some indication of the item's retail value.

OTHER FREE OFFERS

18) **Free Information** - Certainly an inexpensive offer, and a very flexible one. The type of information you provide can range from a simple product catalog sheet to a full-blown series of mailings. Emphasize if the information will not be delivered by a salesperson.

19) **Free Catalog** - Can be an attractive offer for both the consumer and the business market. In the business field, catalogs are often used as buying guides and are saved for future reference. In the consumer field, you can often attach a nominal charge for postage and handling, or offer a full year's catalog subscription.

20) **Free Booklet** - Helps establish your company's expertise and know-how about the specific problems of your industry. Works especially well if the booklet contains helpful editorial material, not just a commercial for your product or service. The booklet should have an appealing title, like "How to Save Money on Heating Costs" or "29 Ways to Improve the Quality Control System."

21) **Free Fact Kit** - Sometimes called an Idea Kit. It's usually put together in an attractive file folder or presentation cover. You can include a variety of enclosures, from booklets to trade paper articles to ad reprints.

22) **Send Me A Salesperson** - This one is included here because the offer is actually a free sales call. The copy includes wording like, have your representative phone me for an appointment. This offer normally produces more qualified inquiries than a free booklet or fact kit. Those who respond are probably ready to order or seriously considering it.

23) **Free Demonstration** - Important for things like business equipment that has to be demonstrated to be fully appreciated. If the equipment is small enough, it can be brought into the prospect's plant or office. If not, they might be invited to a private showing or group demonstration at the manufacturer's facilities.

24) **Free Survey of Your Needs** - Ideal for some industrial products or services, such as a company that sells chemicals for various water treatment problems. Offering a free survey by a sales representative or technical expert is appealing, and gives you the opportunity to qualify a prospect and see if your product or service really fits their needs.

25) **Free Cost Estimate** - Many large industrial sales are only made after considerable study and cost analysis. The offer of a free estimate can be the first step in triggering such a sale.

26) **Free Dinner** - Like the rest of the offers that follow in this section, this one is particularly suited to certain types of direct marketing companies. It's widely used by real estate and land companies, who offer a free dinner at a nearby restaurant. Those who attend also get a sales presentation on the property.

27) **Free Film Offer** - Many mail order film processing companies have been built with some variation of this offer. Either the customer gets a new roll of film when they send one in for processing, or the first roll is offered free, in hopes that it will be sent back to the same company later for processing.

28) **Free House Organ Subscription** - Many industrial companies publish elaborate house organs for customers and prospects which contain a good deal of helpful editorial material. You can offer a free sample issue, or better yet, a year's subscription.

29) **Free Talent Test** - Popular with home study schools. Especially those that offer a skilled course, such as writ-

ing or painting. Legal restrictions require that any such test actually measures real talent or ability, and is not just a door-opener for the salesperson.

30) **Gift Shipment Service -** This is one of the basic appeals of offers used by virtually all mail order cheese and gift food firms. You send them your gift list, and they ship direct to the recipients at no extra cost.

DISCOUNT OFFERS

31) **Cash Discount -** This is the basic type of discount. It's often dramatized by including a discount certificate in the ad or mailing. However, a discount offer will *not* do as well as an attractive free gift with the same value.

32) **Short-Term Introductory Offer -** A popular type of discount used to let somebody try the product for a short period at a reduced price. Offering 10 weeks of the *Wall Street Journal* for only $5.97 or 30 days of accident insurance for only 25¢ are good examples. It's important to be able to convert respondents to long-term subscribers or policyholders.

33) **Refund Certificate -** Technically speaking, this is a delayed discount. You might ask somebody to send $1.00 for your catalog and include a $1.00 refund certificate good on their first order. The certificate is like an un-cashed check -- it's difficult to resist the urge to cash it.

34) **Introductory Order Discount -** A special discount used to bring in new customers. This can sometimes cause complaints from old customers if they're not offered the same discount.

35) **Trade Discount** - Usually extended to certain clubs, institutions, or types of businesses.

36) **Early Bird Discount** - Designed to get customers to stock up before the normal buying season. A great many Christmas cards and gifts have been sold by mail with this offer.

37) **Quantity Discount** - This discount is tied to a certain quantity or order volume. The long-term subscriptions offered by magazines are a type of a quantity discount. The cost-per-copy is usually lower on a two-year subscription because it represents a quantity purchase -- 24 issues instead of 12.

38) **Sliding Scale Discount** - In this case, the amount of the discount depends on the date somebody orders or the size of the order. You might offer a 2% discount for orders up to $50, and a 10% discount for orders over $100.

39) **Selected Discounts** - These are often sprinkled throughout a catalog to emphasize certain items the advertiser wants to push or to give the appearance that everything is on sale.

SALE OFFERS

40) **Seasonal Sales** - Such as Pre-Christmas Sale or Summer Vacation Sale. If successful, they are often repeated every year at the same time.

41) **Reason-Why Sales** - This category includes Inventory Reduction and Clearance Sales. These explanatory

terms help make the sale more believable to the prospect.

42) **Price Increase Notice** - A special type of offer that's like a limited time sale. Price Increase Notices give customers a chance to order at the old prices before increases become effective.

43) **Auction-By-Mail** - An unusual type of sale that has been used to sell such items as lithographs and electronic calculators, when their quantities were limited. Customers send in a "sealed bid" with merchandise usually going to the highest bidder.

SAMPLE OFFERS

44) **Free Samples** - If your product lends itself to sampling, this is a strong offer. Sometimes you can offer a sample made with or by your product. For example, a steel company might offer take-apart puzzles made from their steel wire. Or a printer might offer samples of helpful printed material it has produced for other customers.

45) **Nominal Charge Samples** - In many cases making a nominal charge for a sample--like 10¢, 25¢, or $1.00-- will pull better than a free sample offer. The charges help establish the value of the item and screens out some of the curiosity seekers.

46) **Sample Offer With Tentative Commitment** - This is also known as the "complimentary copy" offer used by many magazines. In requesting the sample, the prospect is also making a tentative commitment for a subscription. But if they don't like the first issue, they just write "cancel" on the bill and sends it back. Legal precautions

are advised, your legal counsel should review this offer before you actually make it.

47) **Quantity Sample Offer** - A specialized offer that's worked well for business services and newsletters. One example is a sales training bulletin, where the sales manager is told to "just tell us how many salesperson you have, and we'll send a free sample bulletin for each one."

48) **Free Sample Lesson** - This has been widely used by home study schools, who offer a sample lesson to demonstrate the scope and content of their course.

TIME LIMIT OFFERS

49) **Limited Time Offers** - Any limited time offer tends to force a quick decision and prevents procrastination. It's usually best to mention a specific date--such as "this special offer expires November 20th" rather than "this offer expires in 10 days."

50) **Enrollment Periods** - Have been widely used by mail order insurance companies, who include a specific cutoff date for the enrollment period. It implies there are savings involved by processing an entire group of enrollments at one time.

51) **Pre-Publication Offer** - Long a favorite with publishers, who offer a special discount or savings before the official publication date of a new book. The rationale is that it helps them plan their printing quantity more accurately.

52) **Charter Membership (or Subscription) Offer** - Ideal for introducing new clubs, publications, and other sub-

scription services. Usually includes a special price, gift, or other incentive for charter members or subscribers. This appeals to those who like to be among the first to try new things.

53) **Limited Edition Offer** - A relatively new direct response offer that has worked well in selling coins, art prints, and other collectable items.

GUARANTEE OFFERS

54) **Extended Guarantee** - Such as letting the customer return a book up to a year later. Or with a magazine, offering to refund the unexpired portion of a subscription any time before it runs out.

55) **Double-Your-Money-Back Guarantee** - Really dramatizes your confidence in the product...but it better live up to your advertising claims if you make an offer like this.

56) **Guaranteed Buy-Back Agreement** - While it's similar to the extended guarantee, this specialized version is often used with limited edition offers on coins and art objects. To convince the prospect of the product's value, the advertiser offers to buy it back at the full price during a specified period that may last as long as 5 years.

57) **Guaranteed Acceptance Offer** - This specialized offer is used by insurance firms with certain types of policies that require no health questions or underwriting. It's especially appealing to those with health problems who might not otherwise qualify.

BUILD-UP-THE-SALE OFFERS

58) **Multi-Product Offers** - Two or more products or services are featured in the same ad or mailing. Maybe you've never thought about it this way, but the best-known type of multi-product offer is a catalog, which can feature a hundred or more items.

59) **Piggyback Offers** - Similar to a multi-product offer, except that one product is strongly featured. The other items just kind of ride along or "piggyback" in the hope of picking up additional sales.

60) **The Deluxe Offer** - A publisher might offer a book in standard binding at $9.95. The order form gives the customer the option of ordering a deluxe edition for only $2.00 more. And it's not unusual for 10% or more of those ordering to select the deluxe alternative.

61) **Good-Better-Best Offer** - This one goes a step further by offering 3 choices. The mail order mints, for example, sometimes offer their medals in a choice of bronze, sterling silver, or 24K gold.

62) **Add-On Offer** - A low-cost item that's related to the featured product can be great for impulse orders. For example, offering a wallet for $7.95, with a matching key case for only $1.00 extra.

63) **Write-Your-Own-Ticket Offer** - Some magazines have used this with good success to build up the sale. Instead of offering 17 weeks for $4.93 - which is 29¢ per issue - they give the subscriber the 29¢ an issue price and let them fill in the number of weeks they want their subscription to run.

64) **Bounce-Back Offer** - This approach tries to build onto the original sale by enclosing an additional offer with the product shipment or invoice.

65) **Increase and Extension Offer** - These are also follow-ups to the original sale. Mail order insurance firms often give policyholders a chance to get increased coverage with a higher-priced version of the same policy. Magazines often use an advance renewal offer to get subscribers to extend their present subscription.

SWEEPSTAKES OFFERS

66) **Drawing Type Sweepstakes** - The majority of sweepstakes contests are set up this way. The prospect gets one or more chances to win, but all winners are selected by a random drawing.

67) **Lucky Number Sweepstakes** - With this type of contest, winning numbers are pre-selected before making the mailing or running the ad. Copy strategy emphasizes "you may have already won." A drawing is held for the unclaimed prizes using all the winning numbers that are actually entered or returned.

68) **"Everybody Wins" Sweepstakes** - No longer widely used, this offer was a real bonanza when it was first introduced. The prize structure is set up so the bottom or low-end prize is a very inexpensive or nominal one. It's awarded to everyone who enters and doesn't win one of the bigger prizes.

69) **Involvement Sweepstakes** - This type requires the prospect to open a mystery envelope, play a game, or

match their number against an eligible number list. In doing so, the prospect determines the value of the grand prize they win *if* their entry is drawn as the winner. Some of these involvement devices have been highly effective in boosting results.

70) **Talent Contests** - Not really a sweepstakes, but effective for some types of direct marketing situations. The mail order puzzle clubs and the "draw me" ad which offers a free scholarship from a home study art school and examples.

Note: Chance promotions are locally and agency regulated. Always be sure your offer is within guidelines. Legal review is advised.

CLUB & CONTINUITY OFFERS

71) **Positive Option** - You join a club and are notified monthly of new selections. To order, you must take some positive action, such as sending back an order card.

72) **Negative Option** - Like the Positive Option, you are still notified in advance of new selections. But under the terms you agreed to when you joined, the new selection is shipped *unless* you return a rejection card by a specific date.

73) **Automatic Shipments** - This variation eliminates the advance notice of new selections. When you sign up, you give the publisher permission to ship each selection automatically until you tell them to stop. It's commonly called a "Till Forbid" offer.

74) **Continuity Load-Up Offer** - Usually used for a continuity book series, like a 20-volume encyclopedia. The
first book is offered free. But after you receive and pay
for the next couple of monthly volumes, the balance of
the series is sent in one load-up shipment. However, you
can continue to pay at the rate of one volume per month.

75) **Front-End Load-Ups** - Commonly used by record and
book clubs, this offer gives you several selections for a
nominal charge if you agree to accept a minimum quantity at a higher price during a specified period. Record
clubs, for example, may give you 4 records for $1.00 if
you agree to purchase 4 more records during the next
year. This is an attractive offer that forces prospects to
make a commitment. Most offers do specify a fixed
time period during which the remaining selections must
be purchased.

76) **Open-Ended Commitment** - Like the Front-End Load-
Up, except that there is no time limit during which additional selections must be purchased.

77) **"No Strings Attached" Commitment**- Like offers 75
and 76, except this offer is more generous because you
are not committed to any future purchases. The publisher gambles that you will find future selections interesting
enough to make a certain number of purchases.

78) **Lifetime Membership Fee** - You pay a one-time fee to
join, usually $5.00 or $10.00, and get a monthly
announcement of new selections. There's no minimum
commitment, and all ordering is done on a positive
option basis.

79) **Annual Membership Fee** - Here you pay an annual fee for club membership. It's often used by travel clubs, where you get a whole range of benefits, including travel insurance. It is also used for fund-raising, where a choice of membership levels is often effective.

80) **The Philanthropic Privilege** - This is the basis of all fund-raising offers. The donor's contribution usually brings nothing tangible in return, but it helps make the world a better place in which to live. This offer is sometimes enhanced by giving gummed stamps, a membership card, or other tokens of appreciation.

81) **Blank Check Offer** - First used in the McGovern fund-raising campaign, supporters could fill out blank, post-dated checks which were cashed one-a-month to provide installment contributions. This offer was later adapted to extend credit to bank charge card customers.

82) **Executive Preview Charge** - An effective offer for such things as sales training films. The executive agrees to pay $25 to screen or preview the film, and if they decide to buy or rent it, the preview price is credited against the full price.

83) **Yes/No Offers** - Asks prospect to let you know their decision either way. In most cases the negative responses have little or no value. But by forcing a decision, you often end up with more "yes" responses.

84) **Self-Qualification Offer** - Uses a choice of options to get the prospect to indicate their degree of interest in your product or service, such as a free booklet or a free demonstration. Those who request the demonstration

qualify themselves as serious prospects and should get more immediate attention.

85) **Exclusive Rights for Your Trading Area** - Ideal for selling some business services to firms who are in a competitive business. An example is a syndicated newsletter that a bank buys and sends to its customers. You give the first bank that responds exclusive rights for their trading area. The percentages that order are such that you seldom have to turn anybody down.

86) **The Super Dramatic Offer** - Sometimes very effective. Such as the offer that challenged, "smoke my new kind of pipe for 30 days. If you don't like it, smash it up with a hammer and send me back the pieces."

87) **Trade-In Offer** - An offer like "we'll give you $10 for your old slide rule when you buy a new electronic calculator" can be very appealing.

88) **Third Party Referral Offer** - Instead of renting somebody's list, you get the list owner to make a mailing for you using their name recommending your product or service. This usually works better than your own promotion because of the rapport a company has with its own customers.

89) **Member-Get-A-Member Offer** - Often used to get customers to send in the names of friends who might be interested. Widely used by book and record clubs, who give their members a free gift if they get new members to sign up.

90) **Name-Getter Offers** - Usually designed for building a prospect list. A firm can offer a low-cost premium at an attractive self-liquidating price.

91) **Purchase-With-Purchase** - Widely used by cosmetic firms and department stores. An attractive gift set is offered at a special price with a regular purchase.

92) **Delayed Billing Offer** - The appeal is: Order now and we won't bill you until next month. Especially effective before the holidays, when people have lots of other expenses.

93) **Reduced Down Payment** - Frequently used as a follow-up in an extended mailing series. If the customer does not respond to the regular offer in previous mailings, you reduce the down payment to make it easier for them to get started.

94) **Stripped-Down Products** - Also used in an extended mailing series. A home study school, for example, that doesn't get the prospect to order the full course might then offer a starter course at a lower price.

95) **Secret Bonus Gift** - Usually used with TV support. The commercial offers an extra bonus gift not mentioned in the corresponding ad or mailing. For example, a record company offers a bonus record if you write the album number in the "secret gold box" on the order form.

96) **Rush Shipping Service** - An appealing offer for things like seasonal gifts and film processing. Sometimes the customer is asked to pay an extra charge for this rush service.

97) **The Competitive Offer** - Can be a strong way to drama-
tize your selling story, like Diner's Club offering to pay
prospects $5.00 to turn in their American Express cards.

98) **The Nominal Reimbursement Offer** - Used for
research mailings. A token payment is offered to get
somebody to fill out and return a questionnaire.

99) **Establish-the-Value Offer** - If you have an attractive
free gift, you can build up its value and establish credibility by offering an extra one for a friend at the regular
price.

Excerpted from *Profitable Direct Marketing* by Jim Kobs,
published by Crain Books, 740 Rush Street, Chicago,
Illinois 60611.

Here's a 100th item to this list: **the perpetual offer**. In business,
this is the offer that provides personal benefit to a buyer when
spending company money. One example of the perpetual offer is
the airlines frequent flyer programs. Similar programs have been
implemented by car rental, hotel, and even catalog companies.

The growth of frequent traveler and frequent user programs has
proven that prospects can become involved with a supplier on an on
going basis. All the supplier need do is remind prospects of their
current "use" status and show them when they will receive an
award. The only drawback to this type of offer program is in cur-
tailing or eliminating it. The plus of this type of program is the
loyal and happy customer database it creates.

Frequent user customers on the database are less expensive to promote because they are known entities. The bonus awards cost less
than promoting the market to stimulate an incremental sale. The
success and continued growth of these types of programs are proof-

positive of how effective marketing to this group of customers has become. In fact, the frequent traveler programs have created substantial joint ventures between airlines, hotels, and car rental companies.

The offer must be in line with program objectives and with the company's operational ability to follow-up on responses. If the objective is lead generation, make an offer that will generate only as many leads as you can effectively handle. Too many leads can be even more destructive to the direct marketing program than not enough leads. Quantity will not be as important as quality.

Whether the offer is for leads or actual orders, make the offer only as enticing as you can afford. It makes no sense to give away profits to generate a response. There are exceptions when you might be willing to not make a profit on an initial order if the potential from future orders can make the customer profitable. This is fairly common in the catalog industry. You will always have to evaluate whether your offer was so lucrative that the quality of the responder was not as good as you had hoped.

When examining the economics of offers you develop, remember that the offers are a variable cost; only respondents are taking advantage of the offer. If a 10,000-piece mailing yields 500 respondents, the cost of the offer is only for the 500 respondents.

When testing a less expensive offer against your control offer, don't assume a lower response rate is less effective. Include the costs for the offer and then review the total direct marketing costs per responder and per order. You may find that the less expensive offer produces a less expensive order. Don't throw out the baby with the bath water because of the difference in response rates.

Lead programs are even more difficult to measure. You have to evaluate not just the responses but the actual orders. Remember, ultimately you're in the sales business. Track your respondents to sales before you decide which offer is best.

As you evaluate which offer will work best for your lead generation effort, consider the personality you're trying to target. Although we have difficulty identifying specific marketing targets, we can often understand the personality of our marketing target. The offer should be targeted to the appropriate personality.

Business Personalities

Successful business-to-business direct marketers try to align the personalities of their promotion with the personalities of the people who are going to receive the promotion. This means marketing to the individual -- not to their position within the company. However, sometimes, as we will explore later, personality type and position can be related. When a company's purchasing procedures involve multiple buyers who use a single purchasing agent, this process becomes more difficult. So we must look to the promotion itself -- through its design, copy and graphics -- to project its personality clearly, one that will match that of the business executive we are targeting.

While all people may be created equal, all people do not make buying decisions for the same set of reasons. People are all driven by an almost unexplainable group of forces. Psychology has developed stereotypes to help categorize the many types of people.

Business purchasers can be defined using four of the major personality types: pragmatic, extroverted, amiable, and analytic. These four stereotypes are determined by the intersection of a person's assertiveness and emotion, from low to high on a set of axis. (See Illustration 6-2)

Now, let's take a look at each of the personality types:

- **Pragmatic** - These people are businesslike; they don't like to waste time or take vacations, and they make quick decisions based on facts. Pragmatic individuals buy condensed books and use a highlighter to emphasize major points. They judge a seminar on its value, not on its presentation; they would prefer to receive an executive summary of its main points. They don't like spectator sports; they would rather participate (except golf, which wastes too much time). Efficiency is important to

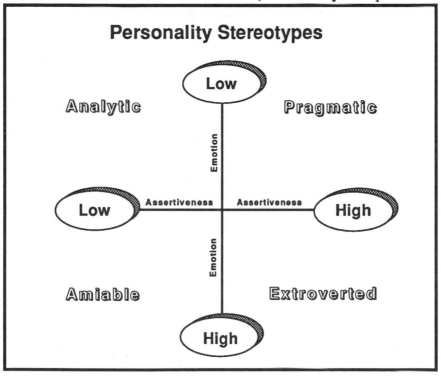

Illustration 6-2: Personality Stereotypes

The four stereotype personalities are charted by the point at which assertiveness intersects with emotion. A highly emotional but unassertive individual, therefore, can be classified as "amiable."

them. They are top managers, or striving to reach that position.

- **Extroverted** - Aggressive, impulsive and very friendly, these people make fast decisions based on excitement or enthusiasm. They go to a seminar and are inspired by the presenters; they don't like charts and graphs, and their desks are usually sloppy. Motivation is a driving force. This is the type of individual most often found in sales and marketing environments.

- **Amiable** - These individuals like to develop relationships with people and things, and are probably in management positions only in larger companies where the system provides barriers against pressure. They drive older cars because they dislike car salespeople. People who fit this stereotype make decisions slowly, based on what will make everybody happy. Their reason for

---

Pragmatic

Do's	**dont's**
• Be clear, specific, brief. • Stick to business. • Provide facts and figures about effectiveness of options. • Call to action by referring to objectives and results. • Provide factual alternatives. • Make ordering easy.	• Don't ramble with long prose. • Don't try to build a personal relationship. • Don't speculate or offer assurances. • Don't try to convince by personal means • Don't dictate or direct. • Don't use complicated merchandising gimmicks or involvement.

Illustration 6-3: Dealing with the Pragmatic Personality.

attending a seminar is simply to be around similar people, and while they are there, they worry about whether or not everyone is having a good time. General traits are openness and friendliness. This type of person is found in personnel, or perhaps as an administrative assistant or staff manager who has protection from dealing with front-line confrontation.

- **Analytic** - A breed apart, these individuals are comfortable with slide rules and calculators, and like to be surrounded by gadgets. Because they can't seem to get enough information, they generally make slow decisions. They can attend a 10-day seminar about coaxial cable, for instance, and feel it was a shallow presentation. Analytical people are often engineers or accountants.

Extroverted

Do's	dont's
• Offer the dream and intentions. • Talk about people and their goals. • Give ideas for implementing action. • Provide testimonials from people seen as important. • Offer special immediate extra incentives for willingness to place orders.	• Don't legislate. • Don't drive facts and figures. • Don't "dream" too much or they will put down the promotion. • Don't be dogmatic. • Don't be impersonal or judgmental.

Illustration 6-4: Dealing with the Extroverted Personality.

Amiable

Do's

- Use personal comments to lead offers.
- Present your case softly, non-threateningly.
- Involve the reader by explaining "how."
- Be casual and informal.
- Provide personal guarantees to minimize risks and give assurances of benefits.

dont's

- Don't stick coldly to business.
- Don't be domineering, demanding or threatening about position or power.
- Don't debate facts and figures.
- Don't patronize or demean.
- Don't offer guarantees or assurances you can't fulfill.

Illustration 6-5: Dealing with the Amiable Personality.

It is important to note that these are broad generalizations. Everyone exhibits pieces and parts of each personality style from time to time. If, however, you have identified yourself with two of these personality types, they are most likely adjacent on the graph, and not diagonal to each other. While you can move up and down the emotional scale and back and forth on the assertiveness scale, you will seldom change styles in adjacent quadrants. This is important to remember as you define your promotion's personality.

If you want to shift your promotion's personality or evaluate whom you are selecting as business customers, take a look at some of the do's and dont's for each personality type. (See Illustrations 6-3 thru 6-6). Then review your (or your competitor's) promotions with these do's and dont's in mind. To whom are you actually directing your promotion?

The common complaint of business-to-business direct marketers is, "We don't know who is doing the buying." A purchasing agent, for

Analytic

Do's	dont's
• Be direct; stick to business. • Support your credibility by listing pros and cons. • Be accurate and allow for ways to verify reliability. • Provide solid, tangible, practical evidence.	• Don't be circuitous, casual or informal. • Don't be too brief. • Don't use testimonials. • Don't use gimmicks or clever, quick manipulations.

Illustration 6-6: Dealing with the Analytic Personality.

example, may place orders for several people or departments. But, if you allow yourself to express some opinions in your promotion, to stereotype a few titles or functions and relate them to your promotion, you can guess fairly accurately who is doing the buying.

As you identify the list and market you're trying to reach, the personality should be fairly easy to identify. Your offer should be aimed at the personality you've identified.

Formats

Format is the method you select to deliver your offer to the market. Many people refer to format as media. This definition is too restrictive since several of the formats do not fall within a media definition. Telemarketing, for example, is not traditionally defined as media. For the purpose of this discussion, we will use formats to encompass all of the ways to deliver a message to a market.

Once you have researched and determined your market segments, and have developed your offers per market segment, you are ready to select the format to deliver your message to your market. This process is often based on previous experience or on recommendations. While it's impossible to provide a fixed formula for selection of formats, it is possible to provide a structure for approaching the format decision.

Illustration 6-7: Personalization of the contact.

There are two major selection criteria to consider when selecting formats:

1) The level of personal contact necessary to gain a sale or to generate a lead that can become a sale.

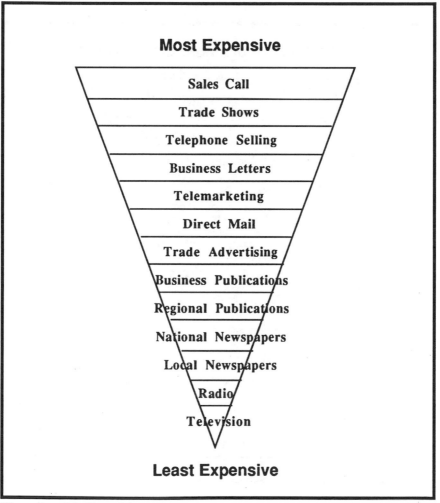

Illustration 6-8: Cost of the contact.

2) The dollars you are willing to spend to gain a sale or to generate a lead that can become a sale.

If we set up a hierarchy of formats (Illustration 6-7) from personal to impersonal contacts, we would see that a sales contact is on the top as the most personal, and network advertising is on the bottom as the most impersonal. I will discuss each of these later in more detail.

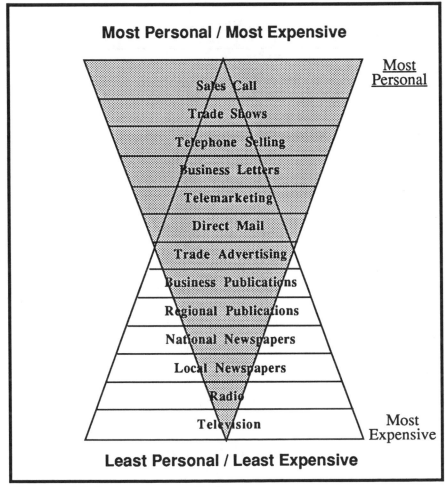

Illustration 6-9: Cost versus personalization.

Now if we examine the associated cost per contact of each of these formats, we see that the higher the level of personal contact, the greater the cost (Illustration 6-8).

Overlaying the triangles (Illustration 6-9) provides a quick reference in helping you make general format selections.

Your experience, knowledge of your selling process and the financial proforma are the guides you should use when selecting formats. Most business-to-business applications use more than one format to deliver their messages to their market. The workhorses of business-to-business direct marketing are telephone, mail, and trade publication space advertising. These three major formats provide the majority of business-to-business leads and orders.

Types of Formats

- **Sales calls.** The most common format used in business-to-business selling to deliver an offer to the market. While the sales call is not direct marketing, it is controllable and measurable in its costs and results, although it is the least controllable format. When you send a sales representative as a promotion, you have no ability to control what will be said. The sales call, the most personal contact, is the most expensive sales contact you can make. You can derive your own cost per sales call, as I discussed in Chapter 3, or use published industry costs as a guideline. The average face-to-face sales call costs more than $250.

    This is not that expensive if you can make a sale on each sales call. Depending on the number of sales calls required per order, you may find that personal selling can cost more than $1,000 per order. The same research that established the average cost per sales call also determined that the average industrial order costs more than $1,100 in sales call expenses. These costs should be part of your marketing plan so you can decide what part of the existing expenses should be displaced by direct marketing.

- **Trade shows.** An alternate format to personal selling where prospects are gathered for the express purpose of reviewing products and services. This is an extension of personal selling with a cost per contact in the $90 to $125 range. This assumes reasonable traffic for the show; otherwise the cost can be thousands of dollars per contact.

  A variation of trade shows are seminars. This technique of group sales situations is becoming more and more popular. It provides an opportunity to spread the sales cost across a group of prospects. Seminars normally require a fair amount of front-end work to drive traffic, but they can be extremely effective in controlling the cost and quality of the sales contact.

- **Telephone selling.** Since this format represents a major opportunity for the business-to-business marketer we have devoted an entire chapter to this subject. For the purposes of evaluating the cost of this format, I will divide telephone into two major segments: telephone selling and telemarketing.

  Telephone selling is when you put a qualified salesperson on the telephone to make sales calls as opposed to having the salesperson meet the prospects face-to-face. The use of telephone selling is fairly expensive per contact. Salespeople will be able to make more calls per day because travel time is eliminated. You probably will not see a rapid increase in sales when you introduce telephone selling because your sales force is already using telephone as a format. Telephone selling costs $50 to $125 per contact.

Telephone selling is difficult to measure in terms of both costs and results. In many businesses, telephone selling is considered a tool and a necessary part of the business. It is often segmented and measured. In many situations, the executive responsible for telephone selling does not even have control, of or responsibility for, the telephone bill. There is usually not a clear understanding of all the expenses involved in telephone selling.

Telemarketing. This telephone format is not dependent on the skill of the communicator but relies on a script, offer, and marketing database to make a contact to the prospect. This format costs between $35 and $65 per hour of activity. Because it is a production activity, it is possible to make a business contact for $7 to $15. The cost per sale will depend on the offer, what is being sold, and the leverage used in the script to increase response (premiums, incentives to the buyer, etc).

- **Business Letters**. These are personal letters written, signed, and mailed one at a time. They are used by sales representatives to communicate proposals, offers, contracts and general information to their accounts. This format costs between $7.50 and $25 per contact.

- **Direct Mail**. This is the workhorse of business-to-business direct marketing. I have provided a complete chapter on this important format. Direct mail can be used as

part of an unsolicited promotion or as a form of fulfillment when a prospect requests more information about a
company and its products. The cost of direct mail can
range from a few cents per contact, in the case of card
decks, to several dollars per contact for fulfillment or
elaborate mail packages. As a general guideline, mail
costs per contact range from .50 to $2.

• **Trade Advertising.** Business-to-business marketers are
the most comfortable with this format. Trade publications are those publications that have circulation to a
specific group. In most cases, subscribers do not pay
for the publication; they receive the publication based on
their industry, area of responsibility and/or position. To
receive the publication, the subscriber completes a qualification card that provides information to the publication.

Direct Mail Formats

Package	Components	$/Piece
Business letter	POE, PLTR, BRE, PRD, #, BR	$1.75
9 x 12	WOE, LTR, BRC, #, BR	$1.60
Promotional letter	WOE, LTR, PBRC, #, BR	$1.05
Invitation	POE, INV, RD, #, BRE	$.95
Self-mailer	BR, PBRC, #	$.90
Catalog	BR, RD, #	$.80
Newsletter	BR, #	$.75
Double Postcard	BR, PBRC, #	$.50
Postcard	BR, #	$.45

BR	= Brochure	PLTR =	Personalized letter
BRC	= Business reply card	POE =	Personalized outer envelope
BRE	= Business reply envelope	PRD =	Personalized response device
INV	= Invitation	RD =	Response device
LTR	= Non-personalized letter	WOE =	Window outer envelope
PBRC =	Personalized business reply card	# =	Phone number

Illustration 6-10: Direct mail formats and associated costs per piece.

Advertisers in this type of publication can review subscriber information before placing print ads in the publication. Depending on circulation and area of concentration, cost per contact may vary. We estimate cost per contact to range between 6 cents and 15 cents. Contacts are based on circulation and are referred to as impressions, assuming that one person will see your ad one time. In addition, trade publications tend to have a high degree of pass-along to other readers. A manager will probably pass a publication to all of their subordinates.

Many trade publications offer reader service cards or "bingo" cards, so called because the reader circles numbers on the card based on the numbers the magazine assigns to each ad in the book. The bingo cards are sent back to the magazine or a service bureau where they are processed. The leads are then passed along to the advertisers. Leads generated from this type of service should be carefully screened prior to being given to the sales force.

- **Business Publications**. These are general interest publications distributed as a result of paid subscriptions. Typically, little is known about their readers except what can be gained from address overlays or subscriber studies. These publications cross industries and are general in nature. If a product crosses many industries and levels of management, these books can work well for it. Like trade publications, business publications normally offer reader service cards to their subscribers. The cost per impression ranges from 3 cents to 10 cents.

- **Regional Business Publications**. When servicing a regional market, regional business publications can be the best print investment. Regional publications are focused on business readers in a circulation area that approximates a given trade area. Regional coverage purchases in national publications may provide greater coverage than regional publications within a trade area, resulting in wasted circulation. While more expensive than national publications, regional publications may be a good alternative. The cost per impression ranges from 9 cents to 20 cents.

- **National Daily/Weekly Newspapers.** There are several newsprint publications written for the business market or that have a business or money section. These newspapers have large circulations intended to cross all types and sizes of businesses. Advertising in these publications can provide large numbers of readers for a relatively low cost. Space ads in these publications can generate a significant number of responders. Leads generated from this type of service should be carefully screened before they are sent to the sales force. The cost per impression can be between 3 cents and 10 cents.

Regional newspapers, like national dailies, can reach large numbers of readers in their business sections. Responders should be carefully screened for qualification. The cost per impression can be the same as in a national daily, however, the circulation contains some people who may not be in the business arena.

- **Local Newspapers.** This is an alternative for the business marketer who is servicing a local area. A national marketer will be concerned about costs, variations of sizes, and submission requirements for ads between all of the local newspapers. Most local papers do not have a business section that will seek out target readers. An ad can be lost in the *ROP* (Run of Press); the publisher can place the ad anywhere in the publication. Costs range from 10 cents to 25 cents per impression.

- **Radio.** This has not proven to be a successful stand-alone format for business-to-business direct marketing. Radio can support a regional or local marketing effort if the listener is going to receive printed material or additional information at a retail location. Costs per impression vary widely depending on the time of day, frequency of airing, and the length of the ad. When planning to use radio, compare the type of listener the radio station represents to the characteristics of your target.

- **Regional or Network Television.** Television has been used from time to time as a response format by companies that have large budgets and strong mark-ups on their products. More often, television is used as an image and awareness-builder. Direct response ads using 800 numbers can generate large quantities of unqualified responders.

  Direct response television has been used successfully in the consumer world where targeting and segmentation are not as critical as in business-to-business. Because there are many people viewing the ad who are not qualified, the cost per *qualified* contact is very high. The cost per contact is very low compared to other formats, but with no way to target the message to a defined group of prospects, the quality of any responder has to be carefully examined. Leads generated from this type of format should be carefully screened before they are sent to the sales force. Most responders will not be qualified. Cost per impression can be from 1/10 to 9/10s of a cent.

Although the cost per impression is attractive, there is a high amount of waste in contacting the wrong people.

Copy/Graphics

This area seems to receive the most attention in the development of the direct marketing promotion. It is clearly an important element within direct marketing, however it will have the least impact on the success of your promotion. At the copy level we spend more time on describing the features of our product rather than the benefits the prospect will receive from acquiring and using the product.

Why is there such a wide variance between what we do and what should be done to produce good direct marketing? Simple. We all love our "**It**."

>   **It**   *(noun) the product or service a company or individ-
>   ual makes available for someone to buy.*

Richard S. Hodgson, in his book, *Direct Mail and Mail Order Handbook* (published by Dartnell, Chicago, Illinois 60640) does an excellent job of providing directions on how to prepare and review direct marketing and direct mail copy. Some of his thoughts and recommendations are given below.

Seek an Expert

The best advice on copy which can be given to any direct mail advertiser is to seek an experienced *direct mail* copy expert. Then work with him or have him work with your copywriters to develop the best techniques to meet the specific communications problems involved. With such guidance, the odds are that you or your copywriting personnel will learn many of the techniques that lead to success, and eventually others will be turning to you for direct mail copy help. Copywriters generally can guide you graphically with ideas or recommend designers than can support your creative efforts. Of course, many good designers work with good copywriters, so you can reverse the entire process if you feel graphic representation of your It is more important than the words that support the graphics.

In the absence of in-person help from an expert, turn to some of the helpful books on direct mail copywriting that are available.

Because there are so many detailed and helpful volumes available on the subject of direct mail copy, it is our primary purpose to provide some basic guidelines for successful promotion design. This material is presented to assist you in evaluating copy and graphics, rather than trying to teach you to be a creative director.

One technical approach to creating effective copy/graphics is to use the AIDA formula (Attention, Interest, Desire, Action). This formula is also used to train sales representatives an approach to selling situations.

Attention - The direct marketing promotion should get the recipient to look at it and focus on its message. This is only accomplished by offering the recipients something of interest to them. Announcing a new product in the opening message does not get anyone's attention unless you relate what the new product is going to do for them. Graphics can also gain the attention of a target.

Interest - Once you have the recipient's attention, you can deliver the benefits and offer of your promotion.

Desire - With the recipient's interest aroused, you can begin to move to close. Restate points of interest in customized terms that are personalized to the recipient's needs. Do not confuse the product's features with the benefits they provide. The classic example is that you are not selling *drill bits,* you are selling *holes.*

It's easy to spend a great deal of time writing about the features of *drill bits*: hardened steel, ground edges, length, weight, etc. What the recipient wants to have is perfect little *holes.* Explain how the *drill bits* will create those perfect little *holes* to satisfy the recipient's needs. If you never make the transition from features to benefits, you will never arouse desire.

Action - This is what it is all about. Many direct marketers never call the prospect to action. You should begin all promotional efforts, including copy, by developing the action you want the recipient to take. Start with the action and weave it through the entire promotion rather than trying to tie it in as an afterthought. Don't be afraid to call the recipient to action frequently throughout the promotion. For example, each time a benefit is mentioned, explain that the

---

Direct Marketing Copy Checklist
Before you start to write

1) Develop the action you want the recipient to take.
2) List all your product's features and associated benefits.
   This is done by listing a feature, followed by the words "What this means to you is..." Answering the statement which provides the benefit.
3) Rank benefits in order of importance to the recipient.
4) Identify someone you know who personifies the recipient you are trying to reach, so that you are writing to a person rather than a concept.

Writing copy

1) Write your action step(s).
2) Using the AIDA formula, create several attention-getting headlines and select the best one.
3) As your message unfolds, keep your copy moving. Frequently remind the reader of the benefits your product will deliver and continually call them to action.
4) Ask for the order. Ask for the order. Ask for the order.
5) If your message is to be printed, make sure it is appealing to the eye. Dense copy and long paragraphs produce little white space where the reader can rest.

Illustration 6-11: A direct marketing copy checklist.

recipient can have it now by going to the action step. This is no different than *trial closing* in face-to-face selling.

Illustration 6-11 gives a method to develop direct response copy. AIDA is only one formula you can use to organize the development of direct marketing copy. Hodgson supplies several other formulas that you might find helpful. No matter what approach to copywriting you use, Illustration 6-12, the checklist by Maxwell Ross can be helpful.

Checklist for Better Direct Mail Copy
Prepared by Maxwell C. Ross

Copy Technique

1) Does the lead sentence get in step with your reader at once?
2) Is your lead sentence more than two lines long?
3) Do your opening paragraphs promise a benefit to the reader?
4) Have you fired your biggest gun first?
5) Is there a big idea behind your letter?
6) Are your thoughts arranged in logical order?
7) Is what you say believable?
8) Is it clear how the reader is to order - and did you ask for the order?
9) Does the copy tie in with the order form - and have you directed attention to the order form in the letter?

Copy Editing

10) Does the letter have "you" attitude all the way through?
11) Does the letter have a conversational tone?
12) Have you formed a "bucket brigade" through your copy?
13) Does the letter score between 70 and 80 words of one-syllable for every 100 words of copy?
14) Are there any sentences which begin with an article - a, an, or the - where you might have avoided it?
15) Are there any places where you have strung together too many prepositional phrases?
16) Have you kept out "wandering" verbs?
17) Have you used action verbs instead of noun construction?
18) Are there any "thats" you do not need?
19) How does the copy rate on such letter craftsmanship points as (a) using active voice instead of passive, (b) periodic sentences instead of loose, (c) too many participles, (d)splitting infinitives, (e) repeating your company name too many times?
20) Does your letter look the way you want it to? (a) placement of page, (b) no paragraphs over six lines, (c) indentation and numbered paragraphs, (d) underscoring and capitalization used sparingly, (e) punctuation for reading ease.

Illustration 6-12: Checklist for better direct mail copy.

Multimedia Synergy

Combining one or more formats or media can dramatically affect your results. Using a combination of media can be planned or accidental. For example, participating in a trade show at the same time you are using direct mail in a particular market can boost direct mail results by three or four times. In addition, the traffic at the trade show booth can be increased. This response is most likely to occur when large companies have separate groups responsible for direct marketing, sales, and trade shows.

It has been proven time and time again that there is a dramatic synergy in combining direct marketing promotions to substantially increase results. If planned properly, the combination of mail and telephone produces three to five times the results of either program individually.

If you are executing telemarketing lead-generation, you should also use direct mail. This may not be immediately apparent, however telemarketing prospects will ask for more information as often as they accept the offer. The direct mail material used to fulfill this request for information will force you into a combined phone and direct mail program. Similarly, you should use direct mail with space advertising, unless you are selling a product directly from the space ad.

These synergistic approaches may not be planned but will be required when you begin to implement any direct marketing promotion. View your prospects who request additional information as people who are beginning to close, not just rejections. Often, particularly in telemarketing, prospects will request information simply to end the dialogue. The prospect does not want to be rude, so they request additional information as a put-off. However, about 25% of this group of people can be converted to orders and sales if they are handled properly.

You may not consider this a synergistic promotion; you may look at it as simply linear common sense. Don't be misled; if you're using multiple formats and multiple media, there is a synergy in the promotions.

These are the types of questions that are most often asked concerning multimedia:

- What happens when you use mail prior to telemarketing?
- What happens when you use direct response print advertising in a market at the same time you are doing a direct mail promotion?
- Does awareness advertising have any affect on the success of your direct mail or telemarketing programs?
- How important is the timing of direct mail followed by telemarketing?

There is a significant increase in response rates when mail is used prior to telemarketing. In Chapter 7, I will discuss several specific programs that combined the use of mail and phone. There is a definite correlation between the time the mail is dropped and the time the phone call is made. When you examine the results of mail and phone together, use the combined totals for the promotion as compared to the individual results of either medium alone.

An example: A direct mail program by itself might produce a 2% response rate. Telemarketing of the same product without direct mail might produce a 6% response rate. While you might think that using mail followed by telemarketing would produce a response rate of 8%, I have seen the combined program produce results as high as 20% and 30%!

Timing is one of the major issues of the synergy of media. You may not be able to wait for all the responses from one medium before you implement another medium within the same program. Since telephone calls are ideally placed about two weeks after the mail is dropped, you may have to start the telemarketing program before you are able to receive all of the mail responses.

I have conducted direct marketing campaigns for cellular telephone companies and high-technology companies while they were also using awareness ads in the same markets. I have also performed the same direct marketing campaigns in different markets with no advertising support. There was an increase in response rate in the markets with the advertising, but it was difficult to determine if the increase in results justified the cost of the advertising. The fact that the campaigns were in different markets tended to distort the results.

I have frequently tested mail followed by telemarketing and found there is a definite correlation between the time the mail is dropped and the time the prospects were called. Telemarketing response rates seem to be at their highest between 11 and 16 days after the mail is dropped.

Media synergy does not always have to be a major program. An example is using two 30-second TV spots on the three network morning programs in the same market while participating in a trade show. The day this was done, the traffic in the booth was three times as high as it was on any other day. The total cost for the advertising was under $3,000.

Time

Today external data is processed using MIPS (million instructions per second), to increase the amount of data that can be processed to provide us with information to make decisions. These decisions will hopefully lead to action. Unfortunately, marketers must often convert data into information hamstrung by tragically slow cycle times of company bureaucrats in data processing and/or accounting. These bureaucracies often have cycle times measured in months, quarters and even years.

You do not have the luxury of time. Many of us have learned that immediate response and rapid cycles of contact improve our chances of gaining and maintaining a customer. Time is an asset that is constant to all competitors and it is fixed and inflexible. Winners in the game will have many contact cycles, while the loser will have a few in the same time frame. The winner will act quickly when requested; the loser will act slowly. The winner will drive the activity of marketing while the loser will be driven.

Many of us spend more time at work than with our families trying to survive in ever more competitive markets. You constantly gather data and try to make decisions that will maintain your market share. Growth has become more an expectation than a reality. You probably struggle with company structures that got their origin from the cycle times of the 50's when centralization was the hallmark of most companies. These antiquated structures are power-based and have grown inflexible. These structures treat time as if it were of no value in the present or for the future. Many of these organizations have fallen in love with their products and their structure instead of their customers.

What is your cycle time for customers to make a decision about acquiring products or services (not what you think, but what you can make happen)? Is it 2 days? 90 days? 120 days? 180 days? This cycle time for action by a customer or prospect is your window of opportunity before a competitor may eclipse your last innovation or beat your last price cut. The only way you can stay in the game is by embracing time as your competitive asset. Reduce your cycle time for decisions, action, and order generation. You cannot become so involved in the process of generating promotional programs that you forget the stakes of the game.

As time is compressed, the costs of delivering a product or a service decrease because the allowable fixed costs per unit can be less. As time is compressed, you can increase the price you charge by being the first in the market with a product or service. As time is compressed, your risks are reduced because you are less exposed to obsolescence and your revenue can go up. As time is compressed, your market-share increases because you are gaining and maintaining customers more rapidly than your competitors.

You can take full advantage of time by including offers in ALL marketing programs so you can begin taking action on initial contact. Quick response and fulfillment to lead programs can mean the difference between success and failure. *Get out of the education business with your promotional materials. Gain involvement and ask for action with every element of your program.*

Generating Leads Summarized

Promotion is defined as the further development and encouragement of prospects to purchase one's products or services. It has two aspects: creative and technical.   The creative elements are the *Big Ideas* that are used to present a product or service to the marketplace. Technical promotion has four parts:

List -   The customers or prospects to whom you plan to target your marketing effort.

Offer -   The proposition you are making to your customers or prospects in order to get them to respond.

Format -   The vehicle for delivering the
                        offer to your market: mail, phone,
                        print or broadcast.

Copy/Graphics -   The words and pictures you use to
                        communicate your offer to the
                        market.

The four parts of technical promotion were explained and the relative importance of each part to the ultimate success of a direct marketing program was discussed. List is 50%, offer is 25%, format is 15% and copy/graphics is 10%.

List selection is the most critical element in the process of developing a direct marketing program. Determining the elements that can be used for better target identification is more difficult in business marketing. Information is not as readily available as it is in the consumer world. Abbreviations and a lack of standards in company name and address information further complicate the selection process. In addition, the high degree of change in business titles and functions makes contacting the correct decision-maker to purchase a product or service difficult.   List selection and testing are critical and should not become an afterthought in direct marketing program development.

I reviewed the different list types and characteristics of each. By understanding lists types and characteristics you'll be able to identify the best opportunity for your lead programs.

Offers were discussed in detail and 100 offer techniques were described. Business offers can appeal to the individual as a business person or a consumer. As a business person, you have to appeal to your prospect's professional motivations. As a consumer, the appeal can be on how the offer will yield the individual personal gratification. Both approaches should be tested to determine the best alternative for your company.

Targeting the correct individual in business marketing is probably the most difficult challenge you will face. A complete review of the types of personalities involved in the business world was discussed. There are four personality stereotypes: analytic, pragmatic, amiable, and extroverted. Each personality stereotype has different likes and dislikes and should be approached separately. You should determine the personality type that is most closely aligned with the environment to which you're trying to sell and develop the direct marketing program around that personality. I discussed the do's and dont's in marketing to each of the personality stereotypes to make creating the direct marketing program easier.

I discussed formats and reviewed how to select the most appropriate for your needs. The cost per contact and personalization of each type of contact were contrasted to help you evaluate the best approach to reach your prospect or customer. Detailed descriptions of many types of formats were provided, along with advantages of each and the average cost per contact

Direct marketing copywriting was discussed. Several formulas were reviewed to help you develop a hard-hitting explanation of your product and offer. One formula, AIDA was examined in detail. Several approaches to reviewing copy to insure that you are taking your best shot at success were also considered. These approaches also focus on the AIDA formula for copy development.

What happens when you use more than one format in the same direct marketing program? Will multiple contacts improve results? Is there synergy in using multiple formats at the same time? Does one format require the use of another format? These questions and their answers were reviewed in some detail.

The question of how to best reach the prospect with the offer is never going to have an easy answer. As time changes so does the best approach to promotion. What is effective today may not be effective tomorrow. You will have to continually evaluate the success of your programs and seek new and better ways to promote your products and services. One of the beautiful things about direct marketing is its testability. This chapter gave you a foundation to build upon.

If you're trying direct marketing for the first time, test multiple approaches to determine the best promotion techniques for your company. Don't rest on your laurels; continue to look for better techniques to improve your results.

Embrace time as part of your promotional materials -- always have an offer that will call for action. Rapid cycles of action will put you in the winners circle more often than having the most well-informed prospects in your markets.

Chapter Seven:
Creating Offers

Like any direct marketing program, next to list, offer is the most important element in a lead generation effort. Unfortunately, little or no time is spent creating the offer. The offer can play a significant role in qualifying respondents and producing high quality leads.

Salespeople will often ignore many leads because the leads they followed up on in the past were low quality. They find it difficult to believe that any new program will be better.

As I discussed in Chapter 3, it is difficult to establish the definition of a qualified lead. Each salesperson seems to have their own perception of the lead they desire. The only characteristic they can agree on is that a good lead is one that closes. You have now been assigned the mission of finding qualified prospects interested in your products, even though your salespeople can't seem to agree on what constitutes a qualified prospect . . . not an attractive mission.

Salespeople will view your actions with skepticism. They have been promised good leads in the past that turn out to be merely information collectors who have no authority or desire to buy.

Illustration 7-1: The Sales Perception.

As you may recall from Chapter 3, there are four issues that need to be addressed in creating a qualified lead:

- Money
- Authority
- Need
- Desire

Remember that the first letter of each word spells MAN with a D. This is a convenient way to remember the four qualification areas. It also spells DAMN!

Hopefully, if the prospect is interested in your product or service, they can afford to purchase from you. In reality, there are three areas that can help financially justify almost any business decision:

1) ***Displaceable Expenses***: Dollars already being expended for similar or like services. You may find displaceable expenses in related areas of the business, as well as in the primary area you're trying to address.

2) ***Avoidable Expenses***: Dollars that the company can avoid having to spend in the future, if they buy your solution.

3) ***Increased Revenue and Business Growth***: Dollars that the company might generate due to better procedures or approaches to their business. This area is often addressed as intangible. Many business decisions are made on emotion based on the intangible value to be derived. For example, a computer that allows instant access to order status will improve customer satisfaction and service. It is very difficult to attribute savings or revenue to improved customer service. However, we cannot overlook these 'intangibles' as a primary justification.

As you try to establish the ability of a company to buy your solution, don't get bogged down with unnecessary details. Sometimes it's nice to have additional facts, but they don't really improve the quality of the lead. Sales managers often forget that the salesperson will generate their own level of information. You invest too much time getting unnecessary details just to qualify the sales lead.

Authority is often difficult to establish. To determine if the person to whom you're trying to sell to has the authority to buy from you, is tough. Ego being what it is, some business people cannot admit to people outside their own company that they have limited power. Lead quality normally suffers the most in this area. Many techniques can be tried to subtly establish buying authority. However, the best method is to ask the prospect directly if they can make the decision to buy your product or service.

Establishing need is the area we all tend to overcomplicate. Try to limit your questions and probes to one or two major criteria. Keep in mind that you're trying to qualify a sales lead that will be followed up by a salesperson. The salesperson will sell the product or service. Many companies perform too much market research under the guise of trying to determine prospect need. In most situations, the salesperson will want to confirm the information and will probably ask the same questions again.

Finally, a lead isn't qualified until the prospect has accepted the offer and agreed to see a salesperson.

The whole process of establishing lead quality should be started on a blackboard with the salespeople. Write the four major categories on the board and ask the sales force what one single question in each area, if answered, would help to confirm the quality of the lead. You'll ultimately get more than one question. To eliminate the other questions, try to determine if the information is absolutely necessary to establish the qualification of the lead.

You can often resolve the money, authority, and desire issues with one question that introduces the price of your product within an offer. Prospects may respond that they can't afford it or that they have to talk to someone else before deciding. Remember, a prospect isn't qualified unless they agree to become a referral.

Common Mistakes

Many lead programs suffer from similar shortcomings. These mistakes will often cause the lead program to fail.

> No measurable objectives: The lead program is often a result of a sales executive telling a communications manager to do some direct mail because the sales force needs leads to

increase their activity and ultimately their results. There are no measurable objectives and therefore it is impossible to measure the success of the effort.

Inconsistent expectations: The lack of measurable objectives will also cause salespeople, sales management, and direct marketing management to have different expectations. Without identifying the quality of the leads required, the number of orders and the leads required per day, week or month, it is almost impossible to satisfy everyone's expectations.

Offers are never considered: The two most common offers used to promote from business to business are; send for additional information or have a salesperson call. Neither of these offers is exciting or descriptive. Most of us have a fear of being sold by a salesperson and will avoid meeting with them if at all possible.

As the lead generation program is planned and implemented, there is little or no thought given to the offer that will be promoted.

Leads are generated ad hoc: Many lead programs are executed to satisfy short-term requirements and are rarely planned in advance. Programs are often executed locally by branch offices with little coordination between headquarters and other field offices. Even when the program is controlled and executed centrally, the leads are typically generated in a single burst with no consideration given to sustaining a constant lead flow to satisfy resource availability.

Lead flow is sporadic and inconsistent. Salespeople may receive a large burst of leads and then no leads for weeks or months. These peaks and valleys will create significant fol-

low-up problems for the salespeople and will ultimately
make them unhappy with lead quality.

Inconsistent communication: Most salespeople manage
their territories from their cars or briefcases. As the lead
program is designed, there is little thought given to the way
leads will be communicated to the salespeople. Each lead
program generates a lead that looks different. Many are created on different sizes of paper. Handling and filing of these
leads becomes a problem for the salesperson.

In Chapters 3 and 4, I discussed how to plan and develop lead programs to avoid these common mistakes. As you begin to develop
the offer for the lead program, don't forget to first resolve the issues
addressed in these earlier chapters.

The common mistakes are directly related to improper planning of
the lead program. Most lead programs are created in reaction to a
sales problem. This places a great deal of pressure on the lead generation efforts and will almost guarantee failure. Lead programs
have to evolutionary to be really successful. You have to learn from
each effort to ultimately produce leads that will satisfy the salespeople and sales management.

Identifying Lead Requirements

As you begin to develop your lead program you will have to first
identify the number of leads required. The number of leads is
directly tied to the number of orders you need, and the number of
orders that the sales force will generate without any lead activity.

In Chapter 4, I suggested you use the Lead Requirements Worksheet
to establish the number of leads you'll have to generate for each
salesperson. Illustration 7-2 shows a completed worksheet. The

average order is $4,660 and the program has to generate 60 orders per salesperson to achieve it's objective. This translates into five orders per month from lead efforts.

The worksheet also identifies that a lead will close 20% of the time, therefore each salesperson will require 300 leads or 60 leads per month. Specific objectives like these make it easier to develop the offer that will provide the quantity and quality of leads required.

Lead Requirements Worksheet

A)	Annual sales quota/objective per salesperson	$712,500
B)	Percent sales quota achieved without leads	60%
C)	Sales revenue achieved without leads *(B x A)*	$427,500
D)	Sales revenue required from leads *(A - C)*	$285,000
G)	Average revenue per order from leads	$4,660
H)	Number of orders from leads required *(F ÷ G)*	60
I)	Percentage of leads that order	20%
J)	Number leads required per salesperson *(H x I)*	300

Illustration 7-2: The Lead Requirements Worksheet

I always suggest that the best way to identify how you'll find leads that can meet your requirements is to really understand how salespeople are currently selling and closing their customers.

An analysis of the customer base can tell you the personality of both the individual buyers and their companies. You can also learn how long the buying decision took and the approach that the salespeople used to convince prospects to buy their products.

Once you know your current customers and successful selling approaches, you can create a respondent profile and ultimately a lead that looks similar.

Quality leads should provide an opportunity to close at least 20% of the time. In my experience, leads that don't close at a rate of at least 1 out of every 5 or 6 generated, are ignored by the salespeople.

You have to use current selling activity information to determine a customer profile that would buy at this rate.

Do not plan lead efforts that will produce so many leads that a salesperson would have to devote 100% of their time to handling them. Salespeople are already handling their current customers and pursuing prospects they have found themselves. If you plan to create more leads than the salesperson can handle, the lead program will fail. Determine the number of orders that a salesperson will generate without the lead program, and you will know how many orders you will need the lead effort to produce.

Make sure you know the number of sales calls a salesperson can make each week. You should also understand the purpose of these calls. How many calls are required to close a sale? If you create a lead program that requires more calls than a salesperson can make, the leads you generate will probably be considered poor quality.

Don't be daunted if you lack the sales staff to follow up on the leads you generate. Instead, focus on producing higher quality leads and use direct marketing to move the prospect closer to a buying decision. Although this may sound impossible, multi-step programs with offers that are perceived as valuable by the prospect can be unbelievably effective.

You can also impact the number of orders and leads required from a lead generation program by changing the average size of the order. Average order size is directly related to the offer made in the promotion. In the earlier example, if the average order was increased to $6,000, the number of orders required is reduced to 48, and the number of leads to about 240. Instead of 5 orders per month, you only need 4. Instead of 25 leads per month you only have to find 20. *Average order size is directly related to the offer you make.*

Offer Motivations

Lead qualification is a dilemma. We often forget that it isn't important what the salesperson thinks, it is only important what the prospect thinks.

When lead programs are developed, most use a series of questions to determine if the prospect is qualified enough to justify having a salesperson contact them. Many managers of lead programs forget how important the perception of the prospect is, and focus on obtaining information to evaluate lead quality from the salesperson's perception.

When qualifying prospects, it really isn't important if we think they have money, authority, need and desire, only that the prospect thinks so.

Illustration 7-3: The Target Area

If you tell a prospect how much your product costs and what it will do for them, and they say, here is my check, I want to buy your product, would you deny their order because they failed to meet your qualifications? This analogy may seem senseless but some of the qualification questions we ask prospects are just as senseless. Your offer can do more to qualify a prospect than almost any other single issue you can control.

Unfortunately, the two offers we know how to make in generating sales leads do very little to qualify the prospect. Companies seldom explain the cost of their products to the prospect for fear that the price may frighten the prospect and cause them not to respond.

There are several problems with offering to send prospects additional information. The information often:

- Is sent before we know if the prospect is truly qualified

- Is not designed to create leads, but is merely sales collateral material

- Is feature-oriented, and does not emphasize the benefits the prospect will realize by purchasing

- Does not contain a call to action which would create a qualified lead

Offers to have a salesperson contact the respondent suffer similar shortcomings. Most people have a natural fear of salespeople and are less inclined to spend time with them. When a prospect does agree to see a salesperson, the participants may not have similar expectations regarding the purpose of the visit. The prospect's expectations of the salesperson's visit are not appropriately set, and

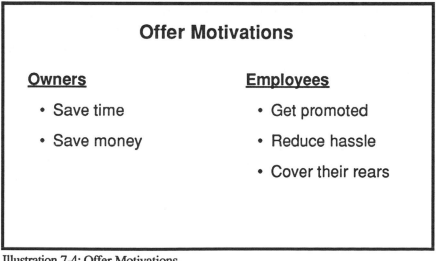

Illustration 7-4: Offer Motivations.

the salesperson does not have a clear idea of what their visit should accomplish.

Offers should address the needs of the person at which the offer is aimed. Remember that prospects will respond best when the offer answers the question -- what's in it for me?

Employees want to get promoted. Yet managers try to motivate employees by speaking in terms of what is good for management, not employees. Managers must find ways to save the company time and money, but to do so, they must offer their employees personal rewards. The employees aren't that interested in saving the company time and money.

Illustration 7-4 shows the different motivations that will affect people based on the role they serve in their company. If you're trying to reach business owners, saving time and money will excite them. On the other hand, employees aren't as concerned about time and money, but react well to getting promoted, reducing the hassle in their lives, and making safe decisions.

Most direct marketing and lead generation programs are geared to employees, yet the offers used are geared to owners. Employees have to make decisions that will help the company save time and money but they will respond best to offers that offer them something personally.

Getting promoted is a very strong motivation to an employee. You can use the actual term *getting promoted* to generate the prospect's interest. For example, this book will give you ideas that if implemented, will set you apart from your peers and may even get you promoted. We are all looking for a personal benefit in everything we do.

Business life is like standing on a slippery rock in water up to your neck in a swiftly moving stream. You're not going to look for a way to put more water in the stream or carry anything on your back. We all tend to avoid decisions that will add more hassle to our lives. This is another of those benefits you can state specifically in your offer. For example, our 7 day free trial will allow you to evaluate our book in your office without the hassle of listening to a salesperson or driving to a retail store.

Perkasie Uniform has the challenge of offering a personal benefit to police department chiefs. Illustration 7-5 shows the approach used by this small uniform company.

Most employees will make the safest decision. When a consumer decides to purchase a product or service they are spending their own money. No one will scrutinize their decision. If they make a bad decision it won't cost them anything but money. On the other hand, when a business person makes a purchase decision it will often be examined by someone else within the company. The buyer may have to justify their decision to others. A bad buying decision can cost the prospect more than money, perhaps even their job or the opportunity for a better job within the company. Many business people avoid purchase decisions for fear of being wrong.

Offers should help the prospect reduce risk and demonstrate a way to get out of the decision. Free trials and money back guarantees will go a long way towards helping the prospect protect their rear. Consider offering guarantees like this: Try our book for 7 days absolutely free. If at the end of 7 days you're not completely satisfied, return the book and owe nothing.

Telephone (215) 257-4544   Established 1922

PERKASIE UNIFORM COMPANY, INC.
Service 'Prestige' Uniforms
520 W. Walnut Street
Perkasie, PA 18944

September 1, 1991

Bernie Goldberg
Chief of Police
Direct Marketing Publishers
1304 University Drive
Yardley, PA 19067

Dear Chief,

Uniforms should be hassle free. Your uniform vendor is expected to provide not only competitive pricing, but also good service and an assortment of quality merchandise that is available when you want it. The last thing you want to deal with is hassle from your officers about uniform problems and concerns.

Perkasie Uniform has been supplying police and fire departments in the Delaware and Lehigh Valleys for over 65 years. Our reputation assures you of excellent service. The departments we serve receive the best service in the area, but most importantly, our chiefs don't have to get overly involved or concerned with uniform issues. We are committed to sustaining our reputation for the best possible service and product selection in the tri-state area.

We not only provide superior service but we assume the responsibility to ensure that you and your officers are kept abreast of the latest changes in uniform clothing. As you may already know, there is a new fibre available from Monsanto (Pil-Trol™) for commando style sweaters that makes them more durable, lighter weight, more comfortable and less expensive.

The commando sweater is becoming more popular. In many police departments, officers on patrol in automobiles or working in an office often remove their coats and wear the sweaters because they look good and are more comfortable. Pil-Trol will help to increase the popularity of this type of sweater. I'd like to give you a sample of this exciting sweater just for allowing me an opportunity to talk to you about your department uniform needs.

And there's more . . .

Illustration 7-5a: Perkasie Uniform Letter - Page 1.

Bernie Goldberg
September 1, 1991
Page 2

The Pil-Trol commando style sweater is made from a new fibre from Monsanto which is an acrylic instead of traditional wool. As a result it is lighter, washable and color fast. Instead of the traditional pilling problem associated with polyester in the past, this new material looks great after every washing without unsightly pilling. Your people will be hearing a lot about this new sweater so why not be the first department in the area to actually use them?

I'd like to discuss your current and future department uniform requirements with you. I may be able to show you how to save money and improve the service you're currently receiving. And when we meet, I'll show you the Pil-Trol commando sweater. In fact, when I call to schedule our meeting, I'll get your size and give you the sweater as a wear-test sample after our meeting.

To get your sample sweater and arrange for our meeting, mail or FAX the enclosed response form today. I'll call to schedule your preview of the Pil-Trol Sweater within a few days. If you have any questions, please don't hesitate to give me a call at (215) 257-4544. I look forward to meeting you in the near future.

Sincerely,

Wes Frith
President

P.S. Your free wear-test sample of the Pil-Trol sweater is available in several different colors. When we schedule our meeting, we'll ensure you receive the color you prefer. FAX the response form to receive your sweater in the next few days.

Illustration 7-5b: Perkasie Uniform Letter - Page 2.

RESPONSE FORM

Yes!   I want to receive a free wear-test sample of the Pil-TrolTM Military Sweater. I understand you'll contact me to get my sweater size and to schedule a no obligation appointment to review my department uniform needs.

Please change as appropriate
Bernie Goldberg
Chief of Police
Direct Marketing Publishers
1304 University Drive
Yardley, PA 19067
Phone: (215) 321-3068

Return this form to:

Wes Frith
President
Perkasie Uniform Company, Inc.
520 W. Walnut Street
Perkasie, PA 18944

Receive your wear-test sample sweater within the next few days -- FAX this form to (215) 453-8733 or call us today at (215) 257-4544!

Illustration 7-5c: Perkasie Uniform Letter - Response form.

Selling the Offer

As you design your promotion, try to sell your offer, your product, and your company. Serdi Corporation, a company selling machine tools to the automobile repair aftermarket, recently used a promotion that made several separate offers. Serdi offered a free demonstration, a free trial, and a special leasing program to ease acquisition. Illustration 7-6 shows the letter used by Serdi to promote the offers.

As you'll notice, Serdi promotes their valve seat machine but the letter promotes the free trial and demonstration. The prospect is aware of what the salesperson will accomplish during their meeting. The expectations are set for both the prospect and the salesperson.

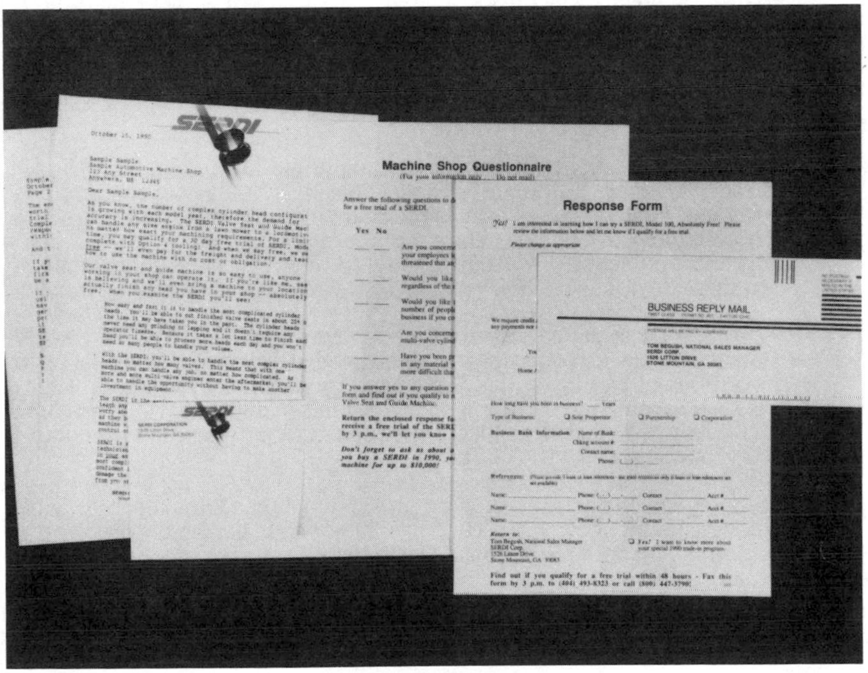

Illustration 7-6a: Serdi direct mail promotion.

October 1, 1990

Bernie Goldberg, President
Direct Marketing Publishers
1304 University Drive
Yardley, PA 19067

Dear Bernie Goldberg,

As you know, the number of complex cylinder head configurations is grow-ing with each model year, therefore the demand for accuracy is increasing. The SERDI Valve Seat and Guide Machine can handle any size engine from a lawn mower to a locomotive -- no matter how exact your machining require-ments. For a limited time, you may qualify for a 30 free trial of the SERDI, Model 100 complete with Option 4 tooling!. And when we say free, we mean free -- we'll even pay for the freight and delivery and teach you how to use the machine with no cost or obligation.

Our valve seat and guide machine is so easy to use, anyone working in your shop can operate it. If you're like me, seeing is believing and we'll even bring a machine to your location and actually finish any head you have in your shop -- absolutely free. When you examine the SERDI you'll see:

- How easy and fast it is to handle the most complicated cylinder heads. You'll be able to cut finished valve seats in about 20% of the time it may have taken you in the past. The cylinder heads never need any grinding or lapping and it doesn't require any operator finesse. Because it takes a lot less time to finish each head you'll be able to process more heads each day and you won't need as many people to handle your volume.

- With the SERDI, you'll be able to handle the most complex cylinder heads, no matter how many valves. This means that with one machine you can handle any job, no matter how complicated. As more and more multi-valve engines enter the aftermarket, you'll be able to han-dle the opportunity without having to make another investment in equipment.

- The SERDI is the easiest machine to learn and use. You can easily teach anyone in your shop to use the SERDI. You won't have to worry about employees holding a gun to your head for higher wages as they become more proficient in machining functions. This machine will make you less dependent on people and put you more in control of your company.

- SERDI is sold and supported by professional, hands-on machine tech-nicians. We'll show you how to use and operate the equipment in your environment doing your jobs. We'll even work with the most compli-cated, valuable cylinder head you have. We're so confident in the quality of our people and products, that if we damage the cylinder head during our demonstration, we'll buy it from you at your full retail price.

Illustration 7-6b: Serdi Direct Mail Letter - Page 1.

Bernie Goldberg
October 1, 1990
Page 2

The enclosed questionnaire will help you determine whether it is worth your time and effort to find out if you qualify for free trial of the SERDI, Model 100. There is no cost or obligation. Complete and return the response form today. If you FAX the response form to us by 3 p.m., we'll tell you if you qualify within 48 hours!

And there's more . . .

If you decide to buy a SERDI before December 31st 1990, you can take advantage of our special lease program and not pay your first payment until April 1st, 1991. In addition, you may even be able to trade your existing machine for up to $10,000!

If you're machining as few as 8 sets per week, you should be using a SERDI. You'll actually experience positive cash flow in savings from consumable materials, additional revenues you'll generate in new work and labor savings created by the improved productivity of your people. You don't have to take my word for it, let us bring a machine to your location and show you the SERDI. Our specially equipped mobile machine shops allow our technicians to come to you and demonstrate how effective the SERDI is doing your work.

Send us the response form as soon as possible to find out if you qualify for a free trial. We want to show you how the SERDI can help you improve your company's results. FAX or mail the response form now and we'll tell you if you qualify within 48 hours of receipt.

Sincerely,

Tom Begush
National Sales Manager

P.S Remember, you can judge for yourself whether you should find out if you qualify for a free trial of the SERDI, Model 100 by simply answering the Machine Shop Questionnaire. Then FAX or mail your response form and you'll know if you qualify within 48 hours of receipt. Don't forget to ask us about our special trade-in program for 1990 orders.

Illustration 7-6c: Serdi Direct Mail Letter - page 2.

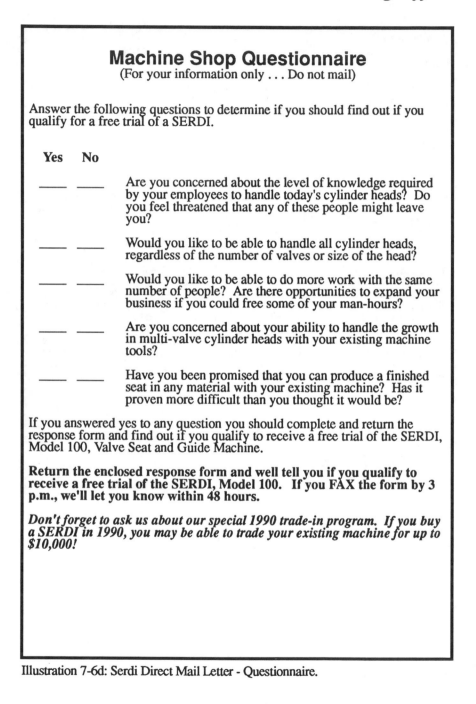

Machine Shop Questionnaire
(For your information only . . . Do not mail)

Answer the following questions to determine if you should find out if you qualify for a free trial of a SERDI.

Yes   No

_____ _____   Are you concerned about the level of knowledge required by your employees to handle today's cylinder heads? Do you feel threatened that any of these people might leave you?

_____ _____   Would you like to be able to handle all cylinder heads, regardless of the number of valves or size of the head?

_____ _____   Would you like to be able to do more work with the same number of people? Are there opportunities to expand your business if you could free some of your man-hours?

_____ _____   Are you concerned about your ability to handle the growth in multi-valve cylinder heads with your existing machine tools?

_____ _____   Have you been promised that you can produce a finished seat in any material with your existing machine? Has it proven more difficult than you thought it would be?

If you answered yes to any question you should complete and return the response form and find out if you qualify to receive a free trial of the SERDI, Model 100, Valve Seat and Guide Machine.

Return the enclosed response form and well tell you if you qualify to receive a free trial of the SERDI, Model 100. If you FAX the form by 3 p.m., we'll let you know within 48 hours.

Don't forget to ask us about our special 1990 trade-in program. If you buy a SERDI in 1990, you may be able to trade your existing machine for up to $10,000!

Illustration 7-6d: Serdi Direct Mail Letter - Questionnaire.

Response Form

Yes!   I am interested in learning how I can try a SERDI, Model 100, Absolutely Free! Please review the information below and let me know if I qualify for a free trial.

Please change as appropriate
Bernie Goldberg, President
Direct Marketing Publishers
1304 University Drive
Yardley, PA 19067
Phone: (___) ___-____   Fax: (___) ___-____

We require credit approval before we'll ship equipment for a free trial. You do not have to make any payments nor are you obligated to buy if you decide to try the SERDI-100.

Guarantor Information

Your Name _____ Social Sec #: _____
Title: _____
Home Address: _____

City _____ State ___ Zip _____ Phone: (___) ___-____

How long have you been in business? ____ Years

Type of Business: ❑ Sole Proprietor ❑ Partnership   ❑ Corporation

Business Bank Information: Name of Bank: _____
Chkng Account #: _____
Contact Name: _____
Phone: (___) ___-____

References: (Please provide 3 lease or loan references - use trade references only if lease or loan references are not available)

Name: _____ Phone: (___) ___-____ Contact _____ Acct# _____
Name: _____ Phone: (___) ___-____ Contact _____ Acct# _____
Name: _____ Phone: (___) ___-____ Contact _____ Acct# _____

Return to:
Tom Begush, National Sales Manager   ❑ *Yes!* I want to know more about your
SERDI Corp.   special 1990 trade-in program.
1526 Litton Drive
Stone Mountain, GA 30083

Find out if you qualify for a free trial within 48 hours - Fax this form by 3 p.m. to (404) 493-8323!   101

Illustration 7-6e: Serdi Direct Mail Letter - Response form.

The Serdi letter may have been even more effective if the price had also been included. You should state your price in the best terms possible. For example, a monthly lease price at least identifies the cost the prospect should be prepared to pay if they decide to buy your product. If the prospect cannot afford the minimum monthly payment, they probably can't afford to buy. The prospect has to believe they have the money to buy.

As you design the offer you should allow the prospect to qualify themselves. Avoid asking a lot of qualifying questions that convince you and the salesperson that a lead is worthwhile. Most of the questions you ask will be asked by the salesperson when they call on the prospect. Most salespeople are suspicious about information provided by the lead program and find it necessary to confirm each data point. If the questions aren't going to be valuable, why ask them?

As you offer a sales visit, promote the benefit that the prospect will receive as a result of seeing the salesperson. Most people have a natural fear and distrust of salespeople. They are afraid they'll be mislead and sold products and services they don't need. You can help overcome this fear by promoting and identifying the benefits the prospect will receive by seeing the salesperson.

Salespeople have their own expectations from different sales leads. By defining the activities that the salesperson will provide to the prospect you are also setting expectations and goals for the salesperson.

Everyone wins.

Serdi promoted a complete on-site demonstration of the Serdi 100. Although this was a sales visit, the prospect understood what was

Illustration 7-7a: Transamerica Fulfillment Kit.

going to happen. The salesperson understood what the prospect had been promised and the expectations they had to meet.

In the computer industry I have also used demonstrations to help define the sales visit. In addition, I have used surveys, proposals and business analysis to define the activity that would be performed by the salesperson.

In Illustration 7-7, Transamerica promoted a proposal by their salesperson. Rather than selling an appointment, they sold the prospect on the benefits they would receive by allowing Transamerica to prepare a personalized proposal.

November 14, 1990

Bernie Goldberg
Direct Marketing Publishers
1304 University Drive
Yardley, PA 19067

Dear Bernie Goldberg,

I don't know the reasons exactly . . .

. . . but I've noticed that some of the most worthwhile, profitable advice you're likely to hear is often exchanged when
sharp-thinking business people socialize outside the office.

That's the idea behind the Executive Video Kit you're requested from Transamerica, and now have in your hands.

It puts you in the middle of a candid conversation among four
good friends after a round of golf. (Each of them is also a
senior executive officer for their company.)

You'll share their insights and experiences in searching for
retirement plans that offer the best benefits for their particular businesses.

When you watch the video tape, you'll listen to comments like
these:

> "Our retirement plan is working better than
> expected. All of my key people have stayed with
> us, and we've got the best administrative staff
> we've ever had," says Mark Peterson, CEO of a $15
> million interior design firm.
>
> to which Earl Green, a CEO of a successful truck-
> ing firm, replies, "I don't know what kind of
> plan you've got, but the one we once had cost a
> lot of money and no one ever understood how it
> worked!"
>
> Ben Lazar, CEO of a family-owned advertising
> agency, expresses caution in dealing with consul-
> tants, "You can't purchase a retirement plan from
> somebody if they don't specialize in the field.
> I called this place once and the guy wanted to
> sell me everything but retirement plans."

Illustration 7-7b: Transamerica Fulfillment Letter - Page 1.

Bernie Goldberg, Direct Marketing Publishers

> But Jack Crowley, founder of a semi-conductor dis-
> tribution company, tells of a different problem,
> saying, "I can't even get someone to come out to
> the office and explain retirement plans, without
> charging me an arm and a leg."

> "I know my defined benefit plans was a big
> headache," adds Earl Green. "It needed so much
> attention, it just took too much of my time. And
> I also didn't have the time to keep answering all
> of my employee's questions."

Don't be surprised if what you hear from Ben, Mark, Jack and
Earl sounds familiar. Like you, these businessmen are concerned about finding the retirement plan that works best for
their companies and employees.

I'm sure you want the same.

But maybe, like Earl, you've found that your company's pension
program requires more time, effort, and attention to detail
than you can dedicate to the task.

Quite simply, we have the experience and ability to handle
every aspect of your retirement program, including:

- Planning a program to meet your needs and budget
- Enrolling and communicating all the details to
  employees
- Recommending and providing investment options
  consistent with your objectives
- Administering the entire program

So let me make a suggestion.

Spend some time with your Executive Video Kit. Share it with
others at your company, if you wish. You'll also find an
executive summary presented in the enclosed brochure.

> After you review this information, fax or mail the
> Response Form in the envelope provided. Or, call
> the Transamerica Pension Line at 1-800-626-2012.

Your completed Response Form will give us the basic facts we
need to develop a sample proposal which will demonstrate an
approach specifically for Direct Marketing Publishers.

The next step is ours.

Illustration 7-7c: Transamerica Fulfillment Letter - Page 2.

Bernie Goldberg, Direct Marketing Publishers

We'll arrange for a Transamerica corporate pension consultant
to meet with you -- at your convenience -- to present this
approach. And that's not all.

You'll be able to freely discuss your corporate retirement
objectives with the Transamerica consultant and receive a cus-
tom-designed recommendation for a plan that's simple to understand and easy to administer.

A plan that truly addresses your needs. One that takes you
quickly and easily to the objective. Your objective.

One final point.

Our consultants are specialists in pension and retirement
plans only. They deal exclusively with executives such as
yourself.

It's our intent to help you make an informed, knowledgeable
decision about choosing a retirement plan which offers the
best potential for your company's future. We promise you'll
be under no pressure to make any commitment whatsoever.

Thanks so much for your consideration. And please send your
Proposal Request Form at your earliest convenience.

Sincerely,

J. Cliffton Masser
V.P./Chief Marketing Officer

JCM/pmc

P.S. If you'd like us to prepare your information even faster,
     simply fax your Response Form to 513-252-9541. Or call
     the Transamerica Pension Line at 1-800-626-2012. You'll
     have no hassle, no obligation . . . just a solid and
     straightforward retirement plan recommendation.

Illustration 7-7d: Transamerica Fulfillment Letter - Page 3.

Response Form

YES! I want to learn more about a retirement plan that's tailored to may company's individual needs.

```
Bernie Goldberg
Direct Marketing Publishers
1304 University Drive
Yardley, PA  19067
Phone: _____
```

I have completed the following questions and would like to receive a retirement plan recommendation, at no cost or obligation.

1. How many non-union employees with over 1 year of service are on your payroll? _____

2. What is the gross annual payroll for your company? $_____

3. What is the estimated percentage of employee turnover at your company during the last three years? _____%

4. Please check the category which best defines your business.
   ❑ Corporation ❑ Sole Proprietorship ❑ Partnership
   ❑ Sub-chapter-S ❑ Other: _____

5. In which month does your Fiscal Year end? _____

6. Please describe your existing retirement plan type.
   ❑ Defined Benefit ❑ Profit Sharing ❑ Target
   ❑ 401(k) ❑ Money Purchase ❑ None
   ❑ Other (describe): _____

7. If you have an existing retirement plan, how much is your annual contribution? $_____

8. Do you feel satisfied that your existing retirement plan is really meeting your current needs? ❑ Yes ❑ No

Mail in the enclosed envelope, FAX this form to (513) 252-9541, or call the Transamerica Pension Line at 1-800-626-2012.

PLEASE CORRECT ANY ADDRESS INFORMATION NECESSARY:	
Name _____	Address _____
Title _____	City _____ State ___ Zip _____
Company _____	Phone (___) _____

Illustration 7-7e: Transamerica Fulfillment Letter - Response form.

As you evaluate the approach you'll take to create high quality leads, don't be afraid to create multiple steps for direct marketing. If you can't move a prospect to seeing a salesperson in one step, consider creating several mail pieces with steps to encourage the prospect to make a logical decision to spend time with your salesperson.

Generating Offers Summarized

Most lead generation programs seem to ignore the necessity of creating an offer to help qualify the sales lead. There are four elements in qualifying sales leads; money, authority, need and desire. These elements can often be validated with a well conceived offer.

Prospects can resolve money, need, and desire issues if the offer identifies the benefits of the product you're selling and a price point.

There are different offer motivations prospects respond to depending on their position in the company. The owner of the business is interested in saving time and saving money. On the other hand, employees are concerned with getting promoted, reducing the hassle in their lives, and covering their rears in any decision they might make. Offers should be made to appeal to the appropriate motivation for the individual and the position they fill. Offers have to answer the question: What's in it for me?

Although you are trying to generate a lead for a salesperson, most people are reluctant to spend time with salespeople. Most have a certain distrust of the sales role and are afraid they'll be sold something. Rather than offering a salesperson visit, offer the benefit that the sales visit will provide. Identify the action that the salesperson will take during the sales visit. Promote the offer instead of the sales visit.

I have some simple rules to follow when creating an offer for a lead generation program.

- It is not important what the salesperson thinks . . . it is only important what the prospect thinks.

- Allow the prospect to qualify themselves . . . avoid asking qualifying questions.

- Present the product benefits and include the price to allow the prospect to establish his own MAND.

- Sell the benefits of the offer. If a salesperson is the offer, sell what the salesperson will do for the prospect.

- Identify what the prospect looks like and what kind of prospect will close at a rate of 1 out of 5 leads.

- Establish a method to provide the best possible lead. Don't be afraid to use multiple steps.

Chapter Eight:
Direct Mail

By *Tracy Emerick, President*
Taurus Direct Marketing
239 Drakeside Road
Hampton, NH 03842   *(603) 926-4477*

Direct Mail Defined

Direct mail is the primary format businesses use to execute direct marketing. Direct mail is often the least expensive and best approach to communicate a message and make an offer to generate a lead. The direct mail format allows the business-to-business marketer to select from a large variety of creative options for soliciting prospects and customers. With direct mail, you can select whatever environment and voice you feel is appropriate. Direct mail allows you to lead the reader through the offer and to the response vehicle using your own tempo and rhythm.

There are other media and formats that may allow similar creative flexibility (such as space advertising), however, none are as targeted as the direct mail format. Direct mail allows you to involve the

reader as no other medium can. A mailing has the unique opportunity of receiving 100% of its reader's attention. A name-directed
mailing can be targeted and personalized more so than any other
medium. Direct mail is the perfect medium to generate high quality
sales leads.

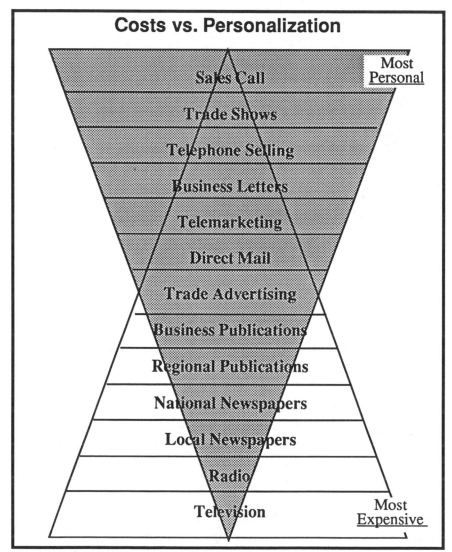

Costs vs. Personalization

Most Personal

- Sales Call
- Trade Shows
- Telephone Selling
- Business Letters
- Telemarketing
- Direct Mail
- Trade Advertising
- Business Publications
- Regional Publications
- National Newspapers
- Local Newspapers
- Radio
- Television

Most Expensive

Illustration 8-1: Cost vs. personalization.

The most effective lead generation programs will require mail either to generate the lead, fulfill information requests, or supplement telephone selling programs.

Direct mail is the most testable of media; you can vary each mailing piece. Each reader can receive a personalized mailing suited to his individual needs, tastes and desires. You can test the positioning of your product and provide research on how to proceed within the entire market. The same flexibility exists with telephone selling which I will discuss in Chapter 9 , but it is not available in print or broadcast promotion.

The advantages of personalizing, targeting, and copy flexibility, cause direct mail to be somewhat expensive on a cost-per-contact basis compared to other formats. As you may recall direct mail is just ahead of telemarketing in the cost-per-contact matrix. Illustration 8-1 reemphasizes the personalization and cost-per-contact comparison.

The additional costs mean that the response rates and closing rates for inquiries generated through direct mail have to be higher than similar inquiries generated in print or broadcast promotions. The higher required quality of leads generated via direct mail will also make them more positively received by the sales force.

Direct mail responders tend to be of high quality because the message they receive in the mail is clear and concise. The prospects understand the offer and are responding to something they are interested in. When evaluating the success of the direct response marketing program, the cost per order will normally prove that direct mail is one of the most economical direct marketing media available.

Lead generation programs are going to be measured based on the ultimate cost per order. If face-to-face selling expenses are included in the ultimate costs derived, direct mail will always compare favorably. The quality of the lead generated is consistently higher in the mail than other similar formats.

Because direct mail is the most frequently used format in lead generation, it deserves special attention. In addition, direct mail tends to produce high quality leads that can easily be implemented by any business and therefore no discussion about lead generation can ignore a detail presentation about direct mail.

Creating a Direct Mail Piece

The varieties of direct mail pieces range from a simple postcard to a full color catalog. Anything mailed to potential customers can be classified as direct mail, even a price list.

By definition, direct marketing is designed to produce a lead or an order. An ad run in a magazine to create awareness and a brochure used as a "leave behind" aren't designed to produce leads or orders. Don't start a direct mail program by taking inventory of existing printed material and deciding what will fit in an envelope.

Many a business manager has mailed a reprint of an ad and decided "direct mail doesn't work!" These managers did not have a direct marketing program; they simply mailed an advertisement. Mailing an existing brochure designed as sales collateral can prove just as unsuccessful. Saving pennies in the cost of producing a mailing can cause the loss of dollars in terms of results.

The design of a direct mail package begins with the business plan you have created and the objectives you want to achieve. In

Chapter 6, we discussed the four elements of a direct marketing program:

- List

- Offer

- Format

- Copy

In your business plan, you defined the target universe you want to reach, focusing on their personalities and buying motivations. As with any direct marketing promotion, these personality issues will govern the format and copy. A brochure designed to be left with the president of a company should not be delivered to a specifying engineer.

The list and offer account for 75% of your success. If your existing materials do not contain your direct response offer, they should not be used. If you use existing materials in a mailing, your list may be correct but your results may not achieve your objectives.

To produce a lead or an order, make your target market an offer that will ask them to take the desired action. Making the offer a second thought will prevent the package from achieving its objectives.

Create the direct mail package as if you are writing a single letter to a well-defined individual. The goal of the creative effort is to move the target to take the action you want. During the planning process you defined an offer that, if accepted, would achieve your objectives. In addition, you identified the personality of the target people in your market. Your creative effort should use a custom format and direct mail copy to reach your targets.

A direct mail piece created to reach an analytical individual will not be as effective when mailed to an extrovert. Such a mailing may generate results because the list is correct. However, the results may not be enough to constitute a successful program.

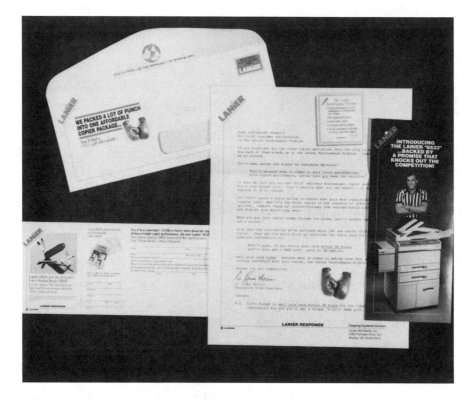

Illustration 8-2: A standard direct mail package.

The standard direct mail package contains:

- an outer envelope
- a letter
- a brochure
- a response device
- a prepaid reply envelope

Except for the outer envelope and the reply envelope, each element of the direct mail package should be able to stand alone. Each element should contain the product benefits, the offer, and instructions for responding by mail and/or phone. A mailing may arrive disassembled in its target's office; the prospect may receive or save only a portion of the mailing. The letter, the brochure, and the response device should all be stand-alone elements creating their own AIDA (Attention, Interest, Desire, Action). This is why existing materials may not fit your direct mail needs.

Copy and Graphics

There are two major areas of consideration within the creative process:

- Copy: The words you use to explain your offer and product.

- Graphic: The visual elements you use to explain your offer and product.

It is unrealistic to try to explain all of the rules of style that pertain to copywriting in this book. For more information about complete texts on copywriting for direct mail, request a bibliography from the Direct Marketing Association, 6 East 43rd Street, New York, New York 10017.

The point I want to make here is that copy should be written with the target in mind. The length of the copy depends on the needs of the target. When writing copy to a person working in a stand-up industry (hair stylist, gas station manager, independent retailer) copy must be short and to the point. This type of individual is not oriented to heavy reading while sitting at a desk. They will probably review a mailing package in the same manner as a consumer standing over a trash can.

If you are writing to a lawyer who is accustomed to reading while sitting, long copy can be successful. In this environment there is a bigger problem: Getting your mailing passed a secretary and to the reader. Remember Bertha Barrier! This problem is independent of the length of copy and must be addressed in the overall strategy of the direct marketing plan.

The length of the copy can be tested. There is a perpetual battle between those who advocate long copy and those who advocate short copy. There is only one rule that applies in either case: copy that interests the reader will be read.

We have all heard and used the term "junk mail." Mail that addresses products of interest to the reader is not junk; mail that addresses products that are of no interest to the reader is junk. If the reader is interested in the copy, its length is insignificant.

Headlines are copy set apart from text by position and size. Headlines and sub-heads are copy used as word graphics. Being set apart and in larger type, headlines pull the eye toward them. Headlines should reach out to the reader with the strongest benefit available. Many people do not read past headlines unless their interest is aroused. Headlines are, therefore, the magnet that will draw people into your offer.

When there are too many headlines and sub-heads on a page, the overall visual effect may put off the reader. Too many headlines mean no headlines, no visual magnet that stands out to draw the reader's eye in. Special nomenclature and terms can also adversely affect a letter. Using a product name containing special characters or numbers frequently in a letter will draw the reader's eyes and impact the flow of the letter.

Using headlines in letters reduces the similarity between promotion and a true business letter. Few people use headlines in business correspondence. Headlines create more of a promotional impression than a business correspondence impression. Headlines are fine in brochures and on reply devices, which are normally viewed with promotional eyes by the reader. If you're trying to convey the image of a standard business letter, headlines may not be effective.

I found that I could not improve on Bob Stone's formula for letter writing. As found in his book, *Successful Direct Marketing Methods*, Third Edition (Crain Books, an imprint of National Textbook Company, Lincolnwood, Illinois), here is Bob Stone's letter writing formula:

> *Promise a benefit in your headline or first paragraph* - your most important benefit. You simply can't go wrong by leading off with the most important benefit to the reader. Some writers believe in the slow buildup. But most experienced writers I know favor making the important point first.
>
> *Immediately enlarge on your most important benefit.* This step is crucial. Many writers come up with a great lead, then fail to follow through. Or they catch attention with their heading, but then take two or three paragraphs to warm up to their subject. The reader's attention is gone! Try hard to elaborate on your most important benefit right away, and you'll build up interest fast.
>
> *Tell the reader specifically what he or she is going to get.* It's amazing how many letters lack details on such basic product features as size, color, weight, and sales terms. Perhaps the writer is so close to his proposition he assumes the reader knows all about it. A dangerous assumption! And when you tell the reader what he or she's going to get, don't

overlook the intangibles that go along with your product or service. For example, he's getting smart appearance in addition to a pair of slacks, knowledge in addition to a 340-page book.

Back up your statements with proof and endorsements. Most prospects are somewhat skeptical about advertising. They know it sometimes gets a little over-enthusiastic about a product. So they accept it only with a grain of salt. If you can back up your own statements with third-party testimonials or a list of satisfied users, everything you say becomes more believable.

Tell the reader what she might lose if she doesn't act. As noted, people respond affirmatively either to gain something they do not possess or to avoid losing something they already have. Here's a good spot in your letter to overcome human inertia -- imply what may be lost if action is postponed. People don't like to be left out. A skillful writer can use this human trait as a powerful influence in his or her message.

Rephrase your prominent benefits in your closing offer. As a good salesperson does, sum up the benefits to the prospect in your closing offer. This is the proper prelude to asking for action. This is where you can intensify the prospect's desire to have the product. The stronger the benefits you can persuade the reader to recall, the easier it will be for him or her to justify an affirmative decision.

Incite Action, Now. This is the spot where you win or lose the battle with inertia. Experienced advertisers know once a letter is put aside or tossed into that file, they're out of luck. So wind up with a call for action and a logical reason for acting now. Too many letters close with a statement like "supplies are limited." That argument lacks credibility. Today's consumer knows you probably have a warehouse full of merchandise. So make your reason a believable one. For example, "It may be many months before we go back to press on this book." Or "Orders are shipped on a first-come basis. The sooner yours is received, the sooner you can be enjoying your new widget."

The old adage "a picture is worth a thousand words" is applicable in direct mail. Graphics can be in two forms: photography and illustration.

Photography is just that: pictures of the product and its use. Use either color or black-and-white depending on the overall design and budget of your package. Color can be a powerful tool to support or defeat your offer. When offering a budget priced product, color can defeat the offer. When offering color-coordinated work clothes, black-and-white can defeat the offer by not showing the benefits color coordination will bring to the buyer.

Graphics should show the reader the benefits of the product. Just showing pictures of the product, without showing a benefit, will not help the selling effort. Using photography because it already exists can do as much damage as using brochures that already exist.

Another decision you make will be whether to use photography, illustrations, or both. This simple concept can help you decide which approach to use:

- photography depicts reality
- illustrations depict illusion or fantasy; the dream of what can be

We can use a combination of photography and illustrations in the same piece to generate both of these impressions in the mind of the reader.

Illustration 8-3: An illustrated graphic.

The overall layout of any direct mail component is also a graphic. A brochure that is copy from top to bottom and from side to side is visually oppressive. Most people will not bother to read such a piece. Because the overall look of the piece is visually unappealing, the copy will never be read.

Graphics can also take the form of small design elements that are used as visual breaks between copy points. Such graphics, like *, give the mind a chance to pause ^ before continuing to read.

An illustrated graphic can be used to present a product and its application. The brochure in Illustration 8-3, shows how a heating system can enhance the comfort of a family.

I have seen cartoon characters used to illustrate personalities in the average office and the mailing piece posted with various names written by many of the characters. The illustration from the mailing lived on long after the mailing was complete. The company name, product, solution and offer were continually selling the prospect.

The Components of a Direct Mail Package

The differences in direct mail packages are as varied as the individuals who create them. A package can include many different pieces. Many companies even include multiple types of components in the same mailing.

Outer Envelope

The outer envelope is the passport that will get the message to the reader, just as a salesperson's appearance is the passport that allows them to make a presentation. You never get a second chance to make a first impression, so do not underestimate the outer envelope.

The most acceptable outer envelope appears as a professional business letter to someone with whom you have a relationship. The envelope has a preprinted *cornercard* (the return address information printed in the upper left-hand corner) with company name and logo, a personal address and first class postage. This type of outer

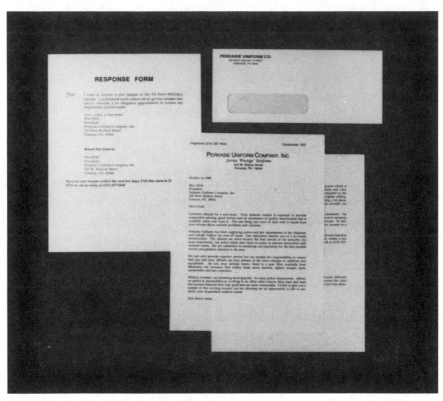

Illustration 8-4: Bill-like format.

envelope is the most expensive since the contents, (the letter and the reply device) should also be personalized where appropriate. Prospects receiving this kind of expensive looking mailing usually open the envelope. Think about the mail you always open and you will typically describe a letter that looks like a personalized business letter or a letter that looks like a bill. Creating this type of personalized mailing is a tedious task for the lettershop and will increase the cost.

If you decide against the business letter format, you can try a variety of creative approaches with the outer envelope. Keep in mind that your goal is to have the prospect open the envelope and read the message.

A bill-like format using a window envelope can often disguise a direct mail package (Illustration 8-4) and ensure a high degree of openability. This format can even fool the post office who will often return a non-deliverable bill-like format even when mailed bulk rate.

If you decide to use window envelopes that don't look like bills to cut costs, there is no point in maintaining the professional letter appearance. No one uses window envelopes for business letters on a day-to-day basis. With a window envelope, you can use bulk postage, oversized envelopes, graphics and/or copy on the outer envelope. You can test these variables to see which outer envelope yields the greatest results. In essence, if you are not going to use the professional letter format, you have no limit on what you can do with the outer envelope so you should experiment.

Quite often, the outer envelope is stripped from the contents by an administrator before the prospect sees it. Unlike consumer mail, Bertha Barrier may strip the contents from the outer envelope as a service to her boss. You therefore have a two-step creative challenge:

- To get the mailing reviewed and accepted by the administrator before it is passed along.

- If the mailing reaches the prospect unopened, to have it opened and reviewed.

It is probably better to use more professional envelopes when mailing to larger businesses that typically have administrators. When mailing to small businesses that do not have such a screen, a more graphic attention-getting outer envelope may improve results.

Letter

The letter should appear as though you were sending a one-of-a-kind letter to each individual, just as though you were mailing a personalized business letter. This process is expensive and may not prove cost effective.

Write your direct mail letters to someone you know, assuming they know nothing about your product or service. Follow the AIDA formula we discussed earlier in Chapter 6.

The elements of the direct mail letter are the same as a normal business letter:

- Printed letterhead
- Date, month and year are sufficient
- Addressee information - name of contact, title, address. It is appropriate to title- or function-address letters when you don't have a contact name.
- Salutation
- Letter body
- Complimentary close
- Signature
- Administrative code
- Postscript

Like most written works, your letter must be readable and attractive to your prospect. If a page is packed from top to bottom and from side to side with prose, the odds are pretty good that it will not get read. Examine the letters you read and enjoy; they are probably written with short paragraphs and contain lots of white space around the copy or prose. Use yourself as a guide and don't mail anything that you wouldn't read.

The reader's interest and eye movement will travel first to the letter-head and addressee information, next to the salutation (those parts that contain the reader's name and title), to the signature block (to see who the letter is from), to the P.S. (unfortunately an uncommon occurrence in a business letter, but when used a real eye-catcher). The P.S. should contain the primary benefit and a call to action since it will probably be read before the body of the letter.

Direct mail letters can contain headlines and sub-heads to get the reader involved with your sales presentation. Be careful not to sell features, but to focus on the benefits the prospect will receive from your product or service. The use of headlines and other eye-catching techniques, such as boldface type, italics and different sizes and styles of type fonts, set direct mail apart from the standard business letter. Unfortunately, these techniques can be overdone to a point that they become a turnoff to the prospect. The best approach will move prospects completely though the presentation and have them feel as though the letter was written to them personally.

Like other direct mail efforts, even in lead generation programs, you must sell the reader on the benefits they'll receive from your offer. It is difficult to convince a prospect that seeing a salesperson will present them with a benefit. Your offer should entice the prospect to want to respond. Offering a salesperson is a sure turn-off, therefore sell what the salesperson will *do* for the prospect not the actual sales call.

Brochure

The brochure may or may not be necessary. If needed support information cannot be put into the letter, a brochure may be required. A brochure is generally required when trying to sell a product or service in a mailing. The brochure can cover all of the information readers may need to satisfy their technical questions prior to making a purchase decision.

A brochure can be multi-color, multi-page with beautiful (and expensive) art and pictures, or it can be a single page of information about a specific product or service.

If you do require a brochure, make sure that it is consistent with the objective of the direct mail program. Excess brochures from a trade show, or sales force collateral material, may not be effective as a direct mail brochure. The brochure must contain all of the information about the offer and a call to action. Remember, it may be used separately by your prospect.

The brochure is also a place to sample the product or service. Prospects can see (using art and photographs) the product and receive a detailed explanation of how the product can meet their needs. Citing testimonials and case histories can help prospects overcome FUD (fear, uncertainty and doubt); and the offer can be reinforced and explained. The brochure can be much more explicit than the letter. In fact, you can even reference the brochure in the letter.

A brochure is not always required or advisable. A brochure that gives an overview of the product or service, may provide insufficient information to make the sale, but enough for the readers to determine that the product or service is not for them. If you are selling a seminar that will give detailed information on a specific product or service, enclosing a brochure in the mailing can actually depress response.

Lead generation programs are designed to have a salesperson visit the prospect and review the product offering. You may not want to give the prospect enough information to determine that they don't need your offering. A detailed brochure could do more damage than good in this situation. On the other hand, you may want only a few good leads and offer a brochure as a fulfillment device with detailed information on your products or services. You may want to offer the brochure as an information kit if the prospect fills out the response vehicle and returns it for fulfillment.

Whether or not your mailing requires a brochure is directly related to the objective you've set for the program. If your objective is the direct sale of your product, the mailing should probably include a brochure explaining the details of your product or service. If you're trying to generate leads, the use of a brochure may be excess baggage in the mailing package.

If you determine that a brochure is appropriate in your mailing package, it may be worthwhile to test a group of prospects who receive no brochure to determine the affect the brochure is having on your program.

Reply Envelope

The prepaid business reply envelope (BRE) has become a standard. Your local post office can supply you with layouts. The preprinted portion of the reply envelope is strictly regulated by the United States Postal Service.

Since this element of the mailing is more of an administrative piece, it is probably not worth the time to overlay your creative efforts in either design or paper selection to enhance it. Black printing on white envelopes will fill the bill if you use a BRE. In fact, you may choose not to include a BRE as a part of your mailing package.

It is not unusual to use a Business Reply Card (BRC) or to request inbound telephone as the response vehicle. Reply envelopes or cards may go largely unused when you provide a telephone number for prospects to use for their response. If your budget permits, use a BRE in your mailing package.

If you are an infrequent mailer, you may not want to go through the process of getting a reply mail number from your servicing post office. You could instead provide prospects with a self-addressed envelope that they could stamp and return. This could save expense, and there is no evidence that prepaid postage in business mailings is as critical as it is in consumer marketing.

The easier you make it for your prospects to respond, the better the odds are that they will take the desired action. If you only offer a telephone response vehicle, the prospects may feel uncomfortable with the pressure of being sold on the phone. A BRC-only response vehicle may make prospects uncomfortable with having the information able to be read by all. A BRE without postage may turn the prospect off because of their financial doubts about your company. You should also allow your prospects to respond via FAX. Evaluate your market and the prospect you're trying to reach to determine the requirement for a response vehicle.

Response Device

The most critical element of a direct mail package is the response device. In fact, you would be well advised to begin your creative process by creating the response device. By creating the response device, you finalize the action you want the prospect to take as a result of the direct mail program.

With the response device designed, you can create the letter and brochure around the action you want the reader to take. This sounds simple enough, but direct mail is not always implemented in this way. More often than not, people spend weeks on the letter copy and put together a response device as an afterthought. The situation is often compounded by a lot of time pressure, as mailings often run behind schedule and have to be finished immediately.

The response device should be easy to understand. People in business are generally careful about what they respond to since they are representing their company when they act. The response device should not be a legal looking document that may frighten the reader. If you are looking for a legal, binding commitment, your response will probably be small.

The flow of the response device should be the same as the flow of the letter and brochure. Do not introduce anything on the response device that has not been covered elsewhere in the mailing. Remember, each piece of the mailing should be able to stand alone.

The concept of no surprises as you ask for the order is not new to the art of salesmanship. Good salespeople know that once you've built your proposition with the prospect, ask for the order and shut up. The next person to talk loses. Never introduce a new idea or concept at the close that gives the prospect something to question or object. This basic approach to selling holds true in direct mail. The response device asks for the order. You may want to reestablish the benefits -- but ask for the order and shut up. Don't try to introduce new concepts on the response device that haven't already been covered in the letter and brochure.

The response device should contain your phone number in several places. And don't forget to include and encourage your prospects to respond via FAX. If a prospect is completing the reply form and the phone number is conspicuous, they may decide to pick up the phone and call. The impulse decision can be important, and you want to make it easy to reach you.

If the prospect does decide to call, you can begin selling and cross-selling during the phone conversation. The phone moves you more quickly into a personal relationship with the prospect and allows you to sell faster with larger orders. In addition, if your phone number is on the response device, the prospect will have information about your product in front of them when they call. You are on their mind, and they are in a positive mood. The prospect took the inertia to call you; this is a great time to move your relationship forward.

Many readers of direct mail breeze through the letter and the brochure and go directly to the response device. They want to determine how much money, if any, the offer will cost if they choose to take advantage of it. They look at the response device as a summary, an outline of the mailing. Many people read the response device to determine whether it's worth their time to read the entire mailing.

If you're asking your prospects to spend $2,000 for your proposition and their buying authority is only $100, you have probably lost the buyer. If they perceived a benefit and value from your proposition and response device, they may read the mailing and refer it to some-one who has authority. In either case, you are not going to make an immediate sale, but the response device sure played an important role in the direction they took.

Response devices take many forms and formats. Business Reply Cards (BRC) are the most common. The prospect is asked to com-plete the card and send it back. The BRC is frequently a self-addressed, prepaid postage mailer. Even if you have a prepaid postage BRC, you should also include a BRE for the prospect to use. Many business people feel more secure in knowing their response will be handled in a confidential manner.

When mailing packages are computer generated to take advantage of the personalization possibilities, it is fairly common to have the BRE as a tear-off portion of the document.

Response devices can be designed to get the prospect involved in the promotion and perform some task as they complete the process.

There are no limits to the format of the response device. The key is involvement by the reader and, most importantly, ACTION.

Postage

One of the most frequently overlooked components of the direct mail format is postage. There are three methods of applying postage to a mailing:

- Preprinted -- where the type of postage is printed on the mailing pieces as part of the printing process.

- Metered -- where a postage meter applies postage directly to the piece.

- Stamped -- where actual stamps are affixed to the mailing.

The preprinted form is fine for promotional mail but may kill the personalized image when using the business letter format.

In the business letter format, use metered postage since most businesses use postage meters in their day-to-day operations. Stamps can be an attention-getting device on a business mailing, since stamps are seldom seen on business letters.

Your target may never see the outer envelope, so in a lot of cases the postage decision may be moot. However, some businesses have instructed their mailrooms not to deliver third class or bulk mail. The mailroom personnel do not look at the postage actually paid, but at the mailing's nature and approach. If mail looks too promotional, it may be discarded by the mailroom staff even if it carries first class postage.

There are two basic postage rates for direct mail:

- First class - cost fixed for the first ounce, and restricted in size to no larger than 6-1/8 by 11-1/2 inches and no smaller than 3-1/2 by 5 inches. Additional weight costs extra per ounce up to 12 ounces maximum.

- Third class or bulk - cost fixed for the first 3.91 ounces with no size constraints. Additional weight costs extra per ounce up to 16 ounces maximum. A minimum number of pieces is required for a third class mailing.

Each of these two classes of postage also has reduced rates for pre-sort, tie and bag preparation before entering the mail stream. Check with your local post office for the regulations that will affect your mailing. A lettershop that prepares mailings will also be able to provide current postal information.

Postage can be a major cost element for direct mail efforts. Almost every conceivable approach to affixing postage and postage rates has been tested. There typically is little difference in response between first or third class rates. Metered mail usually pulls better than stamps, and a well-designed, preprinted permit will pull as well as metered mail.

The decision to use either first or third class postage will be governed by the speed at which you want the mail delivered. First-class mail is normally delivered within three to five days. Third class mail is delivered at the leisure of the post office but can stay in any single facility for a maximum of 48 hours. For a national mailing, it could take as long as 15 work days for third class mail to be delivered.

First class delivery costs almost twice as much, therefore you should evaluate the speed at which you need the mailing delivered in making the postage decision.

There are no rules or known formulas that can govern the best method to affix postage to your mail or determine the best postage rate to use. The way to determine which will be best for you is to test different techniques. However, this is not a major point. After establishing the best lists, offer, and major formats, it may be worthwhile to test postage approaches.

Breaking Through

The biggest challenge in direct mail is breaking through the clutter of mail that a prospect receives each day. As mailers use more standard creative direct mail packages that are sold by various production facilities around the country, the clutter will increase. As you economize more and more, you'll run the risk of becoming part of the clutter rather than beating it.

You can test to determine if frequency will be more important to your direct mail program than creative approaches. Most business publishers and seminar companies have decided that frequency, and not creativity is the key to results. If you are on any business lists you have received the 8-1/2 by 11 inch three-fold, self-mailing brochure from at least one seminar company. This format seems to be the standard.

Breakthrough creative is the development of some type of package that yields the best results for the investment. In some cases, breakthrough can mean just getting a mailing read. This can be a real challenge in markets where there are a few buyers and many sellers. For example, trying to reach MIS managers for the Fortune 1,000 companies.

To reach a difficult and highly mail-cluttered prospect, it may be necessary to develop packages that get attention because of their

size and shape. These are called ***dimensional mailings***.
Dimensional mailings are generally large in a three-dimensional
sense; they are packages or fat letters that have a tendency to get put
on top of the prospect's mail pile. Once delivered, a dimensional
mailing should follow the AIDA rules.

Illustration 8-5: Dimensional mailing.

The use of a dimensional mailing can be effective in breaking
through to a prospect you have been trying to reach. The dimen-

sional can be directly related to the offer or it can just be designed to get the prospect's attention. Illustration 8-5 shows a dimensional mailing to owners of ice cream shops. The scoop in the box created a dimesional that was hard to ignore. Dimensionals appeal to the child in all of us, everyone likes to receive a gift, and curiosity compels us to find out what is inside.

Formats

Business Mail

As discussed earlier in this chapter, business letters are the format generally used for direct communication in business today. The business letter is a closed-faced envelope addressed from one individual to another. It has no promotional copy on the outer envelope. The letter inside is signed by the individual. A brochure may or may not accompany the letter. There is seldom, if ever, a response device. The response device is the difference between a general business communication and a direct response promotion.

Two techniques are available to produce a direct response letter that resembles an actual business letter:

- Full Print

- Match Fill

For either technique, everyday letterhead must be preprinted in sufficient quantity to satisfy the promotion. To avoid signing thousands of letters, preprint the signature on the letter in a blue ink unless the sender normally uses some black or some personal color ink as a hallmark.

Full print is when the addressee and all of the body copy are generated by the printer. There are several options on the quality and
appearance of the print used to generate the letter. The more it looks
like a personalized, typed letter, the more expensive it becomes.
Computer printing can be accomplished with an impact or non-
impact process. The non-impact techniques look close to personalized, typed business letters. Technology continues to expand the
options in this area. Review the image, offer and format you are
using when selecting the production technique.

Match fill means having the letter body copy typeset and preprinted
by a printer, then having the address, salutation and perhaps some
specific information in the body of the letter added during computer
printing. This creates the impression of a fully personalized letter.
The match fill technique is less expensive since there are less lines
to print during the computer run.

Here are a few points to consider to ensure that the match fill letter
resembles a full print letter:

1) The letter body should be generated on the same equipment
   that will be used to complete the match fill. This will ensure
   that the letter is not set in two different fonts-- Like this.

2) The letter body should be printed in a dark grey ink rather
   than black. Printer ribbons tend to fade quickly and often
   appear grey. New laser quality letters can ensure high quality dark print on every letter.

3) Printer alignment is critical. Order extra forms so the computer operators will have all they need for the alignment process.

4) When using a fill-in that varies in length (i.e. a person's
   name inserted in the letter), write copy so the insert will be

at the end of a line. This will ensure enough space for the insert, and it will not appear out of position.

In either case, pre-position the signature on the page before the letterhead is printed. This means the letter must be written before the letterhead is printed. If the letter is not written and printed in the same font and type size before positioning the signature, there may be insufficient space for the signature. There have been situations in which a whole letter was written around a preprinted signature block spaced improperly on the page.

You will need to know which type of paper your printer requires. Computer printers require either continuous form paper (paper connected top to bottom with computer pin-holes on the sides), or single sheets which are fed individually into the printer.

I don't believe there are such things as junk mail and junk telephone. There are poorly implemented uses of the media that get classified as junk. I hope you will think about how your promotion will be classified by your targets. Don't mail anything you wouldn't want to receive. Here are some things to consider:

NO LABELS. Business mail is never sent with an address label. If you must use labels, do not waste your energy on a personalized letter. The label will probably be a different color than the envelope and will probably be affixed to the envelope a little askew. The labeled envelope does not demonstrate the same care given in the preparation of a business letter. If you are going to use labels, spend your money on other elements of the mailing. It will be clear to the target that it is not a business letter, and you will have to use other techniques to ensure that it is read.

NO TEASER. Teaser copy or teaser graphics on the outer envelope are designed to get the reader into the envelope.

Teasers are not normally used on business letters, so do not use them when you are trying to make an envelope look like business mail (as demonstrated in Illustration 8-2).

Making your promotion appear like a business letter increases its chances of being read but also increases the cost.

Letter Packages

A *letter package* is a direct mail promotion that uses the same general size envelope used for business letters. This can range from an invitation size to a number 10, regular business size envelope. The envelope can be closed faced or have a window. A great deal of business direct mail uses the window envelope since it is less expensive to address and mail. Illustration 8-6 shows a letter package in a regular business-size envelope.

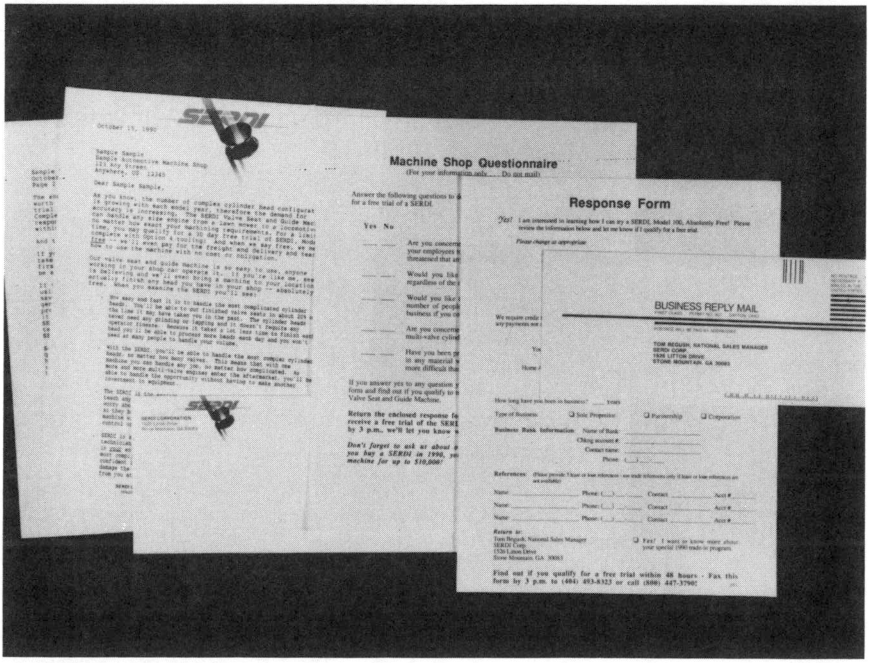

Illustration 8-6: Letter Package.

A mailing in a window envelope costs less because the target address appears only one time and shows through the window. The address often appears on the response device. Addressing on the response device allows you to capture accurate information about the responder. It also makes it easier for the target to respond because they do not have to complete a response device.

I suggest that you personalize the response device. Business promotions are often passed on to other people, so you may receive responses from people you originally did not target. Personalizing the response device ensures that you will be able to establish the coding and source information even if the responder is different from the target.

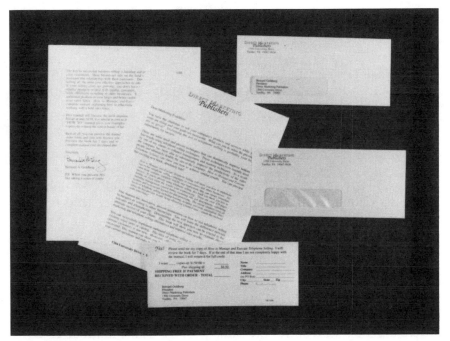

Illustration 8-7: Letter in Window Envelope.

Letter packages generally only carry personalization on one piece within the package. The balance of the mailing includes:

- the letter, which is generically addressed to Dear Executive, or Dear Associate
- a brochure
- a response device
- a business reply envelope (if the response device is not a BRC)

This type of mailing can often prove to be the most productive because of its relatively low cost compared with a business letter format. The cost savings are primarily in the addressing and matching of addresses. The components of the mailing are often the same as the business letter. The personalization, high-quality print and matching of multiple elements in the business letter format tend to be expensive.

The letter package can carry a teaser on the outer envelope. The teaser can be in the form of copy or graphics intended to get the reader into the package and into the offer.

Oversize Packages

The United States Postal Service defines any mailing package that is larger than a number 10 business envelope as an oversized mailing. Fulfillment literature sent in a 9 by 12 inch envelope is an oversized mailing. The advantage of oversized packages is that they receive special handling because everyone thinks there is extra postage involved.

This is true in mailing first class. It is not true in the bulk mail rates where the 9 by 12 requires the same postage as the number 10 envelope. This means you can use the 9 by 12 mailing to gain extra

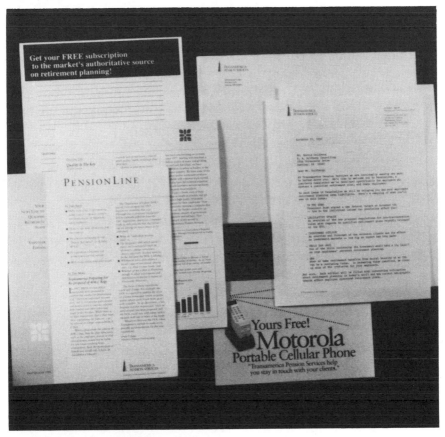

Illustration 8-8: Oversized letter package.

attention in a direct mail promotion. You can go larger or smaller than the 9 by 12 depending on the production techniques being used. Keep postal regulations in mind when producing an oversized package. Illustration 8-8 shows an oversized mailing.

Check with your local post office to determine the appropriate regulations that govern the relationship of your package's height to its length. Regulations govern the ratio of height to length because of postal machines and handling. If your package does not meet the requirements of the postal service, you will be subject to additional postage even for a bulk mailing.

Teasers can be used on oversized mailings when you determine a promotional look is best. If you're not going to use teasers on the envelope, you may want to consider a business-looking label, similar to the concept of the business letter. The more a promotion looks like general business correspondence, the better the chances are that it will be opened and read by your target.

Self-Mailers

You can choose not to use an envelope at all. The elements of your promotion can be printed on a single sheet and folded to a size that can be mailed. Self-mailers can also be brochures or catalogs consisting of multiple sheets bound together and mailed.

The advantages of self-mailers are that they:

- are generally inexpensive to produce
- are easily readable
- get the target involved without opening an envelope
- allow you to quickly state your offer

The main disadvantage of a self-mailer is that the response device is printed on the same weight paper as the entire mailing, unless a heavier weight paper is bound or attached for the response device. This means you must print the entire piece on a seven point paper stock, the minimum the post office allows for a return postcard.

Your choices are:

1) Use seven point stock so the reply device can be mailed back as a card.

2) Use 3.5 point stock so a response device can be made of a sheet folded in two to yield the seven point necessary for mailing. This requires a glue strip or some other form of closure. The post office is getting touchy about staple mail because it hangs in their machines. You could get hit with extra postage if you ask the recipient to use a stapler.

3) Request the reader to insert the reply form in his own envelope. One of the basic rules of direct marketing is to make it easy for your prospect to respond. If you ask prospects to use their own envelopes, you've made it more difficult for them to respond. Most targets will not have an envelope handy and may not make an effort to get one.

4) Ask for telephone response only. Even though you will get a lot of response by phone, some people will not call in order to avoid talking to a salesperson. If you choose this option, I suggest you provide an address for those interested in responding by mail.

5) Require recipients to use their own envelopes and letterheads to respond. This is certainly a qualifier, since you are making it as tough as possible to respond. You will get much fewer responses because of the additional work involved. This is generally not a good idea.

Most self-mailers are designed so the response device does not carry the original address and coding information. The prospect is asked to complete a response device and provide all the pertinent information. Illustration 8-9 shows this approach. One format that works provides personal addressing and coding on the face of the mailing and the same on the response device. This format is generally printed on seven point paper stock.

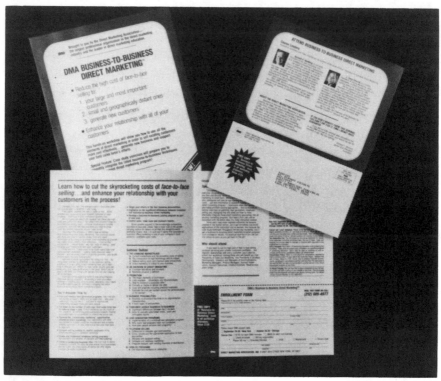

Illustration 8-9: A Self-Mailer.

Dimensionals

The easiest explanation of a dimensional format is any mailing that has more than two dimensions (height and width). A dimensional mailing also has depth. While a regular letter package has the depth of a few layers of paper, a dimensional's depth is noticeable to sight and touch. A box, a tube, or even an envelope containing something fat is considered a dimensional mailing.

The advantages of dimensional mailings are that they generally are not opened during the screening process and that they often are put on the top of the mail pile when it is delivered to the recipient.

A dimensional mailing appeals to two strong motivations of your prospect:

- Ego. We all feel good when we receive a gift.
- Curiosity. It ultimately killed the cat.

These two motivations are the overriding advantages that justify the cost of using the dimensional format. Everyone loves to receive packages they can open and be surprised by. So it is with a dimensional. It will get opened and reviewed and has the highest opening rate of any mailing package. The dimensional will not ensure results; it only ensures that it will be opened. Results will be determined by the offer and list.

Card Decks

In the last few years, the card deck has evolved as a popular form of mailing. The card deck mailing began as a cooperative form of mailing with several marketers sharing the cost of production and mailing. It is still a cost-effective promotional format. Today, many multiple-product companies use card decks as a form of catalog and preclude other companies from participating in their mailing.

A *card deck* is a collection of 3 x 5 cards gathered in a wrap, bound together or placed in an envelope. Each card is a stand-alone sales-and-response device offering to sell or provide information about a product or service. Each participant in the card deck pays a fixed fee for each card in the deck. This form of mailing has proven to be very effective for several types of business mailers when evaluated on a cost-per-inquiry or cost-per-sale basis.

The marketer supplies either camera-ready art in the sizes specified by the printer/mailer or printed pieces in sizes specified by the mailer.

Co-Ops

A card deck is a type of co-operative mailing organized by a printer/mailer to generate a profit. Another form of co-operative marketing is when two or more marketers get together to share expenses and lower the cost of marketing to a common market.

This approach has become common in the travel and entertainment markets. Airlines, hotels, and car rental companies will often get together and promote their individual products in a joint mailing. They may even share offers or the mailing piece with the creative effort unified to improve the overall impression of the mailing package.

The reduced cost and improved results of this type of marketing is being repeated in other markets. Companies dealing in the same vertical markets are beginning to work together to improve their promotional position. For example, service contractors, equipment suppliers, and finance companies will all promote in the same package.

Inserts

Inserts are more a process than a format. The process is when one business uses another business publication or product fulfillment vehicle to carry its promotion. This process delivers the first company's offer to recipients of the host's product. Inserts are most frequently used in the consumer application in which a promotional flyer is inserted in the Sunday newspaper. Another application is placing promotions in invoices for your credit cards and utility services. A fundamental difference between a co-op mailing and an insert is that the user of the insert will pay a fee to the mailer. This fee will be in addition to mail costs and preparation of the mailing material.

This same approach is being used in selling to other businesses. Insurance companies will allow non-competing companies to insert flyers in their mailing packages. The frequent-flyer program mailings from the airlines are often filled with inserts.

The insert process can generate cost-effective leads and sales. However, it can also be uncontrollable and unreliable. For example, if you're paying to have your product promotion inserted in another company's product packages, you are relying on the inserter's shipping department. The insert program in this case is an additional duty for which the shipper's production people are not normally compensated.

Insert programs can be limited in scope. The customer list of most businesses is limited in size. This type of a program may not achieve the contacts you want.

Letter "Grams"

The familiar yellow format of the Western Union Telegram has high delivery and readership because telegrams were the original important or urgent format for delivering information. This format has been copied, expanded, and used by many mailers to achieve a variety of objectives. All of the objectives capitalized on the opening and reading rate of this format.

Inserting a brochure decreases its effectiveness because it makes it more of a letter package. Copy is generally computer generated on continuous form colored stock.

Copy for this format is written in an abrupt form in order to simulate the by-the-word cost of a telegram.

This format, which once ensured high readership, is now experiencing a reduction in readership due to overuse.

Catalogs

Any time you promote more than one product in the same promotion, you have used a catalog. This definition is not completely understood and many companies are actually sending catalogs when they want to use direct mail.

Frequency

Successful salespeople will tell you one of the keys to their success is that they never let go of a qualified prospect. They constantly stay in contact with known qualified prospects through personal contact, telephone selling, and the mail. The salesperson believes that over time the prospect will understand their product or service and will ultimately agree to investigate further. The concept of repetitive contact is also effective in direct marketing techniques.

Frequently in business-to-business selling, products can be sold only when the customer or prospect has an immediate need. A demand cannot be created in all cases. For example, if you are selling light bulbs and the prospect has just purchased a three month supply you want to position your company and products to be the alternative the prospect considers the next time they are acquiring light bulbs.

Consumable products will often only be acquired when there is a need within the company. Sustain your marketing effort so you will be on the prospect's mind when the purchase decision is being made. Being thought of at the time of the purchase decision does not guarantee an order, but not being thought of guarantees no order! In fact, the selling of consumable products is a major area of business-to-business direct marketing today. Consumables generally carry margins and volumes too low to support the use of a field sales force. The challenge is to be in front of the prospects when they are making a buying decision. Customers who have just acquired a new machine may not be in the market for a new or additional machine when you contact them. A frequency program can keep you in the mind of the prospect when they do decide to buy.

If you are selling a capital product which is acquired infrequently, the decision process is prolonged. Successful salespeople of capital products use frequency techniques to move the prospect through the decision process. They *condition* the prospect to move closer to their product. People cannot grasp many concepts at one time. A frequency or conditioning program will allow the salesperson to gradually move the prospect through the selling process.

The lessons the salesperson has learned through experience about multiple contacts and frequency should be applied in direct marketing. The promotional approach you use may vary depending on what you are selling. However, the concept of frequency and multiple contacts will improve results.

To gauge frequency, evaluate cost versus the results achieved. In face-to-face selling, you can't measure the effect of multiple contacts. Because every salesperson does their own thing, you may never know the detail of the contacts. You do know they occurred, but you don't know when, how, or the ultimate results of each contact.

Direct marketing allows you to control the contact, content, method used, and measurability of each contact made. With this in mind, you can continue to contact a customer or prospect until the frequency does not provide a return on the investment.

There are several different issues related to frequency:

- The number of times you contact a prospect

- The length of time between contacts

- The format of the contact

There is no magic formula to determine how frequently to contact a customer or prospect, or how much time to allow between contacts. Each situation is unique. During the planning phase, determine the level of investment you can make in acquiring a lead and/or a sale. Your algorithm, how you measure your programs, for required response will dictate the success you require for each contact.

The format of your contact will vary. However, we suggest you continually test your most successful promotion against any new format. In capital goods selling, it may be worthwhile to develop three different formats delivered over a three-month period. On the other hand, catalogers have found that they can mail the same catalog to the same group 14 times per year and still get acceptable results on the last mailing.

The key to determining the effect of frequency is to test. You can perform multiple, small tests fairly inexpensively when you combine mail and telemarketing follow-up. You can gain readable results in small samples. To effectively measure the results of frequency you will probably require the use of a marketing database.

Each contact you make will condition the prospect to have a better understanding of your company and its products. The conditioning process can be particularly helpful if the prospect is part of a decision-making team. You may even consider mailing to a number of contacts within a single company to help sell your products.

The sales force has learned that people cannot absorb a lot of different points at one time. Salespeople will frequently focus on a key point in each of their contacts. Hopefully, they are relating the features of their products to the benefits that the prospect will enjoy.

Your multiple contacts should also stress a limited series of points. Don't try to take a prospect completely through a complex product and all of its benefits in one mailing. Focus on the primary benefit that will help the prospect relate to your product. Don't lose sight of your objective: to create a lead or an order. If you awaken desire and convince the prospect there is a need, you don't have to fully explain all of the features and run the risk of confusion. Use frequency to help educate, but don't forget to continually ask for the order.

There are some promotions that, by their very nature, are frequency programs. These programs use the formats discussed earlier but require more than one contact.

- **Continuity programs**: As the name implies, these programs use continual or ongoing contacts to a group of customers or prospects. Book or tape clubs and magazine subscriptions are examples of this type of program. The definition of this type of program requires that the marketer continually contact the prospect or customer; the frequency and type of contact may vary.

- **Catalogs**: The economics of catalogs demonstrate that their profits come from the follow-up of catalog sales. A catalog marketer will frequently break-even or lose money on the first catalog sale, in order to acquire that customer for future programs.

- **Newsletters**: These can be sent to prospects or customers. This communication is not often used for direct marketing. If you are using a newsletter or periodic contact to your marketplace, it should be used to help sell products and services.

Newsletters are an excellent opportunity to use frequency to your advantage. Once you design a newsletter as a vehicle to maintain your customer relationship, you can also use it to develop and sustain a relationship with prospects. You can generate interest in products and services and keep your company name in front of your best prospects.

- **Frequent-user programs**: These are the "Executive Green Stamp programs." To be effective, you will want to frequently tell your prospects about their accrued benefits and the opportunities available for additional usage.

- **Showmanship mailings or super-premiums**: This form of dimensional mailing is so expensive you are compelled to follow-up the original mailing with additional contacts.

Schedule

There are a number of factors that have to be considered when planning and scheduling a direct mail program. The most obvious is the time necessary to execute a program. Illustration 8-10 shows a schedule of rough time estimates needed to move through a mailing project. This 14-week schedule shows the steps to implement a program. Your actual time frames will depend on your own program and the capabilities of the vendors you select.

Campaign planning and development is covered in Chapter 4. It is critical that you spend enough time developing a written plan. If you move directly to the creative step without planning, you may exclude proper list and offer development. Without these two elements, the creative execution will probably not achieve your objectives.

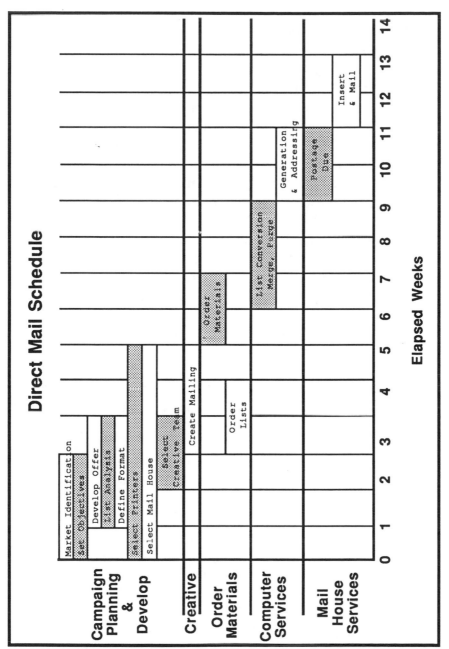

Illustration 8-10: A direct mail schedule

Creative execution is covered in Chapter 9, as well as in this chapter. Your creative staff or outside creative vendor should have a working knowledge of the capabilities of your computer service and your mail house. It is quite possible to create direct mail packages that cannot be assembled by the mail house's machines. This means that the mailing may have to be assembled by hand, causing time delays and substantial increases in mail house charges.

You should do a complete list analysis prior to ordering your lists. Since 50% of the success of the direct mail program depends on the list, you should be comfortable with the available lists before finalizing your target audience. When you are ready to order lists, be sure to provide written instructions to the list vendors including the specifications on list variables plus the technical requirements of your computer service company. There are far too many variables in list ordering not to document your instructions.

Printed materials may be ordered from several printers. There are three major types of printers:

- Continuous form printers. Check with your computer service to see whether they use continuous forms or sheet fed materials.

- Commercial printers that print from one color to full color materials. These printers will print brochures and other non-continuous form materials to insert in the mailing.

- Envelope printers that provide the specialized printing necessary for creating envelopes. Typically, this printer will have the longest lead time for delivery, especially if you order custom envelopes. Beware of envelope lead times.

Computer-generation and mail house service may be offered by a single vendor. More and more mail houses are providing computer-generation services. If you are planning to do a merge/purge, query your mail house to see if they have this capability.

After the mail has dropped, request a Postal Form 3602 if you mailed third class or a Form 3606 if you mailed first class. These forms, prepared by the mail house and then verified by the post office, are your receipt and proof of the mail quantity. Verify that the actual quantity mailed is consistent with the materials and names you provided and the postage you paid.

Fulfillment Kits

Direct marketing requires specialized promotional material seeking to produce a lead or an order. Very often, lead programs fail because material sent to prospects requesting information has been designed for a different purpose.

Virtually every business-to-business selling situation is complicated enough to require several steps. The sales cycle will often take weeks or even months. It is difficult to satisfy the prospect's thirst for information by simply offering a sales visit. Most business people will require you to send additional information before they'll consider meeting with your representative.

Product fact-sheets and flyers which have been designed to provide product information at a trade show or as sales collateral material are not normally effective direct mail materials. The message and offer are not consistent throughout the promotion. These sales collateral and technical support pieces often will not move the prospect closer to meeting with a salesperson. In many situations, these feature-oriented pieces intimidate the prospect with too much information and turn the prospect off.

When you begin to design your lead program, design a fulfillment package that will move the prospect closer to becoming a lead or an order. Make sure that the fulfillment has a call to action that is as strong as the original promotion. Every piece within the kit should include copy that entices the prospect to perform the action that you are promoting. Pieces that have been designed for another purpose should be used for their designed intention and not used to destroy your lead program.

A well conceived fulfillment kit can create a magnificent offer that can be used to generate an initial response prior to offering a sales-

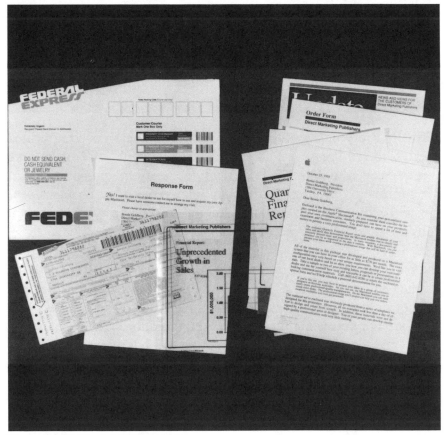

Illustration 8-11: A fulfillment kit.

person. You can offer the fulfillment kit as the first step in the lead program and then make a subsequent offer in the kit to have a salesperson become involved.

Illustration 8-11 shows a fulfillment kit designed by Apple Computer, Inc. to move prospects closer to making a decision to buy the Macintosh^{tm} computer.

Apple is dependent upon computer retailers to sell their products. These same retailers sell products from several manufacturers and have difficulty staying focused on any one program. Lead follow-up has been a constant problem and the quality of the presentation is not consistent from one dealer to another.

Rather than just offering an opportunity to visit with a dealer, Apple decided to move the prospect further along in the sales process by presenting the benefits of their product. Program development began with the design of a fulfillment kit that would allow the prospect to receive a personalized demonstration of the Macintosh in the privacy of their office. An elaborate fulfillment kit was designed, as illustrated, that allowed the output to be personalized based on information provided by each prospect. The kit was sent via Federal Express.

Illustration 8-12 shows the initial letter that was used by Apple to promote the Business Communication Kit. As you can see, there is no effort to generate an appointment with a salesperson in the initial letter.

This was a program where Apple recognized that the prospect couldn't be sold in one step and that additional steps were required. They also were realistic in evaluating their salespeople and the limited resources available to follow-up on each lead. To ensure that each prospect received quality follow-up and would move closer to making a buying decision, a well conceived fulfillment kit seemed to be the answer.

August 1, 1990

Bernie Goldberg, President
Direct Marketing Publishers
1304 University Drive
Yardley, PA 19067

Dear Bernie Goldberg,

We appreciate your interest and inquiry about Apple Computer. As you probably know, a decision to use a Macintosh in your company will significantly impact your communications with customers, prospects and business associates. Perhaps you've considered implementing desktop computing on a Macintosh in your company but have been unable to justify moving forward. We would like to help you evaluate and determine whether you should consider changing now. Complete the enclosed questionnaire to determine whether you should receive our new Business Communication Kit, absolutely free.

The Business Communication Kit is a special package of your own personalized materials produced on the Apple® Macintosh® and it will:

- Provide you with a chance to see several personalized examples in the privacy of your office. If you're like me, you know how difficult it is to visualize and relate to abstract examples of materials from other companies. With this approach you'll be able to not only receive personalized examples, but also to compare them to communications you're currently using.

- Help you identify opportunities for both reducing and avoiding expenses. We'll demonstrate how you can produce professional communication materials while reducing cost or hassle. You will see how these techniques can work in your company today.

- Show you, by producing your own personalized examples virtually overnight, how easily and quickly you or your staff can create professional communication materials. We will not only demonstrate examples that are appropriate for your company, but we'll also help you cost justify your own system. You will be able to relate to how the Macintosh can help you create professional business communications.

Illustration 8-12a: Business Communication Kit offer letter -- Page 1.

Bernie Goldberg
August 1, 1990
Page 2

The enclosed questionnaire will help you determine whether it is worth your time and effort to request the Business Communication Kit. The kit is designed for executives who are trying to make an important decision about how they would like to communicate. There is no cost or obligation. If you answer yes to any question, we can help you. Complete and return the response form to us today. If you FAX the response form to us by 3 p.m., you should receive the kit the very next business day!

The Business Communication Kit will provide you a basis to determine whether you should consider implementing your own system. The kit will enable you to see first hand how you can enhance your image, save time and money, and reduce the number of steps it takes to produce high quality, professional looking communication materials.

The questionnaire will help you evaluate some areas that may offer significant opportunities for your company. The 1990s will require innovative marketing approaches for companies to grow and prosper. As you complete the questionnaire, consider whether you will be able to compete effectively with your current methods for generating communication to your customers and prospects.

Send us the response form as soon as possible to take advantage of the Business Communication Kit. We want to show you how the Macintosh can help you improve your company's results. FAX the response form now and you should have your own personalized examples tomorrow.

Whether you decide to request the Business Communication Kit, we really appreciate your interest in Apple Computer.

Very truly yours,

Patrick S. McVeigh
Marketing Manager

p.s. The Business Communication Kit is absolutely free and if you FAX your response form by 3 p.m., you should receive your own personalized examples tomorrow.

Illustration 8-12b: Business Communication Kit offer letter -- Page 2.

Business Communication Questionnaire

Answer the following questions. If you answer yes to any question a free Business Communication Kit can help you evaluate how desktop computing on the Macintosh can change your company.

Yes   No

____   ____   Are you paying outside professionals or services to create forms, brochures and other communication materials?

____   ____   Would you like to create presentations and proposals that appear to have been professionally developed?

____   ____   Would you like to produce a professional looking newsletter that you can use to periodically contact your customers and prospects?

____   ____   Are you or your staff creating advertisements, slides or overhead transparencies? Would you like to be able to add color, graphics or even sound and animation?

____   ____   Would you like to have the capability to produce your own communication materials for as little as $270 per month?

Return the enclosed response form and we'll rush you a personalized Business Communication Kit absolutely free. If you FAX the form by 3 p.m., you should receive the kit tomorrow.

Illustration 8-12c: Business Communication Kit offer letter -- Questionnaire.

Response Form

Yes!   I want to receive my own personalized examples of business communication. Please rush me a personalized Apple Business Communication Kit.

Please change as appropriate
Bernie Goldberg, President
Direct Marketing Publishers
1304 University Drive
Yardley, PA 19067
Phone: 215-321-3068   Fax:(___) ___-____

To really make your examples meaningful, please answer the following questions completely. The information will be used in the examples we send you.

The name of your company or the company name you'd like to see used in the materials you'll receive:

Company   _____
Address   _____
           _____
City   _____ State ____ Zip _____

Name   _____
Title   _____

Please provide some annual sales and profit information for the three years indicated. This is for your personalized examples and doesn't have to be actual data.

	Sales	Profit
Last Year	_____	_____
This Year	_____	_____
Next Year	_____	_____

Return to:

Pat McVeigh, Marketing Manager
Apple Computer, Inc.
PO Box 751630
Memphis, TN 38175-9967   101-DLR

Receive your Business Communication Kit tomorrow or the next business day - Fax this form by 3 p.m. to (800) 537-9199!

Illustration 8-12d: Business Communication Kit offer letter -- Response form.

The fulfillment kit became the primary offer in the initial mailing. Once the prospect received the kit they would then be offered the opportunity to visit with a salesperson.

Another interesting ingredient in the Apple program was that the fulfillment kit contained pricing information so that the prospect could determine if they could afford to purchase the Macintosh.

I have found that you can effectively design a fulfillment kit to move the prospect closer to a buying decision. In addition, the kit ensures high quality, complete follow-up to each respondent. The kit can also create a terrific offer and allow you to develop a multi-step program that can produce higher quality leads.

Multi-Step Programs

You can use several direct marketing steps, prior to involving a salesperson, to better qualify each prospect. A respondent to multiple steps in a program has indicated a better understanding of the solution to their problem and a stronger interest in moving forward.

Many companies use multiple step promotions to qualify advertising inquiries. According to many salespeople, advertising has always produced leads of suspicious quality. Many salespeople refuse to follow-up these leads, particularly those generated by the reader service cards, often referred to as bingo cards. To better qualify these respondents and produce quality leads a fulfillment kit calling for a second response is often added to the process. Only those prospects responding to the fulfillment kit are considered leads and forwarded to a salesperson.

The technique of using a fulfillment kit to create the lead is often called a two-step program. The first step is the generation of the initial response and fulfillment with an information kit, the second step is the response from the kit.

Unfortunately, many of the fulfillment kits that are used to satisfy the requests for information are designed to convey product features and not to generate high quality sales leads. But those prospects that do respond to these kits are acutely interested and should be relatively high quality leads. Many times these leads suffer only because the respondent does not have the authority to make a decision.

The concept of using the two-step approach to qualify advertising respondents has led us to using multiple step programs to qualify all respondents. More and more of the programs I become involved in use multiple step activities to move the prospect closer to a buying decision and produce higher quality leads.

Offering a fulfillment kit which actively moves the prospect closer to the buying decision and then subsequently following up with either a phone call or another mailing will often produce great leads. Each step serves to eliminate less qualified prospects and encourage those interested and qualified to move closer to buying.

Complicated products like machine tools, electronic equipment, and computer software and hardware, will often require multiple steps to describe the benefits of the product and motivate a prospect to become a lead. Today's computer technology makes it possible to produce personalized letters based on the unique characteristics and status of each prospect. Telephone can be used to augment the direct mail effort and further clarify the offer and generate leads.

Transamerica Pension Services is selling a complicated financial product not easily understood by the average business executive. Most small business owners don't know much about retirement

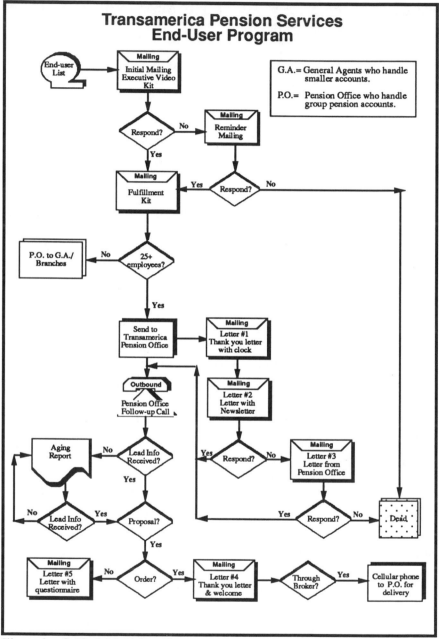

Illustration 8-13: A Multi-Step Program.

plans for their employees and will avoid responding to direct marketing efforts in this area for fear of appearing ignorant.

A special fulfillment kit was designed to explain retirement planning to the prospect. This Executive Video Kit, Illustration 8-13, was offered in the initial mailing. A reminder mailing was also used 10 days later to again offer the kit to those prospects that didn't respond to the initial mailing.

The response form to the letter asked the prospect to identify the number of employees in their company. The Transamerica Pension

Illustration 8-14: The Transamerica Executive Video Kit.

offices have consultants that specialize in dealing with companies having over 25 employees. The smaller accounts are handled by General Agents.

Many prospects took additional time to view the video tape portion of the fulfillment kit and Transamerica wanted to stay in contact with these busy executives until they were ready to visit with a Pension Consultant. A letter series was used to continue to maintain and enhance the relationship and encourage the prospect to respond and become a lead.

This multiple step program recognized the reality of how business executives gradually move to making a buying decision. The program combined direct mail and telephone to ensure that the prospect was ultimately converted to a qualified sales lead.

Current computer technology now makes it possible to manage prospects through different stages and ensure the appropriate communication is created and delivered. Although you can implement this approach internally on your own computer system, the Transamerica project was managed and fulfilled by PMCI, a Dayton Ohio direct marketing firm.

Lead Confirmation

As I have mentioned several times, most leads are not followed up by salespeople. You run the risk of creating long-term image problems in your market when respondents are not contacted.

Prospects who are responding to your direct marketing efforts are indicating a desire to have a relationship with your company. Although you may be dependent on the salesperson to develop, maintain and sustain the relationship, the prospect indicates an interest initially in a relationship with your company not the salesperson.

This is often a difficult concept to explain to the sales force. Many salespeople believe that the prospect is really interested in having a relationship with them personally and these salespeople are often reluctant to allow you to participate in that relationship.

If the salesperson fails to contact the prospect, you will have an unsatisfactory situation which you can't resolve. Rather than allowing this problem to fester, I often suggest that you maintain the relationship directly with the prospect.

As you generate a lead you can maintain the relationship by confirming the lead with the prospect and opening a communication channel between the prospect and your company. If the prospect is not contacted by the salesperson, you can provide the prospect with a name and phone number to reopen the dialogue directly with your company.

Think about your reaction if you were to request information and contact from a potential vendor. No one bothers to contact you. You'll probably have a long memory and never forget how poorly you were treated.

Now imagine your reaction if that same company instead sent you a letter confirming your request and giving you the name and phone number of the salesperson who would be contacting you. The letter also gave you the name of a manager you could contact if your were at all dissatisfied with the salesperson assigned to your account. This kind of lead confirmation opens the dialogue between a company and its prospect. It develops a positive relationship which may encourage the prospect to buy in the future, if not now!

Illustration 8-14 shows a FAX confirmation used by Apple Computer to notify the prospect of the dealer responsible for handling the inquiry. I have effectively used FAX as well as mail to deliver the confirmation.

** Apple Computer, Inc.**
PO Box 751630
Memphis, TN 38175-9967

Date: 9:30 a.m., Wednesday, August 1, 1990

To: Bernie Goldberg, President
              Direct Marketing Publishers
              1304 University Drive
              Yardley, PA 19067
              Phone: (215) 321-3068 Facsimile: (215) 321-9647

From: Pat McVeigh
              Phone (800) 642-8550   Facsimile (800) 537-9199

Pages: Including this cover sheet: 1

I am delighted that you've decided to visit one of our authorized dealers to learn more about business communication and the Apple® Macintosh®. You should be contacted directly by:

              Professional Computer Center
              Summit Square Center
              Langhorne, PA 19047
              Phone (215) 860-5200

The sales manager at Professional Computer Center is Dennis Mehta. If you have not been contacted within the next two days, please call him or call us at (800) 642-8550.

Illustration 8-14: A confirmation contact.

Direct Mail Summarized

Direct mail is the primary tool in business-to-business direct marketing. Direct mail is used as a fulfillment vehicle for other media and formats in direct marketing promotional efforts. It can't be overlooked and should be an important part of your campaign strategy.

Once you have established the list and offer you plan to use, you should begin to consider the format and copy to deliver the message. Direct mail is the most flexible and testable of all media. It is easy to control and to evaluate.

You must have a well-defined set of objectives before you create your direct mail package. The personality of the individual you're trying to reach can substantially alter the creative strategy you choose. Although using existing materials may save money, the objective and target of the direct mail program will probably preclude their use.

The offer and format you use with your audience will dictate the copy and graphics you use in your direct mail package. A photograph depicts reality, and an illustration depicts a dream. The combination can be an exciting visual experience for the reader and an effective support vehicle for the package.

Whatever components the direct mail package contains, each should be able to stand alone. If the package components become separated, you don't want to lose the selling opportunity. The flow of the mail package should continually ask for the order. The old sales adage "close early and close often" applies to direct mail.

The target audience and offer may dictate the use of a special direct mail format, such as a dimensional. These promotions are more expensive, typically take longer to implement, and have greater success in breaking through to the target. Carefully control and test each element of your direct mail program. When working with a small universe, direct mail coupled with telemarketing can be an effective combination to test and evaluate the success of different direct mail formats.

Multiple contacts and the use of a frequency program can significantly increase the effectiveness of your direct mail efforts. Evaluate the techniques being used by the salespeople in your industry. Frequent contact will probably be the key to the success of the better salespeople. Direct marketing results also improve when used in a sustained program. Evaluate, test, and measure the effectiveness of multiple contacts.

The Achilles' heel of direct mail is the time it takes to execute a program. It is not unusual for a program to take 10 to 14 weeks to develop and implement. Trying to short-cut the time frame can negatively affect the program's quality and increase its cost.

Fulfillment materials should be designed and created to ensure that a high quality lead is produced. Lead programs are even more dependent on fulfillment because most business managers will request additional information prior to agreeing to seeing a salesperson. The material you use to fulfill these information requests can significantly impact the results you'll achieve. Material designed for other purposes will not work well in trying to create a quality lead.

A multi-step program can be an interesting method to improve the lead quality and continue to sell a prospect during a lengthy sell cycle. If the product you are selling is complicated, multiple direct marketing steps can allow you to gradually move a prospect closer to a buying decision.

Direct mail is an important and dynamic direct marketing promotional format. You will use direct mail whether you intend to or not. If you plan your direct mail program, it will be more successful.

About Tracy Emerick:

Tracy Emerick's career has included banking, manufacturing, distribution, marketing agency and consulting positions as an owner, president, manager, salesman and as a direct marketer. He is an international consultant and trainer for companies entering or developing direct marketing as a tactical tool or a strategic commitment.

To keep his mind alert, Tracy teaches business policy and marketing planning at the MBA level and Competitive Strategies for the AMA. Tracy co-authored *Business-to-Business Direct Marketing* and has also authored *Desktop Marketing*.

Tracy received his bachelors degree from William and Mary, holds a masters degree from Northeastern and is finishing his Ph.D. in Business Administration. His firm is located in Hampton, New Hampshire where he and his family also reside.

Chapter Nine:
Telephone Selling

We have been discussing the tremendous pressure most companies are dealing with due to escalating selling costs and decreasing profit margins. Less expensive selling techniques must be developed to service smaller customers, sell less expensive products and qualify sales opportunities before introducing the salesperson. Telephone selling is fast becoming one of the most popular methods to attempt to resolve the pressure. Many companies believe that they are using telemarketing, when in fact they are performing telephone selling. There is a substantial difference between the two. Telesales and telemarketing are separate types of telephone selling.

Telephone Selling

The increasing cost of making a sales call in person has created a need for less expensive methods for:

a) Handling smaller customers
b) Setting up appointments for the salesperson

Many companies take some of their outside salespeople and convert them into telephone salespeople. They're paid commissions and make sales calls using the telephone. They do not use a script during these calls. This approach best describes *telesales*.

Telesales can be worthwhile, but it is not telemarketing. Telesales does not conform to our definition of direct marketing because its costs and results may or may not be measurable.

As you may recall from Chapter 2, I believe that direct marketing:

Explores, tests, and substantiates methods of :

- *Prospecting*
- *Qualifying*
- *Closing*

exclusive of a face-to-face contact by a salesperson.

The Definition of Direct Marketing

- **An organized and planned system of contacts**

- **Using a variety of media -- seeking to produce a lead or an order**

- **Developing and maintaining a database**

- **Measurable in costs and results**

- **Effective in all methods of selling**

- **Expandable with confidence**

Illustration 9-1: The definition of direct marketing.

Although the salesperson is using the phone, they are actually still making a face-to-face sales call via the telephone. The key to direct marketing is its measurability and predictability. As you perform an activity and determine its success, you can expect similar results when you duplicate the activity.

Using Illustration 9-1, let's compare telesales to the definition of direct marketing.

Telesales is not an organized and planned system of contacts using a variety of media. In most cases, the salesperson is allowed to schedule and execute the telephone selling on their own. The average salesperson will make about 25 telephone calls per day in the telesales environment.

You're never quite certain of the objective or results of telesales. The salesperson is not scripted and may or may not record the results from the sales call. Performing telesales is like sending a different letter to each customer. It may be a good idea and have very positive results, but it is not measurable direct marketing. Because each contact is personalized and specific to that customer, there is no common standard that is necessary to measure or predict performance.

Some companies have become fairly sophisticated and will allow the telesalesperson to interact with a computerized database. The database software may or may not schedule the telesales activity, record respondents, or record purchases. In essence, it is probably not a direct marketing database.

Measurement of costs and results of the telesales operation is problematic. We can probably establish the costs (in most case they are substantially understated), but measuring the results can be difficult. And as I have mentioned before, measuring the actual orders from lead programs is challenging. Since the offer and actions of the salesperson are not controlled, a true measure of results is hard to determine. Couple the lead measurement problem with the difficulty in measuring telesales and you will have a very frustrating situation involving enormous effort and virtually no identifiable results.

Telesales may not work in all methods of selling. And it is impossible to predict similar results and expand the project. Telesales is based on the effectiveness of the individual salesperson. There will be a wide disparity between good and bad salespeople. Results are based on the competence of the individual, not on the list, offer, promotion, or activity.

I am not discouraging the use of telesales as part of the direct marketing effort. In fact, telesales can work well if it is used as a follow-up to telemarketing. When telemarketing is used first to generate leads, and telesales is then used to close a sale, the combination can be quite effective. This approach can be a cost effective way to sell products and services, but only the first screening call is true telemarketing.

Telemarketing Defined

If telesales isn't telemarketing, what is the definition of this powerful concept?

Telemarketing is performing direct marketing over the telephone. Communicators follow a script to deliver a direct marketing message to a specific group of prospects.

- It is controllable, measurable, and does not depend on the sales ability of the individual communicator to be successful.
- It can be used to support direct mail or advertising, or as a stand-alone campaign.

- It is a planned series of contacts, using a constant message, seeking to produce a lead or an order.
- It yields information to build and maintain a database and is completely measurable in its costs and results.
- It can be outbound or inbound telephone calling.
- It can be used to sell to consumers or to other businesses.

I see frequent use of telemarketing and infrequent use of telesales in lead generation programs. Many telemarketing service bureaus have been used to qualify sales leads but these programs will frequently produce lower quality leads and the activity isn't sustained because the salespeople don't like the leads. Most lead programs using telemarketing, including service bureaus, fail to make an offer that allows the prospect to qualify themselves (Chapter 8).

Telesales and telemarketing can be used on both inbound and outbound telephone calls. However, there are some variations in the way inbound and outbound telemarketing is performed.

Inbound telemarketing involves the systematic handling of a call from a prospect or customer, resulting from a message seen in another medium. The person initiating the call has taken the first step in the sales cycle. If multiple products are being promoted in the advertisement to which the prospect is responding, it is often difficult to script the inbound communicator.

Inbound telemarketing is not controllable since the volume of telephone calls is determined by the prospects or customers. Planning and controlling the inbound telephone effort is difficult because you never know when the calls will occur.

When an inbound call is accepted, you're usually not certain what caused the call. In order to measure the effect of specific direct marketing programs, you'll want to determine the specific source of the

call. However, a prospect or customer often will indicate an advertisement from a medium that never had an ad.

Because inbound telemarketing can occur at any time, staffing and
facility requirements are difficult to determine. Prior response history can be valuable in anticipating activity as a result of new ads or
mailing programs.

Frequently, advertising people will forget to tell the people responsible for handling inbound telephone calls that a new ad has been
placed. Unfortunately, it is not unusual for the inbound telemarketing people to handle calls with no prior warning. It can be embarrassing and damaging to a company to have prospects and customers call in reference to a direct marketing offer if the communicators know nothing about the program.

Many companies fail to anticipate prospect's desire for information
and do not develop adequate fulfillment materials respond to
inbound inquiries. Inbound calls can often be the best source of
high quality leads but will also require high quality fulfillment and
follow-up.

Outbound telemarketing is more controllable. You can plan and execute the telemarketing effort at your leisure. You will know who to
call, when to call, and you can plan to deal with almost every selling
situation. *Outbound telemarketing* is a direct mail message being
delivered over the telephone with you controlling who receives the
message and when the message is delivered.

The outbound call can be timed to take advantage of the synergy
that occurs between various media. If direct mail produces a 1%
response rate and telemarketing produces a 5% response rate, the
use of both media together will produce more than 6% response. In
fact, it is not unusual for the total to be twice the combined results or
in this case, 12%.

There is a critical time frame of about 10 days between the mail drop and follow-up telephone call. This varies by program and should be tested for your environment. There is also synergy possible when print ads and other media are used in conjunction with mail and telemarketing. Testing is the only way to determine your best balance of various media. I have found it almost impossible to produce leads of high enough quality to satisfy field salespeople, using only the telephone to make cold calls. Prospects don't hear the offer or benefits and will often be confused about what they are requesting. When the salesperson follows-up with these prospects, there is very little interest and desire and therefore the lead is perceived as having poor quality.

Within each area of telephone selling, there are two sub-categories of targets that you can reach:

- The *consumer* -- a person who will be contacted at their residence, usually during evening and weekend hours.

- The *business person* -- a person who will be contacted at their office or place of business, usually during the business day.

The time of day and day of week that you attempt to place or receive calls has a major impact on your telemarketing efforts.

Selecting the Best Approach

One of the first decisions you have to make in considering telephone selling is whether you will use telesales, telemarketing or both. If you decide to use telesales, the decision can have far reaching implications to your company, particularly in the personnel area. Staffing telephone selling is one of the critical elements in the ultimate success of the effort.   My book, *How to Manage and Execute Telephone Selling*, published by Direct Marketing Publishers, Yardley, Pennsylvania, has complete instructions on how to select and train telephone selling representatives.

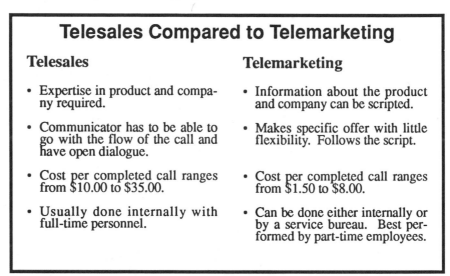

Telesales Compared to Telemarketing

Telesales

- Expertise in product and company required.

- Communicator has to be able to go with the flow of the call and have open dialogue.

- Cost per completed call ranges from $10.00 to $35.00.

- Usually done internally with full-time personnel.

Telemarketing

- Information about the product and company can be scripted.

- Makes specific offer with little flexibility. Follows the script.

- Cost per completed call ranges from $1.50 to $8.00.

- Can be done either internally or by a service bureau. Best performed by part-time employees.

Illustration 9-2: Telesales compared to telemarketing.

The decision to use telesales or telemarketing is dictated by the level of expertise required by the communicator. If the communicator needs to be able to discuss many products, answer questions that cannot be scripted, or sell specific products based on their own judgment of the prospects' needs, telesales is the correct solution. On the other hand, specific offers that allow little or no flexibility on the part of the communicator may be better implemented with telemarketing.

There is a dramatic cost difference between telemarketing and telesales. Telemarketing costs vary based on the target audience. It is less expensive to call consumers than to call businesses.

Telemarketing will cost from $1.50 to $8.00 per completed call. Telesales will cost between $10.00 and $35.00 per completed call.

Telemarketing is best done by a part-time staff, working only 4 to 6 hours per day. Because the telemarketing environment allows the calling presentation to be scripted, you can train people quickly and show results in a short period of time. There are many outside service bureaus available to perform telemarketing at an hourly rate, or even on a per-interaction (PI) or per-order basis.

Telesales typically must be implemented internally within the company. Telesales is also best done only 4 to 6 hours per day, but because of the high level of knowledge required, it is often difficult to attract part-time personnel. Typically, the communicators will spend part of their day performing outbound telephone selling, and the rest of the day performing other functions within the company.

Let's review how telesales is frequently implemented. Many companies already have an inbound telephone support center providing customer service. Frequently, these companies will decide to have their customer service or order processing employees fill their vacant time making outbound telephone calls. This approach rarely works unless the company can fully separate the inbound and outbound calling periods.

If a customer service department is chartered to provide quality service, outbound calling will always suffer. A customer service manager is dedicated to answering calls quickly with little delay, therefore if an inbound call is received, the communicators will always handle that call before making an outbound call.

A high percentage of inbound calls are customers calling to purchase additional products or services. As mentioned earlier, the customer/prospect is calling at their leisure and is much more tolerant and receptive. A high percentage of inbound calls are orders or leads.

Most outbound calling will result in uncompleted calls. Those calls that are completed will most often end in the offer being rejected. Outbound calling is never fun, it's just plain hard work. Communicators tend to avoid outbound calling with a passion. Taking inbound calls is the ideal way to avoid making outbound calls. As a result, inbound customer service departments given the added mission of making outbound calls typically do not produce results.

The typical company I have worked with implemented telesales in one of two ways:

1) Full-time salespeople made sales calls over the telephone. The average communicator dialed the phone about 25 times per day, and completed about 8 to 10 phone calls.

    This wasn't a bad situation when compared to the cost of making face-to-face sales calls. The average industrial sales call costs about $300 and is continuing to increase. A sales call made over the phone (as described above) ranges in cost from $15.00 to $35.00, depending on compensation, overhead, and other expenses.

2) The customer service department, responsible for handling inbound calling activity was asked to spend some time each day making outbound calls. Typically, little or no time or effort was actually devoted to making outbound calls. The results were hard to interpret because so few calls were generated.

In both of these situations, the communicator could still take inbound calls. As a result, it was difficult to sustain planned outbound calling. To improve productivity in either of the above environments, dedicate specific time periods for uninterrupted calling. In addition, manage the outbound calling process to ensure that the communicators are dialing the phone.

It is fairly easy to manage the process of telemarketing because you control the list, offer, script, and the entire process of telephone selling. There will be some difference in each communicators' specific performance, but over time most will perform close to the group average. The key to telemarketing is to manage the calling process and measure the results.

Telesales depends on the individual communicator and, therefore, is more difficult to manage. The success of the communicator depends on their ability to sell. It is still possible to manage the process and track results with an objective of higher productivity, but the ultimate sales results will be determined by the individual.

Existing customer service or order processing departments seem like a natural opportunity to implement telesales. The staff, facilities, and environment already exist for telephone selling. Communicators have daily periods of inactivity that can be used for telephone selling. The expansion into outbound telephone selling seems obvious. However, it is difficult to get the inbound communicators to dedicate time and energy to making outbound calls.

There are some effective techniques that can be used to improve the productivity and results of the telesales operation. Management of the calling process works in telemarketing and telesales, and will help you improve results.

Only commodity products can be sold on the telephone. With that in mind, consumer marketers are extensively using the telephone to sell products directly. In consumer telephone selling, the communicators are scripted, and there is frequent use of telemarketing, and infrequent use of telesales. On the other hand, business marketers are selling more complex products and services with a multi-level decision process. Most business marketers have a difficult time scripting their message. In business marketing, I see telesales used often and telemarketing used infrequently.

Inbound Telephone Selling

To effectively coordinate and control inbound telephone selling, a number of steps must be taken. Inbound telephone can never be used by itself. It is the response vehicle used for some other direct response media. Develop a detailed media plan that projects the number of respondents you anticipate. If you use direct mail or an advertisement with a coupon, project both the total response and the response via telephone.

Every program is different, but in most cases, a company's valuable respondent will come through inbound telephone calls. This makes a lot of sense if you consider that the prospect went out of their way to take immediate action and call the number you provided. Therefore, you want to ensure that your response to that person is of the highest quality, anticipates their needs, and is complete in fulfilling the promise of your offer.

The use of a toll-free 800 number will make it easier and more attractive for your customers and prospects to overcome their resistance to call you. Several companies are against using toll-free numbers because they feel it makes it too easy for people to call and gripe or comparison shop. Evaluate the reason you want people to respond to your company. The toll-free number can be an effective tool to help prospects overcome their fear of responding.

Think of how you react when you see an offer to call to respond to an ad or promotion that you've received. You probably conjure up an image of someone who is waiting for you to respond and is prepared to take your order or answer your inquiry. The marketing challenge is to fulfill this mental picture.

When direct mail offers an inbound telephone response as an option, between 5% and 20% of the total response will come via inbound telephone. This is not a hard and fast rule; your product or service may produce different results. However, prospects are frequently reluctant to call because they don't want to be aggressively sold at that particular time. They may only want to receive information to evaluate at their leisure and then make a decision to purchase or see a salesperson. The group that does respond via telephone represents the cream of the crop and should be handled accordingly.

Knowing that your best responses will probably come through inbound telephone activity, you must ensure that they are handled in a timely and professional way. If you don't plan, the worst will happen: the prospect will be ignored, handled discourteously, or not handled at all. You must plan how you'll accommodate respondents during peak and off-peak hours; how you'll ensure that the telemarketing communicator is prepared for the calls; and how you'll deal with the responder in a timely and professional manner.

Whatever media you've used, you should plan for about 15% of the total response to come via the telephone. This may be more than you'll actually receive, but planning for a higher response rate will ensure that the calls are handled professionally.

A number of considerations are in motion when your prospects call your phone number. If it is a toll-free number, they may have to decide whether to respond to an interstate or an intrastate number. The phone companies have made it much easier and less expensive to have one number for both intrastate and interstate activity. You will have to evaluate your needs and decide on the best approach for your company.

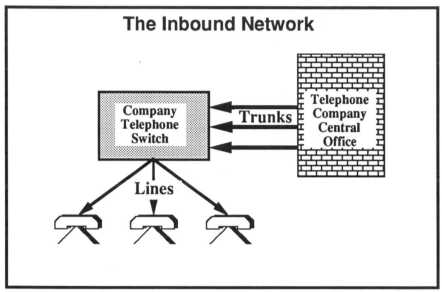

Illustration 9-3: The inbound network.

Some companies prefer to have their local offices handle the inbound telephone respondents. They feel that the local number makes the responder more comfortable. They're responding to someone who is local, as opposed to an unknown person at the end of an 800 number in 'never-never' land.

If you choose to have calls handled by local offices, bear in mind that you will have no control over the quality of the response that will be provided. In addition, it will be difficult to communicate advertising schedules to everyone involved. You also will have a great deal of difficulty measuring the response and the success of your direct marketing program. We have tested both scenarios and found no difference in the level of response between local numbers or 800 centralized facilities. But the centralized facility gave us a lot more control and information about the program.

When the prospect responds, they will either hear the phone ring or get a busy signal. The result is directly tied to the number of 800 trunks you have available to handle the incoming calls. As shown in Illustration 9-3, a *trunk* is the line connecting your business to the phone company. A *telephone line* is the extension or instrument connected to the telephone system within your business. Normally, a company will have 8 to 10 times more lines than trunks. Most phones are not in use all day long, so they do not have to be connected to the external telephone network at all times. Many companies install a telephone switch to handle the switching of the network or trunks to the appropriate line.

Telephone capacity planning is more difficult for inbound telemarketing. You must plan for the high volume peak. If you do not have enough inbound trunks assigned to the 800 number or other inbound numbers, your prospects will receive a busy signal. Hopefully, they'll attempt to call back. But about half never bother according to a recent AT&T study on inbound calling patterns. Your phone bill for the 800 service will confirm how many calls were attempted to your 800 number but ended in a busy signal.

Toll-free telephone usage (800 service) is charged similarly to other WATS (Wide Area Telephone Service) type coverage. The heavier the usage on each line, the less you pay per minute of usage. If you put in excess trunkage to handle the highest volumes you anticipate, you will pay substantially more per minute of actual usage. You'll also pay a monthly access charge per line. Your phone company representative can be of great help in evaluating and recommending the appropriate number of lines. Always compare additional costs against the need for customer service.

Since the phone company will take about one month to install additional 800 trunks, anticipate your volume requirements as accurately as possible. Initially, consider putting in more trunks than you really need and then evaluate the usage. There is an added cost to this safe approach since the phone company will charge to install and remove the trunks.

Busy signals may not achieve the results you want, but at least the prospect may call you back and probably will get the impression that your offer must be pretty good if others are also calling. Not having the phone answered at all can never be perceived positively. There are three primary situations that can cause the phone to ring but not be answered.

1) The prospect is calling when your office is not open for business. As I indicated earlier, you can't control the volume or timing of inbound phone activity. You should anticipate that there will be activity beyond your normal business hours and establish some form of coverage.

    One option is to use a message machine to announce that you're closed, give your normal business hours, and ask prospects to call back. Better yet, also ask them to leave a message and then have them recontacted through an outbound telephone call.

    Another option is to have the number automatically switched to an answering service.   This will give you coverage, but may not ensure the consistency you desire.

2) You have more trunks than people to handle the activity. When the prospect calls there is no one available to handle the inquiry. The same result can occur if you're using a telephone switch and have not programmed the system to handle overflow traffic.

    If your inbound lines terminate individually at a unique telephone, take the empty phone off the hook to send a busy signal to that number. A busy signal is better received than no answer at all.

If it is outside your normal business hours, consider using the tape machine mentioned earlier.

If you're using a telephone switch, ensure that it is programmed to overflow to a tape recording when all lines are busy. If you anticipate higher inbound volumes, consider adding some form of automatic call director to ensure the calls are handled in a professional way.

3) You have a trunk that is not working properly and is not ringing through to your company. Test your inbound lines frequently and have the phone company check them as well. If your phone bill indicates lines with no usage activity, investigate to determine if the line is operating properly. As an aside, if a line is working properly and it has no usage, you have too many inbound trunks and should cut back.

Now that the call is properly coming into your inbound telemarketing operation, make sure that each call is handled in a professional manner. Publish a letter to all employees that explains the promotion so that inbound calls will be expected. Make sure to also inform all of your remote locations.

As I mentioned earlier, in order to conduct true direct marketing your telemarketing program must operate independently of the personalities of the personnel and be measurable in its costs and results. To ensure that each call is handled similarly, you must script or provide a call outline for each communicator.

In the business-to-business selling environment, you must identify the individual calling, their company, title, and business phone number. No matter what the reason for the call, always try to capture this basic information before answering any questions.

When a prospect calls any inbound number, including yours, they expect to be asked for some information. Prospects tend to be fairly tolerant during an inbound call and normally will answer most reasonable questions. Use the prospect's tolerance to your advantage. Unlike outbound telemarketing, the call has not interrupted the prospect and they normally have more patience.

Good AFTERNOON/MORNING -- Thanks for calling ABC Company. My name is _____ (use your full name).

May I have your name and your company name please?

And your company address?

And the zip code?

Mr(s) _____ (use full name from above) may I have your title, please?

And the phone number at which you can be contacted during the day?

Illustration 9-4: An opening for an inbound phone call.

Prepare a form for your communicator to fill out to gather the following basic information:

> Contact Name
> Contact Title
> Company Name
> Company Address (2 lines)
> Company City
> Company State
> Company Zip
> Contact Phone Number (during the day at their business)

```
Date __/__/__    Time __:__    Communicator _____

Contact name    _____
Title           _____
Company         _____
Address         _____
                _____
City            _____ State _____ Zip _____
Telephone No. (___) ___-_____

Reason for response _____
```

Illustration 9-5: A sample form for handling inbound responders.

Also try to source the media and specific ad or mail piece that caused the prospect to call, even though this can often be difficult. Never lose sight of your primary objective: to sell something, not to generate information. If the prospect is uncertain or can't answer the question, quickly move into your sales presentation.

Once you establish a uniform front-end for handling an inbound call, it will be easier to train people. In addition, if a problem occurs during the call, you'll have all the information to recontact the prospect. Getting all of the name and address information at the beginning of the call makes a lot of sense. It isn't difficult to ask a series of non-threatening questions, and doing so often relaxes the responder. Even if the prospect or customer is calling to complain, it is easy to explain that you're capturing this information in case you're cut off and need to recontact them.

Design a form that follows the script so your communicators have a call guide that is easy to follow. Keep this form the same, regardless of the type of response, so it will be easy to train your people. By forcing a uniform approach to handling every inbound call, you are fostering good call quality and professionalism. You will also have a basis to build a database for the future.

Prospects who do not give a company name or phone number are usually of lower quality. They may be good leads or referrals, but your company probably doesn't operate during the hours that these prospects are available. If you're sending a responder to your sales force without a company name, the odds are pretty good that the salesperson will not even attempt to contact the prospect.

I have seen situations where prospects will respond either by mail or phone and give their name and company address but no company name or phone number. There is no way to establish the phone number for these prospects and contact them in the future. In the business-to-business arena, if respondents don't give you a company name, just send them literature (as inexpensively as possible) and consider them suspects.

Because the prospect has taken the initiative to call you, they will be more tolerant of your questions. They also expect you to be able to handle their queries in a professional manner. If your communicators cannot answer every question, they should admit that to the prospect. Establish procedures to have more qualified personnel return calls to prospects who ask difficult questions. If varying levels of prospect qualification will prompt different kinds of fulfillment, ask qualification questions during the phone call. These calls should be scripted and the answers entered on the form used to record the call information.

Don't forget our discussion in Chapter 3 concerning lead qualification -- establish money, authority, need and desire. Don't get trapped by asking market research type questions. These respondents are of the highest quality; don't run the risk of turning them off. They may be more tolerant of questions, but don't lose sight of your objective to generate a sale or a lead. Only get the information necessary to establish the best way to handle the prospect.

Keep a copy of the information gathered from inbound respondents to develop a database. These tend to be your best qualified respondents; they called because they wanted to be handled quickly. Try to fulfill their requests within 48 hours of their call. Consider sending each respondent a letter thanking them for their response and describing how their inquiry will be handled. If you've ever been treated this way, you know how powerful a letter like this can be. One note of caution: Keep the promise delivered in the letter or it can create a terribly negative situation.

Inbound telemarketing is a powerful response tool. However, whenever you offer a phone response option, you should always offer the opportunity to respond through the mail. Some people feel threatened, inhibited, or incapable of using the phone, and will not respond if only a phone option is offered.

If you anticipate a very high volume of responses to your program, consider using an outside telemarketing service bureau that specializes in inbound telemarketing. Another reason to consider an outside service could be your company hours of operation. If you're doing business across the country and only operating eight hours a day, three hours of your non-business hours are business hours for your customers.

The decision to use an outside telemarketing service bureau, or to handle calls in-house is complex:

1) Your company management may be nervous about the quality and customer service issues in sending the inbound activity to a service bureau. In fact, these fears can force management to decide to handle the activity in-house, when a service bureau may be a better alternative.

2) Unless you're selling commodity type products, the service bureau will probably not be able to handle detailed questions. The inbound responder is your best and hottest responder. You may want to strike while the iron is hot. This is a strong argument for keeping the inbound activity in-house.

3) The volume of activity may require a large staff to handle inbound activity only for short periods of time during the day. Even with part-time personnel, this staffing problem can be difficult to address.

4) Non-business hour activity could require you to operate your telemarketing operation at odd hours. This can create management and staffing problems.

5) Scripting and call control tend to be more difficult with in-house staffs.

6) Trunk availability is difficult to plan. If you're not in the telemarketing business, you probably have never planned or evaluated facilities required for handling inbound calls. An outside service has the experience and expertise to guide you through the planning process.

Inbound telemarketing is very complex and planning for it is difficult. It becomes even more complicated if you are targeting the consumer universe as well as the business-to-business arena. The best advice I can give you is to try to provide the same kind of response you would want to receive if you were calling another company.

Outbound Telephone Selling

Outbound telemarketing is one of the fastest growing areas of direct marketing. Selling costs are forcing business executives to find alternatives for selling and servicing their customers.

Where inbound telephone cannot be controlled, outbound is completely controllable. You can plan activity, timing, and set objectives. Outbound telemarketing can be used by itself or in conjunction with other methods of direct marketing. It is a medium to deliver a message over the telephone. Unlike direct mail, telemarketing is interactive and allows you to quickly alter one or more variables, such as the list, offer, or script, while you're still conducting your campaign. You can plan and control outbound telemarketing better than you can control direct mail.

Like other formats of direct marketing, when planning a telemarketing promotion you must consider the same four basic elements:

List	The customers or prospects to whom you plan to target the marketing effort.
Offer	The proposition you make to your customers or prospects in order to get them to respond.
Format	The vehicle to deliver the offer to your market: mail, phone, print, or broadcast.
Copy	The words and graphics you use to communicate your offer to the market.

Telesales eliminates the format and copy variables. This makes the list and offer even more important. Many companies attempt telesales without ever addressing the offer. In Chapter 2, I suggested that the relative importance to the ultimate success of a promotion was distributed among these variables like this:

- List   50%
- Offer   25%
- Format   15%
- Copy   10%

With telemarketing, the format has already been determined, and the only copy variable will be scripting if you're using telemarketing. Therefore, the relative importance of the list and the offer increases substantially.

The **List** is the first element to consider when planning and executing outbound telemarketing. When selecting a universe to use for telephone selling, you will need to establish the availability of telephone numbers.

Businesses are in a constant state of change. People are constantly changing jobs and responsibilities. The larger the company, the more likely it is that the mailing list contact will have changed. You can anticipate about a 30% change in contact and other information each year. Depending on the age of your list, the odds are pretty good that you'll be reaching a different target than you initially pursued.

When you use direct mail to contact businesses, if no contact name is available, you can use title and function addressing. This type of mailing will normally prove successful and not substantially alter the results. When you consider the relatively high degree of turnover, title addressing can be almost as effective as personalized, name-directed mailings. Each company is different and the only

---

List Usage in Telephone Selling

1,000   Names on original list with no phone numbers

60%   Obtain phone numbers

600   Net names for telemarketing

65%   Are reachable on the phone

390   Net offers made

40%   Accept the offer

156   Net acceptances

15.6%   Response rate of original list

Illustration 9-6: An example of telemarketing response rates.

sure way for you to establish the difference between title addressing and name addressing, is to test both and evaluate the results.

Many compiled and response lists have phone numbers, however, most lists do not. If you plan to use outbound telemarketing as a stand-alone medium, or in support of direct mail, you'll need to make sure that you can use the list for telemarketing. Many list owners are reluctant to allow their lists to be used for telemarketing because:

1) They have a negative attitude about telephone selling. Many have received unprofessional and poorly executed calls at home and in their offices. They don't want to have the people on their lists subjected to this kind of activity.

2) List ownership is a major concern. Many list owners
    have heard of telemarketing response rates of 20% to
    40%, and are concerned about losing their list to the tele-
    marketer.

    If the original list doesn't contain phone numbers, typi-
    cally you'll only be able to secure about 60% of the num-
    bers through most phone number appending services.
    Then through the telemarketing effort, you'll be able to
    reach about 65% of the phone numbered list to make
    your offer. If even 40% accept your offer, a great
    response rate, the net acceptance against the list you
    started with is only 15.6%. Yes, this is still a high
    response rate, but it is not so overwhelming as to worry
    the list owner that they will lose their list. We must edu-
    cate the list sellers regarding the true nature of telemar-
    keting and its impact on their lists. It will take time.

As you are probably aware, you normally rent lists for a single
usage. Any responder who accepts your offer, or asks for additional
information, becomes yours for future activity and action. In direct
mail you're only allowed to retain the names of your actual acceptances. In addition, you may have an opportunity to learn about the
quality of the list if you elect to have the non-deliverable (nixie)
mail returned to you. The acceptances and nixies are all you ever
receive back from any mailing.

In telemarketing you'll receive information not only from the acceptances and nixies, but also from other segments of the list. If someone refuses your offer, you can still learn a great deal about their
business. You clearly will own the data captured, which is valuable
market research information. However, in most cases, you can't
keep and re-contact any name that doesn't accept your telemarketing
offer. Review this situation with the list owner prior to starting your
campaign.

Many list owners are now renting their lists for annual or unlimited usage, to enable you to make multiple contacts via mail and phone. Some contracts allow you to use the list for both a mail and phone contact. If you rent a list for a single contact, and plan to use mail followed by a telephone call, that is two contacts. Make sure you review your plans with the list owner.

Outbound telemarketing creates many segments to the original list that must be dealt with independently. The most familiar and obvious segment consists of those who you were able to contact and who made a decision concerning your offer.

The individual names on the lists you use are commonly called *records*. Let's look at all of the ways a record can be used:

1) The record is on the original list, but an outside service cannot obtain a corresponding phone number. This record is never used for telemarketing.

2) The phone number is obtained and you attempt to contact the prospect.

    A) It is a wrong number. You reach a company, but it isn't the correct one. Your prospect may have moved on to a different company. If you attempt to contact their successor, then this record would not be consumed as a wrong number.

    B) The call results in a tape recorded message which states that the number has been disconnected. This is consumed as a technical difficulty.

    C) The company is moving or going out of business and can't make a decision about your offer.

D) Completed Call

1. Prospect refuses to talk and aborts call in the middle of the conversation. In fact, this prospect made a decision concerning your offer; they rejected it.

2. Prospect accepts offer. There are a number of possible ways to accept an offer. These can include a request for literature or a later contact.

3. Prospect rejects offer. A prospect who is unsure about your offer will either reject it or accept it. You should have a plan to handle rejections.

E) The prospect is not reachable after a pre-established number of attempts.

F) The prospect reached is not at a decision making location. This happens from time to time in the business world. You can consume the record, or attempt to get the phone number and appropriate contact at the decision making location, and then call that location.

When measuring telemarketing or telesales you should evaluate the number of dialings made in a specific time frame, normally an hour. In addition, you should also measure the number of completed calls, and the number of acceptances of your offer in that same time frame. When people discuss outbound telemarketing performance standards, many confuse apples and oranges. A constant set of definitions needs to be established that will allow everyone to compare the same thing. Business-to-business calling complicates the situation because additional dispositions are added by the nature of the calling.

In the consumer universe, you normally get through to the prospect or spouse. There is typically no one screening calls and no switchboard to get past. The prospect is normally the decision maker, and most lists used for telemarketing are name-directed.

The business universe is totally different. In most cases, the phone is answered by a receptionist or switchboard operator. The list may not be name-directed, or the name may be wrong. In either case, you'll have to establish your individual prospect's name and title through the switchboard. This prospect probably has a secretary, whose whole mission in life is to prevent calls like yours from reaching their boss. When you finally get to your prospect, there is a good chance that they will not be the person responsible for making the decision and you'll be referred to someone else within the company.

If this scenario occurs in only one call you'll be very lucky. Normally it takes several calls to reach the original prospect and perhaps just as many to contact a referred name. Obviously, the calls tend to be longer due to the multiple contacts required to reach your prospect. In addition, many dialings will have to be rescheduled in order to ultimately consume the record.

Bertha Barrier, the secretary assigned to the mission of screening your calls from her boss, complicates business-to-business telemarketing even further. You must get past her to make your presentation to your prospect. She also performs the same function when she screens face-to-face salespeople and direct mail; she can't be ignored.

In the consumer world, it is fairly common to attempt to reach each record four times before considering the record not reachable. The timing and the way you make these attempts can change, but four attempts seems fairly common. Because of multi-contact problems, the business universe requires a higher attempt threshold. Six attempts is average and it isn't unusual to see as many as eight attempts.

Every program and list differs on anticipated results. In my experience about 25% to 35% of dialings made to the business universe will end in a completed call. This is substantially less than the 50% to 65% completion rate of dialings in the consumer world.

Telemarketing Plan

Total records	1,000
% of records contactable	65%
Total records contactable	650
% of dialings that are able to be contacted	30%
Dialings per hour	25
Contacts per hour	7.5
Planned response rate	10%
Acceptances per hour	.75
Total telemarketing hours for project	86.7
Total acceptances	65

Illustration 9-7: A Typical Telemarketing Plan.

Depending on the type of product and the list being used, whether the list is name-directed, and the length of the script, the number of completed calls per hour ranges from 5 to 13. Dialings range from 20 to 35 per hour. These are not hard and fast standards, but production results that most business-to-business programs seem to operate within.

As part of your business planning process, establish goals that enable you to measure the program at all times. Set dialing, completion, and acceptance objectives for each hour of telemarketing. Once you've established your cost per telemarketing hour, it will be easy to evaluate your cost per lead or cost per order.

Illustration 9-7 shows how a typical outbound telemarketing plan might appear. This plan assumes that we are starting with 1,000 records. Only 65% of the records will be contactable, because many records will either have wrong numbers, not be decision-making locations, be going out of business, or be records that reach the re-call limit after a predetermined number of attempts.

About 30% of dialings will result in a completed call or contact. This plan assumes that we will dial the phone 25 times per hour of telemarketing, with 30% or 7.5 completed calls per hour. The plan also assumes that 10% of the completed calls will accept the offer, or .75 acceptances per hour.

The number of hours required for this project is 86.7 hours. This was derived by dividing the total number of records that were contactable by the number of completed calls per hour. The total number of acceptances was established by multiplying the number of hours by the planned acceptances per hour.

With the cost per telephone calling hour which I will discuss in the next section of this chapter, you can develop the cost per responder and the cost per order.

This type of planning gives you measurable objectives to evaluate the success of your outbound telemarketing project each hour of the project. The model can also be used to measure the success of different lists, offers, and products being sold over the telephone.

Each communicator should make the same presentation to each record on the list. This is one of the basic criteria to telemarketing as opposed to telesales. I recommend the use of scripts that control the complete flow of the telephone call. The communicator is even provided pre-scripted answers to questions and objections.

There are a number of script techniques that you can use.

1) A script outline. This approach uses an outline of the structure that you want the communicator to follow. Every word is not scripted and the communicator has a great deal of flexibility in what is said. Normally a record or form is provided to record the responses from the phone call. The form should be the outline for the call.

   The script outline approach is easy to use, and is not cumbersome during the phone call. It has a stronger dependence on the individual communicator and you're never absolutely certain of what was said on the phone. The communicators have to be well trained to handle questions and objections.

2) A script on pages. This is a typed version of the complete script. This approach scripts virtually every word that you want the communicator to use. It is an easy and quick way to introduce short, easy to learn scripts into the phone operation. It also uses a record or form to record the responses from the phone call.

   The script on pages approach is easy to implement and change in the phone operation. Typically the communicator will memorize the script and then never use it during the phone call. After a period of time, the script becomes personalized to the individual and really isn't a

script at all. As in the outline approach, the record ultimately becomes a call guide and directs the call.

3) A script on flip cards. This script has one or two statements on a flip card. Based on the interaction during the
phone call, the communicator is instructed to proceed to
an appropriate card. In Chapter 3, I used an example of
this type of scripting during the IBM project. It is a
complete script and controls every action and reaction
during the phone call. The communicator says the same
thing all of the time. It also uses a record or form to
record the responses from the phone call.

The script on flip cards approach is a little more difficult
to create and introduce into the phone operation. It takes
more time and effort to produce. You might consider
using a photo album with flip windows that are stag-
gered so you can see the base of the next window. This
type of scripting is dynamic and can change by simply
changing one or two of the cards. Your communicator
will still memorize the script and eventually use it less
and less, but the script on cards approach makes handling questions and objections fairly easy.

4) Computerized scripting. This approach uses a computer
terminal in front of each communicator. As the call pro-
gresses, the reactions to various questions are entered
into the computer and these answers determine the next
part of the script that should be read by the communicator. No paper record is used in this approach as the
information is entered directly into the computer system.

The computerized approach is great but expensive to
implement and difficult to change.   The communicator
may memorize the script but really has no alternative but

to read and view the computer terminal during the phone call. This is probably the most reliable approach to ensuring that the same message is delivered to every person on the list.

Telemarketing is an effective and proven media to ask for an order or commitment from a prospect or customer. However, it is very difficult to sell unfamiliar products or services via telemarketing. The products sold on the telephone almost always must be commodities or well-known items.

A telephone call is disruptive. Think about the calls you've received either at home or in your office. The call probably interrupted something you were doing. You may have been tolerant or even interested, but your patience probably wore pretty thin in a relatively short period of time. This reaction is fairly typical and is the challenge you face when using telemarketing.

Most people will not allow you to sell a product to them over the phone. If they already are familiar with the product or a similar product, they may agree to try yours. You only have between 25 and 45 seconds to generate interest and get your prospect involved in the phone call. The key to the phone call is the offer you make up front to interest the prospect in allowing the call to continue.

This means that you must make your offer easy to understand, risk-free and easy for your prospect to decide on. Multiple offers and choices are difficult to sell over the phone. However, you can make a single offer and then an additional offer after the initial offer has been evaluated and accepted or rejected by the prospect. The best offers allow the prospect to make a simple yes or no decision very early in the phone call.

If you're selling a product directly, consider offering a trial or money-back guarantee. Remember that, you're asking a prospect to purchase something without seeing, feeling, touching, smelling, or tasting the product. The prospect has to evaluate your offer with no sensory support. If the product is a known commodity, depending on the offer, the prospect is more likely to be able to make a buying decision. The less-known the product is, the more difficult, and less likely, the buying decision.

When using direct mail or direct response advertising, you can write longer copy to describe and inform the prospect. If they're interested, prospects can read the material provided and then evaluate and research the information to reach a buying decision. Although you are still asking prospects to make a decision without actually seeing the product, they have more time to consider it.

Telemarketing asks the prospect to make a decision immediately. Because you don't have a lot of time to explain your product or offer, your scripted copy must be short and to the point. On the phone, people do not have time to internalize the words presented. They may not envision what the speaker is trying to convey. Decisions are threatening to most people and they look for reasons to avoid uncomfortable situations. As you are making an offer on the phone, your prospect will be searching for reasons to reject or object to your proposition. They probably will not hear a lot of what you might want to present.

Does this mean that you can't sell over the telephone? Absolutely not. But I have found that you really won't have a lot of time to convey your message. If you're trying to sell a more complicated product or service, a combination of direct mail and telephone will probably be more appropriate.

If you're using the telephone to qualify leads and offer the prospect an opportunity to see a sales representative, similar rules on the offer and length of the message apply. Explain to the prospect why seeing a salesperson will be good for them or their company. This message also must be delivered in a very short and direct presentation. Again, words and copy that work well in other media may not perform as well on the phone.

When designing a telemarketing script, try reading something out loud for 30 to 45 seconds. You'll be surprised how long a period it is. Your prospect will have to be hooked very quickly to allow the call to continue. If you're asking for information to evaluate qualification, you still must get the prospect interested in continuing with the call.

In many cases, the prospects will ask that additional information be sent to them so they can make a decision. Many telemarketers view prospects who request literature as disinterested people simply looking for an easy way to get off of the telephone. Most people do not like to be rude. By asking for additional information, they are deferring the decision and they don't have to be rude to the communicator. A good percentage of these people in fact are simply doing it to get off the phone. However, some of these prospects are legitimately interested in the offer. You must deal with the interested group in a very professional and effective way.

When conducting lead qualification telemarketing programs, I tend to see more prospects requesting additional information than agreeing to seeing a salesperson. And depending on the offer being made in the direct selling programs, they also can have a large number of literature requesters.

As I have continually suggested, promotional material must be designed with prospects who ask for additional information in mind. It must be designed with the specific mission of creating a lead or an order. You can't expect a promotional piece that was designed to be left behind by the salesperson after their sales call to perform the direct marketing mission. Trade show literature won't work any better. What should become obvious is that when you start your telemarketing campaign, you will also need to create some direct mail follow-up material.

You might think that it is easier to treat literature requesters as rejections of your offer who will not care about the material, if any, that you send them. If you're generating enough activity from the prospects accepting your telemarketing offer, this might be a good decision, particularly if your universe is large enough to support your sales and lead requirements for the foreseeable future without dealing with prospects who want additional information.

I have found, however, that when literature requesters are re-contacted by telephone about ten days after the material was sent to them, approximately 25% will convert into a solid lead or an order. The fulfillment material used was specifically designed to move the prospect further along in the buying process.

Evaluate the financial impact to create, produce and fulfill literature. The cost of the second phone call also must be evaluated against the anticipated results to ensure that the program is profitable. If you decide to re-contact the literature requesters, you will be starting down the road towards database marketing.

I am obviously recommending the use of direct mail to support your telemarketing efforts. Telephone selling works best when it is used in conjunction with direct mail. Direct mail followed by telephone will normally yield better results as a combined effort, than when either media is used separately.

I have tested the use of mail and phone separately, and then tested mail followed by phone and the results were very different. The mail produced a 2% response rate and the phone produced at 7.5%. You would therefore expect the combined results to be about 9.5%. The actual result of the combination of the two was almost 13%.

I also tested to determine the best time to follow the mail with tele-marketing. I began telephone selling about five days prior to the mail. The first scripted question asked was, Do you recall seeing the information we sent you? Even before the mail was dropped, about 30% of those asked said that they did remember receiving the mail. This may sound amusing, but some people will respond posi-tively so as not to appear ignorant. After the mail was dropped, we continued to track the answer to this question. The favorable response peaked at almost 70% from day 11 after the mail was dropped and remained there through day 17. The response rate then began to drop. Within 30 days after the mail drop, the favorable response rate dropped to 40% and stayed there for the next 15 days. It ultimately went back to the 30% range.

Answer rates to this question by itself were interesting, but the front-end results were even more informative. The response rate followed the awareness of the mail fairly closely. There was an increase of almost 25% in response rate when the awareness of the mail was at its peak.

Mail and phone work exceedingly well together. To maximize the combined effect of the two media, the phone call should be timed to follow the mail from between 10 to 15 days after the mail is dropped. I have been involved in programs that delayed the phone call to allow for all of the mail responses to be returned. This may make sense, but the results should be carefully evaluated. Test both approaches to determine the best results for your company. If your mail response rate is anticipated at about 2%, you'll only be calling and contacting a very small group who would have already respond-ed by mail. Remember, you will achieve only about a 65% contact rate of all of the records that have phone numbers. Therefore, given a 2% mail response rate you will only duplicate about 1.35% of the list. The only way to find out the impact of phone and mail together is to test... test... test.

Establishing the Costs of Telemarketing

Whether you're planning inbound or outbound telemarketing, you must be able to evaluate the true costs and results of your efforts. The costs for telemarketing are more than just the communicator costs. If you're evaluating whether to keep the function in-house or go to a service bureau, you must know your cost per hour of telemarketing.

Three broad areas should be considered when evaluating the total expenses associated with telemarketing.

  1) The cost of operations - telephone
  2) The cost of operations - clerical support
  3) General and administrative expenses

Use the Telemarketing Expense Worksheet (Illustration 9-8) to help you establish your cost per telemarketing hour. Before you get started, try to determine the amount of telemarketing you're planning to perform. This quantity will be critical in all of your planning and evaluation. I have provided areas to establish both the annual and monthly costs. In many cases you'll find it easier to get either the monthly or annual expense. You can convert either to suit your needs by dividing or multiplying by 12. This will give you a methodology to evaluate all of your costs.

Within the cost area defined as *cost of operations - telephone*, are all the labor expenses. Include the cost of phone center management. If this function will only occupy a percentage of time for an individual, include the total cost and then apply the appropriate percentage. Supervision and communicator costs are obviously an important part of the labor costs.

Telemarketing Expense Worksheet

	Annual	Monthly
Hours of Telemarketing	_____	_____

Cost of Operations - Telephone

	Annual	Monthly
Labor - Mgmt $_____/yr	_____	_____
% of Mgmt needed ___%	_____	_____
Labor - Supv $_____/yr	_____	_____
% of Supv needed ___%	_____	_____
Labor - communicators	_____	_____
Payroll taxes	_____	_____
Fringe benefits	_____	_____
Temporary - outside labor	_____	_____
Telephone equipment	_____	_____
Telephone network - inbound	_____	_____
Telephone network - outbound	_____	_____
Telephone network - local usage	_____	_____
Telephone installation	_____	_____
Total cost of operations - phone	_____	_____

Cost of Operations - Clerical

	Annual	Monthly
Labor - Mgmt $_____/yr	_____	_____
% of Mgmt needed ___%	_____	_____
Labor - Supv $_____/yr	_____	_____
% of Supv needed ___%	_____	_____
Labor - Clerks		
Look-up	_____	_____
Maintenance	_____	_____
Tabulating	_____	_____
Sorting	_____	_____
Payroll taxes	_____	_____
Fringe benefits	_____	_____
Copy machine rental/depreciation	_____	_____
Copy machine supplies	_____	_____
Telephone equipment	_____	_____
Total cost of operations - clerical	_____	_____

Illustration 9-8a: Telemarketing Expense Worksheet

	Annual	Monthly
General & Administrative		
Rent	_____	_____
Heat & electricity	_____	_____
Insurance	_____	_____
Equipment depreciation	_____	_____
Furniture & fixtures depreciation	_____	_____
Telephone equipment	_____	_____
Telephone network	_____	_____
Receptionist/secretarial support	_____	_____
Data processing	_____	_____
Data processing supplies	_____	_____
Repairs & maintenance	_____	_____
General office supplies	_____	_____
Travel & entertainment	_____	_____
Dues & subscriptions	_____	_____
Training & seminars	_____	_____
Advertising & public relations	_____	_____
Bad debt/bad pay/returns	_____	_____
Total cost of operations - G & A	_____	_____
Total Costs	_____	_____
Cost per hour of telemarketing	_____	_____

Illustration 9-8b: (continued): A Telemarketing Expense Worksheet.

In *How to Manage and Execute Telephone Selling*, by Bernie Goldberg, Direct Marketing Publishers, Yardley, PA 19067, detailed cost worksheets have been developed that can help you identify typical selling expenses. Illustration 9-9, which is taken from that book, summarizes typical selling expenses.

Managing the Outbound Telephone Selling Process

It is difficult to manage a person on the telephone to perform exactly as you want. Scripts can go a long way to getting the message

Typical Telephone Selling Expenses

Type of telephone selling	Cost per hour	Cost per contact
Inbound	$35.00 - $65.00	$5.00 - $15.00
Outbound Telemarketing		
Consumer	$18.00 - $35.00	$1.80 - $ 5.00
Business-to-Business	$35.00 - $60.00	$6.00 - $10.00
Outbound Telesales	$50.00 +	$10.00 +

Illustration 9-9: Typical telephone selling expenses from *How to Manage and Execute Telephone Selling*.

delivered exactly as you want it stated. If you're using telesales, you have no control over the message. Training and call monitoring are some of the tools you have available to improve call quality, but unless you listen to every call, you really can't guarantee each specific presentation.

However, you can take complete control of the calling process by managing the flow of records as they pass through the phone operation. The concept of managing the calling records is referred to as managing the process of telephone selling. Process management is appropriate in either telemarketing or telesales. Unfortunately, many telesales operations have not focused on managing the process, and they are at the mercy of the salespeople in both quality and quantity of telephone calling.

Management should control which customers or prospects get called, the frequency of calling, the scheduling of the call, and the recording of the ultimate disposition of the record after the call is made. This process is a way of life in most telemarketing environments. It is relatively new to the inexperienced telesales manager.

Typically, the salespeople manage the calling process similarly to field salespeople. Telesales representatives schedule calls based on their feelings concerning their customers and what they perceive is their next opportunity to sell. This is particularly true if no telephone offers have been created to make the calling process easier and more productive. Many customers are never contacted, and a few select customers receive calls almost weekly.

Telephone selling, particularly business-to-business, works most effectively with current customers. Additional contacts can be made to enhance the company/customer relationship and allow additional products or services to be sold. The customer is familiar with the company and products, so it is not unusual to get a yes or no buying decision during the phone call.

Once you've decided which customers you want to call, these records should be given to the telephone selling operation. As these records are consumed, have them returned and then provide additional records. Provide the calling information for each customer on a card or form, a *unit record* for each call. This approach will allow the communicators to schedule and annotate the record as they are on the phone. I'll discuss unit records and scheduling systems in subsequent chapters.

Illustration 9-10 shows the process of telephone selling. Records are extracted from the database, printed on a unit record, and forwarded to the telephone selling operation. The calls are scheduled and attempted by the communicators. Each dialing attempt is annotated on the unit record and a daily tally sheet. If the call is completed or the record is consumed, the unit record is returned to management for disposition. Records that need rescheduling are handled appropriately. The system is a closed loop with management in control of the calling process.

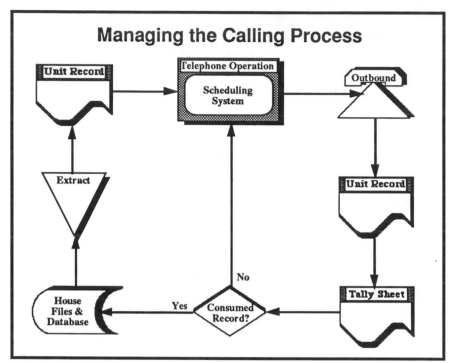

Illustration 9-10: An example of the telephone selling calling process.

Why Use a Unit Record?

The telephone calling process can best be managed by controlling the records to be called. Many people believe they can control the calling records by providing lists of records to the communicators.

However, most calls will have to be rescheduled before the record will be consumed. Remember that a typical business dialing will only result in a completed call about 30% of the time. Consumer calls can be completed as often as 50% of the time. This means that 70% of business and 50% of consumer calls will have to be rescheduled.

If a listing is used by a telephone selling communicator, rescheduling becomes cumbersome and difficult. Think about the lists of calls you maintain of people you want to contact. If the person is not available, you'll probably make a note next to the name with some information to remind you to call again.

In order to re-call that person, you'll have to review the entire list and hope you remember to re-call the person at the appropriate time. Lists have similar deficiencies when they are used to reschedule telephone calls. You have to read the entire list to find records that are due for calling again.

A data processing concept developed many years ago was to store information about a record on a punched card. Each record was referred to as the ***unit record***. The unit record allowed sorting, tabulating, and printing of records and reports. The key to the success of this concept was the ability to manipulate and control all the information because it was stored in a controllable, usable format.

You can see the importance of the unit record when you consider that in many telesales environments, telephone calling and scheduling is left entirely in the hands of the communicator. Each salesperson develops and maintains their own scheduling and record keeping system. Frequently, there are no computer systems used to maintain customer files and calling information.

I've observed several dozens of telesales operations, and with the rare exception, between 30% and 40% of the communicators' time is spent determining who to call next.

In those rare telesales environments where the customer files are maintained on a computer, management provides lists of customers for the communicators to call on a weekly basis. Typically, the calling plan is developed by the telesales representative and the computer is used to keep a diary or calendar. Even with this somewhat sophisticated approach, management and the communicators have not focused on scheduling the call.

When telesales representatives receive lists of customers and prospects to contact from management, frequently the lists only contain name and address information. The telesales representative maintains their own files, either in tubs, draws, or folders on their desk. The communicator will normally locate the appropriate file for the customer prior to making the call.

This can be a time consuming process to locate and review the file prior to making the call. Many communicators consider it vitally important to plan their calls prior to dialing the phone. It becomes quite a waste of time to perform all this activity, when you consider that most dialings will not end in a completed call.

All too often, companies look to automation to cure problems. The fact is that a computer won't solve a problem, but is best used to automate an existing system. Automating your telephone selling will not be easy if you haven't developed a good manual system beforehand.

Most telemarketing service bureaus use a card or form for each call that has to be made. Most calls are made from labels that have been affixed to the cards. The labels contain name, address and telephone information. These cards are, in essence, unit records which allow the calling process to be managed.

As you can see, all of the information required to make the phone call is readily available on the unit record. There is no reason to sort through personal files to locate additional information. The record can be annotated with the next scheduled date of contact and filed appropriately to ensure the contact is made.

DIRECT MARKETING *Publishers*

Telephone Calling Unit Record

Contact Information

Contact _____
Title _____
Company _____
Address _____

City _____ State __ Zip _____
Phone (___)___-_____

Bill To Information

Contact _____
Title _____
Company _____
Address _____

City _____ State __ Zip _____
Phone (___)___-_____

Dialing History

Attempt	Communicator	Date	Time	Dial Result	Today @ (time)	Other Day @ (time)
Morn Aft		/ /	:	DA NA BY	(:)	/ / (:)
Morn Aft		/ /	:	DA NA BY	(:)	/ / (:)
Morn Aft		/ /	:	DA NA BY	(:)	/ / (:)
Morn Aft		/ /	:	DA NA BY	(:)	/ / (:)
Morn Aft		/ /	:	DA NA BY	(:)	/ / (:)
Morn Aft		/ /	:	DA NA BY	(:)	/ / (:)

Calling Information

Completed Call Results

Communicator _____ Date __/__/__ Time__:__

Final Disposition: ☐

1=Wrong number - not in service
2=Wrong person - no referral
3=Reached the re-call limit
4=Refused to talk

5=Completed call - Accepted offer
6=Completed call - Send information
7=Completed call - refused offer

Illustration 9-11: An example of a unit record.

The creation of the unit record in Illustration 9-11 didn't take a great deal of effort. The records to be contacted were still printed in a list, only the list was printed on self-adhesive labels. There was some additional clerical effort involved in affixing the labels to the cards, but the time savings to the communicator and the ability to manage the process far outweigh the disadvantages.

If there is additional information necessary for the communicator to capture during or after the phone contact, the unit record can be easily expanded. If the communicator requires additional information about a customer that might be available in the company's data processing files, the unit record can also be designed to accommodate that requirement.

Because all of the information concerning a customer or prospect is readily available on one record or form, the communicator can easily control the scheduling process. The unit record concept is an effective technique for beginning to manage the process of telephone selling.

There is a fairly dramatic difference between calling customers and prospects from a listing, and calling them from a unit record. If you contact someone on the list and consume the record, the name still stays on the list. It has to be looked at and reviewed each time you are searching for another person to contact. Even if it only takes a few seconds to scan a list to locate a potential contact, the consumed names make the scanning more difficult. With a unit record, you can eliminate those records that have been consumed by simply putting them in a file for consumed records. They don't interfere with records that still have to be contacted.

As I mentioned earlier, the unit record allows management of the process. You can provide a set number of records to the communicators and know at any time the status of those records.

Management controls the inventory of records to be contacted and the work that is already in process.

Call Scheduling

Now that you've designed and created the unit record, managing and controlling records as they move through the calling process is practical. Communicators will not have to peruse lists and spend unproductive time reviewing margin notes to locate appropriate records to contact.

The unit record and, specifically, the Call Scheduling section, give the communicator an area to annotate call attempts and reschedule calls. This section can also effectively limit the number of attempts made to a particular record, and ensure that each record is consumed.

You should establish a scheduling system to either reschedule or consume each record called by the telephone selling staff. By establishing standards and a uniform methodology for scheduling records, you'll be able to more effectively measure the performance of each telephone selling program, each list, and each communicator.

The number of attempts you plan to make and whether you are calling businesses or consumers can substantially change the scheduling approach you'll use. Therefore, you should have a firm understanding of your target audience and how often you plan to call them.

Most computerized schedules are simply diaries. These systems typically provide lists of customers or prospects who should be contacted this week, or in some situations, this day. These so-called scheduling systems do not help the communicator actually schedule the call.

The information typically generated by a diary type scheduling system is a list that requires the communicator to go to another file for other information concerning the customer.

In some scenarios, the diary and the customer information is on-line via a computer terminal. The communicator is given a list of customers to call today. Each record on the list has a unique account number that the communicator uses to access the entire customer record.

As long as the communicator dials the customer and completes the call, this system can work effectively. However, if the communicator calls and finds the customer not available, how do they reschedule the call? Perhaps the system will allow the communicator to enter a future date and the record will appear on that future day's contact listing. The problem gets extremely complicated if the customer asks to be called back later on the same day. This will require the communicator to annotate the listing, and that creates the listing problems I've mentioned before.

Using hanging folders and portable filing systems to control the call scheduling process has been very successful. The hanging folders give you great flexibility in the number of slots you can have, and make it relatively easy to change or modify the system. In addition, the same system can easily accommodate multiple programs, lists, or offers, and the results can be tracked very easily.

In a typical business-to-business program, the following files would be used:

    1)   Schedule anytime
    2)   9:00 to 11:00 a.m.   (0900 to 1100)
    3)   11:00 to 1:00 p.m.   (1100 to 1300)
    4)   1:00 to 3:00 p.m.   (1300 to 1500)

5)   3:00 to 5:00 p.m.   (1500 to 1700)
6)   Reschedule for a future date
7)   Technical difficulty   (Wrong # & not in service)
8)   Accepted offer/order
9)   Requested literature
10) Rejected offer
11) Reached the re-call limit

The first six files provide a way to schedule a call at a specific time during the day. Shortly I will explain a method to automatically reschedule a call when a communicator is unable to establish a particular reschedule time.

Records that have no specific reschedule criteria, and can be called at any time, are found in the first file. New records given to communicators are typically also assigned to the Schedule Anytime file.

The time files are used to schedule records that are to be contacted at a specific time during the current or next business day.

The scheduling approach illustrated for business calling has the day broken down into four equal two-hour periods. These two-hour increments make managing the process easier, and can help you systematize re-scheduling. If your operation provides service 10 or 11 hours per day, you might add another time file for 5:00 p.m. to 8:00 p.m.

The Reschedule for a Future Date file is used to schedule a record for a day other than today. If possible, records in this file should be kept in chronological sequence, with the earliest dates to be rescheduled stored in the front of the file. At the completion of calling each day, this file will have to be reviewed and records scheduled for the next calling day merged and sorted into the current work flow. In addition, the Reschedule for a Future Date file will have to be sorted chronologically.

Many companies will not allow communicators to keep records scheduled beyond two weeks in their scheduling system. Records that are scheduled beyond the limit are returned to phone center management for filing and rescheduling action.

The remaining files are used for records that have been contacted or consumed and will not be rescheduled. These files will vary depending on the final disposition codes you establish for your operation. You should consider establishing a consumed record file for every final disposition code you will use. It may be prudent to combine several final disposition codes in the same file, but the file should be clearly marked with all codes.

Once you've established the system and it is available to each communicator, you've created an environment that can significantly improve productivity. As you distribute unit records to the communicators, these records will be added to the scheduling system.

For a new communicator executing a new telephone selling program, all of the records will be placed in the Schedule Anytime file. The customers have not requested a specific time to receive the call, therefore they can be scheduled anytime.

To begin the telephone effort, the communicator removes a record from the Schedule Anytime file and dials the phone. Most of the time, the contact they are trying to reach is not available. The communicator then annotates the unit record in the call scheduling section (Illustration 9-11) with the date, time, and reason for not completing the call. If the customer's secretary indicated that the target contact would be available at 4:30 p.m. today, that would also be annotated on the unit record.

Without a scheduling system, the re-call time might occur only if the communicator remembered to peruse the list at that time. Instead of leaving the rescheduling to chance, the record is filed in the 3:00 to 5:00 p.m. file. That way the record will be rescheduled for a call at that time.

The communicator continues to dial records and fill out the schedule for each not completed call. The records are either filed in the appropriate time period today, tomorrow, or for some future date. If a customer asks to be called on a future date, the record is filed in the Reschedule for a Future Date file in chronological sequence.

If the record is contacted and consumed, it is filed in the appropriate consumed record file corresponding to its final disposition. The communicator annotates the unit record with the final disposition, and files it in the corresponding file.

As a time period ends, the communicator removes the next time period file, and examines records to be called during the next two hours. The records are sorted by requested re-call time, if one exists. Records with no specific requested time can be called any-time during the time period.

Records in the scheduled time files are called first, prior to calling records in the filing system that can be called anytime. The record that was scheduled earlier to be re-called at 4:30 p.m. will come to the front of the reschedule file pretty close to the exact time that the call should be made. The communicator will not have to peruse a list or remember to call; the records with requested times will be presented almost automatically by the filing system.

Some records might be in a scheduled time file, but not have a spe-cific time to be contacted. This can happen because of automatic rescheduling based on an algorithm you'll establish.

Automatic rescheduling will occur if you are unable to reach a prospect, or the prospect doesn't give you a particular time to call back. Calls that aren't answered will be automatically rescheduled. Alternate attempts between mornings and afternoons. Occasionally, records will be attempted in the afternoon first.   Records attempted between 9:00 and 11:00 a.m. will next be attempted between 1:00 and 3:00 p.m.

Attempt	Next Attempt
9:00 to 11:00 a.m	1:00 to 3:00 p.m.
11:00 to 1:00 p.m.	3:00 to 5:00 p.m.
1:00 to 3:00 p.m.	9:00 to 11:00 a.m
3:00 to 5:00 p.m.	11:00 to 1:00 p.m.

An automatic rescheduling system ensures that every record is attempted at least 3 days in a row (based on 6 attempts). On the average, records will normally be attempted over a 1 to 2 week period.

As the Call Scheduling section is completed, the record will be attempted the number of times that you've pre-determined. The final attempt will force the record to be consumed as having reached the re-call limit.

The Daily Tally Form

Now that you have a system to manage your telephone selling, how do you track and measure the results? Many telephone operations develop tally forms that the communicators complete for each inbound call they take or outbound dialing they make. These forms can be simple lists of types of calls where the communicators make a mark for each call or dialing and put a horizontal line through each set of four lines for each fifth occurrence. We've all used this kind of counting approach at some time.

There is nothing wrong with this approach and it can be very effective. The bigger issue is defining the types of calls and dialings and making it clear to the communicators where to count each occurrence. If you have implemented a unit record and scheduling system, the definition of various calls and dialings is much easier to establish and measure.

Another approach is to design a tally form that makes it easier for the communicators to keep track of their calling and dialing activity and that works in conjunction with the unit record and scheduling system.

The tally form (Illustration 9-12) is used to track each dialing and its result. A separate tally is kept for each program each day. The results of the individual tally reports are consolidated by phone center management to evaluate the overall results of all the telephone selling programs.

The form is divided into several clearly marked sections. The sections with numbered boxes are used to record each dialing. As the dialing is made, the communicator will put a diagonal line through the next number in the appropriate result box. This method will automatically give the total number of dialings and results in any particular area. Note that the numbers start with zero, therefore the next number not crossed off represents the total number of dialings performed.

The tally form should be updated after each dialing just prior to moving the record to the appropriate file of the scheduling system. Each communicator should only update one call on the tally per dialing attempt.

The date of the telemarketing activity and the start and finish times are also provided by the communicator. The communicator will also calculate the total hours used for telemarketing based on the

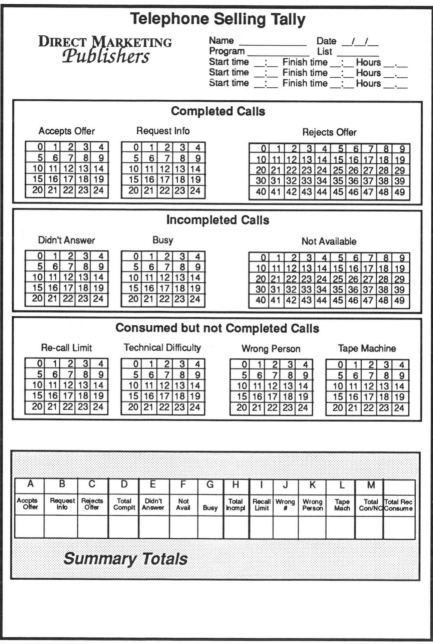

Illustration 9-12: An example of a daily tally form.

elapsed time in the heading of the form. The hours reported should be rounded to the nearest quarter of an hour.

If the communicator starts and stops multiple times during the day, the start and finish time for each session should be recorded on the tally. The communicator should calculate the total hours of calling for the day.

There will be a separate form for each type of telephone selling and for each different list source used. By tracking results by type of telephone selling, you can evaluate the success and performance of the different types of calling. The communicator will identify the source list from which the record came in the heading of the form. Only one type of program results will be recorded per form.

Outbound Telemarketing Results

Every direct marketing and telemarketing program is different and it is dangerous to apply hard and fast rules to all programs. However, I will try to give you some guidelines to help you do a reasonable job in estimating results. I have found that after about 100 hours of business-to-business telemarketing with a list and script, the results will not deviate substantially (more than 10%) for the balance of the program. This assumes that the list, script, and offer remain the same. Consumer calling results also will level off, but after about 250 hours of calling.

If the list is sent to a computer service bureau, normally about 50% of the list will have phone numbers added. This can vary depending on the quality, age, and techniques used to compile the list. You can establish additional phone numbers (about 15%) by sending the remaining unmatched names to a manual telephone look-up service. This tends to be more expensive and take substantially longer. Evaluate the complete information you require on your list prior to sending it to the service bureau. It is possible to have S.I.C. and other sizing information added to your list at the same time as the phone number.

Now that you have the list ready for telemarketing, what kind of results can be expected? My experience says -- it depends. Not a comfortable answer but a truthful one. When you're calling different industry groups or different sized companies the results will vary greatly. It is often difficult to get a doctor on the phone, but fairly easy to reach office managers and purchasing agents. The single biggest factor in altering the calling results will be whether the list is name-directed or not. If you don't have the contact's name, then you must make multiple calls to the same company to first establish the contact, and then to make your presentation.

Long scripts with lots of market research questions can also alter the results significantly. The more questions and the more prospects or customers have to think about their answers, the longer the call will take.

The number of phone attempts made to a particular name on the list can also affect the results. I suggest that the average business-to-business contact be attempted six to eight times and then considered not reachable.

With six attempts, the 65% of the records on the average list will be contacted. In addition, assuming cross industry calling, about 20% of dialings will result in a contact during the first three attempts, 15% will result in a contact in the next two attempts and then 10% or less will result in a contact after six attempts. About 10% to 15% of the list will not be contactable because of wrong number and out of business situations. These will normally be found during the first dialing attempt. Let's examine 1,000 records and identify what happens on six attempts.

1000	Records to start
15%	Not contactable due to wrong numbers and out of business
150	Records not contactable
850	Records contactable
20%	Contacted on 1st attempt
200	Records contacted on 1st attempt
650	Records remaining to contact (200 contacted + 150 not contactable)
20%	Contacted on 2nd attempt
130	Records contacted on 2nd attempt
520	Records remaining to contact
20%	Contacted on 3rd attempt
104	Records contacted on 3rd attempt
416	Records remaining to contact
15%	Contacted on 4th attempt
62	Records contacted on 4th attempt
354	Records remaining to contact
15%	Records contacted on 5th attempt
53	Records contacted on 5th attempt
301	Records remaining to contact
15%	Records contacted on 6th attempt
45	Records contacted on 6th attempt
256	Records remaining to contact and will be treated as not contactable.

As you can see, we will contact 599 records of the original 1,000 or about 60% of the records we started with. Eight attempts will bring the total to about 65%. It gets very expensive to contact records as more attempts are made. A certain percentage of the records will never be reached and they will make up a larger portion of the remaining records after each attempt. You must evaluate the number of attempts you'll make and the results you anticipate.

The dialings and contacts per hour will vary depending on each program. Business-to-business programs average about 20 to 30 dialings per hour and about 20% to 30% as completed contacts. Therefore the average business program will result in about 5 to 8 completed calls per hour. A good planning number for most business programs is about 7 to 7.5 completed calls per hour. If your list is not name-directed, you will lose about 1 completed call per hour.

When executing lead generation programs, I have found for every person that accepts an offer to see a salesperson, about the same number of people request additional information. This group of literature requesters, when followed up with a phone call after the information was sent, converted into a lead about 25% of the time. This seemed to occur in almost every lead program I executed using phone follow-up to the literature requests.

When planning a follow-up call, within 90 days of an earlier phone contact, you can expect to contact 90% of the list in four to six attempts. This is true when the list is name-directed, and you have established a correct phone number and a prior relationship of some sort with the prospect. In fact, you can use this prior relationship as a method to overcome "Bertha Barrier." You can start your call by telling Bertha that you're calling about some information that Mr. Contact requested.

Your response rates will vary significantly based on your offer and script. As you establish your business plan, the required response rates will be established to determine whether your program is successful.

The Telemarketing Plan

Like any other direct marketing program, outbound telemarketing has to have a detailed plan prepared prior to the start of the program. After you develop the business background and the strategy for your direct marketing program, you should review the use of telemarketing. If outbound telemarketing is an appropriate tactic, then you'll have to develop a detailed flowchart and business plan for the use of outbound telemarketing.

As you'll note from Illustration 9-13, the flow chart will start with the tape of records that are being used for the direct marketing effort. We assume the tape was deduplicated against the existing customer file and within itself to ensure that there are no duplicate records.

Frequently, you'll acquire lists that contain several names of people within the same company. Although these can be correct and appropriate names, you may find that all of the records must go through the same switchboard. I have experienced that when you call the same switchboard with a production telemarketing approach, you may overwhelm the attendant. After a number of calls, the attendant may be reluctant to switch the call to the appropriate person. If your list contains duplicate phone numbers, evaluate mixing the records throughout the calling period, or only selecting one record to contact.

Now that you've established the list that you'll use for telemarketing, you may want to eliminate the respondents from direct mail prior to starting the telemarketing. As I mentioned earlier, the number of respondents will be a very small part of the total list. You should evaluate the cost of eliminating the respondents and the additional time it will take before you can start telemarketing.

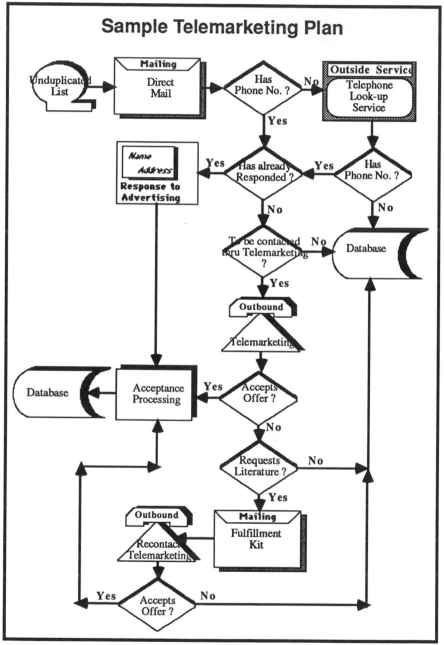

Illustration 9-13: A Sample Telemarketing Flowchart.

As the telephone calls are made, you will determine if the prospect accepts your offer. Acceptances will be processed similarly to other acceptances from direct mail and inbound telephone. The telephone program will generate another group of prospects who will request additional information. This is because outbound telemarketing forces prospects to make an immediate decision.

Don't lose those prospects who request additional information. Although most are asking for information simply to get off the phone, about 25% can be converted into a lead or an order if they are recontacted after the material is sent. You should test this concept with your product in order to determine the number of prospects that can be converted to an order or lead.

This sample flow chart, as illustrated in 9-13, is a simplified approach to a telemarketing program. However, it introduces some interesting concepts in using telemarketing and will give us a practical example to develop a business plan and measurement plan.

The Sample Telemarketing Business Plan

Product Information

Total Revenue per Acceptance	$750.00
% Allowable Expense per Order	10.00%
Allowable Cost per Order	$75.00

Total Records in Test	2,000

List Costs

Direct Mail @ $85 per 1000	$85.00
Telemarketing @ $85 per 1000	$85.00
Total List Costs	$170.00

Direct Mail Costs

Cost per 1000 Pieces of Mail	$750.00	$1,500.00

Phone Number Look-up

% of Records that Find Number	50%	1,000
Cost per Record for Look-up	$0.15	$150.00

Telemarketing Costs

Total Telemarketing Hours	92.3
Cost per Telemarketing Hour	$38.00
Total Telemarketing Costs	$3,507.00

Direct Mail Results

Total Direct Mail Costs	$1,585.00
Total Acceptances Required	21
Required Acceptance Rate	1.10%

Telemarketing Results

% of Total Records Contactable	65.00%
Total Records Contactable	650
Dialings per Hour	25
% of Dialings that Are Contacted	30.00%
Contacts per hour	7.5
Total Initial Call Telemarketing Hours	86.7
Total Telemarketing Costs	$3,530.00
Total Acceptances Required	47.07
Required Acceptance Rate	7.20%
Required Acceptances per Hour	0.54
Planned Request Literature Rate	7.20%
Literature Requests per Hour	0.54
Total Hours	86.7

Total Acceptances	47
Total Literature Requests	47

Send Literature Follow-up Call

% of List Contactable	90.00%
Total List Contactable	42
Contacts per Hour	7.5
Total Hours	5.6
Follow-up Telemarketing Costs	$212.80
Literature Request Fulfillment Costs	$70.50
Total Literature Request Costs	$283.30
Required Acceptances	3.8
Required % of Follow-up Calls that Accept	8.1%

Total Direct Marketing Costs

Direct Mail	$1,585.00
Initial Telemarketing	$3,530.00
Request Lit Fulfillment @ $1.50 each	$70.50
Request Literature Telemktg Follow-up	$213.00
Total Direct Marketing Costs	**$5,398.50**

Acceptances

Direct Mail	21
Initial Telemarketing	47
Request Lit Fulfillment @ $1.50 each	4
Total Acceptances	**72**

Required Response Rate of 2000 Records	**3.6%**
Cost per Acceptance	**$74.98**

Like most business plans or proformas, the revenue and expense that will be allowed for direct marketing needs to be established. In this example, the average order is $750 and the allowable sales expense is 10% or $75 per order.

For the telemarketing test, I will acquire a list of 2,000 records. This list will be sent to a service bureau for phone number look-up and I anticipate that 50% of the original names will be returned with phone numbers. The list is being rented for two contacts, a mail and a phone contact. Therefore, I will have to pay the list owner for using his list two times. The cost for the list is $85 per 1,000 records, therefore my total list costs are $170. Many list owners have minimum charges and small quantities may not meet the minimum charge requirement. You will have to discuss your unique list requirements with your list vendor.

The cost of direct mail is completely variable and will depend on the quantity of material printed, quality, the type of postage and a number of variables that can only be established as you develop your own requirements. Obviously, the more expensive the mailing piece, the higher the results have to be to cover the additional expense. For our example I used $750 per 1,000 pieces mailed as our direct mail costs. I am planning to mail all 2,000 names on the list, even though I will not be able to call all of the names. The mail costs are $1,500. I assumed that the fulfillment kit for people requesting additional information would be more expensive and estimated them at $1.50 per package.

The phone number look-up service will only charge you for those records that match and for which they can provide a telephone number. The telephone look-up services also have minimum charges. The price per phone number look-up record will vary depending on the quantity and turn-around time you require. The smaller the quantity of records sent to the service, the higher the cost per look-up. For the small quantities I used for this test, I estimated the look-up charges at $.15 per record. This probably will not meet the minimum charges at most service bureaus. I estimated, in my example, that only 50% of the records would be found during the phone number search. Therefore, the total expenses are $150.

The cost per telemarketing hour will vary significantly for each company. You can purchase a telemarketing service bureau calling hour for between $35.00 and $60.00 depending on volume and the level of support you require. I have used $38.00 as the cost per hour in my example. As an aside, I have rarely seen the average business conduct in-house outbound telemarketing at $38.00 per hour if all of the costs are reviewed. You should find the telemarketing cost worksheet discussed earlier very helpful in establishing your cost per hour. As you'll see, the total hours required to make the initial calls and perform follow-up calling to the literature requesters amounts to 92.3 hours at $38.00 per hour for a total telemarketing cost of $3,507.00

People use many techniques to estimate the results they expect from direct marketing programs. Most of the time the expectations are unreasonable or are just guesses as to what people would like to have happen. As the first step in my business plan, I established the revenue per order and the allowable sales expense per order. With these "tools" you can establish the required response rate to have a successful program. By establishing required response rates for each step of your program, you'll be able to measure results as the program is being executed.

If you take the mail and list expenses and divide them by the allowable cost per order, you'll establish the number of orders required for the program to be successful. The total required orders divided by the quantity mailed will give you the required acceptance rate.

Establishing telemarketing results is probably a new experience for you. Remember, I only anticipated that 50% of the records would come back from the service bureau with a phone number. Therefore I'll only be starting with 1000 records for telemarketing. As you may recall, the number of attempts you plan to make to each record, the composition of the list, and the length of the script can all significantly affect the results you'll experience in telemarketing.

For this business plan I have assumed 8 attempts per record, and anticipate 25 dialings per hour with 30% of the dialings concluding with a completed call. I have assumed that 65% of the records are contactable. This means that I will complete 7.5 calls per hour of calling. This is arrived at by multiplying the initial number of records on the telemarketing list by 65%. In this case I started with 1000 records in telemarketing and 65% of this list equals 650 records. I then divided the 650 records by 7.5 completed calls per hour and arrived at 86.7 hours required for the initial calls to the prospects.

Now that I have established the number of calling hours, the costs for telemarketing are derived by multiplying the hours by the cost per hour. In my example, 86.7 hours x $38.00 per hour = $3,530.00. As you know I have allowed $75.00 per order in sales expense. I divide the total costs by the allowable sales expense per order and establish the number of orders required in order for this program to be successful. It will take 47.07 orders to have a successful program.

Establishing the required response rates seems pretty easy at first. However, how many records did I really start with? If you assume the 2,000 records that were on the original list I acquired, the required response rate is 2.35% (47.07 ÷ 2,000). The percentage of the 1,000 records available to telemarketing is 4.7% (47.07 ÷ 1,000). The percentage of the 650 records able to be contacted is 7.2% (47.07 ÷ 650).

I suggest you do your planning using both the records available to telemarketing and the records that are contactable. The original list that included names without phone numbers doesn't help measure the program. My plan reflects the percentage of completed calls. This allows me to focus on the per hour results and measure the program while it is in progress.

I established the acceptance rate per hour by dividing the number of acceptances required by the number of hours. In my example this was .54 acceptances per hour (47.07 ÷ 86.7).

I have assumed that for each acceptance I will also generate another person who will request additional information. Therefore, I will have .54 literature requesters per hour in addition to the .54 acceptances of my offer. Literature requesters are important because I plan to fulfill their requests with information and then make an additional phone call to follow-up and attempt to convert them into a lead. It will cost $70.50 to mail fulfillment kits to the literature requesters (47 x $1.50 fulfillment kit expense).

The additional phone call will be made 10 to 15 days after the mail is sent. I have planned a 90% contact of these prospects at the same rate of 7.5 completed calls per hour. Therefore I anticipate 5.6 hours of telemarketing (47 x 90% = 42.3 completed calls) (42.3 ÷ 7.5 = 5.6 hours). The total cost for the literature fulfillment and follow-up calling is $283.30 ($70.50 mail costs + $212.80 phone costs). For this part of the program to be successful, I need 3.8 acceptances ($283.30 ÷ $75.00 allowable sales expense). This is a required response rate of 8.1%. I could have actually planned this segment of the program at a 25% response rate based on my prior experiences. Either approach would be acceptable; if you have no prior experience, the 8.1% planning number is more conservative.

The total direct marketing costs are now easy to establish. I summarize the total direct mail, initial telemarketing, literature request fulfillment, and literature request follow-up telemarketing to establish the total direct marketing costs.

The total acceptances are also summarized. The total costs are then divided by the total acceptances to establish the cost per acceptance for the program. If I had used the required 3.8 acceptances for the follow-up calling, I would have only had 72 acceptances for the project. This means that I need a total response rate of 3.6% of the initial 2,000 records. It may seem contradictory to go back to the 2,000 original records, but this allows you to examine the entire program. I have included all of the costs and if this program performs as planned, I will have a successful direct marketing program.

Mail and Phone Synergy

Mail and phone together can create powerful results. Like any other direct marketing program, the results will depend on your approach, product, and list. I had an opportunity to actually see and measure a program that proved how effective the two media can be together because it allowed us to breakthrough and reach our target contact.

Trillion was a small software company that sold an innovative product to personal computer users. The product established a common interface to several of the most popular software products operating on the PC. The company was in deep financial trouble and looking for a way to contact the major users of PCs in larger businesses.

A direct marketing program was designed to use direct mail and follow-up with a telemarketing call. The telephone call was to follow the mail by 10 days to maximize the synergy of the mail and phone. A special offer was created which allowed the prospect to receive 5 copies of the software product for 30 days absolutely free. At the end of the 30 day trial, the prospect could keep all the copies and pay our invoice, which was substantially discounted, or return the software and owe nothing. In addition, the prospect could keep one copy of the software as an incentive for trying the product.

We acquired a list of 2,000 known large users of PC's. These were mostly larger companies and all had at least 50 PC's in use in their business. Our contact was the PC coordinator or the director of data processing. The list was name-directed and fairly current -- no older than one year.

A mail-gram format was used to make the offer and explain the product to the prospect prior to any telemarketing contact. A response vehicle was included to allow the prospect to accept the offer in the mail. The free trial and free copy premium were high-lighted in bold headlines in the mail-gram format. In addition a small brochure was included to give some limited details about the product. The response in the mail was under 1%.

The phone program started 10 days after the mail was dropped. The telemarketing service bureau actually performed the mail creation, production, and letter-shop services, so we were able to ensure the proper timing of the phone behind the mail.

The results were not very gratifying. The phone produced at about 4% of completed calls and the results were not considered successful. We began to examine the phone results and found that the prospect did not recall our mailing and could not understand the benefit in trying the Trillion product. Our problem was breaking through to the decision makers and making them understand the offer. As I mentioned earlier, it is almost impossible to sell a new concept over the phone. The prospect has to have an understanding of the product for the phone effort to be successful.

We decided to send the prospect a premium that we thought would help our total effort. An inexpensive tee-shirt was designed and cre-ated that said "Be a Trillionaire." We again included a personalized computer generated letter and mailed the tee-shirt, first class to the prospect. Our offer remained the same. There was almost a 30-day delay in the program while the shirts were developed. Due to timing problems, we only offered inbound phone as the response vehicle in this mailing. The outbound telemarketing program remained virtually the same.

The combined mail and phone results on this second approach were over 45%. Almost all the executives we talked to recalled our mailing and were very interested in trying the product.

This program clearly demonstrates the powerful effect of mail and phone. It also proves that we can only get through to our targeted contacts if we create an appropriate mail and phone approach. The data processing executive is overwhelmed by mail from many sources. For your program to succeed in this environment, the offer will have to "break through" the clutter on their desk. We found that a premium (amusing and personalized) could be very effective. The mail and phone combined approach allowed the prospect to have a prior understanding of the product and accept the offer with less reluctance and fear. We had informed the prospect in the second mailing that we intended to call and ask for their acceptance of our offer.

Telephone Selling Summarized

In this chapter, we established a definition of telemarketing that clearly distinguishes telesales from telemarketing. If you are using telesales there are some elements of direct marketing that can significantly improve your results. The database and timely follow-up of information requests can substantially assist the salesperson who is selling on the telephone. However, telesales costs and results are very difficult to measure.

Telemarketing removes dependency on any individual's personality for results in the marketing program. It uses a script and both its costs and results are controllable. Let's again look at the definition of telemarketing I established earlier.

Telemarketing is performing direct marketing over the telephone. Communicators follow a script to deliver a direct marketing message to a specific group of prospects.

- *It is controllable, measurable, and does not depend on the sales ability of the individual communicator to be successful.*
- *It can be used to support direct mail or advertising, or as a stand-alone campaign.*
- *It is a planned series of contacts, using a constant message, seeking to produce a lead or an order.*
- *It yields information to build and maintain a database and is completely measurable in its costs and results.*
- *It can be outbound or inbound telephone calling.*
- *It can be used to market to consumers or to other businesses.*

You will have to evaluate both your inbound and outbound requirements for the effective use of telemarketing. If you're using inbound, make sure that the communicator staff is aware of your advertising and direct mail plan. In addition, plan your efforts to deal with respondents who may call your phone number during your non-business hours.

As you evaluate your inbound requirements, examine your costs to provide the service yourself and then price outside vendors. You may find that an outside service is more economical and efficient.

Outbound telemarketing is a strong promotional format but is dependent on the offer you make. You really can't sell anything new during an outbound call and, after list selection, the strength of the promotion will be your offer. Remember, you will only have about

30 seconds to convince your prospect to listen to the rest of your proposition. Good script writing includes making a compelling offer very early in the phone call.

We examined a number of script approaches including outlines and flip cards. A complete example of a flip card script is available in Chapter 2. Evaluate and decide on the best script approach for your program.

I also explained how to manage the process of telephone selling in a telesales environment. The key to measuring and managing telephone selling is controlling the records and their ultimate disposition.

Illustration 9-14, from *How to Manage and Execute Telephone Selling,* identifies typical productivity expectations in various types of telemarketing. This table can be very helpful in planning telephone selling programs.

Like any direct marketing program, outbound telemarketing is controllable and measurable. You can plan and evaluate your results in a fairly short period of time. The key to measurement is the plan you develop prior to the telemarketing program.

Mail and phone are the ideal combined direct marketing program. In fact, once you commit to telemarketing you will need direct mail to answer requests for additional information. The combination of the two formats typically produces greater results than the sum of each format run independently.

Telemarketing is a powerful weapon in your marketing arsenal. It is one of the fastest growing promotional formats being used by business today. If you haven't tried telemarketing, you're missing a tremendous opportunity.

Telephone Selling Productivity

Type of Calling	Records Dialings /Hour	Consumed /Hour	Completed % Dials Completed	Calls /Hour
Inbound	12-18	12-18	90%	10-16
Outbound Telemarketing				
Consumer	25-35	15-18	40-60%	10-15
Business-to-Business	20-30	8-12	25-35%	5-10
Outbound Telesales-Unmanaged	3-5	2-3	30-40%	1-2
Outbound Telesales-Managed	12-18	5-8	25-35%	4-7

Illustration 9-14: Typical telephone selling productivity from *How to Manage and Execute Telephone Selling*.

Chapter Ten:
Seminar Selling

Direct mail and telephone are the two most popular methods for generating sales leads. The vehicles most frequently used after these are seminars and trade shows. Both of these approaches capitalize on dealing with a group of prospects who have demonstrated an interest in a specific subject. Unlike phone and direct mail lead generation, you can be fairly certain seminar attendees will be interested in your product or service, and they come to you!

In this chapter I will review selling and lead generation through seminars. In Chapter 11, I will discuss trade shows.

Why use Seminar Selling?

The cost of selling products and services has continued to increase unabated. As mentioned in Chapter 1, the cost of making a face-to-face sales call has increased almost 300% in the last ten years. As indicated in Illustration 10-1, the average industrial face-to-face

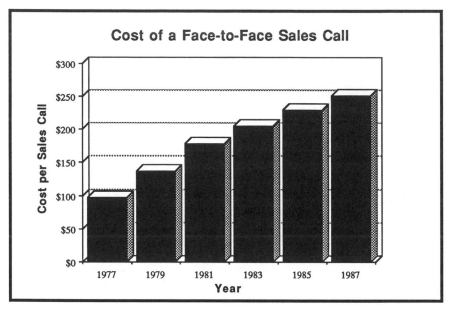

Illustration 10-1: The cost of a face-to-face sales call according to the McGraw Hill Laboratory for Advertising Performance.

sales call costed $96.79 in 1977 and is estimated to cost over $300 in 1991.

This ever increasing cost has caused the business executive to examine alternative methods of delivering their sales message while still maintaining the personal contact afforded by the face-to-face sales call. Seminars present an opportunity to make a face-to-face contact at a significantly reduced cost.

Seminars offer you an opportunity to deliver your sales message to a large group of interested prospects, and capitalize on the group dynamics to increase that interest in your product or service. At seminars, you can create a high quality sales pitch, and be sure that it is delivered consistently to all prospects who attend. You, as managers, can directly control and influence the expectations of your prospects.

Seminars offer strong benefits.

- The use of seminars can be a very subtle way to deliver a powerful sales message. You can conduct seminars about important subjects and just by being the sponsor you will sell your company and products.

- The seminar will allow you to deliver important information in an environment that is totally conducive to your company and product. You can control the environment.

- It may not be necessary to use high power sales techniques because the message delivered by the seminar could be powerful enough to convince prospects and customers to buy. Customer testimonials and demonstrations alone can convince a prospect to buy from you.

- During the seminar presentations you can emphasize the features and benefits of your product offering in a light that will allow you to create uniqueness.

- Within a seminar you not only reinforce your good standing with existing clients and expand into new markets, you also establish yourself as the authority and experienced supplier of solutions to business problems.

- By running a successful seminar, attendees perceive you as a leader, decision-maker and "best contact" on the subjects you present.

While seminars are neither easy or inexpensive to run, they are being more widely used because they are a lot like one-on-one selling. Seminars are much less expensive on a per call or per contact basis than face-to-face sales calls.

A seminar is a selling tool. Your goal is to sell more products and services to your current customers and to add new customers. To accomplish this mission, you are bringing together a small, highly qualified group of selected business people you want as customers. They will come to your seminar because you have correctly identified business problems that are important to them, and you are offering them solutions to those problems.

In other words, you are establishing yourself as an authority, a professional who is knowledgeable and experienced in solving business problems. You control the message, discussions, and the outcome of the seminar, proving just how well you can help them. You are committed to complete success in your seminar because you have aimed high and attracted the very people who can *buy* your solutions, possibly on the spot.

To attract this level person and succeed in your objective, you will have to make an investment. You should expect to spend over $100 per person to make your seminar effective and impressive. You could spend considerably more to promote and attract the proper person to your seminar. In return, you get your prospect's undivided attention for a remarkable length of time, and benefit from the group's spontaneous enthusiasm, interest, and immediately reinforced confidence in you.

Seminars are an interesting and exciting approach to improving sales productivity. Every business that uses this method of selling has established their own formula and definition for a successful program. I will explain some common concepts in developing and implementing seminar programs.

Seminars as a Lead Generation Vehicle

For many years the only direct marketing offers businesses seemed to make were for additional information or to have a salesperson contact the prospect. The high technology, and particularly the computer industry, have introduced another popular offer in the last few years -- attend a seminar.

Seminars continue to grow in popularity and can be excellent opportunities to sell products and services. Unfortunately, the seminar frequently turns into an education session with few orders ever being closed. Many times, management gets a warm fuzzy feeling because of high attendance and loses sight of the ultimate objective which is to generate orders.

To use seminars to generate leads and ultimately orders, treat them like any other lead generation program. Establish specific sales

Illustration 10-2: The misconception about successful seminars.

objectives. Use your seminar costs and selling expenses to establish your cost per order.

As you evaluate seminar costs, make sure you include all of the associated expenses. Often, companies will only include the actual expenses associated with the seminar. The costs associated with generating traffic and lead follow-up to the attendees are ignored.

For example, estimate the time and effort required to plan and prepare for the seminar. Include items such as designing, creating, and mailing invitations; follow-up phone calls to remind prospects to attend; and development and coordination of seminar hand-outs. These are all seminar costs and should be counted separately even if they are performed by people whose time is accounted for in other budgets. When they are performing seminar-related tasks, they are not performing their other duties. Not counting their time in the cost of the seminar will give you inaccurate costs-per-lead and costs-per-order.

The cost-per-lead and cost-per-order are often significantly higher than many companies understand. Consider this example. A company runs an advertisement in a local newspaper promoting the seminar to the local market. The ad costs $1,000.

In addition, a direct mail campaign is executed to about 1,000 businesses in the local market. An invitation-type format is used. To buy the list, and design, produce, and mail the invitations, it costs $1,500.

Finally, to ensure the best turnout, management requires the sales force to personally contact their best prospects. This is the most difficult expense to identify, but each telephone call costs about $50. This may sound high but my experience is that the average salesperson will only make about 1-1/2 completed calls per hour of telephone with the average cost being about $75 per hour. If there are

10 salespeople and each makes 5 calls, the cost for this activity is about $2,500.

The seminar announcement campaign is successful and 30 people agree to attend. Only 20 actually show up at the seminar. This is not unusual because of those who agree to attend a typical seminar, about 30% to 50% will not show up.

The company is uncertain about the actual number of closes from the seminar but estimates that 20% of the attendees will order. Each attendee is considered a lead and therefore turned over to the sales force for follow-up.

Each attendee has associated costs for refreshments, name tags, registration. You may also have expenses for off-site seminars like hotel rooms or catering services. In addition, you must also pay the people who actually conduct the seminar. For our example, we'll assume a seminar cost of $1,000. The actual costs of the seminar are:

Traffic building costs	$5,000
Seminar costs	$1,000
Total costs	$6,000

The cost per attendee is $300 and the cost per order, assuming 20% close, is $1,500. Even with fairly high priced capital equipment, this is an expensive order. And these costs don't include any selling activity after the seminar to convert the attendees to customers.

What is really surprising is how many businesses will make this significant investment without planning a program to ensure the highest possible return. The attendees are turned over to the salespeople for follow-up attention. There is no planned process to ensure follow-up. In most cases only about 30% of the attendees are ever contacted. And the prospects who agreed to attend the seminar but didn't show-up are almost always ignored.

Many seminar planners seem to forget their original mission which is to sell products. The seminars focus on education and the sponsoring company often is reluctant to sell. Don't be afraid to tell your audience pricing, terms, and purchasing alternatives during the seminar. Ask for an order; the attendees expect it.

A planned follow-up program should be developed to contact any prospect who was interested in the seminar. This follow-up program should not not rely on the sales force but be a process that automatically services each of the prospects. Direct mail and telephone are excellent vehicles to implement this kind of process.

Try sending each attendee a follow-up letter which summarizes the benefits identified during the seminar. Make the prospect an offer that encourages them to contact you. Offers that will help the customer move closer to ordering are best.

Make sure you identify how much your solution will cost and encourage the prospect to make a step towards ordering. I've effectively used special kits that further demonstrate the benefits of the product. Another powerful offer is a special purchase plan that will allow the prospect to acquire the product and reduce their risk.

A follow-up phone call can also be extremely effective. Call the prospect 10 to 30 days after the seminar and determine if they got the information they expected at the seminar. You can also find out if the prospect has been contacted by a salesperson.

You will generate additional sales leads and ultimately additional orders if you ensure complete follow-up. In addition, you may win a champion in the future if you leave a good impression with everyone who was interested in the seminar.

Types of Seminars

Once you have identified the appropriate target you're trying to reach, you're faced with some fundamental decisions on the type of seminar you want to conduct. Should you charge for the seminar or offer it for free? Should the audience include customers and prospects? Only customers? Only prospects? What is the ultimate objective of the seminar? Are you going to offer the audience an itinerary selection or is the agenda fixed? Will you use customer or guest speakers? Are you planning to make presentations to large groups or do you want to conduct a small group workshop?

To answer these questions, first you must know why you are conducting the seminar. One primary goal is probably to reduce costs and improve sales productivity. Therefore, the objective of your seminar will be to ultimately sell additional products or services.

If you are the recognized leader in an industry or marketplace you may decide to conduct seminars as a source of revenue. If so you need to determine how much you will charge attendees. Many fee seminars are primarily detailed presentations on how to do something. If you charge an admission fee, make the portion of your seminar designed to increase sales subtle, or you risk irritating your attendees. Prospects and customers who agree to attend a fee seminar expect to gain important information and perceive that your business is qualified to teach on the subject. They are not paying to receive high-pressure sales presentations.

Many business people are constantly seeking additional insight on how to solve their current business problems. Seminars offer them a non-threatening environment to obtain information and keep abreast of the most current business solutions.

Attendees who pay to go to a seminar are making a considerable investment in their education. They not only pay the admission fee, but travel expenses, and the cost of leaving their jobs to attend the seminar. They often expect to gain information at the seminar that they need, that is unique, and that they can't get somewhere else. For example, seminars which teach software applications are often attended because the software owners are uncomfortable with the manual. They look to the seminar to get them started. Knowing these expectations, you owe it to your audience to give them meaningful, practical information that they can apply to their business problems. If you are unable to do that, don't charge an admission fee.

There is a way, however, to sell your product or service at a seminar for which you are charging an admission fee. You simply have to be subtle. When you design the seminar, focus on the expectations of your audience, and then consider how you can use your products or services to demonstrate or present that information. Stress the features and benefits of your products as you use them; don't knock your competition.

Even companies that present seminars as a business offering are using the seminar as a selling platform. They are either trying to sell additional educational offerings or productivity tools that are directly related to the seminar program.

Free seminars are designed to impart information to a group about a particular product or service. Most attendees expect you to sell them. The audience is normally aware that you are using the seminar to reduce selling costs and improve sales productivity. They may have even used the technique themselves to sell their products or services.

Free seminar attendees still incur some expenses: the time they would otherwise have spent at their job, travel, lodging, and food.

Therefore, even though they expect to be sold, they must receive more than just a sales presentation, or they may not think it was worth their time.

Seminars are an increasingly popular sales tool; your competition may even be using them. Many companies hurt rather than help their sales by not planning their seminars or thinking through the content. Don't make that mistake. If you don't have the time and money to present a professional, valuable seminar, don't use seminars as a sales or lead generation tool.

As you establish the seminar content, type, and concept make sure you constantly think of your audience and the need your seminar is trying to fulfill. The participant should walk away from the seminar with something tangible and important. If you plan to use a free seminar, promote the advantage and benefit that the attendee will derive from participating.

The most important decision you will have to make concerning your seminar will be deciding who you want to attend. Once you decide who will be in your audience, you can begin crafting your message. Groups of attendees you may want to consider when choosing an audience include: customers, prospects, and the general public. You also need to identify the experience level of your potential attendees. If managers will be attending, what level of management will they represent?

Customer seminars have attendees who are familiar with you and your products or services. This group of people has established a relationship with you and frequently is trying to learn how to improve their use of your products in their business. In many cases you may be dealing with two different levels within your customer accounts, the user and the decision-maker.

The user is normally familiar with the products and how they operate within the company. They are trying to learn short-cuts and ways to improve the use of the products. Frequently they would like to expand the use so as to increase their relative importance to the company. Seminars aimed at this group of people should be detailed and discuss how to use and operate the products.

On the other hand, the decision maker is frequently more interested in the return on investment that the product has produced for the business. They may not be concerned about the details of how the products work but quite interested in how the product can help improve the business. Decision makers like to associate with people at their same level or higher. They would prefer to discuss higher level problems with peers in other companies.

If you're using the seminar to promote new business and establish new customers, the type of seminar may change substantially. Basically, whether the seminar is free or for a fee, there are three types of seminars:

   1) Vertical Seminar - This seminar is aimed at a specific group of customers or prospects. The group has a common industry or application.   For example, a seminar that deals with third party patient billing would be appropriate for the medical industry.

   2) Horizontal Seminar - This seminar presents information that crosses multiple industries. The attendees will come from many types of businesses and will have a common problem. For example, a seminar on payroll processing might attract managers from all kinds of businesses.

   3) Institute Seminar - This is a new and growing seminar type where the attendee is given a choice of sessions to attend. The program can contain both vertical and horizontal infor-

mation. The program may have agendas for managers/decision makers and a separate agenda for the users. Another variation may have special vertical sessions for specific industries and other sessions that offer information on horizontal areas of interest. The key is that the attendee can choose the appropriate session to attend.

Remember, your audience will determine the type of seminar that you will need. It is a good idea to investigate other seminar offerings in your industry to determine the types of programs that are already being offered to your audience.

In the recent past many larger companies have combined seminars with private trade shows to create an event. This concept typically targets both customers and prospects and uses an institute format. In addition to seminars, the attendee can participate in a trade-show type display area and actually observe products being demonstrated. This type of program is an ideal vehicle for the sponsoring company to announce new products and services. This type of program is being heavily used by the high technology companies such as IBM, Digital Equipment Corporation and Apple Computer.

Large, small and medium size companies are all creating trade show/seminar events for their customers and prospects. The advantages are clear in that the costs are reduced because you can spread fixed expenses for the event and promotion across a larger audience.

Tutorial versus Interactive Seminars

As you determine the type of seminar you will offer, you should also consider the method you will use to convey information. The more involved you get the audience, the better the seminar will be received.

If you evaluate the success of a face-to-face selling situation, the key ingredient that makes this type of selling successful is the interaction between salesperson and prospect/customer. The better salesperson will learn how to probe the prospect and get them talking about their problems. By listening and observing the prospect, the salesperson can personalize the benefits of their products or services to address the needs of the prospect.

At the other end of the spectrum in delivering information to an audience are books and brochures. The information presented requires the reader to identify the solution to their problem. They can't question how the solution will be used in their business. They must rely on word pictures or diagrams to determine how the solution will fit into their business.

There are many methods to convey information that lie between the book and sales call. Seminars, for example allow you to combine the best of both worlds. However, presentations that do not encourage audience participation are difficult to follow and less likely to be remembered in the future. People only retain about 10% of what they hear, but as much as 80% of what they see and participate in. As you design your seminar consider the level of interaction you would like to achieve.

It is difficult to generate a high degree of personal involvement when speaking to a large audience. Smaller groups will allow you to make a group sales call as opposed to a tutorial presentation. Therefore the technique you plan to use to conduct your seminar may limit the size of your audience.

The best techniques used in seminars get the audience involved and participating with the speaker. Games and involvement devices are really effective and help to break the ice. The worst kind of presentation is a speech with no visuals or handouts. This is particularly true if the presenter is uncomfortable in front of the group and reads a script in a monotone voice.

Some material just doesn't lend itself well to interactive presentations. That really becomes a challenge for the seminar presenter. As you develop your material, ask yourself, What will I ask the audience to do here? What kind of questions can I ask the audience to keep them involved? What kind of picture can I use to make my point? What kind of analogy can I draw to help them remember what I am saying? You may want to start an idea file in which you keep pictures, cartoon, and stories you come across that relate to your product or service.

Regardless of the type of seminar you choose, having your attendee perform some task prior to attending can substantially improve their involvement in the session. For example, having a prospect investigate their current procedures in a certain area prior to attending the seminar can greatly enhance their understanding of their need for your solution.

You may want to have a mixture of tutorial and involvement sessions within your seminar to keep the seminar moving and provide a change of pace. Frequently I will see seminars where customer speakers will be featured to provide real-life examples of how a product or service has been used to solve a problem. Testimonials are very effective and can help improve credibility and attendance.

A word of caution about testimonials. Customers are engaged in operating their own businesses and solving their business problems. Most are not experienced speakers and will often present dry and boring presentations. Because they are your customers and quite frequently speaking as a favor, it is difficult to rehearse or critique their presentations. If you are considering using outside speakers keep their presentations short or design round-table formats where you question and they answer. This informal structure will make them more comfortable, give you some control of the presentation and allow you to create audience involvement.

I introduce the concept of tutorial and interactive presentations early in our discussions about seminars because your selection of the approach used can have a significant impact on the size and make-up of the audience you are targeting.

The Elements of Success

The key to success is planning. Every detail must be covered thoroughly and at the right time. Your program topic, agenda, and format must be on target for the audience you have recruited. Then you must execute your plan. That means getting the people there and treating them right once they are in your charge. They are entrusting their time to you, and like yourself, they expect their time to be well spent.

As the "person in charge," you have to keep your attention focused on these seven crucial elements.

1. Know your audience.

    Everything follows from this. Picture the people you have invited, their backgrounds, interests and goals. Ask yourself, What problems does my audience have that I can solve? Define your audience in terms of your business objectives, but understand who your audience is personally as well.

2. Plan your program.

    The program must fit the audience you have profiled exactly. The format, schedule, location, and time, as well as the facility you choose, must all fit the needs of the audience. When promoting your seminar, the title and agenda should strike a responsive chord in the target at first glance.

3. Execute the plan.

    There's an old saying, "Plan your work and work your plan." That's what's needed from now on. Keep deadlines, don't overlook details, don't worry about things later, do them now. Delegate responsibilities, but not control. Don't assume, ask questions constantly and communicate with everyone involved with you in making the seminar go well. Write things down.

4. Promote your program.

    Once you have announced your program, commit yourself to nothing less than unqualified success. Promote only those prospects you genuinely want to attend, and create a sense of urgency in them to attend. Make them think, I have to attend this seminar because I need to find out X. Promote X. Direct mail, telemarketing, telemarketing follow-up and good use of media through advertising and publicity will get the number there. Not only that, they will come prepared to be receptive to your message.

5. Plan for contingencies.

    You may appear to be organized and think everything will go smoothly, but reality is always out there ready to bring you back to earth. Remember, you are committed to success -- there is no such thing as over-planning. Have enough people to handle the unexpected, have back-up equipment, and develop a close working relationship with the facility's manager. Then you will be prepared for the unexpected and unwanted and if something does go wrong no one but you will even notice.

6. Prepare and stick to a realistic budget.

    An important planning tool is your budget. Running a seminar
    requires a substantial investment. You don't want to be extrava-
    gant, and you don't want to be wasteful. But don't skimp where
    it shows either.

7. Follow-through.

    Like the accurate swing in golf, the mark of the professional is
    follow-through. Once you have the good turn out and have run
    a smooth seminar you next have to cash in on the good will and
    impression you have made. You've got to do something with
    that hard-earned confidence and authority.

    Using mail and telephone, contact every attendee immediately
    and thank them for attending. Then follow-up your hottest leads
    with a prepared, personalized presentation. For those prospects
    that aren't quite ready, create a tickler file, and keep your con-
    tacts warm. Persistence pays off.

    Follow-through will turn your time, effort, and investment into
    sales.

I will expand on these critical elements throughout this chapter.
Your attention to the detail referenced in this list will help ensure
that your seminar is a success.

Planning the Seminar

Seminar planning is the process that combines your audience's
needs with your marketing objectives. The process results in a seminar that attracts the people you want, pleases the attendees, and produces sales for you.

There are five major points to focus on when you are responsible for a seminar:

1. Start with the audience.

    Whom do you want to attend this seminar? Presidents?
    General Managers? Purchasing Agents? Engineers? From
    what industry? From this set of questions everything fol-
    lows. You have to develop a complete profile of the person
    you want to attend this seminar: position, age, tastes, educa-
    tion level -- everything you can think of so that the audience
    will be clear and real in your mind.

2. Plan a theme.

    People will attend a seminar that addresses questions and
    problems they have to solve for their company's or their own
    personal success. What is a problem for one group, may be
    merely curiosity for another. It is important to understand
    who it is you want to attend and focus on a problem that
    relates to them.

    This makes your theme compelling. Then it is your job to
    assure that your theme implies practical solutions -- solu-
    tions that, with your help and/or products, they can use.

3. Choose a format.

    Just as form meets function, your seminar format should fit
    the theme, dramatize its importance, and enable you to fully
    present your solutions to the problems you have outlined.
    Illustration 10-3 shows some examples of formats and their
    comparative advantages and disadvantages.

Seminar Formats

Format	Description	Advantage	Disadvantage
Lecture	You and/or your prominent speaker make presentations.	Maintain control; highlights your expertise.	Could get monotonous. Pressure on speaker to be very good.
Panel	Customers, prospects, outside experts comment on problem/solution.	Well-known panelists can *draw*. Could get lively contrast of views.	Loss of control. Substitutions on panel could be fatal. Loss of focus possible.
Case Histories	Problems for which you have actually proposed or sold successful solutions are discussed. Top executives present testimony.	Realistic and convincing third party verification.	Obvious sales pitch. Loss of focus, difficult to keep on the main point and not drift into non-related areas or technical details.

Illustration 10-3: Seminar Formats.

4. Choose a title.

Be careful. It can't be cute, but it has to catch the prospect's attention. One approach is to state a problem in a way that implies your solution, e.g., "Using your Computer to ..."(name a problem or function that may be new, little used or understood). Another approach is to position the dilemma; e.g., "The Personal or Business Computer: Your Choice." Still another is the lure of the unknown (that, of course, is known to you); e.g., "The Automated Office: What's next?" or "Making Small Business More Productive."

5. Select a facility.

Again, have your audience in mind. Where are they coming from? Will they drive, so you'll need parking? Or, will they take public transportation, so the location will have to be accessible? Do you want to serve a meal? Does the facility provide audiovisual equipment in good repair?

Every area has a few hotels or large motels that provide meeting facilities. Check in your telephone directory under the appropriate listing for convention services and facilities. Go visit several. If any facility does not give you a complete tour, and answer all of your questions, cross them off your list. You can't afford to have your seminar receive bad reviews because the facility was unresponsive.

Take the list provided in the logistics section later in this chapter (Illustration 10-6 a and b) and check off what each facility has to offer.

Don't overlook your own facility if it meets all the criteria of your seminar.

As I have mentioned several times the most critical element in the success of your seminar is the selection of your audience. Before you select the audience it would be wise to establish the objectives and goals of the seminar program. Most seminars are designed to ultimately create orders and improve salesperson productivity.

If creating orders is one of your primary goals, you must create a budget to ensure that the investment you make in the seminar is justified by the number of orders the seminar produces.

In Chapter 4, I discussed planning budgets for lead generation programs. The information in that chapter also applies to planning budgets for seminars. Let's review a couple of key formulas from Chapter 4.

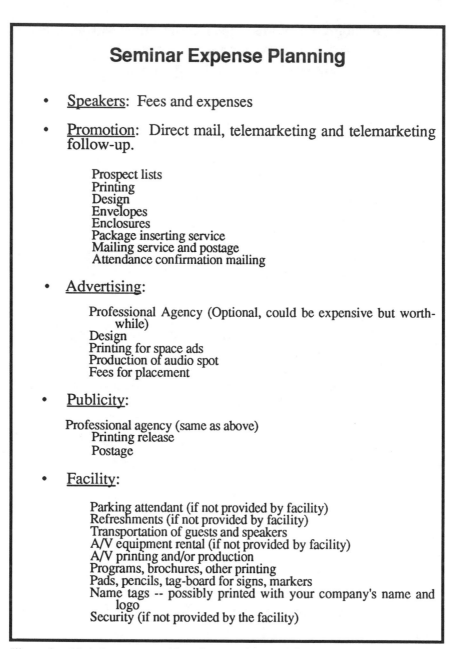

Seminar Expense Planning

- <u>Speakers</u>: Fees and expenses

- <u>Promotion</u>: Direct mail, telemarketing and telemarketing follow-up.

    Prospect lists
    Printing
    Design
    Envelopes
    Enclosures
    Package inserting service
    Mailing service and postage
    Attendance confirmation mailing

- <u>Advertising</u>:

    Professional Agency (Optional, could be expensive but worth-
        while)
    Design
    Printing for space ads
    Production of audio spot
    Fees for placement

- <u>Publicity</u>:

    Professional agency (same as above)
        Printing release
        Postage

- <u>Facility</u>:

    Parking attendant (if not provided by facility)
    Refreshments (if not provided by facility)
    Transportation of guests and speakers
    A/V equipment rental (if not provided by facility)
    A/V printing and/or production
    Programs, brochures, other printing
    Pads, pencils, tag-board for signs, markers
    Name tags -- possibly printed with your company's name and
        logo
    Security (if not provided by the facility)

Illustration 10-4: Items to consider when creating a seminar budget.

Sales Expense ÷ Number of Orders = Sales Cost per Order

Sales Expense ÷ Total Revenue = % of Revenue used for Sales Expense.

Look at Illustration 10-4. It lists the items you must consider when preparing a seminar budget. But before you estimate these costs, ask yourself these questions:

How much do I spend on a face-to-face sales call and how much profit do I make per order?

How much will this seminar cost and how many orders must it produce in order to make it more cost effective than face-to-face selling?

Once you know the answers to those questions, you will have a strong goal toward which to work as you plan your seminar. You can than decide how much you are willing to spend on each item on the list. Knowing your anticipated, or required, return on investment will help you stay focused on your seminar's objectives. It will also help you evaluate its success in terms of actual sales when the seminar is over.

When you evaluate the seminar's success, make sure to follow-up with prospects who were unable to attend the seminar, but who showed an interest in it. If these prospects convert to leads, and ultimately orders, it is appropriate to count them in the amount of revenue generated by the seminar.

One final reason for preparing a detailed seminar budget is to get upper management's buy in. A program to save money and reduce costs is easy to sell. By clearly identifying your anticipated seminar's costs and the return you expect on that investment, you should have no problem getting the support you need to implement a successful seminar.

Once you know how much your seminar will cost and what you will gain by conducting it, you can select a qualified audience that will help you achieve your goal.

Audience Selection

Understanding and selecting the appropriate audience is the largest factor in the ultimate success or failure of the seminar.   You must identify the individuals you are trying to reach.

A description of each major decision maker, including personality similarities and organization reporting structures will be very helpful.   A unique characteristic of the business market is the multiple levels involved in the purchasing decision.

In your review of the individuals involved in the buying process, focus on influencers as well as decision makers. If selling your products involves both decision makers and influencers, try to describe both of their functions and their interaction. A description of how these players fit into the organization and their interaction in the buying decision can be very helpful. The general personalities of all of these individuals can help evaluate new or existing strategies. Keep in mind that different product groups may have different buying decision structures.

As you focus on the individuals you should also try to understand the personalities involved so you can design both the promotion and seminar to appeal to these individuals.

In Chapter 6, I explained four distinct personality types: Pragmatic, Extroverted, Amiable, and Analytic. You may want to review that section when you are selecting your audience. First, identify the primary personality type of the members of your audience. Then design and promote your seminar to meet the interests of that group.

Successful business-to-business direct marketers try to align the personalities of their promotion with the personalities of the people who are going to receive the promotion. This means marketing to the individual -- not to their position within the company. When a company's purchasing procedures involve multiple buyers who use a single purchasing agent, this process becomes more difficult. So you must make the promotion itself, through its design, copy and graphics, project its personality clearly. The promotion's personality must match that of the business executive you are targeting.

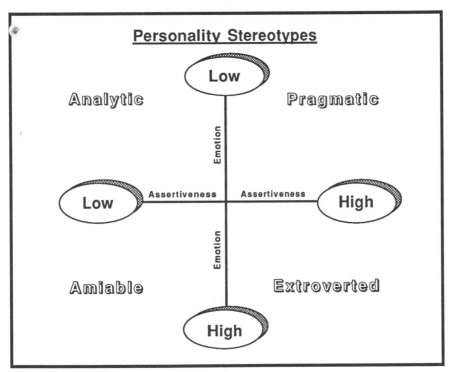

Illustration 10-5: Personality Stereotypes.

To help you recall the primary personality characteristics from Chapter 6, look at Illustration 10-5. The four stereotype personalities are charted by the point at which assertiveness intersects with emotion. A highly emotional but unassertive individual, therefore, can be classified as "amiable".

You have to consider these personality stereotypes in both the promotion of the seminar and the seminar execution. Each of the personalities has different likes and dislikes and the ultimate success of your program will be dictated by how well you match the audience with your approach.

For example, a pragmatic audience will be interested in a seminar filled with summary results. Pragmatics tend to be executives and general managers who aren't interested in a lot of socializing. Your best approach might be to offer a one hour breakfast seminar they can attend on their way to work. Pragmatics won't mind attending an early seminar. And make sure to show them tables, charts, and graphs that illustrate results.

Now that you know who you're addressing, you can name your seminar, develop a theme, and choose a format that will appeal to that audience.

Choosing Title, Theme and Format

The title, theme, and format of your seminar are determined by a combination of your target audience, and the objective of the seminar.

The seminar title must catch the prospect's eye, and promise them information they need. Ask yourself: who is my audience and what do they want that I can deliver?

The theme of your seminar answers the question: What is this seminar about? The format is the way in which the information is presented. The theme and format must reinforce the seminar's objectives and be consistent with the interests of your audience.

For example, if you're trying to sell customers on a new feature for their existing equipment, a demonstration and case history might be effective.

On the other hand, if you're trying to generate sales leads for a new product announcement, you may be forced to use a lecture format.

One consideration when choosing a seminar format is the location and frequency of the seminar. It is easier to promote seminars where you offer the potential attendee the opportunity to select from multiple sessions. This allows the prospect to select a session that is most convenient for them.

There are several advantages to offering multiple sessions:

- The prospect can choose the best session to meet their needs. The odds of having a conflict are reduced.
- You appear to be more sensitive to the prospect's needs.
- You demonstrate a level of intensity and interest in a particular subject. The prospect gets the feeling that you are concerned about the subject material and want to give a larger audience an opportunity to learn.
- You create an impression that the subject is hot and you need multiple sessions to deal with the demand and large audience.

There are disadvantages to offering choices as well:

- The prospect may not be able to decide which session is best and won't select any.

- The prospect may treat the seminar less seriously knowing that if they miss one session, they can attend another.

As you decide to conduct multiple seminars or only one session one time, you also need to decide whether to offer the seminar at multiple locations. If you decide to conduct the seminar at multiple locations, you will have to perform separate planning for each location. Multiple sessions at the same location can be planned in one effort.

Sometimes you can improve the attendance at your seminars by offering multiple sessions at the same location but varying the times that the session is conducted. For example, you can offer a morning, afternoon, and evening session. This allows the prospect to select a time that is most convenient to their schedule. This approach can be enhanced by offering the seminar on one day in the morning, another day in the afternoon, and a final session in the evening. This kind of scheduling will probably work best if done at your own facility.

When you have established the theme and format of your seminar, consider things that can add to the entertainment and enjoyment of your audience. You can rent films and video tapes of short subjects that are great introductions to breaks and special subjects. These materials are professionally developed and designed to improve the overall impression and effectiveness of your seminar. There are a number of film rental companies that specialize in this kind of material.

At this point you know how much the seminar will cost, who will be attending, what you plan to tell them, and how you will tell them. Now you can begin addressing the details, such as, where the seminar will be held.

Selecting the Facility

The facility has to be convenient to get to and provide the necessary amenities to make your seminar successful.

If your seminar is targeted at a large metropolitan center, make sure that the facility is convenient to public transportation and parking is readily available. On the other hand, if your seminar is targeted to suburban or rural areas, ease of access from the major highways can be a critical item.

You might plan a seminar that will require participants to travel from remote areas. In this kind of situation, a facility at an airport with good connecting flights ideal. Airport hotels frequently anticipate this kind of activity and can easily accommodate seminar programs.

As you narrow down the location and begin to focus on the facility, you should have several contingency plans based on the anticipated audience size. The best laid plans often go astray because the turnout isn't what you anticipated. A large room for a smaller audience can be cold and uncomfortable. The participants will focus on the empty space as opposed to the material being discussed.

If your turnout is much larger then you anticipated, the room and other accommodations can be inadequate and create an impression of poor planning.

To avoid facility problems due to unanticipated turnout, you should use some form of confirmation device to verify attendees. Telemarketing a day or two prior to the seminar is an excellent tool to confirm attendance. Mailgrams or telegrams can also be effective devices to confirm attendance.

Make sure you visit each potential seminar site prior to committing your program to that location. Inspect the seminar rooms and audio visual capabilities. Visit each part of the facility that your attendees might use. If the parking garage is poorly lighted or hard to access, your participants will have a bad impression of the seminar before it even begins. If the rest rooms and break areas aren't clean and well maintained your seminar will suffer.

A special note about food service and meals. So often, seminar attendees will judge the quality of a seminar on totally unrelated functions. If you serve a meal or a snack as part of the seminar, the attendees will frequently judge the quality of the seminar by the quality of the food.

When you are screening the facilities, plan to have lunch or dinner so you can judge the quality of the food and service in the restaurant.

If some of your attendees are potentially going to spend the night, inspect the rooms to ensure that they are clean and acceptable.

You will probably be using audiovisual material to aid in the presentation of your seminar. Discuss your audiovisual requirements with the meeting manager at each potential facility. Explore if backup equipment is available should there be a problem. Murphy's Law really comes into play when it comes to audiovisual equipment. So often the bulb will fail at a critical time or the sound system will not be properly adjusted. You want to know how the facility will deal with an audiovisual problem.

If part of your seminar will include the demonstration of equipment, you should understand the delivery, set-up and operation of the equipment. Frequently the facility will require union personnel to participate in some or all phases of the use of your equipment. Discuss your requirements with the facility meeting manager and make sure you both understand the lead times and coordination necessary to perform an equipment demonstration.

Don't overlook the electrical requirements of your equipment for the demonstration. Frequently the facility will have to make special arrangements to have electrical lines installed to meet your requirements.

The facility can help a great deal in making your seminar successful. It can do even more damage if it is not equipped to handle your requirements. Unfortunately, attendees tend to focus on their physical comfort and how they are treated when judging the quality and effectiveness of a seminar. If they were cold, or a facility employee was rude to them, you will be held personally responsible.

Because lead times can often be months or even years for a facility, you can't assume that your desired seminar location will be available when you want it. This is an inherent problems with seminars since a lot of your planning has to be accomplished before you select a location.

When you consider potential locations, think of the distribution of your current prospects and customers. Try to select locations that will be convenient for them to get to. Well known locations or facilities will make promoting your seminar easier. If a prospect is comfortable with a location or facility, it is easier for them to rationalize attending the seminar.

Speaker Selection

Once the participants arrive at your seminar, the success or failure of the program will be heavily dependent on the facility, the subject or theme, and the speakers you've chosen to present the material.

Unless you present the material yourself, you will inevitably be concerned about the quality of the presentation your speakers will give. You may wonder:

- Will the presentation be too basic for your audience?
- Will the audiovisuals be appropriate for the presentation?
- Will the subject be timely and informative?
- Will the speaker have credibility and elicit the confidence of the audience?
- Will the presentation be dry and boring?

As you establish the theme and content of your presentations you should make a list of potential speakers. Do some reference checking to determine if the potential speaker has spoken in front of groups before. Interview the speaker yourself and see if you are comfortable with their style and speaking manner. Sometimes you'll be faced with an extremely credible participant who is not a good public speaker. If you know this in advance there are some techniques you can use to enhance the presentation and still take advantage of the speaker's knowledge:

- If the speaker is nervous or unsure in front of a group, you could use an interview format where a more articulate speaker acts as a moderator and asks the participant a series of questions. This controls the flow of the presentation and will help to relax the speaker.

- Good audiovisuals can help to overcome some of the speaker's short comings. However this is not a cure-all solution.

- Customer testimonial speakers are the greatest risk. A very effective executive or manager may not be an effective speaker. You have to keep these presentations short, crisp, and well rehearsed. You should consider a strong lead-in by a strong speaker and then a debriefing by that speaker after the customer testimonial. In essence you may want to "sandwich" the customer with a professional speaker.

- You can use skits and other amusing anecdotes to lead into or summarize a dry boring subject. An important point to remember in developing any sort of production: Every presentation must have a certain intrinsic entertainment value to be effective.

  The most valuable and interesting material presented by a dry speaker, who uses poor audiovisuals and makes no effort to entertain the audience will be dull and uninteresting. Many participants will leave dissatisfied and unfulfilled, even though the information was important and worthwhile.

  On the other hand, an exciting speaker who gives an entertaining presentation, will be well received, even if their information is weak, and only moderately interesting. So often I will see excellent critiques of presentations that contained virtually no new or exciting information because the presentation was so dynamic.

- Rehearsal can address a lot of the problems of an ineffective speaker. Although it is often difficult to get speakers to actually rehearse their presentations, this may be the single biggest opportunity to ensure the success of the presentation. Speakers are notorious for procrastinating about practicing, and the first live presentation becomes the rehearsal. As a result, they read information directly from the audiovisuals, and appear unprofessional. Your challenge will be to insist that the speakers rehearse as a condition of their selection as a speaker. If you make the speaker aware that rehearsal is mandatory, you will do a lot to ensure the success of your program.

- If you must use a speaker whose speaking ability is questionable, don't schedule them to present after lunch or a long break. People become drowsy after eating and a dull presentation will seem even worse if the audience is tired. As you evaluate the speakers for your seminar, alternate more and less dynamic speakers, as well as short and long presentations.

- Insist that each speaker submit an outline and written objective for their presentation. If your speaker candidate cannot clearly identify the objectives and goals of the presentations concisely, the odds of the speaker being effective are slim to none.

Although outside speakers will often offer the greatest credibility and interest from a seminar promotion point of view, they also offer the greatest risk. You have little or no control over the outside speaker and they are often uncooperative in preparation and rehearsal. As you focus on speaker selection, you should try to limit the number of outside speakers to a minimum, and have a back-up plan if they cancel at the last minute.

Seminar Composition

While the theme of your seminar should be consistent, you don't have to limit yourself to one seminar format. This is particularly true when you are having multiple sessions. You may decide to open the seminar with a lecture highlighting the strong benefits of your products and services. To emphasize the ease of use and real benefits derived, you can have a panel as a follow-up session. To create credibility in you solution, you may even decide to include a case history of your product actually being utilized.

This mixing of formats can be very effective and entertaining. The audience will get to see a variety of styles and concepts. Mixing formats also will keep the pace moving quickly and not allow the attendees to become bored.

Keep in mind the time allocation for each session. Frequently you will plan a presentation to last one hour and the session will actually last much longer. This is a common problem that is frequently caused by a flaw in the planning process.

Presentations tend to take longer when given than they do in rehearsal. Good speakers will pay attention to the audience and slow down if their audience appears confused to allow them to grasp the material. You can read the audience by their expressions and body language. When planning sessions factor time to allow for audience questions and transitions between speakers and subjects.

If you have allocated one hour for a presentation within your seminar, the speaker should plan a 45 minute presentation. This will allow extra time for introductions, transitions and questions. It is better to have a session end early than to run over and inconvenience your audience.

If you promote a four hour seminar, you really don't want it to last five or six hours. The audience may have other commitments after the seminar and could feel pressure if you run over. Whenever I plan a session, I schedule presentations to consume about 75% of the allocated time. The remainder is left for questions and audience discussion.

You must also decide on a format for audience questions. Do you answer questions throughout the session or ask the audience to hold their questions until a particular subject or speaker is finished? There are advantages and disadvantages to both.

If you accept questions throughout the session, the audience becomes more involved and the information tends to flow spontaneously. One question will invite another and so on. You really can get the audience involved. This could instill a lot of enthusiasm in the seminar and be a lot of fun. The questions are timely and the audience tells you when they don't understand a particular point or subject.

There are some serious drawbacks to this approach. Adhering to a time schedule and even sticking to the subject can be a challenge. You may have intended to answer a question later in the presentation and stopping to answer the question early throws off your time and your presentation. You loose control of the seminar and may never be able to regain the momentum you had before you were asked the question. Finally, a spontaneous question can sometimes place you in an embarrassing situation if the answer is negative about your product or company. Having this response in the middle of a session can create credibility problems.

Accepting questions at the conclusion of a subject or speaker gives you great control over the seminar. You get to present the information uninterrupted and flowing the way you designed the presentation. This approach allows you to adhere to your timetable and you can limit the time spent answering questions. Questions that are embarrassing can more easily be tabled to be discussed individually at the next break. You don't run the risk of loosing credibility during the presentation. The key benefit in deferring questions to the conclusion of session is that you maintain control.

Allowing the questions only at the end of a session also has disadvantages. This approach can be insensitive to the audience. If the participants get confused early in the session you may lose their interest permanently. The speakers have to be more sensitive to the reaction of the audience to judge their level of understanding. Attendees have to write their questions down to remember to ask them at the end of the session. Some good points can be lost because they are simply forgotten as the session proceeds. Questions are not spontaneous therefore they may not create the same level of interest and enthusiasm.

The approach you select will be governed by the strength of the speakers, the amount of information you have to cover and the amount of time you have available. The less information you have to cover and the more time you have, the easier it is to take questions spontaneously. The size of the audience can also dictate your ability to address spontaneous questions. A large audience may force you into deferring questions until the end.

The layout of the seminar room can influence the impact of your seminar. Basically there are three layouts for seminars:

- **Auditorium**: This layout is much like that at a theater. The audience sits in rows of chairs, with out tables, and without the benefit of name cards or tags. Normally the room is divided by an aisle or two and smokers are seated in one part of the room.

  This layout works well with large audiences and a lecture format. Bear in mind that the audience doesn't have very much room to spread out and take notes. It is impractical to ask the attendees to participate in a written exercise.

  Most auditorium layouts will place the speaker on a platform or stage at the front of the group. The speakers will normally be restricted to speaking from a lectern, speaker's table, or on the stage at the front of the room. If you have speakers who like to walk through the audience as they present, this environment is more difficult. You'll have to supply the speaker with a cordless microphone.

Because large audiences typically attend auditorium presentations, audiovisuals are limited to slides and films. Overhead, flip-chart, and chalk board visuals may be difficult to see from the rear of the room. Handouts are typically given for reference and not for use during the session.

* **Banquet**. This layout is much like a wedding reception. Eight to ten participants sit at each table. Inevitably, some people will have to turn their chairs 180 degrees away from the table to view the speaker. Tables are designated as smoking or non-smoking, with all the smoking tables grouped together.

    The speaker at a banquet seminar is normally at a lectern and rarely on a stage. This layout requires a larger room even for a relatively small audience. The larger facility will probably require amplification for the speaker.

    If the room is equipped with a stage and lectern, the same constraints that limit the auditorium layout will also limit the banquet layout. That is, overheads, flip-charts, and chalk board visuals may be difficult to see from the rear of the room. Handouts are typically given for reference and not for use during the session. Moving about is difficult for the speaker because there is typically not enough space between tables.

* **Conference**: This layout resembles a classroom. It consists of rows of chairs with each participant or pair of participants having a table or desk surface to work on. Smokers are seated on one side of the room.

    This layout lends itself well to smaller sessions or those in which the attendees will be participating in a practical exercise or taking notes. Conference layouts are more comfortable and tend to give more space to each participant. This additional space may make the attendees feel more at ease and less threatened by strangers.

In traditional conference layouts the speaker may or may not be on an elevated stage. The speaker may elect to write on flip charts or a chalk board and walk through the audience to elicit or answer questions. Depending on the size of the facility, the speaker may not need amplification, so the type of microphone may be a moot point.

In the conference layout, the speaker can usually use almost all of the audiovisual techniques available. Flip-charts, chalk boards, and overheads are commonly used. It is quite common for one speaker to use more than one audiovisual technique to support their presentation.

This is the ideal layout to encourage audience involvement in practical exercises. Practical exercise handouts can be used.

There are several unique configurations of the conference layout. Two of these are the horseshoe and closed horseshoe.

*   *Horseshoe*: This configuration places the tables in a U formation with the stage or speakers lectern at the opening. It is an ideal arrangement for smaller groups so that the speaker can work with the audience in the horseshoe.

    Dynamic speakers who like to force audience involvement prefer this arrangement. If the group is small, this arrangement tends to encourage a relaxed and friendly atmosphere. Each participant can observe the other participants.

- *Closed horseshoe*: This arrangement is similar to the horseshoe above, but there is no open end. All participants, including the speaker, are seated at a large conference table. This is an ideal layout for panels or discussion groups. All of the participants are made to feel like peers, including the session moderator.

Determining the best layout for your seminar will be governed in may ways by the facility you choose and the size of your anticipated audience. You may even be able to use several rooms with different layouts in each room. If possible you should try to use the conference or some variation of the conference layout. This tends to make the participants the most comfortable and offers the most conducive environment for teaching.

Finalize the Agenda

After you've identified the audience, theme, format, and subjects to be covered, you will need to establish a detailed agenda for your program.   You have assumed a certain level of knowledge on the part of the participants when they arrive at your seminar. You expect them to walk away with an enhanced view of the subject. Your agenda should take the attendee from some level of understanding to the objective level of understanding. This sounds so simple.

Earlier I discussed establishing the global objective of the seminar -- Sell, Sell, Sell. Now we have to look at the details of the program and identify the best path to reach our ultimate objective. Depending on the personality and professional level of your audience, the agenda will vary considerably. A seminar about a customer database in data processing will have two very different agendas when given to directors of data processing or to sales managers.

Your agenda has to fit your ultimate goal and the audience you're trying to reach.

You may find it easier to structure the agenda similarly to structuring a sales call. When I teach sales training to new salespeople I instruct them to open the sales call with an initial benefit statement (IBS). This statement is normally the current hot-button of the industry and explains how your product or service will solve the problem. You will only be able to sell a prospect if you can solve their problem. The IBS should gain attention and involve the prospect in your solution immediately.

Your opening session should create interest and involve the attendee in your product's solution. It should relate the benefits of your product to a problem the attendee is experiencing.

The next stage of a typical sales call is to use questioning or probing techniques to determine the problems or hot-buttons of the prospect. This probing technique allows the salesperson to describe the specific features of their products in terms of solutions and benefits to specific problems identified by the customer.

It would be difficult to use probing techniques for everyone in the audience, however there are some interesting techniques that can be used to accomplish the same thing.

- The use of a case study to relate a common problem to the entire group. The case study can describe a problem and then be used to relate the benefits derived from your solution. Another effective technique is to ask the audience to perform an activity that gets them involved in the problem so they can really relate to the solution. Audience involvement gets more difficult with larger audiences.

- Another effective technique is to assign the participants a practical exercise in which they help determine the size of a particular problem. For example, the attendee is provided a worksheet which they complete during the presentation. The instructor shows the attendee how to complete the form and works the audience to help them complete it. The completed form provides an actual assessment of a problem in their business.

  This type of exercise is very effective in smaller groups. I once saw it used at a seminar selling telephone selling telephone equipment. The participants used a computer to enter information. The software then analyzed their telephone network and identified their telephone usage costs. Finally it displayed their potential savings if they bought a new telephone system. The participants remained involved throughout the seminar.

- Asking rhetorical questions can create a particular problem in the mind of the prospect. This is another way of probing the particular needs of a prospect by identifying a problem they might be able to relate to. This technique can also be effective in advertising and direct mail.

The sales technique of translating product features into benefits that will resolve customer needs established during the probing phase of the sales call is called Feature, Benefits and Reaction (FBR). The feature of the product is reviewed in terms of a benefit to the prospect. Hopefully, the benefit will address an area of concern identified during the probing session. The prospect is then asked to react to the feature and benefit. The salesperson constantly tries to close the sale if the reaction is favorable. If the customer's reaction is unfavorable, the salesperson tries to identify the underlying objection, addresses the customer's concern, and once the objection is eliminated, tries to close.

This type of sales presentation can also be delivered during a seminar. Features should always be linked to the benefits that a prospect will derive from the feature. Benefit presentation is the key to selling. The classic explanation of features versus benefits is that of selling shovels. Shovels are features; the holes they dig are benefits. The customer needs a hole not a shovel. Most inexperienced salespeople get so enamored with their products they sell feature and forget to relate specific benefits that the feature will afford.

As you design the seminar agenda keep benefit selling at the forefront of all of your activity. As you present the features of your product, follow each one with a statement such as: And what that means to you is _____. Another way to make sure you are selling benefits is to listen to your presentation from the prospect's perspective. If at any time you make a statement that the prospect might respond to by saying, So what? you have not related the feature to a benefit or that part of the seminar should be deleted from the agenda.

The final part of a sales call is asking for an order or some form of commitment. Salespeople are taught to ask for the order and shut-up. The next person to talk loses.

Seminar selling is no different. Your seminar program should build to a close and you should ask for an order. If you don't ask the attendee to take some action you will have wasted your time and money. You don't just want to feel good after the seminar, you want to get business.

As you finalize the agenda for the seminar keep in mind the structure of the sales call. After all, the seminar is just a sales call being made on a group. The quality of the sales call is yours to determine. You can move a prospect pretty far along the sales cycle by using the seminar to sell. Here are the key elements of a sales call.

- Establish interest by using an Initial Benefit Statement.

- Create desire by probing and presenting material that helps establish need.

- Create a desire for your product by selling the features of your products in relation to the benefits that the prospect will derive. Focus the benefits on the desire created during the probing phase.

- Close, Close, Close. *ASK FOR THE ORDER!*

Seminar Logistics

"Logistics" is a fancy name for the myriad of details that go into making your seminar a success. They all have to be done completely and on time -- some more than once. The key is to keep Murphy's Law in the back of your mind: If something can go wrong, it will. Your job is to increase the odds overwhelmingly in your favor. Planning and attention to detail are the only weapons you have to counter unforeseen problems. Here are some important things to remember:

1. Keep the audience in mind. According to the number of attendees you expect, set the time, place, and date.

2. Be sure to secure a firm commitment from all the speakers, and have a clear idea of their topic, or better yet, have a title and outline, before you start your promotion.

3. Think through your registration procedure carefully. There are basically two types of registration procedures:

Seminar Check-List

Yes No

❑	❑	Have you booked your facility of choice?
❑	❑	Do you have a back-up choice?
❑	❑	Are parking and/or transportation arranged?
❑	❑	Have you made plans for refreshments?
❑	❑	Do you have to rent A/V equipment or does the facility provide well maintained equipment? What about back-up?
❑	❑	Have you arranged for your demonstration equipment to be delivered to the seminar site?
❑	❑	Have you coordinated with the facility for the installation of the demonstration equipment?
❑	❑	Have you arranged with your field support organization to install the demonstration equipment?
❑	❑	Have you arranged for support personnel to conduct the demonstrations?
❑	❑	Have you previewed the demonstrations?
❑	❑	Is the electrical power supply sufficient to run your demonstration equipment?
❑	❑	Will you nccd external communications capability?
❑	❑	Is the ventilation in the room adequate?
❑	❑	Is there a place for coats?
❑	❑	Do you know the facility manager who will be in charge on the day of the seminar and how to get in touch with that person on short notice?
❑	❑	Are the outlets well placed? Are there enough of them?
❑	❑	If there is an in-house sound system/PA system, how does it work?
❑	❑	How do you turn off the "Muzak"?
❑	❑	Do you have enough watcr, cups, ashtrays?

Illustration 10-6a: Seminar Checklist

A. Advance Registration. There are many variations of this preferred technique, including reply cards being inserted in the initial mailing, a form sent out in a follow-up mail piece, and registration by telephone.

B. On-site Registration. This procedure does not let you know in advance how many people to expect and is not

---

Seminar Check-List (Continued)

Know and tell the participants:

- ❑ Fire escape exits and routes.
- ❑ Telephone number for incoming calls.
- ❑ Pay telephone locations.
- ❑ Restroom locations.

Include in seminar kit:

- ❑ Name tags -- made up in advance.
- ❑ Participant list.
- ❑ Agenda.
- ❑ Brochures (company, product).
- ❑ Writing pad, pencil.
- ❑ Give-away (something with your company's name on it).

Miscellaneous:

- ❑ Signs directing people to seminar location.
- ❑ Sign to cover hotel's logo on the podium.
- ❑ First aid kit.

Illustration 10-6.b: Seminar Checklist (continued).

recommended. If you want to have attendees check in when they arrive at the seminar and give them their name tag and seminar kit at that time, that's fine. But be sure to confirm their attendance in advance.

Driving Seminar Attendance

Seminar programs are a form of lead generation but the leads don't flow evenly but occur in a burst. This bubble of activity creates significant problems in follow-up and conversion of leads to orders. As you plan your programs to drive traffic make sure you plan a follow-up program directly to the prospect. Don't rely only on your salespeople to contact the prospects after the seminar.

Direct mail and telephone selling are the two most widely used formats for generating seminars attendance. I have seen virtually every kind of direct mail format used to generate seminar traffic. Like most effective business direct marketing, the most successful campaigns are personalized and will break through to the target.

Multiple mailings seem to be most effective. The initial mailing is sent 4 to 5 weeks prior to the seminar and a follow-up mailing is sent 2 to 3 weeks prior. Telephone can also be effectively included in the program about 2 weeks prior to the seminar. The timing of the follow-up and telephone call can help to create a perception of good service. The prospect will feel that you don't want them to miss an important opportunity.

In selecting your list, try to use name-directed lists, but make sure you also include the title. Your house file of both customers and prospects should be included in the seminar invitation mailing. So often we'll ignore the best list available, our house file, and only mail outside lists.

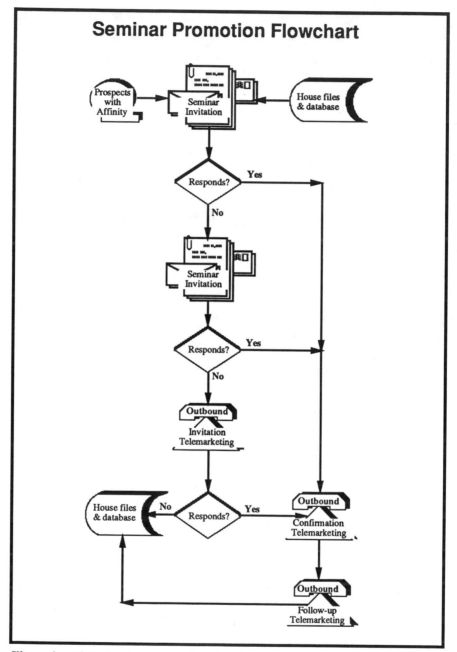

Illustration 10-7: Seminar Promotion Flowchart.

There are literally thousands of lists available for you to rent that will allow you to target your promotion specifically. I discussed lists in great detail in Chapter 6. Once you've identified the audience for the seminar it shouldn't be difficult to obtain a list that meets your requirements. Your local telephone book identifies several list brokers or you can contact the Direct Marketing Association in New York City at (212) 689-4977 for the name of a reputable list broker.

The invitation format that seems to be working well right now is similar to a wedding invitation. If the envelope is personally addressed the odds of delivery increase. The advances in technology will even allow you to use a Calligraphy font and have an invitation that looks hand-written.

Illustration 10-7 shows the flow of direct mail and telemarketing. The initial mailing should be done about 4 weeks prior to the seminar. The wedding invitation format should invite the prospect to attend an important seminar about their business. You understand your audience and what they want to learn. Make sure the invitation describes the benefits that the prospect will realize by attending the seminar.

In most cases you'll be trying to reach a decision maker; sound like a decision maker yourself. The executive-to-executive impression will ensure a higher attendance rate at the seminar.

If you use a letter be brief, direct, and professional in tone. Identify the problem you know the prospect is concerned about and stress that the solutions will be discussed at the seminar. Sell the benefits of the seminar . . . don't attempt to sell your products or services. Build credibility. Be sure it is clear that the seminar, run by your company, is the best way for the prospect to begin to solve their business problems.

If you decide to include additional information with the letter, only insert relevant materials in the envelope. A seminar agenda, case history, or brochure showing how your product solved a company's problems would work best. Don't forget the reply device, either a card or envelope.

About 2 to 3 weeks prior to the seminar you should re-invite those prospects who haven't responded. You can use the same mailer and still be effective. You may want to use a wedding invitation in the initial mailing and a business letter for the reminder mailing. The second mailing should remind the prospect about the seminar and encourage them to enroll now. Try to create a sense of urgency to act now.

Telephone will serve several important roles in this campaign. This is one of those rare situations that telemarketing can be used in a business-to-business area. You should plan to contact each prospect who has agreed to attend 1 or 2 days prior to the seminar to confirm their attendance. You can call and remind them of the seminar, make sure they know how get there, brief them on parking or other pertinent information, and see if they have any questions. About 75% to 85% of the original accepters will confirm their attendance. This call can be scripted and even executed by your clerical staff or an outside telemarketing service bureau.

You can also use telemarketing to contact the best prospects and offer them an opportunity to attend the seminar. The script might go something like this:

> Good morning, Mr. Jones, I'm Bernie Goldberg from XYZ Computer. As you may recall we're having an important seminar on desktop publishing and didn't want you to miss an opportunity to attend.

> As one of the prominent businesses in the area we
> hoped you would participate. Response has been
> very enthusiastic and we have only a few seats still
> open . . . Would you like me to make a reservation
> for you?

The communicator should be prepared to respond to prospects who
are unable to attend but want additional information or to be contacted directly by a salesperson.   In addition some common questions or objections that will probably come up are:

> Is this a sales demonstration?
> Will I be asked to buy something there?
> Will a salesperson be hounding me for weeks if I come?
> Why is the program free?
> Who is your company?
> What is your company's role in the seminar?
> Can someone from my company besides me attend?
> Is there a cut-off date or limit on the number of attendees?
> I'll be away that week. Can I get a transcript or something?

As I discussed in Chapter 9, telephone selling is significantly more
expensive than direct mail. You want to use it where it can produce
the best results. You can start your phone campaign about 2 weeks
prior and continue until about 5 days prior with great effectiveness.
In most situations, a business can't afford to call every prospect,
therefore you should try to target your largest and best sales opportunities.

You'll notice that the flowchart in Illustration 10-7 contains a follow-up phone call. I like to use telephone to determine the outcome
of the seminar and measure the results. This call was described in
Chapter 3 and again in Chapter 9. It helps you get feedback about
your program, and also makes the prospect feel good about your
company.

I think the biggest problem in seminar programs is getting salespeople to follow-up with each attendee. This is the typical problem associated with lead generation programs but it is compounded when leads are generated in a single burst as they are at seminars. It is impossible for the sales force to contact each prospect and do a quality selling job.

You should include some direct contact with each attendee after the seminar. A thank you letter can be extremely effective in sustaining the business relationship and helping to pave the way for a future sale. Another effective technique is a questionnaire asking the prospect to evaluate the seminar and provide you with feedback on how you can improve your offerings.

Advertising and Publicity

As you know by now, I have never been a big advocate of using advertising. The leads generated are usually too expensive and poor quality when compared to those leads gained through well executed direct marketing. Advertising can however be extremely effective in building awareness and creating an environment that will allow direct marketing to be even more successful.

Advertising and publicity can play an important role in the overall promotion of your seminar. Used well and timed properly, they are powerful ways to bolster attendance and call attention to the stature and value of your company. Although publicity and advertising should be tightly coordinated with your direct response promotion, one does not replace the other. If your budget will allow it, you should plan to do both.

Publicity is distinct from advertising. For one thing, publicity consists of information that is deemed newsworthy, so you don't pay to get space or air time. But free is not easy. Your seminar may be interesting and newsworthy to some, and may mean nothing to others.

Your target audience will likely read trade magazines or newsletters where events of interest in their field are published. That is where you want to send a news release about your seminar. Many newspapers publish listings that contain just the title, date, time, place, and price of a meeting or seminar. Make sure you send a short notice to these publications.

If you have a major industrial figure or famous person speaking at your seminar, that will be of more interest to more people. You can send news releases to general consumer publications or even write a letter to the editor explaining the event and its importance. If you find a widespread enthusiastic response, you might consider holding a press conference prior to the seminar. Attempt the press conference only if you're convinced there is genuine enthusiasm about the news value of your seminar.

A feature story won't get people to your seminar because the story will probably appear after the seminar has taken place. But this can be a priceless tool for credibility and image building. Since one of the prime objectives of conducting the seminar is to build credibility and enhance your image, don't overlook this opportunity.

Here are some tips for getting publicity:

- Send out as many press releases as necessary to cover the trade and general interest publications . . . but send only one per publication.

- Be absolutely sure to have the name and telephone number of a contact person at your company on the release.

- Leave adequate lead time. Trade publications and newsletters, for instance, are usually monthlies and releases have to be in the editor's hands weeks before the publication date. Weeklies have their own deadline day so you can check with their editors. Daily newspapers work on closer deadlines and should not present a problem.

- For the publications you deem to be the most important, a follow-up phone call to the editor could be appropriate. If you are trying to get a feature story published, a call is essential.

- Include a black and white glossy photograph if at all possible; the guest speaker or relevant system makes a newsworthy photograph.

Like publicity, advertising is a tool to create awareness about the seminar and your company and can be an effective way to increase attendance. Unlike publicity, you pay to place your message.

While advertising is expensive, it can be very effective for reaching a wide audience with a well thought-out message to promote your seminar.

You should use an advertising agency or free-lance creative specialist to create the advertisement you will use.   You can use space advertising in both newspapers and magazines. You may also want to consider using radio.

Each advertisement media has its own unique set of strengths and weaknesses. Based on the nature of the seminar and the relative cost of each medium you will have to determine the best medium to use. You should distribute your advertising dollars among the following:

- Use local, daily newspapers as your primary medium, concentrating space in the business and financial pages.

- The market you're trying to reach will dictate how you will advertise in regional trade magazines and newsletters. Decide whether you are trying to reach one industry (vertical marketing), or many businesses in a geographical area (horizontal marketing), and adjust your plans accordingly.

- Use some radio as a general awareness mechanism, and end the spot by directing the listener to the print ads and/or giving them a phone number to call.

The Benefits Table

One way to involve your prospects in your seminar is to ask them to complete a Benefits Table during the presentation. The Benefits Table is a tool that helps prospects evaluate your product offering, and lets you know that they clearly understand the benefits of purchasing your product. It also helps the prospect justify the cost of the purchase by helping them envision exactly how your product will solve their problem.

One way to use the Benefits Table at your seminar is to have two presenters: one explains The Benefits Table and monitors the audience's understanding and completion of it, and the other presents the topic of the seminar. Let me explain how The Benefits Table works.

The Benefits Table assumes that there are three areas that a prospect can experience return on investment in making a buying decision:

The Benefits Table

	Total Expenses	Potential Savings	Probability		
			High	Med	Low
Displaceable Expense Current hardware Service bureau Hardware maintenance Software maintenance Related personnel Environment Supplies Outside services Accounts receivable Inventory Other _____			1	3	6
Avoidable Expense Anticipated % growth in next 3 years _____% Current hardware Service bureau Hardware maintenance Software maintenance Related personnel Environment Supplies Outside services Accounts receivable Inventory Other _____			2	5	8
Increased Revenue or Profit Inceased customer service Detail sales analysis Timely job costing Accurate estimating Additional customer serv Other _____ _____ _____			4	7	9

Illustration 10-8: The Benefits Table.

- Displaceable expense savings
- Avoidable expense savings
- Increased revenue or profit

In Illustration 10-8, the three areas for financial justification are listed with related expenses under each one.

Displaceable expenses are those current expenses that will be eliminated as a result of implementing a new procedure. Current expenses for equipment, personnel, services, supplies and other direct costs that will be reduced or eliminated belong in this category.

Avoidable expenses are those expenses that the company will not have to experience if they make a change. Many times the displaceable expenses are repeated in this category. The savings in this category can often be identified by asking prospects to estimate how much the company will have to add in various areas if it continues to sustain its current rate of growth.

The final category is often called intangible, however, if it is intangible you can't assign it a value. I prefer to identify this category as *increased revenue or increased profit*. You can often identify potential dollars in this area by focusing on a specific opportunity and establishing a value. For example, you might ask, have you ever had a potential customer call you only to find you were out of stock of a particular item? Would you say that this situation occurs 2 out of every 100 calls your receive? If you agree, you have just identified 2% in lost sales that you might be able to recapture with a better inventory control system.

We have long been aware of the different areas that can afford cost justification in a business acquisition. I used to teach The Benefits Table to new salespeople as a method to ensure they focused on all of the justification opportunities. The technique also allowed the prospect to examine each category and to weigh the savings opportunity against the risk and believability.

Instead of just identifying the total savings or total opportunity dollars, the prospect can distribute them based on their confidence in each category. For example, if they identify that the potential displaceable expense for equipment rental is $1,000 per month, they may think that only $500 will actually be saved. They could assign 500 to the high probability cell and perhaps $250 to medium and $250 to low. By spreading the potential savings based on their own comfort level, the prospect has more confidence in the analysis.

The total expenses and potential dollar savings are identified and recorded on the table in the total column. The remaining three columns provide a vehicle for the prospect to assign the amount they feel has a high probability, a medium probability and low probability for actually occurring. Prospects can allocate all or any portion of potential savings for each item in any probability area they feel most comfortable.

Let's say you are about to give a seminar in which you are selling computers. You are going to use The Benefits Table. First you need to list all the associated expenses associated with purchasing and owning a computer. Those items include current hardware, service bureau, hardware maintenance, software maintenance, related personnel, environment, supplies, and outside services.

Next you need to assign each of those items to one of the three categories on The Benefits Table: Displaceable Expenses, Avoidable Expenses, and Increased Revenue. My opinion on how those items should be listed on the The Benefits Table is shown in Illustration 10-8.

Now pretend you're the prospect who is going to complete The Benefits Table. We have just discussed current hardware costs and you've agreed to spending $1,000 per month as the total expense. We write that amount on the chart in the total expenses column for current hardware.

During the discussion about the current hardware expense you were confident that part of the equipment would be eliminated when you acquired a new computer. However you were concerned that a portion of the system might have to be retained and decide to allocate $500 as high probability, while you allocate $250 to the medium and $250 to the low columns. You may even believe that a portion of the system is never going to be eliminated and not allocate that part of the total expenses as savings potential.

After going through the entire exercise The Benefits Table has potential dollars identified in each of the columns. Notice that the 3 categories and 3 levels of probability form 9 cells. I have assigned a relative order to the 9 cells. These relative values rank each cell in the importance that most prospects rank them. You can ask your prospect to rank the cells or explain the illustrated ranking as the most common approach.

The values from each cell can easily be transposed to a summary work sheet (Illustration 10-9). This makes it easy to examine the potential benefits at a glance.

Now that you've established the order of the cells, ask the prospect to identify the cells they will use to cost justify a purchase decision. You should try to convince them to include the high probability from each of the three categories. In my example this would include the first four cells which should be used to justify a buying decision.

The Benefits Table Summary

Category	Probability	Cell Rank	Potential Dollars	Cumulative Dollars
Displaceable	High	1		
Avoidable	High	2		
Displaceable	Medium	3		
Inc Rev/Profit	High	4		
Avoidable	Medium	5		
Displaceable	Low	6		
Inc Rev/Profit	Medium	7		
Avoidable	Low	8		
Inc Rev/Profit	Low	9		

Illustration 10-9: The Benefits Table Summary.

The Benefits Table can ensure that your seminars focus on benefits and help participants identify benefits they can relate to and use to make a buying decision. Armed with this form, presentations and demonstrations can be executed with an eye towards establishing the potential savings or increased revenue a particular feature may bring the prospect.

Each seminar participant could be given a blank form. You can identify the specific items that will be impacted by your products or services. The summary chart above should be printed on the back of the table to allow the prospect to tally their potential. The cumulative summary allows them to identify the potential at various levels.

The seminar presenter should explain how to use the table and provide actual examples that the participants can understand. They should execute an example, customized to the industry and audience in attendance. Actual savings should be explained. The total expenses and potential savings should be explained and then, using an example, the savings should be allocated to the appropriate column.

Using two presenters, one person can present features of a product, while the other can focus on the benefits actually derived from the features presented. These benefits can be explained in terms of savings or additional opportunity. The prospects can privately write their own potential savings or additional revenue on the form. The presenter responsible for highlighting benefits can tailor the results to specific companies in attendance and help the audience achieve the highest impact from the activity.

I think this approach would be best executed in small audiences and will not be effective unless the ultimate decision maker participates in the exercise. This process can help reduce the selling effort required per order and also help eliminate those prospects that are never going to buy. If the prospect does not have believable cost justification it is almost impossible to sell them.

This workshop approach also changes the offer you're making to the prospect. You can offer a complete workshop where the prospect will be able to determine for themselves that a buying decision is worthwhile, affordable, and something they should be making now. In addition, by promoting the outcome as an important step that an executive should take to enable them to make this important computer decision, the appropriate executives will be encouraged to attend.

The field sales representatives should be encouraged to sell participation in this workshop right from the onset of their selling activity. It should be presented as a step that every executive should participate in prior to making their computer decision. If the

August 1, 1991

Mr. John Q. Sample, President
Sample Company
123 Any Street
Anywhere, US   12345

Dear Mr. Sample,

When you decided to install your computer system it was one of the most important decisions you made for your company. Your system has probably been an important reason for your success and growth. Perhaps you've considered changing systems and have been unable to justify purchasing another computer. We would like to help you evaluate and determine whether you should consider changing now. Fill out the enclosed questionnaire to determine whether you should attend our new workshop on how to evaluate and justify a computer purchase.

This special workshop, which is limited to no more than 3 companies at a time will:

- Provide you with a proven cost justification technique that can be used for all decisions you make in your business. We will teach you a technique developed by a major business school for evaluating any business decision. You'll be able to not only identify potential savings or opportunities but also to contrast risk and probability for success of each potential benefit of the decision.

- Help you identify opportunities for both reducing and avoiding expenses. Using actual case studies, examples, and demonstrations, we will show you how other companies, similar to Sample Company, are using technology to save money. You will see how these techniques can help work in your company today.

- Show you, with a complete demonstration, how you can take advantage of an XYZ solution in your business today. We will not only demonstrate solutions that are appropriate for your company, but will provide you with detailed cost justification information on each feature of the system. You will understand the specific implication of each element of the solution.

Illustration 10-10a: A promotion letter selling benefits table workshop.

Sample Company
August 1, 1991
Page 2

This session is designed for executives who are trying to make an important computer purchase decision. The enclosed questionnaire will help you determine whether it is worth your time and effort to participate in this important workshop. If you answer yes to any question, we can help you. Complete the questionnaire and return it to us today!

The results of the workshop will provide you a basis to determine whether you should consider enhancing your system. The workshop is not a sales call but an opportunity for both of us to determine how purchasing a computer can help your company.

The questionnaire will help you evaluate some areas that may offer significant opportunities for your company. In the past, computers were used primarily to enhance accounting. In the 1980's, operations was the important application thrust for many businesses. This decade will require innovative marketing approaches for companies to grow and prosper. As you complete the questionnaire, consider whether your existing system will allow you to face these new marketing challenges.

Send us the questionnaire as soon as possible to take advantage of the workshop. We can help you determine how your computer system can help you improve your company's results.

We look forward to working with you in the near future.

Very truly yours,

Bernie Goldberg
Marketing Manager

P.S.   The cost justification workshop is absolutely free and will provide you a technique that can be used for all business decisions. Complete the questionnaire today!

Illustration 10-10b: A promotion letter selling benefits table workshop (continued).

Current System Questionnaire

Answer the following questions. If you answer yes to any question we can help you with a free cost justification workshop.

Yes **No**

❑   ❑   Are your customers or suppliers requesting services you are unable to provide because of limited computer capabilities or resources? For example, bar-coding, electronic data interface, or database services?

❑   ❑   Are you unable to expand your business or satisfy current requirements because of insufficient computer resources? For example, are you limited by storage, processing capacity, or the number of users you can support?

❑   ❑   Are your competitors offering services that you are unable to provide?

❑   ❑   Would you like to better utilize your computer to improve sales and marketing functions?

❑   ❑   If it were cost justified, would you make installing another XYZ system in your company a priority?

Yes!   Please have someone call me to schedule a free cost justification workshop. I can be contacted at:

John Q. Sample, President
Sample Company
123 Any Street
Anywhere, US 12345

Illustration 10-10c: A promotion letter selling benefits table workshop (continued).

workshop is sold to the executive as an expectation in the decision process it will also ensure participation.

Seminar Selling Summarized

I explained why seminar selling has become such a popular mechanism and is expanding so rapidly. The cost of face-to-face selling continues to escalate and many companies view seminars as an alternative method of making a face-to-face contact. They offer significant benefits to the company and can help create credibility and awareness.

A seminar is a selling tool. Your goal is to sell more products and services to your current customers and to add new customers. To accomplish this mission, you are bringing together a small, highly qualified group of selected business people you want as customers. They will come to your seminar because you have correctly identified business problems that are important to them, and you are offering them solutions to those problems.

In other words, you are establishing yourself as an authority, a professional who is knowledgeable and experienced in solving business problems. You control the message, discussions, and the outcome of the seminar, proving just how well you can help them. You are committed to complete success in your seminar because you have aimed high and attracted the very people who can *buy* your solutions, possibly on the spot.

To attract this level of person and succeed in your objective, you will have to make an investment. You should expect to spend over $100 per person to make your seminar effective and impressive. You could spend considerably more to promote and attract the proper person to your seminar. In return, you get your prospect's undivided attention for a remarkable length of time, and benefit from the

group's spontaneous enthusiasm, interest, and immediately reinforced confidence in you.

Seminars are an interesting and exciting approach to improving
sales productivity. Every business that uses this method of selling
has established their own formula and definition for a successful
program.

Seminars continue to grow in popularity and can be excellent opportunities to sell products and services. Unfortunately, the seminar
frequently turns into an education session with few orders ever
being closed. Many times, management gets a warm fuzzy feeling
because of high attendance and loses sight of the ultimate objective
which is to generate orders.

If you are using or plan to implement seminar activity to generate
leads and ultimately orders, these programs should be treated like
any other lead generation program. You should establish specific
sales objectives. The seminar costs and selling expenses should be
used to establish the cost per order.

The seven key elements to conducting a successful seminar are:

1) Know your audience.
2) Plan your program.
3) Execute the plan.
4) Promote your program.
5) Plan for contingencies.
6) Prepare and stick to a realistic budget.
7) Follow-through.

There are several different types of seminars. All seminars could be
offered for free or for a fee. The three seminar types I discussed are:

1) Vertical
2) Horizontal
3) Institute

I also explained the prospect's perception of free and fee seminars and how you might evaluate which is most appropriate for you.

Planning the seminar is important and I discussed five important steps to cover as you plan the activity:

1) Start with the audience.
2) Choose a title.
3) Plan a theme.
4) Choose a format.
5) Select a facility.

Speaker selection was discussed. There is always some risk associated with a speaker other than yourself. You are faced with some basic issues:

- Will they be too basic for your audience?
- Will the audiovisuals be appropriate for the presentation?
- Will the subject be timely and informative?
- Will the speaker have credibility and elicit the confidence of the audience?
- Will the speaker be dry and boring?

You have to select one of three seating arrangements for your seminar:

- Auditorium
- Banquet
- Conference

Seminar Countdown by Weeks

Task Module	8	7	6	5	4	3	2	1
I. Program Planning and Organization	1. Analyze Audience. 2. Identify potential problems and issues. 3. Plan budget.	4. Devise Theme. 5. Choose format, Title. 6. Select speakers. 7. Draft, mail letters of invitation to speakers	8. Gain commitment from speakers. 9. Revise theme, title. 10. Set agenda.	11. Draft or select materials for seminar kit. 12. Assess speakers' A-V needs, materials	13. Materials to printers. 14. Begin A-V production.	15. Verify speakers' topics, A-V needs. 16. Proof all materials.	17. Rehearse your seminar scripts. 18. Revise scripts as needed.	19. Dress Rehearsal.
II. Logistics	1. Analyze Audience. 2. Assess facility needs. 3. Request headquarters seminar support, if required.	4. Plan registration procedure. 5. Scout facilities. 6. Choose facility, reserve it. 7. Keep a back-up in mind.	8. Explore A-V services availability. 9. Locate and coordinate shipment of required computer or other demo equipment.	10. Order A-V equipment, if necessary. 11. Confirm availability of field service technical support, if required.			12. Order refreshments.	13. Make all signs. Directional, registration. 14. Test all A-V equipment. 15. Assemble seminar kits. 16. Know facility and facility manager. 17. Start packing pencils, pads, name tags, etc. 18. Rehearse registration procedure. 19. Reconfirm field service technical support.

Illustration 10-11a: Seminar Countdown by Weeks.

Seminar Countdown by Weeks

Task Module	8	7	6	5	4	3	2	1
III. Direct Marketing Promotion	1. Analyze Audience.	2. Create message for mailing piece.	3. Compile or order lists. 4. Draft contract. 5. Finalize all mail copy, agenda, letter.	6. Research and obtain telephone registration, 7. Send material to printer or load on word processor.	8. Mail initial inviation. to prospects. 9. Prepare call scripts and unit records.	10. Mail reminder to prospects.	11. Begin phone campaign.	12. Confirm attenders. Don't forget a follow-up campaign after the seminar.
IV. Advertising and Publicity	1. Analyze Audience.	2. Create headline 3. Contact ad reps of magazines, newspapers and radio stations for commitment and closing dates.	4. Research media for publicity. 5. Compile list including name, editor, address, phone no. 6. Draft press release, radio spot. 7. Set deadlines for releases. 8. Produce space ad and send to trade magazines to meet closing dates.	9. Mail release to monthly trades. 10. Begin radio spot production.	11. Mail release to weeklies. 12. Call trades. Confirm production schedule on space ad and press releases.	13. Mail to dailies. 14. Set spot for radio. 15. Follow-up calls to weeklies.	16. Follow-up calls to dailies.	

Illustration 10-13b: Seminar Countdown by Weeks.

The agenda and information that will be presented during the seminar was discussed next. Involvement techniques and audience participation were also discussed. Remember that your objective is to sell, not just to educate.

I presented a plan for driving attendance to your seminar using direct mail and telephone selling. I also included some techniques for creating awareness of your seminar and company using advertising and publicity.

The Benefits Table allows you to convince the seminar attendee that there are quantifiable benefits to be gained from your solution. Using the Benefits Table can also help you compensate for less effective speakers or clarify technical subjects.

Putting all the elements together and executing a successful seminar is no small feat. Illustration 10-11 will give you a plan of attack and identify some of the items you should try to accomplish each week prior to the seminar.

Chapter Eleven:
Trade-Shows

Like seminar selling, trade shows also bring together a group of prospects who have demonstrated an interest or affinity in a specific subject. This affinity gives you the opportunity to sell products or services directly related to the interests of the prospects.

In the seminar environment you have to drive the traffic in order to create leads. In essence, the offer you are making is the seminar and direct marketing can be used to drive the traffic, qualify the lead, and maintain the relationship after the seminar.

Driving traffic is not an issue in trade-shows. Typically a group of prospects is attending a trade-show and your objective is to generate sales opportunities from those who attend. Your challenge is to create a display that is interesting, so that the attenders will automatically visit with your sales staff at the show.

Why use Trade Shows?

Trade show attendance is big business. According to the Trade Show Bureau, an association that monitors and promotes exhibitions, 65 million people attend trade shows in North America every year.

The average trade show participant travels 400 miles, stays three to four days and spends over $850 each trip (not counting airfare or the cost of the booth).

Business Marketing Magazine estimated that over $21 billion dollars was spent by companies promoting and using trade shows in 1990.

Why are businesses so aggressively using this format for reaching customers and prospects? Trade shows offer an exhibitor the opportunity for multiple face-to-face contacts to a targeted and qualified group of potential buyers. Considering the increasing cost of the face-to-face sales call, trade shows make good business sense.

Trade shows offer some great benefits.

- You can demonstrate and show your products and services.

- The buyer has come to you and typically pre-qualifies their interest in your company and products.

- You can get a good feel for customer and prospect interest in your products and company. Trade shows are an ideal environment to gain market research.

- It is easy to arrange high level meetings between your executives and important customers and prospects.

- You can review competitive offerings and understand better how to position your products and services.

- Trade shows are a terrific place to meet and recruit potential employees.

- It is a great place to announce new products and ensure you achieve maximum impact and publicity. You can even hold a press conference and ensure maximum coverage from the appropriate trade and local publications.

Too many companies participate in trade shows and don't attempt to get the most from their investment. They will often treat the show like a three day event, when they should be treated as marketing campaigns that could start as much as 3 months before the show and extend to 3 or 4 months after the show.

Trade shows share a disadvantage of seminars. They create leads in a burst and, sales follow-up becomes difficult. Most trade show leads are never contacted by a salesperson.

If you're considering participating in trade shows, you have to determine the best ones for your business. Trade magazines in the exposition industry, magazines to your industry or the industry you want to reach, and the appropriate trade associations are all excellent sources of information about trade show opportunities. Trade Show Week Data Book and the Trade Shows and Professional Exhibits Directory, provide a wide range of information about major shows including dates, locations, past attendance, and number of exhibitors.

Regional or local shows typically will draw 40% to 50% or more of the audience from approximately a 200-mile radius. National shows draw 70% or more from outside the 200-mile radius.

Trade Show Bureau studies support the contention that the right people are attending. Figures from the Bureau show that 86% of those attending shows have buying influence, 90% of them buy within nine months, and 91% plan to buy within 12 months.

There are three phases to participating in a show:

- Pre-show
- At-show
- Post-show

Each phase requires hard work and careful planning to take advantage of the opportunity and increase your return on investment. Unfortunately, too many businesses only concern themselves with the at-show phase and often waste the investment they've made. I have had many clients generate leads at a trade show and never attempt to follow-up. In some cases the trade show is viewed as awareness advertising and is not even considered a lead generation opportunity.

Pre-Show Planning

The first thing you have to do in any marketing campaign, and trades shows are no different, is establish the objective. Are you trying to sell products directly? Introduce a new product? Generate sales leads? Establish credibility in a market?

If you're planning to generate sales leads, you should establish a specific lead and order objective from the show. Like any lead generation effort, remember you're not in the business to generate activity, you're in the business to sell something. I always suggest creating a special offer that will help the prospect qualify themselves in their own mind. You may want to refer to the discussion in Chapter

7 about creating offers. At trade shows you simply use a different format or vehicle to deliver your offer to the market.

Once you have identified the lead and order objective, you'll have to determine which show can produce the kind of activity you need to meet your objectives.

Remember, you don't have to drive attendance at trade shows. Your objective is to drive participants at the show to your booth. One exception might be to invite your house file of customers and prospects. You may want to personally invite these important prospects to attend the show and visit your booth.

There is an enormous difference between participating in a show by simply renting the space, building the booth and staffing it and actively using the show to sell your products and services. At trade shows, you have a captive audience who is genuinely interested in your product or service. Entertain them. Sell them. Liven your display with:

- Technical demonstrations and discussions.
- Mini-seminars on relevant topics.
- Games and contests that focus on product features and benefits.

The objective is to provide a reason for a prospect to enter your exhibit area. Your corporate name alone won't do it. With the tremendous interest and use of trade shows, you have to find a way to stand out in the crowd. One of the biggest challenges is getting the trade show audience across the invisible carpet line that separates your booth space from the rest of the show floor.

Once you've set your objectives and selected the show you need to decide how you'll promote your exhibit so attenders will visit your booth. Most shows will offer exhibitors a list of reserved attenders.

Many show managers even offer their list of prior attenders for direct marketing activity.

You should develop a direct marketing campaign, making an offer, that encourages prospects to visit your booth. As you develop the campaign, include a way for the prospect to respond even if they are not planning to attend the show. Include a response form in the mailing.

Timing on the direct mail campaign can be important. If you mail too far in advance of the show, the prospect may discard the promotion and not remember it. If you want to mail early, consider mailing a file or hanging folder that can be placed in the prospect's desk and used to store other promotional mailings about the show they might receive.

You can send a coupon for a special premium that is only offered in the mail. Make the prospect bring the coupon to the booth to receive the premium. This type of promotion can be targeted to specific businesses or executives within a business and encourage them to visit the show and your booth. You can use this type of promotion to get your best prospects to visit your booth.

Another successful technique is to send a series of mailings to anticipated attenders, providing them with different valuable information prior to the show. You can send a program or agenda of the show. Pocket sized program are particularly useful. You can then send information about restaurants or areas of special interest in the show location. Along with these useful tools, you can promote your products and company and encourage the prospect to visit your booth.

You should send a mailing to your entire house file. Even if most of these prospects don't typically attend the show, you get an opportunity to reinforce your relationship and you may even create a sales opportunity.

As you design the direct marketing promotion, use the techniques I've explained throughout this book. If you're trying to generate sales leads, use lead generation techniques.

The Booth

You now have to decide how you'll exhibit at the show. Prospects walking through the aisles are in information overload. Unless you see them early in the day, they're typically tired and bored. You have to break the pattern and create excitement and interest in your booth.

According to Curt Schleier in his article The Business of Trade Shows, *US Air Magazine*, (Volume XIII, Number 1, January 1991), there are basically five kinds of booths:

- *Drape and Table* is the simplest and least expensive approach. This is typically the type booth provided by the trade show sponsor. This exhibit can be customized by using special drapes (with the company's logo, for example), but they are still the simplest booths.

- *Tabletop Display*, as the name implies, these displays are typically small enough to fold into a carrying case, hand-carry into the exposition hall, and be set up by the exhibitor. This is a big advantage for tabletop and portable exhibits, since it avoids delays, not to mention the often steep bills that often occur when skilled labor is required to set up the booth.

- *Portable Exhibits* are prefabricated, lightweight and pack-aged in containers that can be shipped as airline baggage and

hand-carried to a show. They come in a variety of configurations and usually can be put together by the exhibitor.

- *Custom Exhibit* are designed and built to the company's
  specifications. They almost always must be crated or blan-
  ket-wrapped, shipped to the show, and set up by skilled
  labor. Of course, the more customized your display, the
  more it costs to create and set up each time you use it. But it
  may be more effective. Because they are generally larger
  than surrounding booths, customized exhibits tend to attract
  more attention than drape and table stands.

- *Exhibit Systems* fall somewhere between portable and customized exhibits. Like portables, they are lightweight, prefabricated, and can be used to create exhibits of varying
  sizes. However, they are usually far more elaborate, and
  often are too large to be hand-carried to an exhibit, and generally require skilled labor to set up.

The best booth for you is the one that best fits your strategy and plan
including your budget. You have to decide which products and services are going to be promoted at the show and the best way to display them. You should also consider your image. Major corporations go to major shows, and they need big areas. If you're occupy-
ing a large area, say 20' x 20', a portable is not appropriate.

Size, color, shape, texture, and lighting can all be used to draw
attention to your booth. In addition, the costumes or uniforms your
staff wears on the show floor can also draw attention to the booth.

In one show I worked on we required the entire staff, both men and
women, to dress in tuxedos with tails. The booth played classical
music and the theme was based on a promotion we developed called
the Orchestrator. The company had a record number of high quality
leads but also got terrific publicity and recognition in the trade and

local publications. Very little was done to change the appearance of the booth.

Your objective for participating in the show will influence the theme and ultimately the composition of the booth. All the elements that contribute to capturing the attention of the show attenders while walking down the aisle should be factored into the booth design. If you can't afford a large booth with an elaborate display, use sight and sound elements to make your booth stand out from the crowd.

Make it a personal challenge to get prospects to cross the invisible carpet line from the show floor to your booth space. I have always operated on the premise that once someone enters your booth, it is almost impossible for them not to examine the products and services you display.

I will frequently advise companies to consider giving a premium away or holding a raffle for a prize. Make the display fun to visit and people will stop. Remember that the prospect is probably dealing with sensory overload and is looking for an opportunity to learn and have some fun. Most attendees are tired and will stop at different booths if they appear interesting and promise a chance to rest and take a breather.

You always walk a delicate balance in the quantity and quality of prospects you attract in the trade show environment. You can drive unqualified prospects into your booth as well as really qualified individuals. If you give away an expensive premium, you run the risk of encouraging unqualified prospects to visit your booth just to receive the gift.

Some trade shows distribute embossed name badges to attendees and small machines to exhibitors. The small machines work like those used in retail outlets to secure credit card information. The exhibitor can ask booth guests for their name badge, and run it through the machine to quickly obtain the name, company, and address of the prospect. This is a convenient system, but it often generates many unqualified leads. Often, it is difficult to determine appropriate follow-up after the show because the information you obtained from the prospect is so limited. The same thing happens if your merely ask prospects for their business cards.

I advocate having the prospect complete a request card. You can provide a place to attach their business card and then ask them to answer one or two simple questions. Don't forget to make them an offer and see if they want to respond.

Remember, that it isn't important what the salesperson thinks, it is only important what the prospect thinks. The prospect should qualify themselves. If your offer explains how much your product costs, its benefits, and asks for a response, prospects who request action are qualified.

As you may recall, lead qualification involves four elements:

- Money
- Authority
- Need
- Desire

Rather than asking a lot of detailed questions to qualify the prospect, make an offer that resolves money, need, and desire. That way the only question you need to ask is:

Which of the following best describes your involvement in a decision to acquire _____?

1) You make the decision
2) You investigate and recommend
3) The decision is made elsewhere in the company

If made elsewhere, can you tell me who is responsible for these type of decisions:

Name _____
Title   _____
Phone (___) ___-____

Once you have someone who has accepted your offer and is involved in the decision, you have a qualified respondent.

Why should a prospect stop at your booth and complete a response card? They would have to be extremely interested in your products or services. By requiring them to complete the card, you are actually making it more difficult to stop at your booth and request information.

One way to get prospects to complete the card is to offer a prize drawing similar to a raffle. This technique encourages prospects to enroll at your booth. You purchase a VCR or CD Player and offer to give it away at the end of the show. You can even play music on the CD player to gain attention during the show. Some companies have developed looped video tapes which constantly play during the show. You can have a drawing to give both the VCR and TV monitor away after the show.

The drawing will attract attention and increase the traffic in your booth. It also makes it easier to invite prospects into your booth. Salespeople can ask the strolling audience if they've already entered to win their free VCR. This technique will drive traffic into the booth. And once prospects enter a booth they will probably examine the products and services displayed.

A give-away will attract more unqualified prospects and therefore, you want each prospect to qualify themself without involving your booth staff. Make it clear that only cards completely filled out will be eligible for the drawing.

If you decide to have a drawing, you will have to design your booth to contain a bowl or ballot box to allow prospects to enter the drawing. You should also create signs announcing the drawing. The ideal booth design will display the prize clearly so that prospects can see what they might win.

In some situations I have seen companies hire professional models to walk through the display floor, circulating enrollment cards to attenders and inviting them to visit the booth to enroll in the drawing. Once you decide to pursue an avenue to drive traffic into the booth, you can have a lot of fun.

If you are planning to offer demonstrations in your booth, make sure there is enough space to allow several people to observe. Very often prospects will be walking by while the demonstration is in progress. Make it easy for them to observe and participate. If you're using computer terminals to demonstrate, use video monitors to allow the audience to follow along with the operator. Obviously this type of demonstration requires additional space.

Telephones in booths can be very distracting. If you are planning to have a phone in the booth, try to have it behind the display and don't allow your staff to use the phone while the display area is open to prospects. Nothing can be more discouraging to a prospect than to visit a booth and find the sales staff not available because they are on the telephone.

<u>Staffing</u>

Working a trade show may be the most demanding and physically tiring sales effort you'll ever encounter. Salespeople are required to stand on their feet for hours on end and hopefully talk to an endless stream of prospects. The selling skills required in a trade show booth are different then traditional face-to-face skills. People who are extremely effective in selling face-to-face will often fail when asked to sell in a booth.

Direct selling is a long, involved process that permits the salesperson to build and sell through a relationship. The salesperson can establish credibility and trust with the prospect. They will often have made several calls and presentations to the prospect allowing both the prospect and salesperson to know one another.

At a trade show, you get only a few moments to create a favorable impression and sell your product. You have to display enthusiasm, be friendly and knowledgeable all at once. Very often the superstar salesperson is not the best person to work a show. High powered salespeople are often too preoccupied with generating sales in their territories. They can't sell many of the show participants because they aren't located in their territories. These highly effective salespeople often fail at trade shows.

It is better to have too many people than to have too few. The work is exhausting and no one should be required to work the booth more than four to six hours per day. After about four hours people begin to tire and lose their effectiveness. Burnout is a real problem and working the booth too long can be counterproductive.

Many times the exhaustive effort required to work the show is compounded by time zone changes. If a salesperson lives on the east coast and has traveled to the west coast to participate in the show, he will be physically and mentally exhausted by the middle of the day.

Once a trade show staffer becomes tired, they begin to treat the prospects with disdain. They feel imposed upon and convey that feeling to the show attenders. An overtired salesperson can make your investment in the trade show worthless.

Trade show salespersons should be trained on how to work a booth. They should be discouraged from grouping together among themselves and having meetings and conversations. They're participating in a show to meet prospects and sell your products.

As I mentioned earlier, the appearance of the salespeople can draw attention to your booth. If you decide to have your staff dress in a uniform or costume, enforce the requirement to all participants. You should set dress standards for all show participants, even if you don't use a uniform or costume. Professional image starts with appearance and prospects will draw conclusions about your company based on how your staff looks.

The way people dress will send a clear message to the show participants about your company. The way the people act in the booth will also send a message. If activity slows down, salespeople shouldn't sit and read magazines or books. Here are some simple rules for staffing the booth:

- Never sit. Stand with an open stance without folding your arms.
- Don't talk with other staffers.
- Don't smoke or eat in the booth.

Very often salespeople will stand in the back of the booth and wait for prospects to stop by and ask them a question. Prospects need to be invited into your booth and sold on learning more about your products and services. Some salespeople are afraid to be too aggressive and consider working a booth beneath their status in life. Their egos force them to stand back and wait.

The worst question a salesperson can ask a prospect is May I help you? Prospects are intimidated by salespeople and avoid interacting with them for fear they'll be sold something. Salespeople will have to break the ice and make the prospect feel comfortable with the booth, the environment, and themselves.

Having a drawing is a great way to initiate conversation and draw traffic into your booth. Salespeople can stand on the corner of the booth or even in the aisle and ask attenders if they have had a chance to sign-up for their free CD player. Once a prospect enters a booth, it is fairly easy to start a meaningful conversation.

Like telephone selling, you only have a few seconds to get the attention of the prospect. Show attenders are trying to sort through enormous amounts of information and breaking through the clutter is a real problem. You want to be noticed and remembered. Your staff should clearly understand the objectives in participating in the show and work to meet those objectives. In most situations, the booth salespeople will be talking to prospects that are handled by other salespeople. They should be aware that their actions can make or break a sale for one of their associates.

Salespeople have to appear anxious to help prospects. Their job is get acquainted, get the name and title of the prospect, and determine their qualification. If the prospect is interested and qualified, the booth salesperson has to pass on the pertinent information to the field salesperson. They can't rely on memory. If possible, booth salespeople should take notes as well as obtain the prospect's business card. Your booth should contain prospect qualification forms and a stapler to allow the booth salespeople to attach business cards.

Many companies will staff their booths with two different types of people. Salespeople hawk prospects into the booth and then more technical customer service people answer questions and demonstrate products. I prefer to have salespeople who are capable of demonstrating the product as well as driving traffic into the booth. You can still have technical people available in case you have a malfunction or require more technical discussions with a prospect. The more self-sufficient the booth salesperson, the better the impression the prospect will have of your other salespeople.

Driving Booth Attendance

Advertising and publicity can play an important role in the overall promotion of your booth. Used well and timed properly, they are powerful ways to bolster attendance and call attention to the stature and value of your company. Although publicity and advertising should be tightly coordinated with your direct response promotion, one does not replace the other. If your budget will allow it, you should plan to do both.

Publicity is distinct from advertising. For one thing, publicity consists of information that is deemed newsworthy, so you don't pay to get space or air time. But free is not easy. Your seminar may be interesting and newsworthy to some, and meaningless to others.

Your target audience will likely read trade magazines or newsletters where events of interest in their field are published. That is where you want to send a news release about your booth. Many newspapers list the title, date, time, place, and price of meetings, seminars and trade shows. Make sure you send a short notice to these publications.

In your press releases, describe the products you will exhibit at the show. New products or service announcements are even more newsworthy and justify a release. You can send news releases to general consumer publications or even write a letter to the editor explaining the announcement and its importance. If you find widespread enthusiastic response, you might consider holding a press conference prior to the show. Schedule a press conference only if you're convinced there is genuine enthusiasm about the news value of your show.

Here are some tips for getting publicity.

- Send out as many press releases as necessary to cover the trade and general interest publications, but send only one per publication.

- Be absolutely sure to have the name and telephone number of a contact person at your company on the release.

- Leave adequate lead time. Trade publications and newsletters, for instance, are usually printed monthly, and releases have to be in the editor's hands weeks before the publication date. Weeklies have specific deadline dates; check with their editors. Daily newspapers often accept press releases until only hours before printing.

- For the publications you deem to be the most important, a follow-up phone call to the editor might be appropriate. If you are trying to get a feature story published, a call is essential.

- Include a black and white glossy photograph if at all possible; the product announcement is a publishable item.

Like publicity, advertising is a tool to create awareness about your exhibit and your company and can be an effective way to increase traffic. Unlike publicity, you pay to place your message.

While advertising is expensive, it can be very effective for reaching a wide audience with a well thought-out message to promote your booth.

You should use an advertising agency or a creative free-lancer to create the advertisement you will use You can use space advertising in both newspapers and magazines. Many trade shows have directories in which you can place ads. These directories are normally given to each attendee and will be seen by your specific target market.

Some larger shows also have trade show newspapers that can allow you to reach the attendee for several days. You can use the trade press, conference journal and show newspaper by inserting your existing advertisement and adding a tag line, Come See Us at the ABC Show, Booth 123. This will tell people where to find you and enhance the image of your company and products.

Many shows offer an opportunity to purchase advertising time on the hotel TV systems. This can be another effective way to reach the target audience of attenders.

Here are some other interesting advertising opportunities that you might consider to reach the show attenders.

- Local radio and television stations.
- Billboards on the way into town or from the hotel to the convention center.
- Skywriting in the morning or evening when prospects are arriving or leaving the show.
- Flyers or ad reprints in the enrollment area for prospects coming to the show.
- Flyers or ad reprints in or around the trade show.

- Floor-walker models to hand flyers or brochures to the attenders encouraging them to visit your booth.
- A large balloon that announces your booth location. You should also consider having a similar balloon in the show to make it easier to find your booth.

The list of advertising and promotional opportunities is virtually endless and your budget and show rules will dictate what you can do. Each advertisement media has its own unique set of strengths and weaknesses.

Direct mail and telephone selling are also terrific traffic building techniques for your trade show exhibit. Many trade show sponsors will publish enrollment lists and list of prior attenders. These lists can offer you an excellent opportunity to pre-sell the attendee and invite them to visit your booth.

Don't forget your house file. Your current prospects and customers will probably offer you the greatest short-term sales potential. The show gives you a reason to contact them and enhance the relationship. You can also make them a special offer for visiting the booth.

As you design your direct marketing promotion, try to follow the guidelines I've discussed throughout this book. Here are some other considerations about trade show direct mail.

- Other companies, including your competition, will be mailing the same lists. Your promotion should be specialized and segmented. Make an offer and sell benefits.

- Help drive traffic to the event as well as to your booth. Describe the session as an important event, one that shouldn't be missed. Make sure your exhibit is described in similar terms.

- Show how the prospect will get information in a unique way and stress the benefits of visiting your booth. Be careful not to stress features. Features are what your product does; benefits are what your prospect gains by having your product do something. Sell holes, not shovels.

- Provide statistics that demonstrate how attendance at the event is a good investment of their time and resources. Prove that coming to the event will offer high return on investment.

Trade shows are similar to most lead programs but because the activity centers around driving traffic to a specific date, the leads occur in a burst. This bubble of activity creates significant problems in follow-up and conversion of leads to orders. As you plan your programs to drive traffic make sure you plan a follow-up program directly to the prospect. Don't rely only on your salespeople to contact the prospect after the trade show.

In most cases you'll be trying to reach a decision maker. Sound like a decision maker yourself. The executive-to-executive impression will ensure a higher attendance rate at the show.

If you use a letter, be brief, direct, and professional in tone. Identify the problem you know the prospect is concerned about and stress that they can see the solutions at the trade show.

Telephone will serve several important roles in this campaign. Contact prospects and invite them to your booth. This really works well if you have created a unique offer that the prospect will receive when visiting the booth.

As I discussed in Chapter 9, telephone selling is significantly more expensive than direct mail. You want to use it where it can produce the best results. Calling prospects after trade shows is a good investment. These calls can let you know how effective your exhibit was, and will make your prospect feel good about your company at the same time. Details on how to conduct these calls can be found in Chapters 3 and 9.

I think the biggest problem with trade shows is getting salespeople to follow-up with each attendee. This is the typical problem associated with every lead generation effort, but it is compounded when leads are generated in a single burst. They will almost always overload the sales force. It is impossible for them to contact each prospect and do a quality selling job.

You should plan some direct contact with each attendee after the show. A thank you letter go a long way to sustaining the business relationship and helping to pave the way for a future sale. Another effective technique is a questionnaire asking the prospect to evaluate the show and provide you with feedback on how you can improve your offerings.

At-Show Activity

Now the hard physical work really begins. Trade show work is physically gruelling. It doesn't let up and booth staff has to stay up every minute they're working the exhibit.

Promotional efforts shouldn't stop once the show begins. Use any method you can to drive traffic to the booth during the show. Many companies will have contests or giveaways and even in-booth celebrities. Skits, shows, and live music are also popular methods to attract attention to trade show booths.

Many concepts have been used over and over and you might think they wouldn't work anymore. But so many trade show exhibitors don't do anything that if you make your booth a little different, you can easily stand out in the crowd.

A war room or control suite is an ideal vehicle to turn your trade show into a selling event. This room should be a place where the booth support staff can meet and discuss daily activity, plan and schedule booth staffing, and process leads generated during the show.

The war room should be away from the hustle and bustle of the trade show pressure. It's a place where sales management can meet with the show staff and discuss issues that arise during the show, and plan the activity for the coming day. Management can bring life and enthusiasm back into the staff in the war room.

Think about the last show you attended. You probably were in information overload. What did you do with all of the promotional material you acquired at the show? Did it even make it to your office? If it did make it home, what ultimately became of the material?

Trade shows are popular because an attendee can visit multiple vendors in a short period of time and collect large amounts of information at a minimal cost. As trade show participants, your challenge is to make sure the material you distribute isn't lost in the information the attendees take away. If you're actually selling products and accepting orders at the show, it is appropriate to distribute complete product literature.

But if you are using the trade show as a lead generation event, distributing product information can be expensive and counterproductive.

The ideal situation is to have appropriate material delivered to a prospect in their office immediately after the show.

You just attended a show and visited ABC company's booth. You were interested in their new computer and desktop publishing system. You visited the booth on Tuesday and it's now Thursday and you're back in your office. About mid-morning you receive an overnight express delivery with a complete information package and special offer to test the product in your office. How would you react?

I think you can be more effective if you don't provide all your information in the booth. Demonstrate products, and qualify prospects by showing what the product will do and what it will cost. Make the prospects qualify themselves. If you make a strong offer in the booth, the prospect can accept the offer by enrolling or completing a card and you can fulfill using direct mail.

The war room is the ideal facility to process the requests from prospects. If you're using an outside fulfillment service, you can complete the information requests each evening and express mail to the fulfillment house and ensure timely mailing to your prospect. If you're doing your own fulfillment, you can mail directly from the war room to the prospect and they'll receive the information package immediately upon returning from the show.

You can even install a computer in the war room and print personalized letters, update your database, and generate the sales lead while you're still at the show.

The technology now makes it possible to FAX the information from a desktop computer to the prospect while the prospect is still at the show. You can even FAX the lead directly to the salesperson in the prospect's territory and ensure immediate follow-up.

I think that the more timely your response the better opportunity you have to sell. You can set yourself aside from competition by providing information soon after the show. This approach will add some expense but will ensure that the prospect sees your material in his office and thinks about you in the most positive way.

If you decide to follow-up on leads after the show, you will have to accurately capture information at the show. Use a registration system that the prospect is responsible for completing. You will get the most accurate and complete information directly from the prospect.

If you use a raffle or giveaway system, you will have a reason to contact the prospect via direct mail after the show and tell them who won. This direct mail contact can make another offer and start a two step process that can generate highly qualified leads.

Try to limit the time your staff works the show floor to one or two hour increments. I think that trade show activity is physically the most tiring of all selling endeavors. If the staff is doing their job, they don't get a chance to sit or rest during their booth time.

As a staff member leaves the booth, encourage them to visit the war room and complete a debriefing. If they have met hot prospects, ask them to make complete notes to ensure timely and accurate follow-up.

Your staff should be selling and encouraging show traffic to stop and visit your booth. They should understand that their mission is to sell, not to just answer questions. A trade show will usually place competition side-by-side. You can either win or lose the sale based on how well the booth and staff are perceived on the trade show floor. If your staff is standing together having friendly discussions among themselves, prospects may get the idea that your company is stand-offish and pursue competition.

Get your staff dispersed and talking to prospects. If prospects aren't entering your booth, have the staff sell them on visiting. **Don't**

allow smoking, drinking, eating, or internal meetings to take place in your booth, no matter how slow the show may seem.

A telephone in the booth can be a real productivity tool. If you're using equipment in demonstrations and a problem should arise, the telephone can be a real life-saver. Unfortunately, the telephone becomes a convenience for staff to contact customers, prospects or internal staff members. It also becomes an easy way for people to contact the booth. Someone on the phone in your booth isn't talking to prospects at the show. The telephone can be a distraction and valuable sales opportunities can be missed. There are several alternatives for telephone communications that you might want to consider:

- Install the phone behind your display and only allow emergency calls to be made or received.

- Provide a portable cellular telephone for emergency communication. When a call has to be made or received, it should be done away from the booth where it won't distract prospects.

- Install the phone in the war room and then have communication relayed to the staff in the booth. This is the best solution to the problem. Consider having the war room staffed at all times during the show. This will provide a central communication and coordination facility.

As you generate activity in the booth, and hopefully generate sales leads, make sure you add every name to your database. Although some of the leads won't be qualified, every visitor to your booth is important and deserves a high quality follow-up. You decided to participate in the show because the audience met the criteria of your sales target. You want to make a favorable impression on as many attenders as possible. Prospects who visit your booth should receive high quality follow-up because they may be your customers in the future.

Post-Show Activity

Once the show ends, you begin an equally hard job of making your efforts pay off. If you decided to participate in the trade show to generate sales leads, you must contact each prospect and offer them something of value. Like advertising and seminars, trade shows develop leads in a single burst. If you have limited sales resources, it will be difficult to ensure timely follow-up. **Your efforts should not be totally dependent on salespeople to follow-up.**

I have seen many trade show programs generate a large number of leads that are never even distributed to the sales force. The leads are brought back from the trade show and stored in a box and never contacted by anyone. When these companies are questioned why this occurred, the standard answer seems to be that the salespeople don't like the quality of trade show leads and refuse to follow-up.

I suggest you design a complete information kit that can be easily sent after the show to every respondent. You may want to create two different versions for qualified and less qualified prospects. Remember that qualification should be determined by the prospect, not by you or your salespeople.

As I mentioned earlier, providing expensive fulfillment material at the show can be a waste of money. Send the material after the show. Sending the material promptly will be the single most impressive aspect of your fulfillment.

Make each prospect an offer. Most lead programs suffer from not having a real offer. As you design the fulfillment material develop an offer that allows the prospect to qualify themselves and encourages them to request additional activity. In essence, create a two step program. The first step was the prospect visiting your booth. Step two should encourage the prospect to request additional contact from your company. The prospect should have an understanding of the benefits they will derive from the next contact and also have an idea of the costs involved in your product solution. Prospects who know what a solution will give them and how much it costs and still request additional contact are qualified.

Prospects who met with your staff and have been identified as being high quality leads -- hot prospects -- should be immediately forwarded to a local salesperson for handling. You may want to FAX the lead information to the salesperson after the information has been added to your database. You can then also forward a copy through your normal distribution system. The FAX lead will prompt the salesperson to give the prospect immediate and special attention.

If you used a raffle or contest approach to capture the interest of a larger number of prospects, you have an excellent reason for contacting this group after the show. You can notify all of the show participants of the winner. This notification vehicle gives you a solid reason for contacting the prospect, developing a relationship, and making an additional offer.

With constant profit pressure on most businesses, customer (prospect) service seems to be one of the first areas in which companies reducing expense. You can immediately improve the perception of your company if you pay attention to a prospect. Most of us have grown accustomed to poor service and apathetic people handling our inquiries. If you provide good service with knowledgeable, friendly people, prospects will want to do business with your company. A friendly follow-up letter can go a long way towards creating a relationship built on a foundation of good service.

You may not be able to afford to have salespeople contact every prospect, but you cannot afford no contact at all. Direct mail is the ideal vehicle to ensure 100% follow-up of every prospect who visited your booth.

As we discussed earlier you can use direct marketing to promote attendance at the trade show booth. Illustration 11-1 demonstrates one approach to generating a mail campaign. You can include a special coupon or invitation that the prospect can redeem for a free prize or gift when they visit the booth. As you design the campaign you'll be able to create several dynamic offers that will attract attendance to the booth and allow you to generate high quality leads. You can even extend the flow and add a phone call to confirm a

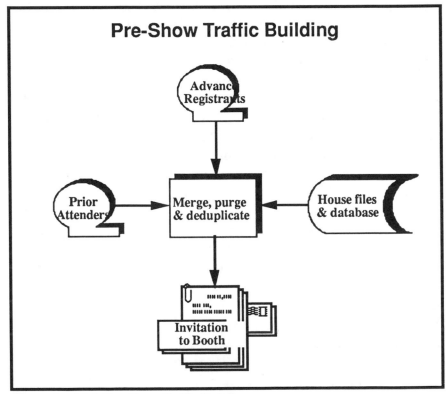

Illustration 11-1: Pre-Show Traffic Building.

prospect's attendance at the show and perhaps offer your best prospects free tickets to the show.

Once the show is over and you have generated the leads, direct marketing becomes even more important. If you have used an enrollment card with an incentive for the prospect to provide additional information, you can have the prospect qualify themselves.

As Illustration 11-2 shows, the respondent information should first be entered into your database. You can use time to your advantage if you capture the information while still at the show and then mail the fulfillment kit so it arrives when the prospect returns to their office from the show.

You should consider creating two different fulfillment kits based on different qualification levels. For example, if a prospect indicates they are not involved in decisions to acquire products like yours, it wouldn't be appropriate to expend significant effort and resources selling that individual. The fulfillment kit should contain an offer that encourages the appropriate person in the prospect's business to respond if the attendee passes the information along to that person.

Encourage qualified prospects to respond by making them a valuable offer. Use telephone selling to develop the highest response rate possible from the attenders group. The telephone call can enhance the relationship and develop immediate leads.

Once the prospect has agreed to further contact, the lead should be sent to the salespeople as fast as possible. FAX or electronic mail are ideal methods to get the lead out quickly. Remember the discussion about territory management in Chapter 5? If you decide to send the leads out for immediate follow-up, you should also send a copy in the territory management format to help the salesperson control and manage their territory.

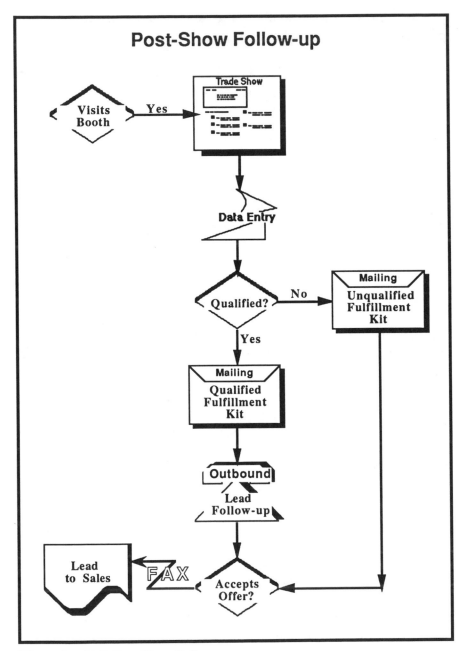

Illustration 11-2: Post-Show Follow-up.

While I was writing this section I received a phone call from a company that recently attended a trade show. The telephone selling specialist called for some advice on how to follow-up on the prospects identified at the show. The show was held about 90 days ago and the leads were just turned over for follow-up. I don't think that the prospect who attended the show will remember anything about the company or their products. The telephone call will be just a cold phone call and the results will be disappointing. This will probably convince the company that the quality of leads generated at a trade show isn't very good. I cannot emphasize enough the importance of timely follow-up to generating successful trade show activity.

Like all lead generation programs, measurement and follow-up are difficult, but critical. You need to make it your personal mission to make sure all prospect's identified at the show are contacted afterward.

Salespeople will find it difficult to reach the prospects on the telephone and some may never be contacted. This situation is common in most lead generation programs but because of the volume of leads developed in a short period of time at trade shows, it is exacerbated. You can implement an independent telephone follow-up to ensure that each lead is contacted. This phone call can provide valuable measurement information and ensure that good selling opportunities don't slip through the cracks. This is similar to the follow-up phone call program described in Chapters 3 and 4.

Trade Shows Summarized

Trade shows, like seminars, are growing in popularity as lead generation vehicles. Both of these approaches bring together a group of prospects who have demonstrated an interest or affinity in a specific subject. This affinity gives you an opportunity to sell products or services directly related to the interests of the prospects.

Driving traffic is not an issue in trade-shows. Typically a group of prospects is attending a trade-show and your objective is to generate sales opportunities from those who attend. Your challenge is to create a display that is interesting, so that the attenders will automatically visit with your sales staff at the show.

Trade shows offer some great benefits.

- You can demonstrate and show your products and services.

- The prospects are pre-qualified.

- They are an ideal environment to gain market research.

- It is easy to arrange high level meetings between your executives and important customers and prospects.

- You can review competitive offerings and understand better how to position your products and services.

- Trade shows are a terrific place to meet and recruit potential employees.

- They are a great place to announce new products and ensure you achieve maximum impact and publicity.

There are three phases to participating in a show:

- Pre-show
- At-show
- Post-show

The first thing you have to do in any marketing campaign, and trades shows are no different, is establish the objective. Are you trying to sell products directly? Introduce a new product? Generate sales leads? Establish credibility in a market?

There is an enormous difference between participating in a show by simply renting the space, building the booth and staffing it and participating to sell your products and services. You can entertain or sell a captive audience on your products and services. You can liven your display by:

- Technical demonstrations and discussions.
- Mini-seminars on relevant topics.
- Games and contests that focus on product features and benefits.

The objective is to provide a reason for a prospect to enter your exhibit area. Your corporate name alone won't do it. With the tremendous interest and use of trade shows, you have to find a way to stand out in the crowd.

There are basically five kinds of booths:

- *Drape and Table*
- *Tabletop Display*
- *Portable Exhibit*
- *Exhibit Systems*
- *Custom Exhibit*

The best booth for you is the one that best fits your strategy and plan including your budget. You have to resolve which products and services are going to be promoted at the show and what is the best way to display them.

I advocate having the prospect complete a request card. You can provide a place to attach their business card and then ask them to answer one or two simple questions. Don't forget to make them an offer and see if they want to respond.

One way to get prospects to complete the card is to offer a prize drawing similar to a raffle. This technique encourages prospects to enroll at your booth. The drawing will attract attention and increase the traffic in your booth.

A giveaway will attract more unqualified prospects and therefore, you want each prospect to qualify themself without involving your booth staff. Make it clear that only cards completely filled out will be eligible for the drawing. Prospects now have a reason to complete the card. The enrollment card should make an offer and verify the prospect's buying authority.

Very often salespeople will stand in the back of the booth and wait for prospects to stop by and ask them a question. Prospects need to be invited into your booth and sold on learning more about your products and services.

Here are some simple rules for staffing the booth.

- Never sit. Stand with an open stance without folding your arms.
- Don't talk with other staffers.
- Don't smoke or eat in the booth.

Advertising and publicity can play an important role in the overall promotion of your booth. Used well and timed properly, they are powerful ways to bolster attendance and call attention to the stature and value of your company. Although publicity and advertising should be tightly coordinated with your direct response promotion, one does not replace the other. If your budget will allow it, you should plan to do both.

Direct mail and telephone selling are also terrific traffic building techniques for your trade show exhibit. Many trade show sponsors will provide enrollment lists and a list of prior attenders. These lists can offer you an excellent opportunity to pre-sell the attendee and invite them to visit your booth.

Don't forget your house file. Your current prospects and customers will probably offer you the greatest short-term sales potential. The show gives you a reason and opportunity to contact them and enhance the relationship. You can also make them a special offer for visiting the booth.

Some other thoughts about trade show direct mail:

- Other companies, including your competition, will be mailing the same lists. Your promotion should be specialized and segmented. Make an offer and sell benefits.

- Help drive traffic to the event as well as to your booth. Describe the session as an important event, one that shouldn't be missed. Make sure your exhibit is described in similar terms.

- Show how the prospect will get information in a unique way and stress the benefits of visiting your booth. Be careful not to stress features. Features are what your product does; benefits are what your prospect gains by having your product do something. Sell holes, not shovels.

- Provide statistics that demonstrate how attendance at the event is a good investment of their time and resources. Prove that coming to the event will offer high return on investment.

A war room or control suite is an ideal vehicle to turn your trade show into a selling event. This room should be a place where the booth support staff can meet and discuss daily activity, plan and schedule booth staffing and process leads generated during the show.

Trade shows are popular because an attendee can visit multiple vendors in a short period of time and collect large amounts of information at a minimal cost. As trade show participants, your challenge is to make sure the material you distribute isn't lost in the information the attendees take away. If you are using the trade show as a lead generation event, distributing product information can be expensive and counterproductive. Most of the information will probably not even make it back to the attender's office. The ideal situation is to have appropriate material delivered to a prospect in their office immediately after the show.

Like advertising and seminars, trade shows develop leads in a single burst. If you have limited sales resources, it will be difficult to ensure timely follow-up. Your follow-up efforts should not be totally dependent on salespeople.

Prospects who met with your staff and have been identified as being high quality leads -- hot prospects -- should be immediately forwarded to a local salesperson for handling. You may want to FAX the lead information to the salesperson after the information has been added to your database. You can then also forward a copy through your normal distribution system. The FAX lead will prompt the salesperson to give the prospect immediate and special attention.

This chapter focused on how to participate in a trade show and ensure the best production of leads. Like any lead program, the real effort starts once you develop interest and create the lead. Sales follow-up is difficult and will require committment from you and your staff. Seminars, advertising, and trade shows generate leads in a burst and make it even more difficult to ensure timely, quality follow-up.

Chapter Twelve:
Customer Lead Generation

The best list you have available for any direct marketing, including lead generation, is your house file. This database should consist of customers and prior respondents. In virtually every test I've ever participated in, the house file has performed better than all other lists by almost 2 to 1. In this chapter I'll discuss programs that can help you generate leads from your house file.

As you develop your house file, you should begin to add prior respondents to it as well as any prospect or customer with whom you have a relationship. Business selling is traditionally done through sustained relationships. Any customer who has spent money with your company, regardless of how little, has established a relationship that you can use to generate additional business.

Remember that a *Customer* is any individual who has purchased products or services from you. It doesn't matter how little they have purchased. This group is different than the rest of the world. They know who you are and have paid money to your company. In addition, you know who they are and have dealt with them in the past.

You have a relationship with them and they are certainly different than prospects and referrals.

In most cases you have invested money in building the relationship with your customers. If they were sold by a face-to-face salesperson, you may have invested thousands of dollars. It is often said that the most valuable asset in a business is the house file. If you consider both the acquisition and selling expenses associated with each name on your customer file, the database is probably your most expensive asset as well.

Respondents to your direct marketing efforts are also extremely expensive and valuable. Besides the costs associated with acquiring the response, you may have also invested money in fulfillment and even in face-to-face selling activity. If your lead programs are extremely effective, you may be able to close one out of every 5 leads generated. In addition, if you're qualifying each respondent prior to sending them to the sales force, you may only be sending 1 out of every 2 respondents as leads.

As you can see, the number of non-buyers is significantly greater than the actual customers created by a lead program. What happens to these respondents? Have they all purchased from someone else? Are they no longer prospects for your company?

Respondents are also different than the rest of the business universe because they have a relationship with your company. It is up to you to sustain and enhance that relationship. Let's assume that you generated a lead 8 months ago and the prospect never purchased. You can make an interesting offer that might help the prospect decide to make a decision now.

You can have as much invested in a prior respondent as you have in a customer. If you send the lead to the sales force and they make face-to-face calls on that prospect, it is easy to invest several hundred or even thousands of dollars in that prospect. These valuable and expensive prospects should be included in your house file.

The Customer Opinion Survey

The relationship you enjoy with your customers is as much perceived as it is reality. Customer satisfaction is dependent on many things, not the least of which is the level and quality of communication you have sustained with them. I have found that a customer opinion survey is an excellent vehicle to rekindle customer relationships, create valuable information and generate high quality leads.

Illustration 12-1 is an example of a letter used to announce an integrated telephone selling staff. The letter is designed to enhance the relationship and open dialogue between the Sample Company and the customer. The communication responsibility is going to be less dependent on the salesperson.

Illustration 12-2 is the customer opinion survey that was included with the letter. You can learn a lot about how your customers feel about your company, products, service, and people from an opinion survey. But you can also develop terrific sales leads when you include an open area for customers to tell you what their requirements are today.

As you'll notice, the survey on page 593 asks the customer to provide their answers with a quantitative response. This kind of information can be very useful in establishing customer satisfaction objectives and measurements. If you make the survey an annual event, you can track the change in customer satisfaction and develop programs with an objective to improve satisfaction. I have found that when customer satisfaction is increasing, business is growing. On the other hand if satisfaction is declining, sales also seem to decline.

Mr. Joe Sample, President
Sample Company
123 Any Street
Grand Rapids, MI 49501

Dear Mr. Sample,

You are an important customer and we are committed to our continued relationship. In an effort to provide you even better customer service, I am introducing a new program to provide you better service and support. In addition
to the sales, systems, and service personnel assigned to your account, we are
now introducing an inside salesperson who will contact you from time to
time on the telephone. This inside representative will work closely with our
other personnel who service your account to ensure you receive an even
higher level of support and attention.

I am experimenting with an inside representative because I know it is difficult to provide you with the level of support you require. Like most companies, we don't have enough resources to remain in contact with all of our customers as often as we'd like. As a result, you may have some problems that
we could help solve, that we simply aren't aware of. The periodic calls you'll
receive will allow you to learn about new announcements and give us an
opportunity to determine how we can better serve you. The inside salesperson will not replace your current sales and systems personnel, but is an addition to your support team. If you require support, please feel free to contact
any of the people assigned to your account.

We are interested in how you feel about our current relationship and would
appreciate your completing and returning the enclosed questionnaire. This
information can help us develop better programs to support you.

If you have any questions, please feel free to give me a call. I appreciate
your continued business and would like to work with you to enhance our
relationship.

Sincerely,

Branch Manager

Illustration 12-1: Letter Announcing Opinion Survey.

Customer Opinion Survey

We want to provide you with the best possible customer service and we are committed to your satisfaction. To help us help you, please answer each question with one of the following responses which best represents your feelings:

> 1=Very Satisfied
> 2=Satisfied
> 3=Neither satisfied nor dissatisfied
> 4=Dissatisfied
> 5=Very Dissatisfied

❑ 1) Are you happy with the level of support you receive directly from this branch office?

❑ 2) Do you feel you receive enough contact from us?

❑ 3) How do you feel about the quantity of information you receive from us?

❑ 4) How about the quality of that information?

5) Are you satisfied with:

❑ Your equipment?

❑ Your maintenance services?

❑ The software you are using?

❑ The value you receive from your equipment?

❑ The marketing personnel that support your account?

❑ 6) How satisfied are you overall?

7) Please help us improve our service to you. Can you think of any areas you would like us to change that would help us give you better service?

_____

8) Is there a particular area that we can be of assistance with right now?

_____

123456789

Illustration 12-2: Customer Opinion Survey.

You can print the customer's account number in the margin of the survey to allow you to track each customer. Because you have asked each answer to be coded with a relative level of satisfaction, you can develop specific satisfaction indexes for each customer and each question.

In the example on page 579, there are 10 questions that the customer would respond to using the 1-5 scale (Questions 1-6). A simple method for establishing an index would be to value each question as 10% of the overall level of satisfaction.

The five possible responses also make it easy to establish the relative satisfaction of each question. A very satisfied response would be worth 100% while a very dissatisfied response is worth 0. The values to use for each question are:

1=Very Satisfied	100%
2=Satisfied	75%
3=Neither satisfied nor dissatisfied	50%
4=Dissatisfied	25%
5=Very Dissatisfied	0%

Once you have established the value of each question and the relative value of each answer, you can establish satisfaction indexes. I recommend you establish a satisfaction index for each customer, a combined index for each salesperson or territory, and one for each question.

Illustration 12-3 on page 581 shows how a typical customer might respond to the survey. Using this example we'll calculate the satisfaction index for this customer. Each question has a relative value of 10 points (10% of the total) and the value for each answer will be based on the table.

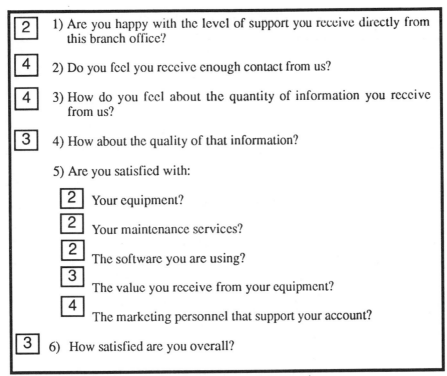

Illustration 12-3: The completed customer opinion survey.

Question 1 is worth 7.5 points.   (10 x 75%)
         2   =   2.5   (10 x 25%)
         3   =   2.5   (10 x 25%)
         4   =   5.0   (10 x 50%)
        5a   =   7.5   (10 x 75%)
        5b   =   7.5   (10 x 75%)
        5c   =   7.5   (10 x 75%)
        5d   =   5.0   (10 x 50%)
        5e   =   2.5   (10 x 25%)
         <u>6</u>   =   <u>5.0</u>   (10 x 50%)
Satisfaction   =   52.5   (Sum of each)

As you can see, with this approach it is fairly easy to combine the answers from all the surveys and develop a satisfaction level for each salesperson or territory. You can also evaluate each question and get a feeling for the average satisfaction in that area.

If you use the survey over time, you can compare satisfaction and determine programs to help it improve.

When you use an opinion survey many customers will voice concerns that need immediate attention and some will also identify sales opportunities you can capture today.

You may decide that one question is a better indicator of satisfaction than others and want to make it more important than the other questions. In the example above, you might decide that question 6 is the true measurement of satisfaction. Another approach is to increase the relative value of that question in the overall analysis. For example, let's assume that question 6 is considered 3 times as valuable as any other response. Each response is worth 8.3 points and questions 6 is worth 25 points.

Question 1 is worth 6.2 points.	(8.3 x 75%)
2	2.1	(8.3 x 25%)
3	2.1	(8.3 x 25%)
4	4.2	(8.3 x 50%)
5a	6.2	(8.3 x 75%)
5b	6.2	(8.3 x 75%)
5c	6.2	(8.3 x 75%)
5d	4.2	(8.3 x 50%)
5e	2.1	(8.3 x 25%)
6	12.5	(25 x 50%)
Satisfaction	52.0

Once you develop the questionnaire you can experiment with different methods of calculating the satisfaction index until you find the method that works best for you. You don't have to re-mail the questionnaire.

I have mailed this type of opinion survey many times with great success. In every situation the response rate has been over 30%. The key to generating high response is to keep the survey simple, short and easy to use. Don't turn a customer opinion survey into a market research vehicle. The survey should be used to reestablish the business relationship and let your customers know that you care about them.

Limit the number of questions on your survey to the minimum number that will allow you to determine customer satisfaction. There are 5 or 6 areas that you may want to ask about:

- Product satisfaction - How does the customer feel about the quality and availability of the products you're selling?

- Service satisfaction - Is the customer satisfied with hardware, software, and customer support?

- Communication - Is the customer satisfied with the level and quality of the communication they receive from your company? This question can include field sales, telesales, and direct marketing communication. You may want to add a question about field sales support and service.

- Product questions - Is the customer satisfied with the specific features and functions of one or two specific products they purchased?

- Value received from investment made - There can be a difference between satisfaction and value received. I tend to make this question intentionally open-ended so the customer will establish their own definition and level of satisfaction.

October 5, 1990

Mr. Bernard A. Goldberg
President
Direct Marketing Publishers
1304 University Drive
Yardley, PA 19067

Dear Bernie:

I hope you'll use the enclosed dollar to have a cup of coffee on us as you complete the enclosed customer satisfaction survey. I promise it will take you less than three minutes.

We would like to provide you with the best possible service and your input will help us understand our current performance. I'm extremely interested in how you feel about our products, support, and service. The information will be kept confidential and used only to help us help you.

Use the enclosed postage paid envelope to return the questionnaire or you can fax it to (201) 231-8934. If you have any questions, please feel free to give me a call at (800) 421-8042.

Thanks for your continued support.

Sincerely,

Kevin Keegan
President

Illustration 12-4: Marshall & Swift opinion survey letter.

MARSHALL & SWIFT
THE BUILDING COST PEOPLE

Customer Satisfaction Questionnaire

Please answer each question with one of the following responses:

1=Excellent
2=Very satisfied
3=Satisfied
4=Dissatisfied
5=Very dissatisfied

❑ How satisfied are you with Marshall & Swift products? Do we have the product you need?
Comments:_____

❑ How satisfied are you with the service provided by Marshall & Swift? We're interested in your opinion of customer support as well as technical support.
Comments:_____

❑ How satisfied are you with the level and quality of communication you receive from Marshall and Swift. Your opinion may include field sales contact and sales communication as well as other material you receive from us.
Comments:_____

❑ Are you satisfied with the accuracy of the information we provide? This includes the data you use, either in print or from our computerized estimating systems.
Comments:_____

❑ How satisfied are you with the value you receive from your Marshall & Swift products?
Comments:_____

❑ What is your overall satisfaction with Marshall & Swift?
Comments:_____

Recommendations and suggestions:

109017

Illustration 12-5: Marshall & Swift customer opinion survey.

- Overall - How satisfied is the customer overall with your company?

Page 585 contains an opinion survey from Marshall & Swift. The company provides construction cost estimating products. Their customers include some of the largest insurance companies. m When the survey was conducted Marshall & Swift was launching several new products and services. This opinion survey was used to enhance the customer relationship and give the company a promotional platform to build from for the future.

The survey produced over 50% response. Most of the responses were returned via FAX. As illustrated in 12-4, the letter included $1.00 to encourage response. Many of the bills were returned because of a customer's internal rules against accepting gifts, but even those questionnaires were often completed.

The company decided to follow-up with any customer who responded with a 4 (dissatisfied) or 5 (very dissatisfied) response to any question. These follow-up calls were only to be made by a manager or senior executive in the company.   The follow-up calls were used to resolve problems as well as provide additional feedback. In addition, the company was making a concerted effort to improve customer satisfaction.

This survey was intentionally kept short and easy to use. The company plans to use the same survey for the next few years so they can measure the current satisfaction level and the change over time. The survey is specific enough to provide meaningful information and general enough to allow it to be used for a long time.

Transamerica Pension Services was interested in developing lead generation programs and enhancing their existing customer relationship. A customer opinion survey was developed in conjunction with the field sales force. The survey (Illustration 12-7) was kept as short

September 28, 1990

Mr. Bernard A. Goldberg
President
Direct Marketing Publishers
1304 University Drive
Yardley, PA 19067

Dear Mr. Goldberg:

It has been a pleasure to serve you over the past year and I look forward to working together over the years ahead to meet all of your pension and retirement needs. In order to ensure that we are doing the best job for you, please complete the brief questionnaire enclosed. Although it will take a few minutes of your time to complete, it will go a long way to help us meet your needs as effectively as possible.

Thanks again for the opportunity to serve you.

Sincerely,

Richard J. Eskoff
President and Chief Executive Officer
Transamerica Life Insurance and Annuity Company

Illustration 12-6: Transamerica Pension Services opinion survey letter.

(4055-005026000)

CUSTOMER QUESTIONNAIRE

1. How would you rate our performance over the last year?
   (1 = Excellent, 2 = Very Good, 3 = Satisfactory, 4 = Marginal, 5 = Unsatisfactory)

	1	2	3	4	5
a. Investment Performance	___	___	___	___	___
b. Service from Home Office	___	___	___	___	___
c. Service from your Transamerica field rep	___	___	___	___	___
d. Overall satisfaction	___	___	___	___	___

2. Is your current retirement plan meeting your expectation and objectives?
   ____Yes   ____No

3. In what areas would you like us to improve? (Please be specific, and use additional pages if desired.)
   _____
   _____
   _____

4. Would you like us to contact you immediately about a particular issue?
   ____Yes   ____No

5. Please verify the following information, and make changes where appropriate:

   Company Name: Direct Marketing Publishers, Inc.
   Address: 1304 University Drive

   City: Yardley
   State: PA
   Zip Code: 19067

   Telephone Number: (215) 321-3068 (including area code)

   No. of employees: ____ Less than 25   ____ 100 - 249
                        ____ 25 - 49   ____ 250 or more
                        ____ 50 - 99

   Name of Primary Contact: Mr. Bernard Goldberg
   Title: _____

   Name of Plan Administrator:
   (if not Transamerica)
                        _____
                        (Specify Name of Company)

   Thanks for your cooperation!

Illustration 12-7: Transamerica Pension Services opinion survey.

as possible and mailed to the chief executive in each of the customer accounts.

The survey's accompanying letter (Illustration 12-6) was from the president of Transamerica Pension Services and was designed to enhance the relationship between the company and the customer and open dialogue at a higher level.

The survey produced over a 35% response. To get even more customers to respond, a second reminder mailing along with the questionnaire was sent to the non-responding customers about 2 weeks after the initial mailing. The reminder produced another 20% response. The total response to the mailing was almost 60% of all customers. This gave an excellent sample from which to evaluate customer satisfaction.

If your satisfaction survey demonstrates outstanding levels of satisfaction you can develop strong copy platforms for future promotions that highlight the results. You can even use the information as a press release item in the appropriate trade publications.

Virtually every time I have used a second or reminder mailing it has produced 1/2 the response rate of the first mailing. This is an easy and inexpensive method to increase response and make the program even more meaningful.

Transamerica was concerned about the accuracy of their customer database and used the survey to enhance and update the information. Most of the customer information was maintained in the local offices and the central data files contained accounting and contract information. The opinion survey offered a perfect opportunity to verify the correct information and gather other important data to allow precise targeting and promotion. You will have to be selective when writing your survey questions. Information is absolutely necessary for you to establish satisfaction and maintain the business relationship, and some information is nice to have, but is really only market research.

A customer opinion survey is an excellent vehicle to generate immediate sales and lead opportunities within your customer base. It can help you reestablish and enhance the relationship with your customers and find out how your customers feel about your company. It is an inexpensive technique that can serve many purposes and every company should execute a similar program at least once each year.

Sustaining Customer Relationships

Once the relationship with customers has been established, ongoing dialogue can lead to increased satisfaction and revenue. Too many companies place the responsibility of the company/customer relationship in the hands of the salespeople. There is no attempt to sustain any communication link between the company and the customer. When sales costs escalate to the point where it becomes too costly to maintain smaller accounts, the company must begin servicing customers with whom they have not had an ongoing relationship. If the company had maintained communication with all its customers, this problem would not exist.

The pressure on businesses to find alternative methods for selling to their smaller customers has increased substantially in the last decade. The cost of face-to-face sales calls continues to rise forcing businesses to examine ways to cut costs and increase revenue. There are a number of ways to deal with this continuing problem. The easiest method is to increase prices to maintain profits. However, competitive pressures make it difficult to increase prices at a level high enough to offset the escalating costs of selling. Another more popular method, has been to curtail or abandon selling efforts to smaller customers, or for less expensive products.

Historically, it was the salesperson's responsibility to maintain the relationship with a company's customers. Successful salespeople maintain a vast inventory of information about their customers. Each sales representative maintains a file containing the historical relationship of their company and their customers. In fact, these files are handed down from one salesperson to another as territories or responsibilities change. In some cases, the salesperson's file is the most complete historical record available detailing the relationship between the customer and the company.

Good salespeople will continue to maintain the history of their relationships in their own files. The real question is: How can we, as companies, maintain the same historical record for all our customers? This question becomes more critical as we assess alternative methods of dealing with various customer segments.

It is interesting that there tends to be a direct relationship between how frequently a customer is contacted and how often they buy. The best customers are often those who have received the best sales and support services from the company.

As selling costs continue to grow, the number of customers that a company can afford to have salespeople call on, will continue to decline. Smaller customers become too expensive to service with a salesperson. As a result, the historical record of the relationship with that customer, maintained by the salesperson, is lost.

It is almost a self-fulfilling prophecy that smaller customers remain small or even become non-customers over time. The company ultimately loses its relationship with these customers. Does this mean that businesses cannot afford to deal with smaller customers?

Not necessarily. Direct marketing, telemarketing, and telesales are ideal methods to sustain and enhance the relationship between a company and its customers; all customers, small and large. However, in business-to-business selling, some form of database will be required to record and identify the marketing relationships.

This database can be as simple as sales files. It doesn't always have to be executed on a large mainframe computer and cost hundreds of thousands of dollars. In Chapter 2, I stated that a direct marketing database will:

- Contain the names, addresses, titles, and phone numbers of contacts you want to reach via direct mail, telephone or some other direct marketing format.
- Have the capability to record all responses.
- Have the capability to record all purchases.
- Provide the capability to sustain communication and selling activity for all names on the database and record each contact.

This is done by the salesperson in their desk file. It just makes good business sense to develop a history of the relationship between a company and its customers. Unfortunately, as the company grows, the ability to maintain a manual database becomes impossible. And, because most companies have data processing report to the financial area of the company, computerized databases for marketing purposes become a low priority.

This is not to suggest that each company develop a sophisticated database immediately. However, every business selling to other businesses should plan to develop a complete marketing database over time. It should not suspend any current marketing efforts to enhance general customer relationships for the sake of database development. It should be evolutionary. The customer opinion survey, discussed earlier, is an excellent starting point.

Recently, a number of effective, inexpensive and easy-to-use computerized database programs have become available that allow the marketing and sales department to use personal or desktop computers to satisfy their database needs. These programs make it relatively easy to implement the database described above. Armed with a marketing database, albeit manual or fully automated, relationship marketing can be expanded to include all customers.

Newsletters

One cost effective technique for maintaining customer communication is a newsletter. It should have the ultimate objective of selling products and services. It shouldn't contain pictures of buildings and information about the personnel of the business. The newsletter should help the customer understand additional benefits they can derive by using the company's products and services. Most importantly, it should continue to ask the customer to order throughout the document. You may also want to consider using the newsletter as a mini-catalog followed by periodic telesales.

Whenever I introduce the subject of a newsletter to clients, they all agree it would be worthwhile but can't seem to find the resources to accomplish the ongoing effort. You can alleviate many of the problems inherent in implementing a newsletter by contracting the development to an outside firm or free-lance writer. The return on investment could be higher than anything else you might do in your business.

If you decide to develop a newsletter don't include stories or pictures about people or buildings unless they are about customers or prospects using your products. Develop an information oriented document that conveys how the customer can better use your equipment or services. Don't be embarrassed to sell, and call the customer to action throughout the document. Include a response form that allows the customer to request action from you.

You should develop and mail the newsletter as often as your resources allow. A quarterly newsletter is timely and will help you maintain a reasonable relationship.

Most newsletters are printed on 17" by 11" stock. The paper is folded in the middle producing four 8-1/2" x 11" pages. You can use 15-1/2" by 11" paper to produce a six page newsletter. The paper is then folded twice. As you design the newsletter, leave a lot of white space and try to use illustrations, cartoons, or photographs to make the material interesting.

To make it easier to read and use, you should develop several standard columns and then you will only have to develop new copy to fill the columns for each issue. Although it may sound like a lot of work, each department can coordinate their activity and be responsible for the various columns. By apportioning out the work, it takes a minimum effort to produce the newsletter. By using an outside professional to edit the newsletter you'll ensure continuity and a professional document. You'll also be able to ensure timely completion and avoid using jargon specific to your company or industry.

Some interesting sections that might be included are:

- New product news: This section should highlight products announced since the last issue, focusing on their benefits. It should not be a presentation of feeds and speeds. Encourage the customer to request additional information if they are interested.

- Local calendar of events: Seminars, workshops and classes being offered locally and nationally.

- Technical and helpful hints: Some short, crisp ideas and suggestions that can help prospects better use their equipment or your products and services.

- Supplies and services news: A section which sells related supplies and services that prospects and customers may not be aware of.

- Financial news: Short articles explaining how prospects and customers can take better advantage of innovative financing and terms and conditions.

- Industry spotlight: A case history of a local company explaining how they have been able to take advantage of your product solution.

- Education: A section on how to select a computer system or whatever product or service you're selling. This section can be ongoing or a one time article which helps customers and prospects determine whether they need a new product. If they are in the process of considering a new product, explain the key areas they should consider.

- Administrative news: It may seem strange to include a section about administration, but some administrative areas are extremely confusing to customers. Terms and conditions are one administrative item that can be explained in each issue.

As you can see, there is an awful lot of information that can and should be included in your newsletter. This information should help your customers and enhance the customer relationship.

You can also ask other organizations or experts to create special articles for inclusion in your newsletter. Some of your vendors can even create special articles about how their products are used with your products and services.

Once you have developed and implemented a newsletter you will also have created an exciting direct marketing approach to prospects and prior respondents. You can even use the newsletter as an offer and encourage prospects to request an ongoing subscription.

Credibility

Mel Jaffe, President of M.A.S. Consulting, 535 North Michigan Avenue, Chicago, IL 60606 (312) 644-5818, wrote the following article for The Business Marketing Notepad, February, 1991.

During the last 22 years of consulting I have come to the conclusion that credibility is a very important ingredient in successful business relationships. By credibility, I mean the willingness of one person to believe another.

No business relationship can be successful if the person you're dealing with doesn't believe you. In the social sciences, the specialists in communication believe that there can be no true communication without trust. As a consultant, credibility is the basis for success, it is in essence the product we sell to our clients.

Credibility isn't just a concern of consultants, it is the basis for selling, business relationships, business communication and any relationship one becomes involved in. I think there are four sources of credibility.

The first source of credibility is **personal experience**. If you have had positive personal experience with an individual, he will have credibility in your eyes. Your positive experience will lead you to accept him as believable in future dealings.

Personal experience is one of the main reasons that customers continue to deal with certain vendors. The vendor has established credibility and the customer is comfortable with the relationship. As you think about the companies you continue to use as vendors, you'll probably discover that the person you deal with has credibility with you.

Problems arise when dealing with strangers. In the case of strangers, we must rely on the second source of credibility, **referential credibility**. Referential credibility is when something connected with the stranger allows you to infer his credibility.

Third party credibility is the first type of referential credibility and is established through a third party personal relationship. You may be dealing with a stranger, but you know that the stranger is known and trusted by someone who you know and trust. This will allow you to accept the stranger as credible.

Although credibility is established between individuals, it is easy for a customer to transfer the personal credibility from one individual to the company the individual works for. This is probably the most common type of third party credibility. A company and its employees will be given an opportunity to sustain the credibility established by other individuals in prior dealings.

Salespeople have long understood that if they have credibility with a customer, they can transfer this credibility by reference and sell to the customer's associates. Reference selling is one of the most valuable tools used by salespeople. In the insurance industry, salespeople often use their relationship with one customer to gain access to another customer.

Another example of third party credibility can occur when the customer refers an associate directly to the salesperson. This new relationship may be initiated by the customer who has decided to refer the salesperson to their associates without any impetus from the salesperson. This is probably the best transfer of credibility a stranger (the salesperson) can hope for. Imagine how you feel when a friend or associate suggests you contact one of their friends or associates . . . instant credibility.

Institutional credibility, the third source of credibility, is another form of referential credibility. Universities, professional clubs, social clubs, even charitable organizations can provide a vehicle for establishing credibility. If an individual believes in an institution, they will tend to give credibility to anyone associated with that institution. This is sometimes called the old school tie or old boy network.

Degrees, titles and other honors are symbols of institutional credibility. Many people will invest significant time and money acquiring these types of institutional relationships because of their inherent credibility.

Books, articles, and speaking engagements are also forms of institutional credibility.

Self-generated, the fourth source of credibility, is different than the other sources. It is more psychological and harder to describe. When two strangers meet and there is no third-party or institutional credibility, one person will tend to give credibility to another to the degree that the person inspires credibility. An individual inspires credibility based upon their attitude towards themself and the image they portray to others.

You will give credibility to someone who you believe is like you. There are many ingredients to this perception. They can be as simple as dress or jewelry. Or as subtle as speech pattern, vocabulary, slowness to commit oneself or controlled enthusiasm. Many of these traits have been discussed under the subject of first impressions. There are some people you meet who you extinctively like and trust. The question is why? The reason this question is so difficult to answer is because it varies depending on how the individual portrays himself.

Examples of this concept carried to an extreme, would be charismatic personalities such as Franklin D. Roosevelt, John F. Kennedy, Ronald Reagan and the news anchor on the 10 o'clock news. These people have credibility with an enormous audience of people. There is no personal experience or referential opportunity to help these personalities establish credibility. They instill credibility because of how they carry and project themselves. They believe in themselves and what they represent, therefore you tend to also believe them. The same phenomenon exists in one-to-one relationships.

Although you can use the first three types of credibility, they are not in your immediate control when you meet people for the first time. Self-generated credibility becomes an important ingredient in every relationship. We as business managers have to remember that customers buy from people they trust. Trust is earned through an individual's credibility and is often transferred to their company. Therefore we have a responsibility to ensure that all people within our company help develop credibility with our prospects and customers.

Appearance, enthusiasm and sincerity can be important elements in establishing credibility and earning trust. One of the reasons that business people dress a certain way is to establish credibility with their associates and customers. Everything we do in our professional relationship with prospects and customers can help create or destroy credibility. It is something that shouldn't be taken for granted. Successful companies make a concerted effort to earn and sustain credibility. We should all make an effort to instill self-generated credibility.

We can never be sure how a stranger will perceive us. If we could be certain of the expectations of each person before meeting them, we could prepare and act accordingly. But most first meetings occur unplanned.

In face-to-face discussions, appearance and personal reactions will be important to creating credibility. We have to learn to listen well and react to the situation.

Telephone removes the appearance issue but places more emphasis on our listening and communication skills. Enthusiasm and self-assuredness will be extremely important in establishing credibility.

Direct mail and other direct contacts will create credibility based on the perception of professionalism and honesty created in the mind of the recipient. Handling inquiries quickly and completely will help establish credibility. The more professional we appear in the mind of the prospect, the higher our credibility. Self-generated credibility can be created by the company before a person ever becomes involved if the inquiry is professionally and completely handled.

Friend-Get-A-Friend

When I was a salesperson for IBM I used to ask my customers if they knew of any other prospect I should be selling. They would often not only give me the names of businesses but often make a phone call to the appropriate executive and arrange for an appointment. These were always my best leads.

Every successful salesperson knows that their best sales leads come from existing customers. They can use referential credibility to build a relationship with a new prospect.

If you work hard to create a strong relationship with your customers, you can use the relationship and credibility to generate additional selling opportunities just like the face-to-face scenario. This approach works in all kinds of businesses and even in the consumer world.

You can use direct marketing to accomplish the same thing as the salesperson asking a customer for a lead. A well written letter asking customers for friends or associates who they feel would welcome an opportunity to learn about your products or services is usually well received.

Satisfied customers usually like to tell others about their good fortune. When a business person makes a good decision, they are anxious for others to learn about it. It makes them feel good and demonstrates their intelligence. You can use this to your advantage.

If you have developed a relationship with a company, you can use it to generate activity with other departments or divisions. These are known as Friend-get-a-friend promotions.

There are many ways to execute Friend-get-a-friend promotions and the only creative constraints are those you would have with any direct marketing program. You've already selected the list in targeting your customers, therefore the next most important element is the offer. You're going to offer your customers an incentive to provide you with a lead.

As you consider the promotion and offer you might want to have two different offers. One for providing a lead to whom you can

June 28, 1989

Dear Valued Customer:

Hewlett-Packard would love to give you one of our new lap-top computers, absolutely free, for your business use. Read on to find out how you can qualify.

You probably are aware of Hewlett-Packard's reputation for quality. You might even be aware that we've been ranked #1 in customer support satisfaction in Datapro User Surveys <u>six years in a row</u>! The fact is, people that buy HP computers like them -- a lot. Once a company buys their first Hewlett-Packard computer, they usually buy more. This makes new customers especially valuable to us. For that reason, we can make this offer to you.

If you provide us with the name of someone who buys a Hewlett-Packard multi-user computer before October 31, 1989, we will give you a Hewlett-Packard LS12 lap-top computer!

It's that simple. The referral you give can even be someone in your own company. To achieve our goal of gaining new customers, some restrictions apply. The computer purchased must be an HP9000 or HP3000 multi-user computer, and the company must not have purchased one of these models already.

So fill in the enclosed reply card and send it in now. But hurry -- only one computer will be given away per order, and the first person to provide the referral will receive the free lap-top computer.

Best regards,

David E. Smith
Marketing Services Manager

P.S. Increase your chance of being the first to provide a referral by calling me at: (800) 288-4267.

Illustration 12-8: Hewlett-Packard customer lead mailing.

make a sales presentation. And another, more elaborate offer for those leads that convert to orders.

The travel industry has, from time-to-time, offered premium awards to customers for recommending friends to join their programs. Some of the frequent traveler programs will offer bonus miles or points for getting others to join their program. If the nominated name accumulates a minimum level of points or miles, the original customer is given an even larger bonus.

This program not only motivates a customer to provide another prospect for you to sell, but also rewards their effort in helping the prospect to make a buying decision. Even customers who purchase products from a different division of your company can be excellent prospects for you.

Illustration 12-8 shows a program executed by Hewlett-Packard to encourage their customers to provide names of prospects who might be interested in an HP 3000 computer system. The customer list not only included existing HP 3000 customers but also customers who bought instruments and other HP products.

Some companies are reluctant to offer premiums to their customers for providing a sales lead. Some of the senior executives become nervous that the customers will perceive the effort as tacky and be offended. There is even a concern that the offer might hurt or destroy the company/customer relationship.

Illustration 12-9 demonstrates a technique for requesting leads from existing customers while still enhancing the customer relationship. You'll notice that the customer opinion survey was used first to enhance the relationship. This next letter alludes to the survey, further strengthening the relationship, and then asking for a sales lead.

September 1, 1991

Bernie Goldberg, President
Direct Marketing Publishers
1304 University Drive
Yardley, PA 19067

Dear Mr. Goldberg,

I'm writing to thank you for being a client of Transamerica
Pension Services, and to tell you how much we appreciate your
participation in our survey earlier this year.

As a result of the response we received from executives like
yourself, we've already taken several steps to enhance the
services we offer to our clients. For instance, we've started
publishing our new PensionLine Newsletter as part of our
effort to improve communications with you.

Our primary goal is to respond to each of our clients with
special attention to their individual needs. And during the
months ahead you'll see an even greater commitment to customer
support.

That's why I've sent the enclosed clock. It's our way of
thanking you for the time you've spent with our survey. Your
responses have helped to make Transamerica Pension Services
even better.

With that in mind, Mr. Goldberg, I'd like to take this opportunity to request your help in telling our story to a friend
or colleague of yours. We've developed a brief, 10 minute
Video overview that could be very useful to someone you know
who may be looking into a corporate pension plan. We'll
gladly send them a copy at no obligation.

If you know someone who might benefit from this informative
video, please take a moment to jot their name and address on
the enclosed card and drop it in the mail to us. I'll see
they get their personal copy with our compliments. Thanks so
much, and thanks for being a friend of Transamerica.

Sincerely,

J. Clifton Masser
VP/Chief Marketing Officer
Transamerica Pension Services

Illustration 12-9: Transamerica Pension Services customer lead mailing.

Lead programs to your customer base can be used to enhance the relationship and generate sales activity. The customer relationship is often based on perception. The more you contact your customers, the better they are going to feel about your company. Of course, this can be carried to an extreme and create a negative effect. I am aware of several mail-order catalogers who mail their customers more than 50 times per year. If your promotion is relevant and appropriate, your customers will react favorably.

Most business-to-business selling is done to existing customers. Almost any account I work with generates over 50% of their sales and profits from existing customers. Most of this activity is handled by direct sales and most companies have not asked their customers for additional sales leads.

You can experiment with lead generation from your customers in your inbound telephone operation. Ask your communicators to ask customers calling to place orders or for customer service if they have a friend or associate who they think might be interested in your products or services. You can train the communicators to deal with any problems this question might create. I think you'll be very pleasantly surprised at how many of your customers will anxiously provide you with additional selling opportunities.

House File Activity

I am always surprised when I hear a company delaying a lead generation program because the salespeople want to review the mailing list and ensure that none of their customers or active prospects will be targeted for the promotion. Unfortunately this situation is a commonplace occurrence in some of the largest companies. Many salespeople are afraid that their relationship with the customer or prospect will be injured by the promotion.

It is naive to think that a group of customers or prospects will not become aware of the promotion. As I discussed in Chapter 2, the art of list maintenance in the business-to-business world is imperfect and you will not be able to eliminate all customers. The problem is compounded because many executives from different businesses will often share ideas and information. Customers and active prospects will become aware of your promotional efforts. Your program should be designed to accommodate and take advantage of this situation.

It is also interesting that even after an attempt is made to eliminate customers and prospects from a promotional list, you will receive responses from the group you're trying to avoid. This proves that customers and prospects are your best list to promote. The proof is dramatic. If you make an attempt to eliminate a group of businesses from your promotion list, the number of targets who are mailed the promotion but who you intended to eliminate is very small. If you get any response from the group you were trying to avoid, the response rate has to be significant.

Even with overwhelming evidence, many companies will discontinue a lead program because customers and active prospects are responding and upsetting the sales force. Perhaps these companies should examine why this group is responding and learn how to capitalize on the situation.

Customers and prospects are your best list source for additional leads and orders.

- You have an established relationship. Both customers and its prospects know your company and products. If they respond they will be easier to sell or eliminate as buying opportunities.

- Customers have indicated an affinity for your company and its products. Most customers would like to enhance their purchase and learn how to make it more effective. They will eagerly respond for additional information and opportunities to enhance their purchase.

- You have probably spent significant selling dollars (face-to-face) convincing them that they should buy from your company. Most names on your house file have received multiple contacts and a sustained selling effort.

- Customers are loyal. They will try to help you be successful. If they receive a lead generation mailing, they'll often respond with interest for additional products or with leads for new and additional sales.

- You may have sold one department or division within a company and there are additional opportunities within the same company. Customers and prior respondents will often let you know about these additional opportunities.

- Timing may be in your favor. This is particularly true of a prior respondent who didn't purchase during the last response. Your promotion may hit the prospect at just the right time or your offer may be perfect for their needs.

With all these advantages, a list of companies eliminated from a lead generation mailing by the sales force should be the *first* list you mail. It will be the most successful for both your company and its salespeople.

Serdi Corporation contacted me in October 1990 and was interested in implementing a lead generation program that had to produce over 70 orders by December 31, 1990.

October 15, 1990

Bernie Goldberg
President
Direct Marketing Publishers
1304 University Drive
Yardley, PA 19067

Dear Bernie Goldberg,

As you know, the number of complex cylinder head configurations is growing with each model year, therefore the demand for accuracy is increasing.
The SERDI Valve Seat and Guide Machine can handle any size engine from a
lawn mower to a locomotive -- no matter how exact your machining requirements. For a limited time, you may qualify for a 30-day free trial of the
SERDI, Model 100 complete with Option 4 tooling! And when we say free,
we mean free -- we'll even pay for the freight and delivery and teach you
how to use the machine with no cost or obligation.

Our valve seat and guide machine is so easy to use, anyone working in your
shop can operate it. If you're like me, seeing is believing and we'll even bring
a machine to your location and actually finish any head you have in your
shop -- absolutely free. When you examine the SERDI you'll see:

- How easy and fast it is to handle the most complicated cylinder heads.
  You'll be able to cut finished valve seats in about 20% of the time it
  may have taken you in the past. The cylinder heads never need any
  grinding or lapping and it doesn't require any operator finesse.
  Because it takes a lot less time to finish each head you'll be able to process more heads each day and you won't need as many people to handle your volume.

- With the SERDI, you'll be able to handle the most complex cylinder
  heads, no matter how many valves. This means that with one machine
  you can handle any job, no matter how complicated. As more and
  more multi-valve engines enter the aftermarket, you'll be able to handle
  the opportunity without having to make another investment in equipment.

- The SERDI is the easiest machine to learn and use. You can easily
  teach anyone in your shop to use the SERDI. You won't have to worry
  about employees holding a gun to your head for higher wages as they
  become more proficient in machining functions. This machine will
  make you less dependent on people and put you more in control of
  your company.

- SERDI is sold and supported by professional, hands-on machine technicians. We'll show you how to use and operate the equipment in your
  environment doing your jobs. We'll even work with the most complicated, valuable cylinder head you have. We're so confident in the quality of our people and products, that if we damage the cylinder head
  during our demonstration, we'll buy it from you at your full retail price.

Illustration 12-10.a: Serdi lead generation letter - page 1.

Bernie Goldberg
October 15, 1990
Page 2

The enclosed questionnaire will help you determine whether it is worth your time and effort to find out if you qualify for a free trial of the SERDI, Model 100. There is no cost or obligation. Complete and return the response form today. If you FAX the response form to us by 3 p.m., we'll tell you if you qualify within 48 hours!

And there's more . . .

If you decide to buy a SERDI before December 31st 1990, you can take advantage of our special lease program and not pay your first payment until April 1st, 1991. In addition, you may even be able to trade in your existing machine for up to $10,000!

If you're machining as few as 8 sets per week, you should be using a SERDI. You'll actually experience positive cash flow in savings from consumable materials, additional revenues you'll generate in new work, and labor savings created by the improved productivity of your people. You don't have to take my word for it, let us bring a machine to your location and show you the SERDI. Our specially equipped mobile machine shops allow our technicians to come to you and demonstrate how effective the SERDI is doing your work.

Send us the response form as soon as possible to find out if you qualify for a free trial. We want to show you how the SERDI can help you improve your company's results. FAX or mail the response form now and we'll tell you if you qualify within 48 hours of receipt.

Sincerely,

Tom Begush
National Sales Manager

P.S. Remember, you can judge for yourself whether you should find out if you qualify for a free trial of the SERDI, Model 100 by simply answering the Machine Shop Questionnaire. Then FAX or mail your response form and you'll know if you qualify within 48 hours of receipt. Don't forget to ask us about our special trade-in program for 1990 orders.

Illustration 12-10.b: Serdi lead generation letter - page 2.

Machine Shop Questionnaire
(For your information only . . . Do not mail)

Answer the following questions to determine if you should find out if you qualify for a free trial of a SERDI.

Yes   No

____ ____   Are you concerned about the level of knowledge required by your employees to handle today's cylinder heads? Do you feel threatened that any of these people might leave you?

____ ____   Would you like to be able to handle all cylinder heads, regardless of the number of valves or size of the head?

____ ____   Would you like to be able to do more work with the same number of people? Are there opportunities to expand your business if you could free some of your man-hours?

____ ____   Are you concerned about your ability to handle the growth in multi-valve cylinder heads with your existing machine tools?

____ ____   Have you been promised that you can produce a finished seat in any material with your existing machine? Has it proven more difficult than you thought it would be?

If you answer yes to any question you should complete and return the response form and find out if you qualify to receive a free trial of the SERDI, Model 100, Valve Seat and Guide Machine.

Return the enclosed response form and we'll tell you if you qualify to receive a free trial of the SERDI, Model 100. If you FAX the form by 3 p.m., we'll let you know within 48 hours.

Don't forget to ask us about our special 1990 trade-in program. If you buy a SERDI in 1990, you may be able to trade in your existing machine for up to $10,000!

Illustration 12-10.c: Serdi lead generation letter - Questionnaire.

Response Form

Yes! I am interested in learning how I can try a SERDI, Model 100, Absolutely Free! Please review the information below and let me know if I qualify for a free trial.

Please change as appropriate

Bernie Goldberg, President
Direct Marketing Publishers
1304 University Drive
Yardley, PA 19067
Phone: (___) ___-____   Fax: (___) ___-____

We require credit approval before we'll ship equipment for a free trial. You do not have to make any payments nor are you obligated to buy if you decide to try the SERDI-100.

Guarantor Information

Your Name _____   Social Sec #: _____
Title: _____
Home Address: _____

City _____ State ___ Zip _____   Phone: (___) ___-____

How long have you been in business? ____ Years

Type of Business: ❑ Sole Proprietor   ❑ Partnership   ❑ Corporation

Business Bank Information: Name of Bank: _____
Chkng account #: _____
Contact name: _____
Phone: (___) ___-____

References: (Please provide 3 lease or loan references - use trade references only if lease or loan references are not available)

Name: _____ Phone: (___) ___-____ Contact _____ Acct #_____
Name: _____ Phone: (___) ___-____ Contact _____ Acct #_____
Name: _____ Phone: (___) ___-____ Contact _____ Acct #_____

Return to:
Tom Begush, National Sales Manager
SERDI Corp.
1526 Litton Drive
Stone Mountain, GA 30083

❑ Yes! I want to know more about your special 1990 trade-in program.

Find out if you qualify for a free trial within 48 hours - Fax this form by 3 p.m. to (404) 493-8323!
101

Illustration 12-10.d: Serdi lead generation letter - Response Form.

Serdi sells a milling machine for approximately $35,000 to automobile machine shops and maintenance facilities. The machine enjoys a terrific reputation but is over 3 times as expensive as the leading competitor's. The Serdi machine is easier to use, more versatile and is able to perform more complex operations. In addition, automobile engines are becoming more complex and the Serdi is the only machine that can handle some of the newer engines.

The Serdi sales force consisted of 6 field representatives. Each was equipped with a truck-mounted machine shop that allows on-site demonstrations. In addition, the salespeople are all technicians who have worked in machine shops. They are not skilled salespeople.

Initially the company was interested in using telemarketing to develop the sales leads because of the limited time frame of the project. I discouraged the company from telephone activity and was extremely pessimistic about the project. As I discussed in Chapter 9, telephone is an offer medium; it is difficult to sell anything on the phone.

Even if you are willing to pay a premium price, it is difficult to execute a direct mail campaign in less than 4 weeks. It didn't seem possible to create an offer, acquire a list, create and produce the direct mail, generate the sales lead and follow-up and close in less than 2 months. And this was at the end of the year in the throws of the holiday season.

In addition, lead generation programs done in desperation typically don't work. If you put too much pressure on the lead program it usually fails because you can't learn from your mistakes and grow the program over time. There is no margin for error.

As we began to discuss the program, list sources were reviewed. The sales executive mentioned that the company had developed a house file of prior respondents over the last two years that had been

November 1, 1990

Bernie Goldberg
President
Direct Marketing Publishers
1304 University Drive
Yardley, PA 19067

Dear Bernie Goldberg,

As you may recall, I recently sent a letter offering you a unique opportunity to experience first hand the power and effectiveness of the SERDI Valve Seat and Guide Machine. The SERDI can handle any size engine from a lawn mower to a locomotive -- no matter how exact your machining requirements. For a limited time, you may qualify for a 30-day free trial of the SERDI, Model 100 complete with Option 4 tooling! And when we say free, we mean free -- we'll even pay for the freight and delivery and teach you how to use the machine with no cost or obligation. Since we haven't heard from you, I wanted to ensure you didn't miss the opportunity to take advantage of this exciting offer.

Our valve seat and guide machine is so easy to use, anyone working in your shop can operate it. If you're like me, seeing is believing and we'll even bring a machine to your location and actually finish any head you have in your shop -- absolutely free. When you examine the SERDI you'll see:

- How easy and fast it is to handle the most complicated cylinder heads. You'll be able to cut finished valve seats in about 20% of the time it may have taken you in the past. The cylinder heads never need any grinding or lapping and it doesn't require any operator finesse. Because it takes a lot less time to finish each head you'll be able to process more heads each day and you won't need as many people to handle your volume.

- With the SERDI, you'll be able to handle the most complex cylinder heads, no matter how many valves. This means that with one machine you can handle any job, no matter how complicated. As more and more multi-valve engines enter the aftermarket, you'll be able to handle the opportunity without having to make another investment in equipment.

- The SERDI is the easiest machine to learn and use. You can easily teach anyone in your shop to use the SERDI. You won't have to worry about employees holding a gun to your head for higher wages as they become more proficient in machining functions. This machine will make you less dependent on people and put you more in control of your company.

- SERDI is sold and supported by professional, hands-on machine technicians. We'll show you how to use and operate the equipment in your environment doing your jobs. We'll even work with the most complicated, valuable cylinder head you have. We're so confident in the quality of our people and products, that if we damage the cylinder head during our demonstration, we'll buy it from you at your full retail price.

Illustration 12-11.a: Serdi reminder letter - page 1.

Bernie Goldberg
November 1, 1990
Page 2

Find out if you qualify for a free trial of the SERDI, Model 100. There is no cost or obligation. Complete and return the response form today. FAX or mail the response form so we can tell you if you qualify as soon as possible!

And there's more . . .

If you decide to buy a SERDI before December 31st 1990, you can take advantage of our special lease program. After initiating the lease, your next payment won't be due until April 1st, 1991. In addition, you may even be able to trade in your existing machine for up to $10,000!

If you're machining as few as 8 sets per week, you should be using a SERDI. You'll actually experience positive cash flow in savings from consumable materials, additional revenues you'll generate in new work, and labor savings created by the improved productivity of your people. You don't have to take my word for it, let us bring a machine to your location and show you the SERDI. Our specially equipped mobile machine shops allow our technicians to come to you and demonstrate how effective the SERDI is doing your work.

Send us the response form as soon as possible to find out if you qualify for a free trial. We want to show you how the SERDI can help you improve your company's results. FAX or mail the response form now and we'll tell you if you qualify.

Sincerely,

Tom Begush
National Sales Manager

P.S.   FAX or mail your response form and you'll know if you qualify for a free trial of a SERDI. Don't forget to ask us about our special trade-in program for 1990 orders.

Illustration 12-11.b: Serdi reminder letter - page 2.

sent to the salespeople as leads. The house file consisted of 4,700 records. I began to be more optimistic about the effort and convinced Serdi to mail the house file to develop their required leads.

As I have mentioned throughout this book, most sales leads are never contacted by a salesperson. Although the names on the file had been distributed to the sales force as leads, only a small percentage were actually contacted.

The letter, questionnaire, and response form in Illustration 12-10 was created, produced and mailed to the house file of customers and prior respondents. The mailing was done in an extremely compressed time-frame and mailed via first class in less than 3 weeks.

The results of this program were unbelievable. Serdi began to receive responses via fax 2 days after the mail dropped. Two of the first five responses were not requests for a free trial but actual orders! The initial letter produced almost 90 responses and a reminder letter (Illustration 12-11) was sent two weeks later. It produced over 55 responses and the total number of responses from the program was around 150. The response form was the same as the original letter but contained a different source code. A follow-up mailing seems to produce about 1/2 the response of the original mailing.

I was surprised by the overall effectiveness of the program. The program produced 77 orders by the end of the year. There were so many responses that the company couldn't follow-up on each one effectively. Prospects who were not prepared to make an immediate decision were sent a letter and deferred for follow-up until 1991.

Every lead was sent a letter (Illustration 12-12) to allow the company to maintain the relationship with the prospect. Having seen the tremendous response from names that were originally sent to the sales force, the company decided to sustain the relationship and not

October 22, 1990

Bernie Goldberg
President
Direct Marketing Publishers
1304 University Drive
Yardley, PA 19067

Dear Bernie Goldberg,

I appreciate your response to our demonstration and free trial offer and as we explained, the interest in this exciting offer has been overwhelming.

As you may recall:

If you decide to buy a SERDI before December 31st 1990, you can take advantage of our special lease program and not pay your first payment until April 1st, 1991. In addition, you may even be able to trade in your existing machine for up to $10,000!

I understand that you will shortly be receiving your demonstration and hope that you become as excited about the SERDI as the other 150 new users did in the last 12 months. I think you'll agree after seeing the demonstration, there is no other machine as easy to use or operate, no matter how exact your machining requirements.

I have forwarded a complete analysis of the information you provided to Joe Salesperson. He will demonstrate the machine, set-up your free trial and review the information with you. If you purchase the machine prior to December 31st, you can take advantage of our special trade-in and financing plan.

Joe can be reached at (404) 999-1234. If you have any questions, or you are unable to reach Joe, please feel free to contact me at (800) 447-3790.

Again, thanks for your interest and we look forward to convincing you that there is no other machine quite like a SERDI.

Sincerely,

Tom Begush
National Sales Manager

Illustration 12-12: Serdi lead follow-up letter.

rely only on the salesperson. The prospect was given the name and phone number of the assigned salesperson and was also provided the name of the sales manager should the salesperson not fulfill properly.

Serdi was able to accomplish a difficult short-term objective because of the house file. The customers and prospects the file represented had some relationship with the company and therefore made it easier to sell. The company had already invested selling dollars to make them more likely to buy.

The direct marketing campaign included every name on the file, including existing customers. By the way, several customers did respond and buy additional equipment.

The Serdi example isn't unique. Every time I have worked with clients and included their house files in a lead generation program, the house file is the best producing list. As I discussed at the onset of this chapter, customers, prior respondents and former leads should comprise your house file. The Serdi example demonstrates the value of maintaining a complete house file.

Apple Computer experienced similar results when it executed a direct marketing campaign. Apple has relied on computer resellers to service and support inquiries and all leads are sent directly through the distribution channel. Research had demonstrated that only about 15% of the leads were actually contacted by a salesperson.

A database of prior respondents and customers was developed and it was used to mail an offer letter (Illustration 12-13). The response was over 15% requesting the kit and a large percentage of those converted to appointments for the sales force. Many existing customers also requested the kit which alerted Apple to a marketing opportunity.

April 1, 1991

Bernie Goldberg
President
Direct Marketing Publishers
1304 University Drive
Yardley, PA 19067

Dear Bernie Goldberg,

We appreciate your interest and inquiry about Apple Computer. As you probably know, a decision to use a Macintosh in your company will significantly impact your communications with customers, prospects, and business associates. Perhaps you've considered implementing desktop computing on a Macintosh in your company but have been unable to justify moving forward. We would like to help you evaluate and determine whether you should consider changing now. Complete the enclosed questionnaire to determine whether you should receive our new Business Communications Kit, absolutely free.

The Business Communications Kit is a special package of your own personalized materials produced with desktop publishing on the Apple® Macintosh® and it will:

- Provide you with a chance to see several personalized examples of desktop publishing in the privacy of your office. If you're like me, you know how difficult it is to visualize and relate to abstract examples of materials from other companies. With this approach you'll be able to not only receive personalized examples, but also to compare them to communications you're currently using.

- Help you identify opportunities for both reducing and avoiding expenses. We'll demonstrate how you can produce professional communication while reducing cost or hassle. You will see how these techniques can work in your company today.

- Show you, by producing your own personalized examples virtually overnight, how easily and quickly you or your staff can create professional communication materials. We will not only demonstrate examples that are appropriate for your company, but we'll also help you cost justify your own system. You will be able to relate to how the Macintosh can help you create professional business communication.

Illustration 12-13.a: Apple lead generation letter - page 1.

Bernie Goldberg
April 1, 1991
Page 2

The enclosed questionnaire will help you determine whether it is worth your time and effort to request the Business Communications Kit. The kit is designed for executives who are trying to make an important decision about how they would like to communicate. There is no cost or obligation. If you answer yes to any question, we can help you. Complete and return the response form to us today! If you FAX the response form to us by 3 p.m., you should receive the kit in the next day or so!

The Business Communications Kit will provide you a basis to determine whether you should consider implementing your own system. The kit will allow you to see first hand how you can enhance your image, save time and money, and reduce the number of steps it takes to produce high quality, professional looking communication materials.

The questionnaire will help you evaluate some areas that may offer significant opportunities for your company. In the past, computers were used primarily to enhance accounting and operations. The 1990's will require innovative marketing approaches for companies to grow and prosper. As you complete the questionnaire, consider whether you will be able to compete effectively with your current methods for generating communication to your customers and prospects.

Send us the response form as soon as possible to take advantage of the Business Communications Kit. We want to show you how the Macintosh can help you improve your company's results. FAX the response form now and you should have your own personalized examples tomorrow.

Whether you decide to request the Business Communications Kit, we really appreciate your interest in Apple Computer.

Very truly yours,

Patrick S. McVeigh
Marketing Manager

P.S. The Business Communications Kit is absolutely free and if you FAX your response form by 3 p.m., you should receive your own personalized examples tomorrow.

Illustration 12-13.b: Apple lead generation letter - page 2.

Business Communication Questionnaire

Answer the following questions. If you answer yes to any question a free
Business Communications Kit can help you evaluate how desktop publishing
can change your company.

Yes   No

____ ____   Are you paying outside professionals or services to create
              forms, brochures, and other communication materials?

____ ____   Would you like to create presentations and proposals that
              appear to have been professionally developed?

____ ____   Would you like to develop and implement a professional
              looking newsletter that you can use to periodically contact
              your customers and prospects?

____ ____   Are you or your staff creating advertisements, slides, or
              overhead transparencies?   Would you like to be able to add
              color, graphics, or even sound and animation?

____ ____   Would you like to have the capability to produce your own
              communications materials for less than $160 per month?

**Return the enclosed response form and we'll rush you a personalized
Business Communications Kit absolutely free. If you FAX the form by 3
p.m., you should receive the kit tomorrow.**

Illustration 12-13.c: Apple lead generation letter - Questionnaire.

Response Form

Yes!   I want to receive my own personalized examples of business communication. Please rush me a personalized Apple Business Communication Kit.

Please change as appropriate
Bernard Goldberg
President
Direct Marketing Publishers
1304 University Drive
Yardley, PA 19067
Phone: (215) 321-3068   Fax: (215) 321-9647

To really make your examples meaningful, please answer the following questions completely. The information will be used in the examples we send you.

The name of your company or the company name you'd like to see used in the materials you'll receive:

Company   _____
Address   _____

City   _____ State ____ Zip _____

Name   _____
Title   _____

Please provide some annual sales and profit information for the three years indicated. This is for your personalized examples and doesn't have to be actual data.

	Sales	Profit
Last Year	_____	_____
This Year	_____	_____
Next Year	_____	_____

What type of desktop computer are you currently using:
   ❑ Macintosh   ❑ MS/DOS   ❑ Other   ❑ None

Return to:

Pat McVeigh, Marketing Manager
Apple Computer, Inc.
PO Box 751630
Memphis, TN 38175-9967

Receive your Business Communications Kit tomorrow or the next day - Fax this form by 3 p.m. to (800) 537-9199!

Illustration 12-13.d: Apple lead generation letter - Response Form.

Apple then sent the same mailing to their house file. The house file contained respondents from several programs over a one year period. The most recent responses were about 3 months old. The oldest responses were about 1 year old. The more recent respondents on the house file responded the best to the new offer. But those respondents who were close to a year old also responded, and many converted to leads and orders.

The house file should be used for ongoing contact and lead generation activity. Serdi and Apple are only two examples. I have experienced similar results with almost every company I have worked with. The house file of customers and prospects is the best performing list you can use.

Even an aged list of inactive customers and prior respondents will probably out-produce a new list. Apple Computer found that even their older prior respondents produced significant results.

In both the Serdi and Apple programs a significant effort was expended on developing a meaningful offer. In addition, both programs sustained the relationship even if the salesperson didn't fulfill the offer completely. The promotional campaign included prospects and customers and both responded with equal success.

Customer Lead Generation Summarized

In this chapter I discussed using your house file for lead generation activity. The house file, in many companies, only includes customers. It should also include prior respondents and leads previously sent to the sales force.

A customer is any individual who has purchased products or services from you. It doesn't matter how little they have purchased.

This group is different than the rest of the world. They know who you are and have paid money to your company. In addition, you know who they are and have dealt with them in the past. You have a relationship with them and they are certainly different than prospects and referrals.

Respondents to your direct marketing efforts are also extremely expensive and valuable and therefore different than then the universe of prospects. Besides the costs associated with acquiring the response, you may have also invested money in fulfillment and even in face-to-face selling activity.

I discussed using a customer opinion survey as a method of enhancing the relationship, determining the level of satisfaction, and as a way to identify high quality sales opportunities.

Using several practical examples I demonstrated how to establish a satisfaction index and evaluate satisfaction of individual customers, salespeople, territories, and the entire company.

The most effective satisfaction survey programs limit the number of questions to the minimum number to determine customer satisfaction. There are six areas that you may want to ask about:

- Product satisfaction
- Service satisfaction
- Communication
- Products
- Value received from investment made
- Overall

A customer opinion survey is an excellent vehicle to generate immediate sales and lead opportunities within your customer base. You can reestablish and enhance the relationship with your customers and find out how your customers feel about your company. It is an inexpensive technique that can serve many purposes and every company should execute a similar program at least once each year.

Once the relationship with customers has been established, ongoing dialogue can lead to increased satisfaction and revenue. Too many companies place the responsibility of the company/customer relationship entirely in the hands of the salespeople.

As selling costs continue to grow, the number of customers that a company can afford to have salespeople call on, will continue to decline. Smaller customers become too expensive to service with a salesperson. As a result, the historical record of the relationship with that customer, maintained by the salesperson, is lost.

A cost-effective technique for maintaining customer communication is a newsletter. It should have the ultimate objective of selling products and services. It shouldn't contain pictures of buildings and information about the personnel of the business. If you decide to develop a newsletter don't include stories or pictures about people or buildings unless they are about customers or prospects using your products. Develop an information oriented document that conveys how the customer can better use your equipment or services. Don't be embarrassed to sell, and call the customer to action throughout the document. Include a response form that allows the customer to request action from you.

To make it easier to read and use, you should develop several standard columns and then you will only have to develop new copy to fill the columns for each issue. Some interesting columns that might be included are:

- New product news
- Local calendar of events
- Technical and helpful hints
- Supplies and services news

- Financial news
- Industry spotlight
- Education
- Product selection
- Administrative news

You can also ask other organizations or experts to create special articles for inclusion in your newsletter. Some of your vendors can even create special articles about how their products are used with your products and services.

Once you have developed and implemented a newsletter you will also have created an exciting direct marketing approach to prospects and prior respondents. You can even use the newsletter as an offer and encourage prospects to request an ongoing subscription.

Mel Jaffe's discussion on credibility helps clarify why the house file can be so valuable in sustained marketing programs. No business relationship can be successful if the person you're dealing with doesn't believe you. In the social sciences the specialists in communication believe that there can be no true communication without trust. Credibility is the basis for success, it is in essence the product we sell to our clients.

There are four types of credibility:

- Personal experience
- Referential credibility
- Institutional credibility
- Self-generated

Although you can use the first three types of credibility, they are not in your immediate control when you meet people for the first time. Self-generated credibility becomes an important ingredient in every relationship. We as business managers have to remember that customers buy from people they trust. Trust is earned through an individual's credibility and is often transferred to their company. Therefore we have a responsibility to ensure that all people within our company help develop credibility with our prospects and customers.

Direct mail and other direct contacts will create credibility based on the perception of professionalism and honesty created in the mind of the recipient. Handling inquiries quickly and completely will help establish credibility. The more professional we appear in the mind of the prospect, the higher our credibility. Self-generated credibility can be created by the company before a person ever becomes involved if the inquiry is professionally and completely handled.

Every successful salesperson knows that their best sales leads come from existing customers. They can use referential credibility to build a relationship with a new prospect.

If you work hard to create a strong relationship with your customers, you can use the relationship and credibility to generate additional selling opportunities just like the face-to-face scenario. This approach works in all kinds of businesses and even in the consumer world.

A well written letter asking customers for friends or associates who they feel would welcome an opportunity to learn about your products or services is usually well received. Satisfied customers usually like to tell others about their good fortune. When a business person makes a good decision, they are anxious for others to learn about it. It makes them feel good and demonstrates their intelligence. You can use this to your advantage.

These are known as Friend-get-a-friend promotions. If you have developed a relationship with a company, you can use it to generate activity with other departments or divisions within that same company.

I used several examples of friend-get-a-friend promotions. Hewlett-Packard offered their customers a significant premium for providing sales leads that could convert to a computer order. Transamerica was concerned about the perception of soliciting for leads and coupled a customer opinion survey designed to enhance the relationship with a request for names of prospects.

You can experiment with lead generation from your customers in your inbound telephone operation. Ask your communicators to ask customers calling to place orders or for customer service if they have a friend or associate who they think might be interested in your products or services. You can train the communicators to deal with any problems this question might create. I think you'll be very pleasantly surprised at how many of your customers will anxiously provide you with additional selling opportunities.

Customers and prospects are your best list source for additional leads and orders.

- You have an established relationship.
- Customers have indicated an affinity for your company and products.
- You have probably spent significant selling dollars (face-to-face) convincing them that they should buy from your company.
- Customers are loyal.
- You may have sold one department or division within a company and there are additional opportunities within the same company.
- Timing may be in your favor.

With all these advantages, a list of companies from a lead generation mailing by the sales force should be the *first* list you mail. It will be the most successful for both your company and its salespeople.

The house file should be used for ongoing contact and lead generation activity. Serdi and Apple were used as examples of house file activity. The house file of customers and prospects is the best performing list you can use. Even an aged list of inactive customers and prior respondents will probably out-produce a new list.

Chapter Thirteen:

Building a Lead Generation Database

Database may be the most misused term in direct marketing. Database has become the new buzz word and concept for direct marketing. Everyone uses and embraces the term, but few people understand what it means. The concept is so new that most dictionaries do not even include a definition for it. *The World Book Dictionary* defines database as "a large collection of records stored on a computer system from which specialized data may be extracted or organized as desired."

Historical Development

Let's review database within the context of a quick history of data processing. In the evolution of data processing, information was originally captured on punched cards. Each card was only able to hold 80 characters of information. The machines that processed this information were initially limited to a series of registers that could perform arithmetic functions. Additional information created during the processing was printed or punched into another card.

The first computer system, ENIAC, developed in the late 1940s, weighed several tons and filled a large room. Today that same computing power is available on a microchip. It is mind boggling how far and fast data processing technology has come. Our ability to store, retrieve, and process data has grown exponentially over the last 40 years.

In the 1960s the storage of information progressed from punched cards to magnetic tape. The magnetic tape had many advantages over punched cards. However, tape processing was limited in its ability to store and retrieve data.

Information in punched cards was limited to 80 characters of data per card. Files could contain more than one card per record. However, multiple cards per record made the processing slower and more difficult. In order to read and process information, you had to read the cards sequentially. If multiple cards were used, they had to be sorted and merged prior to processing. If new information was created as a result of processing, a new card or series of cards had to be created.

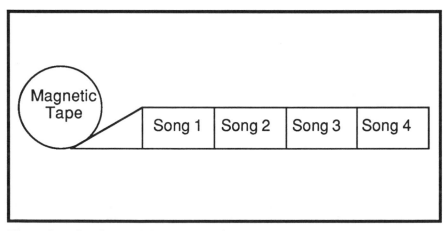

Illustration 13-1: Sequential Tape Processing.

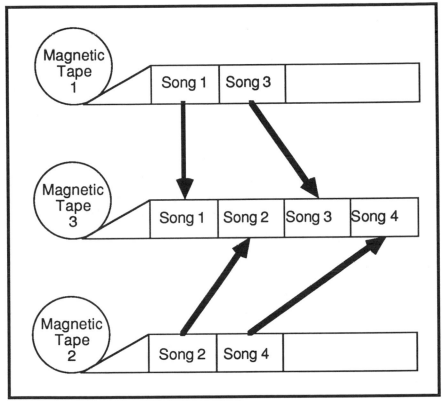

Illustration 13-2: Sequential Tape Processing.

You are probably familiar with the use of magnetic tape for storing and playing music. If you want to play a song on the center of the tape you have to play through or fast forward to the appropriate part of the tape. This type of information storage, reading one item at a time, is called *sequential processing*. Having to move through all the preceding songs is one of the primary limitations of sequential processing. To play song 4 in Illustration 13-2, you first have to play or fast forward through songs 1, 2, and 3.

Besides the difficulties in reading a song in the middle of the tape, imagine the difficulty in combining songs from multiple tapes.

Illustration 13-2 shows that in order to write or record in the center of a tape, you must first erase any existing information on the tape. Creating a new tape of information or music then requires reading information from one device and writing information on a different device. So while tape processing allows you to store more than 80 characters of information in each record, it has limitations in reading, writing, and processing.

Tape processing permits almost unlimited strings of data. Therefore, you can store all pertinent information in one record. Still, processing and creating new information required creating a new tape on a different device. If only one record was processed, the whole tape had to be read and a new tape created.

During the 1970s, the data storage medium changed significantly to allow for the direct access of information. Using the music exam-

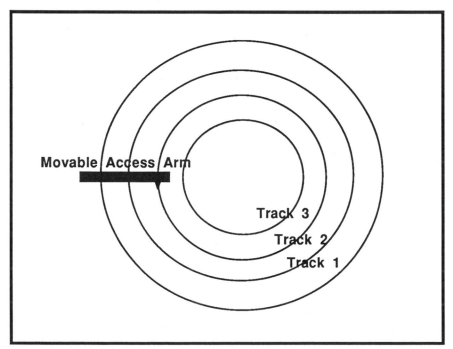

Illustration 13-3: Disk Processing.

ple, if you were listening to a record and wanted to play the fourth song on that record, you could lift the arm and place it directly on that song. This technique is similar to *disk processing* in data processing. Illustration 13-3 shows how data is stored in tracks on a rotating magnetic surface. A movable arm is directed to a specific track location. As the rotating surface passes under the access arm, the required data is read.

Disk processing allows the computer to randomly access information. It enables information to be retrieved randomly. In addition, disk processing also permits the writing and updating functions to be accomplished simultaneously. We no longer have to read sequentially and then write the processed information onto a new tape. We can now read, write, and update simultaneously.

Disk processing permits the random processing of information. The introduction of *random direct access processing* has allowed for the development of dynamic databases. The rapid introduction of new and innovative technology now makes direct access processing widely and easily available.

With tape processing, lists could be compiled that contained more than 80 characters of information per record. The larger size of the record permitted the addition of demographic and psychograpic information to these lists, further enabling better segmentation and targeting techniques. Tapes also facilitate the interchanging and exchanging of list information with other companies.

The technological advancements in data storage and retrieval have significantly improved our ability to conduct sophisticated direct marketing. Unfortunately, many companies today are still using tape and punched card processing as the basis for most of their programs. This is not because the equipment required to upgrade to newer techniques is too expensive, but rather because it is perceived that the change to the newer technologies would be too difficult and risky.

Computer programs are traditionally written to manage files whose records have specific characteristics. If the record format is changed, the computer programs that are used with that record will all have to be modified. It is not unusual, as a system evolves, to have hundreds of computer programs involved in the processing of information. Introducing a new piece of information, such as the average earnings per household, could require a major programming effort. This big "change" is not to create the new information, but to modify the existing programs to handle this new piece of data.

Traditional computer programs deal with fixed length and formatted files. Your data processing department is probably using programs and files. In addition, if your company is a long-time user of data processing, you probably have a number of program applications based on tape processing. This doesn't mean that your data processing system is antiquated, but just reflects the natural business perspective of, if it isn't broken, don't fix it. Your data processing department is never starved for things to do. Updating an application that is working always will be assigned a lower priority than installing new applications or fixing existing programs that are not functioning properly.

As data processing equipment technology has improved, so have the programming and processing techniques. In the 1980s, the state-of-the-art has evolved to computer programs that can deal with data independently of the software programs. This means that the computer programs don't care about the format of the information. These database management systems (DBMS) allow the data processing departments to write programs that will not have to be modified when information is added or changed within the system.

These database managers operate independently of the application programs. Most database management systems will allow an unsophisticated user to perform his own inquiries into the computer without the aid of the data processing department. This new technology promises to reduce the backlog of new applications the data processing department would otherwise develop. More importantly, it will put the power of the computer into the hands of the end-users without having to make them computer programmers.

A computer database program to manage information is a relatively new concept. Many companies are not yet using this new technique; more than likely they are still using application programs and files to manage their information. It is ironic that while the cost and effort to convert existing applications to a database management system may be prohibitive, the cost of the actual DBMS program is fairly modest.

Technological enhancements over the last few years have produced a whole new set of applications. Because the data is now randomly available and the computer is powerful enough to process one transaction at a time, *on-line transaction processing applications* have evolved. This new application series has placed added demands on data processing to provide data instantly.

When many computer programs originally were written, the available data and necessary reports were perceived to be relatively fixed. If the programmer who initially designed the system didn't anticipate a requirement for information in the future, that information became very difficult to obtain. Data availability was controlled by the computer and data processing department, not the user of the information. This accounts for the usage explosion of personal computers within business. End-users were frustrated with the "long" delivery time from data processing. They wanted to control their own information and not be limited in what information they could receive.

Database management systems offer a way to solve the problems of both the user and the data processing department. Still, business decision-makers are faced with some very difficult questions:

1) Which database management system suits our needs?

2) Does the economic benefit of transferring information to the user outweigh the additional computer power needed for rapid information delivery?

3) How difficult will it be to convert to a database management system?

I have provided this background to demonstrate the different meanings for database. As you probably have noticed, data processing people use the term database to mean a management system to control data. The direct marketing definition of database is totally different.

Because most data processing centers are still using programs and files to process information, greater care in planning for the data requirements of your direct marketing database will be needed. As we discussed in Chapter 2, you must have five specific elements (Illustration 13-4) for a successful direct marketing program.

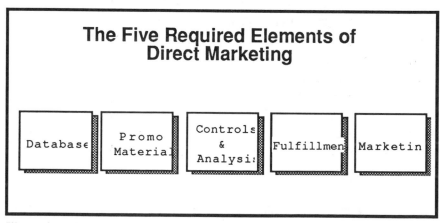

The Five Required Elements of Direct Marketing

Database   Promo Material   Controls & Analysis   Fulfillment   Marketing

Illustration 13-4: The elements of direct marketing.

Two of these elements are directly related to our discussion:

- **Database**

- **Controls & Analysis**

Illustration 13-5 reviews the definition of direct marketing including a definition of database. Let's again examine the various parts of the direct marketing database:

The Definition of Direct Marketing with Database Defined

- An organized and planned system of contacts

- Using a variety of media -- seeking to produce a lead or an order

- Developing and maintaining a database

  - **Providing names of customers and prospects**

  - **Vehicle for storing and measuring responses**

  - **Vehicle for storing and measuring purchases**

  - **Vehicle for continuing direct communication**

- Measurable in costs and results

- Effective in all methods of selling

- Expandable with confidence

Illustration 13-5: The definition of database.

- **A database provides names of customers or prospects.**

  The original name and address list is an important part of the database, but all of the activity relating to each of the names on that list is also essential.

- **A database is a vehicle for storing and measuring responses.**

  Once you reach the targets you identified and they respond to your offer, the database should provide the ability to track each contact and each response.

- **A database is a vehicle for storing and measuring purchases.**

  Now that you know if a prospect has responded to your direct marketing program, you want to track whether these respondents actually become buyers.

  The back-end conversion of respondents to orders is the key measurement in evaluating the success of the direct marketing program. By tracking the actual respondents who purchase, you can establish the cost per order and the average order size.

- **A database is a vehicle for continuing direct communication to the prospects, respondents, and customers.**

  The database should allow you to have a sustained and complete ability to contact the initial list of prospects, the group that responded, and the group that became customers.

As you can see, the measurement and controls of the direct marketing program are directly tied to the database. It is very challenging to anticipate the information you'll have to capture to measure and evaluate the program, prior to starting the project. Because many data processing departments are using programs and files as opposed to database management systems, adding or changing data is more difficult.

Database Requirements

Your direct marketing database has to fulfill the four functions described in Illustration 13-5.

First the database must provide a list to promote. As I discussed in Chapter 6, there are four kinds of lists:

- House or Customer lists
- Compiled lists
- Respondent lists
- Subscription or Membership lists

Each list has different characteristics that may make it a worthwhile list for your business to use. The lists you select for your direct marketing effort will be the single most important decision in determining the success or failure of the project.

In real estate, there are three things that are important in a piece of property:

1) Location
2) Location
3) Location

Direct marketing has a similar series of important elements:

1) List
2) List
3) List

To underscore the importance of the list, carefully consider this direct marketing axiom: an outstanding offer made in an outstanding package to a poor list will produce poor results. On the other hand, a mediocre offer, in a mediocre package made to a good list will probably produce good results.

In the business-to-business environment there are over 40,000 lists available. It is impossible to know about every list. As part of your direct marketing business plan, you will identify the most likely prospect for your products. After you define your marketing program, you may want to consider using a list broker to help you select and evaluate the most useful lists.

Once you select the various lists you plan to use, your database effort will begin. Using various computer routines, you'll want to combine the lists and eliminate duplicate records to the best of your ability. As you may recall from Chapter 2, de-duplication in the business-to-business environment is more difficult than when marketing to consumers.

Even screening by telephone number, which you may or may not have, will not guarantee the elimination of duplicate records. Many businesses provide direct phone numbers for individuals and a different phone number for the company. On the other hand, some businesses only have a central phone number. It is impossible to use the phone number to accurately eliminate duplicates.

Based on my experience, the best de-duplication routines will be only about 60% effective in the business-to-business environment. Consider using an outside service to eliminate duplicates and combine the lists. Each record should be updated to reflect the list from which it came. This will allow you to perform an analysis of each list source.

If you're planning to use telemarketing, you may want to send the combined, de-duplicated list to a service bureau to have the phone numbers appended to the record. These same service bureaus can also add industry, sizing, and other demographic information to your list.

What started as a simple mailing list, is now growing into a database containing other valuable pieces of information. At this point, you can fulfill the first requirement of the direct marketing database - - you can reach a group of prospects or customers. Frequently, this is where the database effort ends. I often find internal databases that have no measurement information about respondents or purchasers. It is also fairly common to find that the respondents from a mail campaign were never recorded and sent to the sales force for follow-up.

The database must be able to store information about respondents. Your data processing department may not be able to handle additional information because of the modifications required by their existing programs. If an application system is being designed to support your needs, you should evaluate all of the additional information required for your database.

The database should be capable of measuring that group of people who responded to the direct marketing promotion. This sounds simple, but it can prove to be very difficult depending on your direct marketing program type. As you define your database requirements for the data processing department, make sure they understand that you'll need to identify respondents and, ultimately, buyers.

Lead generation results are difficult to measure. You may have to design a special method to capture respondent information. Special coupons or premium offers that are only available as a result of the direct marketing program can be useful in establishing measurement information.

As you identify your database requirements, you may want to include:

Type of contact
Date of contact
Response date
Response request (what did the prospect ask for)
Response source (mail, phone)

This information can be helpful in evaluating the success of your program, and determining your next logical step. By building a transaction file detailing the activity and results, you'll be able to follow the sales cycle from start to finish.

If you are only making one contact per prospect, this information is not difficult to record. The situation gets more complex and difficult if multiple contacts and types of contacts are used for the same list. For example, you may decide to mail to several different titles in the same business. Tracking responses from this program can become difficult.

The real measurement of the success of any direct marketing program is the ultimate cost per order and the profitability of the program. But if the measuring of a respondent can get difficult, the measuring of a purchase can become impossible.

Frequently, a prospect will respond to a direct marketing program with a different company name than the name used during the purchase. A prospect may respond to the offer as an individual yet the purchase is then actually made by the company.

Your database must first measure respondents and then those respondents that ultimately convert to orders. Several methods can help you measure the actual purchases made because of the direct marketing program.

- Make a special offer only available through the direct marketing program. If this offer is fulfilled, you'll know that the order came as a direct result.

- Ask the customer after they buy, how they heard of your company and the primary reason they purchased.

- Pay special incentives to the distribution channel for ordering through the direct marketing program.

- Use a computer matching routine to identify orders from direct marketing.

- If you are using a sales force, ask the salespeople what has happened.

Don't limit your measurement program to these ideas. Include measurement as part of the creative process in designing your direct marketing program.

As I have continued to discuss, in a lead generation program, the problem of measuring sales is frustratingly complicated. The salespeople do not like to admit that you helped them. They are reluctant to give credit to the direct marketing program for the sale. In addition, many leads are not even followed up by the salespeople. The same techniques described above for measuring orders can also be used to measure the effectiveness of your salespeople. Frequently, direct marketers elect to ask the sales force to evaluate the quality of the leads. This seems to be the least effective technique for evaluating the success of the direct marketing program.

You may want to add the following information to your database to help you evaluate purchases:

Date of purchase
Product purchased
$ Amount purchased
Method of purchase (retail, salesperson, direct)

Any respondent to your direct marketing programs -- whether for information or actual purchases -- will become your best opportunity for additional response in future programs. Remember that the house file of customers and respondents could become one of your most valuable assets.

Illustration 13-6 shows the difference between information maintained by salespeople about their customer relationships and the information typically kept by the company. The database you develop will probably have to accommodate information that has not been kept in the past.

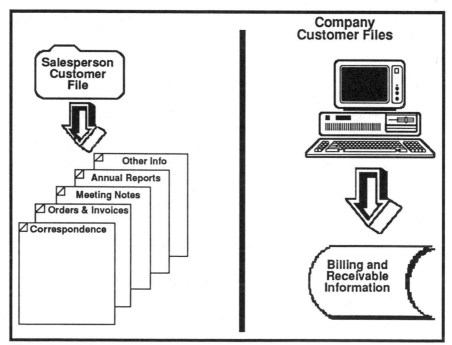

Illustration 13-6: The elements of direct marketing.

As you use direct marketing programs to contact your "house" list, be sure you provide a way to keep the list up-to-date. If names, addresses, phone numbers, or contact information change, your database should reflect the most current information.

Your least expensive respondent, lead, or order will be generated from your "house" list of prior respondents and customers. That means this list will represent your most profitable universe for selling products or services.

Very often I'll see lists of respondents to direct marketing programs stacked in boxes with nothing being done to further the sales effort. As I discussed in the last chapter, other than existing customers, those "bad" leads represent your best selling opportunity.

Building a Relational Database

Relational database technology now allows you to separate your data into unique elements and only store one version of information for multiple uses. For example, you can create a single company name and address that can be used for contacting multiple people within that company. If the address changes, you only have to make the address change once for all contacts within the company.

Information in a relational database is stored in *tables.* The database table contains *columns*, that are similar to the fields in a normal data processing file. The members of the table are called *rows.* These are similar to the records in standard data processing files. Key fields are data elements that link information in separate files to make updating easier.

In the past, if you needed to capture multiple options for a specific question that allowed more than a single response, you probably created a separate 'bucket' for each possible response. Illustration 13-7 depicts a single record that has been designed to accommodate

3 orders. The 3 sets of information about the 3 orders becomes a part of each customer record. As you can see, to capture this information with traditional file processing, a separate bucket for each order is necessary. Additionally, if the customer purchases a 4th time, you would have to either eliminate one of the prior orders or change all the programs and files involved.

In a relational database, you would create a separate table for orders and link them together using a common key.

For example, suppose you have given your prospects the following response choices in a mailing: receive additional information; attend a seminar; be contacted by a salesperson; or be added to a mailing list. Prospects will often select more than one option. To capture this information with traditional file processing, a separate bucket for each option was necessary. Additionally, if you offered another option on a subsequent program, you would have to change all of the files and programs involved.

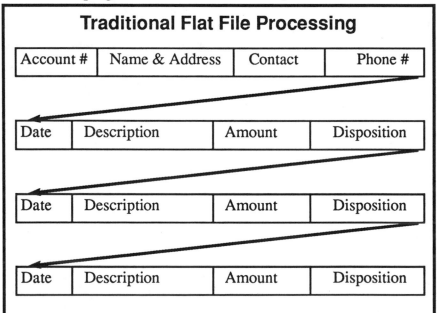

Illustration 13-7: Flat File Processing.

Using a relational database (Illustration 13-8), a table for prospect requests is created and linked via a common element in the *Names* table. Normally, the common element is an account number. Each separate request is entered into the activity table. New or additional requests are added independent of prior activities.

Location addresses are stored in a separate table and individuals are related to the location table by a common location identifier. If the address changes, only the location table needs to be changed. Each individual's contact address is automatically updated by the change.

Relational Processing

Location Table

Account #	Name & Address	Phone #
Account #	Name & Address	Phone #
Account #	Name & Address	Phone #

Names Table

Account #	Contact	Phone #
Account #	Contact	Phone #
Account #	Contact	Phone #

Activity Table

Account #	Contact	Date	Description	Amount	Disposition
Account #	Contact	Date	Description	Amount	Disposition
Account #	Contact	Date	Description	Amount	Disposition

Illustration 13-8: Relational Processing.

A Database Model

Illustration 13-9 is a database model that establishes commonly used information for direct marketing purposes. Your needs may vary significantly, but this model gives you a basis for creating a database.

The following table layout will help you set up your own database. In the Format column, the letter identifies the field elements as being alphabetic or numeric; the number shows how many characters that field can contain.

The *Names* table is used to store the marketing contact name, title, and telephone number for marketing purposes.

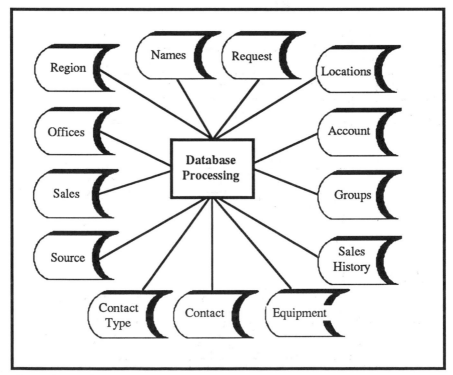

Illustration 13-9: A direct marketing database model.

The *Names* table will be related to the *Location* table to get address information to contact the individuals in the *Names* table.

The *Names* table will be related to the *Source* table to verify the specific format of the names.

1.0 Names Table Layout

	Column Name	Description	Format
1.1	Names_ID	Unique Identification #	N6
1.2	Loc_ID	Location Identification # - this identifier will link the *Names* table to the *Location* table. It is the key to the *Location* table.	N4
1.3	Lname	Last name	A15
1.4	Fname	First name	A14
1.5	MI	Middle initial	A1
1.6	Salt	Salutation - (Mr/Mrs/Ms)	A3
1.7	Title	The functional business title used by the individual like DP/Manager or VP/MIS.	A15
1.8	Phone	The phone number of the prospect. The phone number may include up to a 4 position extension. Any field may include special editing characters such as parentheses, dashes, or periods.	A17

Column Name		Description	Format
1.9	Dec_status	Decision status. This represents the individual's involvement in the decision to add or change vendors.	A1
		1=Makes the decision	
		2=Investigates and recommends	
		3=Not involved in the decision	
1.10	Source_ID	A code that identifies the source that added this particular name to the *Names* table. The Source_ID is the link to the *Source* table. It is the key to the *Source* Table.	N4
1.11	Update	The last date this row of the table was updated or changed.	A8

The *Request* table is used to store the detailed information about each name in the *Names* table and the disposition of that name. Names may have multiple dispositions.

The *Request* table is related to the *Names* table.

1.0 Request Table Layout

Column Name		Description	Format
1.1	Names_ID	Unique Identification # for a particular Account.	N4
1.2	Request	The description of the particular request made by the prospect.	A25
		Send Additional Information	
		Attend a Seminar	
		Have Sales Rep Call	

The *Locations* table is used to store the company name, address, and other master information about a particular company or location.

The *Locations* table is related to the *Sales* table and is used to record the information about the salesperson assigned to a particular location.

1.0 Locations Table Layout

	Column Name	Description	Format
1.1	Loc_ID	Unique Identification # for a particular location.	N4
1.2	Sales_ID	Salesperson Identification # - this identifier will link the *Locations* table to the *Sales* table. It is the key to the *Sales* table.	N4
1.3	Company	Company name	A35
1.4	Address1	First line of street/mailing address	A25
1.5	Address2	Second line of street/mailing address	A25
1.6	City	Address city	A16
1.7	State	The standard two position state code	A2
1.8	Zip	The zip code containing 5 or 9 characters.	A10
1.9	Phone	The phone number of the company	A12

Column Name	Description	Format
1.10 Parent	The location_ID of the parent company, if the company is a subsidiary or division of another company.	N4
1.11 SIC	The Standard Industrial Classification (SIC) code.	A5
1.12 Update	The last date this row of the table was updated or changed.	A8

The *Account* table is used to store the details about accounts within different locations. A location can have several account records for different applications or opportunities. The *Account* table should be created to contain your own specific qualification information. It is where you store the unique data about a specific account. Remember, if you are storing multiple types of similar data, you should create a separate table for each type of data. In this example, we will have multiple types of equipment, so we have created a separate *Equipment* table.

The *Account* table is related to the *Names* table to establish the primary sales contact with the prospect business.

The *Account* table is related to the *Location* table to establish the company address and master information.

The *Account* table is related to the *Equipment* table to establish the quantity and type of equipment installed at each account.

1.0 Account Table Layout

Column Name	Description	Format
1.1 Account_ID	Unique Identification # for a particular account.	N4

Column Name	Description	Format
1.2 Names_ID	The primary sales contact. The Names_ID is used to identify the Name Identification # - this identifier will link the *Names* table. It is the key to the *Names* table.	N6
1.4 Unique	The rest of this table will contain the unique data you're capturing for a specific account.	

The *Groups* table is used to store the details about each name in the *Names* table and relate names to particular accounts in the *Account* table.

The *Groups* table is related to the *Names* table. This table will enable you to establish all of the individual names involved in a specific account.

1.0 Groups Table Layout

Column Name	Description	Format
1.1 Account_ID	Unique Identification # for a particular Account.	N4
1.2 Names_ID	Names_ID is the unique identification number that links the *Names* table.	N4

The *Sales history* table is used to store the details about a salesperson's activity or history with a specific account. If you are using a sales force, you will store prospect activity in this table.

The *Sales history* table is related to the *Account* table to establish the salesperson's historical selling activity with a specific account.

1.0 Sales History Table Layout

	Column Name	Description	Format
1.1	Account_ID	Unique Identification # for a particular account.	N4
1.2	Date	Date of activity	A8
1.3	Activity	Type of activity I=Init Call Q=Stage 1, Qualification P=Stage 2, Proof S=Stage 3, Proposal/Sale O=Stage 4, Order	A1
1.4	Disposition	Disposition of the account as a result of the contact activity. 1=Actively Working 2=Account Rejection 3=Sales Rep Rejection	A1
1.5	Odds	Odds that this account will order.	N2
1.6	Nxt_Date	The anticipated date to move to the next sales stage.	A8
1.7	Order	The account has ordered and is now a customer. Y=Customer	A1

The *Equipment* table is used to store the details about equipment or other unique products or services used in each account.

The *Equipment* table is related to the *Account* table to establish the account at which the equipment is installed.

1.0 Equipment Table Layout

	Column Name	Description	Format
1.1	Account_ID	Unique Identification # for a particular account.	N4
1.2	Vendor	The manufacturer of the equipment.	A15
1.3	Model	The model of the equipment.	A10
1.4	Description	A description of the installed equipment.	A50
1.5	Quantity	The quantity installed.	N5

The *Contact* table is used to store the details about each sales contact. It contains a description of the contact, cost information and the specific direct marketing or selling program that is related to this contact.

1.0 Contact Table Layout

	Column Name	Description	Format
1.1	Contact_ID	Unique Identification # for a particular Contact.	N4
1.2	Names_ID	The name of the target contacted. The Names_ID is used to identify Name Identification # - this identifier will link the *Names* table. It is the key to the *Names* table.	N6
1.3	Type_ID	The contact_ID # that is used to identify the type of contact that was made to this name. The Contact_ID is the identifier that will link the	N4

Column Name		Description	Format
		Contact_ID table. It is the key to the *Contact_ID* table.	
1.4	Date	The contact date.	A8
1.5	Disposition	The result of the contact. 01=Responded 02=Rejected-Not Qualified 03=Rejected-Prospect not interested 04=Lead Generated 05=Ordered 06=Requested Literature 07=Requested Seminar 08=Complaint	N2

The *Contact type* table is used to store the details about each sales contact. It contains a description of the contact, costing information and the applicable direct marketing program.

1.0 Contact Type Table Layout

Column Name		Description	Format
1.1	Type_ID	Unique Identification # for a particular contact.	N4
1.2	Project	The name of the project that is being supported with this type of contact.	N6
1.3	Program	The program of which this project and contact are a part.	N6
1.4	Description	A complete description of the contact.	A50

Column Name	Description	Format
1.5 Costs	The estimated or actual costs of the contact.	A8

The *Source* table is used to store the details about lists and other sources of names. This table will be used to determine the effectiveness of various list sources, and to determine the best sources for new names.

1.0 Source Table Layout

Column Name	Description	Format
1.1 Source_ID	Unique Identification # for a particular source.	N4
1.2 Name	The name of the source.	A15
1.3 Description	A description of the source.	A50
1.4 Date	The date that the source was acquired.	A8
1.5 Count	The number of records this source contained.	N8

The *Sales* table is used to store the information about each of the salespeople. The table will contain information on salespeople and sales managers. This table will contain home addresses and phone numbers that will be added to direct marketing programs. The start date and last date will allow you to evaluate the sales performance over time.

The *Sales* table is related to the *Offices* table to establish the address information to contact the individuals in the *Sales* table. Consolidation of information by sales office will also be possible with the *Offices* table.

The *Sales* table will be related to the *Region* table to establish the reporting structure of each individual.

1.0 Sales Table Layout

Column Name		Description	Format
1.1	Sales_ID	Unique Identification # for each salesperson.	N6
1.2	Office_ID	Office Identification # - this identifier will link the *Sales* table to the *Office* table. It is the key to the *Office* table.	N4
1.3	Lname	Last name	A15
1.4	Fname	First name	A14
1.5	MI	Middle initial	A1
1.6	Salt	Salutation - (Mr/Mrs/Ms)	A3
1.7	Title	The functional business title used by the individual like Senior Sales or Account Executive.	A15
1.8	Phone	The phone number of the sales rep. The phone number may include up to a 4 character extension.	A17
1.9	Addr1	Home address	A25
1.10	City	Home city	A16
1.11	State	The standard two position state code.	A2

Column Name	Description	Format
1.12 Zip	The zip code containing 5 or 9 characters.	A10
1.13 Phone	The employee's home phone number.	A12
1.11 Start	The start date of the employee.	A8
1.12 Finish	The last day of employment.	A8
1.13 Region	The Region_ID. This establishes the affiliation of the individual with their immediate manager.	N4

The *Office* table is used to store information about each of the offices to make contacting the personnel in each office possible.

1.0 Office Table Layout

Column Name	Description	Format
1.1 Office_ID	Unique Identification # for each field office.	N6
1.2 Street	Address	A25
1.3 City	City	A16
1.4 State	The standard two position state code.	A2
1.5 Zip	The zip code containing 5 or 9 characters.	A10
1.6 Phone	The phone number.	A12

The *Region* table is used to store information about each branch office or sales region. It establishes the reporting structure of the individual salespeople.

The *Region* table is related to the *Sales* table to capture the name and address information of the regional manager.

1.0 Region Table Layout

Column Name	Description	Format
1.1 Region_ID	Unique Identification # for each field office.	N6
1.2 Name	The name of the region.	A25
1.3 Manager	Sales_ID of the regional manager. The Sales_ID will link the *Region* table to the *Sales* table. Sales_ID is the key to the *Sales* table.	A16

This database model may not fit your business. However, it demonstrates how involved the database becomes. You must keep repetitive data in separate tables to permit maximum flexibility. This database model will give your data processing department an idea of your requirements, and allow you to perform the database functions inherent in the direct marketing definition.

A number of relational database management systems (DBMS) are available that make implementing this approach easier. In the PC market, Paradox and Dbase IV are two alternatives. Oracle and Ingres are DBMS alternatives on some mini-computers and mainframes. The IBM AS400 and System/38 have database managers as part of their operating systems.

Database Marketing

This is the newest marketing concept and the current buzz word that everyone is using to describe their marketing efforts. As you have already seen, a database means different things to different people. This marketing concept presumes that each marketing contact is stored on the computer database. The prior contact history will be used to establish the next logical contact and marketing activity. This almost sounds like *Star Wars*. Because most businesses are still using programs and data files, they are probably unable to implement database marketing today.

To properly implement database marketing, you must be able to change your data requirements as your needs change. It is possible to require a change based on each contact you make to the database. This could mean dedicating a computer programming staff to the direct marketing project. The use of a dynamic database probably requires a database management system. Again, it is very difficult to operate and control database marketing using computer programs and fixed files.

Your need to capture information about each contact and the results of that contact will require a significant amount of computer storage and the flexibility to change the files each time you introduce a new marketing program. If you have this capability, you will be able to automatically generate contacts to your customers and prospects based on the results of the last contact.

The real question becomes: does database marketing offer you an opportunity to generate a less expensive order and increase your profits? Based on my experience, database marketing substantially improves results. The challenge is to use a database to support, maintain and enhance the relationship between your company and its customers . . . the database is only a tool to help you achieve these objectives.

Every direct marketing function in which I participate inevitably has a session on database marketing. These sessions focus on computer techniques and how to create a database but spend almost no time on how to develop, build, and enhance the relationship between your company and its customers. In this chapter I've tried to bridge the technical discussions and show you how to build the database.

Historically, it was the salesperson's responsibility to maintain the relationship with a company's customers. Successful salespeople maintain a vast inventory of information about their customers. Each maintains a file containing the past and current relationship of their company and their customers. In some cases, the salesperson's file is the most complete historical record available within the company concerning the relationship between the customer and the company.

The underlying reason salespeople maintain customer files is to establish and maintain a relationship with their customers and prospects. The files document that sustained relationship. This is the fundamental key to sales success.

Good salespeople will continue to maintain the history of their relationships in their own files. The real question is: How can we as companies maintain the same historical record for all our customers?

Existing company data files contain information related to billing and accounting. There is virtually no information about the selling and marketing activity that has occurred in the past.

Documenting customer/company relationships becomes more critical as we assess alternative methods of dealing with various customer segments. Some companies instruct their clerical staffs to develop and maintain complete customer files. Over time there are limits to the amount of information these files can contain and older information is often purged. In addition, these files often only contain contact information in which the customer has initiated the contact. The file may not contain all contact initiated by the company.

The files maintained by accounting and sales administration will generally be well organized and standardized. However, they will not be complete. The salesperson's files will be complete but individualized by the salesperson and hard to use by someone else -- there will be little organization or standardization. There may be scarce information available on smaller customers.

It is also interesting that there tends to be a direct relationship between how frequently a customer is contacted and how often they buy. The best customers are often those that have received the best sales and support services from the company.

As selling costs continue to grow, the number of customers that a company can afford to have salespeople call on, will continue to decline. Smaller customers become too expensive to service with a salesperson. As a result, the historical record of the relationship with that customer, maintained by the salesperson, is lost.

Traditional consumer selling is frequently a one-shot approach. That is, the company makes an offer for a product, and does or does not sell the product. Often, there is no need or desire to maintain a sustained relationship with the customer. Like retail selling, the consumer marketer will attempt to drive a new customer for each order. Because of the relatively large size of the consumer universe, it is both reasonable and affordable to drive a new customer for each order.

Business marketers can't afford to regenerate new customers for each order. Most businesses are selling to a limited universe, which tends to be relatively small. The best opportunity for a company is to establish long term relationships with their customers.

Some form of database is necessary to sustain the relationship in business-to-business marketing. This database can be as simple as the sales files described earlier. It doesn't always have to be executed on a large mainframe computer and cost hundreds of thousands of dollars.

A direct marketing database will:

- Contain the names, addresses, titles, and phone numbers of contacts you want to reach via direct mail, telephone or some other direct marketing format.
- Have the capability to record all responses and purchases.
- Provide the capability to sustain communication and selling activity for all names on the database and record each contact.

The results of one marketing activity should dictate the next marketing activity. The ongoing transactions in the relationship should control the ongoing marketing activity.

When a marketer is aware of all the products purchased by a customer, they can design a direct mail program or telesales program to contact customers and solicit them for additional sales based on what they have purchased in the past. Direct mail can be personalized and created via a word-processing system. Telesales contacts can review prior activity and develop new needs based on the relationship. The customer will feel like they are receiving personal attention. The 'relationship' will be sustained.

Database Marketing Case Study

Let's examine a lead generation program that ultimately evolved into a significant database marketing program. In Chapter 5, I used the Cellular Company as an example of how direct marketing could be used to develop a successful measurement approach for lead generation. That same case study also demonstrates database marketing.

As you may recall, Cellular Company is a major supplier of cellular telephone equipment and was interested in generating sales leads for their independent distributors in several market areas. Broadcast, radio, television, space ads in both newspapers and magazines, and direct mail were used to generate responses. Illustration 13-10 shows how the responses were handled by an independent telemarketing service bureau. The independent firm was fully automated and handled both mail and phone responses. If the response was via telephone, the inbound communicators were scripted and fully interactive with a computer.

The prospect was considered of lower quality if they did not provide a company name. These prospects were sent a less expensive fulfillment package. Cellular Company did not feel that a salesperson could effectively follow-up a responder at their home. Salespeople have a tendency to prejudge the quality of leads. Respondents who only provide their home address are frequently judged to be tire kickers and not buyers. The company decided to use a two-step approach to better qualify these incomplete respondents.

All respondents were added to a database and each contact was tracked. As new respondents were received, they were checked against the database to ensure that they hadn't already been handled in the last 90 days. Quite often, a prospect who hasn't received a timely follow-up will respond a second time. Cellular Company was selling through outside distributors and there were several distributors in each market. An attempt was made to ensure that the same prospect wasn't sent to two different distributors. We also tried to eliminate prior respondents. As discussed earlier, de-duplication routines in business-to-business are not very effective.

All respondents were qualified via telephone. If a mail respondent did not provide a telephone number, and the number wasn't available through directory assistance, the record was considered not qualified and sent the less expensive information package.

At the onset of the project, Cellular Company recognized that their product was unique and there would be a lot of interest from people who were not qualified. In addition, Cellular Company had a limited geographic area in which they offered services. In order to deal with the unqualified prospect, either through geography or qualification criteria, a less expensive generic fact kit was developed.

The qualified prospects, those with business addresses and phone numbers, were contacted via outbound telemarketing. Each prospect was screened for qualification and offered a call by a salesperson. The telephone screening approach is detailed in Illustration 13-11.

The same lead qualification script was used for both inbound and outbound telemarketing. If the prospect wasn't qualified, meaning they didn't meet the criteria for money, authority, need, and desire, they were sent the inexpensive mail kit. Qualified prospects were offered the opportunity to be contacted by a salesperson.

I know that many prospects request literature before they agree to be contacted by a salesperson. I also know that a substantial percentage of prospects who request information can be converted to a lead if they are contacted after they receive the material.

In telemarketing, prospects will frequently request additional information. Some people respond to telephone offers then request information as an easy way to terminate the call. However, people are interested in the offer, but want more information prior to making a commitment. All prospects who request additional information should be considered legitimate prospects. In my experience, about 25% of these literature requesters can be converted into leads.

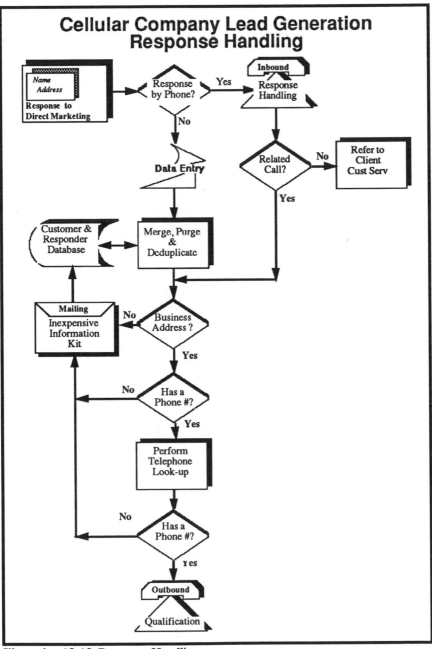

Cellular Company Lead Generation Response Handling

Illustration 13-10: Response Handling.

Keeping track of who requested literature; when the literature was fulfilled; and when the prospect should be re-contacted will require some form of database. Small volumes will only require a manual database. However as the volumes become larger, the database will require a computerized approach.

Initially, Cellular Company management wasn't concerned about the return of information from the sales force. Management was convinced that the sales force would follow-up on every lead and provide feedback about lead quality. Cellular Company didn't feel that a lead management and control system was necessary.

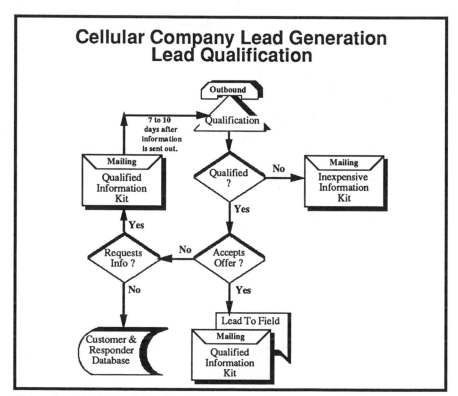

Illustration 13-11: Lead Qualification.

After several months of lead generation and several thousand leads, only 5% of the leads had been returned with any information. Cellular Company couldn't evaluate the success of the lead program. Senior management received verbal feedback that lead quality was not very good. They were considering shutting down the project.

To evaluate the success of the lead program, a mail questionnaire was sent to all leads to determine their disposition. The respondent database made re-contacting the leads very easy.

The results were startling. Forty percent of the leads had been contacted by the sales force. In my experience, this is a good follow-up rate. I have seen lead follow-up as low as 8% in other campaigns. In this instance the leads proved to be very high quality. Of the leads contacted by a salesperson, over 60% had purchased a product.

Management was alarmed about the business opportunity that had been lost because the sales force had not followed-up. Several action programs were implemented to ensure that Cellular Company could capitalize on the opportunity within their current and future respondent database.

A complete lead management and tracking system was implemented to ensure that the sales force followed up on all leads. The leads were only given to a distributor salesperson for 30 days. Cellular Company used telemarketing to re-contact prospects 30 days after the leads were generated to determine their disposition. The follow-up call determined if the prospect had received the information requested and if they had been contacted by a salesperson. If the lead was not contacted, it was regenerated and sent to another distributor salesperson. Illustration 13-12 reflects the flow of activity in the lead tracking and follow-up system.

The results of the project were very rewarding. Follow-up improved to almost 80% of leads generated. More importantly,

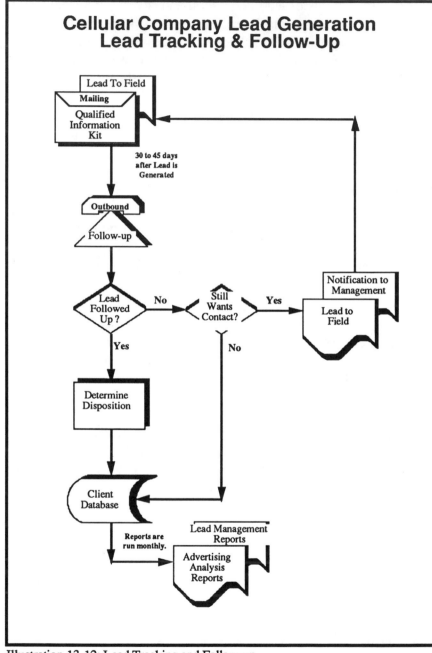

Illustration 13-12: Lead Tracking and Follow-up.

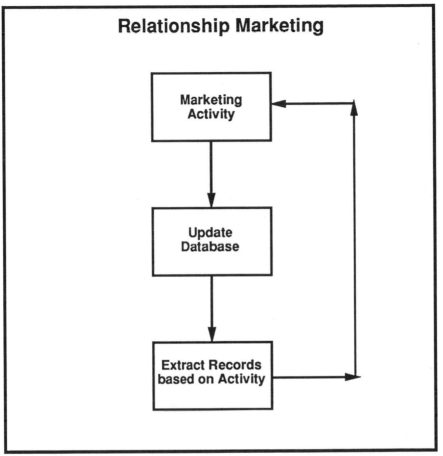

Illustration 13-13: Relationship Marketing.

30% of all leads generated resulted in orders. The cost per lead and cost per order were substantially less than originally anticipated.

The database allowed ongoing contact with the respondent. It also allowed an accurate measurement system to be developed to evaluate the success of the lead generation program.

Additional direct mail followed by outbound telemarketing programs were developed and the database was naturally used as a list source. Prospects on the database were contacted three additional times in the first year to generate more leads. Only those prospects who had already purchased were not included in the continuing direct marketing program. Not surprisingly, the least expensive leads and orders were derived from the database because these database names performed at a higher level of response than other lists.

Each time a contact was made, it was added to the database to track and evaluate the effectiveness of each step of the direct marketing effort. The database also contained all of the information captured during the telemarketing contacts, and this data became valuable market research.

The results of each contact established the next activity for the prospect. The storage, retrieval and updating of the information as a result of each contact developed a dynamic marketing database. As I discussed in Chapter 2, the ongoing database activity is the basis for relationship marketing (Illustration 13-13). The results of each contact had to be evaluated to determine the next step.

The use of this information to condition the next selling activity is the essence of database marketing.

These results and benefits justify the investment to implement a dynamic database. You can experiment with database marketing by handling your literature requesters similarly to the methods we discussed earlier. Send the information to the respondent and then follow-up with a telephone call to attempt to convert the prospect to a lead or an order. I think you'll find the results very encouraging.

Database Summarized

The term database may be the most misused and misunderstood term in our marketing language. It means different things to different people.

Data processing people think about a database in terms of how the computer information is going to be managed and controlled. To them, database means database management systems (DBMS).

The conversion of existing files and programs to a DBMS is a large effort and has substantial impact on data processing. Computer programs are written to deal with data that is formatted in a specific way. Changing the format of the data normally means having to change any computer program that will deal with that data. Even adding a small piece of information to existing systems can mean a massive change to computer programs.

Database management systems separate the data from the computer programs and make changing and adding information relatively easy. DBM systems allow you to add or change information independently of computer programs. They also move the control of information from the data processing department to the end-user.

The list industry defines database as an expanded list. Several list companies now offer databases that are the result of combining several lists and then adding demographic, geographic, and psychograpic data to them. These combined lists are referred to as databases. They arc a significant improvement over prior list sources because you can be more effective in selecting and segmenting your target audience.

Other departments within your business can probably give you additional definitions of database. All of the definitions may be correct for their particular application. For the purposes of business-to-business direct marketing, the definition I've been using throughout our discussion is most appropriate.

Direct marketing will develop and maintain a database which:

- Provides names of customers or prospects.

- Is a vehicle to store and measure responses.

- Is a vehicle to store and measure purchases.

- Is a vehicle for ongoing communication with customers and prospects.

I explained how to combine lists to create a target universe for your direct marketing promotion.   Once you begin direct marketing, your database needs to be able to measure responses and then measure purchases. I listed the minimum elements needed for both of these functions.

A complete relational database model was provided to allow you to evaluate the amount of information you may need for direct marketing. The model could be used to work with your data processing department to design your own direct marketing database.

Database marketing offers great promise in reducing costs and increasing results. A complete program was reviewed to demonstrate the elements of database marketing. I emphasized how the database was used to condition additional contacts to the prospects and customers.

The explanation of database in this chapter will allow you to effectively communicate with data processing and direct marketing. Database is one of the required elements of direct marketing. If you don't have control of the database, your efforts will probably fail. If you can't automate the database with your data processing department, consider using another alternative that will give you control.

Chapter Fourteen:

The Lead Planning Model

During our seminars about business-to-business direct marketing we develop a case study that is ultimately used to show the participants how to plan a lead generation program. We use a computer model to demonstrate how changing various elements affects the results of a lead generation program. The model is such an effective tool that I wanted to include the information in this book. Appendix I provides you with the calculations to create the model on your own computer using a spreadsheet program.

I am often asked to project the results of a direct marketing program before the first piece is mailed or the first call is made. Clients believe that consultants are blessed with a special gift that enables them to predict the future. Although most direct marketing experts have executed hundreds or even thousands of programs, none can predict what will happen with a new program. In addition, any change to an existing program can significantly alter the results you experienced in the past. Any program change is almost like starting a new campaign and result projections will not be reliable.

Rather than attempting to project results based on feelings or intuition, I have found that projecting results on break-even or allowable budget criteria is more effective. This approach allows you to establish the return on investment you require. You can then use that information to identify the number of orders, number of leads, and number of responses you require from a program. The expectations set for the program will produce the required results for the company to meet objectives.

As I have mentioned throughout this book, one of the biggest problems inherent in lead programs is inconsistent expectations at various levels of the organization. Salespeople and sales managers expect everyone to respond to a direct marketing program. Many, when asked, will indicate they expected 10% to 20% of those contacted to respond. These unreasonably high expectations will often cause a successful campaign to be scrapped.

The lead planning model we're going to discuss is an excellent way to establish realistic objectives and evaluate the ultimate effectiveness of a campaign. You may have to modify the model to meet your unique requirements, but it does give you a starting point.

Let's first examine the case study company used in our seminars to set the tone for the model.

The ABC Company Case Study

The ABC Company was started about 10 years ago by John Q. Smythe. Initially the company sold Commodore Computers. Smythe started the company from his home by selling products personally. The business grew dramatically in the first year and a store was opened in a small shopping mall. The store consisted of about 3,500 square feet and has expanded to its current 6,000 square feet. The company continues to operate from the single location.

Initially the staff consisted of Smythe, his wife, and his son, who was a computer hobbyist. The store maintains business hours six days a week with expanded hours on Thursday and Friday. The initial customer base consisted of consumers who purchased systems for home and educational purposes.

The company became an authorized Apple reseller in 1980 and has evolved into a full service computer store selling Apple, Commodore, Compaq, IBM, and IBM look-alike products. In addition, the company sells peripherals and computer related furniture and supplies from various manufacturers.

ABC Company offers a broad selection of software across all of the various product lines. Networks and communications are becoming more important in the current selling environment.

Currently the company offers supplies and services that include scanning, laser output, and seminar type training on word processing, spreadsheets and desktop publishing. ABC offers complete maintenance services on all the products sold. ABC also offers maintenance and extended warranty type contracts.

Sales, service, and support had initially been accomplished from the store location with little or no outside sales support. Initially, ABC Company was the only store selling computer products in the area.

Today, at least three other sources are available locally for consumers and businesses to acquire computer products. The increased availability of products from other sources and the expanding product line in the last few years has caused sales to expand their target market from one segment to five different segments.

These segments are:

Market Segment	Description	Average Order	% of ABC Gross Sales
Consumers	Parents whose children use the computer for education. Professionals working at home.	$ 2,000	10%
Education	Schools and educators	$ 6.000	10%
Small Businesses	Single system sales to businesses. System usually includes monitor, disk drive, printer and software. ABC does not try to make subsequent sales to these customers and doesn't know why these sales are limited to single systems.	$ 4,500	40%
Large Businesses	Multiple system sales to businesses. Sale includes system, peripherals, and software.	$ 6,000	35%
Supplies & Services	Consumable supply sales and maintenance services.	Unknown*	5%

* Average order is difficult to estimate but gross sales from this segment can be obtained through cash register records.

ABC Company's past sales have been accomplished in the retail store and most traffic was developed through advertising. The sales organization had typically reacted to the demand of the marketplace. In certain market segments, this sales approach continues to be successful. However, selling to businesses (education sales included) has forced ABC to be more aggressive in contacting the customers and prospects and soliciting for an appointment or seminar. The use of 'outside' salespeople has intensified and become a major part of the selling scenario.

When ABC recently reviewed their sales to businesses, they found that each business order took an average of three face-to-face contacts to close These face-to-face contacts could be either in the retail store or at the customer location, and most frequently at least one contact was made at the customer location. In addition, there were several lengthy telephone contacts to coordinate the selling activity.

The face-to-face contacts were:

- Face-to-face #1 - Initial demonstration and fact finding sought by the customer usually at the retail store location.

- Face-to-face #2 - A second demonstration for additional people from the customer site to reaffirm that the product is appropriate for the business. Many times ABC would have to give estimates on costs and performance during this contact. This contact is sometimes done at the customer location.

- Face-to-face #3 - The salesperson calls on the customer at their location and the decision to buy is confirmed. Sometimes the system is even delivered to the customer location.

Each face-to-face contact takes about one hour.

The salespeople average four face-to-face contacts per day. This doesn't include telephone selling, direct mail and letter writing activity, order processing, and travel.

ABC Company Volumes

Total Revenue	$6,000,000
Cost of Goods	$4,200,000
Gross Margin	$1,800,000
Selling Expenses	$900,000
Contribution to Profit & General & Administrative Expenses (G/A)	$900,000

ABC has developed a customer file on one of their IBM computers. The file includes a customer's name, title, company name, address, and phone number. There are about 4,000 customers on the file but no information is available about purchases or products acquired.

The complexity of the product line and expanding marketplace has significantly changed the qualifications of the people ABC employs. Initially the company could be staffed and operated by the family with some minimal augmentation to work the retail store. The expertise required was not as extensive and required no more than one 'tekkie'.

Today, the salesperson has to be more and more knowledgeable in hardware, software, and business computer applications. The one tekkie support organization has been replaced by applications and equipment specialists.

In the past, the costs to hire, train, and retain people were moderate. Turnover wasn't really a concern. Today, because of the higher expertise level and increased training required, personnel and associated costs have grown dramatically.

The organization today consists of:

Executives/owner	2
Sales manager	1
Salespeople	8
Support/training	2
Clerical/Administration	2
Technical/Maintenance	3

The Salesperson Cost Worksheet

As you may recall from Chapter 4, I suggested that you complete a salesperson cost worksheet as one of the first elements in planning a lead program. The lead planning model requires certain pieces of information that will be easily available if you completed the worksheet. The worksheets in this chapter contain data from ABC Company. In this section, I will explain the steps to complete the lead planning model using the data from your company.

First, establish the total revenue and marketing costs for the period you will use to establish the cost per sales call. Try to use a 12 month period so you'll have to plan your results on an annual basis.

In ABC we were able to identify the number of orders for everything except services and supplies. I suggest you ignore those issues that you can't establish exact information about. Illustration 14-1 shows how each market segment's percent of sales and average order size was used to establish the revenue and number of orders.

Establishing ABC Order Volume

	Percent Business	Revenue	Average Order	Number Orders
Consumer	10%	$600,000	$2,500	240
Education	10%	$600,000	$6,000	100
Small Business	40%	$2,400,000	$4,500	533
Large Business	35%	$2,100,000	$6,000	350
Total		$5,700,000		1,223

Illustration 14-1: Establishing ABC order volume.

The order volume was calculated by multiplying the total revenue ($6 million) by the percent of revenue in each segment. The revenue for each segment was then divided by the average order to establish the number of orders per segment. Because there was no average order size for supplies and services, that segment was excluded and the total sales used for analysis is only $5,700,000 ($6,000,000 less the 5% for supplies and services).

As I discussed in Chapter 4, you can use the actual marketing expenses available from your operating reports to establish the cost per salesperson per year. Marketing costs will usually include all of the field selling expenses as well as advertising, sales and marketing support, marketing research, and other channels of distribution support. Field selling expenses should include sales, management, clerical and technical support labor expenses as well as all of their associated fringe and G/A expenses.

Once you've established the marketing expenses, identify the total number of salespeople you have in your company. Do not include management or field support personnel. These and other 'overhead' costs will be included within the total marketing costs.

Salesperson Cost Worksheet

A)   Total annual revenue $5,700,000

B)   Total annual marketing expenses $900,000

C)   Total number of orders 1,223

D)   Total number of salespeople..8

E)   Revenue per salesperson per year $712,500
     $(A \div D = E)$
F)   Cost per salesperson per year $112,500
     $(B \div D = F)$
G)   Average order size..$4,660
     $(A \div C = G)$
H)   Average # of orders per salesperson...........................153
     $(C \div D = H)$
I)   Average # of sales calls per day 4
     (Based on assumption)
J)   Number of business days per year 220
     per salesperson (Normally 200-220)
K)   Number of sales calls per year per 880
     salesperson $(J \times I = K)$
L)   Cost per sales call...$128
     $(F \div K = L)$
M)   Number of sales calls per order.................................5.8
     $(K \div H = M)$
N)   Closing rate 17.3%
     $(H \div K = N)$

Illustration 14-2: The Salesperson Cost Worksheet for ABC.

*Total Marketing Costs ÷ Number of salespeople =
Cost per Salesperson*

By dividing the total marketing costs by the number of salespeople, you'll establish the cost per salesperson per year. Many sales executives maintain that they're paying their sales forces strictly on a commission basis, therefore the commissions are the only cost for the salespeople. This ignores the other costs involved in promoting and supporting the products.

If you're only using a sales force, the only time you have an opportunity to sell is when the salesperson makes contact with your customers or prospects. Marketing expenses should be apportioned to all of the salespeople, since this will give you a much better indication of your true selling costs. Illustration 14-2 shows that ABC Company's total marketing expenses are $900,000.

Establish the average order size next by dividing the total revenue by the number of orders. We established the number of orders in Illustration 14-1.

Now determine the average revenue and the average number of orders per salesperson. To do this, divide the revenue by the number of salespeople. Then divide the total revenue by the total number of orders.

Now that you know the average cost per salesperson, the average number of orders per salesperson, and the average revenue per order, you can begin to establish cost per sales call.

You should also establish the average number of face-to-face sales calls made per business day. Salespeople perform many other activities besides making sales calls. They travel to and from calls, plan calls, and create call reports and orders. And while most companies believe each of their salespeople average between 3 and 4 face-to-face sales calls per day, McGraw-Hill research estimates an average of 2.1 sales calls per day per salesperson is more accurate. However, we used 4 calls per day for ABC Company's Salesperson Cost Worksheet and you may want to do the same thing.

The actual number of selling days per year is an interesting and sometimes very depressing fact of business. There are 365 days per year. 104 are weekends (52x2). This leaves 261 available selling days. When you subtract vacations (average 10 days) and holidays (average 10 days) and personal days (average 6 days) you'll have only 235 potential selling days per year.

This 235 days equals only 19.6 selling days per month. Now estimate the number of days taken from selling time for meetings, administrative work in the office, training, and recognition events and you'll probably end up with 200 to 220 days available for selling per year. I used 220 selling days in completing the worksheet for ABC Company.

Using the 4 sales calls per day there are 880 sales calls per year. Although this is usually far fewer than the number of calls management thought were being made, it is probably overstated. Averaging 3 or 4 calls per day doesn't recognize the independence of the sales force and their tendency to play golf, tennis, and socially spend time with their customers.

Using the worksheet I established ABC's cost per sales call at $128, the number of sales calls per order at 5.8, and the closing ratio at 17.8%

Knowing the facts -- the costs and the budgets -- can help you establish a better direction for your program. You'll also establish some measurement criteria that can help you evaluate the success of your program. Next I'll use this information to examine various elements in a lead generation program and establish objectives.

Lead Planning Model Variable Elements

	1	2	3	4	Total
A Current Cost per Sales Call					$128
B Allowable Cost per Qualified Lead					$128
C Gross Margin					30%
One-Time Costs					
D Creative costs/project					$1,500
E Management Costs/project					$1,000
List Information					
F List Identification Code	101				
G List Name	Rented				
H Quantity Mailed	5000				
I Average Order Size	4500				
Variable Costs per Name Mailed or Contacted					
J Fulfillment Costs per Respondent	$0.00				
K Phone Follow-up Costs	$0.00				
L Premium or Incentive	$0.00				
M List Cost or Minimum per Name	$0.090				
N Print/Production/Mail	$0.650				
P Postage	$0.181				
Q Fulfillment (formula based on J,K,L)					
Response Rates and Conversion Rates					
R % of respondents qualified as leads	100.0%				
S % of resp not qualify converting to leads	0.0%				
T % of leads that order	18.0%				
Sales Calls					
U Number of Sales Calls per Close	3				
V Number of Sales Calls to Lose Order	2.5				

Illustration 14-3: Lead planning model variable elements.

Lead Planning Model Variable Elements

The computer model we'll use allows you to control certain variable elements of information. Based on your input the spreadsheet calculates the results and allows you to test different "what if" scenarios.

The model I've created requires you to provide different pieces of information and will calculate totals for up to four different test cells. A *test cell*, or, *cell*, refers to a variation of a direct marketing program in which one variable is changed at a time. The four columns on the Lead Planning Model marked 1 through 4 allow you to compare the projected results of a program if you change a specific element of the program.

Certain elements of information will be used generically by each test cell, while other elements are exclusive for that test cell only. Illustration 14-3, shows the test cells or programs number 1 through 4 and a column for the total of the program. You can use the model to evaluate up to four programs or cells within a single program.

In the model and all of the worksheets I have identified each row or line item by alphabetical lettering. This will make it easier to understand the calculations and results. To help explain the elements required and how to input information into the model, let's use the data from ABC Company to complete one example. Throughout this chapter I'll show you how changing various elements impacts the overall results.

The following items, which are fully described, are used by all 4 programs you may decide to evaluate.

A. <u>Current Cost per Sales Call</u>. As I demonstrated in the previous section, this cost can be easily established by completing the salesperson cost worksheet.

This information is entered only once and is used in any of the 4 scenarios you elect to develop. The value used will not affect the required response rate but can have a major impact on the contribution. The cost per sales call will be used to determine the total selling expenses.

ABC's cost per sales call is $128.

B. <u>Allowable Cost per Qualified Lead</u>. This is the cost you are prepared to spend to develop a qualified lead that you can give to a salesperson. A reasonable cost per qualified lead in business marketing is upwards of $150.

I advocate that a qualified lead is worth about the same thing as one sales call. After all, the salesperson frequently has to make a face-to-face call to determine if a prospect is truly qualified.

You can test a number of scenarios using different allowable cost-per-lead values. Cost per lead is required for each cell as well as in the total analysis columns.

The allowable cost per qualified lead determines the required response rate for each scenario you test. It is the basis for determining cost per respondent and the overall number of responses and leads required for the program. This is one of the key ingredients in determining the required response rate you'll need from the program to meet your objectives.

For our discussions, I'm going to use the cost-per-sales call as the allowable cost per lead. Therefore, you'll notice that B is also $128.

C. <u>Gross Margin</u>. This is the percentage of revenue you have to work with after you pay for the cost of goods. Every spreadsheet requires you to input percentages as decimal equivalents. For example 30% would be entered as .3.

The gross margin is used for each of the scenarios you choose to evaluate as well as for the totals of all programs. Gross margin % is the basis for determining the gross margin dollars and ultimately the dollar contribution for each scenario and the overall program.

ABC's gross margin was identified as 30%.

<u>One-time Costs</u>. This section contains information that is not used in the program analysis. It is only provided to ensure that you are aware that there is an investment requirement on a one-time basis to move into direct marketing lead generation.

The one-time investment is not considered in the evaluation of each scenario because it would be difficult to determine an approach to allocating the expense. And, if the program is continued beyond the initial phase, there may be no one-time costs in subsequent rollout of the initial effort. If you try to include development or one-time costs each iteration of the program will become less expensive distorting the results.

D. <u>Creative Costs/project</u>. These are the costs involved in developing the creative concept for the project. If you are testing multiple creative concepts these costs can grow substantially.

For ABC Company I used $1,500 for creative costs. Again, this amount will not be used in the analysis and is only included for informational purposes.

E. <u>Management Costs/project</u>. Every project will require time to manage and evaluate the effort. Whether it is done internally or by an outside service, the costs should be determined and allocated prior to implementing the direct marketing effort.

ABC Company estimated $1,000 for management costs. This amount will not be used in the analysis and is only included for informational purposes.

So far we've examined the information that will be used by each cell or program included in the analysis. If you change any of these items it will effect every program included.

Now let's examine those elements that allow you to develop individual programs and evaluate their results. The variable individual program information is divided into 4 sections:

- List Information
- Variable Costs per Name Mailed or Contacted
- Response Rates and Conversion Rates
- Sales Calls

<u>List Information</u> - In this section you can identify the characteristics and size of each test cell. You can identify a unique name or code that you might actually use when the program is executed.

F. <u>List Identification Code</u>. As you develop different direct marketing scenarios, you may want to assign a code that can appear on the direct marketing piece for measurement purposes. This code can be used in the evaluation and planning phase as well.

The code is not used in the analysis. I favor using simple numeric codes assigned sequentially. The initial program we're discussing has been coded 101.

G. <u>List Name</u>. This is a 7 character abbreviation of the name of the list that will be used for each scenario. You assign the name and it is not used in analysis. This is just a convenience so you will know which list was used for the program or cell in question. I used the name *rented* in the example. This could have just as easily been D&B or some other list.

H. <u>Quantity Mailed</u>. Now we're really getting into the information that will drive the results and analysis of this specific cell or program. This is the number of names that will be mailed or contacted for each scenario. This quantity will be used to determine the itemized costs as well as the response rates and results.

For the example I have decided to promote to 5,000 names from an outside rented list.

I. <u>Average Order Size</u>. This is the average size of the order that is anticipated from the direct marketing program. The size of the order will tie directly to the offer and target list selected.

The average order size at ABC is 4,660. I have rounded this to $4,500 for ease of use.

<u>Variable Costs per Name Mailed or Contacted</u> - This section contains the individual cost items for each piece of mail or phone contact. You will have to determine the individual item costs because many suppliers will estimate charges for their services and products based on quantities of 1,000.

J. <u>Fulfillment Costs per Respondent</u>. If you are planning to send each respondent an information kit or brochure the total costs of each piece should be established.

If you are planning to send a salesperson each respondent as a lead and not fulfill with information, there are no fulfillment costs. On the other hand, if you plan to pre-qualify the leads and only send the most qualified to the salesperson, you will incur some fulfillment expenses.

ABC doesn't use fulfillment information and sends each respondent to their salespeople as leads. Therefore I have not listed any fulfillment costs.

K. <u>Phone Follow-up Costs</u>. If you are planning to pre-qualify leads, you will probably use telemarketing or telesales. These costs should be established on a cost per contact basis.

The model calculates the cost of multiple phone calls based on the conversion percentage you will provide as the % of respondents not qualified who convert to leads (S). This is an algorithm that assumes one phone call for each respondent and an additional phone call for those requesting additional information.

With all respondents being supplied to the salespeople as leads and no fulfillment, there is no requirement for telephone follow-up. Therefore I have not allocated any expense for phone follow-up costs.

L. <u>Premium or Incentive</u>. This item is used if you are planning to use a premium or incentive to increase response. A premium expense in this category assumes you are going to give a premium to each respondent. If you are planning to send a premium in the initial mailing package, you would include the cost of the premium in the cost of the mail package (N).

ABC Company did not use a premium, therefore, I have not allocated any expenses in this area.

M. <u>List Cost or Minimum per Name</u>. Determine the cost per name for the list you will use for each scenario. Some lists have minimum order amounts and therefore can substantially increase the cost per name in smaller quantity mailings.

ABC Company planned to use a rented list that costed $90 per thousand names. The minimum quantity they could purchase was 3,000, which we exceeded. Even though the list rents for $85.00 per thousand we paid an additional $5.00 in selects and processing, bringing our total to $90.00. I divided the $90 by 1,000 to arrive at a cost of $.09 per name.

N. <u>Print/Production/Mail.</u> This is the cost per piece mailed including printing, data processing, labeling, lettershop, and handling costs.

For the example, I planned to use a standard letter package with a non-personalized letter. The cost was $65.00 per 1,000 or $.65 for each name mailed.

P. <u>Postage</u>. This is the cost per piece for postage or shipping charges.

In the example, we planned to use third class bulk postage at $.181 per name mailed.

Q. <u>Fulfillment</u>. This section is automatically calculated based on the cost per piece for fulfillment, telephone contact, and premiums developed earlier (J + K + L).   The automatic calculation assumed an average response rate of 1.5%.

ABC Company did not anticipate any expense for fulfillment costs per respondent, telephone follow-up costs, or premium costs, therefore there were no fulfillment expenses.

Response Rates and Conversion Rates. This section contains your anticipated lead percentages and closing rates for your program. The model will calculate the anticipated response. However, you have to determine what percent of respondents will be qualified leads, what percent of those not initially qualified can be converted to leads, and what percentage of qualified leads you expect to become customers after the salespeople have an opportunity to follow-up on the leads. The values will be used to determine the required response rates and cost per lead and response.

R. % of respondents qualified as leads. This is the percentage of respondents for each scenario that you expect to send to the salespeople as leads. If you are planning to send all of the respondents to the salespeople, the value for this should be 100%.

If you are planning to send 100% of the respondents to the sales force, the value for fulfillment (J) and phone follow-up (K) will probably be 0.

All of the respondents at ABC were sent to the salespeople therefore we used 100% for this element.

S. % of resp not qualify converting to leads. If you are planning to pre-qualify your respondents and only send to the sales force those meeting your qualification criteria, there will be a group of respondents remaining. You can use fulfillment and re-contact these respondents to attempt to re-qualify them into leads. This value is the percentage of respondents not formerly qualified that you expect to now qualify as leads. In many lead generation programs, I have experienced about 25% of prospects who request additional information will convert to a qualified lead if they are contacted after the information has been fulfilled.

If you are planning to send re-qualified respondents a fulfillment piece, you should enter a value for fulfillment (J) and phone follow-up (K).

In the example we are planning to send all of the respondents out to the salespeople as leads, therefore there are no respondents for us to re-qualify.

T. <u>% leads that order</u>. This is the percentage of the leads that you anticipate will order. You may have previous closing ratios that you can use for this element.

ABC's Salesperson Cost Worksheet indicated a closing ratio of 18% of all calls.

<u>Sales Calls</u>. This section contains the anticipated number of calls that will be made to the average respondent. Both those respondents who order and those who do not order will have to be included.

Items U and V will be used to establish the total number of sales calls required for each scenario. The total estimated number of sales calls will be used to establish the selling expenses for each scenario.

U. <u>Number of Sales Calls per Close</u>. The average number of sales calls estimated to close an order.

ABC estimated 3 sales calls for each order.

V. <u>Number of Sales Calls to Lose an Order</u>. Most companies think in terms of the number of calls it takes to sell but seldom examine the number of calls to lose. In my experience it will frequently take more calls to lose than to sell.

For the example we estimated 2.5 calls to lose.

The various elements explained so far will enable the spreadsheet software to project required response rates and develop the costs and profitability of each program.

<u>Results and Analysis</u>

The model now uses the information to create a second page of results and analysis. Illustration 14-4 shows the type of output developed by the model. The list identification code and list name are duplicated on the results report to make it easier for you to analyze and evaluate. The quantity mailed is also duplicated.

Using the cost per item provided and the quantity promoted, the model calculates the various cost elements for each program. For ABC Company the list costs were $450; print/production/mail was $3,250 and the postage was $905. The total direct marketing expense was $4,605 which was used to determine the number of leads and respondents required to meet the objectives of the program.

The allowable cost per sales lead established for all the programs is used to calculate the number of respondents and the number of leads. A series of calculations is used to establish leads from the initial promotion and additional leads that might be generated from follow-up promotions. We sent 100% of the respondents to the salespeople and therefore leads and respondents were equal.

Lead Planning Model Results & Analysis

	1	2	3	4	Total
List Identification Code	101				
List Name	Rented				
AA Quantity Mailed	5,000				5,000
BB List Costs (M x AA)	450				450
CC Print/Prod/Mail (N x AA)	3,250				3,250
DD Postage (P x AA)	905				905
EE Fulfillment (Q x AA)					
FF Total Direct Marketing Expenses	4,605				4,605
GG Allowable cost per qualified lead (B)	$128				
HH % of responders qualified as leads (R)	100.0%				
II % of resp not qualified as leads (1 - HH)	0.0%				
JJ % of not qual resp convert to lead (II x S)	0.0%				
KK Total Lead/Response % (II + JJ)	100.0%				
LL Allowable Cost per Responder (GG x KK)	$128.00				
MM Required Responses (FF ÷ LL)	36				36
OO Required response % (MM ÷ AA)	0.72%				0.72%
PP Leads Initially (MM x HH)	36				36
QQ Responders for Fulfillment (MM - PP)		0			
RR Leads from Fulfillment (QQ x S)	0				
SS Total Leads (PP + RR)	36				36
TT Orders (T x SS)	6				6
UU Number of Sales Calls-Orders (U x TT)	18				18
VV No Sls Calls-Non-orders (V x (SS - TT))	75				75
WW Total Sales Calls	93				93
XX Revenue (I x WW)	27,000				27,000
YY Gross Margin (XX x C)	8,100				8,100
ZZ Sales Call Expenses (WW x A)	11,904				11,904
BA Direct Marketing Expenses (FF)	4,605				4,605
BB Total Selling Expenses (ZZ + BA)	16,509				16,509
BC Contribution (YY - BB)	-8409				-8409
BD % Contribution (BC ÷ XX)	-31.1%				-31.1%

Illustration 14-4: Lead planning model results & analysis.

This represents a required response rate of .72% to meet the cost-per-lead objective.

> Required Responses (36) ÷ Quantity Mailed (5,000) =
> Required Response Rate (0.72%)

The closing ratio is used to determine the number of orders produced by the program. Both the number of sales calls to leads that don't close and the calls on actual orders are calculated based on the information provided earlier.

Our model indicated that ABC would generate 36 leads and produce 6 orders.

> Orders (6) x Number of Sales Calls per Close (3) =
> Number of Sales Calls per Order (18)

The 6 new customers would require 18 sales calls and the leads that don't produce orders will require another 75 sales calls

> Leads (35) - Orders (6) = Leads that don't produce order s (30)

> Leads that don't produce order s (30) x Number of Sales Calls to
> lose order (2.5) = Number of Sales Calls for Leads that don't
> order (75)

The number of sales calls to both the customers that order and the prospects that don't is 93.

Total revenue for the program is $27,000.

> Orders (6) x Average Order Size ($4,500) = Revenue ($27,000)

Gross margin for the program is $8,100.

Revenue ($27,000) x Gross Margin (30%) =
Gross Margin Dollars ($8,100)

Sales call expenses are calculated by multiplying the cost of a face-to-face sales call by the total sales calls.

Total Sales Calls (93) x Cost per Sales Call ($128) =
Sales Call Expenses ($11,904)

As you can see, ABC Company had sales call expenses of $11,904. The direct marketing expenses (FF) were identified as $4,605. The total selling expenses are then calculated by subtracting the sales call expense and direct marketing expense from the gross margin to establish the net contribution to profit and general and administrative expenses.

Revenue - (Sales Call Expense ($11,904) + Direct Marketing Expenses ($4,605)) = Contribution (-$8,409)

As you can see, this program lost $8,409 or 31.1%.

Appendix I contains the formulas for you to create your own model. The examples I'm using may not be appropriate for your business, but you can use your own data to create results and analysis that more closely represent programs you have or plan to execute.

Now that I have set the stage and defined the elements of the model and how they work, let's take a look at what happens when various elements are changed or modified.

Changing the List

Let's review the relative importance of the four direct marketing elements:

- List   50%
- Offer   25%
- Format   15%
- Copy   10%

Since the list you promote will dictate the success of your direct marketing efforts more than any other single element, you cannot select your list casually.

And when choosing a list remember that you make a significant investment in leads that don't close. It takes as many sales calls to lose an order as it does to win one. In fact, it is not unusual to spend more face-to-face effort on a prospect that doesn't buy than on one who does.

With that in mind, let's turn our attention to the value and importance of the house file.

You have established a relationship with the people on your house file. They know who you are, know your products and have identified an interest in belonging to your house file. If you promote to your house file and they respond, their odds of closing are probably higher and they should require fewer sales calls to close. All of the preliminary selling effort has been done. Remember that a house file outperforms an outside list by 2 to 1. Customers and prior respondents raise their hands time and time again.

Let's now use the model to evaluate the results of adding the house file to the direct marketing program. You'll be able to see the results of conducting the program by promoting to the rented list, the house list, and the two lists combined.

As we add or make changes to the model, traditional direct marketing testing techniques will be used. The best performing program will be used as a control and any new program will be compared to the control. The model allows up to four test cells to be evaluated within a total program. Therefore you can see each cell individually as well as the total of the four cells.

In Illustration 14-5, I've added another program and coded it as 102. This is the 4,500 record house file identified earlier in the case study. I have also assumed that the average order will remain the same at $4,500. All of the variables from the prior program have remained the same. The rented list program we discussed earlier is still part of the overall program.

I haven't added fulfillment or premiums to the promotion, but notice that there is no list cost in cell 2. Your house file is your property and you don't have to pay anyone for its use. I am planning to mail the same package as the rented list using third class postage.

You'll notice a significant change in the overall conversion rate (T). Members of the house file already know your company and products. If they respond a second or third time they should be better qualified and more likely to buy. You have already expended significant selling effort in prior promotions. Their odds to close are significantly better than a name from a cold list. If you discuss sales results with your salespeople, you'll find that many of their current orders come from prospects they identified a long time ago. Over time, these prospects are convinced to buy. Additional responses from the house file should be at least twice as likely to buy, hence I have increased the conversion rate to 35%.

I have also reduced the number of sales calls required to close to 2 (V) or to lose a respondent from the house file to 1.5 (V). These changes are based on the proven tendency for house lists to produce better results than other lists. You have already made over 2.5 calls to each member of the file. They are informed about your company and products. It should take less effort to sell these prospects and less selling effort for them to decide not to buy.

Lead Planning Model Adding the House File

	1	2	3	4	Total
A Current Cost per Sales Call					$128
B Allowable Cost per Qualified Lead					$128
C Gross Margin					30%
One-Time Costs					
D Creative Costs/project					$1,500
E Management Costs/project					$1,000
List Information					
F List Identification Code	101	102			
G List Name	Rented	House			
H Quantity Mailed	5000	4500			
I Average Order Size	4500	4500			
Variable Costs per Name Mailed or Contacted					
J Fulfillment Costs per Respondent	$0.00	$0.00			
K Phone Follow-up Costs	$0.00	$0.00			
L Premium or Incentive	$0.00	$0.00			
M List Cost or Minimum per Name	$0.090	$0.000			
N Print/Production/Mail	$0.650	$0.650			
P Postage	$0.181	$0.181			
Q Fulfillment (formula based on I + J + K)					
Response Rates and Conversion Rates					
R % of respondents qualified as leads	100.0%	100.0%			
S % of resp not qualif converting to leads	0.0%	0.0%			
T % of leads that order	18.0%	35.0%			
Sales Calls					
U Number of Sales Calls per Close	3	2			
V Number of Sales Calls to Lose Order	2.5	1.5			

Illustration 14-5: Lead planning model adding the house file.

Results & Analysis with the House File

		1	2	3	4	Total
	List Identification Code	101	102			
	List Name	Rented	House			
AA	Quantity Mailed	5,000	4,500			9,500
BB	List Costs (M x AA)	450	0			450
CC	Print/Prod/Mail (N x AA)	3,250	2,925			6,175
DD	Postage (P x AA)	905	815			1,720
EE	Fulfillment (Q x AA)					
FF	Total Direct Marketing Expenses	4,605	3,740			8,345
GG	Allowable cost per qualified lead (B)	$128	$128			
HH	% of responders qualified as leads (R)	100.0%	100.0%			
II	% of resp not qualified as leads (1 - HH)	0.0%	0.0%			
JJ	% of not qual resp convert to lead (II x S)	0.0%	0.0%			
KK	Total Lead/Response % (HH + JJ)	100.0%	100.0%			
LL	Allowable Cost per Responder (GG x KK)	$128.00	$128.00			
MM	Required Responses (FF ÷ LL)	36	29			65
OO	Required response % (MM ÷ AA)	0.72%	0.64%			0.68%
PP	Leads Initially (MM x HH)	36	29			65
QQ	Responders for Fulfillment (MM - PP)	0	0			
RR	Leads from Fulfillment (QQ x S)	0	0			
SS	Total Leads (PP + RR)	36	29			65
TT	Orders (T x SS)	6	10			16
UU	Number of Sales Calls-Orders (U x TT)	18	20			38
VV	No Sls Calls-Non-orders (V x (SS - TT))	75	29			104
WW	Total Sales Calls	93	49			142
XX	Revenue (I x WW)	27,000	45,000			72,000
YY	Gross Margin (XX x C)	8,100	13,500			21,600
ZZ	Sales Call Expenses (WW x A)	11,904	6,272			18,176
BA	Direct Marketing Expenses (FF)	4605	3740			8345
BB	Total Selling Expenses (ZZ + BA)	16,509	10,012			26,521
BC	Contribution (YY - BB)	-8409	3488			-4921
BD	% Contribution (BC ÷ XX)	-31.1%	7.8%			-6.8%

Illustration 14-6: Model results & analysis with the House File.

Illustration 14-6 shows the results of adding the house file to this program. The lack of expense associated with list acquisition reduces the overall expense and therefore the required response rate. Although the required response rate is lower, most house file activity will out-perform outside list promotions by about 2 to 1.

The conversion % is higher therefore the number of orders generated from the leads is also higher. And the number of sales calls to sell and to lose to prospects on the house file is less, therefore the selling expense is significantly lower.

As you can see the results from the house file promotion produce a profit of almost $3,500 or a contribution of 7.8% to profit and general and administrative expenses.

When you combine the results of both the rented list (101) and the house file (102) the overall program still loses money, but the loss has been reduced by almost half.

The impact of using a better list is graphic. Your house file is available in your format and costs you nothing to use. You'll probably be pleasantly surprised by the results it will produce both in initial responses and conversion to orders. You have everything to gain and nothing to lose.

So far we've examined adding another, higher quality list to the program and evaluating the results. Another way to improve the results by controlling the list is to not send every respondent to the salesperson as a lead.

Fulfillment

Instead of sending every responder to your salespeople as a lead, in this example I'll show you the impact of qualifying each lead and using a fulfillment kit with those prospects who don't immediately appear to have money, authority, need, or desire.

In Chapter 3 I talked about regeneration and conditioning and in Chapter 8 Tracy Emerick talked about fulfillment kits. Both concepts recognize that not every respondent will immediately be qualified. You may have to sustain a direct marketing program to ultimately convince the prospect that they should consider buying from you.

I have successfully used a fulfillment kit followed by a telephone call to produce better quality leads. The fulfillment kit is sent to prospects requesting additional information and then a follow-up phone call is used to convert interested prospects into qualified sales leads.

Illustration 14-7 shows two test cells being added which include fulfillment. As you'll notice I have kept as a control the current winning test (although the combined programs weren't profitable they are the best performance and therefore the champion) program which include the rented list and house file (101 & 102). The model will analyze each individual cell as well as the total combined program.

I have retained all of the list information from the control and will only change those areas affected by fulfillment. Both the rented list of 5,000 as well as the house file of 4,500 records will be evaluated.

I am going to use a fulfillment kit which costs $3.00 including processing and postage. The kit will be mailed to all those prospects that aren't immediately qualified. In addition, I plan to follow-up to the fulfillment recipients with a telephone call about 7 days later. This phone call will cost $6.00.

Lead Planning Model Adding Fulfillment

	1	2	3	4	Total
A Current Cost per Sales Call					$128
B Allowable Cost per Qualified Lead					$128
C Gross Margin					30%
One-Time Costs					
D Creative Costs/project					$1,500
E Management Costs/project					$1,000
List Information					
F List Identification Code	101	102	103	104	
G List Name	Rented	House	Rented	House	
H Quantity Mailed	5000	4000	5000	4000	
I Average Order Size	4500	4500	4500	4500	
Variable Costs per Name Mailed or Contacted					
J Fulfillment Costs per Respondent	$0.00	$0.00	$3.00	$3.00	
K Phone Follow-up Costs	$0.00	$0.00	$6.00	$6.00	
L Premium or Incentive	$0.00	$0.00	$0.00	$0.00	
M List Cost or Minimum per Name	$0.090	$0.000	$0.090	$0.000	
N Print/Production/Mail	$0.650	$0.650	$0.650	$0.650	
P Postage	$0.181	$0.181	$0.181	$0.181	
Q Fulfillment (formula based on J, K, L)			0.171	$0.162	
Response Rates and Conversion Rates					
R % of respondents qualified as leads	100.0%	100.0%	60.0%	70.0%	
S % of resp not qualif converting to leads	0.0%	0.0%	25.0%	25.0%	
T % of leads that order	18.0%	35.0%	25.0%	35.0%	
Sales Calls					
U Number of Sales Calls per Close	3	2	3	1	
V Number of Sales Calls to Lose Order	2.5	1.5	1.5	1	

Illustration 14-7: Lead planning model adding fulfillment.

Results & Analysis Adding Fulfillment

		1	2	3	4	Total
	List Identification Code	101	102	103	104	
	List Name	Rented	House	Rented	House	
AA	Quantity Mailed	5,000	4,000	5,000	4,000	18,000
BB	List Costs (M x AA)	450	0	450	0	900
CC	Print/Prod/Mail (N x AA)	3,250	2,600	3,250	2,600	11,700
DD	Postage (P x AA)	905	724	905	724	3,258
EE	Fulfillment (Q x AA)			855	648	1,503
FF	Total Direct Marketing Expenses	4,605	3,324	5,460	3,972	1,7361
GG	Allowable cost per qualified lead (B)	$128	$128	$128	$128	
HH	% of responders qualified as leads (R)	100.0%	100.0%	60.0%	70.0%	
II	% of resp not qualified as leads (1 - HH)	0.0%	0.0%	40.0%	30.0%	
JJ	% of not qual resp convert to lead (II x S)	0.0%	0.0%	10.0%	7.5%	
KK	Total Lead/Response % (HH + JJ)	100.0%	100.0%	70.0%	77.5%	
LL	Allowable Cost per Responder (GG x KK)	$128.00	$128.00	$89.60	$99.20	
MM	Required Responses (FF ÷ LL)	36	26	61	40	163
OO	Required response % (MM ÷ AA)	0.72%	0.65%	1.22%	1.00%	0.91%
PP	Leads Initially (MM x HH)	36	26	37	28	127
QQ	Responders for Fulfillment (MM - PP)	0	0	24	12	36
RR	Leads from Fulfillment (QQ x S)	0	0	6	3	9
SS	Total Leads (PP + RR)	36	26	43	31	136
TT	Orders (T x SS)	6	9	11	11	37
UU	Number of Sales Calls-Orders (U x TT)	18	18	33	11	80
VV	No Sls Calls-Non-orders (V x (SS - TT))	75	26	48	20	169
WW	Total Sales Calls	93	44	81	31	249
XX	Revenue (I x WW)	27,000	40,500	49,500	49,500	166,500
YY	Gross Margin (XX x C)	8,100	12,150	14,850	14,850	49,950
ZZ	Sales Call Expenses (WW x A)	11,904	5,632	10,368	3,968	31,872
BA	Direct Marketing Expenses (FF)	4,605	3,324	5,460	3,972	17,361
BB	Total Selling Expenses (ZZ + BA)	16,509	8,956	15,828	7,940	49,233
BC	Contribution (YY - BB)	-8,409	3,194	-978	6,910	717
BD	% Contribution (BC ÷ XX)	-31.1%	7.9%	-2.0%	14.0%	0.4%

Illustration 14-8: Model results & analysis with fulfillment.

The remaining mail costs are exactly the same as the control test cells. The only change I am making to the promotion is the addition of fulfillment.

You'll notice that the model automatically calculated the cost per name fulfilled. The amount is calculated based on the cost per piece for fulfillment (J) and the cost of the follow-up phone call (K). These costs are used in conjunction with the percentage of names you send directly to the sales force (R). The remaining names not sent directly to the sales force are sent the fulfillment. Finally I have used a fixed response rate of 1.5%. The cost identified (Q) represents the fulfillment cost per name that you promote.

You'll notice that I am only sending 60% of the rented name respondents directly to the sales force (HH). In addition, I have found through experience that it is possible to convert about 25% of literature fulfillment respondents into leads via telephone contact. Therefore, I used the 25% (T) as the conversion amounts. Finally I assumed that the leads are of a better quality because we have eliminated some immediately and used fulfillment to move others closer to making a buying decision.

The quality of the leads should be better because 40% aren't being forwarded to the salespeople. Therefore the percentage of the leads that do turn into orders should be higher. I have increased the closing percentage to 25%. If you consider 100 respondents of which only 60 (60%) are leads and 25% convert to orders it will yield 15 orders. In the control scenario, using the same 100 respondents, 18 converted to orders (18%). The 25% is actually pretty conservative.

The number of orders it takes to close really won't change. However, the number to lose could be reduced significantly. The fulfillment package makes it easier for the prospect to evaluate the offer without spending as much sales time. In addition, the less qualified respondents will not even be initially sent to the salespeople.

Only those respondents who qualify after receiving the fulfillment kit will be sent to the salespeople. This group will be better informed and able to make a decision more easily.

The house file will take a lot less selling effort to sell or to lose. As I described earlier, this group is knowledgeable about your company and products. If prospects respond a second time, a higher percentage should be qualified as leads. I used 70%. Those that are not qualified will also receive a fulfillment kit and follow-up call to re-qualify them and I assumed the same 25% conversion from the literature requests to leads. Notice the higher projected closing rate of 35%.

House file records that qualify as leads will be the best leads and the easiest to close. It shouldn't take much more than 1 call to close or to lose prior respondents. I estimated 1 call to sell or lose.

The results are significantly different for the fulfillment test cells. Overall the promotion expenses are elevated and therefore a higher initial response rate is required. As you can see the rented list costs $5,460 compared to the $4,605 without fulfillment. The house file costs $3,972 compared to $3,324. To cover the higher promotion costs, the rented list program will have to generate 1.22% response (OO) while the house file requires 1.00%.

Because all of the respondents are not going to be sent to the salespeople, there is a difference in the allowable cost per response (LL) and the allowable cost per lead (GG). The rented list program needs to produce 61 respondents and 43 leads while the house file will have to produce 40 respondents and 31 leads.

Because the leads are of higher quality and require less calls to lose, the number of sales calls are reduced. Even though the program produces almost one-third more leads, the total number of sales calls required is about 10% less.

Many companies fail to analyze lead generation programs to include the selling expenses associated with selling and qualifying. The model considers these costs as well as the promotion expenses in determining the contribution of the program. The promotion expenses were higher because of the fulfillment activities, but the overall costs were lower.

Overall the control program lost almost $5,000 (-$4,921 Illustration 14-6) even with the house file. Using fulfillment the program now produces a profit of almost $6,000 (-$978 + $6,910 = $5,932, Illustration 14-8). The two programs tested together produce an overall profit ($717, Illustration 14-8) .

You can have a terrific impact on your lead generation programs by sending higher quality leads to the salespeople using fulfillment techniques to handle the less qualified respondents. It is much less expensive to use direct marketing to handle lower quality respondents than to expend valuable sales resources.

Modifying the Offer

I have continued to stress that one of the most overlooked elements in most lead generation programs is the offer. This section will demonstrate the importance and value of the offer. Illustration 14-9 shows the changes I've made to illustrate the impact of varying the offer.

I have used the results of adding fulfillment (test cells 103 & 104) as the control. Two new test cells have been created (105 & 106). Everything in this new test will remain the same except that a new offer promoting a larger computer has been created. I believe that the larger offer can easily be accepted by the outside list, however, some of the house file may still request the less expensive product based on their prior knowledge.

All of the other elements will remain the same which will allow us to compare the impact of only changing the offer.

The larger order being offered may not be as radical as it might appear. The average order established earlier is based upon selling the entire product line to all kinds of prospects. You can significantly change the results of a promotion by controlling the list and the offer you're making.

As you can see in Illustration 14-10, the results required to have this program meet the objectives in cost-per-lead are exactly the same as the prior program. The outside rented list requires 1.22% response while the house file has to produce 1.00% response.

The number of leads and orders as well as the cost of promotion and cost of selling are identical between the two different programs. There isn't any difference until you examine the revenue generated by the two programs. The rented list generates $71,500 compared to the $49,500 of the original offer. The house file generates $60,500 compared to the $49,500 of the control.

The results of additional revenue with no additional expenses falls right to the bottom line. Changing the offer increases the contribution from about $6,000 to almost $16,000 ($5,622 + $10,210 = $15,832, Illustration 14-10). The impact of changing the offer is dramatic.

Offer is one of the most overlooked elements in many direct marketing programs and is almost totally ignored in lead generation. You shouldn't rely on the salesperson to create the need for a specific product. You can use the offer to establish the order size right from the start.

Lead Planning Model Changing the Offer

	1	2	3	4	Total
A Current Cost per Sales Call					$128
B Allowable Cost per Qualified Lead					$128
C Gross Margin					30%
One-Time Costs					
D Creative Costs/project					$1,500
E Management Costs/project					$1,000
List Information					
F List Identification Code	103	104	105	106	
G List Name	Rented	House	Rented	House	
H Quantity Mailed	5000	4000	5000	4000	
I Average Order Size	4500	4500	6500	5500	
Variable Costs per Name Mailed or Contacted					
J Fulfillment Costs per Respondent	$3.00	$3.00	$3.00	$3.00	
K Phone Follow-up Costs	$6.00	$6.00	$6.00	$6.00	
L Premium or Incentive	$0.00	$0.00	$0.00	$0.00	
M List Cost or Minimum per Name	$0.090	$0.000	$0.090	$0.000	
N Print/Production/Mail	$0.650	$0.650	$0.650	$0.650	
P Postage	$0.181	$0.181	$0.181	$0.181	
Q Fulfillment	$0.171	$0.162	$0.171	$0.162	
Response Rates and Conversion Rates					
R % of respondents qualified as leads	60.0%	70.0%	60.0%	70.0%	
S % of resp not qualif converting to leads	25.0%	25.0%	25.0%	25.0%	
T % of leads that order	25.0%	35.0%	25.0%	35.0%	
Sales Calls					
U Number of Sales Calls per Close	3	1	3	1	
V Number of Sales Calls to Lose Order	1.5	1	1.5	1	

Illustration 14-9: Lead planning model changing the offer.

Results & Analysis Changing the Offer

		1	2	3	4	Total
	List Identification Code	103	104	105	106	
	List Name	Rented	House	Rented	House	
AA	Quantity Mailed	5,000	4,000	5,000	4,000	18,000
BB	List Costs (M x AA)	450	0	450	0	900
CC	Print/Prod/Mail (N x AA)	3,250	2,600	3,250	2,600	11,700
DD	Postage (P x AA)	905	724	905	724	3,258
EE	Fulfillment (Q x AA)	855	648	855	648	3,006
FF	Total Direct Marketing Expenses	5,460	3,972	5,460	3,972	18,864
GG	Allowable cost per qualified lead (B)	$128	$128	$128	$128	
HH	% of responders qualified as leads (R)	60.0%	70.0%	60.0%	70.0%	
II	% of resp not qualified as leads (1 - HH)	40.0%	30.0%	40.0%	30.0%	
JJ	% of not qual resp convert to lead (II x S)	10.0%	7.5%	10.0%	7.5%	
KK	Total Lead/Response % (HH+ JJ)	70.0%	77.5%	70.0%	77.5%	
LL	Allowable Cost per Responder (GG x KK)	$89.60	$99.20	$89.60	$99.20	
MM	Required Responses (FF ÷ LL)	61	40	61	40	202
OO	Required response % (MM ÷ AA)	1.22%	1.00%	1.22%	1.00%	1.12%
PP	Leads Initially (MM x HH)	37	28	37	28	130
QQ	Responders for Fulfillment (MM - PP)	24	12	24	12	72
RR	Leads from Fulfillment (QQ x S)	6	3	6	3	18
SS	Total Leads (PP + RR)	43	31	43	31	148
TT	Orders (T x SS)	11	11	11	11	44
UU	Number of Sales Calls-Orders (U x TT)	33	11	33	11	88
VV	No Sls Calls-Non-orders (V x (SS - TT))	48	20	48	20	136
WW	Total Sales Calls	81	31	81	31	224
XX	Revenue (I x WW)	49,500	49,500	71,500	60,500	231,000
YY	Gross Margin (XX x C)	14,850	14,850	21,450	18,150	69,300
ZZ	Sales Call Expenses (WW x A)	10,368	3,968	10,368	3,968	28,672
BA	Direct Marketing Expenses (FF)	5,460	3,972	5,460	3,972	18,864
BB	Total Selling Expenses (ZZ + BA)	15,828	7,940	15,828	7,940	47,536
BC	Contribution (YY - BB)	-978	6,910	5,622	10,210	21,764
BD	% Contribution (BC ÷ XX)	-2.0%	14.0%	7.9%	16.9%	9.4%

Illustration 14-10: Model results & analysis changing the offer.

Changing the Format

Most people seem to spend too much of their time creating the best words and pictures and way to deliver them to their audience. In almost every seminar or meeting I present, there is inevitably a group of attendees who have copy with them that they are working to modify and improve. This is particularly true if these people are working with their general advertising agency, who encourages improving the creative effort to improve results.

So far I have used the lead planning model to demonstrate how changing the list and offer can improve results. Let's now examine how changing the format and its associated copy and graphics will influence the results of the program.

Illustration 14-11 shows the comparison of a winning program (the improved offer) with a different approach to delivering the message to the audience. I decided to use a personalized letter and to send via first class mail.

The winning test cells from the offer program have been used as the control for the format test. I have created two additional test cells (107 & 108) to the rented and house files. The list and offer remain the same. The only change made in the new test is the cost for print/production/mail from $.65 to $1.05 and the cost for postage from $.181 to $.290. All of the response rate and sales call information remains the same from the previous test.

If you took a quick look at the contribution % you might think the program didn't change significantly, but don't be misled. The promotion costs increased from $5,460 to $8,005 to the rented list and from $3,972 to $6,008 to the house file. The increased costs require significantly more leads and therefore more responses to produce the same allowable cost per lead.

The control requires 1.22% response from the rented list while the change in format now requires 1.78% response from the same list. The house file requires 1.53% compared to the previous 1.00%.

The elevated response rates produce more leads and more orders and therefore the revenue and required sales calls are also increased significantly. The bottom line contribution dollars are increased but the cost has also increased and therefore the contribution % is about the same.

If this program were believable you would probably opt for changing the format because of the larger bottom line revenue contribution. However, the required response rate is very high and may not be possible.

I think that required response rates over 1.00% from an outside list could be difficult to achieve. The highest response rate you should allow a program to require is about 1.5%, and you may be unable to attain that objective. Your house file can require 1.5% to 2.5% and still be realistic.

The change in the format requires the rented list to produce a 1.78% response. I would be nervous about this expectation and begin to examine changing the offer or adding a premium to increase the response rate.

Throughout the example I've used so far, only one element has been changed at a time. This is the best way to test direct marketing so you can evaluate the change and determine the results. It is impossible to evaluate more than one change at a time. You can create a testing approach that will allow you to test multiple elements but each test cell will have only one element you're trying to evaluate.

You can often increase the response rate by offering a premium to the prospect for responding. Many people who may not be really interested in your products and services will respond to receive the

Lead Planning Model Changing the Format

	1	2	3	4	Total
A Current Cost per Sales Call					$128
B Allowable Cost per Qualified Lead					$128
C Gross Margin					30%
One-Time Costs					
D Creative Costs/project					$1,500
E Management Costs/project					$1,000
List Information					
F List Identification Code	105	106	107	108	
G List Name	Rented	House	Rented	House	
H Quantity Mailed	5000	4000	5000	4000	
I Average Order Size	6500	5500	6500	5500	
Variable Costs per Name Mailed or Contacted					
J Fulfillment Costs per Respondent	$3.00	$3.00	$3.00	$3.00	
K Phone Follow-up Costs	$6.00	$6.00	$6.00	$6.00	
L Premium or Incentive	$0.00	$0.00	$0.00	$0.00	
M List Cost or Minimum per Name	$0.090	$0.000	$0.090	$0.000	
N Print/Production/Mail	$0.650	$0.650	$1.050	$1.050	
P Postage	$0.181	$0.181	$0.290	$0.290	
Q Fulfillment	$0.171	$0.162	$0.171	$0.162	
Response Rates and Conversion Rates					
R % of respondents qualified as leads	60.0%	70.0%	60.0%	70.0%	
S % of resp not qualif converting to leads	25.0%	25.0%	25.0%	25.0%	
T % of leads that order	25.0%	35.0%	25.0%	35.0%	
Sales Calls					
U Number of Sales Calls per Close	3	1	3	1	
V Number of Sales Calls to Lose Order	1.5	1	1.5	1	

Illustration 14-11: Lead planning model changing the format.

Results & Analysis Changing the Format

		1	2	3	4	Total
	List Identification Code	105	106	107	108	
	List Name	Rented	House	Rented	House	
AA	Quantity Mailed	5,000	4,000	5,000	4,000	18,000
BB	List Costs (M x AA)	450	0	450	0	900
CC	Print/Prod/Mail (N x AA)	3,250	2,600	5,250	4,200	15,300
DD	Postage (P x AA)	905	724	1,450	1,160	4,239
EE	Fulfillment (Q x AA)	855	648	855	648	3,006
FF	Total Direct Marketing Expenses	5,460	3,972	8,005	6,008	23,445
GG	Allowable cost per qualified lead (B)	$128	$128	$128	$128	
HH	% of responders qualified as leads (R)	60.0%	70.0%	60.0%	70.0%	
II	% of resp not qualified as leads (1 - HH)	40.0%	30.0%	40.0%	30.0%	
JJ	% of not qual resp convert to lead (II x S)	10.0%	7.5%	10.0%	7.5%	
KK	Total Lead/Response % (HH + JJ)	70.0%	77.5%	70.0%	77.5%	
LL	Allowable Cost per Responder (GG x KK)	$89.60	$99.20	$89.60	$99.20	
MM	Required Responses (FF ÷ LL)	61	40	89	61	251
OO	Required response % (MM ÷ AA)	1.22%	1.00%	1.78%	1.53%	1.39%
PP	Leads Initially (MM x HH)	37	28	53	43	161
QQ	Responders for Fulfillment (MM - PP)	24	12	36	18	90
RR	Leads from Fulfillment (QQ x S)	6	3	9	5	23
SS	Total Leads (PP + RR)	43	31	62	48	184
TT	Orders (T x SS)	11	11	16	17	55
UU	Number of Sales Calls-Orders (U x TT)	33	11	48	17	109
VV	No Sls Calls-Non-orders (V x (SS - TT))	48	20	69	31	168
WW	Total Sales Calls	81	31	117	48	277
XX	Revenue (I x WW)	71,500	60,500	104,000	93,500	329,500
YY	Gross Margin (XX x C)	21,450	18,150	31,200	28,050	98,850
ZZ	Sales Call Expenses (WW x A)	10,368	3,968	14,976	6,144	35,456
BA	Direct Marketing Expenses (FF)	5,460	3,972	8,005	6,008	23,445
BB	Total Selling Expenses (ZZ + BA)	15,828	7,940	22,981	12,152	58,901
BC	Contribution (YY - BB)	5,622	10,210	8,219	15,898	39,949
BD	% Contribution (BC ÷ XX)	7.9%	16.9%	7.9%	17.0%	12.1%

Illustration 14-12: Model results & analysis changing the format.

premium. The conversion % may be lower, but the increased response rate can often overcome this phenomenon.

Illustration 14-13 shows the results of offering a $10.00 premium to respondents. I also lowered the % of prospects who convert to leads after fulfillment from 25% to 20%. I decided not to add the premium to the house file promotion. This may not be realistic because your house file will become aware of the premium offer and you'll ultimately give it to them as well. But for the example, I have decided not to offer the premium to the house file.

The promotion expenses increase from $8,005 (FF, Illustration 14-12) to $8,755 (FF, Illustration 14-13). The additional promotion costs will raise the required response rate to 2.02%. This is an aggressive program but the premium should allow you to achieve a significantly higher response.

The program produces about $24,000 ($7,883 + $15,898 = $23,731) in contribution compared to the almost $16,000 of the control. The contribution percentage is lower for the rented list, and about the same for the house file. In this program, changing the format will require you to make a significantly larger investment in the promotion. You will have to spend 60% more to promote the rented list. If the program is successful, you'll certainly reap more contribution, but will the risk be worth the reward?

Many people will spend more time creating format and copy because they are easy to evaluate and understand. Variations in the format and copy are based on personal experiences with other direct mail pieces the individual has observed. Everyone seems to be an expert in making judgments on the best format and copy. But as you've seen, these elements will most often have only a marginal impact on the overall success of the direct marketing program.

Changing the Format with a Premium

		1	2	3	4	Total
	List Identification Code	105	106	107	108	
	List Name	Rented	House	Rented	House	
AA	Quantity Mailed	5,000	4,000	5,000	4,000	18,000
BB	List Costs (M x AA)	450	0	450	0	900
CC	Print/Prod/Mail (N x AA)	3,250	2,600	5,250	4,200	15,300
DD	Postage (P x AA)	905	724	1,450	1,160	4,239
EE	Fulfillment (Q x AA)	855	648	1,605	648	3,756
FF	Total Direct Marketing Expenses	5,460	3,972	8,755	6,008	2,4195
GG	Allowable cost per qualified lead (B)	$128	$128	$128	$128	
HH	% of responders qualified as leads (R)	60.0%	70.0%	60.0%	70.0%	
II	% of resp not qualified as leads (1 - HH)	40.0%	30.0%	40.0%	30.0%	
JJ	% of not qual resp convert to lead (II x S)	10.0%	7.5%	8.0%	7.5%	
KK	Total Lead/Response % (HH + JJ)	70.0%	77.5%	68.0%	77.5%	
LL	Allowable Cost per Responder (GG x KK)	$89.60	$99.20	$87.04	$99.20	
MM	Required Responses (FF ÷ LL)	61	40	101	61	263
OO	Required response % (MM ÷ AA)	1.22%	1.00%	2.02%	1.53%	1.46%
PP	Leads Initially (MM x HH)	37	28	61	43	169
QQ	Responders for Fulfillment (MM - PP)	24	12	40	18	94
RR	Leads from Fulfillment (QQ x S)	6	3	8	5	22
SS	Total Leads (PP + RR)	43	31	69	48	191
TT	Orders (T x SS)	11	11	17	17	56
UU	Number of Sales Calls-Orders (U x TT)	33	11	51	17	112
VV	No Sls Calls-Non-orders (V x (SS - TT))	48	20	78	31	177
WW	Total Sales Calls	81	31	129	48	289
XX	Revenue (I x WW)	71,500	60,500	110,500	93,500	336,000
YY	Gross Margin (XX x C)	21,450	18,150	33,150	28,050	100,800
ZZ	Sales Call Expenses (WW x A)	10,368	3,968	16,512	6,144	36,992
BA	Direct Marketing Expenses (FF)	5,460	3,972	8,755	6,008	24,195
BB	Total Selling Expenses (ZZ + BA)	15,828	7,940	25,267	12,152	61,187
BC	Contribution (YY - BB)	5,622	10,210	7,883	15,898	39,613
BD	% Contribution (BC ÷ XX)	7.9%	16.9%	7.1%	17.0%	11.8%

Illustration 14-13: Model results & analysis changing format with a premium.

The Lead Planning Model Summarized

In this chapter I used a computer model to demonstrate the impact the various elements of direct marketing promotion can have on the results of a program. I used a case study company to develop the information required to develop a lead program. The model I used is included in Appendix I.

Using the Salesperson Cost Worksheet, I identified the cost per sales call, the closing ratio, and available sales calls. Many lead programs don't include the cost of the salesperson follow-up and selling activities. You should identify all the costs in a lead generation program to allow an accurate comparison of one to another.

You will need to identify your allowable cost per lead. I often advocate that a company should be willing to spend the cost of one face-to-face sales call for each lead. With the cost of a face-to-face call constantly escalating and now being close to $300, many companies find this too much to spend for a lead. I still maintain that if the lead is worthwhile, it should be able to save at least one sales call, and therefore it should be worth the value of one call.

Using the results of the case study, I set up the model with the appropriate information. I explained each item and how the information was evaluated by the spreadsheet software.

Once the initial information was provided, I explained how the model used the information to identify the required response rate, the number of leads, and the number of orders. This information was used to determine revenue, promotion expenses, and selling expenses. The model calculated the dollars of contribution to profit and general and administrative expenses, as well as the percent contribution.

Using the information from the case study, I then changed one element of the program at a time to demonstrate the impact each has on the ultimate results of the program.

The initial information showed over a 30% loss. When I added the house file it produced a profitable contribution of over 7%, and the overall program only lost 7%. This began to demonstrate the value of the list.

I next took the model a step further in trying to produce higher quality leads by using fulfillment. Throughout this chapter, whenever I made change to the program, I tested against the best producing program to that point. This is the traditional way to test direct marketing; always use your current champion as the control.

Fulfillment improved the results of the program from a 7% loss to a 12% gain.

I next changed the offer to increase the average size of the order. Everything else in the program remained the same and the best performing effort was again used as a control. The results were again dramatic and the overall contribution increased from 12% to almost 25%.

Finally I changed the format and there wasn't a significant change in the contribution %. There was a significant increase in contribution dollars, but the required response rate became unreasonable. I added a premium to demonstrate one approach to dealing with unusually high response rates.

In direct marketing we rely less on creative approaches and more on technical execution to produce significantly better results. The four elements in direct marketing promotion and their relative importance to the ultimate results of the program are:

List	50%
Offer	25%
Format	15%
Copy/Graphics	10%

The lead planning model graphically demonstrates the importance of the list and offer in lead generation efforts. Rather than spending so much time creating the format and copy, you should allocate your time and effort to the elements that will produce the highest level of results.

Chapter Fifteen:

Sales Compensation

By   *Dick Vink*
         High Tech Marketing
         1842 Port Taggert
         Newport Beach, CA 92660
         (714) 720-9950   FAX: (714) 720-0612

An integral part of any lead generation program is how the sales-people are compensated and motivated. As has been continually stressed throughout this book, lead programs are designed to produce orders not just activity. Your sales compensation program should be developed to be consistent with your business objectives as well as the lead generation objectives. This may sound like a strange comment because both objectives should be complementary, but I have observed many situations where this is not true.

If you are responsible for a lead generation program and have not examined the sales compensation plan because it is the responsibility of another department or function in your company, you are making a terrible mistake. You could develop a lead program that will ask the salesperson to sell in an area where the compensation plan doesn't reward his efforts.

Sales Compensation Plan Development - The 7 Step Process

A well-designed and implemented Sales Compensation Plan (SCP) will communicate the business direction and priorities. It will meet the sales objectives of the company and motivate the sales force to achieve these objectives. It also achieves the pay objectives set by the company.

A good Sales Compensation Plan alone will not guarantee sales success. It is, however, one of the critical cornerstones of an environment in which a salesperson is motivated to excel.

Over the years I have reviewed and developed over 200 SCPs and found that there is a seven step process to follow when putting together a SCP.

1. **Prioritize Company Sales Objectives**

   Establish/review the company's sales and marketing objectives - short and long term. These objectives should already have been described in the marketing plan. Examples are market penetration (= New Account Bonus); building a strong backlog (= Booking Incentive); push strategic products (= Product Emphasis Bonus).

   All key executives should be involved in the objective setting process, not just the person heading up sales. A major side benefit of this process is the consensus it builds among the executives. Having a consensus increases the chance for success.

This step yields the types of incentives and their relative size.

2. Determine Earning Levels and Base Salaries

The total compensation at 100% attainment is often market driven or, in other words, determined by what the competition pays. Knowing the earning levels in your industry (preferably of your competitors) helps attract and keep top performers. Knowing how your competition pays discloses much about their strategic objectives.

When sales performance exceeds 100% of quota, accelerators are normally applied to the incentives for key objectives. First you have to decide how much you want to pay at certain attainment levels over 100%. For example at 150% of quota attainment you may decide to pay 1.3 X the earnings at 100% of quota attainment. A spreadsheet will then help you determine the size of the accelerators.

Some companies put a cap on the earnings. I do not favor this. In certain situations, however, it may be necessary to implement decelerators over certain attainment levels.

3. Quotas

Without quotas it is hard to measure success. Quotas should be a natural result of the business plan. Proper emphasis on the achievement of quotas as a way of life is key to attaining your sales objectives. Salespeople thrive on quota attainment and on their ranking within their peer group.

On what basis are quotas assigned? This depends on the sales objectives. Quotas may be expressed in Revenues,

Units, New Accounts, Points, Margin Dollars, etc. It is important to specify qualification criteria (revenues from supplies and spare parts don't count; the minimum for New Account is 1 CPU or a $40,000 initial order at a new enterprise). Only a few companies express quota in bookings, but many pay a commission advance at the time of booking.

Quotas can be assigned monthly, quarterly, semi-annually, or annually. Annual quotas are appropriate when the sell/ship cycle is long and the business is stable. Quarterly quotas make sense if the business is seasonal, the sell/install cycle is short, or the company is fast growing. Short time periods may cause sandbagging of orders. Forecasts should be frequently compared to performance to test how realistic the quotas are.

Consideration should be given to over-assignment of quotas. This will create a buffer for attrition and illness, causing territories not to be covered for a certain period of time. Remember that it is always easier to lower quotas later in the year than to increase them.

4. Compensation Method

Most companies pay their salespeople a guaranteed (base) salary + incentives; this method seems to be the trend. A base salary helps create a professional image and it shows a commitment to the salespeople. In return for paying a base salary you can expect the salesperson to perform certain job functions (attend training classes, help junior salespeople, submit sales reports, forecasts, computerize the prospect/customer database, focus on customer satisfaction, etc.). In other words paying a base salary gives you control over the activities of the salesperson.

Base salaries should preferably be expressed as a percentage of the total compensation at 100% of quota attainment. This percentage tends to be smaller if greater personal skills are required and/or the salesperson has less company support and/or has a high degree of personal control over the selling cycle and the territory.

There are basically two ways to pay incentives: Incentives may be based on sales volume performance or quota attainment performance.

SCPs based on sales volume performance pay an incentive which is a fixed amount, such as $75 per product, $300 for a New Account, 3% of the revenues attained up to 100% of quota attainment and 5% of revenues over 100% of attainment. This method works well when territories can be created that all have equal potential.

SCPs based on quota attainment performance pay an incentive which is dependent on the attainment of quota. One salesperson may be making more for selling $1 million of products than the next salesperson. This method is used when the same skills and efforts yield different results in different territories, or when territories with equal earning potential cannot be created for all salespeople.

5. Incentives

A good SCP is clear and simple. It will pass the following two tests:

- Does the salesperson know what the incentive is for the solution they are trying to sell?

Can you explain your SCP to an outsider in less than 10 minutes?

When you reach this step you have determined total compensation and base salaries. Now the question is how to develop meaningful incentives. The incentives you pay depend on your company objectives as well as what makes sense for your industry and sales channel.

The most common incentives we see are incentives for attainment of revenues, unit gross margins and new accounts. Less common, but not necessarily less meaningful are product bonuses, a bonus for being 100% year-to-date at the end of the quarter, milestone bonuses and bonuses, for achieving management objectives (MBOs).

Step levels may be created to tie commissions more closely to results. For example, a lower percentage might be paid for under 50% of quota attainment, and an accelerator for attainment over 100%.

One successful approach to develop incentives I observed was when the company explained its objectives and incentives budget to its top performers and asked them to put together the package.

Whatever the incentives are, keep some money in the budget for non-scheduled incentives to promote the achievement of specific objectives during the year, such as moving inventory, cutting down accounts receivable, or just to keep up the morale of the sales force. Don't overlook non-cash incentives such as travel and merchandise. At a cost of one-third of cash incentives, they can be just as effective.

6. Budget

To understand the impact of the incentives, develop several scenarios using a spreadsheet. Don't assume everyone will be at 100% of attainment. Assume a mix of attainment figures as accelerators will drive the sales expense upward. When it is simple to put the SCP in a spreadsheet, the SCP is probably easy to understand.

Compare your SCP budget as a percentage of revenues with other companies in your industry, especially those using similar sales channels. Researching this information is not easy because financial reports usually bundle sales and marketing expenses as well as G&A expenses into one figure. High Tech Marketing and several other firms are able to provide you with this information.

7. Document and Communicate

Sales Compensation Plans must always be documented. If you don't document them, they will be the cause for misunderstandings or worse. The back-end of the SCP is too often ignored. A well-documented SCP should clearly spell out the incentives, definitions, examples, and terms and conditions.

Salespeople tend to resist change and therefore the key to a fast start of the new sales year is to clearly explain the new SCP and its underlying objectives in a group session. Then, motivate the salespeople through the use of realistic examples.

Prioritize Company Objectives

To direct the sales force effectively, the company's sales objectives have to be clearly defined for the short and long term, even if the company does not plan to pay incentives. How else can one measure sales success?

Involve executives from various departments in this process. This will help in keeping an open perspective and assures management consensus on objectives during the fiscal year. To avoid endless discussions, ask your executives to write down the objectives and their priority and submit them to the sales plan coordinator before any meetings are held on the subject.

Keep in mind that the purpose of this phase of sales compensation plan development is to establish sales objectives and their priority. It is too early to establish the actual details about the incentives. This will be done in Step 5.

Start by listing all objectives, and discuss their priority and trade-offs, for example:

- For a given revenue number that your company projects, would you rather have this revenue come from a large number of new accounts or a smaller number of large accounts? Or should it be a mixture? This will have an impact on whether or not you want to establish a New Account Bonus.

- Is margin more important than revenues? If so, you probably want to pay at least a part of the commissions based on margin contributions. How do you define margins to the sales force?

- Is it vital, from a strategic standpoint, to push certain products? If so, you probably want to pay an extra bonus for the sale of these products. Products here can include service, maintenance, training, upgrades/add-ons, etc.

- Is it important to maintain a healthy backlog and is the book-to-ship cycle long? If so, an incentive at time of booking may be necessary.

- Is cashflow an overriding factor? If it is, you may want to pay an incentive for collecting payment, or not pay a part of the incentive until customer payment has been received.

Some objectives include penetration of competitive accounts, success at strategic accounts, employment of additional sales channels, market share, and product mix. There are probably some objectives you want to achieve this year that have a long term strategic value. For example establishing new accounts, which will eventually yield the needed upgrade/add-on revenue stream. Another example is objectives that will not bring in any revenue in the coming year, but which have to be achieved for long term survival.

It is not the intent of this article to try to guess what your sales objectives are. The objectives listed above are only intended to give you some ideas.

Below are examples of incentives I have worked with as well as a brief description of the objectives they try to accomplish.

Shipment Dollar Revenues - This objective is in almost every sales compensation plan, in one form or another. Xerox used a point system, where a point was equivalent to a certain dollar value. Assigning points has advantages:

-   Extra points can be assigned to products that are of strategic importance.

-   Emphasis can be placed on high margin products. Normally, revenues are broken down by category, such as hardware, software, maintenance, consulting, and education services. The numbers come straight from the business plan. Bundling all revenues in one objective number may be acceptable to the salespeople (so they can make up for the lack of attainment in one category with extra sales in another). But for line managers the goals should be kept separate, if feasible, to keep a management focus on all company objectives.

Gross Margins - This objective is especially popular with the computer resellers and other vendors that face an industry where discounting is becoming the norm. Prime Computer is currently in the process of switching from revenue incentives to incentives based on gross margins.

Companies have tried to reduce revenue incentives if prices are discounted. This, however, complicates the incentives calculations tremendously and still does not get the message across to the sales people that the company can only survive by making profits.

Revenue Bookings - This used to be a popular objective, but is disappearing. IBM, over the years, went from paying most incentives for bookings to paying all incentives for activities related to shipment of products.

If the book-to-ship cycle is longer than three months, a booking incentive is certainly recommended. The salesperson thrives on getting the order signed and being recognized for it. Some companies do not pay for bookings but measure bookings as a criteria for the 100% Club, an annual event for salespeople achieving 100% of quota.

Some companies pay incentives for shipment revenues as opposed to booking revenues but advance half of the incentives at the time of booking.

New Accounts - An incentive for new accounts can be expensive, but accomplishes the following:

> It establishes an "installed base" that yields repeat and/or upgrade revenues and therefore is essential for company growth. Without a new account incentive the salespeople tend to go for the easy sales (from existing customers).

> It focuses the company's sales efforts on increasing market share.

Balanced Performance - Companies typically desire to achieve a balanced performance in sales of their product lines/services for strategic and manufacturing reasons.

Accounts Receivable - Salespeople don't like to be measured on Days of Sales Outstanding (DSO). Very few companies have been successful in reducing DSO by offering incentives, such as a quarterly bonus if the DSO is under 45 days. Administration of DSO incentives can be a nightmare.

A good SCP should encourage productivity and discourage unproductive activities. Does the salesperson really have control over DSO?   If not, DSO may be a more appropriate measurement for second line (and up) managers who tend to be measured more on the profitability of the business. Put the accounts receivable goals in the salesperson's performance plan to help develop their business acumen. Do not put a DSO incentive in place for the salespeople until it has been tried at a sales manager's level first.

Product Emphasis - The marketing plan may emphasize the sales of certain products for strategic importance. Bonuses for these products, especially if accelerated incentives are offered for subsequent sales of product units, always get the attention of the sales force. Limit the number of product lines subject to bonuses to increase strategic focus. For example, a company that wants to start focusing on local area networking may want to offer a bonus only for the network software (if sold with hardware). The software will pull the hardware with it, therefore other network product bonuses may not be necessary.

Consistent Sales Achievement - Or how to avoid getting most of the business in the last quarter of the fiscal year. Divide the salesperson's quota over four quarters and provide a bonus for attaining the quarterly quota in each of the first two quarters. Or, provide a bonus for being 100% year-to-date at the end of each of the first two quarters. The bonus for the first quarter is usually the highest to motivate the sales force to start running at full speed on the first day of the new year.

Management By Objectives - Also called Target Objective Bonuses. Sometimes it is hard to generalize the objectives (and therefore the incentives) so that they fit all salespeople. For example, you may want to encourage a salesperson to call on certain accounts with no immediate revenue potential. Here you may want to establish certain milestones (with incentives for achievement) that are likely to lead toward the sale. Try to keep objectives measurable rather than subjective, to avoid arguing with the salespeople over attainment.

This type of incentive may be just a part of the total incentive package. IBM provides in its 1989 sales plan a "Customer Solution Bonus." Specific objectives for the territory are agreed upon by the salesperson and the sales manager at the beginning of the year and a dollar value is attached to each.

The key is to keep it simple. Unfortunately I have seen too many well-intended sales compensation plans that were too complicated because companies wanted to accomplish too much or they were so badly patched-up over the years that nobody could see the forest for the trees.

Whatever the objectives and resulting incentives are that you decide on, try to keep them to an absolute minimum to establish a clear focus. Less important objectives can be achieved by emphasizing them in the salesperson's performance plan.

Determining Target Earnings

The total compensation a salesperson who attains 100% of quota receives should be market driven. In other words it should match or beat the competition. For this reason, many companies do not provide merit increases to their salespeople. Make it a point to keep track of what your competition pays. By finding out how their incentives break down, you will also get a good picture of their sales objectives. Knowing what your competition pays helps you avoid losing your top performers and attract top quality salespeople.

Target earnings at 100% of quota attainment vary by sales channel, average order size, inside versus outside sales, customer type, and product type. For example:

> According to the 1990 Reseller Management Survey, reseller outside salespeople earned an average of $40,400, and inside salespeople earned an average of $28,860.

The Culpepper Study in 1990 showed that the average annual total compensation of salespeople in the software industry varied depending on the average order size.

Order Size	Earnings
>$80K	$70,000
$40K - $80K	$55,000
<$40K	$45,000

Salespeople selling hardware to OEM's earn an average of $90,000 per year. All of these examples assume the salesperson is at 100% of quota attainment.

The average annual earnings of salespeople employed by larger computer companies selling directly to end-users is from $50,000 to over $100,000. IBM and DEC pay between $50,000 and $65,000; Stratus and Tandem pay about $75,000; Amdahl pays more than $100,000.

In 1990 *The Wall Street Journal* stated average annual earnings of salespeople to be very close and independent of product: hardware $44,000; software $43,800; and service $43,000.

Computer Product Selling also in 1990, showed an average annual earnings of $42,960 in the high tech industry (independent stores; $27,960; franchises: $34,560; company-owned stores: $40,200; small VAR's: $39,840; and larger VAR's: $52,200).

Target earnings at 100% are generally based on the complexity of the product, the market, or both. They should not depend on the size of the average order, although they often do. It takes the same amount of skill, time, and effort to sell (and install) a turnkey system to a travel agency, whether the system costs $20,000 or $90,000.

To determine the target earnings, first decide what you have to pay a salesperson who attains 100% of the objectives (quota) you have set.

Next determine what the earnings should be at different levels, perhaps 50%, 150%, and 200% of quota attainment.

Some companies do not pay any incentives until the salesperson achieves 50% of quota. They also typically assign quotas for short time periods, such as per month or per quarter. Generally, I do not recommend this approach. If the salesperson does not perform, fire them. If you keep them, they may start sandbagging their orders until the next time period to comfortably pass the 50% milestone. If you feel strongly about paying a lower incentive for performance under 100%, consider paying milestone bonuses. For example, a $5,000 bonus for reaching 100% of quota.

Deciding what to pay at 150% quota attainment is challenging. Consider this example in which all figures are annualized.

A salesperson is targeted to make $60,000 when they reach 100% of quota. Their base salary is $30K. There are no bonuses or accelerators. If this salesperson reaches 150% of quota, what is their total compensation?

Answer: $75,000

$30,000 base salary
$30,000 for achieving first 100%
$15,000 for achieving next 50% (from 100% to 150%)

So here you have a successful salesperson achieving 150% and being paid 125% ($75,000 divided by $60,000). You also save money for having relatively less overhead for this person. However, you don't want to lose this high performer to your competition. Therefore, you increase the commission rate by applying an accelerator.

To apply an accelerator, first decide how much you want the salesperson who achieves 150% of quota to make. Let's assume that upon achieving 150% of quota, you want the salesperson to make 1.5 times what they would have earned at 100% of quota. (In this case, two of these top performers still cost you less than three performers who achieve 100% of quota each.) Given this example, the salesperson would make $90,000 upon reaching 150% of quota.

The accelerator, then, is a factor of 2 because the commission rate for performance over 100% is twice that for performance under 100%.

Calculating the accelerator becomes more difficult if there are also some other bonuses in the compensation plan. They usually increase the accelerator. Also, if you pay 50% of the commissions for bookings, and 50% of the commissions for shipments, and you do not want to pay an accelerator for commissions paid on bookings (most companies don't), the accelerator in the above example is 4.

I use a PC with a spreadsheet to calculate the accelerators. The formula may be so long that it runs off the spreadsheet. But the spreadsheet allows you to evaluate different assumptions on the total sales expense as well as expense/revenue ratios.

We assume here, of course, that the quotas have been set correctly. Sometimes companies believe it is necessary to put a cap on earnings. Some spread payments of commissions beyond a certain amount over a couple of years. I do not favor this approach. A high performer earning lots of money usually stimulates their peers to perform better.

However, it may be necessary to stop the accelerator at a certain attainment level (e.g. for performance over 175%) and start paying the same commission rate you pay for performance under 100%. The only environment in which I have to (reluctantly) agree to this is when accurate quota setting is almost impossible but still necessary. An example may be salespeople selling to OEMs, where the salesperson has little influence over the success of their customer (Compaq vs. Kaypro).

I recommend you not apply accelerators against commissions until 100% of the annual quota has been attained. Use caution if you assign quotas for shorter time periods than one year. I have seen several companies with quotas for quarterly periods pay undeserved high commissions to salespeople who made a "killing" in the first quarter and did not perform for the rest of the year. If you have to assign quotas for short time periods, for example in a seasonal business or fast growing company, do not start accelerators until the third or fourth quarter.

It is hard to come up with general rules for establishing earning levels. Once you determine the average for your industry, develop a model to ensure your compensation program helps you meet your objectives.

Salespeople thrive on Achievement of Quota

Establish the Quotas

Without quotas it is hard to measure success. Proper management emphasis on quota attainment as a way of life is a key to achieving your sales objectives. Ongoing recognition of top performers, based on quota attainment, will focus the salespeople's attention on this criteria. Salespeople thrive on their ranking within their peer group.

Some companies post the relative ranking of salespeople in the sales office, for everybody to see. To be listed at or near the top often becomes as important to a salesperson as the monetary rewards. Many companies hold an annual recognition event ("Hundred Percent Club") for the salespeople who attain quota. The event ranges from a dinner attended by corporate executives to a trip with a companion to an exotic resort. Whatever format the event may have, qualifying for the Hundred Percent Club should be the main goal of each salesperson.

There are four aspects to setting quota that have to be considered: Basis, event, time frame, and over-assignment. Each will be discussed in more detail.

The basis of quota depends on the sales objectives. Quotas may be expressed as revenues, units, new accounts, points, margin dollars, etc. A quota for revenues is probably the most common. Strict management control on pricing is necessary to ensure profitability. The current trend is to establish quota objectives in the form of margins to make the salespeople aware of the impact of discounting on the bottom line.

Quotas in the form of specific product sales rarely work well. Sales people sell what the market wants, not what the marketing or engineering department thinks the market needs. If certain products have to be pushed, try using bonuses, not specific product quotas which can demotivate the sales force.

A quota expressed in points, crediting for example 3 points for product A and 7 points for product B is another design that may excite the marketing department but not the sales force. Salespeople relate to dollars and units. An example of units is New Accounts.

It is important to specify what sales transactions qualify for quota credit. For example, to qualify for a New Account, you may want to stipulate that the initial order has to be greater than $25,000, has to contain a CPU, and has to be from an enterprise to which no sales have occurred in the prior three years. Or, revenues may be defined as to not include sales of supplies, training, and service.

The event of quota credit can be upon booking of the order, credit verification, order shipment, or receipt of customer payment. When the salesperson closes the sale, some recognition should be given in the form of commission, quota credit, or both. Keep in mind that commission payment and quota credit do not have to occur at the same time. In the extreme case, quota credit for an order could be given at the time of booking, while commission payment could occur when customer payment is received. A better approach would be to pay an advance of half the commission at the time of booking, and the other half at the time of order shipment, while the order is fully credited at the time of shipment. The commissions advanced can be considered an interest-free loan. Of course, if the order is canceled, quota credit is reversed and the commissions advanced are charged back.

The time frame for a quota assignment is normally from a month to a year and varies by sales channel. Annual quotas are appropriate when sales cycles are longer and the business is pretty much the same over the year. Quarterly quotas make sense if the business is seasonal, the sell/ship cycle is short, or the business is fast-growing. Watch out for sandbagging of orders when the quota time frames are short: If the bonuses in the sales compensation plan are paid for performance over short time periods, salespeople tend to keep orders in their drawers until they are sure that they have enough to qualify for the bonus.

Over-assignment of quotas means that the total of the quotas of the salespeople is higher than what the business plan calls for. The reason for over-assignment is that territories may not be covered for periods of time due to sickness and attrition.

Typically, over-assignment ranges from 10% to 30%. The higher the number of salespeople, the lower the percentage of quota over-assignment.

Setting quotas is more complicated when cross-selling is involved. For example: A salesperson sells direct to end-users while resellers also sell the company's products in the same territory. To avoid cross-channel conflict, the salesperson may get duplicate quota credit (and incentives) for reseller's sales in the territory. The salesperson's quota should identify the portion of their own direct sales responsibility. At least the direct sales portion of the quota should be attained to qualify for the Hundred Percent Club, although preferably both portions of the quotas should be achieved. Without this requirement, the result may be that all the salespeople are in the Hundred Percent Club, while the company as a whole has not made its goals. It also would be difficult to measure the salesperson's real performance.

Quota setting is an art, not a science. Often, the quotas for the new year are based on performances in the past, plus a significant bit of guess work. This is the reason quotas for salespeople vary so much from company to company in the same industry. The guessing part of the quota setting process, new products coming out, and a changing market, can have a major impact on whether or not the quotas are realistic. Actual sales attainment and new sales forecasts should be frequently reviewed to determine how realistic the quotas are. Being able to manage quotas and quota attainment is a key to running a business successfully.

It is easier to assign quotas on the high side at the beginning of the year and then lower it later, than to increase quotas during the year. The kick-off meeting may be your only opportunity to set higher quotas because of new, but still unannounced products, and markets that will be tapped into during the coming year.

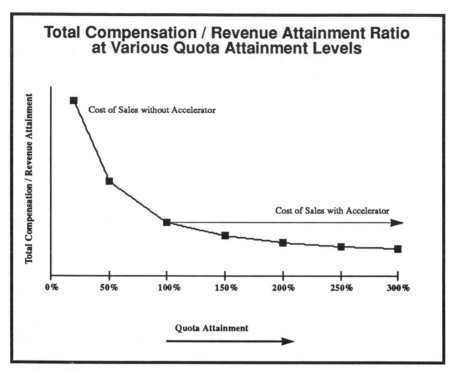

Increasing the commission rate for quota attainment over 100% does not have to increase the cost of sales - as illustrated above - and allows you to create an attractive compensation package to hire and keep top performers!

Determine the Compensation Method

There are three aspects of determining a method of compensation. The base salary as a component of the total compensation, types of draws, and incentive methods will be discussed in this section.

There are various ways to structure the compensation package. The following are the three most common compensation methods:

- Base salary plus incentives
- Incentives only (with or without a draw)
- Straight salary

The current trend is to pay salespeople a base salary plus incentives. Paying a base salary gives you control over the activities of the salespeople. In return for paying a base salary you can require the salesperson to perform certain job functions that are difficult to demand with an incentives-only compensation method. Examples of these job functions are: assist at trade shows, attend training classes, help junior salespeople, submit sales forecasts, focus on customer satisfaction, and computerize the prospect/customer database. In addition, paying a base salary creates a professional image for your company and shows a commitment to your salespeople.

Base salaries should be expressed as a percentage of total compensation at 100% of quota attainment. This percentage tends to be smaller if greater personal skills are required, the salesperson has little company support, or the salesperson has a high degree of personal control over the selling cycle and the territory. The base salary is a higher percentage of total compensation if the selling cycles are very long, sales success is hard to measure, or sales accomplishments are the result of team work. Base salaries range typically from 50% to 80% of the total compensation at 100% of quota attainment.

Most companies selling computers to end-users pay a base salary plus incentives. Digital Equipment is an exception; this company pays a salary only, although in the last few years it has offered a bonus to top performers. Companies paying no base salary, just incentives, are found in the computer retail, distribution, and manufacturer's representatives segments. I know of very few companies paying their salespeople a straight salary with no incentives. Salespeople earning a straight salary often have an engineering or support function in addition to their sales responsibilities.

Most companies that pay incentives also provide a draw. A ***draw*** is an advance payment against future earnings. The reasons for providing a draw vary, but normally they are paid to smooth the peaks and valleys of the salesperson's cash flow stream, or to take care of a salesperson starting out in a new territory. It is important to clearly define the type of draw to your sales force, because draw provisions that are not clearly defined often become the source of disagreements. There are three types of draws:

- Recoverable draw. This draw is an advance against incentives. Incentives are normally paid only when they exceed the draw. If no incentives are earned, the salesperson owes the company the amount of draws that were advanced. I advise you to carefully think through the consequences of this type of draw for the salesperson and your company before offering it. For example, what will you do at year-end about draw balances owed by salespeople? Do you forgive the balances or do you carry them over into the new year?

- Non-recoverable draw. This draw is also an advance against incentives and, like recoverable draws, incentives are paid only when they exceed the to-date draw amount. However if the commissions earned are less than the draw paid, the salesperson does not owe the company any money. Hewlett-Packard provides a non-recoverable draw to salespeople who have attained 100% of quota in the prior year. The company pays the monthly non-recoverable draw all year. Other companies pay the non-recoverable draws only for a specified number of months to provide the salespeople an opportunity to get up to speed.

- Guaranteed draw. This draw is not netted against incentives. Any incentives earned are paid over and above the draw (and base salary). This type of draw is often used to hire a professional salesperson and provide them with an immediate income equivalent to that of their prior job. The draw is normally paid for three to six months. Another example of the use of the guaranteed draw is when a salesperson has fallen on hard times because of circumstances beyond their control. In this situation the normal sales compensation plan is replaced with a guaranteed draw and the salesperson is not eligible for any incentives.

There are two types of Sales Compensation Plans: Incentives may be based on sales volume performance (Revenue Based) or on quota attainment performance (Quota Based).

Sales compensation plans based on sales volume performance pay an incentive as a fixed portion of the sales volume. For example, the incentive might be 3% of the net revenues shipped, or $75 per product. This method is normally used when territories can be created that have equal potential for all salespeople. The advantage of this method is that sales compensation expenses can be budgeted, at least as a percentage of sales.

Sales compensation plans based on quota attainment performance pay an incentive as a portion of the total incentives, also called the *Incentive Base*. The incentive base is normally the total of incentives for revenues. For example, assume that the total annual compensation for a salesperson at 100% of quota attainment is $60,000; the base salary is 50% of total compensation, or $30,000; bonuses are projected to amount to $5,000. The remaining incentives are for revenues, or in other words, the Revenue Incentive Base is $25,000. For every 1% of quota attainment, the salesperson gets paid 1% of the $25,000 Incentive Base or $250. The amount of money received for the sale of $1 of products is called the *Revenue Multiplier*. The revenue multiplier is calculated by dividing the incentive base by the quota. Note that the incentive payment is independent of quota or actual revenue attainment. The incentive payment is a function of the attainment as a percentage of quota and the incentive base. This method is used when territories cannot be created with the same potential, so that salespeople having the same skills and working the same number of hours would have different earning potentials. The Quota Based compensation plan allows you to set different quotas for different salespeople and pay them the same incentives at 100% of quota attainment. The disadvantage of this method is that the sales manager has great influence over the earnings of the salespeople. Setting the quota wrong can make or break the salesperson. Also, this method makes it more difficult to budget for sales compensation expenses.

The final factor of total compensation is the merit increase. Most companies do not provide merit increases for their salespeople. Instead, they adjust the total compensation at 100% of quota attainment to what the market pays. These figures are adjusted annually based on competitive research. Not providing merit increases should not mean that appraisals can be abandoned. It is still important to sit down at least annually with each salesperson to conduct a formal performance review.

Develop the Incentives

When you get to this step, you already have determined target earnings at various quota attainment levels and outlined your sales objectives (steps 1 & 2). Now the challenge is to quantify the incentives that will motivate your sales force to achieve the objectives you have set forth. The most common incentives I see are incentives for attainment of revenues, gross margin, and new accounts. Less common, but not necessarily less meaningful are product bonuses, milestone bonuses, and Management By Objective bonuses.

Revenue incentives are usually straightforward and easy to calculate. First the components of revenues must be determined. Not included are, of course, discounts and freight. But you have to decide what revenue streams are included, for example training and support. The percentage of revenue paid as commissions depends on the annual quota and the type and price of the product, I have seen rates varying from 1% to 15%.

Gross margin is normally defined as the selling price minus the cost of goods sold. It is important that the salesperson knows up-front the cost from which the gross margin is calculated, so that they know what the commissions are for the solution they sell. Normally the SCP specifies a gross margin or a product cost basis. They may vary by product line and come straight from the business plan. When prices fluctuate too much, the gross margins and/or product cost basis should be adjusted periodically. The attractive aspect of paying commissions based on gross margins is that the salesperson penalizes his own income when he offers discounts.

New Account Bonuses are needed when a key sales objective is the attainment of additional customers. New Account Bonuses can make up as much as 40% of the total incentives. Sometimes a company loses money on the initial New Account order because of the high bonus, but considers it a good investment because of the future revenue expected from the new account. Care should be taken to define what constitutes a new account. For example, the customer should not have purchased any products in the last three years, or the order should contain at least one key product, or the order should have a certain minimum dollar value.

When certain products are of key importance to the strategic direction of the company, product bonuses will get the attention of the sales force. Incentives for product bonuses, if existent, rarely exceed 20% of the total incentives. Keep the number of different product bonuses to a minimum so that each bonus is big enough to get the salesperson's attention.

Sometimes it is difficult to quantify objectives, for example: What kind of incentives can you offer a salesperson who has a large account with a sales cycle that can be expected to be more than a year? Here Management by Objectives (MBO) bonuses can be effective. Examples would be arranging an executive briefing or placing a product for evaluation with the prospect. Care has to be taken to be specific about the objectives. Too often objectives are written such that the achievement is dependent on subjective judgment; or, they are so nebulous that their achievement is hard to determine.

Milestone bonuses are normally used to reward salespeople for going the extra mile, such as achieving 110% of quota or achieving a balanced performance between revenues and gross margins, or revenues and new accounts, or revenues for each of several specified product lines.

Incentives vary by channel. Large hardware and software manufacturers selling direct to end-users, companies selling to OEMs, and most VARs pay commissions, based for the largest part, on revenues. Most of the incentives offered by computer retailers and distributors are based on gross margins.

For example, surveys of VARs paying a base salary show that 41% pay commissions on net revenues, with an average commission of 4%. Thirty-eight percent of the VARs pay commissions on gross margins only, averaging 15%. Twenty percent of the VARs pay commissions on net profits only, averaging 23%. The same surveys show that of VARs who pay no base salary, the commission averages 9% of net revenues, or 17% on gross profits, or 33% on net profits.

Awards and recognition are other effective ways to motivate sales-people to achieve sales objectives. Some companies have indicated that offering cash and prizes have achieved the same results for less money. Every company understanding the psyche of a salesperson organizes an annual event for top achievers and/or salespeople attaining 100% of quota. The most appropriate event would be a trip, with companion, to a resort. The trip can be combined with business meetings in the mornings designed to provide the salespeo-ple with a better perspective of the business and provide company executives an opportunity to better understand the salespeople's challenges and opinions.

Last, but not least, before you present your sales force with the Sales Compensation Plan, make sure it passes the following two tests:

- Is it easy for the salespeople to understand the incentives for the solutions they are trying to sell?

- Can you explain your SCP to an outsider in less than 10 min-utes?

If you can answer yes to both questions, you have succeeded. The best SCPs are the ones that are clear and simple!

Review the budget, document, and communicate the plan

These two steps are combined because they are so closely related. As you document and communicate the Plan, you will have to review the plan and budget.

To measure the impact of various sales performance scenarios on the budget, I recommend that you use a spreadsheet. Assume a mix of attainment figures rather than assuming that everybody will be at

The test for a good Sales Compensation Plan:
Can you explain the plan in less than 10 minutes?

100%, because accelerators in the Plan will drive the sales expense upward.

By the way, if it is simple to put the Sales Compensation Plan (SCP) into a computerized spreadsheet it should be easy for the sales force to understand. If you have to figure out how to computerize the plan, you'll also have to figure out how to explain the features of the plan to the salespeople.

In addition, you will identify all of the special incentive opportunities making it easy to figure incentives during the sales year. It will also require less time to calculate and issue the incentive pay checks.

It is usually a good idea to have the incentives administrator work with you to develop the spreadsheet because they may discover inconsistencies and may have suggestions that simplify the calculations.

Your administrator will also become thoroughly familiar with the Plan. They can help you develop comparisons between the current compensation program and the new SCP.

Compare your SCP budget as a percentage of revenues with other companies in your industry. You want to specifically compare your SCP with other companies who are using similar sales channels. Researching this information is not easy because financial reports usually bundle sales and marketing expenses as well as general and administrative (G&A) expenses into one figure.

The SCP budget (including base salaries, if any, plus incentives) as a percentage of revenues varies widely, depending on the type of products, customers, and sales channels used.

For example, for companies selling their products mainly to OEMs and large distributors the figure is usually low, like around 2%.

For companies selling to end-users, I have seen the figures range from 5% to 25%.

For software vendors, the figure may be 25% or higher.

You can use outside sources to verify sales compensation in your industry. Employment agencies can offer some help. Classified advertisements and networking can also be helpful sources of information. Outside consultants, like High Tech Marketing, have also provided consulting services to help identify compensation information in other companies.

The last step in sales compensation development is documenting the Plan.

While this is a time-consuming task, it is a necessary one. If no documented Plans are in place, signed by each salesperson at the start of the sales year, there will be misunderstandings and arguments. By having each employee certify a written explanation of the plan, you can avoid hassle in the future.

Disgruntled former employees often challenge SCP issues as they exit a company. If a case goes to court, the company normally loses. You can avoid costly and lengthy litigation with a well documented SCP.

A well-documented Plan should contain the following:

- All incentives, clearly spelled out, with effective dates and time of payment. There should be a paragraph on what happens to orders from last year that will be shipped in the new year.

- Examples of calculations.

- Sales provisions and terms and conditions, including definitions, such as what revenues are commissionable and what revenues are not and what constitutes a New Account. It is helpful to have a glossary attached to the Plan to avoid the problem of semantics.

- Conditions of employment, describing the company policy on moonlighting, accepting gifts from prospects, etc.

- Job duties.

- Pricing authority.

- Provisions for termination, transfer, leave of absence, and change in position.

- The company's right to modify anything at any time during the year.

- Provisions for incentives and credit sharing or splits, if applicable.

- An attachment stating the territory, quota, and the base salary.

- Acknowledgments to be signed by the salespeople.

Salespeople resist change of compensation plans. Therefore it is important to set up a sales meeting at the start of the year to explain the plan and communicate the objectives that the Plan is intended to accomplish.

As part of the plan, create a cover sheet that allows the salesperson to acknowledge receipt and understanding of the plan.

I would suggest you schedule a one-on-one meeting with each salesperson to answer their questions about the plan. As part of this meeting, you should get each salesperson to sign the cover sheet and file a copy in their personnel file. This will help you avoid many problems in the future.

Sales Compensation Summarized

A good sales compensation plan may be the most important ingredient in ensuring that corporate objectives are communicated to the field organization. Everyone will be marching to the tune of the same drummer.

There are three key criteria of a good Sales Compensation Plan:

- A well-designed and implemented Sales Compensation Plan (SCP) will communicate the business direction and priorities.

- It will meet the sales objectives of the company and motivate the sales force to achieve these objectives.

- It achieves the pay objectives set by the company.

You can follow a 7-step process to developing a good SCP, and ensure that your SCP includes all of the ingredients necessary to meet the three criteria.

The 7 steps are:

1. Prioritize company sales objectives
2. Determine earnings levels and base salaries
3. Establish sales quotas
4. Determine the compensation method
5. Develop the incentives
6. Create the budget
7. Document and communicate the plan

About Dick Vink:

Dick Vink spent almost 10 years with the IBM Corporation in marketing and sales of small business computers. Dick was a top salesman, and sales manager in addition to being an instructor in their marketing training organization.

After IBM, Dick helped start an independent sales organization specializing in small business computers for the first time computer user.

During the past 10+ years Dick has managed his own consulting firm, High Tech Marketing, specializing in marketing, investment research, sales compensation and business development. He is a leading consultant to many computer equipment manufacturers as well as many other high technology firms.

A native born Dutchman, Dick holds a Masters degree from Delft University in the Netherlands. His firm is located in Newport Beach, California where he and his family also reside.

Chapter Sixteen:

Creating a Unique Selling Proposition

By   *Lane Wolbe*
   Wolco, Inc.
   3030 Holcomb Ridge Road
   Atlanta, GA 30071
   (404) 729-2506 FAX: (404) 729-2523

Why the Need to be Unique

Whether you're selling face-to-face, on the telephone, through retail, or via mail order, positioning your company and product to be unique and valuable is one of the most difficult challenges.

Chapter 1 explained how your company and products are in one of four conditions. Illustration 16-1 reviews those four conditions. Your objective is to become known and unique. Rapidly changing technology has given us increased efficiency, and more accurate, immediate access to information. But it has also presented us with new challenges. Selling costs have continued to increase, while profit margins decline, (Illustration 16-2). In this chapter, I will dis-

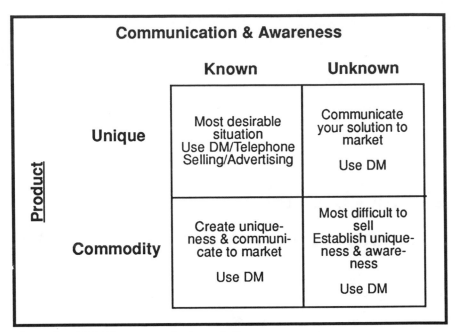

Illustration 16-1: The communications challenge.

cuss how you can address these challenges using unique selling techniques.

The Changing Environment

The competitive selling world has changed dramatically over the past several decades. In the past your primary concern was whether or not you could win the order. Today, you not only have to be concerned about winning the order, but whether winning the business will create enough profit to justify making the sale.

I will discuss how the environment has changed; what common solutions have been implemented and why some of them haven't worked; what the customer is really looking for in making a buying decision; how to use the customer's buying criteria to set yourself

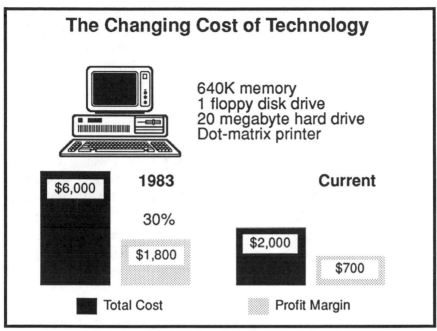

Illustration 16-2: The changing cost of technology.

apart from your competition; and how to begin increasing both revenues and gross profit margins.

A good deal of the pressure in generating adequate profit margin is caused by selling products that are perceived by the buyer as commodities. *Commodity products* are those products whose function is readily available in the marketplace from multiple vendors at about the same price. Examples of such products abound: computers, from PCs to mainframes, phone systems, and heavy equipment. Just about anything that is manufactured and subsequently sold through a third-party or in-house dealer/distributor network, may be classified as a commodity.

In today's marketplace, most successful commodity products have been cloned. The Japanese first approached our shores with inexpensive but poorly made products. American business looked with amusement as the Japanese worked to bring quality in line with American expectations. Some of us are old enough to remember our sense of amusement when we discovered a product stamped *Made in Japan.* We even helped the Japanese improve their manufacturing processes so they could turn out better quality goods. Many businesses felt immune from the competitive threat these products might present.

All of a sudden, the quality of Japanese products was not only as good as comparable U.S. items, but in many instances, it was better. For the first time American companies were presented with a new and perplexing question: How do we compete with imported products? We're no longer amused when a product is made in Japan. If an imported product is at least as good as the American made product and it costs less, shouldn't the customer buy the import? Don't you?

The success of the Japanese has made cloning a game in which anyone can play. Manufacturers can now wait until a new product is introduced and established in the market. Once the product has gained success and developed demand, a cloned version becomes a natural progression.

By reverse engineering, a similar product can be brought to market without the costly burden of product development or the financial risk of product failure. Obviously, these cloned new products can be priced substantially less than the original. The original developer and manufacturer must reduce his price to compete with the clone.

Soon other clones hit the market and the price, and profit margin, go into free fall. Orders go to the supplier willing to sell at the lowest price and/or to take the least profit. Many companies will make sales to avoid inventory carrying costs or to maintain market share.

The art of selling simply becomes who can provide the product at the lowest price.

Other factors contribute to the changing face of the competitive marketplace. Buyers now have the idea that price should be the primary criteria for selecting a vendor for a commodity product. As I have already discussed, this concept is reinforced by the vendors. When faced with a competitive situation, salespeople will attempt to sell their management on lowering their price to *win* the business and to maintain a relationship with their customer. Many companies give the buyers just what they want . . . a lower price. In other words, the selling company gets lazy and takes the order as easily as possible.

When your price and margin are reduced, you often lose the extra profit needed to create true product differences. As a result, many products look and act alike.

We've all seen the commercial in which the salesperson says, "It's just as good as a Xerox." The key phrase in this commercial, *It's just as good as*, really describes the problem we're all facing.

Many product lines are produced by generic manufacturers and are often given private labels. In fact, often similar products from competing companies are exactly the same. There is no functional difference in these products, only in the packaging and merchandising.

We as vendors are doing a great job of convincing customers that price is the most important issue. With all other factors being the same, the customer should buy the least expensive item available because all the competing brands do the same thing. Imagine what this approach to selling is doing to the salesperson. Instead of the salesperson taking the fight to the customer's location, the new arena for the battle becomes the sales manager's office where they fight to have the price reduced.

Sales skills deteriorate because selling is not part of the equation if the buying decision is made strictly on price. Instead of trying to convince prospects and customers to buy their products, many salespeople spend most of their energy attempting to engineer the lowest possible price.

Everything I've discussed so far seems to paint a hopeless picture of gloom, doom, and consistently declining profits. The following changes are placing tremendous pressure on traditional sales activity.

- Cloning can rob products of their uniqueness.

- Reduced profit margins make it more difficult to develop true product differentiation.

- Customers and vendors are using price as the primary buying criteria.

- Sales skills are deteriorating due to lack of use.

The most successful companies work hard to establish unique offerings to surround their products. These companies bundle their products into packages which serve to differentiate them from their competition and give the customer a reason to buy on something besides price.

The bundle can consist of anything the seller feels will make their package attractive to the buyer. The bundle is supposed to make the difference.

The concept of bundling is often referred to as ***added value***. We have all heard this term and virtually every industry uses it. I wonder if added value doesn't often turn into added cost.

Value Added

One of the biggest challenges a salesperson faces is creating a perception in the mind of the buyer that their product is unique. Most successful salespeople have found methods of communicating a unique selling proposition that allows them to win in most situations. Customers treat many products as commodities. That is, the product function required by the customer is available from multiple vendors for about the same price. In trying to win the sale of the commodity product, the selling company is often forced to compete primarily on price.

Price merchandising robs you of the margins required to either enhance the selling offering or to develop true product differentiation between you and your competition. Either of these steps could move your product from the commodity status and allow you to create a true sales edge.

In addition, sales skills are deteriorating as customers and vendors alike use price as the primary buying criteria. As a result, prospects are forced to choose between similar products, usually marketed in similar ways, to fill their needs. Given this scenario, the prospect makes the "from whom to buy" decision primarily based on price.

However, creative marketers expend a great deal of effort trying to establish meaningful reasons why a prospect should buy their product as opposed to a similar product offered by competition. Merchandising, advertising, and sales presentations are used creatively to build product differentiation in the minds of potential buyers. The claims made in merchandising campaigns address either the function of the product itself, or the support package that comes with the product.

In some industries, heavy investments in *value add* services are made in an effort to distinguish one total package from a similar product offered by the competition. These bundled value added packages will often help win the business. However, for value add to have long term benefit, you should understand the long range implications of creating a package of services to surround your products.

Most value add services typically require substantial investment. The value added package must be created; often over a long period of time. Depending on what goes into the package, the decisions about the contents will often have to be made long before the package is ready for delivery. We live and work in an extremely dynamic world -- What seems to be of great value today may carry little perceived value tomorrow. Therefore, investments in a value added package must be immediately available to the market. This immediacy is the only way to capture the responsiveness of the market and generate the volumes required to recoup the investment.

Even if you can create a timely value add offering, prospects will still be able to take advantage of market forces working against you. In a market of competitive offerings, value add services are often used as part of the buying criteria for only the initial purchase. Once the value added functions have been acquired as part of a transaction, they will often be ignored in subsequent purchase decisions.

Many value added functions tend to make the customer self-sufficient. These types of services enable the customer to ignore your offerings in future purchases. In addition, customers will often develop internal support systems, thus further reducing the dependency and benefit of your value added package.

It may also be difficult for a customer to assign a monetary weight to your value added services. This is not because the services have no value, but the benefits may be too subjective to establish a real dollar value.

Intangible benefits are often the most emotional and hardest hitting. But many prospects refuse to convert their emotions into tangible dollar values and will avoid involving themselves in this exercise.

Most business decisions involve a manager spending company funds. Their buying decisions will often be scrutinized by someone else in the company. Many of these managers are reluctant to pay for additional services that the company's internal departments are supposed to be supplying. As a result, it is difficult to sell value added services, with intangible benefits, to company employees.

The real clincher is that if a value added service is of true significance to the marketplace, most competitors will be forced to offer the same service. What starts as a way to distinguish one vendor from another, becomes an *I've got it too* offering available from any legitimate supplier. This cloning of a value added package has the same impact as the cloning of a product.

But there is a significant difference when an added value is duplicated. When similar services are offered by competition there is no uniqueness to the added value service, therefore, the value added service becomes part of the commodity product. In other words, the value added service doesn't help win any business after the initial blush comes off the rose. Once the service is introduced, it becomes very difficult to remove it from your product package. At least with product cloning, you don't have to incur additional costs. Value added cloning can raise your costs and ultimately still force you to compete on price.

Let me give you a personal example. Several years ago I purchased a mobile telephone for my wife's car. She drove to the vendor's location and had the phone installed. Last year I called the same vendor to have a phone installed in my car. I was pleased to find that the vendor would now come to my place of business and install the phone on-site. While calling other vendors to compare the price of this commodity product, I found that all vendors would install on-site for about the same price.

This is an example of a unique value added offered by one vendor which has now become a commodity practice offered by all vendors. The net result is that all the vendors have incurred additional expenses and reduced their profit margins. There is no uniqueness to this service. As I said earlier, if a service has true value it will be duplicated in the market.

To test the true value of an offering, you should try to market the service on its own. By that I mean, customers should be willing to pay independently for the service if it is worthwhile. The easiest way to prove the real value of the service is to offer it to purchasers of your competitor's similar products. If your competitor's customers will buy your value add, you've really got something. If they won't, you should rethink your strategy.

You should also test your own customers to see if they will buy your value add as a stand alone purchase. It's one thing to accept a service as a bundled offer; quite another to buy the service as an individual product.

After the preceding, you might think that I am against value added offerings as a means to distinguish you from your competition. Quite the opposite is true. I believe that adding value is the **only way** to create demand for your product in a price focused marketplace.

I am opposed to bundling items to make sales that will not have lasting individual worth. If the value added is offered at the same price at which the product used to be sold, then you are only adding expense.

How then do you compete? What can your organization do to distinguish itself from competitors offering similar products to the same prospects at the same price?

The answer is to create value that is:

- In constant demand from your customers

- No or low cost to create and implement

- Dynamic and responsive to the needs of the marketplace

- Easy to understand and use

Decision Criteria

So far, I have explained the commodity-like attitude purchasers and salespeople have toward many products. I pointed out how value add when used to differentiate one vendor from another has a very short usable life. It has a short life because a service or package which truly adds value will be duplicated by competitors. As a result, value add as it is most commonly used today quickly becomes added cost while offering no real competitive edge.

Value add, however, is the key to being competitive. In order to compete profitably, value add must meet the criteria explained above.

Before you can develop a formula that will meet these criteria, you should understand what typically motivates people to buy. After discussions with hundreds of salespeople I have concluded that there are 7 major factors in a prospect's buying decision.

1) <u>Function</u> - Will the product offered do the job required by the prospect?

2) <u>Availability</u> - Is the product available in the time frame acceptable to the customer?

3) <u>Price</u> - How much does it cost?

4) <u>Terms</u> - When and how does the vendor expect payment?

5) <u>Service</u> - How quickly can it be repaired if it breaks?

6) <u>Quality</u> - How often is it going to break?

7) <u>Salesmanship</u> - How much can the "from whom to buy decision" be influenced by the sales representative?

You can probably add other criteria that may influence the "from whom" decision in your market. As an example, some salespeople feel that location, or proximity to the prospect, plays a major role in the "from whom" decision.

As you develop your own list of buying decision criteria, rank them in relative importance to the customer's decision. Many salespeople, when faced with the ranking decision, immediately rank price as most important.

In many cases, price *is* the deciding factor. However, price can be a distant second if the customer must have the product today, but the least expensive source cannot deliver for two weeks. In this situa-

Buying Criteria

Criteria	Importance to Customer	Sales Ability to Impact
Function	1	1
Availability	3	2
Price	2	2
Terms	5	2
Service	6	3
Quality	4	1
Salesmanship	7	5

Illustration 16-3: Buying Criteria.

tion, availability will probably be number one. The laws of supply and demand will overcome price if the need is great enough.

In fact, several companies have gotten rich using just this philosophy. They stock seldom used, but critical items and charge a premium price when a customer places an order. They can get their price for a potential commodity product because availability creates uniqueness.

For our discussion let's assume that there are no special circumstances. As you rank the buying decision criteria, remember you're evaluating the importance of each element as it is perceived by the prospect. Illustration 16-3 shows a typical ranking of the seven criteria according to their importance to the customer.

If two or more of the items were equal in their importance, you could rank them both the same.

You'll also notice that I have ranked the salesperson's ability to impact each criteria. The sales ability to impact the criteria should be ranked on a scale of 1 to 5. The higher the rating the more the salesperson can influence the prospect's buying decision in that area. Therefore, a 1 rating indicates criterion over which a salesperson has no control. For example, Function is rated a 1 because, regardless of the salesperson's efforts, they cannot make the product do something it was not designed to do. A 5 identifies criteria that is entirely in the seller's control.

For our discussion, salespeople are assumed to be territory representatives. Managers and senior executives can also complete this exercise but they may not be objective. Their desire to increase profits may introduce more opinion than fact in the scoring.

The table ranks both the customer's perception of what is important and the salesperson's belief of how significantly they can impact each criteria. Notice that the items most important to the customer are those over which the salesperson has the least control. The following summarizes why each criteria received its individual rating.

1) Function - The salesperson has little ability to impact the function of the current product line.

2) Availability - The salesperson can influence this criteria by understanding the customer's needs and anticipating future purchase requirements.

3) Price - Surprisingly, salespeople have little control over pricing if a constant profit percentage is required. The cost of goods is relatively fixed and businesses have to sell at certain prices in order to cover expenses and make a reasonable profit. While price can be lowered, it will affect the profit objective and change the impact of the sale.

4) Terms - Terms suffer from the lack of flexibility imposed by price. The more lenient the terms, the greater the profit suffers.

5) <u>Service</u> - Salespeople can impact service by helping to solve customer problems. Although this sounds great conceptually, most salespeople don't become involved in service problems until it is too late. Very often the salesperson is asked to become involved in a service problem to smooth ruffled feathers or to get a customer to pay a service bill. It is almost like getting the salesperson to close the gate of the corral after the horse has escaped.

6) <u>Quality</u> - Product quality is determined, in most cases, by the manufacturing process.

7) <u>Salesmanship</u> - At last . . . an item that can be controlled and impacted by the salesperson. Before you get too excited, look where salesmanship falls on your ranking in importance to the customer. And this is further complicated when selling commodity products. In many situations, salesmanship is often reduced to one simple question . . . who got there first?

These are the most frequently used criteria in the buying decision, and how most salespeople identify their ability to influence these factors.

On the surface, it doesn't appear that there is an awful lot the salesperson can do to control the buying decision other than get there first. I don't believe that is the case.

Financial Selling

The salesperson can have a significant impact if they are given the motivation to reach and exceed goals; if the tools necessary to make them unique in the marketplace have been put into place; and if they are trained to use these tools. True salespeople can sell what they believe in, but they must understand the subject before they can truly believe in it. Training is the key to this understanding. In this section I'll discuss the sales tools and the training. Motivation is a topic all its own that will not be covered here.

In order to create the tools necessary to become unique in the eyes of the customer, you will have to combine the buying criteria with the requirements for real added value. Let's take an easy one first -- salesmanship. Remember, salesmanship is the least important element in the eyes of the customer but the one over which we have the greatest control.

Because salesmanship in a commodity product is often a case of "who got there first" you must implement specific business-to-business programs to constantly get information about your product and its unique value in front of the customer or prospect. In effect, direct marketing becomes a catalyst demonstrating your desire to earn the prospect's business. By letting direct marketing make the *prospect* call your sales force, productivity can be expanded and the odds of getting their first can be increased. The face-to-face salespeople can concentrate on using the value add package to close profitable business in situations where interest and desire have been stimulated.

Face-to-face selling cannot be totally replaced with a direct marketing strategy. However, sales productivity can be improved and enhanced with direct marketing, and getting there first is one of the most important factors in salesmanship when selling a commodity product.

Salesmanship can be enhanced with direct marketing, training, motivation, and management. These elements are within your control. Addressing the other elements is more difficult. As I discussed earlier, you want value add that is:

- In constant demand from your customers
- No or low cost to create or implement
- Dynamic and responsive to the needs of the marketplace
- Easy to understand and use

I have discussed how salesmanship can be enhanced and used to sell a value add. Let's now look at the other criteria and how they can be used to create and sell a value add.

- Function - Cannot be controlled by the salesperson.

- Availability - In many situations the salesperson can use this element if they have been involved and working with the prospect. If the customer doesn't need the product immediately, or if it is readily available from other sources, this element will not be as important as price. In some situations this element can make a commodity product a unique offering. The downside to maintaining a product's availability is the extraordinary investment required in inventory. You may have to carry excess quantities or line items which increase carrying costs and impede your ability to remain price competitive.

- Price - This is a tough element to impact, particularly if it only refers to the invoice price. You can often change the perception of price by how it is defined and what is included. You need to discuss price in terms that are favorable to your selling effort. I'll discuss this in more detail shortly.

- Terms - This is definitely an opportunity for value add. You can use terms to create a value added unique selling proposition. I'll discuss this in more detail later in this section.

- Service - This is another definite opportunity for value add. However, if service translates to something that costs you extra, make sure your customers can identify a specific value for the service they are receiving. If you don't establish a recognized value for the service, it will become an added expense without giving you a unique value add when it is copied by your competitors. Don't reduce your margin with no real sales advantage.

- <u>Quality</u> - This refers to product quality that a salesperson has little control impacting. Once a product is included in your inventory, you can't control its quality.

Based on these elements, price and terms are the two factors impacting the customer's buying decision. For the sake of this discussion I'll blend the two together and discuss them as price. As I mentioned earlier, price is usually dealt with by lowering it. I want to show you how price can be used to generate additional revenue and also make you unique.

The most productive way to create unique selling solutions and compete and win profitably is to use third party financing or leasing to sell price. In essence, use financial marketing to sell price.

Many companies will react to this idea by saying, Leasing. . . We offer leasing today, but it's not winning any business for us! They're probably right! But it's because they're offering leasing and not using financing to compete and win. In most cases, they offer financing based on a customer request, and the discussion takes place after the sale has been made. By then it's too late to use this marvelous tool to impact the sale or the margin made from the sale. Or they go to financing as a last ditch effort before losing the business.

It's easy to understand why financial marketing is not being used as the powerful sales tool it presents . . . most salespeople are not comfortable with financial marketing. They are not trained in how to use financial marketing and there are not marketing programs designed around the concept. Not being conversant in financial marketing, most salespeople and managers turn the deal over to a leasing company when the subject comes up.

The most important first step toward more profitable sales is to integrate a financial marketing approach into your day to day selling activity. This can be achieved by realizing that most small to medium size businesses are concerned with monthly cash flow. The ability to meet monthly cash requirements is always on the mind of the small business owner. By presenting your product in monthly cost terms to which your customer can relate, you will make it easier for them to buy from you.

For example, assume your product sells for $10,000, but that you regularly discount to $8,500. If your customer only has $7,000 in the bank they can't make a buying decision because the money isn't available. However, if you offer your product for less than $500 per month, you have created a different buying decision for your customer to make, and probably increased the odds of getting the order. In addition, because the small business is so concerned with cash flow, by making the buying decision easier and compatible with the owner's environment, you will increase your odds of winning.

You can also increase the revenue you realize from each transaction. Instead of computing the monthly rate based on the discounted price, use the list price. It's important to lead with a monthly fee that covers the lease price because your customers will probably want to negotiate to feel like they got a deal. You want to leave some room for negotiation.

Financial selling creates other inducements or offers you can make to your customer. For example, rather then discounting the purchase price, you could offer to make a month or two of the lease payments. This will give the customer an opportunity to use the product, generate revenue and incur no expense. This offer will probably be less expensive than the traditional discount you're already giving, therefore you'll actually generate more revenue and profit.

When you offer a financed approach you make it easier for the prospect to say yes while increasing the profit opportunities for your company.

Financial selling will allow you to make attractive offers to your prospects and customers that identify price in terms they can afford and understand. You can use direct marketing to attract prospects without fear of "sticker shock."

Financing is a unique value that meets the criteria for success and has been in your hip pocket all along. All you have to do is to turn it into a sales tool. You can do this by recognizing the opportunity to use lease based financial marketing to:

- Build a competitive edge
- Create demand
- Build the sale
- Compete on price

You and your competitors sell commodity products. As we have been discussing it is difficult to create a reason for your prospects to buy from you. You can use financial selling to build a competitive edge. All of your competitors are offering products for a price -- for a lump sum price. Why not begin to quote your price in terms of dollars per month?

As soon as you propose a financed purchase, you will immediately differentiate yourself from competition. You will probably find it easier to get your prospect to fill out a credit application than it is to close a sale.

Leasing, or monthly selling costs, make it easier to create desire for your product. Think about how you make decisions . . . you relate acquisition costs to your cash flow. This approach is even more important if your prospects are small businesses. And you can usually relate benefits that your product provides directly to monthly savings . . . whether the savings are displaceable, avoidable, or from increased revenue. Savings and revenue increases are more easily understood in terms of monthly savings and the costs associated with generating these opportunities are more easily explained in the same terms.

Lease based financial marketing can also help you create demand for your products by expanding the prospect base who may be able to purchase your products. Consider this: no matter how much you discount your product, if the customer doesn't have the cash or a line of credit available to purchase, it's impossible for them to make a buying decision. You can expand your selling opportunities by showing prospects how they use financing tools like leasing to acquire your products even when they don't have the funds immediately available. A discount may create additional interest, but an easy way to acquire your product with limited cash will create orders.

Using financial selling you can sell the complete configuration, or an advanced model with all of the nice to have features, by quoting the price in terms the prospect can afford. You can include service, support, and software in the total transaction and still be price competitive. And by building the total sale into an affordable monthly payment, the customer will get everything they need. You'll create higher margin. It's a true win/win situation.

Even when you sell based on a monthly lease price, customers who want to purchase outright can still buy your product. But by promoting and selling using a financed price, you'll position yourself closer to the way the prospect thinks. You'll be there first. And you'll have better credibility because you understand how their business operates which will produce a closer working relationship between you and the customer.

Your competitors are working on being the cheapest place to buy. You should work on being the easiest place to buy!

Financial marketing can be used to set your commodity product apart from your competition while increasing your profits. Easy buying terms are always in demand from your customers, and it will cost you little or nothing to implement. Terms can be altered to react to the changing needs of the marketplace or the changing needs of a particular customer. The key is to make the approach easy to understand and implement.

Getting the Salespeople Involved

I've described lease based financial marketing as a solution for creating a value add without risk. The real key to the success of this approach is selling your salespeople on *selling*. I have worked with several companies, from very large Fortune 500 corporations to small independently owned operations, and this approach works equally as well across a broad spectrum of businesses and industries.

The first obstacle to the success of financial based marketing is convincing the salesperson that this approach is *different*. They may not perceive financial based marketing as being different than their current approach to selling. Many salespeople believe that their current approach to selling is just as effective and unique. Therefore it is extremely important that your sales force understand my earlier discussion about the marketplace. You have to gain their agreement that what is being used today to differentiate and establish a competitive advantage is not getting the job done at the highest possible profit margin.

Many salespeople will argue that they don't need to understand this type of selling. If you don't get them to agree that they have to generate higher margins and improve their competitive advantage, you'll hear a lot of complaints like: why bother? or Nobody else is doing it this way! If you get this kind of feedback after setting the stage, then you have to work harder on selling them on the importance of being unique and generating as much profit as possible. It is important that they agree that there has to be a better way to compete than by simply giving away all of the profit in the transaction.

Now that you've got their attention and involvement, find out what your sales force thinks are their customer's buying criteria. You'll probably be surprised by this conversation. Having conducted several of such training sessions, I have learned to sit back and let the salespeople fight until they have tired themselves out. I was initially shocked to see experienced salespeople, selling the same product to the same types of customers, violently disagree about the true decision criteria in their marketplace.

I now believe, after several years of observation and analysis, that salespeople identify the customers buying criteria based on the areas:

a) They are most comfortable dealing with, or
b) That won or lost a sale for them the last time they were in a competitive situation

Once you're able to establish agreement on the buying criteria, ask the salespeople to rank them in order of importance. You will probably have to lead the group to complete the list of criteria. You may recall my discussion and the example in Illustration 16-3 on page 787.

Work with the group on ranking the list of criteria first on its importance to the customer and then on their ability to impact the customer's perception and reaction to each criteria. In every situation I've observed the salespeople identify very little ability to influence price. During all discussions about price, you should stress the requirement that the item sold must produce enough profit to justify making the sale.

With the criteria listed and ranked, you can now begin to have fruitful conversations about how you can sell around the various criteria. Price is always ranked high by the salespeople and low in their ability to impact, so you'll have the perfect environment to introduce financial marketing. You can expect a great deal of skepticism, perhaps similar to your reaction when this idea was first introduced.

However, once the salespeople begin to evaluate the opportunity and results this approach can yield, they'll be more receptive to learning more. If you relate how they make their own buying decisions using their home and car as practical examples, they'll become strong believers.

You can get the salespeople fully involved by using practical examples to prove your point. The best way to demonstrate the value of financial marketing is to create live examples using situations you recently lost. Work with the group on how much better you could have presented the price if you had used a lease and packaged offering.

Your leasing company or broker can help you prepare for this training session by creating the examples prior to the meeting. Many leasing company representatives and brokers prefer to provide just the rate and documentation. You should demand more. Most of these people are professionals and can help you create unique and innovative value added offerings.

If you're not getting this kind of service, ask your leasing representative or broker to assist you. If the performance is not satisfactory,
get another representative, even if you have to change companies.
Remember, a leasing company or broker is selling a commodity
product -- money -- and it's up to them to make it unique for you.
They have to sell value add too.

Several things you should remember in dealing with a leasing
company or broker:

- Once you decide to use a leasing company, they should
  become your partner. You both should be fully committed
  to one another. Work with them on developing unique solutions for your customers.   Loyalty can buy a lot of flexibility on the part of the leasing company.

- No company wants to spend its creativity on you only to
  have you go elsewhere to get a lower rate. Most financial
  transactions are not rate sensitive because most rates are
  about the same. Exceptions to this occur in a very large
  lease or if a very large company is requesting the lease.
  Creativity can overcome small rate differences.

- Leases can be configured differently. Creative ways of
  packaging the offer include adjusting the down payment,
  term (number of months), buy out rules, or periodic payment vacations to account for the seasonality of your customers business. These configuration differences can be
  extremely important for you to be responsive to the needs of
  your customer. They can make you unique and add value to
  the transaction. Your leasing company or broker plays an
  active and important role in making financial marketing a
  value add.

If your leasing company cannot or will not work with you on creating an individualized package that allows you to be unique, change companies. The leasing representative or broker that only drops off the rates and documentation is of no use to you. You have to work with someone who can blend their background of financial marketing with your product, sales team, and customers to create the proper offer that will make a difference for you.

Implementing this approach will take hard work. As I mentioned earlier, success is directly related to your ability to sell your sales people on selling. The salespeople have to believe in and sell using financial marketing.

Too many salespeople are comfortable calling on the same people and competing in the same way. Financial marketing decisions may not be able to be made at the current contact level. Your salespeople will have to learn how to find and sell the appropriate person within the company. Most of the time the current contact can introduce you to the appropriate person. This can help the person look good inside the company and help you meet another contact within the company.

This sounds so easy, but many salespeople are not comfortable going within a company to talk about a subject they're not really comfortable with. You can take some of the pressure off initially by having the leasing representative or broker go along with your salesperson on the first call or two. This is another area where loyalty to one financing source can pay dividends to you.

You'll need to to assist the day-to-day territory implementation of financial marketing as well. You should develop marketing support materials that also tell the financial marketing story specific to your product(s). Again, the leasing company can help you create these materials.

Tracking the salespeople can help you complement success and correct weaknesses. Create a prospect tracking form. Include on it a section on financial marketing containing questions like:

1. What is the monthly cost of the purchase?
2. What is the monthly financial benefit, agreed to by the prospect, of buying the product?
3. Using only agreed upon dollars, tell me why the prospect should buy the product.
4. What is the competitions cost per month?
5. What financial terms are important to the customer?

You'll continue to search for other ways to be unique and add value. Virtually anything you do will add expense and ultimately be copied by your competitors. Financial marketing can address what is perceived as the most important decision criteria by salespeople while adding profit margin.

Convincing your sales force that financial selling is different and adds value is difficult. Training your salespeople to be comfortable can be painful. Implementing and managing financial marketing will add work in managing the outside financial provider. But no other effort can produce as much differentiation and uniqueness that can be implemented relatively quickly without radically changing your company and products.

Creating a Unique Selling Proposition Summarized

Companies are being continually challenged on how to become known and unique in their markets. Most can't afford to develop totally unique products and are often selling commodities that are offered by other companies. The challenge is to create the perception of being known and unique in the mind of the prospect.

This communication challenge is further compounded by the price performance of technology. The dramatic reduction in the price of technology in the last few years has adversely effected the margin dollars in many industries. This phenomenon has occurred while the cost of selling has continued to escalate. Companies are struggling with how to sustain profits in light of this two edged sword.

The following changes are placing tremendous pressure on traditional sales activity.

- Cloning can rob products of their uniqueness.

- Reduced profit margins make it more difficult to develop true product differentiation.

- Customers and vendors are using price as the primary buying criteria.

- Sales skills are deteriorating due to lack of use.

Even products that are initially unique and different only enjoy a short period with a competitive advantage. Many companies will quickly create clones of the original product and then sell them at a fraction of the cost. Therefore, most products quickly become commodities with the only differentiation being price.

Companies combat this commodity syndrome by attempting to add additional ingredients to the product package. Unfortunately, any value add that is worthwhile, is quickly copied by competition. Price again becomes the differentiation.

The result is added cost with no incremental revenue. The real clincher is that if a value added service is of true significance to the marketplace, most competitors will be forced to offer the same service. What starts as a way to distinguish one vendor from another, becomes an *I've got it too* offering available from any legitimate supplier. This cloning of a value added package has the same impact as the cloning of a product.

How then do you compete? What can your organization do to distinguish itself from competitors offering similar products to the same prospects at the same price?

The answer is to create value that is:

- In constant demand from your customers
- No or low cost to create and implement
- Dynamic and responsive to the needs of the marketplace
- Easy to understand and use

Before you can develop a formula that will meet these criteria, you should understand what typically motivates people to buy. After discussions with hundreds of salespeople I have concluded that there are 7 major factors in a prospect's buying decision.

1) <u>Function</u> - Will the product offered do the job required by the prospect?
2) <u>Availability</u> - Is the product available in the time frame acceptable to the customer?
3) <u>Price</u> - How much does it cost?
4) <u>Terms</u> - When and how does the vendor expect payment?
5) <u>Service</u> - How quickly can it be repaired if it breaks?
6) <u>Quality</u> - How often is it going to break?
7) <u>Salesmanship</u> - How much can the "from whom to buy decision" be influenced by the sales representative?

Based on these elements, price and terms are the two factors most susceptible to sales influence in impacting the customer's buying decision. For the sake of this discussion I'll blend the two together and discuss them as price. The most productive way to create unique selling solutions and compete and win profitably is to use third party financing or leasing to sell price. In essence, use financial marketing to sell price.

When you offer a financed approach you make it easier for the prospect to say yes while increasing the profit opportunities for your company.

Financial selling will allow you to make attractive offers to your prospects and customers that identify price in terms they can afford and understand. Financing is a unique value that meets the criteria for success, and you can use lease based financial marketing to:

- Build a competitive edge
- Create demand
- Build the sale
- Compete on price

Your competitors are working on being the cheapest place to buy. You should work on being the easiest place to buy!

The first obstacle to the success of financial based marketing is convincing the salesperson that this approach is *different*. They may not perceive financial based marketing as being different than their current approach to selling.

You can get the salespeople fully involved by using practical examples to prove your point. The best way to demonstrate the value of financial marketing is to create live examples using situations you recently lost. Work with the group on how much better you could have presented the price if you had used a lease and packaged offering.

Implementing this approach will take hard work. As I mentioned earlier, success is directly related to your ability to sell your sales people on selling. The salespeople have to believe in and sell using financial marketing.

You'll continue to search for other ways to be unique and add value. Virtually anything you do will add expense and ultimately be copied by your competitors. Financial marketing can address what is perceived as the most important decision criteria by salespeople, while adding profit margin.

About Lane Wolbe:

Lane Wolbe spent 20 years with the IBM Corporation in marketing and sales of business computers. He was a Regional Manager in the Product Center organization after successful stints as a salesperson, sales manager, sales training instructor, marketing planning manager, and branch manager.

Lane moved to Nynex when they purchased the product centers from IBM. He created and implemented the first chain backed national trade-in program for PCs. During the past several years he has managed his own consulting and financial services firm, WOLCO. He specializes in working with both small and large companies showing them how to use financial terms and conditions to improve sales and profits.

A native of Atlanta, he is a graduate of Vanderbilt University and a former captain of their football team. Lane's company is in Atlanta where he and his wife reside.

Appendix I

Creating a Lead Planning Model

This section provides the formulas for you to create your own lead planning model using a standard spreadsheet program like Lotus 1,2,3 or Microsoft Excel.

Chapter 14 explained how to use the model and the various elements. You may find it useful to create the model on your own computer system and then follow the examples illustrated in the chapter. This will show you how various elements work and you can also check your results.

The following templet allows you to create the spreadsheet in a similar format to the examples. The first three pages represent the data entry section, while the following four pages are the results calculated based on your input. The last page of this section contains the formatting for the various cells.

	A	B	C	D	E	F	G
1							
2		**Assumptions and Known Variables**					
3			1	2	3	4	Total
4	A	*Current Cost per Sales Call*					
5							
6	B	*Allowable Cost per Qualified Lead*					
7							
8	C	*Gross Margin*					
9							
10		*One Time Costs*					
11	D	Creative costs/project					
12	E	Management Costs/project					
13							
14		*List Information*					
15	F	List Identification Code					
16	G	List Name					
17	H	Quantity Mailed					

	A	B	C	D	E	F	G
18	I	Average Order Size					
19							
20							
21		*Variable Costs per Name Mailed or Contacted*					
22	J	Fulfillment Costs per Responder					
23	K	Phone Follow-up Costs					
24	L	Premium or Incentive					
25	M	List Cost or minimum per name					
26	N	Print/Production/Mail					
27	P	Postage					
28	Q	Fulfillment	=IF(C$22<>" ", IF(C22+C23-C24>0, (C$22+(C$23*(1+(1-C31)))+C$24)*0.015," "), " ")	=IF(D$22<>" ", IF(D22+D23+D24>0, (D$22+(D$23*(1+(1-D31)))+D$24)*0.015, " "), " ")	=IF(E$22<>" ", IF(E22+E23+E24>0, (E$22+(E$23*(1+(1-E31)))+E$24)*0.015, " "), " ")	=IF(F$22<>" ", IF(F22+F23+F24>0, (F$22+(F$23*(1+(1-F31)))+F$24)*0.015, " "), " ")	
29							
30		*Response Rates and Conversion Rates*					
31	R	% of responders qualified as leads					
32	S	% of resp not qualif converting to leads					

	A	B	C	D	E	F	G
33	T	% of leads that order					
34							
35		*Sales Calls*					
36	U	Number of Sales Calls per Close					
37	V	Number of Sales Calls to lose order					
38							
39							
40		© 1991 Direct Marketing Publishers, Inc.	(215) 321-3068				
41							
42							

	A	B	C	D	E	F	G
43		**Program Analysis**					
44			1	2	3	4	Total
45		List Identification Code	=C15	=D15	=E15	=F15	
46		List Name	=C16	=D16	=E16	=F16	
47	AA	Quantity Mailed	=C17	=D17	=E17	=F17	=IF(SUM(C47:F47)>0, SUM(C47:F47)," ")
48	BB	List Costs (M x AA)	=IF(C47<>"", ROUND(C25*C$47,0), " ")	=IF(D47<>"", ROUND(D25*D$47,0), " ")	=IF(E47<>"", ROUND(E25*E$47,0), " ")	=IF(F47<>"", ROUND(F25*F$47,0), " ")	=IF(SUM(C48:F48)>0, SUM(C48:F48)," ")
49	CC	Print/Prod/Mail (N x AA)	=IF(C47<>"", ROUND(C26*C$47,0), " ")	=IF(D47<>"", ROUND(D26*D$47,0), " ")	=IF(E47<>"", ROUND(E26*E$47,0), " ")	=IF(F47<>"", ROUND(F26*F$47,0), " ")	=IF(SUM(C49:F49)>0, SUM(C49:F49)," ")
50	DD	Postage (P x AA)	=IF(C47<>"", ROUND(C27*C$47,0), " ")	=IF(D47<>"", ROUND(D27*D$47,0), " ")	=IF(E47<>"", ROUND(E27*E$47,0), " ")	=IF(F47<>"", ROUND(F27*F$47,0), " ")	=IF(SUM(C50:F50)>0, SUM(C50:F50)," ")
51	EE	Fulfillment (Q x AA)	=IF(C47<>"", ROUND(C28*C$47,0), " ")	=IF(D47<>"", ROUND(D28*D$47,0), " ")	=IF(E47<>"", ROUND(E28*E$47,0), " ")	=IF(F47<>"", ROUND(F28*F$47,0), " ")	=IF(SUM(C51:F51)>0, SUM(C51:F51)," ")
52	FF	*Total Direct Marketing Expenses*	=IF(SUM(C48:C51)>0, SUM(C48:C51)," ")	=IF(SUM(D48:D51)>0, SUM(D48:D51)," ")	=IF(SUM(E48:E51)>0, SUM(E48:E51)," ")	=IF(SUM(F48:F51)>0, SUM(F48:F51)," ")	=IF(SUM(G48:G51)>0, SUM(G48:G51)," ")
53							

	A	B	C	D	E	F	G
54	GG	Allowable Cost per Qualified Lead (B)	=If(C47<>"",G6,"")	=If(D47<>"",G6,"")	=If(E47<>"",G6,"")	=If(F47<>"",G6,"")	
55	HH	% of Responders qualified as leads (R)	=If(C47<>"",C31,"")	=If(D47<>"",D31,"")	=If(E47<>"",E31,"")	=If(F47<>"",F31,"")	
56	II	% of Resp not qual as leads (1-HH)	=If(C47<>"",1-C55,"")	=If(D47<>"",1-D55,"")	=If(E47<>"",1-E55,"")	=If(F47<>"",1=F55,"")	
57	JJ	% of of not qual resp conv leads (II x S)	=If(C47<>"", C56*C32,"")	=If(D47<>"", D56*D32,"")	=If(E47<>"", E56*E32,"")	=If(F47<>"", F56*F32,"")	
58	KK	Total Lead/Response % (II + JJ)	=If(C47<>"", C55+C57,"")	=If(D47<>"", D55+D57,"")	=If(E47<>"", E55+E57,"")	=If(F47<>"", E55+E57,"")	
59	LL	Allowable Cost per Response (GG x KK)	=If(C47<>"", ROUND(C54*C58,2), "")	=If(D47<>"", ROUND(D54*D58,2), "")	=If(E47<>"", ROUND(E54*E58,2), "")	=If(F47<>"", ROUND(F54*F58,2), "")	
60	MM	*Required Responses* (FF + LL)	=If(C55<>"", ROUND(C52/C59,0), "")	=If(D55<>"", ROUND(D52/D59,0), "")	=If(E55<>"", ROUND(E52/E59,0), "")	=If(F55<>"", ROUND(F52/F59,0), "")	=If(SUM(C60:F60)<> "",SUM(C60:F60), "")
61	OO	Required response % (MM + AA)	=If(C60<>"", ROUND(C60/C47,4), "")	=If(D60<>"", ROUND(D60/D47,4), "")	=If(E60<>"", ROUND(E60/E47,4), "")	=If(F60<>"", ROUND(F60/F47,4), "")	=If(G60<>"", ROUND(G60/G47,4), "")
62							
63	PP	Leads Initially (MM x HH)	=If(C60<>"", ROUND(C60*C55,0), "")	=If(D60<>"", ROUND(D60*D55,0), "")	=If(E60<>"", ROUND(E60*E55,0), "")	=If(F60<>"", ROUND(F60*F55,0), "")	=IF(SUM(C63:F63<>0, SUM(C63:F63), "")

	A	B	C	D	E	F	G
64	QQ	Responders for Fulfillment (MM - PP)	=If(C60<>"", C60-C63,"")	=If(D60<>"", D60-D63,"")	=If(E60<>"", E60-E63,"")	=If(F60<>"", F60-F63,"")	=If(SUM(C64:F64)<>"",SUM(C64:F64),"")
65	RR	Leads from Fulfillment (QQ x S)	=If(C64<>"", ROUND(C64*C32,0),"")	=If(D64<>"", ROUND(D64*D32,0),"")	=If(E64<>"", ROUND(E64*E32,0),"")	=If(F64<>"", ROUND(F64*F32,0),"")	=If(SUM(C65:F65)<>"",SUM(C65:F65),"")
66	SS	Total Leads (PP + RR)	=If(C63<>"", C65+C63,"")	=If(D63<>"", D65+D63,"")	=If(E63<>"", E65+E63,"")	=If(F63<>"", F65+F63,"")	=If(SUM(C66:F66)<>"",SUM(C66:F66),"")
67							
68	TT	Orders (T x SS)	=IF(C47<>"", ROUND(C66*C33,0),"")	=IF(D47<>"", ROUND(D66*D33,0),"")	=IF(E47<>"", ROUND(E66*E33,0),"")	=IF(F47<>"", ROUND(F66*F33,0),"")	=If(SUM(C68:F68)<>"",SUM(C68:F68),"")
69							
70	UU	Number of Sales Calls-Orders (U x SS)	=IF(C47<>"", ROUND(C68*C36,0),"")	=IF(D47<>"", ROUND(D68*D36,0),"")	=IF(E47<>"", ROUND(E68*E36,0),"")	=IF(F47<>"", ROUND(F68*F36,0),"")	=If(SUM(C70:F70)<>"",SUM(C70:F70),"")
71	VV	No. Sls Calls-Non-orders (V x (SS-TT))	=IF(C47<>"", ROUND((C66-C68)* C37,0),"")	=IF(D47<>"", ROUND((D66-D68)* D37,0),"")	=IF(E47<>"", ROUND((E66-E68)* E37,0),"")	=IF(F47<>"", ROUND((F66-F68)* F37,0),"")	=If(SUM(C71:F71)<>"",SUM(C71:F71),"")
72	WW	Total Sales Calls	=IF(C47<>"", C71+C70,"")	=IF(D47<>"", D71+D70,"")	=IF(E47<>"", E71+E70,"")	=IF(F47<>"", F71+F70,"")	=If(SUM(C72:F72)<>"",SUM(C72:F72),"")
73							

	A	B	C	D	E	F	G
74	XX	*Revenue* (I x WW)	=IF(C47<>"", C68*C18,"")	=IF(D47<>"", D68*D18,"")	=IF(E47<>"", E68*E18,"")	=IF(F47<>"", F68*F18,"")	=If(SUM(C74:F74)<>"", SUM(C74:F74),"")
75							
76	YY	Gross Margin (XX x C)	=IF(C47<>"", C74*G8,"")	=IF(D47<>"", D74*G8,"")	=IF(E47<>"", E74*G8,"")	=IF(F47<>"", F74*G8,"")	=If(SUM(C76:F76)<>"", SUM(C76:F76),"")
77							
78	ZZ	Sales Call Expenses (WW x A)	=IF(C47<>"", C72*G4,"")	=IF(D47<>"", D72*G4,"")	=IF(E47<>"", E72*G4,"")	=IF(F47<>"", F72*G4,"")	=If(SUM(C78:F78)<>"", SUM(C78:F78),"")
79	BA	Direct Marketing Expenses (FF)	=IF(C47<>"", C52,"")	=IF(D47<>"", D52,"")	=IF(E47<>"", E52,"")	=IF(F47<>"", F52,"")	=If(SUM(C79:F79)<>"", SUM(C79:F79),"")
80	BB	Total Selling Expenses (ZZ + BA)	=IF(C47<>"", C78+C79,"")	=IF(D47<>"", D78+D79,"")	=IF(E47<>"", E78+E79,"")	=IF(F47<>"", F78+F79,"")	=If(SUM(C80:F80)<>"", SUM(C80:F80),"")
81	BC	Contribution (YY - BB)	=IF(C47<>"", C76-C80,"")	=IF(D47<>"", D76-D80,"")	=IF(E47<>"", E76-E80,"")	=IF(F47<>"", F76-F80,"")	=If(SUM(C81:F81)<>"", SUM(C81:F81),"")
82	BD	% Contribution (BC + XX)	=IF(C47<>"", C81/C74,"")	=IF(D47<>"", D81/D74,"")	=IF(E47<>"", E81/E74,"")	=IF(F47<>"", F81/F74,"")	=If(SUM(C82:F82)<>"", SUM(C82:F82),"")

In most spreadsheet programs you can also format each cell to present numeric information. The columns of the spreadsheet are identified by the alphabetic character. Rows are identified by number.

Cell	Format	Method of Calculation

The following cells will contain fixed information that you will develop and enter:

Cell	Format	Method of Calculation
G4	$0,000 ($, no decimal)	None
G6	$0,000	None
G8	0.00% (%, no add'l decimals)	None
G11	$0,000	None
G12	$0,000	None

Columns C, D, E, F will have information entered for each test cell you are creating.

Cell	Format	Method of Calculation
Row 15	Text	None
Row 16	Text	None
Row 17	0,000 (comma no decimals)	None
Row 18	$0,000	None
Row 22	$0,000.000	None
Row 23	$0,000.000	None
Row 24	$0,000.000	None
Row 25	$0,000.000	None
Row 26	$0,000.000	None
Row 27	$0,000.000	None
Row 28	$0,000.000	Automatic
Row 31	00%	None
Row 32	00%	None
Row 33	00%	None
Row 36	0.0	None
Row 37	0.0	None

The results section of the spreadsheet (Rows 43 to 82) contains information calculated from the data you provided. These rows should be formatted to display the information so it's easy to read and understand.

Cell	Format	Method of Calculation
Row 45	Text	Automatic
Row 46	Text	Automatic
Row 47	$0,000	Automatic
Row 48	$0,000	Automatic
Row 49	$0,000	Automatic
Row 50	$0,000	Automatic
Row 51	$0,000	Automatic
Row 52	$0,000	Automatic
Row 54	$0,000	Automatic
Row 55	00.0%	Automatic

Cell	Format	Method of Calculation
Row 56	00.0%	Automatic
Row 57	00.0%	Automatic
Row 58	00.0%	Automatic
Row 59	00.0%	Automatic
Row 60	000	Automatic
Row 61	00.00%	Automatic
Row 63	000	Automatic
Row 64	000	Automatic
Row 65	000	Automatic
Row 66	000	Automatic
Row 67	000	Automatic
Row 68	000	Automatic
Row 69	000	Automatic
Row 70	000	Automatic
Row 71	000	Automatic
Row 72	000	Automatic
Row 74	$0,000	Automatic
Row 75	$0,000	Automatic
Row 76	$0,000	Automatic
Row 77	$0,000	Automatic
Row 78	$0,000	Automatic
Row 79	$0,000	Automatic
Row 80	$0,000	Automatic
Row 81	$0,000	Automatic
Row 82	00.0%	Automatic

Glossary

Access Charge: A fee for the use of local telephone lines.

Access Line: A telephone circuit that links a customer location to a network switching center.

Access Time: The time it takes a computer to locate a piece of information in memory or storage and to take action, i.e., the "read" time. Also, the time it takes a computer to store a piece of information and to complete action, i.e., the "write" time.

ACD: *See Automatic Call Director.*

Action Devices: Items and techniques used in a mailing to initiate the response desired.

Active Buyer: A buyer whose latest purchase was made within the last 12 months. *(See also Buyer.)*

Active Customer: A term used interchangeably with "active buyer."

Active Member: Any member who is fulfilling the original commitment or who has fulfilled that commitment and has made one or more purchases in the last 12 months.

Active Subscriber: One who has agreed to receive periodic delivery of magazines, books or other goods or services for a period of time that has not yet expired.

Actives: Customers on a list who have made purchases within a prescribed time period, usually not more than one year; subscribers whose subscriptions have not expired.

Added Value: Offering a service to your product to distinguish it from your competitor's. For example, a software distributor who offers training on the software they sell is offering added value.

Additions: New names, either of individuals or companies, added to a mailing list.

Add-On Service: A service of the Direct Marketing Association (DMA) which gives consumers an opportunity to request that their names be added to mailing lists.

Address Coding Guide (CG): A guide which contains the actual or potential beginning and ending house numbers, block group and/or enumeration district numbers, zip codes, and other geographic codes for all city delivery service streets served by 3,154 post offices located within 6,601 zip codes.

Address Correction Requested: An endorsement which, when printed in the upper left-hand corner of the address portion of the mail-ing piece (below return address), authorizes the U.S. Postal Service, for a fee, to provide the new address of a person no longer at the address on the mailing piece.

A.I.D.A.: The most popular formula for the preparation of direct mail copy. The letters stand for Get Attention, Arouse Interest, Stimulate Desire, Ask for Action.

Alphanumeric: A contraction of "alphabetic" and "numeric". Applies to any coding system that provides for letters, numbers (digits), and special symbols such as punctuation marks. Synonymous with Alphameric.

Assigned Mailing Dates: The dates on which the list user has the obligation to mail a specific list. No other date is acceptable without specific approval from the list owner.

Assumptive Close: When a communicator assumes the customer is going to buy and begins asking questions about the order. *You use twelve ribbons per year. Would you like them shipped monthly, or quarterly?*

Audience: The total number of individuals reached by a promotion or advertisement.

Authorization Code: An identification number the caller enters when placing a call. The number is generally used for billing purposes, customer/user validation and/or security.

Automatic Call Director or Distributor (ACD): A computerized approach to handling inbound calls. The ACD directs calls, in the order they are received to an inbound communicator. If all communicators are busy, the ACD plays a tape recording and directs the call to the next available communicator. This system typically will generate extensive production reports.

Average Order Size: A simple arithmetic formula used to establish the average order size. The total revenue generated from a program divided by the total number of orders will establish the average order size.

Avoidable Expenses: Dollars that a prospect can avoid spending if they purchase your product or service.

Back-End: The conversion of a direct marketing respondent to a buyer, and a buyer to a repeat buyer. Also, the activities to complete a mail order transaction. Can define the measurement of: a buyers performance after he has ordered the first item in a series; prospects who become leads; performance toward purchasing. (*See also Front-End.*)

Batch Processing: Techniques of executing a set of computer programs/selections in batches as opposed to executing each order/selection as it is received. Batches can be programmed or created manually by collecting data in groups.

Batched Job: A job that is grouped with other jobs as input to a computer system, as opposed to a transaction job entry where each job is run individually to completion.

Bill Enclosure: Any promotional piece or notice enclosed with a bill, an invoice or a statement not directed toward the collection of all or part of the bill, invoice or statement.

Bingo Card: A reply card inserted in a publication and used by readers to request literature from companies whose products and services are either advertised or mentioned in editorial columns.

Bounce Back: An offer enclosed with a mailing sent to a customer in fulfillment of an offer.

BRC: Business Reply Card.

BRE: Business Reply Envelope.

Breakeven: The point in a business transaction when income and expenses are equal.

Broadcast Media: A direct response source that includes radio, television and cable TV.

Broadside: A single sheet of paper, printed on one side or two, folded for mailing or direct distribution, and opening into a single, large advertisement.

Brochure: A high-quality pamphlet, with specifically planned layout, typography and illustrations. This term is also used loosely to describe any promotional pamphlet or booklet.

Bulk Mail: A category of Third Class Mail involving a large quantity of identical pieces which are addressed to different names for mailing before delivery to post office.

Business List: Any compilation or list of individuals or companies based upon a business-associated interest, inquiry, membership, subscription or purchase.

Business-Person: Telemarketing; A person who will be contacted at his office or place of business, usually during the business day.

Business Planning: Putting on paper all the facts you have at your disposal.

C/A: Change of Address.

Call Detail Reporting (CDR): An automated approach to capturing and reporting on the detail telephone activity by extension in a business. In essence, CDR creates a detailed phone bill by extension.

Card Deck: A collection of 3" x 5" cards gathered in a wrap, bound together or placed in an envelope.

Carrier Route: Grouping of addresses based on the delivery route of each letter carrier. The average number of stops is 400 but does range from under 100 to 3,000. There are about 180,000 carrier routes in the United States.

Cash Buyer: A buyer who encloses payment with order.

Cash Rider: Also called "cash up" or "cash option" wherein an order form offers installment terms, but a postscript offers the option of sending full cash payment with order, usually at some saving over credit price as an incentive.

Catalog: Any promotion that offers more than one product. Frequently, a catalog is described as a book or booklet showing merchandise with descriptive details and prices.

Catalog Buyer: A person who has bought products or services from a catalog.

Catalog Request: (Paid or Unpaid). One who sends for a catalog (prospective buyer). The catalog may be free; there may be a nominal charge for postage and handling, or there may be a more substantial charge that is offer refunded or credited on the first order.

CDR: *See Call Detail Reporting.*

Cell(s): In list terminology, a statistical unit or units. A group of individuals selected from a file on a consistent basis.

Centrex: A service offered by most local telephone companies which provides the features and functions of a PBX, but the actual equipment is installed in the phone company's central office, rather than at the customer site.

Cheshire Label: Specially prepared paper (rolls, fanfold or accordion fold) on which names and addresses are printed to be mechanically affixed, one at a time, to a mailing piece.

Circulars: General term for printed advertisement in any form, including printed matter sent out by direct mail.

Cleaning: The process of correcting and/or removing a name and address from a mailing list because it is no longer correct or because the listing is to be shifted from one category to another.

Closed Face Envelope: An

envelope that is addressed directly on the face, and does not have a die-cut window.

Closing Rate: The percentage of sales calls that result in a an order.

Coding: (1) Identifying marks used on reply devices to identify the mailing list or other source from which the address was obtained. (2) A structure of letters and numbers used to classify characteristics of an address on a list.

Collate: (1) To assemble individual elements of a mailing in sequence for inserting into a mailing envelope. (2) A program which combines two or more ordered files to produce a single ordered file. Also the act of combining such files. Synonymous with merges as in Merge/Purge.

Commission: A percentage of sale, by prior agreement, paid to the list broker, list manager, or other service arm for their part in the list usage.

Commodity Products: Products whose function is readily available in the market-

place from multiple vendors at about the same price.

Common Carrier: A government regulated long-distance telecommunications company that provides the general public with telecommunications services and facilities.

Compile: The process by which a computer translates a series of instructions written in a programming language into actual machine language.

Compiled List: Names and addresses derived from directories, newspapers, public records, retail sales slips, trade show registrations, or other sources, which identify groups of people with something in common.

Compiler: Organization which develops lists of names and addresses from directories, newspapers, public records, registrations, and other sources, identifying groups of people, companies, or institutions with something in common.

Completed Calls: An outbound call in which the target had been contacted and had made a decision concerning the offer. The prospect either accepted the offer, rejected the offer, requested additional information, remained uncertain, or refused to complete the call and, in essence, refused the offer.

Completed Cancel: One who has completed a specific commitment to buy products or services before cancelling.

Comprehensive: Complete and detailed layout for a printed piece. Also: "Comp," "Compre."

Completed Contact: Contacting the prospect and getting a decision on the offer.

Computer Letter: Computer-printed message providing personalized, fill-in information from a source file in pre-designated positions. May also be full-printed letter with personalized insertions.

Computer Personalization: Printing of letters or other promotional pieces by a computer using names, addresses, special phrases, or other information based on data appearing in one or more computer records. The

objective is to use the information in the computer record to tailor the promotional message to a specific individual.

Computer Program: Series of instructions or statements prepared to achieve a certain result.

Computer Record: All the information about an individual, company, or transaction stored on a specific magnetic tape or disk.

Computer Service Bureau: An internal or external facility providing general or specific data processing services.

Computerized Scripting: Software which displays appropriate script copy on a cathode ray tube based on the responses entered into the terminal by a communicator.

Conditioning: Sustained selling activity directed toward a prospect by both marketing and sales.

Consumer: Telemarketing; A person who will be contacted at his residence, usually during evening and weekend hours.

Consumer List: A list of names (usually at home

addresses) compiled, or resulting, from a common inquiry or buying activity indicating a general or specific buying interest.

Continuation: The next step after a list test. If the test proved responsive within established financial parameters, the list should be reordered.

Continuity Program: Products or services bought as a series of small purchases, rather than all at one time. Generally based on a common theme and shipped at regular or specific time intervals.

Contribution: A term that describes the amount of gross profit made by a specific activity. In essence, it is the gross profit of a project after allowing for cost of goods and cost of selling including commissions

Contributor List: Names and addresses of persons who have given to a specific fund-raising effort. *(See also Donor List.)*

Controlled Circulation: Distribution of a publication at no charge to individuals or companies on the basis of their titles or occupations. Typically, recipients are asked from time to time to verify the information that qualifies them to receive the publication.

Controlled Duplication: A method by which names and addresses from two or more lists are matched (usually by computer) in order to eliminate or limit extra mailings to the same name and address.

Controlled Subscription: *See Controlled Circulation.*

Conversion: (1) Process of changing from one method of data processing to another, or from one data processing system to another. Synonymous with reformatting. (2) To secure specific action such as a purchase or contribution from a name on a mailing list or as a result of an inquiry.

Co-op Mailing: A mailing of two or more offers included in the same envelope or other carrier, with each participating mailer sharing mailing costs according to some predetermined formula.

Copy: The words and graphics used to communicate offers

to a market.

Cornercard: The return address information printed in the upper-left had corner of an envelope.

Cost Per Inquiry (C.P.I.): A simple arithmetical formula derived by dividing the total cost of a mailing or an advertisement by the number of inquiries received.

Cost Per Order (C.P.O.): A simple arithmetical formula derived by dividing the total cost of a direct marketing campaign by the number of orders received. Similar to Cost per Inquiry, except based on actual orders rather than inquiries.

Cost Per Thousand (C.P.M.): Refers to the total cost-per-thousand pieces of direct mail "in the mail".

Coupon: Part of an advertising promotion piece intended to be filled in by the inquirer or customer and returned to the advertiser.

Coupon Clipper: One who has given evidence of responding to free or nominal-cost offers out of curiosity, with little or no serious interest or buying intent.

C.P.I.: *See Cost Per Inquiry.*

C.P.M.: *See Cost Per Thousand.*

C.P.O.: *See Cost Per Order.*

Creative Aspects: The big ideas that clothe your information to make it more appealing to its market.

C.T.O.: Contribution to overhead (profit).

Customer: Individuals who have purchased products or services from you.

Data: A representation of facts, concepts, or instructions in a formal manner suitable for communication, interpretation, or processing either manually or automatically.

Database: The structure for storing and controlling the relationship information between a company and its customers. Within direct marketing, a database will provide a means to contact a group of prospects, a method to measure respondents to the direct marketing effort, a method to measure purchasers, and a method to provide continuing communications.

Decoy: A unique name especially inserted in a mailing list for verifying usage.

Demographics: Socio-economic characteristics pertaining to a geographic unit (county, city, sectional center, zip Code, group of households, education, ethnicity, income level, etc.).

Dimensional Mailings: Generally large mailings in a three-dimensional sense; they are packages or fat letters that have a tendency to get put on the top of a prospect's mail pile.

Direct Access: An access mode in which records are obtained from, or placed into, a mass storage file in a non-sequential manner so that any record can be rapidly accessed. Synonymous with Random Access.

Direct-inward-dialing (DID): A telephone capability providing individual's direct lines to the their office's, while still permitting calls to go through the company switchboard.

Direct Mail Advertising: Any promotional effort using the postal service, or other direct delivery service, for distribution of the advertising message.

Direct Marketing: An organized and planned system of contacts, using a variety of media, seeking to produce a lead or an order. It requires the development and maintenance of a database, is measurable in costs and results, and is effective in all methods of selling.

Direct Marketing Association (DMA): The primary trade association for direct marketing.

Direct Response Advertising: Advertising, through any medium, designed to generate a measurable response by any means, such as mail, telephone, or telegraph.

Directive Questions: Questions which guide a customer's talking that cannot be answered with a 'yes' or 'no'. *Who do you get your various cleaning supplies from now?*

Disk Processing: In data processing, data is stored in tracks on a rotating magnetic surface. A movable arm is directed to a specific track location. As the rotating surface passes under the access arm, the required data is read.

Displaceable Expenses: Dollars already being expended

for similar or like services that can be eliminated if they purchase your product or service.

DMA: *See Direct Marketing Association.*

DMA Mail Preference Service: *See Mail Preference Service.*

Donor List: A list of persons who have given money to one or more charitable organizations. *(See also Contributor List.)*

Dummy: (1) A mock-up giving a preview of a printed piece, showing placement and nature of the material to be printed. (2) A fictitious name with a mailable address inserted into a mailing list to check on usage of that list.

Dupe: Duplication. Appearance of identical or nearly identical entities more than once.

Duplication Elimination: A specific kind of controlled duplication which provides that: no matter how many times a name and address is on a list, and how many lists contain that name and address, it will be accepted for mailing only once by that mailer. Also referred to as "dupe elimination" or "deduplication" or "merge/purge."

Editing Rules: Specific rules used in preparing name and address records that treat all elements the same way at all times. Also, the rules for rearranging, deleting, selecting, or inserting any needed data, symbols and/or characters.

Electronic Mail: Also called E-Mail, it provides the ability to create, store or forward messages by computer.

End-User: Generally refers to the customer or caller. In data processing this can also mean the person using the computer or terminal.

Envelope Stuffer: Any advertising or promotional material enclosed in an envelope with business letters, statements or invoices.

Exchange: An arrangement whereby two mailers exchange equal quantities of mailing list names.

Expire: A former customer who is no longer an active buyer.

Expiration: A subscription which is not renewed.

Expiration Date: Date a subscription expires.

Field: Reserved area in a computer which services a similar function in all records of the file. Also, location on magnetic tape or disk drive which has definable limitations and meaning: For example, position 1-30 is the Name field.

File Maintenance: The activity of keeping a file up-to-date by adding, changing, or deleting data (all or part). Synonymous with list maintenance *(See also Update.)*

Fill-In: A name, address or other text added to a preprinted letter.

First-Time Buyer: One who buys a product or service from a specific company for the first time.

Fixed Field: A way of laying out, or formatting, list information in a computer file that puts every piece of data in a specific position relative to every other piece of data, and limits the amount of space assigned to that data. If a piece of data is missing from an individual record, or if its assigned space is not completely used, that space is not filled (every record has the same space and the same length). Any data exceeding its assigned space limitation must be abbreviated.

Flip-card: A method of scripting in which the script copy is printed on randomly accessible pages which can be "flipped" to display the next logical portion of the script based on the response of the customer.

Forced-Choice Questions: Questions which force the customer to make a decision. *Do you want your order shipped on the 10th or 15th?*

Format: The vehicle used to deliver an offer to a market: mail, phone, print, or broadcast.

Former Buyer: One who has bought one or more times from a company but has not purchased in the last twelve months.

Free-Standing Insert: A promotional piece loosely inserted or nested in a newspaper or magazine.

Frequency: The number of times an individual has ordered within a specific period of time. *(See also Monetary Value* and *Recency.)*

Friend-of-a-Friend: Friend Recommendations. The result of one party sending in the name of someone who might be interested in a specific advertiser's product or service; a third party inquiry.

Front-End: Activities performed to produce responses to a direct marketing program and the measurement of those activities.

Fulfillment: Delivering the offer made in a direct marketing promotion.

Full Print: The addressee's name and all of the body copy are generated by the printer.

FX: Foreign Exchange. A telephone technique of having an exchange added to your network that is not in the same exchange as your business. This approach can have a significant impact on phone toll charges.

Geo Code: Symbols used to identify geographic entities (state, county, zip code, SCF, tract, etc.).

Geographics: Any method of subdividing a list, based on geographic or political subdivisions (zip codes, sectional centers, cities, counties, states, regions).

Gimmick: Attention-getting device, usually multi-dimensional, attached to a direct mail printed piece.

Guarantee: A pledge of satisfaction made by the seller to the buyer and specifying the terms by which the seller will make good his pledge.

Gross Margin: The selling price minus the cost of goods sold.

Half-Duplex: A circuit for transmitting or receiving signals in one direction at a time.

Hot-Line List: The most recent names available on a specific list, that are no older than three months. In any event, use of the term "hot-line" should be further modified by "weekly," "monthly," etc.

House List: Any list of names owned by a company as a result of compilation, inquiry or buyer action, or acquisition, that is used to promote that company's products or services.

House-List Duplicate: Duplication of name and address

records between the list user's own lists and any list being mailed by him on a one-time use arrangement.

Inbound Telemarketing: The systematic handling of a call from a prospect or customer, resulting from a message seen in another medium.

Incentive Base: Usually the total of incentives for revenues. Sales compensation plans based on quota attainment performance pay an incentive as a portion of the total incentives, also called the Incentive Base.

Incompleted Calls: Outbound calls in which the caller was unable to speak with the prospect or customer because either the prospect didn't answer, was not available, or the line was busy.

Indicia: A symbol imprinted on the outgoing envelope to denote payment of postage.

Influencer: In the business-to-business environment, a person who is involved in the buying decision process but is not the decision maker.

Inquiry: One who has asked for literature or other information about a product or service. Unless otherwise stated, it is assumed no payment is required for the literature or other information. *(Note: A catalog request is generally considered a specific type of inquiry.)*

Insert: A promotional piece inserted into an outgoing package or invoice.

Installment Buyer: One who orders goods or services and pays for them in two or more periodic payments after their delivery.

Intensive Planning: A concept that encourages communication, problem definition, and problem resolution.

Interactive Database: Enables callers to access a database for specific information electronically by phone or remote computer.

Interactive FAX: The ability to request and respond to requests for faxed material electronically.

Inter-List Duplicate: Duplication of name and address records *between* two or more lists, other than house lists, being mailed by a list user.

KBN: Kill Bad Name. Action taken on undeliverable addresses (nixies). You

KBN a nixie.

Key: One or more characters within a data group that can be used to identify it or control its use. Synonymous with Key Code in mailing business.

Key Code (Key): A group of letters and/or numbers, colors, or other markings, used to measure the specific effectiveness of media, lists, advertisements, offers, or any parts thereof.

Keyline: Any one of many partial or complete descriptions of past buying history coded to include name and address information and current status.

Key-Pad Response: Callers can choose options from a menu by pressing numbers on a touch-tone telephone.

Label: Piece of paper containing the name and address of the recipient which is applied to a mailing for address purposes.

Layout: (1) Artist's sketch showing relative positioning of illustrations, headlines, and copy. (2) Positioning subject matter on a press sheet for most efficient production.

Lead: *See Referral*

Least Cost Routing: A feature on a PBX telephone system which automatically selects the least expensive route for a telephone call to travel based on distance, other calls, and the time of day.

Letter Package: A direct mail promotion that uses the same size envelope used for business letters.

Letterhead: The printing on a letter that identifies the sender.

Lettershop: A business organization that handles the mechanical details of mailings such as addressing, imprinting, collating, etc. Most lettershops offer some printing facilities and many offer some degree of creative direct mail services.

Lifetime Value: A measurement of the long-term dollar value of a customer, subscriber, donor, etc. This figure is essential when evaluating initial costs to bring in a customer against the lifetime proceeds.

Line: The extension or line of a telephone system within a company. Lines connect telephone instruments to the outside trunks usually through a PBX or key system.

List: Mailing List. Names and addresses of individuals and/or companies having in common an interest, characteristic or activity. The customers or prospects to whom a marketing program will be targeted.

List Broker: A specialist who makes all necessary arrangements for one company to use the list(s) of another company. A broker's services may include most, or all, of the following: research, selection, recommendation and subsequent evaluation.

List Buyer: Technically, this term should apply only to one who actually buys mailing lists. In practice, however, it is usually used to identify one who orders mailing lists for one-time use: a List User or Mailer.

List Cleaning: The process of correcting and/or removing a name and/or address from a mailing list because it is no longer correct. Term is also used to describe identifica-

tion and elimination of duplicates on house lists.

List Compiler: One who develops lists of names and addresses from directories, newspapers, public records, sales slips, trade show registrations and other sources for identifying groups of people or companies with something in common.

List Exchange: A barter arrangement between two companies for the use of mailing list(s). May be, list for list, list for space, or list for comparable value - other than money.

List Maintenance: Any manual, mechanical or electronic system for keeping name and address records (with or without other data) up to date at any specific point(s) in time.

List Manager: One who, as an employee of a list owner or as an outside agent, is responsible for the use, by others, of a specific mailing list(s). The list manager generally serves the list owner in several or all of the following capacities: list maintenance (or advice thereon), list promotion and marketing, list clearance and record keeping, collection of fees for use of the list by others.

List Owner: One who, by promotional activity or compilation, has developed a list of names having something in common; or one who has *purchased* (as opposed to rented, reproduced, or used on a one-time basis) such a list from the developer.

List Rental: An arrangement whereby a list owner furnishes names to a mailer, together with the privilege of using the list on a one-time basis only (unless otherwise specified in advance). For this privilege, the list owner is paid a royalty by the mailer. "List Rental" is the term most often used although "List Reproduction" and "List Usage" more accurately describe the transaction, since "Rental" is not used in the sense of its ordinary meaning of leasing property.

List Royalty: Payment to list owners for the privilege of using their lists on a one-time basis.

List Sample: A group of names selected from a list in order to evaluate the responsiveness of that list. *(See also List Test.)*

List Segmentation: *See List Selection.*

List Selection: Characteristics used to define smaller groups within a list (essentially, lists within a list). Although very small, select groups may be very desirable and may substantially improve response; minimum set-up costs, however, often make them expensive.

List Sequence: The order in which names and addresses appear on a list. While most lists today are in zip code sequence, some are alphabetical by name within the zip code; others are in carrier sequence (postal delivery); and still others may (or may not) use some other order within the zip code. some lists are still arranged alphabetically by name and chronologically, and in many other variations or combinations.

List Sort: Process of putting a list in specific sequence or no sequence.

List Source: The media used to acquire names: direct mail, space, TV, radio, telephone, etc.

List Test: Part of a list selected to try to determine the effectiveness of the entire list. *(See also List Sample.)*

List User: One who uses names and addresses on someone else's list as prospects for the user's product or service; similar to Mailer.

Live-Operator Interaction: This service lets callers access professional operators who can provide or receive information..

Load Up: Process of offering a buyer the opportunity of buying an entire series at one time after the customer has purchased the first item in that series.

Local Area Network (LAN): Intra-office communication system generally used for voice and data transmission.

Mail Date: Date a list user, by prior agreement with the list owner, is obligated to mail a specific list. No other date is acceptable without specific approval from the list owner.

Mailer: (1) A direct mail advertiser who promotes a product or service using lists of others, or house lists,

or both. (2) A printed direct mail advertising piece. (3) A folding carton, wrapper, or tube used to protect materials in the mail.

Mailgram: A combination telegram-letter, with the telegram transmitted to a postal facility close to the addressee and then delivered as first class mail.

Mailing Machine: A machine that attaches labels, addresses envelopes, inserts printed pieces into any style envelope, affixes postage to mailing pieces and otherwise prepares such pieces for deposit in the postal system.

Mail Order Action Line (MOAL): A service of the Direct Marketing Association which assists consumers in resolving problems with mail order purchases.

Mail Order Buyer: One who orders, and pays for, a product or service through the mail. Generally, an order telephoned in response to a direct response advertisement is considered a direct substitute for an order sent through postal channels.

Mail Preference Service (MPS): A service of the

Direct Marketing Association wherein consumers can request to have their names removed from, or added to, mailing lists. These names are made available to both members and non-members of the association.

Margin: The gross profit on sales after subtracting cost-of-goods from the gross revenue.

Marketing: All activities which move goods and services from seller to buyer.

Master File: File that is of a permanent nature or regarded in a particular job as authoritative, or one that contains all sub files.

Match: A direct mail term used to refer to the typing of addresses, salutations or inserts onto letters with other copy imprinted by a printing process.

Match Code: A code determined either by the creator or the user of a file for matching records contained in another file.

Match Fill: Having the letter body copy typeset and preprinted by a printer to achieve the appearance of a fully personalized letter.

The address, salutation and perhaps some specific information in the body of the letter are added during computer printing.

Message Unit: A local telephone toll rate calling plan based on time and distance.

MOAL: *See Mail Order Action Line.*

Monetary Value: Total expenditures by a customer during a specific period of time, generally twelve months.

MPS: *See Mail Preference Service.*

Multimedia: The use of a variety of media in promotional efforts such as direct mail, space, TV, or radio.

Multiple Buyer: One who has bought two or more times (not one who has bought two or more items, one time only); also a Multi-Buyer or Repeat Buyer.

Multiple Regression: Statistical technique used to measure the relationship between responses to a mailing with census demographics and list characteristics of one or more selected mailing lists. Used to direct mail to the best types of people or areas. This technique can also be used to analyze customers, subscribers, etc.

Name: Single entry on a mailing list.

Name Acquisition: Technique of soliciting a response to obtain names and addresses for a mailing list.

Name-Removal Service: Portion of Mail Preference Service offered by the Direct Marketing Association wherein consumer is sent a form which, when filled in and returned, constitutes a request to have the individual's name removed from all mailing lists used by participating members of the association and other direct mail users.

Need: A problem that a prospect has to address.

Negative Option: A buying plan in which a customer or club member agrees to accept and pay for products or services announced in advance at regular intervals unless the individual notifies the company, within a reasonable time after each announcement, not to ship the merchandise.

Nesting: Placing one enclosure within another before insert-

ing them into a mailing envelope.

Net Name Arrangement: An agreement, at the time of ordering or before, whereby the list owner agrees to accept adjusted payment for less than the total names shipped to the list user. Such arrangements can be for a percentage of names shipped or names actually mailed (whichever is greater) or for only those names actually mailed (without a percentage limitation). The list owner may or may not provide for a running charge.

Nixie: A mailing piece returned to a mailer (under proper authorization) by the postal service because of an incorrect, or undeliverable, name and address.

Novelty Format: An attention-getting direct mail format.

OCR: *See Optical Character Recognition.*

Offer: The terms promoting a specific product or service. The proposition made to customers or prospects to elicit a response.

One-Time Buyer: A buyer who has not ordered a second time from a given company.

One-Time Use Of A List: An intrinsic part of the normal list usage, list reproduction, or list exchange agreement in which it is understood that the mailer will not use the names on the list more than one time without specific prior approval of the list owner.

Open Account: A customer record that, at a specific time, reflects an unpaid balance for goods and services ordered, without delinquency.

Open questions: Questions designed to get a customer talking that cannot be answered with a 'yes' or 'no'. *Who do you get your various cleaning suppliers from now?*

Optical Character Recognition (OCR): Machine identification of printed characters through use of light sensitive devices.

Order Blank Envelopes: An order form printed on one side of a sheet, with a mailing address on the reverse. The recipient simply fills in the order, then folds and seals it like an envelope.

Order Card: A reply card used to initiate an order by mail.

Order Form: A printed form on which a customer can provide information to initiate an order by mail. Designed to be mailed in an envelope.

Outbound Telemarketing: A direct mail message being delivered over the telephone. The communicator is fully scripted.

Overflow Calls: Calls from people who dialed an 800 number and encountered a busy signal making it impossible to get through to the company they were calling.

Package: A term used to describe all of the assembled enclosures (parts or elements) of a mailing effort.

Package Insert: Any promotional piece included in a product shipment. It may be for different products (or refills and replacements) from the same company or for products and services of other companies.

Package Test: A test of part or all of the elements of one mailing piece against another.

Paid Cancel: One who completes a basic buying commitment, or more, before cancelling the commitment. *(See also Completed Cancel.)*

Paid Circulation: Distribution of a publication to individuals or organizations which have paid for a subscription.

Paid During Service: Term used to describe a method of paying for magazine subscriptions in installments, usually weekly or monthly, and, usually, collected in person by the original sales person or a representative of that company.

Paid Subscription: *See Paid Circulation.*

PBX: Private Branch Exchange. The equipment used to switch telephone calls within a company. Most PBX units are computerized and handle many telephone related functions. Some vendors refer to their PBX's as CBX meaning Computerized Branch Exchange.

Peel-Off Label: A self-adhesive label attached to a backing which is attached to a mailing piece. The label is intended to be removed from the mailing piece and attached to an order blank or card.

Penetration: Relationship of the number of individuals or families on a particular list (by state, zip code, SIC code, etc.) compared to the total number possible.

Personalization: Individualizing of direct mail pieces by adding the name or other personal information about the recipient.

Phone List: Mailing list compiled from names listed in telephone directories.

P.I.: *See Per Interaction.*

Piggy-Back: An offer that hitches a free ride with another offer.

Poly Bag: Transparent polyethylene bag used in place of envelopes for mailing.

Pop-Up: A printed piece containing a paper construction pasted inside a fold and which, when the fold is opened, "pops up" to form a three-dimensional illustration.

Positive Option: A method of distributing products and services incorporating the same advance notice techniques as Negative Option but requiring a specific order each time from the member or subscriber. Generally, it is more costly and less predictable than Negative Option.

Postal Service Prohibitory Order: A communication from the postal service to a company indicating that a specific person and/or family considers the company's advertising mail to be pandering. The order requires the company to remove from its own mailing list and from any other lists used to promote the company's products or services all names listed on the order. Violation of the order is subject to fine and imprisonment. Names listed on the order are to be distinguished from those names removed voluntarily by the list owner at an individual's request.

Post Card: Single sheet self-mailers on card stock.

Post Card Mailers: Booklet containing business reply cards which are individually perforated for selective return, to order products or obtain information.

Premium: An item offered to a buyer, usually free or at a nominal price, as an inducement to purchase or obtain for trial a product or service offered via mail order.

Premium Buyer: One who buys a product or service to get another product or service (usually free or at a special price), or who responds to an offer of a special product (premium) on the package or label (or sometimes in the advertising) of another product.

Preprint: An advertising insert printed in advance and supplied to a newspaper or magazine for insertion.

Pressure: The disparity felt by business as a result of face-to-face selling expenses increasing disproportionately to pricing and other cost items.

Private Mail: Mail handled by special arrangement outside the postal service.

Private Use Network: Two or more private line channels contracted for by a customer and restricted for use by that customer only.

Program: (1) A sequence of steps to be executed by the

computer to solve a given problem or achieve a certain result. (2) A sequence of direct marketing activities that identify a direct marketing effort to sell products or generate leads.

Programming: Designing, writing and testing of a computer program.

Promotion: The further development and encouragement of prospects and customers to purchases one's products or services without the aid of a sales representative.

Prospect: (1) A name on a mailing list considered to be a potential buyer for a given product or service, who has not previously made such a purchase. (2) That group of prospects that meet your predetermined qualification criteria making you want to include them in an ongoing marketing program.

Prospecting: Mailing to get leads for further sales contact rather than to make direct sales.

Protection: The amount of time, before and after the assigned mailing date, that a list owner will not allow the same names to be mailed by anyone other than the mailer cleared for that specific date.

Psychographics: Any characteristics or qualities used to denote the lifestyle(s) or attitude(s) of customers and prospective customers.

Publisher's Letter: A second letter enclosed in a mailing package to stress a specific selling point.

Purge: The process of eliminating duplicates and/or unwanted names and addresses from one or more lists.

Questionnaire: A printed form to a specified audience to solicit answers to specific questions.

Question Close: A question asked with the intent of getting the customer talking about why he is reluctant to buy. *Sir, if you agree that this system will satisfy your need, and I believe you do, is there any reason to delay?*

Random Access: An access mode in which records are obtained from, or placed into, a mass storage file in a non-sequential manner so that any record can be rapidly accessed. Synonymous with Direct Access.

Recency: The latest purchase or other activity recorded for an individual or company on a specific customer list. *(See also Frequency and Monetary Value.)*

Records: The individual names on a list.

Referral: (1) That group of prospects that is of such high quality that it should be referred for immediate handling by a salesperson or customer support organization. Sometimes called leads. (2) Usually derived form the Friend-get-a-Friend program, where a member is offered a record or book to suggest the names of friends who might be interested in joining the club.

Reflective Questions: Questions that cause a customer to consider a statement he made or a possible thought which was unexpressed. *Do you feel that automatic shipments limit your flexibility?*

Reformatting: Changing a magnetic tape format from one arrangement to another, more usable format. Synonymous with Conversion (list or tape).

Regeneration: Repeated attempts to get a prospect to respond through direct mail and telephone selling once these prospect have indicated an interest in your product or service.

Remote Access: The ability to electronically gain access to a computer at another location.

Renewal: A subscription that has been renewed prior to, or at, expiration time or within six months thereafter.

Rental: *See List Rental.*

Repeat Buyer: *See Multiple Buyer.*

Reply Card: A sender-addressed card included in a mailing on which the recipient may indicate his response to the offer.

Reproduction Right: Authorization by a list owner for a specific mailer to use that list on a one-time basis.

Response Rate: Percentage of returns or inquiries from a mailing.

Return Envelopes: Addressed reply envelopes, either stamped or un-stamped as distinguished from business reply envelopes which carry a postage payment guarantee included with a mailing.

Return On Investment (ROI): The evaluation of return on invested capital. In direct mail, often loosely described as the return (income) based on the dollars expended in a direct mail campaign.

Return Postage Guaranteed: A legend imprinted on the address face of envelopes or other mailing pieces when the mailer wishes the postal service to return undeliverable third class bulk mail. A charge equivalent to the single piece, first class rate will be made for each piece returned. *(See also List Cleaning.)*

Returns: (1) Responses to a direct mail program. (2) Returns of products shipped to customers on free or limited trials that are not purchased.

Revenue Multiplier: The amount of incentive dollars received for the sale of $1.00 of products. The revenue multiplier is calculated by dividing the incentive base by the quota.

RFMR: Acronym for Recency-Frequency-Monetary Value Ratio, a formula used to evaluate the sales potential of names on a mailing list.

R.O.I.: *See Return On Investment.*

Rollout: To mail the remaining portion of a mailing list after successfully testing a portion of that list.

R.O.P.: *See Run Of Paper.*

Rough: Dummy or layout in sketchy form with a minimum of detail.

Royalties: Sum paid per unit mailed or sold for the use of a list, imprimatur, patent, etc.

Running Charge: The price a list owner charges for names run or passed, but not used by a specific mailer. When such a charge is made, it is usually to cover extra processing costs. However, some list owners set the price without regard to actual cost.

Sample Buyer: One who sends for a sample product, usually at a special price or for a small handling charge, but sometimes free.

Sample Package: Mailing Piece. An example of the package to be mailed by the list user to a particular list.

Such a mailing piece is submitted to the list owner for approval prior to commitment for one-time use of the list. Although a sample package may, due to time pressure, differ slightly from the actual package used, the list owner agreement usually requires the user to reveal any material differences when submitting the sample package.

SCF: *See Sectional Center.*

Script-on-paper: A method of scripting in which copy is typed on pages and posted or available at the communicator station.

Script-on-record: A method of scripting in which the script is printed directly on the unit record.

Sectional Center (SCF or SCF Center): A postal service distribution unit comprising different post offices whose zip codes start with the same first three digits.

Selection Criteria: Definition of characteristics that identify segments or sub-groups within a list.

Self-mailer: A direct mail piece mailed without an envelope.

Sequence: An arrangement of items according to a specified set of rules or instructions. Refers generally to zip codes or customer number sequence.

Sequential Processing: Type of information storage, reading one item at a time, having to move through all the preceding records to get the next record in sequential order.

SIC: *See Standard Industrial Classification.*

Single Number Routing: This allows 800 or 900 calls to be directed to the closest service bureau to the caller's home. It offers convenience to the caller and receiver and cuts long-distance costs.

Silent Monitoring: Listening directly to a phone call while at least one party has given permission to allow a third party to listen.

SMSA: *See Standard Metropolitan Statistical Area.*

Soft Close: *See Trial Close.*

Solo Mailing: A mailing promoting a single product or a limited group of related products. Usually it consists of a letter, brochure and reply device enclosed in an envelope.

Source Code: Unique alphabetical and/or numeric identification for distinguishing one list or media source from another. *(See also Key Code.)*

Source Count: The number of names and addresses, in any given list, for the media (or list sources) from which the names and addresses were derived.

Split Test: Two or more samples from the same list -- each considered to be representative of the entire list -- used for package tests or to test the homogeneity of the list.

Standard Industrial Classification (SIC): Classification of businesses, as defined by the U.S. Department of Commerce.

Standard Metropolitan Statistical Area (SMSA): Major metropolitan areas as set forth by the government.

State Count: The number of names and addresses, in a given list, for each state.

Statement Stuffer: A small, printed piece designed to be inserted in an envelope carrying a customer's statement of account.

Step Up: The use of special premiums to get a mail order buyer to increase his unit of purchase.

Stock Art: Art sold for use by a number of advertisers.

Stock Formats: Direct mail formats with pre-printed illustrations and/or headings to which an advertiser adds his own copy.

Stopper: Advertising slang for a striking headline or illustration intended to attract immediate attention.

Strategic: use of direct marketing; the long term efforts and results that will be experienced.

Strategy: The "map" that defines where you would like to go over the longer term.

Strategies: Definitions of long term goals.

Stuffer: Advertising enclosures placed in other media such as newspapers, merchandise packages, or mailings for other products.

Subscriber: Individual who has paid to receive a periodical.

Suspect: The name of a business in business-to-business direct marketing.

Syndicated Mailing: Mailing

prepared for distribution by firms other than the manufacturer or syndicator.

Syndicator: One who makes available prepared direct mail promotions for specific products or services to a list owner for mailing to his own list. Most syndicators also offer product fulfillment services.

Tabloid: A preprinted advertising insert of four or more pages, usually about half the size of a regular newspaper page, designed for inserting into a newspaper.

Tactical: use of direct marketing; how you will implement direct marketing with the current approach to selling.

Tactics: The things one does to execute a strategy.

Tag: To mark a record with definitive criteria which allows for subsequent selection or suppression.

Tape Recording: A type of monitoring in which a phone call is tape recorded while both parties are aware of the taping, and there is an audible beep present at least every 15 seconds during the recording.

Teaser: An advertisement or promotion planned to excite curiosity about a later advertisement or promotion.

Technical Difficulties: A broad description of records that had been attempted and for some reason, were not able to be contacted. These records will not be attempted again

Technical Elements: Those elements that are critical to any successful direct marketing effort; product information, a reply devise, etc.

Telecommunications: (1) Data transmission between a computer system and remotely located devices via a unit that performs the necessary format conversion and controls the rate of transmission over telephone lines, microwaves, etc. Synonymous with Transceive. (2) The management and control of the routing that a voice or data communication takes when leaving one location and traveling to another.

Telemarketing: A medium used to perform direct marketing using a scripted or message-controlled communicator to deliver a direct marketing message over the telephone.

Telephone Line: The extension or instrument connected to the telephone system within your business.

Telephone Preference Service (TPS): A service of the Direct Marketing Association for consumers who wish to have their names removed from national telemarketing lists. The name-removal file is made available to subscribers on a quarterly basis.

Telephone Switch: A computer designed to control the telephone activity within a business. Phone calls are received or routed automatically. Often referred to as a PBX, private branch exchange, or CBX, computerized branch exchange.

Telesales: Telephone selling where the communicator has open dialogue with the prospect. Typically the communicator is a qualified salesperson.

Terminal: Any mechanism which can transmit and/or receive data through a system or communications network.

Test Panel: A term used to identify each of the parts or samples in a split test.

Test Tape: A selection of representative records within a mailing list that enables a list user or service bureau to prepare for reformatting or converting to a form more efficient for the user.

Tie-In: Cooperative mailing effort involving two or more advertisers.

Til Forbid: An order for continuing service which is to continue until specifically cancelled by the buyer. Also "TF".

Time Sharing: Multiple utilization of available computer time, often via terminals, usually shared by different organizations.

Tip-on: An item glued to a printed piece.

Title: A designation before or after a name to more accurately identify an individual.

Title Addressing: Usually refers to functional titles used in compiling business lists, where there is no individual name.

Token: An involvement device, often consisting of a perforated portion of an order card designed to be removed from its original position and placed in another designated area on the order card, to signify a desire to purchase the product or service.

Town Marker: A symbol used to identify the end of a mailing list's geographical unit. Originated for "towns" but now used for zip codes, sectional centers, etc.

TPS: *See Telephone Preference Service.*

Traffic Builder: A direct mail piece intended primarily to attract recipients to the mailer's place of business.

Trial Buyer: One who buys a short-term supply of a product, or buys the product with the understanding that it may be examined, used, or tested for a specified time before deciding whether to pay for it or return it.

Trial Close: A question that forces a customer to indicate that he is interested in pursuing one's offer. *How many will you be needing?*

Trial Subscriber: A person ordering a publication or service on a conditional basis. The condition may relate to: delaying payment, the right to cancel, a shorter than nor-

mal term and/or a special introductory price.

Trunk: The telephone line connecting a business to the telephone company local central office. Typically a company will have dedicated inbound and outbound trunks.

Uncollectible: One who hasn't paid for goods and services at the end of a normal series of collection efforts.

Unit of Sale: Description of the average dollar amount spent by customers on a mailing list.

Unit Record: A form designed to record information about individual calls to make it possible to sort, tabulate, and print records and reports.

Universe: Total number of individuals that might be included on a mailing list; all of whom fit a single set of specifications.

Update: Recent transactions and current information added to the master (main) list to reflect the current status of each record on the list.

Up Front: Securing payment for a product offered by mail order before the product is sent.

UPS: Acronym for United Parcel Service.

Variable Field: A way of laying out list information for formatting that assigns a specific sequence to the data, but doesn't assign it specific positions. While this method conserves space, on magnetic tape or disk, it is generally more difficult to work with.

Verification: The process of determining the validity of an order by sending a questionnaire to the customer.

Voice Mail: The ability to create, store and forward messages through voice processing.

Voice Recognition: The ability to electronically recognize and respond to human words.

Volatile: A telephone automation application in which the call cannot continue if the computer fails to perform properly.

WATS: Acronym for Wide Area Telephone Service. A service providing a special line allowing calls within certain areas to be called at significantly lower rates.

White Mail: Incoming mail that is not on a form sent out by the advertiser. All mail other than orders or payments.

Window Envelope: Envelope with a die-cut portion on the front that permits viewing the address printed on an enclosure. The "die-cut window" may or may not be covered with a transparent material.

Wing Mailer: Label-affixing device that uses strips of paper on which addresses have been printed.

Zip Code: A group of five digits used by the U.S. Postal Service to designate specific post offices, stations, branches, buildings or large companies.

Zip Code Count: The number of names and addresses on a list, within each zip code.

Zip Code Sequence: Arranging names and addresses on a list according to the numeric progression of the zip code in each record. This form of list formatting is mandatory for mailing at bulk third class mail rates, based on the sorting requirements of postal service regulations.

Index